Gore Vidal

A Comprehensive Bibliography

S. T. Joshi

Foreword by Jay Parini

The Scarecrow Press, Inc.
Lanham, Maryland • Toronto • Plymouth, UK
2007

SCARECROW PRESS, INC.

Published in the United States of America
by Scarecrow Press, Inc.
A wholly owned subsidary of
The Rowman & Littlefield Publishing Group, Inc.
4501 Forbes Boulevard, Suite 200, Lanham, Maryland 20706
www.scarecrowpress.com

Estover Road
Plymouth PL6 7PY
United Kingdom

Copyright © 2007 by S. T. Joshi

British Library Cataloguing in Publication Information Available

Library of Congress Cataloging-in-Publication Data

Joshi, S. T., 1958–
  Gore Vidal : a comprehensive bibliography / S.T. Joshi ; foreword by Jay Parini.
    p. cm.
  Includes indexes.
  ISBN-13: 978-0-8108-6001-8 (alk. paper)
  ISBN-10: 0-8108-6001-5 (alk. paper)
  1. Vidal, Gore, 1925—Bibliography. I. Title.

Z8942.19.J67 2007
[PS3543.I26]
016.8185'4—dc22   2007009223

Contents

Foreword

By Jay Parini

There is something exhilarating about a good bibliography of a major writer, one that takes the measure of this writer in his or her full complexity and amplitude, listing and annotating the obvious publications as well as those that have dropped unnoticed into the deep, dark well of literary history. That is, it puts the whole writer before us. We can see the splashes and waves this writer has made in the world, as his or her work has been published, translated, adapted, criticized, admired, ignored. S. T. Joshi does all of this, and more, in *Gore Vidal: A Comprehensive Bibliography*.

This is the first fully comprehensive bibliography of Vidal, replacing the admirable start made by Robert J. Stanton. In this case, Joshi has come at just the right moment, when Vidal stands close to the end of his career, with almost everything of consequence already written: a vast shelf of books that rivals the production of any of his contemporaries. And what a remarkable shelf it is, encompassing massive historical novels like *Burr, Lincoln,* and *Julian* as well as brief satires like *Myra Breckinridge* and *Duluth*. It includes witty plays like *Visit to a Small Planet* or *The Best Man,* film scripts and teleplays, hundreds of book reviews, shimmering essays on literary subjects, fierce political and cultural critiques, diatribes against the establishment, coolly reasoned pamphlets against the war in Iraq, against the Bush/Cheney junta, affecting memoirs and countless autobiographical musings from a life lived deeply and broadly. As Joshi notes, there were even a few poems in there, and short stories as well. It seems that Vidal has left no literary form untried.

In fact, it's hard to imagine another single life as complete as Vidal's. He has known Washington and Hollywood, Greenwich Village and London, Rome and Paris—all from the inside. He has run for public office in New York and California, has written and acted in films, produced hits on Broadway, appeared on countless radio and television programs in dozens of countries. He has lectured widely. His name is known around the world, his voice heard in many languages. And he has done all of this for nearly sixty years, unceasingly, with apparent ease.

Joshi takes the measure of the man in this work of considerable scholarship and imagination. After a shrewd introduction, he puts before us everything that Vidal has published and most of what was not published. He digs into the translations and adaptations. He provides a thorough and reliable guide to what critics have said about Vidal in reviews, in books and essays, in commentaries in various forms. A list of the interviews is here: a genre in which Vidal excels, and one that he has almost turned into a literary art. He offers a guide to news items about Vidal, to web resources as well as repositories of Vidal manuscripts, letters, and memorabilia. Future biographers—and their will be many—must remain forever in Joshi's debt.

In all, this is a marvelous book, a work of scholarship that affords readerly pleasures of a most unexpected kind. I would recommend it to Vidal's many readers and to libraries and collectors as well. It is a good book to browse in the most casual way, or to study closely, or to use as a reference work. All of us who admire Gore Vidal should be grateful to its compiler.

Introduction

To say that Gore Vidal (b. 1925) occupies a distinctive place in American literature is unhelpfully vague and imprecise. Few authors can combine so impressive a family heritage with such substantial and consistent achievement over more than half a century; few can match his mastery of multiple modes of expression—the novel, the short story, the essay, the play, the screenplay, even the letter and the clever riposte; and few have mastered the ability to achieve celebrity and notoriety, as a novelist, playwright, political commentator, and even as an actor in film and televison, while at the same time demonstrating the undoubted richness and substance of his work. Vidal has been a best-selling writer for decades, but his work is certain to endure longer than that of the transient popular writers of the day; he has raised the historical novel to literary heights rarely achieved in that difficult genre; but he has also been the acquaintance of presidents and influenced the course of political thought and action in this country and the world. On occasion it seems that Vidal is not just a single individual but, as one critic noted, "a score of authors existing on some cultural astral plane."

It would seem, therefore, that the compilation of a bibliography of such a well-known literary and public figure would present few difficulties, since his early celebrity ensured the publication of his work in well-known venues and in substantial quantities. But it is a token of our throwaway society, especially where nonprint media are concerned, that many of the details of Vidal's career, especially in regard to his work in drama, film, and television, are already in danger of being lost. The purveyors of these media have not always been scrupulous in the preservation of their past, and it now requires considerable scholarly excavation to ascertain even the traces of Vidal's—and others'—work in them.

Gore Vidal was born Eugene Luther Vidal Jr. on 3 October 1925. The grandson of the well-known blind senator from Oklahoma, Thomas P. Gore, and the son of Eugene Vidal, an early pioneer in aviation who became director of the Bureau of Air Commerce under Franklin D. Roosevelt, Vidal was early acclimated to the corridors of political power in the United States. Although born at West Point, Vidal spent most of his youth at two different homes near Washington, D.C., where he developed an enthusiasm for literature by reading to his grandfather. He was educated at a succession of private schools in the area, including the exclusive St. Albans Academy, and then at Phillips Exeter Academy in New Hampshire. It was at this time that Vidal's first surviving writings appeared: his first publication was apparently a letter to the editor of the *Exonian,* the academy's newspaper, published on 1 March 1941. Shortly thereafter, stories and poems began appearing in the school's literary magazine, the *Phillips Exeter Review.* Vidal later noted that many other contributions were rejected by the editors.

After graduating from Phillips Exeter, Vidal, rather than attending college, decided to enter the army. An indifferent student, bored with academic routine, Vidal perhaps saw in the army a means of social and political advancement. It was not, indeed, that he was especially patriotic or that he felt a burning desire to defeat Nazism; rather, he believed that the prospects of future political office—a goal he had already set for himself—would be advanced by a stint in the military. During his three years in the army (1943–1946), Vidal suffered a serious illness and saw action, of a sort, in Alaska. He also began seriously writing, producing an entire volume of poetry and a draft of his first novel, *Williwaw.* Through family connections, the novel was read by an editor at E. P. Dutton, who felt it a strong work and published it in the spring of 1946. Vidal was not yet twenty-one years old.

Williwaw received generally favorable reviews as a tightly woven, laconic novel of the war. A second novel, *In a Yellow Wood* (1947), was not as well received, but Vidal's career took a very different turn with his third novel, *The City and the Pillar* (1948). One of the first novels that frankly discussed homosexuality—and, more significantly, portrayed its lead character, Jim Willard, as indistinguishable in physique and character from heterosexuals—it became a best-seller and established Vidal as a vibrant young postwar talent. Reviews of the novel ranged from enthusiastic to hostile, many reviewers treating the central subject with caution and even a bit of queasiness. His editors at Dutton (where Vidal was now working) had urged him not to publish the work, stating that it might damage both his literary and his political prospects; but Vidal was determined to give a voice to a homosexual character, and he is now seen as a pioneer in gay literature, even though Vidal himself has maintained that the categories "homosexual" and "heterosexual" are meaningless and that all human beings are, in varying degrees, bisexual.

The exact degree to which *The City and the Pillar* damaged Vidal's career in the short term is now difficult to gauge. He continued to publish novels at a regular rate of one a year; indeed, he was now writing so voluminously that his novels were completed years before their publication. Over the next five years (1949–1954), Vidal published an array of novels, each of which attempted to break out of the Hemingway/James T. Farrell mode of spare prose realism that had typified his early work: *The Season of Comfort* (1949), his first political novel (and, perhaps, even his first historical novel, as it opens in the year 1928), an unflinching portrayal of his tormented relationship with his mother, Nina; *A Search for the King* (1950), a historical fantasy set in the Middle Ages; *Dark Green, Bright Red* (1950), a grim, cynical novel of political chicanery in a Latin American nation (derived from a year-long stay in Guatemala); *The Judgment of Paris* (1952), a languid novel of heterosexual and homosexual love; and *Messiah* (1954), perhaps Vidal's finest novel of his early period, a cataclysmic tale of religious fanaticism and one of several that bravely exhibited his atheism. Critics such as John W. Aldridge, who had initially identified Vidal as a promising war novelist, did not know what to make of the thematic and stylistic variety of these works, but clearly Vidal had attracted a following.

And yet, Vidal himself would later maintain that *The City and the Pillar* had closed a number of editorial doors and made him persona non grata in the publishing community. Although by this time he had already developed close friendships with Anaïs Nin, Tennessee Williams, and other leading literary figures of the day, Vidal felt that sales of the novels published under his own name were not sufficient to support him as a full-time writer, and so he turned to the writing of pseudonymous potboilers. Three of these—the detective novels written under the pseudonym Edgar Box—are now widely known and are regarded charitably by devotees of the detective story; but two others—*A Star's Progress* (1950), published as by "Katherine Everard," and *Thieves Fall Out* (1953), as by "Cameron Kay"—have only recently come to light. The latter in particular, published only in paperback, is among the rarest of Vidal's writings. (Another pseudonymous novel, "Some Desperate Adventure," was never completed; the manuscript survives in the Gore Vidal Papers at the Houghton Library, Harvard University.)

Around 1954 Vidal made an even more dramatic decision to escape the opprobrium caused by *The City and the Pillar:* he would abandon novel-writing altogether and enter the world of television and film. Already convinced that the novel was a dying form—not because of the lack of capable writers but because of the gradual decline of educated readers capable of understanding and being moved by literary fiction—Vidal decided to exercise his talents as a screenwriter. At this time television presented substantial opportunities in this regard, as all the major networks featured live dramas written by leading playwrights of the period, including Paddy Chayefsky and Rod Serling. Vidal slipped naturally into this role, apparently writing dozens of teleplays, although only about twenty have been identified as his work. Some of these appeared in print in the collection *Visit to a Small Planet and Other Television Plays* (1956). In film, his first screenplay was *The Catered Affair* (1956), based on a teleplay by Chayefsky. He quickly produced other screenplays, including those for José Ferrer's *I Accuse!* (1958) and for *The Scapegoat* (1959), based on a novel by Daphne du Maurier. His most celebrated work in this regard—although it was acknowledged only years later—was his contribution to the screenplay of the blockbuster *Ben-Hur* (1959).

Vidal felt confident enough of his abilities as a dramatist—and, more significantly, had developed sufficient contacts in the film and drama industries—to generate a full-length play, *Visit to a Small Planet,* designed for production on Broadway. An expansion of a 1955 television play, it premiered in early 1957 and became an immediate hit, proving that satire—even if, as here, masquerading as farce—could be a success in the United States. Holding the Broadway stage for more than a year, it was later made into an indifferent film, becoming a vehicle for the comic talents of Jerry Lewis. A few years later, *The Best Man* (1960) was an even more triumphant success, remaining on Broadway for a remarkable 520 performances and being repeatedly revived—as recently as 2004. When plans were developed for making it a film, Vidal this time did not make the mistake of entrusting the screenplay to others but wrote it himself; he has also written amusingly that he gently dissuaded his producers from hiring Frank Capra as director of the film, rightly feeling that Capra's naïve enthusiasm would prove catastrophic in this cynical account of machinations at a political convention. Vidal had by this time already become an intimate of political heavyweights, including Jack and Jackie Kennedy, as Jackie was a stepdaughter of Vidal's own stepfather, Hugh D. Auchincloss, who had married Vidal's mother, Nina, after her divorce from Eugene Vidal.

From as early as 1950, however, Vidal had cultivated the essay as a literary mode, and this work continued even after his abandonment of the novel. The majority of his essays began life as reviews, but Vidal developed the knack of using a given book to probe broader issues related to literature, the drama, politics, and society. By 1962 he had amassed a substantial body of work in this mode, and when *Rocking the Boat* was published in that year it created a sensation. Many reviewers not only felt that Vidal was one of the most skillful and polished of modern American essayists, but—a refrain that Vidal would come to disdain—maintained that his essays were on the whole superior to his novels. The founding in 1963 of the *New York Review of Books* opened up an ideal venue for Vidal's ruminative essay-reviews. Liberal in political orientation and permitting its authors to write at length about a given subject or book, the magazine provided Vidal the opportunity to write some of his finest essays, and for more than thirty years he took up the challenge with vigor.

What readers did not know was that, by around 1960, Vidal was tentatively contemplating a return to the novel. The curious paperback omnibus *Three* (1962) included a reprint of *Williwaw* and of his collection of seven short stories, *A Thirsty Evil* (1956)—after which Vidal abandoned the short story as a preferred mode of literary utterance—as well as a novella entitled "Julian the Apostate." This proved to be an early draft of the beginning of his substantial novel *Julian* (1964), which triumphantly heralded his return to the novel by becoming a best-seller. In spite of unimaginative reviewers' comparisons of it to Robert Graves's *I, Claudius,* the novel established Vidal as one of the most accomplished of historical novelists, one who could use the historical novel not merely to re-create a remote era vividly but to fashion it as a vehicle for the expression of his profoundest philosophical views—in this case, his increasingly hostile view of organized religion in general and Christianity in particular.

But Vidal was by this time much more than a novelist writing in a secluded garret. Having purchased a beautiful house near Hyde Park, New York, thereby becoming the neighbor and friend of Eleanor Roosevelt, Vidal found himself inexorably attracted to political activity. He and others became convinced that *The City and the Pillar* was not necessarily the kiss of death for a political career, and he was persuaded to run for Congress on the Democratic ticket in the heavily Republican district in which he lived. In the election of 1960, he took pride in the fact that, although he lost, he received more votes than John F. Kennedy in his district. Needless to say, much media attention was devoted to Vidal during this period, and he became a frequent and recognized figure on television talk shows, hosting one himself ("Hot Line") for a short period and appearing on such national programs as "What's My Line?" and "The Tonight Show." Strikingly handsome, gifted with a rapier wit that seemed the perfect liberal antidote to his later nemesis, William F. Buckley Jr., Vidal had become a celebrity in addition to a well-known writer, playwright, and politician.

His playwriting career, however, was in jeopardy. *Romulus* (1962), an adaptation of a play by Friedrich Duerrenmatt about the end of the Roman Empire, was a relative critical success but closed after sixty-nine performances on Broadway. The unjustly neglected play *On the March to the Sea* (an expansion of the television play *Honor*), an emotionally searing treatment of the Civil War, never reached Broadway at all, being staged only in Hyde Park and in Germany. *Weekend*

(1968), a political comedy, closed after twenty-one performances and could legitimately be deemed a flop. It seemed as if Vidal's literary work would be restricted to novels and essays. *Washington, D.C.* (1967), a riveting novel of politics that left readers wondering whether it contained a covert portrayal of Jack Kennedy, received generally positive reviews and was also a best-seller, as virtually every Vidal novel thereafter would be.

Vidal's life would change yet again in 1968, when the scandalous *Myra Breckinridge* appeared. Kept under wraps by the publisher, with no advance review copies being sent out, the novel sold prodigiously, especially in paperback, probably because readers sensed a prurience in it that Vidal had inserted only as an element of satire. In this novel Vidal showed that he could appeal to many levels of readership: the novel did not lack supporters among highbrow critics (notably Brigid Brophy) who understood the profound social and political satire at its heart. The notorious film adaptation of 1970, starring Raquel Welch, Rex Reed, and Mae West, only augmented Vidal's reputation as the bad boy of American literature.

But it was another event in 1968 that made Vidal a household name in a nation where few writers become household names. He had been asked by ABC to appear as a commentator, along with William F. Buckley Jr., during the Republican and Democratic national conventions. Vidal himself had already served in a similar capacity during the 1964 conventions, but the 1968 sessions—in a year when the nation was torn by the seemingly unending conflict in Vietnam, when hippies and other liberals were ushering in a new age of sexual, social, and political freedom and conservatives were responding with alarm at the apparent crumbling of American society, and when such a divisive figure as Richard Nixon was running against a Democrat tainted by his association with the Johnson administration's failed Vietnam policy—promised to be more electrifying. They certainly were that: constantly bickering and attempting to trump the other with verbal abuse, Vidal and Buckley descended to name-calling, Vidal referring to Buckley as a "crypto-Nazi" and Buckley lashing out, "You queer!" In competing essays published the next year in *Esquire,* the two writers continued their verbal sparring; but the matter got out of hand when Buckley sued Vidal and *Esquire* for libel. The case dragged on for years and was finally settled out of court; but Buckley continued his misrepresentations of the outcome for years or decades, claiming falsely that the court had sustained a judgment of libel against Vidal, when in fact the libel charge had been dismissed by the presiding judge.

Vidal's second essay collection, *Reflections upon a Sinking Ship* (1969), cemented his reputation as one of America's leading literary and political commentators, especially his notorious essay "The Holy Family" (1967), a jaundiced look at the deification of the Kennedy family. Vidal had been a familiar figure in the Kennedy White House until, for complex reasons, he earned the enmity of Robert F. Kennedy—a circumstance that would have repercussions some years later. The autobiographical novel *Two Sisters* (1970), featuring a transparent reflection of his relations with Anaïs Nin, was received generally unfavorably as a somewhat self-indulgent work in which Vidal was attempting to capitalize on his own celebrity. As early as 1960, in an essay on Norman Mailer, Vidal had rightly identified Mailer as having become famous for being famous; and now some critics felt that Vidal was falling into the same syndrome. A later essay, "Women's Liberation: Feminism and Its Discontents" (1971), seemed to compare Mailer to Charles Manson, and this led to another celebrated literary feud on television, this time on "The Dick Cavett Show." In reality, the actual fisticuffs had occurred offstage prior to the airing of the show, as Mailer had butted Vidal in the head in the dressing room. But Vidal went on stage as if nothing had happened, presenting his usual unflappable self while Mailer seethed and glowered. The episode brought much disrepute to Mailer. (Years later, in 1977, the two authors again came to blows: at a dinner party in New York, Vidal and Mailer exchanged several punches before being separated by other guests.) Mailer and Vidal finally made peace in the 1980s by appearing jointly at writers' conferences and other events. Still later, their mutual hostility to the trend of American politics under Republican administrations would bind them even closer.

Meanwhile, literature was not forgotten. The late 1960s and early 1970s were a period of tremendous fertility for Vidal, who has in fact always maintained a steady flow of publications of remarkably uniform quality. Excluding his final drama, *An Evening with Richard Nixon* (1972), a dismal failure that closed after sixteen performances, Vidal captivated audiences with an omnibus of his essays, *Homage to Daniel Shays* (1972), and especially with the novel *Burr* (1973), which perhaps remains his most accomplished and riveting historical novel. This vivid account of the complex political and military activities of such revered figures as George Washington, Thomas Jefferson, and Alexander Hamilton, all seen through the eyes of the "traitor" Aaron Burr, displayed Vidal's gift at historical re-creation and historical research, and showed once again how he could use the historical novel to make pointed comments on contemporary American life. *Myron* (1974), a sequel to *Myra Breckinridge,* was received poorly, although a few critics felt that it was superior to its predecessor. With the appearance of *1876* (1976), a loose sequel to *Burr,* readers became aware that Vidal was embarking upon an ambitious program whereby the entirety of American history—and, in particular, its seamy underbelly—was exposed by means of historical novels that seamlessly fused real and imaginary figures. It was already becoming evident that Vidal took a dim view of the transformation of the United States from a republic of limited ambitions to an empire whose tentacles would seek to span the world. His disappointment with the increasing militarism and conservatism of his native land was perhaps symbolized by his purchase of a villa near the town of Ravello, Italy, named La Rondinaia, in 1972; it would become his primary residence for more than three decades, although Vidal maintained several homes in the United States and remained an American citizen. But his departure from the United States had no effect on his celebrity—witness the cover story he received from *Time* magazine (1 March 1976), timed for the publication of *1876.*

The later 1970s were highlighted by a scintillating essay collection, *Matters of Fact and of Fiction* (1977), and the unclassifiable novel *Kalki* (1978), in one sense a reprise of *Messiah* as a warning on the dangers of religious fanaticism but in another sense a much darker, even misanthropic work in which Vidal appears to relish the annihilation of the entire human race. Vidal seemed to establish a pattern whereby he would alternate his weighty historical novels with shorter, lighter "inventions" in the antic vein of *Myra Breckinridge.* Years would pass before his next novel, *Creation* (1981)—an immense account of the Persian Cyrus Spitama's search for philosophical truth in the ancient world—appeared, but Vidal remained in the limelight in several ways. One of the more unfortunate ways was his litigation with Truman Capote, who had stated in an interview in *Playgirl* that, years before, Vidal had been physically carried out of the White House by security guards after a contretemps with Robert F. Kennedy. The facts were far otherwise, and Vidal sued Capote for libel. This case, like that with Buckley, dragged on for years, but the ultimate results were again satisfactory to Vidal: Capote, faced with clear evidence that his account was both false and malicious, was forced to apologize publicly. Vidal made one final foray into politics by running a shoestring campaign for the United States Senate in California in 1982, attempting to unseat the Democratic incumbent, Jerry Brown. In spite of low finances and some gaffes during the campaign, Vidal came in a respectable second, polling a far higher percentage of voters than most commentators had predicted.

Few readers knew what to make of the bizarre, surrealistic novel *Duluth* (1983), but by this time Vidal was already working on the novel that perhaps has brought him the greatest admiration of any single work he has written: *Lincoln* (1984). Although some reviewers responded unfavorably, feeling that Vidal had kept too close to the historical sources for this riveting novel of Abraham Lincoln's presidency, the majority of critics praised the novel enthusiastically, and it became one of Vidal's largest and most consistent sellers. Its stylish adaptation as a television miniseries, starring Sam Waterston and Mary Tyler Moore, only enhanced its reputation. The novel was followed by *Empire* (1987), set in the McKinley-Roosevelt period, and by *Hollywood* (1989), in which the administrations of Woodrow Wilson and Warren G. Harding are dissected (the novel had originally been titled *Harding*).

Vidal continued to write essays of increasing weight and substance, gathered in *The Second American Revolution* (1982), *Armageddon?* (1987), and *At Home* (1988). By this time Vidal had come to believe that his work was receiving more sensitive appreciation in England than in his native land, and he established the pattern of allowing much of his work to appear first in the United Kingdom and only later in the United States. *Armageddon?* included several essays that once again brought Vidal into the limelight as a notorious gadfly. By this time confirmed in his liberal political outlook, he addressed the issue of American imperialism pointedly in "Requiem for the American Empire," published in that bastion of liberalism, the *Nation,* for 11 January 1986, and retitled "The Day the American Empire Ran out of Gas" in his essay collections. Heated responses to the essay by a husband-and-wife team of conservative commentators, Norman Podhoretz and Midge Decter, impelled Vidal to write a pungent reply, "The Empire Lovers Strike Back" (*Nation,* 22 March 1986), later titled "A Cheerful Response." Vidal had already accused Decter and other conservatives of prejudice against homosexuals in the essay "*Some* Jews and *the* Gays" (*Nation,* 14 November 1981; later titled "Pink Triangle and Yellow Star"), but the new essay, accusing these figures of putting their allegiance to Israel ahead of their devotion to the United States, incited predictable accusations of anti-Semitism, although Vidal was defended by numerous commentators who objected to many American Jews' reflexive accusations of anti-Semitism directed at anyone who criticized the actions of the Israeli government and of those who supported it. The contretemps played itself out in a wide variety of newspapers and magazines, Podhoretz later writing a long-winded article in which he expressed dismay that only a relatively small number of intellectuals condemned Vidal. Buckley got into the act with a tendentious book, *In Search of Anti-Semitism* (1992), in which he predictably whitewashed conservative commentators of anti-Semitism but condemned Vidal.

Vidal's work in the media continued apace, although somewhat more sporadically than in the 1950s or 1960s. He developed a two-part documentary about Venice, aired as *Vidal in Venice,* but in the subsequent book (1985) he wrote only the preface; the rest of the book was ghostwritten by his "editor," George Armstrong. In 1987 Vidal worked on the film *The Sicilian,* based on a novel by Mario Puzo; but, denied screenwriting credit, he took the unprecedented step of suing the Writers' Guild, and eventually prevailed. The film *Dimenticare Palermo,* shown in the United States as *The Palermo Connection,* passed almost entirely unnoticed. Two television films, *Dress Gray* (1986) and *Gore Vidal's Billy the Kid* (1989), received mixed reviews. In 1992 he took the remarkable step of appearing in a major acting role in the film *Bob Roberts.* Although Vidal had appeared as a bit player in films from as early as 1946, this was his first significant role, and his performance met with considerable favor. One of his most recent works in film is a five-minute pseudo-trailer, *Trailer for a Remake of Gore Vidal's Caligula* (2005), a tongue-in-cheek rebuke of the pornographic excesses that had caused him to remove his name from the film *Caligula* (1979), which was to have been titled *Gore Vidal's Caligula.*

The year 1992 also saw the publication of three smallish books by Vidal: *Screening History,* a series of lectures given at Harvard telling of his fascination with film and its significance in providing Americans with their view of history; *Live from Golgotha,* an outrageous satire on Christianity that evoked predictable howls from the pious, including Pat Robertson, who equated Vidal with the Antichrist, much to Vidal's delight; and *The Decline and Fall of the American Empire,* a slim collection of essays that would herald Vidal's later work as a political pamphleteer. The next year saw the appearance of *United States: Essays 1952–1992,* an immense gathering of Vidal's collected essays (although many essays from previous collections were excluded, along with dozens of uncollected essays and reviews published in magazines and newspapers) that emphatically established Vidal as the premier American essayist of his era. Two years later the memoir *Palimpsest* appeared, also to nearly universal acclaim. Vidal had earlier protested that he would never write an autobiography; but he appears to have been inspired to do so by the failure of Walter Clemons, a journalist deemed his authorized biographer, to produce a biography even after years of research. That biography would later be produced by the veteran Fred Kaplan.

The appearance of the collected essays and the memoir created the impression that Vidal, by this time seventy years of age, was attempting a kind of summation of his literary career—an impression fostered by the publication of *The Essential Gore Vidal* (1999), a volume assembled by Kaplan as a companion to his biography. But Vidal was by no means ready to retire, either literarily or personally. Although his later essays became increasingly elegiac, as he devoted himself to recollections of the numerous friends and colleagues who had died—Tennessee Williams, Christopher Isherwood, Anthony Burgess—Vidal himself was still vigorous and productive. *The Smithsonian Institution* (1998) demonstrated that the imaginative vitality of his "inventions" remained high: in a sense, this novel could be said to represent a fusion of his "inventions" and his historical novels, as it is set largely in the early years of the Second World War. *The Golden Age* (2000), probably Vidal's last novel, encapsulates his long-held view that the five years following the end of World War II represented, in America, a "golden age" both politically and literarily—an age abruptly ended when Truman and his successors put the United States on a permanent war footing and rendered social amelioration difficult by immense military expenditures.

During the past decade Vidal has become an increasingly outspoken critic of American foreign and domestic policy. The small pamphlet *The American Presidency* (1998) is an expansion of a British television program in which Vidal casts a skeptical eye on certain presidents who, in his judgment, unwisely fostered the growth (and later decay) of the American empire. His latest essay collection, *The Last Empire* (2001), underscores these concerns, also devoting much space to the ill-fated Republican effort to impeach President Bill Clinton. The terrorist attacks of 2001, and the subsequent efforts by the George W. Bush administration to combat terrorism by poorly conceived military adventures and a restriction of civil liberties, brought Vidal to a white-hot pitch of indignation, exhibited in the volumes *Perpetual War for Perpetual Peace* (2002), *Dreaming War* (2002), and *Imperial America* (2004). Vidal in turn evoked much indignation by expressing guarded sympathy for the political views of Timothy McVeigh, convicted of masterminding the Oklahoma City bombing of 1995. Vidal incurred still more anger by accepting McVeigh's invitation to witness his execution in 2001, although Vidal did not in fact attend the event. While some commentators—not all from the right—have accused Vidal of becoming addicted to conspiracy theories and of hurling wild accusations against the Bush administration, it can perhaps be said that, while he is often wrong on particulars, his general view—notably that Bush and his cohorts have used the terrorist attacks as an excuse to make an unprecedented, and perhaps unconstitutional, grab for presidential power and to advance radically conservative causes that have little to do with terrorism—appears sound and, in fact, receives increasing corroboration with each passing day.

In early 2003, because of health considerations, Vidal and his longtime companion Howard Austen at last departed from their villa in Ravello; they settled full-time in the Los Angeles area, where Austen died later in 2003. Aside from his political pamphlets, Vidal has written the rather slight *Inventing a Nation* (2003), a cursory survey of the presidencies of Washington, Adams, and Jefferson, and a follow-up to *Palimpsest,* entitled *Point to Point Navigation* (2006), breezily covering the last fifty or so years of his life. His essays have decreased in frequency but not in pungency, as his witty dissection of John Updike ("Rabbit's Own Burrow") and his careful analyses of James Purdy and others attest. Most of his political essays now appear in the *Nation,* and Vidal has always been generous in writing prefaces, introductions, or afterwords to books by other writers with whose theses—whether they be literary, sexual, or political—he agrees. If it is too early to assess Vidal's ultimate place in American literature and thought, there is little reason to doubt Anthony J. Hall's recent evaluation that "Vidal will emerge in the intellectual histories of the future as one of the most original and enduring figures of 20th-century Americana."

———

As has been suggested above, the majority of criticism devoted to Vidal over the past half-century or more takes the form of reviews, some slight but many quite substantial. Because Vidal has for so long occupied a unique status as both a popular best-seller and a writer of depth and substance, his work has been reviewed by illustrious critics in both the United States and England, ranging from Leslie A. Fiedler, Mark Schorer, Edward Wagenknecht, Muriel Spark, and Robert Penn Warren in the 1940s and 1950s to Peter Ackroyd, Brigid Brophy, Angela Carter, Martin Amis, Stephen Spender, William H. Pritchard, C. P. Snow, V. S. Pritchett, Edmund White, Clive James, Mary Renault, Thomas M. Disch, Denis Donoghue, and Frank Kermode in the 1970s, 1980s, and 1990s. And yet, certain trends in these reviews are worth noting. Vidal and others are probably correct in believing that homophobia was a factor in some of the hostile reviews of *The City and the Pillar* and later works, even those without a homosexual element. Vidal has stated that the novel so outraged Orville Prescott, the reviewer for the *New York Times,* that he refused even to read, let alone review, another work by Vidal. (Vidal's books, however, were consistently reviewed in the *New York Times Book Review.*) Famously hostile reviews of some of his plays by Robert Brustein may have to do with Brustein's resentment of Vidal's celebrity status, something that other commentators have regarded as an excuse not to take his work seriously. It is particularly noticeable that conservative journals such as the *National Review,* the *American Spectator,* and the *New Criterion* persistently single out Vidal's books for malicious censure, even those (such as *United States* and *Palimpsest*) that were reviewed with unequivocal approval elsewhere. Religious or religiously based journals, such as *America,* the *Catholic World,* and even the blandly titled *Best Sellers* (whose reviews were written largely by Jesuits), display an analogous prejudice against Vidal for his outspoken atheism. In this context, it is interesting to note that reviews in liberally oriented journals, such as the *New York Review of Books* or the *Nation,* tend not only to be more penetrating and insightful, but are by no means uniformly adulatory; the *Nation,* for example, published a harsh review of *Lincoln* by Nicholas von Hoffman.

Vidal has not been entirely well served by those who have written monographs on his work. On the whole they tend to be superficial and cursory, and of course become quickly outdated. Most of these monographs, when they are not mere surveys of his entire oeuvre, tend to focus rather mechanically either on Vidal's writings on sex or on his historical novels. Vidal himself has spoken somewhat disparagingly of Fred Kaplan's biography, feeling that Kaplan, for all his diligence in producing a detailed chronicle of his life, has failed to understand his work or his motives as a writer and thinker. A full-scale portrayal of Vidal, uniting biography with literary and political criticism, has yet to be written.

In spite of Vidal's frequently repeated condemnation of the pedantries and obscurities of academic criticism (especially in the essay "The Hacks of Academe"), which in his judgment has helped to destroy the American novel, Vidal has been discussed at length in academic journals. He has perhaps not received the volume of criticism that other such writers as Norman Mailer or Toni Morrison have received, but he is certainly a presence. Vidal's own role as a leading literary and cultural critic may have intimidated others, as they perhaps fear verbal reprisals for comments at which he takes umbrage. Vidal has certainly engendered any amount of commentary from his many literary friends and colleagues, and from the biographers of those colleagues; much of this constitutes the raw material of biography and is accordingly of considerable value. Vidal has predictably become the subject of dissertations, given his role in the currently fashionable confluence of literature and gender, but little of this work is of lasting value, with the rare exception of the work of Heather Neilson, who has gone on to write several penetrating articles on Vidal.

Whatever the ultimate place of Gore Vidal in American and world literature, there is no denying that at least a small proportion of the criticism of his work is penetrating, insightful, and profound. Vidal's multifaceted talents as novelist, essayist, playwright, screenwriter, actor, and political commentator make an exhaustive or comprehensive assessment of his achievement a matter of great difficulty, but certain phases of his work and thought have been treated illuminatingly by those who have managed to put aside literary, sexual, and political prejudices and gauge his work as a contribution to the culture of which it is a part. Later students of Vidal's writing can build upon this scholarship, which lays the groundwork for a proper understanding of what Gore Vidal has meant to his contemporaries and what he will mean to future generations.

Explanatory Notes

This bibliography has been compiled in a substantially different manner from that of the previous Vidal bibliography, by Robert J. Stanton (see III.A.2), especially in regard to Vidal criticism. Some notes on the methodologies used in compiling this bibliography, and on the nature of the information to be found in it, are here provided.

In Part I (Works by Gore Vidal), all items in sections A (Books and Pamphlets), B (Short Stories and Poems), C (Essays and Reviews), D (Plays), E (Screenplays), and F (Published Letters) are arranged chronologically by date of first publication or production or screening, which in all likelihood roughly corresponds to date of composition. In A, all separate publications by Vidal are included. Lowercase letters indicate a new edition; numbers indicate a new printing within an edition. Since the majority of Vidal's books appeared after he had become a best-selling author, it has been very difficult to ascertain the exact number and date of the printings of his various books, especially the paperback editions of such novels as *Myra Breckinridge* or *Burr.* Online book catalogs have been of some help in this regard, but the results must be deemed tentative. As this is a bibliography for students and scholars rather than collectors, I have not thought it useful to provide detailed information on bindings, dust jackets, and other collectors' "points."

In B, Vidal's relatively few poems have been annotated to indicate stanzas and lines; no specific annotation has been made for his short stories. Also included in this section are extracts from Vidal's novels appearing in books or periodicals. In C, aside from essays and reviews (the distinction between these two categories being itself problematical in many cases), Vidal's prefaces, introductions, and forewords to books by himself and others are listed, as well as contributions to symposia and other nonfictional miscellany. All items are annotated to give an idea of their content. In D, a distinction has been made between Vidal's theatrical plays (most, but not all, staged on Broadway) and his television plays. Information has been given on the leading cast members of premieres where known; for some of his television plays this information is not known. Information on revivals of his stage plays has been given, although no doubt his more popular plays have been revived in lesser venues on any number of occasions not listed here. Unpublished, unstaged, or unbroadcast plays are not listed (some can be found in section G). In F, the letters are listed in order of publication, not order of composition; most of these are letters of comment to reviews of Vidal's books, or letters commenting on other letters (listed in III.E) by those commenting on Vidal's essays and reviews. No book of Vidal's letters has yet appeared.

In G (Manuscripts), manuscripts by Vidal in all known public repositories are listed. The repositories are listed alphabetically by state, and by city within a state; overseas repositories are listed at the end. The major Vidal collection, of course, is at the Houghton Library, Harvard University; this collection includes separate drafts of many of Vidal's works, but no attempt to enumerate these drafts has been made here. The repository has not been fully catalogued, and all facets of it may not be available to researchers.

In H (Media Adaptations), information is supplied on adaptations of Vidal's works as recorded books, e-books, film (including videocasettes and DVDs), television, theater, and recordings. Section I (Vidal in the Media) should be considered highly preliminary. In this section an attempt has been made to enumerate Vidal's appearances as an actor in films and television (including his serving as host or narrator of talk shows and documentaries), media programs specifically about Vidal, filmed or taped interviews, and appearances on radio. Given that, since at least 1960, Vidal has been a regular fixture in film, television, and radio, it is likely that the number of such appearances is substantially greater than what is listed here; but current reference works in film, television, and radio (including online databases such as imdb.com and tv.com) are not sufficiently detailed or exhaustive to allow for a comprehensive tabulation.

In Part II (Gore Vidal in Translation), section A lists books by Vidal in languages other than English, arranged alphabetically by language and chronologically within the language; section B lists contributions to books and periodicals. The latter list should be regarded as preliminary, as Vidal has probably appeared more widely in foreign periodicals than it is currently possible to enumerate.

Part III (Works about Gore Vidal) has been compiled with the purpose of assisting students and scholars of Vidal's life, work, and thought, both in regard to arrangement and in regard to annotation. In A (Bibliographies), the two bibliographies of Vidal are listed. In B (News Items and Encyclopedias), news items about Vidal are listed; these items are distinguished from those in section E by their relative lack of critical analysis and their reporting in a generally factual manner of Vidal's activities or of the publication of his work. In this section, reports pertaining to Vidal's two campaigns for public office are listed. Encyclopedias or other reference works including Vidal are listed in the second part of the section, but are not annotated, since the great majority of them supply only the surface facts pertaining to Vidal's life and work.

A case could be made that Vidal's interviews (section C) should be regarded as works by him; but since they contain considerable self-commentary on his life and work, and also substantial writing by the interviewer, I have decided to place them among works about Vidal. The interviews are arranged alphabetically by the name of the interviewer; included here are Vidal's two "self-interviews." For each interview, a brief synopsis of the major topics covered is supplied; many of the interviews, of course, cover the same ground over and over again. In D (Books about Vidal), monographs, collections of essays, and collections of interviews are included; reviews of these books are listed, but the reviews are not annotated, even though a few of them are quite substantial. The most prominent book about Vidal is Fred Kaplan's biography (D.10), which was no doubt reviewed very widely in newspapers around the country; but these reviews are now difficult to locate. Section E (Criticism in Books and Periodicals) includes essays on Vidal in academic journals and general-interest magazines, letters commenting on Vidal's essays and reviews, portions of books discussing Vidal, books or articles by Vidal's friends and associates discussing him, and the like. In a few cases, I have determined that some interviews contain so much discussion of Vidal by the interviewer that they constitute a critical article rather than an interview. Vidal, as is well known, was acquainted with many leading literary, social, and political figures of his day, and many biographies of these figures mention him either briefly or extensively; only the most prominent of these biographies, containing substantial discussion of Vidal, have been listed.

Section F (Book Reviews) is the largest single section of this bibliography; and, as book reviews still constitute the most voluminous facet of criticism of Vidal's work, these reviews have been annotated with some care. Reviews are listed chronologically by the book reviewed and alphabetically within a given book; unsigned reviews are placed at the end. Only reviews of some substance and length have been annotated; these annotations appear in paragraph form following the reviews for each book, with the author's name printed in boldface for ease of identification. No distinction is made between reviews of the first edition of a work and reviews of a later reprint. In this section are included reviews of the premieres (and revivals) of Vidal's plays, as well as book publications of the plays. The term "multiple review" is used when a review discusses works by several authors; it can therefore be assumed that the discussion of the Vidal work constitutes only a portion of the total review. Reviews in which several books by Vidal himself are covered are listed separately under each work reviewed. It is worth noting that the online edition of the *Times Literary Supplement* now identifies the authors of many (but not all) of the reviews that, during most of its tenure, appeared anonymously.

Section G (Media Reviews) lists reviews of films, television shows, and other media programs for which Vidal was the author or coauthor of the screenplay (no reviews of the films *Ben-Hur, Night of the Generals,* or *The Sicilian* are listed, since Vidal's contribution to the screenplays was not credited at the time, so that reviews would not include any substantive discussion of him), reviews of film or other media adaptations of his work (e.g., the film of *Myra Breckinridge*), and the like.

Section H (Websites) is self-explanatory. There is only one website pertaining to Vidal that is of any consequence, but some others are of ancillary importance. Section I (Academic Papers) lists master's theses and doctoral dissertations devoted in whole or in part to Vidal. Circumstances have prevented the examination of more than a few of these items, and so they are not annotated. Section J (Miscellany) lists such things as Vidal's appearance as a character in books by other writers and other information that cannot conveniently be placed elsewhere.

I am grateful to David E. Schultz for his skill in preparing the camera-ready pages of this book. I have received assistance from Massimo Berruti, Robert N. Bloch, Kitty Chibnik (Avery Library, Columbia University), Edouard L. Desrochers (Assistant Librarian and Academy Archivist, Phillips Exeter Academy), Stefan Dziemianowicz, Marco Frenschkowski, Philippe Gindre, John Haefele, Fred Kaplan, T. E. D. Klein, Harry B. Kloman, Rob Latham, Sean McLachlan, Leslie A. Morris (Houghton Library, Harvard University), and Monica Wheeler (Stanford University). Most of my research was conducted at the Cornell University Libraries, and I have done other research at the New York Public Library, the Library of Congress, and the libraries of Brown University, Ithaca College, Johns Hopkins University, and the University of Buffalo.

I. Works by Gore Vidal

A. Books and Pamphlets

1.   *Williwaw.*
     a.   New York: E. P. Dutton, [April] 1946.
     b.   New York: Editions for the Armed Services, 1946.
     c.1. New York: New American Library, 1953 (as *Dangerous Voyage*).
     c.2. New York: New American Library, 1968.
     c.3. New York: New American Library, 1978.
     d.1. St. Albans, UK: Panther Books, 1965.
     d.2. St. Albans, UK: Panther Books, 1968.
     d.3. St. Albans, UK: Panther Books, 1970.
     d.4. St. Albans, UK: Panther Books, 1976.
     e.   London: Heinemann, 1970.
     f.1. New York: Ballantine Books, 1978.
     f.2. New York: Ballantine Books, 1986.
     f.3. New York: Ballantine Books, 1992.
     g.   San Francisco: Arion Press, 1996.
     h.   Chicago: University of Chicago Press, 2003.
     i.1. London: Abacus, 2003.
     i.2. London: Abacus, 2004.
         Vidal's first novel, written when he was nineteen, dealing with tensions aboard a navy boat during World War II. "Williwaw" is the Eskimo word for a storm at sea.

2.   *In a Yellow Wood.*
     a.   New York: E. P. Dutton, [January] 1947.
     b.   London: New English Library, 1967.
     c.   London: Heinemann, 1979.
     d.   St. Albans, UK: Panther Books, 1980.
     e.1. London: Abacus, 2004.
     e.2. London: Abacus, 2005.
     e.3. London: Abacus, 2006.
         Vidal's second novel, dealing with the life of Robert Holton, a stockbroker in New City, and his personal and professional involvements. One scene, describing a gay club visited by Robert and his girlfriend Carla, anticipates Vidal's later work.

3.   *The City and the Pillar.*
     a.1. New York: E. P. Dutton, [January] 1948.
     a.2. New York: E. P. Dutton, 1948.
     a.3. New York: E. P. Dutton, 1948.
     a.4. New York: E. P. Dutton, 1948.
     a.5. New York: E. P. Dutton, 1948.
     a.6. New York: E. P. Dutton, 1948.
     b.   New York: Grosset & Dunlap, 1948.
     c.1. New York: New American Library, 1948.
     c.2. New York: New American Library, 1950.
     c.3. New York: New American Library, 1955.
     c.4. New York: New American Library, 1961.
     d.1. London: John Lehmann, 1949.
     d.2. London: John Lehmann, 1950.
     d.3. London: John Lehmann, 1950.
     d.4. London: John Lehmann, 1950.

Revised edition:
e.   New York: E. P. Dutton, 1965.
f.   New York: New American Library, 1965.
g.   London: Heinemann, 1965.
h.   London: New English Library, 1967.
i.1. St. Albans, UK: Panther Books, 1972.
i.2. St. Albans, UK: Panther Books, 1973.
i.3. St. Albans, UK: Panther Books, 1978.
j.1. New York: Ballantine Books, 1979.
j.2. New York: Ballantine Books, 1986.
j.3. New York: Ballantine Books, 1992.
k.   London: Andre Deutsch, 1994.
l.1. London: Abacus, 1997.
l.2. London: Abacus, 1998.
m.   New York: InsightOutBooks, 2001.
n.   New York: Vintage International, 2003.

Vidal's third novel and his first best-seller, a controversial study of Jim Willard, whose homosexual experience as a teenager with a close friend, Bob Ford, colors his entire life. He later enters the navy, becomes the lover of a celebrated movie star, and, after finally reuniting with Bob (who has now married and forgotten all about his gay episode), kills him after being rejected by him. In the revised edition (e.) Vidal, aside from rewriting the prose throughout, eliminates this sensational ending. This edition includes the essay "Sex and the Law" (C.62) and an afterword (= "*The City and the Pillar* After Twenty Years" (C.63). Vidal later admitted that the general scenario describes his own relations with his teenage friend Jimmie Trimble.

4.   *The Season of Comfort.*
a.   New York: E. P. Dutton, [January] 1949.
b.   London: Andre Deutsch, 1996.
c.   London: Abacus, 1997.

Vidal's fourth novel and perhaps his first historical novel, as it begins in 1928. It concerns the family of William Hawkins, a former vice president, and focuses ultimately on the relations between his daughter, Charlotte, and her son, William—an echo of Vidal's troubled relationship with his own mother.

5.   *A Search for the King: A 12th Century Legend.*
a.   New York: E. P. Dutton, [January] 1950.
b.   London: New English Library, 1967.
c.1. New York: Pyramid Books, 1968.
c.2. New York: Pyramid Books, 1973.
d.   New York: Ballantine Books, 1978.
e.   London: Heinemann, 1979.
f.   St. Albans, UK: Panther Books, 1980.
g.   London: Abacus, 1993.

Vidal's fifth novel and a strong departure from his previous work, an almost fairytale-like account of the troubadour Blondel and his involvement with Richard the Lion-Hearted. Supernatural episodes involving vampires and unicorns lend an unwonted tone of fantasy to the work.

6.   *A Star's Progress* (as by Katherine Everard).
a.   New York: E. P. Dutton, [February] 1950.
b.   New York: Pyramid Books, 1950 (as *Cry Shame!*).

The first of Vidal's pseudonymous novels, a work he has only recently admitted to writing. It is the story of Graziella Serrano, who later adopts the stage name Grace Carter and becomes a celebrated movie star but never achieves happiness and dies by suicide. Vidal was compelled to write several pseudonymous novels because the hostile reception of *The City and the Pillar* made it difficult for him to publish work under his own name.

7. *Dark Green, Bright Red.*
    a.   New York: E. P. Dutton, [August] 1950.
    b.   London: John Lehmann, 1950.
    c.   London: New English Library, 1968.
    d.   New York: New American Library, 1968.
    e.   New York: Ballantine Books, 1978.
    f.   London: Heinemann, 1979.
    g.   St. Albans, UK: Panther Books, 1980.
    h.   London: Andre Deutsch, 1995.
    i.1. London: Abacus, 2005.
    i.2. London: Abacus, 2006.
        A novel about political chicanery in an unnamed Latin American country, where a general, Jorge
        Alvarez, a dictator who had been forced out of power, wishes to regain control and is supported
        by an American corporation. The novel is a reflection of Vidal's brief stay in Guatemala.

8. *The Judgment of Paris.*
    a.   New York: E. P. Dutton, [February] 1952.
    b.   London: Heinemann, 1953.
    c.   New York: Ballantine Books, 1961.
    Revised edition:
    d.   Boston: Little, Brown, 1965.
    e.   New York: New American Library, 1965.
    f.   London: New English Library, 1966.
    g.   London: Heinemann, 1968.
    h.1. New York: Ballantine Books, 1978.
    h.2. New York: Ballantine Books, 1984.
    i.   St. Albans, UK: Panther Books, 1984.
        Vidal's seventh novel (under his own name), about Philip Warren, a Harvard graduate who
        decides to spend a year traveling in Europe and encounters three women—Regina Durham, a
        married woman; Sophia Oliver, an archeologist; and Anna Morris, another married woman—
        who exemplify the character traits of the three goddesses (Hera, Athena, and Aphrodite)
        involved in the Greek myth of the judgment of Paris.

9. *Death in the Fifth Position* (as by Edgar Box).
    a.   New York: E. P. Dutton, [May] 1952.
    b.1. New York: New American Library, 1953.
    b.2. New York: New American Library, 1957.
    b.3. New York: New American Library, 1964.
    c.   London: Heinemann, 1954.
    d.   London: Ace Books, 1960.
    e.1. London: New English Library, 1965.
    e.2. London: New English Library, 1968.
    f.   New York: Bantam Books, 1972.
    g.1. New York: Vintage Books, 1979.
    g.2. New York: Vintage Books, 1982.
    h.   London: Heinemann, 1979.
    i.   London: Granada, 1982.
    j.   Bath, UK: Chivers Press, 1984.
    k.1. New York: Armchair Detective Library, 1991.
    k.2. New York: Armchair Detective Library, 1991.
        Vidal's first detective novel, introducing Peter Cutler Sargeant II, a public relations consultant
        who investigates several murders in a ballet company in New York.

10. *Death Before Bedtime* (as by Edgar Box).
    a.   New York: E. P. Dutton, [March] 1953.

    b.   London: Heinemann, 1954.
    c.1. New York: New American Library, 1954.
    c.2. New York: New American Library, 1958.
    c.3. New York: New American Library, 1964.
    d.   London: Ace Books, 1960.
    e.   London: New English Library, 1965.
    f.   New York: Bantam Books, 1973.
    g.   New York: Vintage Books, 1979.
    h.   London: Heinemann, 1979.
    i.   London: Granada, 1982.
    j.   London: Chivers Press, 1985.
    k.1. New York: Armchair Detective Library, 1990.
    k.2. New York: Armchair Detective Library, 1991.
    Vidal's second detective novel, in which Peter Cutler Sargeant II investigates the death of Leander Rhodes, a conservative senator who was contemplating a run for the presidency.

11.   *Thieves Fall Out* (as by Cameron Kay).
    a.   Greenwich, CT: Fawcett, 1953.
    Probably Vidal's scarcest work, a pseudonymous novel about Peter Wells, who becomes enmeshed in a convoluted adventure in Egypt involving smuggling. Vidal wrote the novel by dictaphone.

12.   *Messiah.*
    a.   New York: E. P. Dutton, [February] 1954.
    b.1. New York: Ballantine Books, 1954.
    b.2. New York: Ballantine Books, 1961.
    c.   London: Heinemann, 1955.
    Revised edition:
    d.   Boston: Little, Brown, 1965.
    e.1. New York: Ballantine Books, 1965.
    e.2. New York: Ballantine Books, 1968.
    e.3. New York: Ballantine Books, 1979.
    e.4. New York: Ballantine Books, 1984.
    e.5. New York: Ballantine Books, 1987.
    f.   London: New English Library, 1966.
    g.   London: Heinemann, 1968.
    h.   New York: Bantam Books, 1972.
    i.1. St. Albans, UK: Panther Books, 1973.
    i.2. St. Albans, UK: Panther Books, 1977.
    j.   Boston: Gregg Press, 1980 (with introduction by Elizabeth A. Lynn).
    k.   London: Abacus, 1993.
    l.   New York: Penguin, 1998.
    Vidal's eighth novel, about John Cave, a charismatic figure who devises a new religion that ultimately overwhelms the world but proves to be a death cult. The novel is told as a flashback by Eugene Luther (a name coined from Vidal's own name), a former follower of Cave's.

13.   *Death Likes It Hot* (as by Edgar Box).
    a.   New York: E. P. Dutton, [March] 1954.
    b.1. New York: New American Library, 1955.
    b.2. New York: New American Library, n.d.
    b.3. New York: New American Library, 1958.
    b.4. New York: New American Library, 1964.
    c.   London: Heinemann, 1955.
    d.   London: Ace Books, 1960.

  e.1. London: New English Library, 1965.

  e.2. London: New English Library, 1968.

  f. New York: Bantam Books, 1973.

  g. New York: Vintage Books, 1979.

  h. London: Granada, 1982.

  i. London: Chivers Press, 1985.

  j.1. New York: Armchair Detective Library, 1990.

  j.2. New York: Armchair Detective Library, 1991.

   Vidal's third and final detective novel, in which Sargeant investigates murders at the East Hampton home of a wealthy heiress.

14. *Best Television Plays* (edited by Gore Vidal).

  a.1. New York: Ballantine Books, 1956.

  a.2. New York: Ballantine Books, 1963.

  a.3. New York: Ballantine Books, 1965.

   Contents: *The Mother* by Paddy Chayefsky; *Thunder on Sycamore Street* by Reginald Rose; *My Lost Saints* by Tad Mosel; *Man on the Mountaintop* by Robert Alan Aurthur; *A Young Lady of Property* by Horton Foote; *The Strike* by Rod Serling; *The Rabbit Trap* by J. P. Miller; *Visit to a Small Planet* by Gore Vidal (D.ii.11). For the introduction that was to have appeared in this volume, see C.9.

15. *Visit to a Small Planet and Other Television Plays.*

  a. Boston: Little, Brown, [December] 1956.

   Contents: "Foreword" (= "Writing Plays for Television" [C.10]); *Dark Possession* (D.ii.2); *A Sense of Justice* (D.ii.6); *Summer Pavilion* (D.ii.10); *Visit to a Small Planet* (D.ii.11); *The Death of Billy the Kid* (D.ii.13); *Smoke* (D.ii.3); *Barn Burning* (D.ii.4); *The Turn of the Screw* (D.ii.7).

16. *A Thirsty Evil: Seven Short Stories.*

  a. New York: Zero Press, [December] 1956.

  b. London: Heinemann, 1958.

  c.1. New York: New American Library, 1958.

  c.2. New York: New American Library, 1968.

  d. London: Ace Books, 1960.

  e. London: New English Library, 1967.

  f. Freeport, NY: Books for Libraries Press, 1970.

  g.1. St. Albans, UK: Panther Books, 1974.

  g.2. St. Albans, UK: Panther Books, 1978.

  h. San Francisco: Gay Sunshine Press, 1981.

  i. Helsinki: Eurographica, 1985 (as *The Ladies in the Library and Other Stories*).

  j. London: Andre Deutsch, 1994.

  k. London: Abacus, 2004.

  l. London: Little, Brown, 2005.

  m. New York: Carroll & Graf, 2006 (as *Clouds and Eclipses: The Collected Short Stories*).

   Contents: "Three Stratagems" (B.10); "The Robin" (B.15); "A Moment of Green Laurel" (B.14); "The Zenner Trophy" (B.16); "Erlinda and Mr. Coffin" (B.11); "Pages from an Abandoned Journal" (B.17); "The Ladies in the Library" (B.13). Vidal's only collection of short stories. In e., the essay "On Pornography" (C.64) is included. In m., "Clouds and Eclipses" (B.31) is added.

17. *Visit to a Small Planet: A Comedy Akin to a Vaudeville.*

  a. Boston: Little, Brown, [January] 1957.

  b. New York: New American Library, 1960.

  c.1. New York: Dramatists Play Service, 1959.

  c.2. New York: Dramatists Play Service, 1987.

   Contents: "Preface" (= *"Visit to a Small Planet"* [C.12]); *Visit to a Small Planet* (D.i.1). An expansion of Vidal's television play (included in A.15) into a stage play.

18.   *The Best Man: A Play about Politics.*
      a.   Boston: Little, Brown, [August] 1960.
      b.   New York: Dramatists Play Service, 1962.
      c.   New York: New American Library, 1964.
      Revised edition:
      d.1. New York: Dramatists Play Service, 1977.
      d.2. New York: Dramatists Play Service, 1996.
      d.3. New York: Dramatists Play Service, 1998.
      d.4. New York: Dramatists Play Service, 2001.
             Contents: "Notes on *The Best Man"* (= "A Note on *The Best Man"*); *The Best Man* (D.i.2).
             Vidal's most substantial and most successful stage play.

19.   *Romulus.*
      a.1. New York: Dramatists Play Service, [January] 1962.
      a.2. New York: Dramatists Play Service, 1990.
      b.   New York: Grove Press, 1966 (as *Romulus: The Broadway Adaptation*).
             A play about the fall of the Roman Empire. In b., Friedrich Duerrenmatt's play *Romulus the*
             Great (translated by Gerhard Nellhaus), of which Vidal's is an adaptation, is included.

20.   *Three: Williwaw; A Thirsty Evil; Julian the Apostate.*
      a.   New York: New American Library, June 1962.
             Contents: *Williwaw* (A.1); *A Thirsty Evil* (A.16) ["Three Strategems" (B.10); "The Robin"
             (B.15); "A Moment of Green Laurel" (B.14); "The Zenner Trophy" (B.16); "Erlinda and Mr.
             Coffin" (B.11); "Pages from an Abandoned Journal" (B.17); "The Ladies in the Library" (B.13)];
             "Julian the Apostate" (B.19). An omnibus including Vidal's first novel, his collection of short
             stories, and an early segment of the novel *Julian* (A.23).

21.   *Rocking the Boat.*
      a.   Boston: Little, Brown, [July] 1962.
      b.   London: Heinemann, 1963.
      c.   New York: Dell, 1963.
             Contents: "Foreword" (C.39); "John Kennedy: A Translation for the English" (C.26); "Barry
             Goldwater: A Chat" (C.29); "The House Un-American Activities Committee" (C.31); "HUAC
             Revisited" (C.35); "Closing the Civilization Gap" (C.32); "The Future of Conservatism" (C.36);
             "Love Love Love" (C.18); "Eugene O'Neill's *A Touch of the Poet"* (C.16); "Bernard Shaw's
             Heartbreak House" (C.21); "The Commercialites" (C.20); "The Couch in the Shrine: Dore
             Schary and Paddy Chayefsky" (C.22); "Strangers at Breakfast: *Five Finger Exercise"* (C.24);
             "Ladders to Heaven: Novelists and Critics of the 1940's" (C.6); "A Note on the Novel" (C.8);
             "The Demotic Novel: John Dos Passos" (C.27); Norman Mailer: The Angels Are White" (C.23);
             "Carson McCullers's *Clock without Hands"* (C.33); "In the Shadow of the Scales: Friedrich
             Duerrenmatt" (C.17); "Book Report: Robert Penn Warren's *Band of Angels"* (C.7); "The
             Making of a Hero and a Legend: Richard Hillary" (C.2); "Footnote to the Dreyfus Case" (C.11);
             "Robert Graves and the Twelve Caesars" (C.41); "Social Climbing, According to the Books"
             (C.28); "Two Immoralists: Orville Prescott and Ayn Rand" (C.30); "Evelyn Waugh" (C.37);
             "The Unrocked Boat: Satire in the 1950's" (C.14); "Writing Plays for Television" (C.10);
             "Putting On *Visit to a Small Planet"* (C.12); "A Note on *The Best Man"* (C.25); "Notes to the
             Chapters." Vidal's first collection of essays, gathering many (but not all) of the essays and
             reviews he had written between 1952 and 1962.

22.   *Three Plays.*
      a.   London: William Heinemann, [October] 1962.
             Contents: "Preface to the British Edition" (C.43); *Visit to a Small Planet* (D.i.1); "[Preface to]
             On the March to the Sea" (C.44); *On the March to the Sea* (D.i.3); "Preface to *The Best Man"* (=
             "A Note on *The Best Man"* [C.25]); *The Best Man* (D.i.2); "Love, Love, Love" (C.18);
             "American Preface to *Visit to a Small Planet"* (= "*Visit to a Small Planet"* [C.12]).

23.   *Julian.*
   a.   Boston: Little, Brown, [May] 1964.
   b.   London: Heinemann, 1964.
   c.   New York: New American Library, 1965.
   d.   London: Reprint Society, 1965.
   e.   London: New English Library, 1966.
   f.   New York: Modern Library, 1970.
   g.1. St. Albans, UK: Panther Books, 1972.
   g.2. St. Albans, UK: Panther Books, 1976.
   h.   Geneva: Edito-Service, 1974.
   i.   New York: Vintage Books, 1977.
   j.   Franklin Center, PA: Franklin Library, 1981.
   k.   New York: Modern Library, 1984.
   l.1. New York: Ballantine Books, 1985.
   l.2. New York: Ballantine Books, 1991.
   m.   London: Abacus, 1993.
   n.   New York: Vintage International, 2003.
      Vidal's ninth novel and the first since *Messiah* (A.12), written over several years and after Vidal had spent nearly a decade working in television and theater. An impressive novel of ancient Rome, focusing on the emperor (r. 363–365 C.E.) who attempted to stop the spread of Christianity. It is chiefly told from the standpoint of Libanius and Priscus, two colleagues of Julian who are editing his memoirs after his death.

24.   *Washington, D.C.*
   a.   Boston: Little, Brown, 1967.
   b.   London: Heinemann, 1967.
   c.   New York: New American Library, 1968 (5 printings).
   d.   London: World Books, 1968.
   e.1. St. Albans, UK: Panther Books, 1968.
   e.2. St. Albans, UK: Panther Books, 1969.
   e.3. St. Albans, UK: Panther Books, 1976.
   e.4. St. Albans, UK: Panther Books, 1977.
   e.5. St. Albans, UK: Panther Books, 1985.
   e.6. St. Albans, UK: Panther Books, 1988.
   f.1. New York: Ballantine Books, 1976.
   f.2. New York: Ballantine Books, 1978.
   f.3. New York: Ballantine Books, 1979.
   f.4. New York: Ballantine Books, 1981.
   f.5. New York: Ballantine Books, 1983.
   f.6. New York: Ballantine Books, 1984.
   f.7. New York: Ballantine Books, 1985.
   f.8. New York: Ballantine Books, 1986.
   Revised edition:
   g.   London: Abacus, 1994.
   h.   New York: Modern Library, 1999.
   i.   New York: Vintage International, 2000.
      The first installment of what would become Vidal's American Chronicle, although clearly such a series was not contemplated at this time. It is told largely from the perspective of Peter Sanford, the son of a newspaper owner in Washington, D.C., Blaise Delacroix Sanford, who witnesses the alarming political ascendancy of a demagogue, Clay Overbury, who ardently seeks the presidency. A pirated edition from Taiwan (probably dating to 1967 or 1968) has been reported. See a similar pirated edition of *1876* (A.35.c).

25.   *Myra Breckinridge.*
      a.1. Boston: Little, Brown, [February] 1968.
      a.2. Boston: Little, Brown, 1968.
      a.3. Boston: Little, Brown, 1968.
      b.   London: Anthony Blond, 1968.
      c.   New York: Bantam Books, 1968 (22nd printing 1974).
      d.1. St. Albans, UK: Panther Books, 1969.
      d.2. St. Albans, UK: Panther Books, 1970.
      d.3. St. Albans, UK: Panther Books, 1971.
      d.4. St. Albans, UK: Panther Books, 1976.
      d.5. St. Albans, UK: Panther Books, 1977.
      d.6. St. Albans, UK: Panther Books, 1986.
      d.7. St. Albans, UK: Panther Books, 1989.
      e.   London: Collins, 1986.
      f.   New York: Vintage Books, 1987.
            Vidal's outrageous novel (his eleventh) about Myron Breckinridge, who undergoes a sex change
            operation and becomes Myra Breckinridge, whose goal is to achieve physical and psychological
            victory over men. Also involved are Buck Loner, the grotesque owner of an acting school, and
            Rusty Godowsky, a naïve young student of the school whom Myra (in one of the most celebrated
            scenes in the book) anally rapes. An immense best-seller, it was made into an equally notorious
            film (see H.ii.3) with Raquel Welch and Mae West.

26.   *Weekend: A Comedy in Two Acts.*
      a.1. New York: Dramatists Play Service, 1968.
      a.2. New York: Dramatists Play Service, 1981.
            Vidal's fourth Broadway play. See D.i.5.

27.   *Sex, Death and Money.*
      a.   New York: Bantam Books, November 1968.
            Contents: "Preface" (C.77); "On Pornography" (C.64); "Sex and the Law" (C.62); "Robert
            Graves and the Twelve Caesars" (C.41); "The *Sexus* of Henry Miller" (C.56); "*The City and the
            Pillar* After Twenty Years" (C.63); "Tarzan Revisited" (C.49); "Love Love Love" (C.18);
            "Writing Plays for Television" (C.10); "The Television Blacklist" (C.53); "Public Television"
            (C.72); "Novelists and Critics of the 1940's" (C.6); "A Note on the Novel" (C.8); "French
            Letters: Theories of the New Novel" (C.70); "John O'Hara's Old Novels" (C.52); "The
            Revelation of John Horne Burns" (C.55); "The Demotic Novel: John Dos Passos" (C.27);
            "Norman Mailer: The Angels Are White" (C.23); "Book Report: Robert Penn Warren's *Band of
            Angels*" (C.7); "Writers and the World" (C.61); "Closing the Civilization Gap" (C.32); "The
            Future of Conservatism" (C.36); "Barry Goldwater: A Chat" (C.29); "The Holy Family" (C.67);
            "The Manchester Book" (C.68); "God's Country: The American Empire's Beginning" (C.66);
            "The Liberal Dilemma" (C.78). A paperback collection meant to capitalize on the notoriety of
            Myra Breckinridge and including some essays from *Rocking the Boat* and others written
            subsequently, but quickly superseded by the following item.

28.   *Reflections upon a Sinking Ship.*
      a.1. Boston: Little, Brown, [March] 1969.
      a.2. Boston: Little, Brown, 1969.
      a.3. Boston: Little, Brown, 1969.
      b.   London: Heinemann, 1969.
            Contents: "Preface" (C.77); "Writers and the World" (C.61); "French Letters: Theories of the
            New Novel" (C.70); "Miss Sontag's Second New Novel" (C.69); "John O'Hara's Old Novels"
            (C.52); "The Revelation of John Horne Burns" (C.55); "John Hersey's *Here to Stay?*" (C.45);
            "The Wit and Wisdom of J. K. Galbraith" (C.50); "E. Nesbit's Use of Magic" (C.54); "The
            Waking Dream: Tarzan Revisited" (C.49); "Notes on Pornography" (C.64); "Sex and the Law"
            (C.62); "The *Sexus* of Henry Miller" (C.56); "*The City and the Pillar* After Twenty Years"
            (C.63); "On Revising One's Own Work" (C.60); "God's Country: The American Empire's
            Beginning" (C.66); "Edmund Wilson, Tax Dodger" (C.48); "Public Television: A Meditation"

(C.72); "Byzantium's Fall" (C.59); "The Holy Family" (C.67); "The Manchester Book" (C.68); "A Passage to Egypt" (C.42); "The Liberal Dilemma" (C.78); "Gore Vidal: Subject" (C.74); "The Twenty-ninth Republican Convention, Miami Beach, Florida, August 5–8, 1968" (C.75); "A Manifesto" (C.76). A strong collection gathering together essays and reviews published subsequent to *Rocking the Boat.*

29.   *Two Sisters: A Memoir in the Form of a Novel.*
       a.1. Boston: Little, Brown, 1970.
       a.2. Boston: Little, Brown, 1970.
       b.   London: Heinemann, 1970.
       c.   New York: Bantam Books, 1971.
       d.1. St. Albans, UK: Panther Books, 1972.
       d.2. St. Albans, UK: Panther Books, 1976.
       d.3. St. Albans, UK: Panther Books, 1977.
       e.   New York: Ballantine Books, 1987.
       f.1. London: Abacus, 2004.
       f.2. London: Abacus, 2006.
       A complex novel (Vidal's twelfth) in which the narrator is clearly Vidal himself, as he tells of his involvement with Marietta Donegal (manifestly an echo of Anaïs Nin) and with Murray Morris, who is making a film entitled *The Two Sisters of Ephesus.* The Vidal character for a time thinks he has had a child by Erika Van Damm, the sister of a deceased filmmaker. The dust jacket of a.1 gives the subtitle as "A Novel in the Form of a Memoir."

30.   *An Evening with Richard Nixon.*
       a.   New York: Random House, [July] 1972.
       b.   New York: Vintage Books, 1972.
       Contents: "Note" (C.92); *An Evening with Richard Nixon* (D.i.6). Vidal's fifth and final Broadway play.

31.   *Homage to Daniel Shays: Collected Essays 1952–1972.*
       a.   New York: Random House, [October] 1972.
       b.   New York: Vintage Books, 1973.
       c.   London: Heinemann, 1974 (as *Collected Essays 1952–1972*).
       d.   St. Albans, UK: Panther Books, 1976 (as *On Our Own Now*).
       Contents: "Note" (C.94); "Novelists and Critics of the 1940's" (C.6); "A Note on the Novel" (C.8); "Book Report" (C.7); "Writing Plays for Television" (C.10); *"Visit to a Small Planet"* (C.12); "Satire in the 1950's" (C.14); "Love Love Love" (C.18); "Bernard Shaw's *Heartbreak House"* (C.21); "The Twelve Caesars" (C.41); "Norman Mailer's Self-Advertisements" (C.23); "President Kennedy" (C.26); "John Dos Passos at Midcentury" (C.27); "Barry Goldwater: A Chat" (C.29); "Police Brutality" (C.32); "Nasser's Egypt" (C.42); "Edmund Wilson, Tax Dodger" (C.48); "Tarzan Revisited" (C.49); "John O'Hara" (C.52); "E. Nesbit's Magic" (C.54); "John Horne Burns" (C.55); "Sex and the Law" (C.62); "The *Sexus* of Henry Miller" (C.56); "Byzantium's Fall" (C.59); "Writers and the World" (C.61); "Pornography" (C.64); "The Holy Family" (C.67); "The Manchester Book" (C.68); "Paranoid Politics" (C.66); "French Letters: Theories of the New Novel" (C.70); "Miss Sontag's New Novel" (C.69); "Gore Vidal" (C.74); "The Twenty-ninth Republican Convention" (C.75); "Manifesto and Dialogue" (C.76); "Literary Gangsters" (C.81); "An American Press Lord" (C.82); "Meredith" (C.83); "Doc Reuben" (C.84); "Drugs" (C.85); "The Death of Mishima" (C.87); "Women's Liberation Meets Miller-Mailer-Manson Man" (C.84); "The Fourth Diary of Anaïs Nin" (C.89); "Eleanor Roosevelt" (C.90); "H. Hughes" (C.91); "Homage to Daniel Shays" (C.93). An omnibus gathering many (but not all) of the essays in *Rocking the Boat* and *Reflections upon a Sinking Ship,* along with some new items.

32.   *Burr.*
       a.1. New York: Random House, 1973.
       a.2. New York: Random House, 1973.
       a.3. New York: Random House, 1973.
       a.4. New York: Random House, 1973.

a.5. New York: Random House, 1973.

a.6. New York: Random House, 1973.

a.7. New York: Random House, 1973.

a.8. New York: Random House, n.d.

b.　London: Heinemann, 1974.

c.1. New York: Bantam Books, 1974.

c.2. New York: Bantam Books, 1975.

c.3. New York: Bantam Books, 1976 (15th printing).

c.4. New York: Bantam Books, 1980.

c.5. New York: Bantam Books, 1981 (19th printing).

c.6. New York: Bantam Books, 1985.

d.1. St. Albans, UK: Panther Books, 1974.

d.2. St. Albans, UK: Panther Books, 1976.

d.3. St. Albans, UK: Panther Books, 1977.

d.4. St. Albans, UK: Panther Books, 1984.

e.　Franklin Center, PA: Franklin Library, 1979.

f.1. New York: Ballantine Books, 1982.

f.2. New York: Ballantine Books, 1983.

f.3. New York: Ballantine Books, 1985.

f.4. New York: Ballantine Books, 1986.

f.5. New York: Ballantine Books, 1988.

f.6. New York: Ballantine Books, 1989.

f.7. New York: Ballantine Books, 1990.

f.8. New York: Ballantine Books, 1991.

f.9. New York: Ballantine Books, 1993.

g.　Norwalk, CT: Easton Press, 1990.

h.1. London: Abacus, 1994.

h.2. London: Abacus, 1998.

h.3. London: Abacus, 2003.

i.　New York: Modern Library, 1998.

j.　New York: Vintage International, 2000.

Perhaps Vidal's most substantial and well-respected historical novel, as the reputed traitor Aaron Burr tells the story of his life to a young disciple, Charles Schermerhorn Schuyler, and of his involvement with Thomas Jefferson (whose vice president he was) and other figures in early American history. A pirated Taiwanese or Hong Kong edition (Asia Printing, c. 1973) has been reported.

33.　*A Conversation with Myself.*

a.　New York: Bantam Books, 1974.

A separate publication of a self-interview about *Burr* (see III.C.130).

34.　*Myron.*

a.1. New York: Random House, [November] 1974.

a.2. New York: Random House, 1974.

a.3. New York: Random House, 1974.

b.　London: Heinemann, 1975.

c.　New York: Ballantine Books, 1975.

d.1. St. Albans, UK: Panther Books, 1975.

d.2. St. Albans, UK: Panther Books, 1977.

A sequel to *Myra Breckinridge,* in which Myron, now married, attempts to maintain a vigorously heterosexual (and politically conservative) existence, but finds that Myra is increasingly possessing his body, until finally she thrusts him into an old movie, *Siren of Babylon,* being filmed in 1948.

35. *1876.*
   - a.1. New York: Random House, [February] 1976.
   - a.2. New York: Random House, 1976.
   - a.3. New York: Random House, 1976.
   - b.   London: Heinemann, 1976.
   - c.   Taipei: Chung-shan Shu Chü, 1976.
   - d.1. New York: Ballantine Books, 1977.
   - d.2. New York: Ballantine Books, 1977.
   - d.3. New York: Ballantine Books, 1981.
   - d.4. New York: Ballantine Books, 1982.
   - d.5. New York: Ballantine Books, 1987.
   - d.6. New York: Ballantine Books, 1988.
   - e.1. St. Albans, UK: Panther Books, 1977.
   - e.2. St. Albans, UK: Panther Books, 1988.
   - f.   Norwalk, CT: Easton Press, 1990.
   - g.1. London: Abacus, 1994.
   - g.2. London: Abacus, 2000.
   - h.   New York: Modern Library, 1998.
   - i.   New York: Vintage International, 2000.

   Vidal's fifteenth novel and a loose sequel to *Burr*. Charles Schuyler has spent much of his life in France but now returns to the United States to report on the presidential election of 1876, the nation's centennial year. He is appalled by the corruption of the Grant administration and generally takes the side of the Democratic candidate, Samuel J. Tilden; but Tilden is robbed of the presidency by chicanery that lands the nonentity Rutherford B. Hayes into the White House. The Taipei edition (c.) is pirated from the Heinemann edition (b.).

36. *Matters of Fact and of Fiction: Essays 1973–1976.*
   - a.1. New York: Random House, [March] 1977.
   - a.2. New York: Random House, 1977.
   - a.3. New York: Random House, 1977.
   - a.4. New York: Random House, 1977.
   - b.   London: Heinemann, 1977.
   - c.   New York: Vintage Books, 1978.
   - d.1. London: Panther, 1978.
   - d.2. London: Panther, 1980.

   Contents: "Note" (C.118); "The Top Ten Best Sellers According to the Sunday *New York Times* as of January 7, 1973" (C.96); "The Great World and Louis Auchincloss" (C.104); "Calvino's Novels" (C.103); "Professor V. Nabokov" (C.102); "French Letters: Theories of the New Novel" (C.70); "The Hacks of Academe" (C.113); "American Plastic: The Matter of Fiction" (C.115); "Some Memories of the Glorious Bird and an Earlier Self" (C.112); "Contagious Self-Love" (C.101); "The Four Generations of the Adams Family" (C.110); "President and Mrs. U. S. Grant" (C.109); "West Point" (C.99); "The Art and Arts of E. Howard Hunt" (C.100); "What Robert Moses Did to New York City" (C.105); "Conglomerates" (C.97); "Political Melodramas" (C.95); "The State of the Union" (C.107). Vidal's fourth collection of essays (not counting *Sex, Death and Money*), gathering the essays and reviews published since *Homage to Daniel Shays.*

37. *Kalki.*
   - a.   Franklin Center, PA: Franklin Library, [March] 1978.
   - b.1. New York: Random House, [March] 1978.
   - b.2. New York: Random House, 1978.
   - b.3. New York: Random House, 1978.
   - c.   London: Heinemann, 1978.
   - d.1. New York: Ballantine Books, 1979.
   - d.2. New York: Ballantine Books, 1989.
   - d.3. New York: Ballantine Books, 1991.

e.1. St. Albans, UK: Panther Books, 1979.

e.2. St. Albans, UK: Panther Books, 1990.

f.   London: Abacus, 1993.

g.   New York: Penguin, 1998.

Vidal's sixteenth novel, and in some ways a reprise of *Messiah:* the story of Theodora (Teddy) Ottinger, a celebrated aviatrix who investigates the claims of James K. Kelly, a man claiming to be the Hindu messiah, Kalki. He persuades Ottinger to scatter paper lotuses around the world—these lotuses have been infected with bacteria that kills off the entire human race, leaving only Kalki and a few of his followers alive; but Kalki and his chosen mate, Lakshmi, cannot reproduce because their blood is incompatible, so the human race is doomed.

38.   *Three by Box: The Complete Mysteries of Edgar Box.*

a.   New York: Random House, [June] 1978.

Contents: *Death in the Fifth Position* (A.9); *Death Before Bedtime* (A.10); *Death Likes It Hot* (A.13).

39.   *Sex Is Politics and Vice Versa.*

a.   Los Angeles: Sylvester & Orphanos, 1979.

A separate publication of Vidal's essay (see C.127). Limited to 330 copies.

40.   *Julian; Williwaw; The Judgment of Paris; Messiah; The City and the Pillar.*

a.1. New York: Octopus Books; London: Heinemann, 1979.

a.2. New York: Octopus Books; London: Heinemann, 1982.

An "instant remainder" omnibus.

41.   *Creation.*

a.   New York: Random House, [February] 1981 (limited edition).

b.1. New York: Random House, 1981.

b.2. New York: Random House, 1981.

c.1. London: Heinemann, 1981.

c.2. London: Heinemann, 1989.

d.1. New York: Ballantine Books, 1982.

d.2. New York: Ballantine Books, 1983.

d.3. New York: Ballantine Books, 1984.

d.4. New York: Ballantine Books, 1986.

d.5. New York: Ballantine Books, 1990.

e.1. London: Panther Books, 1982.

e.2. London: Panther Books, 1989.

f.1. London: Abacus, 1993.

f.2. London: Abacus, 1998.

Restored edition:

g.   New York: Vintage International, 2002 (with a foreword by Anthony Burgess and an "Author's Note 2002" by Vidal [C.289]).

Vidal's seventeenth novel and one of his most impressive, a panoramic account of a Persian ambassador, Cyrus Spitama, who travels much of the known world (with his nephew, the Greek philosopher Democritus) in search of wisdom; along the way he meets Zoroaster, Buddha, Confucius, and others. The limited edition (a.) is a signed, numbered, and slipcased edition limited to 500 copies.

42.   *The Second American Revolution and Other Essays (1976–1982).*

a.1. New York: Random House, [April] 1982.

a.2. New York: Random House, 1982.

b.   London: Heinemann, 1982 (as *Pink Triangle and Yellow Star and Other Essays 1976–1982*).

c.   New York: Vintage Books, 1983.

    d.   St. Albans, UK: Panther Books, 1983 (as *Pink Triangle and Yellow Star and Other Essays 1976–1982*).

        Contents: "F. Scott Fitzgerald's Case" (C.134); "Edmund Wilson: This Critic and This Gin and These Shoes" (C.136); "Christopher Isherwood's Kind" (C.117); "On Prettiness" (C.124); "The Oz Books" (C.119); "Lessing's Science Fiction" (C.131); "Sciascia's Italy" (C.129); "V. S. Pritchett as 'Critic'" (C.128); "Thomas Love Peacock: The Novel of Ideas" (C.138); "Who Makes the Movies?" (C.116); "Sex Is Politics" (C.127); "Pink Triangle and Yellow Star" (C.142); "How to Find God and Make Money" (C.125); "Rich Kids" (C.123); "Theodore Roosevelt: An American Sissy" (C.141); "The State of the Union Revisited (1980)" (C.135); "The Real Two-Party System" (C.137); "The Second American Revolution" (C.139); "A Note on Abraham Lincoln" (C.140). Vidal's fifth collection of essays, including work published since *Matters of Fact and of Fiction*.

43.   *Duluth.*

    a.1. New York: Random House, [May] 1983.

    a.2. New York: Random House, 1983.

    b.   London: Heinemann, 1983.

    c.1. New York: Ballantine Books, 1984.

    c.2. New York: Ballantine Books, n.d.

    c.3. New York: Ballantine Books, n.d.

    c.4. New York: Ballantine Books, n.d.

    c.5. New York: Ballantine Books, 1988.

    c.6. New York: Ballantine Books, 1991.

    d.1. St. Albans, UK: Panther Books, 1984.

    d.2. St. Albans, UK: Panther Books, 1989.

    e.   London: Abacus, 1993.

    f.   New York: Penguin, 1998.

        Vidal's eighteenth novel and perhaps his most outrageous, an indescribable fantasy purportedly set in the city of Duluth (which, however, is near the Mexican border) and involving a television show also named "Duluth" (a parody of "Dallas"), a spaceship that has landed nearby, the antics of a policewoman, Darlene Ecks, and much else.

44.   *Lincoln.*

    a   Franklin Center, PA: Franklin Library, [April] 1984.

    b.1. New York: Random House, [May] 1984.

    b.2. New York: Random House, 1984.

    c.   London: Heinemann, 1984.

    d.1. New York: Ballantine Books, 1985.

    d.2. New York: Ballantine Books, 1987.

    d.3. New York: Ballantine Books, 1988.

    d.4. New York: Ballantine Books, 1989 (13th printing).

    e.1. St. Albans, UK: Panther Books, 1985.

    e.2. St. Albans, UK: Panther Books, 1986.

    f.   Norwalk, CT: Easton Press, 1990.

    g.1. New York: Modern Library, 1993.

    g.2. New York: Modern Library, 1998.

    h.1. London: Abacus, 1994.

    h.2. London: Abacus, 1997.

    i.   New York: Vintage International, 2000.

        Vidal's nineteenth novel and perhaps his most impressive historical novel, focusing upon the presidency of Abraham Lincoln and his actions during the Civil War, as well as those of his secretary of state, William H. Seward, and other leading political and military figures. It was filmed as a television miniseries (see H.iii.2). In a. there is a special introduction by Vidal.

45.   *Vidal in Venice* (ed. George Armstrong).
      a.1. London: Weidenfeld & Nicolson/Antelope, 1985.
      a.2. London: Weidenfeld & Nicolson/Antelope, 1987.
      b.   New York: Summit Books/Antelope, 1987.
           Contents: "Preface"; "The Face of Venice"; "In the Beginning"; "The Birth of an Empire"; "The
           Mercantile City and Its People"; "The Turning of the Tide"; "The Flowering of the Arts";
           "Coryate in Seventeenth-Century Venice"; "Carnival and Decline"; "Venice and the Romantics";
           "The City Today"; "Behind the Camera" by Tore Gill; "Map of Venice"; "Selected
           Bibliography"; "Photographic Acknowledgments"; "Index." A survey of the history, topography,
           and culture of Venice, based upon the television show hosted by Vidal (see E.ii.2). Vidal,
           however, wrote only the "Preface"; the rest of the book was written by George Armstrong.

46.   *Myra Breckinridge; Myron.*
      a.   New York: Random House, 1986.
      b.   London: Andre Deutsch, 1987 (as *Myra Breckinridge and Myron*).
      c.   New York: Vintage Books, 1987.
      d.   London: Grafton, 1989 (as *Myra Breckinridge and Myron*).
      e.   London: Abacus, 1993 (as *Myra Breckinridge and Myron*).
      f.   New York: Penguin, 1997.
           An omnibus of the two novels.

47.   *Empire.*
      a.   Franklin Center, PA: Franklin Library, [May] 1987.
      b.1. New York: Random House, [May] 1987.
      b.2. New York: Random House, 1987.
      b.3. New York: Random House, 1990.
      c.   London: Andre Deutsch, 1987.
      d.   New York: Ballantine Books, 1988.
      e.   London: Grafton, 1989.
      f.   Norwalk, CT: Easton Press, 1990.
      g.   London: Abacus, 1994.
      h.   New York: Modern Library, 1998.
      i.   New York: Vintage International, 2000.
           Vidal's twentieth novel, a sequel to *1876,* focusing on the presidency of Theodore Roosevelt and
           told largely from the perspective of John Hay, who had been one of Lincoln's secretaries and is
           now secretary of state. Blaise Sanford and his half-sister Caroline operate rival newspapers in
           Washington. By this time Vidal's thesis that the original American republic has declined and all
           but ceased to exist, in the wake of an overseas empire, is manifest.

48.   *Armageddon? Essays 1983–1987.*
      a.1. London: Andre Deutsch, [November] 1987.
      a.2. London: Andre Deutsch, 1987.
      a.3. London: Andre Deutsch, 1987.
      a.4. London: Andre Deutsch, 1987.
      a.5. London: Andre Deutsch, 1987.
      a.6. London: Andre Deutsch, 1990.
      b.   London: Grafton, 1989.
           Contents: "Preface" (C.172); "At Home in Washington, D.C." (C.144); "On Flying" (C.156);
           "Frederic Prokosch: The European Connection" (C.148); "Tennessee Williams: Someone to
           Laugh at the Squares With" (C.157); "Richard Nixon: Not *The Best Man*'s Best Man" (C.151);
           "Hollywood!" (C.145); "Ronnie and Nancy: A Life in Pictures" (C.149); "Armageddon?"
           (C.170); "The Day the American Empire Ran out of Gas" (C.161); "A Cheerful Response"
           (C.162); "Vidalgate" by Andrew Kopkind (III.E.177); "Mongolia!" (C.147); "At Home in a
           Roman Street" (C.158); "The Bookchat of Henry James" (C.163); "William Dean Howells"
           (C.150); "The Golden Bowl of Henry James" (C.153); "Logan Pearsall Smith Loves the Adverb"
           (C.154); "Paul Bowles's Stories" (C.131); "Calvino's Death" (C.151); "Why I Am Eight Years

Younger Than Anthony Burgess" (C.164). Vidal's sixth collection of essays, including work published subsequent to *The Second American Revolution.*

49.   *At Home: Essays 1982–1988.*
      a.1. New York: Random House, [November] 1988.
      a.2. New York: Random House, 1988.
      a.3. New York: Random House, 1988.
      a.4. New York: Random House, 1988.
      a.5. New York: Random House, 1988.
      b.   New York: Vintage Books, 1990.
           Contents: "Preface" (C.178); "At Home in Washington, D.C." (C.144); "On Flying" (C.156); "Frederic Prokosch: The European Connection" (C.148); "Tennessee Williams: Someone to Laugh at the Squares With" (C.157); "Richard Nixon: Not *The Best Man's* Best Man" (C.151); "Hollywood!" (C.145); "Ronnie and Nancy: A Life in Pictures" (C.149); "Armageddon?" (C.170); "The Day the American Empire Ran out of Gas" (C.161); "A Cheerful Response" (C.162); "Ollie" (C.166); "The National Security State" (C.175); "Mongolia!" (C.147); "At Home in a Roman Street" (C.158); "The Bookchat of Henry James" (C.163); "William Dean Howells" (C.150); "The Golden Bowl of Henry James" (C.153); "Logan Pearsall Smith Loves the Adverb" (C.154); "Oscar Wilde: On the Skids Again" (C.168); "Paul Bowles's Stories" (C.131); "Calvino's Death" (C.151); "Why I Am Eight Years Younger Than Anthony Burgess" (C.164); "Dawn Powell: The American Writer" (C.169); "How I Do What I Do If Not Why" (C.179); "Appendix." A slightly expanded edition of *Armageddon?*

50.   *Hollywood.*
      a.   London: Andre Deutsch, [November] 1989.
      b.   New York: Random House, [January] 1990 (limited edition).
      c.1. New York: Random House, [January] 1990.
      c.2. New York: Random House, 1990.
      c.3. New York: Random House, 1990.
      d.   Norwalk, CT: Easton Press, 1990.
      e.   New York: Ballantine Books, 1991.
      f.   London: Grafton, 1991.
      g.1. London: Abacus, 1994.
      g.2. London: Abacus, 1996.
      g.3. London: Abacus, 1999.
      g.4. London: Abacus, 2000.
      g.5. London: Abacus, 2004.
      h.   New York: Modern Library, 1999.
      i.   New York: Vintage International, 2000.
           Vidal's twenty-first novel, telling of how Caroline Sanford becomes a celebrated early film star under the name Emma Traxler. Much of the novel, however, concerns the Harding administration and its descent into corruption. Vidal wishes to suggest that "almost everyone nowadays had two lives, his own and his life at the movies." On the dust jacket of the Andre Deutsch edition appears a subtitle ("A Novel of the Twenties"); on the Random House editions (b. and c.) appear a different subtitle ("A Novel of America in the 1920's"). Neither of these subtitles appears anywhere in the book proper. The limited edition is a signed, numbered, and slipcased edition limited to 200 copies.

51.   *A View from the Diners Club: Essays 1987–1991.*
      a.   London: Andre Deutsch, [November] 1991.
      b.   London: Abacus, 1993.
           Contents: "Preface" (C.194); "Every Eckermann His Own Man" (C.177); "Pen Pals: Henry Miller and Lawrence Durrell" (C.176); "Dawn Powell: The American Writer" (C.169); "Remembering Orson Welles" (C.180); "Maugham's Half & Half" (C.184); "Ford's Way" (C.185); "Oscar Wilde: On the Skids Again" (C.168); "How I Do What I Do If Not Why" (C.179); "H. L. Mencken the Journalist" (C.192); "The National Security State" (C.175); "Ollie"

(C.166); "Cue the Green God, Ted" (C.181); "God & Greens" (C.182); "On the Last Day of the 1980's" (C.183); "Italian Footnote" (C.171); "Reflections on Glory Reflected and Otherwise" (C.189). Vidal's seventh collection of essays, containing work published subsquent to *Armageddon?/At Home.*

52.   *Myra Breckinridge; Myron; Kalki; Duluth.*
      a.   New York: Quality Paperback Book Club, 1992.
           A book club edition.

53.   *Screening History.*
      a.1. Cambridge, MA: Harvard University Press, [July] 1992.
      a.2. Cambridge, MA: Harvard University Press, 1994.
      b.   London: Andre Deutsch, 1992.
      c.   London: Abacus, 1993.
           Contents: "The Prince and the Pauper"; "Fire Over England"; "Lincoln." The William E. Massey Sr. Lectures in the History of American Civilization. Vidal's informal account of growing up watching films. He suggests that American and British films played a critical role in drumming up support for American intervention in World War II.

54.   *Live from Golgotha.*
      a.1. New York: Random House, [September] 1992.
      a.2. New York: Random House, 1992.
      b.1. London: Andre Deutsch, 1992.
      b.2. London: Andre Deutsch, 1992.
      b.3. London: Andre Deutsch, 1992.
      c.   New York: Penguin, 1993.
      d.1. London: Abacus, 1993.
      d.2. London: Abacus, 2003.
           Vidal's twenty-second novel and his most unrestrained lampoon of Christianity. Narrated by Timothy, who was born a few years after the death of Jesus Christ, it tells of Timothy's attempt to write a gospel telling what actually happened to Jesus. The matter is the more pressing because, as a result of a computer hacker, all the texts of the Bible in our own time are being wiped out. A subtitle appears on the dust jacket of the Random House (a.) edition, "The Gospel According to Gore Vidal," but this appears nowhere in the book proper.

55.   *The Decline and Fall of the American Empire.*
      a.   Berkeley, CA: Odonian Press, [October] 1992.
           Contents: "Preface" (C.202); "The Day the American Empire Ran Out of Gas" (C.161); "The National Security State" (C.175); "Cue the Green God, Ted" (C.181); "Time for a People's Convention" (C.197); "Should Our Intelligence Services Be Abolished?" (C.198); "Monotheism and Its Discontents" (C.201); "Recommended Reading"; "Books by Gore Vidal"; "Index." The first of Vidal's pamphlets collecting his essays on current political events.

56.   *United States: Essays 1952–1992.*
      a.1. New York: Random House, [April] 1993 (hardcover).
      a.2. New York: Random House, 1995 (paperback).
      b.   London: Andre Deutsch, 1993.
      c.   London: Abacus, 1994.
      d.   New York: Broadway Books, 2001.
           Contents: "Author's Note" (C.208); *State of the Art:* "Every Eckermann His Own Man" (C.177); "Novelists and Critics of the 1940s" (C.6); "A Note on the Novel" (C.8); "Satire in the 1950s" (C.14); "Norman Mailer's Self-Advertisements" (C.23); "Writers and the World" (C.61); "Literary Gangsters" (C.81); "Love, Love, Love" (C.18); "The Top Ten Best Sellers" (C.96); "French Letters: Theories of the New Novel" (C.70); "The Hacks of Academe" (C.113); "American Plastic: The Matter of Fiction" (C.115); "Thomas Love Peacock: The Novel of Ideas" (C.138); "Meredith" (C.83); "The Bookchat of Henry James" (C.163); "The Golden Bowl of Henry James" (C.153); "Logan Pearsall Smith Loves the Adverb" (C.154); "William Dean Howells" (C.150); "Oscar

Wilde: On the Skids Again" (C.168); "Bernard Shaw's *Heartbreak House"* (C.21); "Maugham's Half & Half" (C.184); "Ford's Way" (C.185); "The *Sexus* of Henry Miller" (C.56); "Pen Pals: Henry Miller and Lawrence Durrell" (C.176); "Edmund Wilson: This Critic and This Gin and These Shoes" (C.136); "F. Scott Fitzgerald's Case" (C.134); "Dawn Powell: The American Writer" (C.169); "John O'Hara" (C.52); "John Horne Burns" (C.55); "John Dos Passos at Midcentury" (C.27); "Book Report" (C.7); "V. S. Pritchett as 'Critic'" (C.128); "The Great World and Louis Auchincloss" (C.104); "Miss Sontag's New Novel" (C.69); "Lessing's Science Fiction" (C.131); "Christopher Isherwood's Kind" (C.117); "On Prettiness" (C.124); "Why I Am Eight Years Younger Than Anthony Burgess" (C.164); "Frederic Prokosch: The European Connection" (C.148); "Professor V. Nabokov" (C.102); "Paul Bowles's Stories" (C.131); "Tennessee Williams: Someone to Laugh at the Squares With" (C.157); "The Death of Mishima" (C.87); "Sciascia's Italy" (C.129); "Calvino's Novels" (C.103); "Calvino's Death" (C.151); "Montaigne" (C.199); *State of the Union:* "The Twelve Caesars" (C.41); "Sex and the Law" (C.62); "Sex Is Politics" (C.127); "Police Brutality" (C.32); "Pornography" (C.64); "Doc Reuben" (C.84); "Women's Liberation: Feminism and Its Discontents" (C.84); "Pink Triangle and Yellow Star" (C.142); "The Birds and the Bees" (C.193); "How to Find God and Make Money" (C.125); "Rich Kids" (C.123); "Drugs" (C.85); "The Four Generations of the Adams Family" (C.110); "First Note on Abraham Lincoln" (C.140); "Lincoln, *Lincoln,* and the Priests of Academe" (C.209); "Last Note on Lincoln" (C.191); "President and Mrs. U. S. Grant" (C.109); "Theodore Roosevelt: An American Sissy" (C.141); "Eleanor Roosevelt" (C.90); "H. L. Mencken the Journalist" (C.192); "Paranoid Politics" (C.66); "What Robert Moses Did to New York City" (C.105); "Conglomerates" (C.97); "Edmund Wilson, Tax Dodger" (C.48); "President Kennedy" (C.26); "The Manchester Book" (C.68); "The Holy Family" (C.67); "Barry Goldwater: A Chat" (C.29); "The Twenty-ninth Republican Convention" (C.75); "Political Melodramas" (C.95); "The Art and Arts of E. Howard Hunt" (C.100); "An American Press Lord" (C.82); "H. Hughes" (C.91); "Richard Nixon: Not *The Best Man's* Best Man" (C.151); "Homage to Daniel Shays" (C.93); "The State of the Union: 1975" (C.107); "The State of the Union: 1980" (C.135); "The Real Two-Party System" (C.137); "The Second American Revolution" (C.139); "Ronnie and Nancy: A Life in Pictures" (C.149); "Armageddon?" (C.170); "The Day the American Empire Ran out of Gas" (C.161); "A Cheerful Response" (C.162); "The National Security State" (C.175); "Cue the Green God, Ted" (C.181); "Gods & Greens" (C.182); "Patriotism" (C.190); "Monotheism and Its Discontents" (C.201); *State of Being:* "At Home in Washington, D.C." (C.144); "On Flying" (C.156); "West Point" (C.99); "The Oz Books" (C.119); "E. Nesbit's Magic" (C.54); "Tarzan Revisited" (C.49); "Some Memories of the Glorious Bird and an Earlier Self" (C.112); "The Fourth Diary of Anaïs Nin" (C.89); "Writing Plays for Television" (C.10); *"Visit to a Small Planet"* (C.12); "Who Makes the Movies?" (C.116); "Gore Vidal" (C.74); "Hollywood!" (C.145); "Remembering Orson Welles" (C.180); "Contagious Self-Love" (C.101); "Nasser's Egypt" (C.42); "Mongolia!" (C.147); "At Home in a Roman Street" (C.158); "Reflections on Glory Reflected and Otherwise" (C.189); "Index." An immense collection of Vidal's collected essays, divided into literary essays, political essays, and personal essays. Vidal states that he has gathered about two-thirds of the essays that have appeared in his previous collections, but much other work remains uncollected.

57.   *The City and the Pillar and Seven Early Stories.*
   a.   New York: Random House, [July] 1995.
       Contents: "Preface" (= "A Note on *The City and the Pillar* and Thomas Mann" [C.223]); *The City and the Pillar* (rev. ed.); "Three Strategems" (B.10); "The Robin" (B.15); "A Moment of Green Laurel" (B.14); "The Zenner Trophy" (B.16); "Erlinda and Mr. Coffin" (B.11); "Pages from an Abandoned Journal" (B.17); "The Ladies in the Library" (B.13).

58.   *Palimpsest: A Memoir.*
   a.1. New York: Random House, [October] 1995.
   a.2. New York: Random House, 1995.
   a.3. New York: Random House, 1995.
   a.4. New York: Random House, 1995.
   b.   London: Andre Deutsch, 1995.
   c.   New York: Penguin, 1996.
   d.1. London: Abacus, 1996.
   d.2. London: Abacus, 1997.

d.3. London: Abacus, 1999.

d.4. London: Abacus, 2002.

> An exhaustive memoir, even though Vidal had earlier stated that he would never write one; it proceeds only up to the year 1964. He apparently undertook it after becoming irritated that Walter Clemons, deemed Vidal's official biographer, spent years researching a biography of Vidal but failed to produce it (see III.B.94). The title (referring to a parchment that has been erased and written over) suggests that Vidal's recollection of the events he is recounting is colored by later events, and we receive scattered glimpses of Vidal's present-day life. For the sequel, see *Point to Point Navigation* (item 70 below).

59.   *Virgin Islands: A Dependency of* United States: *Essays 1992–1997.*

a.   London: Andre Deutsch, [July] 1997.

b.   London: Abacus, 1998.

> Contents: "Preface" (C.242); "Edmund Wilson: Nineteenth-Century Man" (C.213); "Dawn Powell: Queen of the Golden Age" (C.228); "The Romance of Sinclair Lewis" (C.204); "Twain on the Grand Tour" (C.230); "Reply to a Critic" (F.39); "Rabbit's Own Burrow" (C.229); "A Note on *The City and the Pillar* and Thomas Mann" (C.223); "Anthony Burgess" (C.215); "Pride" (C.211); "George" (C.243); "FDR: Love on the Hudson" (C.220); "Truman" (C.203); "Goin' South: Clinton-Gore I" (C.205); "Bedfellows Make Strange Politics" (C.217); "Bubba Rules: Clinton-Gore II" (C.233); "R.I.P., R.M.N." (C.216); "Kopkind" (C.222); "How We Missed the Saturday Dance" (C.207); "In the Lair of the Octopus" (C.221); "With Extreme Prejudice" (C.198); "Time for a People's Convention" (C.197); "The Union of the State" (C.218); "Mickey Mouse, Historian" (C.232); "US out of UN—UN out of US" (C.231); "Race against Time" (C.212); "Chaos" (C.235); "Stop Press: Through a Vote, Darkly" (C.238); "Appendix" (C.240). Vidal's eighth collection, gathering material published subsequent to *United States.* The subtitle indicates that the collection is an adjunct to that volume.

60.   *The Smithsonian Institution.*

a.   New York: Random House, [February] 1998.

b.   Franklin Center, PA: Franklin Library, [March] 1998.

c.   [Rockland, ME:] Compass Press, 1998 (large print).

d.   London: Little, Brown, 1998.

e.   London: Abacus, 1999.

f.1.   San Diego: Harvest/HBJ, 1999.

f.2.   San Diego: Harvest/NBJ, 2003.

> Vidal's twenty-third novel and another outrageous "invention," once again dealing with time travel. In the spring of 1939, a thirteen-year-old named only T. (perhaps meant to refer to Vidal's boyhood friend Jimmie Trimble) goes to the Smithsonian and becomes enmeshed in a bizarre fantasy world where presidents and their wives come to life. T. glimpses the future and becomes involved in a quest to reverse the motion of particles so that World War II never occurs.

61.   *The American Presidency.*

a.   Monroe, ME: Odonian Press, [October] 1998.

> Contents: "Dawn"; "High Noon"; "Twilight"; "Index." An encapsulated history of the United States, focusing on the role of key American presidents in establishing the American empire. An expansion of a television program (see I.ii.11).

62.   *The Essential Gore Vidal* (ed. Fred Kaplan).

a.   New York: Random House, [January] 1999.

b.   London: Little, Brown, 1999.

c.   London: Abacus, 2000.

> Contents: "Introduction" by Fred Kaplan (III.E.168); *Early Fiction:* From *The City and the Pillar* (A.3); "The Ladies in the Library" (B.13); From *The Judgment of Paris* (A.8); *Theater Writings: The Best Man* (D.i.2); *Inventions: Myra Breckinridge* (A.25); From *Duluth* (A.43); *Religion:* From *Julian* (A.23); From *Creation* (A.41); From *Live from Golgotha* (A.54); *Chronicles of American History:* From *Burr* (A.32); From *Lincoln* (A.44); From *1876* (A.35); From *Empire* (A.47); From *Hollywood* (A.50); From *Washington, D.C.* (A.24); *Essays:* "At

Home in Washington, D.C." (C.144); "On Flying" (C.156); "West Point" (C.99); "The Twelve Caesars" (C.41); "The Birds and the Bees" (C.193); "Women's Liberation: Feminism and Its Discontents" (C.84); "Pink Triangle and Yellow Star" (C.142); "Drugs" (C.85); "The Day the American Empire Ran Out of Gas" (C.161); "Bad History" (C.249); "President and Mrs. U. S. Grant" (C.109); "Theodore Roosevelt: An American Sissy" (C.141); "Eleanor Roosevelt" (C.90); "The Holy Family" (C.67); "Ronnie and Nancy: A Life in Pictures" (C.149); "Remembering Orson Welles" (C.180); "Who Makes the Movies?" (C.116); "French Letters: Theories of the New Novel" (C.70); "Edmund Wilson: This Critic and This Gin and These Shoes" (C.136); "Montaigne" (C.199); "Thomas Love Peacock: The Novel of Ideas" (C.138); "The Bookchat of Henry James" (C.163); "William Dean Howells" (C.150); "Calvino's Death" (C.151); "Some Memories of the Glorious Bird and an Earlier Self" (C.112); "Chronology"; "Bibliography." A volume designed to accompany Fred Kaplan's biography.

63. *Sexually Speaking: Collected Sex Writings* (ed. Donald Weise).
    a.1. San Francisco: Cleis Press, [September] 1999.
    a.2. San Francisco: Cleis Press, 2001.
    Contents: "Preface" (C.262); *Essays:* "Sex and the Law" (C.62); "The *Sexus* of Henry Miller" (C.56); "Pornography" (C.64); "Doc Reuben" (C.84); "Women's Liberation: Feminism and Its Discontents" (C.84); "Eleanor Roosevelt" (C.90); "Christopher Isherwood's Kind" (C.117); "Sex Is Politics" (C.127); "Pink Triangle and Yellow Star" (C.142); "Tennessee Williams: Someone to Laugh at the Squares With" (C.157); "Oscar Wilde: On the Skids Again" (C.168); "Maugham's Half & Half" (C.184); "The Birds and the Bees" (C.193); "J'Accuse!" (C.258); *Interviews:* "Introduction" by Donald Weise; "The *Fag Rag* Interview" by John Mitzel and Steven Abbott (III.C.1); "The *Gay Sunshine* Interview" by Steven Abbott and Thom Willenbecher (III.C.2); "The Sadness of Gore Vidal: An Interview" by Larry Kramer (III.C.78); "Index." A collection of Vidal's writings on sex, homosexuality, bisexuality, and related issues.

64. *The Golden Age.*
    a. New York: Doubleday, [September] 2000.
    b. Norwalk, CT: Easton Press, 2000.
    c. London: Little, Brown, 2000.
    d. New York: Random House Large Print, 2000.
    e. New York: Vintage International, 2001.
    f. London: Abacus, 2001.
    Vidal's twenty-fourth and last novel, focusing on the years 1939–1950, and especially on 1945–1950, which Vidal believed to be a golden age of American culture. Vidal maintains that Franklin D. Roosevelt's actions in the Pacific left the Japanese no option but to attack Pearl Harbor. Many of the characters from Vidal's earlier novels—including Blaise, Caroline, and Peter Sanford—are featured, and the young Vidal himself makes a cameo appearance. The Easton Press edition is a signed, numbered edition limited to 1100 copies.

65. *The Last Empire: Essays 1992–2000.*
    a. New York: Doubleday, 2001.
    b. London: Abacus, 2002.
    c. New York: Vintage International, 2002.
    Contents: "Edmund Wilson: Nineteenth-Century Man" (C.213); "Dawn Powell: Queen of the Golden Age" (C.228); "Lost New York" (C.248); "The Romance of Sinclair Lewis" (C.204); "Twain on the Grand Tour" (C.230); "Reply to a Critic" (F.39); "Twain's Letters" (C.237); "Rabbit's Own Burrow" (C.229); "A Note on *The City and the Pillar* and Thomas Mann" (C.223); "Anthony Burgess" (C.215); "Pride" (C.211); "Lindbergh: The Eagle Is Grounded" (C.256); "Sinatra" (C.250); "C. P. Cavafy" (C.278); "George" (C.243); "Amistad" (C.245); "FDR: Love on the Hudson" (C.220); "Wiretapping the Oval Office" (C.264); "Clare Boothe Luce" (C.239); "Truman" (C.203); "Hersh's JFK" (C.247); "Nixon R.I.P." (C.216); "Clinton-Gore I" (C.205); "Bedfellows Make Strange Politics" (C.217); "Clinton-Gore II" (C.233); "Honorable Albert A. Gore, Junior" (C.259); "Kopkind" (C.222); "Bad History" (C.249); "Blair" (C.238); "How We Missed the Saturday Dance" (C.207); "The Last Empire" (C.244); "In the Lair of the Octopus" (C.221); "With Extreme Prejudice" (C.198); "Time for a People's Convention" (C.197); "The Union of the State" (C.218); "Mickey Mouse, Historian" (C.232);

"U.S. out of UN—UN out of U.S." (C.231); "Race against Time" (C.212); "Chaos" (C.235); "Shredding the Bill of Rights" (C.257); "The New Theocrats" (C.241); "Coup de Starr" (C.255); "Starr Conspiracy" (C.252); "Birds and Bees and Clinton" (C.261); "A Letter to Be Delivered" (C.271); "Democratic Vistas" (C.273); "Three Lies to Rule By" (C.269); "Japanese Intentions in the Second World War" (F.42). Vidal's ninth collection of essays, including work published subsequent to *United States* and incorporating the essays included in *Virgin Islands.*

66.   *Perpetual War for Perpetual Peace: How We Got to Be So Hated.*
      a.   New York: Thunder's Mouth Press/Nation Books, [March] 2002.
      b.1. Forest Row, UK: Clairview Books, 2002.
      b.2. Forest Row, UK: Clairview Books, 2003.
           Contents: "Introduction" (C.280); "September 11, 2001 (A Tuesday)" (C.281); "How I Became Interested in Timothy McVeigh and Vice Versa" (C.282); "Shredding the Bill of Rights" (C.257); "The Meaning of Timothy McVeigh" (C.275); "Fallout" (C.283); "The New Theocrats" (C.241); "A Letter to Be Delivered" (C.271). A pamphlet collecting essays dealing with the terrorist attacks on the United States and their political aftermath.

67.   *Dreaming War: Blood for Oil and the Cheney-Bush Junta.*
      a.1. New York: Thunder's Mouth Press/Nation Books, [December] 2002.
      a.2. New York: Thunder's Mouth Press/Nation Books, 2003.
      b.   Forest Row, UK: Clairview Books, 2003.
           Contents: "Note" (C.286); "Democratic Vistas" (C.273); "Goat Song: Unanswered Questions—Before, During, After 9/11" (C.284); "Meandering toward Armageddon" (C.287); "Three Lies to Rule By" (C.269); "Japanese Intentions in the Second World War" (F.42); "How We Missed the Saturday Dance" (C.207); "The Last Empire" (C.244); "In the Lair of the Octopus" (C.221); "Mickey Mouse, Historian" (C.232); "With Extreme Prejudice" (C.198); "The Union of the State" (C.218); "The Last Defender of the American Republic? An Interview with Gore Vidal" by Marc Cooper (III.C.35). A further pamphlet condemning the George W. Bush administration for actions taken subsequent to the terrorist attacks of 2001.

68.   *Inventing a Nation: Washington, Adams, Jefferson.*
      a.1. New Haven: Yale University Press, [November] 2003.
      a.2. New Haven: Yale University Press, 2004.
      b.   Prince Frederick, MD: RB Large Print, 2004.
      c.   Melbourne, Australia: Melbourne University Publishing, 2004 (foreword by Bob Carr). A somewhat informal account of three of the important figures in early America and their role in shaping the course of American history.

69.   *Imperial America: Reflections on the United States of Amnesia.*
      a.1. New York: Thunder's Mouth Press/Nation Books, [May] 2004.
      a.2. New York: Thunder's Mouth Press/Nation Books, 2005.
      b.   Forest Row, UK: Clairview Books, 2004.
           Contents: "State of the Union: 2004" (C.293); "The Privatizing of the American Election" (C.294); "The Day the American Empire Ran out of Gas" (C.161); "A Cheerful Response" (C.162); "Armageddon?" (C.170); "Notes on Our Patriarchal State" (C.186); "The National Security State" (C.174); "The State of the Union: 1980" (C.135); "The Second American Revolution" (C.139); "We Are the Patriots" (C.290); "Interim Report: Election 2004" (C.292); "Index." Vidal's latest pamphlet condeming the Bush administration and the trend of American politics over the past two decades.

70.   *Point to Point Navigation: A Memoir 1964 to 2006.*
      a.   New York: Doubleday, [November] 2006.
      b.   London: Little, Brown, 2006.
           Vidal's second memoir, purportedly a sequel to *Palimpsest,* although it covers some of the same ground as its predecessor. Vidal discusses his relationships with Johnny Carson, Paul Bowles, Saul Bellow, and others, and in particular speaks poignantly of the death of his longtime companion, Howard Austen. He also discusses some recent books about him, including those by Dennis Altman (III.D.1) and Marcie Frank (III.D.6).

B. Short Stories and Poems

1. "To R. K. B.'s Lost Generation."
   a. *Phillips Exeter Review* 9 (Fall 1941): 17 (as by "Gene Vidal").
      Poem in 5 stanzas of rhyming quintrains with a final stanza of 8 lines; 33 lines total.

2. "Tower of Stone."
   a. *Phillips Exeter Review* 9 (Fall 1941): 24 (as by "Gene Vidal").
      Poem in 10 stanzas of rhyming quatrains; 50 lines total.

3. "Semisonnet."
   a. *Phillips Exeter Review* 9 (Spring 1942): 14 (as by "Gene Vidal").
      Poem in 14 lines in rhyming pseudo-sonnet form.

4. "Mostly about Geoffrey."
   a. *Phillips Exeter Review* 10 (Fall 1942): 7–9.
   b. In Paul Mandelbaum, ed. *First Words: Earliest Writings from Favorite Contemporary Authors.* Chapel Hill, NC: Algonquin Books of Chapel Hill, 1993, pp. 474–77.
      Short story.

5. "New Year's Eve."
   a. *Phillips Exeter Review* 10 (Winter 1943): 3–4.
   b. In Paul Mandelbaum, ed. *First Words: Earliest Writings from Favorite Contemporary Authors.* Chapel Hill, NC: Algonquin Books of Chapel Hill, 1993, pp. 478–81.
      Short story.

6. "The Bride Wore a Business Suit."
   a. *Phillips Exeter Review* 10 (Winter 1943): 14–16.
      Short story.

7. "Union Station."
   a. *Phillips Exeter Review* 10 (Winter 1943): 23 (as by "G. V.").
      Poem in 24 lines of free verse.

8. "Five Poems."
   a. *Voices* No. 126 (Summer 1946): 27–29.
      Contains: "Modernity" (27; 5 irregular stanzas of free verse; 11 lines total), "The Lover and the Juniper Tree" (27; 2 irregular stanzas of free verse; 15 lines total), "Stone Block" (28; 4 irregular stanzas of free verse; 12 lines total), "Moving Picture" (28; 3 irregular stanzas of free verse; 13 lines total), and "The Mirror" (28–29; 7 irregular stanzas of free verse; 19 lines total).

9. "Walking."
   a. *Harper's Bazaar* 80 (November 1946): 362.
      Poem in 3 irregular stanzas of free verse; 15 lines total.

10. "The Robin."
    a. *Tomorrow* 8, no. 6 (February 1949): 20–22.
    b. In A.16.
    c. In A.20.
    d. In A.57.
       Short story.

11. "Three Strategems."
    a. *New Directions in Prose and Poetry* 12 (1950): 92–104.

    b.   In A.16.

    c.   In A.20.

    d.   In Stephen Wright, ed. *Different: An Anthology of Homosexual Short Stories.* New York: Bantam Books, 1974, pp. 1–15.

    e.   In A.57.

        Short story.

12.   "Erlinda and Mr. Coffin."

    a.   *New World Writing* no. 1 (1952): 130–39.

    b.   In A.16.

    c.   In Richard A. Condon and Burton O. Kurth, eds. *Writing from Experience.* New York: Harper & Brothers, 1960, pp. 265–77.

    d.   In A.20.

    e.   In Kevin McCarthy, ed. *Florida Stories.* Gainesville: University of Florida Press, 1989, pp. 270–82.

    f.   In A.57.

        Short story.

13.   "The Winter River."

    a.   *Voices* no. 149 (September–December 1952): 13.

        Poem in 2 stanzas of 6 lines; 12 lines total.

14.   "The Ladies in the Library."

    a.   *New World Writing* No. 4 (1953): 119–35.

    b.   In A.16.

    c.   In A.20.

    d.   In A.57.

    e.   In A.62.

        Short story.

15.   "A Moment of Green Laurel."

    a.   *Encounter* 7, no. 6 (December 1956): 39–42.

    b.   In Themistocles Hoetis, ed. *Zero No. 8 Anthology of Literature and Art.* New York: Zero Press, 1956, pp. 140–48.

    c.   In A.16.

    d.   In A.20.

    e.   In Oliver Evans and Harry Finestone, eds. *The World of the Short Story: Archetypes in Action.* New York: Alfred A. Knopf, 1971, pp. 243–48.

    f.   In A.57.

        Short story.

16.   "The Zenner Trophy."

    a.   In A.16.

    b.   In A.20.

    c.   In A.57.

    d.   In Nina Baym, ed. *The Norton Anthology of American Literature.* 5th ed. New York: W. W. Norton & Co., 1998, Vol. 2, pp. 2035–38.

        Short story.

17.   "Pages from an Abandoned Journal."

    a.   In A.16.

    b.   In A.20.

    c.   In John Hollander, ed. *American Short Stories Since 1945.* New York: Harper & Row, 1968, pp. 267–82.

  d. In Seymour Kleinberg, ed. *The Other Persuasion: An Anthology of Short Fiction about Gay Men and Women.* New York: Vintage Books, 1977, pp. 203–15.

  e. In Edmund White, ed. *The Faber Book of Gay Short Fiction.* London: Faber & Faber, 1991, pp. 171–85.

  f. In A.57.
    Short story.

18. *Myra Breckinridge* (extracts).

  a. *Cosmopolitan* 165, No. 2 (August 1968): 111–15.

  b. In Leonard Michaels, David Reid, and Raquel Scherr, eds. *West of the West: Imagining California.* San Francisco: North Point Press, 1989, pp. 44–47.

19. "Julian the Apostate."

  a. In A.20.
    Early draft of the opening section of *Julian* (A.23).

20. *Two Sisters* (extracts).

  a. *Esquire* 73, No. 5 (May 1970): 106–16, 169–72, 174–75 (as "A Memoir in the Form of a Novel").

  b. *Partisan Review* 37, No. 1 (1970): 33–40 (as "All Our Lives").

21. *Washington, D.C.* (extract).

  a. In Whit Burnett, ed. *This Is My Best in the Third Quarter of the Century.* Garden City, NY: Doubleday, 1970, pp. 76–89 (as "Ex-Senator").

22. *Burr* (extract).

  a. *Times* (London) (9 March 1974): 9, 13 (as "A Dinner at the White House").

23. *1876* (extract).

  a. *Times* (London) (13 March 1976): 8 (as "A Dinner Engagement").

24. *Kalki* (extracts).

  a. *Playboy* 25, no. 3 (March 1978): 94, 96, 106, 156, 189–97; 25, no. 4 (April 1978): 132, 134, 140, 224, 226, 230, 232, 234, 236, 238, 240, 242.

25. *Lincoln* (extracts).

  a. *Atlantic Monthly* 253, no. 5 (May 1984): 37–39, 42–46, 49–53, 55–58, 60, 65–66, 69, 71–74.

26. *Empire* (extract).

  a. *Harper's Magazine* 274 (May 1987): 31–34 (as "The Making of the President").

27. *Hollywood* (extract).

  a. *Los Angeles Times Magazine* (28 January 1990): 14 (as "The Perils of Caroline").

28. *Creation* (extract).

  a. In Barbara Baker, ed. *Chinese Ink, Western Pen.* New York: Oxford University Press, 2002.
    Not seen.

29. *Live from Golgotha* (extract).

  a. *Granta* no. 32 (Spring 1990): 189–201 (as "Epistle to the New Age").

30. *The Golden Age* (extract).

  a. *Independent* (8 October 2000): Review, pp. 63–64 (as "The End of an Era").

31.   "Clouds and Eclipses."
       a.   *Harvard Review* No. 29 (2005): 75–82 (afterword by Vidal, p. 83).
       b.   In I.A.16.m.
             Short story, written around 1953. Vidal withheld publication at the time at the request of
             Tennessee Williams, who believed the incident recounted in the story was based upon an event
             in the life of his material grandfather.

C. Essays and Reviews

1. "Gore Vidal: Quick Start."
   a. *New York Herald Tribune Book Review* (8 October 1950): 18.
   Brief autobiographical sketch, also supplying information on his character traits and overall philosophy.

2. "The Making of a Hero and a Legend: Richard Hillary."
   a. *New York Times Book Review* (11 February 1951): 5 (as "The Making of a Hero and a Legend").
   b. In A.21.
   Review of Lovat Dickson's *Richard Hillary,* a biography of the Australian-born R.A.F. pilot. Vidal also has praise for Hillary's autobiographical work, *The Last Enemy.*

3. "Murder of Innocence."
   a. *Saturday Review of Literature* 34, no. 8 (24 February 1951): 13–14.
   b. In Fritz Peters. *Finistère.* New York: New American Library (Plume), 1986, pp. [ix–x] (as "Preface").
   Review of *Finistère* by Fritz Peters, deemed a "remarkable novel" in its character sketch of Matthew Cameron, a homosexual.

4. "Did a Machine Write 'Moby Dick'?"
   a. *New York Times Book Review* (5 August 1951): 9.
   Review of *The Arts in Renewal,* edited by Sculley Bradley, a collection of essays about the state of contemporary art. Vidal has particualr praise for an essay by Lewis Mumford about "the dehumanization of the arts from the seventeenth century to the present day."

5. "Disaster and Flight."
   a. *New York Times Book Review* (22 March 1953): 6.
   Review of *Nine Days to Mukalla* by Frederic Prokosch, a novel that embodies Prokosch's chief theme: "disaster and flight, anticipation and arrival."

6. "Novelists and Critics of the 1940s."
   a. *New World Writing* no. 4 (1953): 303–16 (as "Ladders to Heaven: Novelists and Critics"; as by "Libra").
   b. In A.21 (as "Ladders to Heaven: Novelists and Critics of the 1940's").
   c. In Richard Kostelanetz, ed. *On Contemporary Literature.* New York: Avon Books, 1964, 1969; Freeport, NY: Books for Libraries Press, 1971, pp. 29–35 (as "Ladders to Heaven"; abridged).
   d. In A.27.
   e. In A.31.
   f. In A.56.
   Vidal's assessment of the status of literature in the preceding decade. Among critics, he speaks with praise of Edmund Wilson, Malcolm Cowley, John W. Aldridge. No novelists are discussed in specific detail, but Vidal declares that "Carson McCullers, Paul Bowles, Tennessee Williams are, at this moment at least, the three most interesting writers in the United States."

7. "Book Report."
   a. *Zero* no. 7 (Spring 1956): 95–98.
   b. In A.21 (as "Book Report: Robert Penn Warren's *Band of Angels*").
   c. In A.27 (as "Book Report: Robert Penn Warren's *Band of Angels*").
   d. In A.31.
   e. In A.56.

Satirical review of Robert Penn Warren's historical novel, set during and after the Civil War. The review is written as if by a not overly educated woman in a reading club presenting a book report.

8.   "A Note on the Novel."
   a.   *New York Times Book Review* (5 August 1956): 2 (as "Speaking of Books").
   b.   In A.21.
   c.   In A.27.
   d.   In A.31.
   e.   In A.56.
         One of Vidal's first statements that the novel is in decline because poor education, television, and other factors are reducing the audience for the serious novel.

9.   "Television Drama, circa 1956."
   a.   *Theatre Arts* 40, no. 12 (December 1956): 65–66, 85–86.
         An essay originally written as the introduction to *Best Television Plays* (A.14) but not published there, because (as Vidal notes at the end of the essay) one of the contributors to the book felt that Vidal had "slighted the television writer's essential 'dignity'" and refused to allow his play to be included unless Vidal's introduction was removed. In the essay Vidal speaks of the unprecedented opportunity for playwrights to display their talents on television in the 1950s; but Vidal is wary of assuming that there is "a new renaissance in dramatic writing, brought about by television."

10.   "Writing Plays for Television."
   a.   *New World Writing* no. 10 (1956): 86–91 (as "Notes on Television").
   b.   In A.15 (as "Foreword").
   c.   In A.21.
   d.   In A.27.
   e.   In A.31.
   f.   In A.56.
         Vidal speaks of his own shift from novel writing to television writing in the early 1950s, even though "I had not watched television until the winter I decided to write for it." He speaks of the aesthetic opportunities in television writing, in spite of censors, advertisers, and the need to work with a large group of collaborators. He concludes: "All things considered, I suspect that the Golden Age for the dramatist is at hand."

11.   "Footnote to the Dreyfus Case."
   a.   *Reporter* 16, no. 7 (4 April 1957): 48 (as "Somber Lunacy, Stern Illogic").
   b.   In A.21.
         Review of Maurice Paléologue's *An Intimate Journal of the Dreyfus Case,* a diary that Paléologue had kept while the Dreyfus case was in progress (1894ff.). Vidal concludes: "This journal is certainly the most interesting record published so far of the Dreyfus case." Cf. his own film about the case, *I Accuse!* (E.i.2).

12.   *"Visit to a Small Planet."*
   a.   *Reporter* 17, no. 1 (11 July 1957): 33–36 (as "The Perils and Rewards of Going into Trade").
   b.   *Cosmopolitan* 143, no. 2 (August 1957): 58–59.
   c.   In I.A.17 (as "Preface").
   d.   In A.21 (as "Putting On *Visit to a Small Planet*").
   e.   In A.22 (as "American Preface to *Visit to a Small Planet*").
   f.   In A.31.
   g.   In A.56.
         Vidal speaks of transforming his television play of 1955 into a stage play and discusses its reception in its pre-Broadway opening in New Haven (16 January 1957) and its Broadway premiere on 7 February 1957. He also discusses the difficulty of writing satire for an audience generally incapable of appreciating it.

13. "Ideas and Theatre."

    a. *Tulane Drama Review* 2, no. 1 (November 1957): 45.
       A one-paragraph statement that the theatre is, "intellectually," not worth "a hill of beans in any country."

14. "Satire in the 1950s."

    a. *Nation* 186, no. 17 (26 April 1958): 371–73 (as "The Unrocked Boat").
    b. In A.21 (as "The Unrocked Boat: Satire in the 1950's").
    c. In A.31.
    d. In A.56.
       A brief history of literary satire from classical antiquity onward and a rumination on the unreceptiveness of Americans to satire. But satire is needed today because "we are in a new age of conformity."

15. "*Death of a Salesman:* A Symposium."

    a. *Tulane Drama Review* 2, no. 3 (May 1958): 63–69.
       Symposium featuring Vidal, Arthur Miller, Richard Watts, John Beaufort, Martin Dworkin, David W. Thompson, and Phillip Gelb (moderator). Vidal makes relatively few remarks, asserting that Miller's play is "more concerned with a human being who tries to live by a certain set of standards to which he cannot measure up and what happens to him as he fails."

16. "Eugene O'Neill's *A Touch of the Poet.*"

    a. *Nation* 187, no. 13 (25 October 1958): 298–99 (as "Theatre").
    b. In A.21.
    c. In John H. Houchin, ed. *The Critical Response to Eugene O'Neill.* Westport, CT: Greenwood Press, 1993, pp. 234–36 (as "Theatre").
       Review of the play—"a beautiful play, beautifully presented." Set in the year 1828, it deals with an Irishman, Cornelius Melody, who came to the United States and opened a tavern. "What makes the play work thematically is the examination of Melody's dream world."

17. "In the Shadow of the Scales: Friedrich Duerrenmatt."

    a. *Reporter* 20, no. 9 (30 April 1959): 40–41 (as "In the Shadow of the Scales").
    b. In A.21.
       Survey of Duerrenmatt's novels (Vidal has read three out of eight) and plays (Vidal has read two out of six), most of which deal with murder and other crimes. The play that Vidal would later adapt (*Romulus*) is not mentioned.

18. "Love, Love, Love."

    a. *Partisan Review* 26, no. 4 (Fall 1959): 613–20.
    b. In A.21 (as "Love Love Love").
    c. In A.22.
    d. In William Phillips and Philip Rahv, eds. *The Partisan Review Anthology.* New York: Holt, Rinehart & Winston, 1962; London: Macmillan, 1962, pp. 231–37.
    e. In A.27.
    f. In A.31 (as "Love Love Love").
    g. In A.56.
       Celebrated essay in which Vidal maintains that "Our popular theater ponders, to the exclusion of all else, the pathos of Love withheld, of Love lost, of Love found after three acts of jittery footling . . ." Ideas are almost wholly lacking in the stage, especially in the work of Arthur Miller; all is subordinated to "the cult of feeling." Vidal concludes with some mixed praise for the theater criticism of Mary McCarthy.

19. "Sir John, by a Nose."

    a. *Reporter* 21, no. 6 (15 October 1959): 38–39.
       Review of a production of Shakespeare's *Much Ado about Nothing* starring Sir John Gielgud and Margaret Leighton, with some background on Shakespeare's play. Gielgud's direction "is at best

serviceable, at worst desultory. Leighton "moves exquisitely through the plot as though it was not there, and I can think of no higher compliment."

20.   "The Commercialites."
       a.   *Reporter* 21, no. 8 (12 November 1959): 36–37.
       b.   In A.21.
             Another attack on the commercial theater, in particular such works as Arthur Miller's *The Crucible,* Jerome Lawrence and Robert E. Lee's *Auntie Mame,* and *The Gang's All Here;* these and other works simply cater to audience expectations instead of challenging them.

21.   "Bernard Shaw's *Heartbreak House.*"
       a.   *Reporter* 21, no. 9 (26 November 1959): 33–35 (as "Debate in the Moonlight").
       b.   In A.21.
       c.   In A.31.
       d.   In A.56.
             Examination of Shaw's play, a rumination about the British ruling class, some of it written before World War I and some of it after. The production was directed by Harold Clurman, who was "enormously helped by Diana Wynyard and Pamela Brown, who are beautifully right for this kind of thing." Vidal also has praise for the acting of Maurice Evans.

22.   "The Couch in the Shrine: Dore Schary and Paddy Chayefsky."
       a.   *Reporter* 21, no. 10 (10 December 1959): 39 (as "The Couch in the Shrine").
       b.   In A.21.
             Review of Dore Schary's *The Highest Tree* (about the atomic bomb) and Paddy Chayefsky's *The Tenth Man* (a love story between an atheist and a Jewish woman). Of the latter, although his "admiration for Mr. Chayefsky . . . [is] real," Vidal writes: "I didn't believe a word of it."

23.   "Norman Mailer's Self-Advertisements."
       a.   *Nation* 190, no. 1 (2 January 1960): 13–16 (as "The Norman Mailer Syndrome").
       b.   In A.21 (as "Norman Mailer: The Angels Are White").
       c.   In A.27 (as "Norman Mailer: The Angels Are White").
       d.   In Robert F. Lucid, ed. *Norman Mailer: The Man and His Work.* Boston: Little, Brown, 1971, pp. 95–107 (as "Norman Mailer: The Angels Are White").
       e.   In A.31.
       f.   In Harold Bloom, ed. *Norman Mailer.* New York: Chelsea House, 1986, pp. 7–16 (as "The Angels Are White").
       g.   In A.56.
             Significant early essay on Mailer, analyzing Mailer's first novel, *The Naked and the Dead* (which Vidal first thought was a "fake"—"a clever, talented, admirably executed fake") and discussing his encounters with Mailer (they first met in 1954) and proceeding to a detailed review of Mailer's new book (never mentioned by name in the essay), *Advertisements for Myself,* which Vidal characterizes as prototypical of modern American literature in that the author has become his own subject. "Despite a nice but small gift for self-destruction, he is uncommonly adroit, with an eye to the main chance." And yet, "of all my contemporaries I retain the greatest affection for Mailer as a force and as an artist."

24.   "Strangers at Breakfast: *Five Finger Exercise.*"
       a.   *Reporter* 22, no. 1 (7 January 1960): 36–37 (as "Strangers at Breakfast").
       b.   In A.21.
             Review of a play by Peter Shaffer, "as depressing a bit of playwriting as one will ever encounter." It is a family drama, and Shaffer seems to be suggesting that "the family in the West is finished."

25.   "A Note on *The Best Man.*"
       a.   *Theatre Arts* 44, no. 7 (July 1960): 8–9 (as "Notes on 'The Best Man'").
       b.   In A.18 (as "Notes on *The Best Man*").
       c.   In A.21.

d. In A.22 (as "Preface to *The Best Man*").
Discussion of the writing and purpose of *The Best Man*. "I use the theater as a place to criticize society, to satirize folly, to question presuppositions."

26. "President Kennedy."
   a. *Sunday Telegraph* (London) (9 April 1961): 4 (as "A New Power in the White House").
   b. In A.21 (as "John Kennedy: A Translation for the English").
   c. In A.31.
   d. In A.56.
   Rumination on the newly elected president, both physical ("Close to, Kennedy looks older than his photographs") and psychological ("Kennedy's relationships tend to be compartmentalized"). Kennedy is not a full-fledged liberal, but "a pragmatist with a profound sense of history, working within a generally liberal context." Vidal discusses his own encounters with Kennedy both in and out of the White House.

27. "John Dos Passos at Midcentury."
   a. *Esquire* 55, no. 5 (May 1961): 56–59 (as "A Couple of Demotic Novels and a Few Solipsistic Moments").
   b. In A.21 (as "The Demotic Novel: John Dos Passos").
   c. In A.27 (as "The Demotic Novel: John Dos Passos").
   c. In A.31.
   d. In A.56.
   Review of Dos Passos's *Midcentury,* a book about the American labor mvoement from the New Deal to the present. Vidal "never cared much for his early work even at its best," but he has "enjoyed, even admired, the dottiness of his politics." The documentary style that Dos Possos had used his his previous works does not work well here, and his concluding attack on the youth of today is misguided.

28. "Social Climbing, According to the Books."
   a. *Esquire* 55, no. 6 (June 1961): 132–35 (as "Social Climbing, and How").
   b. In A.21.
   A review of two books. Lucy Kavaler's *The Private World of High Society* is a gushing account of upper-class American life. In reality, Kavaler is "writing not about High Society, but about the ever-enlarging, ever more affluent middle class." Cleveland Amory's *Who Killed Society?* is a study of the decay of American social and family life. Amory "makes a strong but inconclusive case that the old High Society is dead and that only the current half-world of Celebrity holds the fort." There is also some discussion of Louis Auchincloss's new novel, *The House of Five Talents.*

29. "Barry Goldwater: A Chat."
   a. *Life* 50, no. 23 (9 June 1961): 106, 108, 111–12, 114, 117–18 (as "A Liberal Meets Mr. Conservative").
   b. In A.21.
   c. In A.27.
   d. In Herbert Gold, ed. *First Person Singular: Essays for the Sixties.* New York Dial Press, 1963, pp. 232–50.
   e. In A.31.
   f. In A.56.
   Pungent interview with and study of Barry Goldwater, already emerging as a leading conservative candidate for president. Vidal notes that, although Goldwater's views appear to have shifted a bit toward the center since the publication of his book *The Conscience of a Conservative* (1960), he is nonetheless attracting a number of far-right groups, such as the John Birch Society. Vidal meets Goldwater in his office in the Senate Office Building, and they discuss the John Birch Society, communism (Goldwater is in favor of it being taught in schools: "Show the kids what we're up against"), aid to education, farm subsidies, the nature of conservatism, his impressions of John F. Kennedy ("He thinks the government should do a lot

more for people than I do"), medical care for the aged (Goldwater is against it), and other issues. Vidal concludes that "in his simplifying of great issues Goldwater has a real appeal for a nation which is not at all certain about its future either as a society or as a world power."

30.   "Two Immoralists: Orville Prescott and Ayn Rand."
a.   *Esquire* 56, no. 1 (July 1961): 24, 26–27 (as "On a Few Personal Horizons: Colorful, Limited, Limitless").
b.   In A.21.
Discussion of Orville Prescott (book reviewer for the *New York Times*), who merely caters to the sexual and social prejudices of his middle-class readers; and Ayn Rand, novelist and philosopher, whose attack on altruism Vidal finds objectionable ("That it is right to help someone less fortunate is an idea which has figured in most systems of conduct since the beginning of the race").

31.   "The House Un-American Activities Committee."
a.   *New York Herald Tribune* (14 July 1961): 13 (as "The Whole Sordid Story").
b.   In A.21.
A review of Frank J. Donner's *The Unamericans,* "a brilliant case against HUAC." Vidal notes that HUAC has focused only on "un-American" activities on the left, not the right. The anti-Communist hate groups proliferating in the United States are worse than the Communists themselves.

32.   "Police Brutality."
a.   *Esquire* 56, no. 2 (August 1961): 120, 123 (as "The Race into Grace, or the Civilization Gap").
b.   In A.21 (as "Closing the Civilization Gap").
c.   In A.27 (as "Closing the Civilization Gap").
d.   In A.31.
e.   In A.56.
A rumination on a crime in Washington, D.C., that Vidal witnessed: four men came out of a YMCA with two other men in tow, whom they then began to beat up. Vidal, in a taxicab, approaches the group; one of the four men is a police detective, who shouts obscenities at him. Vidal suggests that every major city should have a permanent committee to investigate police brutality.

33.   "Carson McCullers's *Clock without Hands.*"
a.   *Reporter* 25, no. 5 (28 September 1961): 50, 52 (as "The World Outside").
b.   In A.21.
c.   In Harold Bloom, ed. *Carson McCullers.* New York: Chelsea House, 1986, pp. 17–19.
A review of McCullers's new novel and a discussion of her writing overall in the context of Southern literature. In her first novel, *The Heart Is a Lonely Hunter,* "her prose was chaste and severe, and realistic in the working out of the narrative." The new novel is "odd" in its attempt to portray social and political changes in the South in the wake of the Supreme Court's desegregation of public schools. "But even this near failure of McCullers is marvelous to read."

34.   "Comment."
a.   *Esquire* 56, no. 5 (November 1961): 202–4.
Vidal begins with a discussion of the cautiousness of American politicians, who are afraid of tackling tough issues because it may endanger their quest for higher office. He proceeds to "the grim state of our public education": the lack of good teachers (chiefly a result of poor pay) and the dangers of reactionary and ignorant school boards. Vidal suggests that the government "should set minimum academic standards for the entire country."

35.   "HUAC Revisited."
a.   *Esquire* 56, no. 6 (December 1961): 40 (as "The Wrath of the Radical Right").
b.   In A.21.

An account of the reaction to Frank Donner's *The Unamericans* and to Vidal's favorable review of it (see item 31 above). The "Radical Right" went ballistic over the book and the review, claiming that Donner's assertions should be discredited because he was an admitted former Communist. Vidal is attacked by several politicians on HUAC, including Gordon Scherer (who is "as beautifully fatuous a creature as ever swung down out of the tangled trees of American politics").

36.　"The Future of Conservatism."
　　a.　Associated Press (10 December 1961).
　　b.　In A.21.
　　c.　In A.27.
　　One of the first occasions on which Vidal asserts that "there is no important liberal movement in the United States." There are really only two parties: conservative and reactionary ("A reactionary is one who wishes to reverse an existing state of affairs and to return to a previous condition of society"). Although reactionaries (such as Barry Goldwater) "can never win, because clocks go forward, not backward," they are nonetheless bolstered by wide public support.

37.　"Evelyn Waugh."
　　a.　*New York Times Book Review* (7 January 1962): 1, 28 (as "The Satiric World of Evelyn Waugh").
　　b.　In A.21.
　　A surprisingly uncharitable assessment of the British satirist, chiefly devoted to his war trilogy, *Men at Arms* (1952), *Officers and Gentlemen* (1955), and *The End of the Battle* (1961), of which this essay is nominally a review. Waugh is only on solid ground when he is attacking; "even his prose . . . grows solemn and hollow when he tries to celebrate goodness and love and right action."

37A.　"The Role of the Writer in America" [symposium].
　　a.　*Michigan's Voices* 2, no. 3 (Spring 1962): 18–21.
　　The text of a speech delivered at the University of Michigan in a symposium sponsored by *Esquire.* Other participants were Vance Bourjaily, William Styron, and Nelson Algren. Vidal discusses the "defection of the public" from novel reading, but thinks that a renaissance of drama via television is still possible.

38.　"Comment."
　　a.　*Esquire* 57, no. 5 (May 1962): 159–62.
　　Vidal discusses adapting the play *Romulus* from Duerrenmatt's original. He discusses reading other plays by Duerrenmatt, then meeting the playwright. In opposition to the naturalism dominant in the theater, *Romulus the Great* is a fantasy, and plays of this sort "have a difficult time on Broadway." Nevertheless, the play "is a speaking picture of some of our day's follies and foibles."

39.　"Foreword."
　　a.　In A.21.
　　Vidal speaks of the rationale of writing his essays and reviews, and of the ambiguous nature of his political affiliations.

40.　"Comment."
　　a.　*Esquire* 58, no. 2 (August 1962): 25–26.
　　b.　In Robert Gover. *From One Hundred Dollar Misunderstanding.* [New York: Grove Press, 1962?].
　　Beginning with an ironic paean to ex-President Eisenhower, who has condemned the "filth" in modern society, Vidal goes on to discuss Robert Gover's *One Hundred Dollar Misunderstanding,* a novel about a college boy who visits a young African American prostitute. b. includes a chapter from the novel, preceded by a reprint of Vidal's comments.

41.   "The Twelve Caesars."
      a.   In A.21 (as "Robert Graves and the Twelve Caesars").
      b.   In A.27 (as "Robert Graves and the Twelve Caesars").
      c.   In A.31.
      d.   In John Gross, ed. *The Oxford Book of Essays*. Oxford: Oxford University Press, 1991, pp. 634–40 (abridged).
      e.   In A.56.
      f.   In A.62.
           Essay on Suetonius' *The Twelve Caesars*. Suetonius, in Vidal's view, shows the crippling psychological effects of absolute power upon the Roman emperors, chiefly embodied in their sexual proclivities. In A.21 Vidal gives the date of composition as 1959; in A.56 he gives it as 1952.

42.   "Nasser's Egypt."
      a.   *Esquire* 58, no. 4 (October 1962): 138, 140, 142–44, 146, 148, 150, 152, 155–57.
      b.   In A.28 (as "A Passage to Egypt").
      c.   In A.31.
      d.   In A.56.
           Lengthy essay on Vidal's trip to Egypt, where he visited Cairo, Aswan (where many Russians are assisting in the building of the dam), and elsewhere. Throughout the trip he attempts to discuss President Nasser with the various individuals (both Egyptians and foreigners) whom he meets, but with relatively little success. Vidal makes a succession of appointments to see Nasser himself, but is always put off. He notes that "The principal source of irritation between Nasser and the United States is Israel."

43.   "Preface to the British Edition."
      a.   In A.22.
           Vidal speaks in general terms of the three plays in the book.

44.   "[Preface to] *On the March to the Sea.*"
      a.   In A.22.
           Vidal refers to the play as "faulty" and discusses the circumstances of its composition.

45.   "John Hersey's *Here to Stay?*"
      a.   *New York Review of Books* 1, no. 1 (27 February 1963): 22–23 (as "Tenacity").
      b.   In A.28.
      c.   In Robert B. Silvers and Barbara Epstein, eds. *Selections from the First Two Issues of* The New York Review of Books. New York: Rea S. Hederman, 1988, pp. 51–53 (as "Tenacity").
           Negative review of a collection of articles by Hersey, who is "almost always dull." Hersey's journalistic method is to collect an enormous amount of data and then to editorialize about it.

46.   "The Best Man 1968."
      a.   *Esquire* 59, no. 3 (March 1963): 59–62, 136.
           A rumination about the probable candidates for president in 1968 (Vidal assumes that John F. Kennedy will be elected to a second term in 1964). Robert F. Kennedy is the most likely Democratic candidate, as "it would be almost like granting John a third term." But Robert is not temperamentally suited to be president, because he sees everything in black-and-white terms and is a zealot. On the Republican side, Vidal goes through a number of possibilities—Nelson Rockefeller, George Romney, William Scranton, Mark Hatfield, Barry Goldwater—before deciding on Rockefeller.

47.   "Un-American Activities."
      a.   *Observer* (London) no. 8964 (21 April 1963): 23.
           A review of *The American Establishment* by Richard Rovere, a collection of political and cultural essays. Vidal states that Rovere "does splendid work" on several subjects, including

Douglas McArthur and the Truman-Dewey campaign; "Mr. Rovere possesses not only wit and grace but a shrewd moral sense."

48.   "Edmund Wilson, Tax Dodger."
   a.   *New York Herald Tribune Book Week* (3 November 1963): 3 (as "Indicting the Piper").
   b.   In A.28.
   c.   In A.31.
   d.   In A.56.
       A review of Wilson's *The Cold War and the Income Tax,* in which Wilson admitted that he filed no tax returns between 1946 and 1955 and was subsequently in trouble with the IRS for years thereafter. Vidal agrees with Wilson that our taxes are, in general, high because they are being used to support an immense military buildup.

49.   "Tarzan Revisited."
   a.   *Esquire* 60, no. 6 (December 1963): 193, 262, 264.
   b.   In A.27.
   c.   In A.28 (as "The Waking Dream: Tarzan Revisited").
   d.   In A.31.
   e.   In The Editors of Esquire, ed. *Esquire: The Best Forty Years.* New York: David McKay, 1973, pp. 252, 254–55.
   f.   In Edgar Rice Burroughs. *Tarzan of the Apes.* New York: New American Library, March, 1990, pp. 9–14.
   g.   In A.56.
       Affectionate essay on Vidal's early reading of the Tarzan novels by Edgar Rice Burroughs, "an archetypal American dreamer." Vidal has now reread several of these books, which, although subliterary, nevertheless have some merits (Burroughs "can describe action vividly"). Tarzan is in essence "a daydream figure."

50.   "The Wit and Wisdom of J. K. Galbraith."
   a.   *New York Review of Books* 1, no. 8 (12 December 1963): 4 (as "Citizen Ken").
   b.   In A.28.
       A review of Galbraith's *The McLandress Dimension,* a collection of essays written under the pseudonym "Mark Epernay." The seven articles are all "based on a single joke" and are highly uneven.

51.   "Primary Vote for a 'Best Man.'"
   a.   *New York Times* (5 April 1964): Section 2, p. 7.
       Discussion of the increasing number of political films being made, including *Dr. Strangelove* and *Seven Days in May,* followed by remarks about the play *The Best Man* and its film adaptation.

52.   "John O'Hara."
   a.   *New York Review of Books* 2, no. 5 (16 April 1964): 5–9 (as "Appointment with O'Hara").
   b.   In A.27 (as "John O'Hara's Old Novels").
   c.   In A.28 (as "John O'Hara's Old Novels").
   d.   In A.31.
   e.   In A.56.
       Overview of O'Hara's work, focusing on two recent books: the novel *Elizabeth Appleton* and *The Hat on the Bed,* a collection of short stories currently on the best-seller list. O'Hara's work is in the naturalist tradition; his "prose is plain and rather garrulous." The novel seems "improvised," and many of the realistic details seem to have no bearing to the work as a whole. But O'Hara does possess "the narrative gift."

53.   "The Television Blacklist."
   a.   *New York Herald Tribune Book Week* (15 November 1964): 1, 24–25 (as "Night of the Vigilantes").

b.   In A.27.
A review of *Fear on Trial* by John Henry Faulk, a discussion of the blacklist of supposed Communists in the 1950s. Faulk speaks of accusations that he was a Communist sympathizer, which resulted in the damaging of his career for years but finally led to the punishment of the McCarthyite organization (AWARE) that had brought the accusations.

54.   "E. Nesbit's Magic."
a.   *New York Review of Books* 3, no. 8 (3 December 1964): 12–13 (as "E. Nesbit").
b.   In A.28 (as "E. Nesbit's Use of Magic").
c.   In A.31.
d.   In A.56.
Warm essay on E. Nesbit's novels about children (Vidal states that, like Lewis Carroll, she did not write "*for* children"). "To my mind, it is in the 'magic books' that Nesbit is at her best." Vidal's favorites are *The House of Arden* and *Harding's Luck.* He believes that children would be better off reading books of the imagination like these rather than "practical books with facts in them."

55.   "John Horne Burns."
a.   *New York Times Book Review* (30 May 1965): 2, 22 (as "Speaking of Books: John Horne Burns").
b.   In A.27 (as "The Revelation of John Horne Burns").
c.   In A.28 (as "The Revelation of John Horne Burns").
d.   In Francis Brown, ed. *Page 2: The Best of "Speaking of Books" from* The New York Times Book Review. New York: Holt, Rinehart & Winston, 1969, pp. 256–60.
e.   In A.31.
f.   In A.56.
Essay on Burns, a novelist who wrote several novels about World War II and its aftermath, including *The Gallery* (1947), referred to as "the best book of the Second War." "Burns's style is energetic, very much that of the forties."

56.   "The *Sexus* of Henry Miller."
a.   *New York Herald Tribune Book Week* (1 August 1965): 1, 10 (as "Oh, Henry").
b.   In A.27.
c.   In A.28.
d.   In A.31.
e.   In A.56.
f.   In A.63.
Discussion of Miller's *Sexus:* "only a total egotist could have written a book which has no subject other than Henry Miller in all his sweet monotony." Although Miller's accounts of his sexual escapades are monotonous and self-indulgent, he did help "make a social revolution" in breaking down barriers for those who wished to write honestly about sex.

57.   "American Fiction: The Postwar Years, 1945–65" [symposium].
a.   *New York Herald Tribune Book Week* (26 September 1965): 6.
One-sentence comment by Vidal stating that the period in question was "Easily the richest period in the history of the American novel."

58.   "The Novel in the Age of Science."
a.   *Quarterly Journal of the Library of Congress* 22, no. 4 (October 1965): 288–99.
Major uncollected essay discussing the role of science in modern society and the pernicious influence of "scientism" in the arts, including the novel, the theater, and film. The essay is a lecture delivered at the Library of Congress on 11 June 1965.

59.   "Byzantium's Fall."
a.   *Reporter* 33, no. 6 (7 October 1965): 54–57 (as "Byzantine Mosaic").
b.   In A.28.
c.   In A.31.

A review of Sir Steven Runciman's *The Fall of Contantinople, 1453,* and a rumination on the end of the Byzantine Empire.

60.   "On Revising One's Own Work."
    a.   *New York Times Book Review* (14 November 1965): 2, 82 (as "Speaking of Books: Making and Remaking").
    b.   In A.28.
    Vidal speaks of the revision of his three early novels, *The City and the Pillar* (A.3.e), *The Judgment of Paris* (A.8.c), and *Messiah* (A.12.d).

61.   "Writers and the World."
    a.   *Times Literary Supplement* no. 3326 (25 November 1965): 1042–43 (as "Writers in the Public Eye"; unsigned).
    b.   In A.27.
    c.   In A.28.
    d.   In A.31.
    e.   In A.56.
    On the effect of celebrity upon writers, and the need for good writers to be politically and culturally engaged.

62.   "Sex and the Law."
    a.   *Partisan Review* 32, no. 1 (Winter 1965): 79–87 (as "But Is It Legal?").
    b.   In A.3.e.
    c.   In A.27.
    d.   In A.28.
    e.   In A.31.
    f.   In A.56.
    g.   In A.63.
    Vidal provides a potted history of governmental attempts to legislate sexual morality and the gradual realization that such attempts almost always fail.

63   *"The City and the Pillar* After Twenty Years."
    a.   In A.3.e (as "Afterword").
    b.   In A.27.
    c.   In A.28.
    Brief account of the writing of his celebrated novel and a discussion of the ways in which sexual mores have been liberalized since its publication.

64.   "Pornography."
    a.   *New York Review of Books* 4, no. 5 (31 March 1966): 4–6, 8, 10 (as "On Pornography").
    b.   In A.16.e.
    c.   In A.27 (as "On Pornography").
    d.   In A.28 (as "Notes on Pornography").
    e.   In A.31.
    f.   In A.56.
    g.   In A.63.
    A discussion of Maurice Girodias, publisher of the Olympia Press, and his recent book, *The Olympia Reader,* and a consideration of the effects of pornography on society. For Girodias's response to the review, see III.E.127.

65.   "Tennessee Williams."
    a.   *McCall's* 94, no. 1 (October 1966): 107.
    A brief and impressionistic portrait of Williams. For Williams's similar portrait of Vidal, see III.E.306.

66. "Paranoid Politics."
  a. *New Statesman* 73 (no. 1870) (13 January 1967): 49–50 (as "God's Country").
  b. In A.27 (as "God's Country: The American Empire's Beginning").
  c. In A.28 (as "God's Country: The American Empire's Beginning").
  d. In A.31.
  e. In A.56.
      A review of Richard Hofstadter's *The Paranoid Style in American Politics* and an examination of political fanaticism on both the right and the left.

67. "The Holy Family."
  a. *Esquire* 67, no. 4 (April 1967): 99–102, 201–4.
  b. In A.27.
  c. In A.28.
  d. In Harold Hayes, ed. *Smiling through the Apocalypse:* Esquire's *History of the Sixties.* New York: McCall Publishing Co., 1969; New York: Dell, 1971, pp. 111–26. New York: Crown Publishers, 1987, pp. 57–72.
  e. In A.31.
  f. *Esquire* 99, no. 6 (June 1983): 210 (as "Dynastic Ambitions"; extract).
  g. In A.56.
  h. In A.62.
  i. In Ian Hamilton, ed. *The Penguin Book of Twentieth-Century Essays.* London: Allan Lane/Penguin Press, 1999; London: Penguin, 2000; New York: Fromm International, 2000 (as *The Book of Twentieth-Century Essays*), pp. 387–405.
      Celebrated essay on the Kennedys and on the scholars who have, in Vidal's view, acted as their toadies, including William Manchester (*The Death of a President*), Pierre Salinger (*With Kennedy*), Paul B. Fay Jr. (*The Pleasure of His Company*), and others who have sought to elevate the Kennedys to the status of secular saints.

68. "The Manchester Book."
  a. *New York World Journal Tribune Book Week* (9 April 1967): 1–3 (as "A Twist of History").
  b. In A.27.
  c. In A.28.
  d. In A.31.
  e. In A.56.
      A closer examination of William Manchester's *The Death of a President* and its account of Kennedy's assassination.

69. "Miss Sontag's New Novel."
  a. *Washington Post Book World* (10 September 1967): 5, 34 (as "The Writer as Cannibal").
  b. In A.28 (as "Miss Sontag's Second New Novel").
  c. In A.31.
  d. In A.56.
      A review of Susan Sontag's *Death Kit* and its failed attempt to mimic the French "New Novelists."

70. "French Letters: Theories of the New Novel."
  a. *Encounter* 29, no. 6 (December 1967): 13–23 (as "French Letters: The Theory of the New Novel").
  b. In A.27.
  c. In A.28.
  d. In A.31.
  e. In A.36.
  f. In A.56.

g.   In A.62.
      A lengthy and largely censorious account of the work of Alain Robbe-Grillet, Nathalie Sarraute, Michel Butor, and other experimental writers whose work is excessively theoretical and marred by shoddy writing and inconsistent theorizing.

71.   "Books They Liked Best" [symposium].
      a.   *Washington Post Book World* (3 December 1967): 7.
            Three titles listed by Vidal as among his favorite books of 1967.

72.   "Public Television: A Meditation."
      a.   *New York Review of Books* 9, no. 10 (7 December 1967): 24–29 (as "See It Later").
      b.   In A.27 (as "Public Television").
      c.   In A.28.
            A rumination on the difficulties that public television faces in competition with commercial television.

73.   [Untitled.]
      a.   In Cecil Woolf and John Bagguley, eds. *Authors Take Sides on Vietnam.* London: Peter Owen, 1967; New York: Simon & Schuster, 1967, p. 187.
            A two-paragraph statement expressing opposition to "American intervention in the Vietnamese civil war."

74.   "Gore Vidal."
      a.   *New York Times Book Review* (1 September 1968): 1, 19 (as "The Subject Doesn't Object").
      b.   In A.28 (as "Gore Vidal: Subject").
      c.   In A.31.
      d.   In A.56.
            A charitable review of Ray Lewis White's *Gore Vidal* (III.D.16), stating that it is "a most interesting book, astonishingly exact in detail and often shrewd in judgment."

75.   "The Twenty-ninth Republican Convention."
      a.   *New York Review of Books* 11, no. 4 (12 September 1968): 5–6, 8 (as "The Late Show").
      b.   In A.28 (as "The Twenty-ninth Republican Convention, Miami Beach, Florida, August 5–8, 1968").
      c.   In A.31.
      d.   In A.56.
            A satirical description of the Republican convention, in which Richard M. Nixon was nominated, although Ronald Reagan made a strong showing.

76.   "A Manifesto."
      a.   *Esquire* 70, no. 4 (October 1968): 156, 158, 252.
      b.   In A.28.
      c.   In A.31 (as "Manifesto and Dialogue").
            A rumination on the impending overpopulation of the planet and a plea for an ill-defined "Authority" to "have the power to limit births by law." The latter part of the essay is a dialogue between a "Private Self" and a "Public Self" on the wisdom and practicability of this idea.

77.   "Preface."
      a.   In A.27.
      b.   In A.28 (revised).
            A brief explanation of why "sex, death and money . . . are the essential interests of the naked ape." Vidal notes that American sexual morality is being liberalized and that "the American political system is running down." In b. a new opening paragraph has been written.

78.   "The Liberal Dilemma."
     a.   In A.27.
     a.   In A.28.
     A study of the decline of liberalism and the rise of conservatism in the wake of the Vietnam War and the attempt to bestow equality upon African Americans.

79.   "Books I Liked Best in 1968" [symposium].
     a.   *Washington Post Book World* (1 December 1968): 4.
     Three titles listed by Vidal as his favorite books of 1968.

80.   "A Distasteful Encounter with William F. Buckley, Jr."
     a.   *Esquire* 72, no. 3 (September 1969): 140–43, 145, 150.
     b.   In Harold Hayes, ed. *Smiling through the Apocalypse:* Esquire's *History of the Sixties.* New York: McCall Publishing Co., 1969; New York: Dell, 1971, pp. 947–63. New York: Crown Publishers, 1987, pp. 572–88.
     Pungently satirical response to Buckley's "On Experiencing Gore Vidal" (III.E.48), and a detailed examination of their television debate at the Republican and Democratic national conventions of 1968, followed by an account of Vidal's earlier dealings with Buckley. He defends *Myra Breckinridge* against Buckley's charges that it is pornographic, and discusses Buckley's family, including an incident in 1944 when some of his sisters vandalized an Episcopal church in Connecticut. It was this article that led to Buckley's suit against Vidal and *Esquire,* which presumably accounts for why Vidal never reprinted the article in any of his essay collections.

81.   "Literary Gangsters."
     a.   *Commentary* 49, no. 3 (March 1970): 61–64.
     b.   In A.31.
     c.   In A.56.
     Harsh attack on such critics and reviewers as John W. Aldridge, Robert Brustein, John Simon, and Richard Gilman, who engage in *ad hominem* attacks for the purpose of getting noticed.

82.   "An American Press Lord."
     a.   *New York Review of Books* 14, no. 7 (9 April 1970): 4–6 (as "Ambassador Erect").
     b.   In A.31.
     c.   In A.56.
     Study of Walter Annenberg (under the guise of reviewing Gaeton Fonzi's *Annenberg: A Biography of Power*), Nixon's ambassador to England and the owner of numerous popular newspapers and magazines, including *TV Guide* and the *Philadelphia Inquirer,* which Annenberg used to attack his political enemies.

83.   "Meredith."
     a.   *Times* (London) (2 May 1970): Saturday Review, I, IV (as "King Meredith").
     b.   In A.31.
     c.   In A.56.
     Study of George Meredith and his peculiar place in the history of the English novel.

84.   "Doc Reuben."
     a.   *New York Review of Books* 14, no. 11 (4 June 1970): 8, 10, 12–14 (as "Number One").
     b.   In A.31.
     c.   In A.56.
     d.   In A.63.
     Satirical review of David Reuben's *Everything You Always Wanted to Know about Sex (But Were Afraid to Ask)*, criticizing him for superficial Freudianism and for prejudice against gay sex.

85.   "Drugs."
       a.   *New York Times* (26 September 1970): 29 (as "Drugs: Case for Legalizing Marijuana").
       b.   In A.31.
       c.   In A.56.
       d.   In A.62.
             Argues that legalizing all drugs and selling them at cost will do more to end drug addiction than spending enormous amounts of money attempting to interdict them.

86.   "The Best Man '72."
       a.   *Esquire* 75, no. 6 (June 1971): 102–5.
             Discussion of the New Party, formed by Dr. Benjamin Spock, and the prospects of this third party if it were to nominate Ralph Nader for president.

87.   "The Death of Mishima."
       a.   *New York Review of Books* 16, no. 11 (17 June 1971): 8–10 (as "Mr. Japan").
       b.   In A.31.
       c.   In A.56.
             Study of the Japanese writer Yukio Mishima and the death-imagery pervading his novels. Vidal concludes that Mishima is a "minor artist."

88.   "Women's Liberation: Feminism and Its Discontents."
       a.   *New York Review of Books* 17, no. 1 (22 July 1971): 8, 10–12 (as "In Another Country").
       b.   In A.31 (as "Women's Liberation Meets Miller-Mailer-Manson Man").
       c.   In Michael S. Kimmel and Thomas E. Mosmiller, eds. *Against the Tide: Pro-Feminist Men in the United States, 1776–1990: A Documentary History.* Boston: Beacon Press, 1992, pp. 375–78 (extract; as "Women's Liberation Meets Miller-Mailer-Manson Man").
       d.   In A.56.
       e.   In A.62.
       f.   In A.63.
             Study of the feminist movement (Eva Figes, Kate Millett, Betty Friedan, Germaine Greer) and such opponents of feminism as Sigmund Freud, Norman Mailer, and Irving Howe. The essay particularly infuriated Mailer because it seemed to liken him to Charles Manson.

89.   "The Fourth Diary of Anaïs Nin."
       a.   *Los Angeles Times Book Review* (26 September 1971): 1, 5, 23 (as "Taking a Grand Tour of Anais Nin's High Bohemia via the Time Machine").
       b.   In A.31.
       c.   In A.56.
             A review of the fourth volume of Nin's diary (see III.E.234), covering the years 1944–1947, when Vidal first encountered her. Vidal records his own impressions of Nin and claims that many of the statements in her diary are false or misleading.

90.   "Eleanor Roosevelt."
       a.   *New York Review of Books* 17, no. 8 (18 November 1971): 3–4, 6, 8 (as "Eleanor").
       b.   In A.31.
       c.   In A.56.
       d.   In A.62.
       e.   In A.63.
             Nominally a review of Joseph Lash's *Eleanor and Franklin,* allowing Vidal to discuss Eleanor Roosevelt, with whom Vidal was acquainted in the 1950s. He studies her relations with Franklin D. Roosevelt and records his own memories of her.

91.   "H. Hughes."
- a.   *New York Review of Books* 18, no. 7 (20 April 1972): 11–12 (as "Hughes' Tool").
- b.   In A.31.
- c.   In A.56.
  Review of *Howard: The Amazing Mr. Hughes* by Noah Dietrich and Bob Thomas, discussing Howard Hughes's involvement in the film industry, the airline industry, and politics.

92.   "Note."
- a.   In A.30.
  Vidal notes that he came to write the play *An Evening with Richard Nixon* after "much brooding on the national amnesia."

93.   "Homage to Daniel Shays."
- a.   *New York Review of Books* 19, no. 2 (10 August 1972): 8–12.
- b.   In A.31.
- c.   In A.56.
  Review of G. William Donhoff's *Fat Cats and Democrats*. Vidal writes a paean to Shays, who led a tax revolt in the early nineteenth century, and a proceeds to a discussion of tax policies in the United States, noting that even the Democrats are in the pockets of a small elite of wealthy individuals and corporations.

94.   "Note."
- a.   In A.31.
  Explains the purpose of gathering most (but not all) of the essays he had written up to this point.

95.   "Political Melodramas."
- a.   *New Statesman* 85 (no. 2198) (4 May 1973): 639–40 (as "Politics, Washington DC").
- b.   In A.36.
- c.   In A.56.
  Vidal begins with a discussion of his political works (*The Best Man, Washington, D.C., An Evening with Richard Nixon*) and proceeds to a discussion of Robert N. Winter-Berger's *Washington Pay-Off,* an exposé of influence-peddling in Washingon.

96.   "The Top Ten Best Sellers According to the Sunday *New York Times* as of January 7, 1973."
- a.   *New York Review of Books* 20, no. 8 (17 May 1973): 12–16 (as "The Ashes of Hollywood I: The Bottom 4 of the Top 10"); 20, no. 9 (31 May 1973): 15–18 (as "The Ashes of Hollywood II: The Top 6 of the Top 10").
- b.   In A.36.
- c.   In A.56.
  Piquant review of best-selling novels, including Marjorie Holmes's *Two from Galilee,* Trevanian's *The Eiger Sanction,* Victoria Holt's *On the Night of the Seventh Moon,* Herman Wouk's *The Winds of War,* Robert Crichton's *The Camerons,* Mary Renault's *The Persian Boy,* Alexander Solzhenitsyn's *August 1914,* Dan Jenkins's *Semi-Tough,* Frederick Forsyth's *The Odessa File,* and Richard Bach's *Jonathan Livingston Seagull.*

97.   "Conglomerates."
- a.   *New Statesman* 86 (no. 2209) (20 July 1973): 87–88 (as "Linkage Is All").
- b.   In A.36.
- c.   In A.56.
  On ITT's influence upon contemporary American politics through lobbying and campaign contributions.

98.   "Philip French Presents an Appreciation of Edmund Wilson, 1895–1972" [symposium].
- a.   *Listener* 90 (no. 2321) (20 September 1973): 371–74.
  Vidal, along with Lionel Trilling, Stephen Spender, V. S. Pritchett, John Wain, Jason Epstein, George Steiner, Yigael Yadin, and Philip French (moderator) discuss the life and work of

Edmund Wilson. Vidal notes Wilson's importance as a critic in post–World War II America and states that "I certainly had enormous sympathy" with him.

99.   "West Point."
   a.   *New York Review of Books* 20, no. 16 (18 October 1973): 21–22, 24, 26–28 (as "West Point and the Third Loyalty").
   b.   In A.36.
   c.   In A.56.
   d.   In Robert Pack and Jay Parini, eds. *American Identities: Contemporary Multicultural Voices.* Hanover, NH: University Press of New England, 1994, pp. 322–34.
   e.   In A.62.
        Nominally a review of *West Point: America's Power Fraternity* by K. Bruce Galloway and Robert Bowie Johnson. Vidal speaks of being born at West Point (his father had attended the military academy) and the peculiar loyalties that emerge from its culture.

100.   "The Art and Arts of E. Howard Hunt."
   a.   *New York Review of Books* 20, no. 20 (13 December 1973): 6, 8, 10, 12–19.
   b.   In A.36.
   c.   In A.56.
        Satirical account of E. Howard Hunt, the Watergate conspirator, and the numerous political and military novels he wrote from the 1940s to the 1970s.

101.   "Contagious Self-Love."
   a.   *New Statesman* 87 (no. 2242) (8 March 1974): 327 (as "British Worthy no. 4").
   b.   In A.36.
   c.   In A.56.
        Review of *The Grain of Wheat: An Autobiography* by the Earl of Longford, with whom Vidal had a debate about sex (see III.C.39). The book details, among other things, Longford's "crusade against pornography."

102.   "Professor V. Nabokov."
   a.   *Observer* (London) no. 9537 (12 May 1974): 36 (as "Black Swan's Way").
   b.   In A.36.
   c.   In A.56.
        Review of Nabokov's memoir *Strong Opinions,* which reveals that Nabokov "is still very much a part of the American academic machine."

103.   "Calvino's Novels."
   a.   *New York Review of Books* 21, no. 9 (30 May 1974): 13–21 (as "Fabulous Calvino").
   b.   In A.36.
   c.   In A.56.
        Lengthy discussion of Italo Calvino, including personal recollections and a survey of his novels and stories. The essay was a significant landmark in Calvino's critical recognition.

104.   "The Great World and Louis Auchincloss."
   a.   *New York Review of Books* 21, no. 12 (18 July 1974): 10–14 (as "Real Class").
   b.   In A.36.
   c.   In A.56.
        Study of the novels of Auchincloss, a friend and remote relation of Vidal's and one of the few modern American novelists to discuss the issue of class in his work.

105.   "What Robert Moses Did to New York City."
   a.   *New York Review of Books* 21, no. 16 (17 October 1974): 3–4, 6–9 (as "Emperor of Concrete").
   b.   In A.36.
   c.   In A.56.

Review of Robert A. Caro's *The Power Broker*, a biography of Robert Moses, Parks Commissioner for New York City. Vidal believes Moses damaged New York by corrupt dealings and by ruthlessly uprooting mostly impoverished residents to make way for his grandiose building projects.

106. "Epilogue."
    a. In Roloff Beny. *Roloff Beny in Italy*. London: Thames & Hudson, 1974; New York: Harper & Row, 1974; Toronto: McClelland & Stewart, 1974, pp. 408–9.
       Vidal speaks of why he lives in Rome and some of its distinctive characteristics.

107. "The State of the Union: 1975."
    a. *Esquire* 83, no. 5 (May 1975): 61–68, 137 (as "The State of the Union").
    b. In A.36 (as "The State of the Union").
    c. In A.56.
       Vidal discusses American politics and society and thinks that neither political party (really branches of the same party) can offer a solution to the numerous problems facing the nation: drugs, excessive defense spending, overpopulation, political corruption.

108. "The Meaning of Vietnam" [symposium].
    a. *New York Review of Books* 22, no. 10 (12 June 1975): 24.
       Vidal contributes to a symposium pondering the fate of Vietnam and the United States at the conclusion of the war.

109. "President and Mrs. U. S. Grant."
    a. *New York Review of Books* 22, no. 14 (18 September 1975): 6, 8–12 (as "The Grants").
    b. In A.36.
    c. In A.56.
    d. In A.62.
       Nominally a review of *The Personal Memoirs of Julia Dent Grant*, and a study of Grant during the Civil War and as president. Many of the conclusions reached in the essay are also found in the novel *1876*.

110. "The Four Generations of the Adams Family."
    a. *Sunday Times Magazine* (London) (2 November 1975): 50, 56, 58–59, 61, 63, 65–66, 68 (as "The First Family").
    b. *New York Review of Books* 23, no. 4 (18 March 1976): 18–20 (as "Adamses: The 'Best' People I"; 23, no. 5 (1 April 1976): 20–23 (as "The Adams' Fall: II").
    c. In *Great American Families* by Gore Vidal et al. London: Times Books, 1977; New York: W. W. Norton, 1977, pp. 9–27 (as "Adams").
    d. In A.36.
    e. In A.56.
       Discussion of John Adams, John Quincy Adams, Charles Francis Adams, Henry Adams, and their roles in American politics and culture. Some paragraphs from item 120 below were incorporated into the book versions of the essay.

111. "Praefazione."
    a. In Gianfranco Corsini and Franco Ferrarotti. *America duecento anni dopo*. Rome: Editori Riuniti, 1975, pp. 7–8.
       In Italian. Vidal states that Proteus should be the titular deity of the United States.

112. "Some Memories of the Glorious Bird and an Earlier Self."
    a. *New York Review of Books* 23, no. 1 (5 February 1976): 13–18 (as "Selected Memories of the Glorious Bird and the Golden Age").
    b. In A.36.
    c. In A.56.
    d. In Phillip Lopate, ed. *The Art of the Personal Essay*. New York: Anchor Books/Doubleday, 1994, pp. 623–38.

    e.   In A.62.
        Extensive and affectionate memoir of Tennessee Williams (nominally a review of Williams's
        Memoirs), relating their visits to Europe and their responses to each other's writings.

113.   "The Hacks of Academe."
    a.   *Times Literary Supplement* no. 3858 (20 February 1976): 182–83 (as "The Fall of the
        House of Fiction").
    b.   In A.36.
    c.   In A.56.
        A review of *The Theory of the Novel: New Essays,* edited by John Halperin, and a searing
        condemnation of academic critics who write in obfuscatory jargon and are incapable of assessing
        literature as a living force.

114.   "I Hear America Silenced."
    a.   *Penthouse* 7, no. 11 (July 1976): 75–76.
        Brief essay condemning recent Supreme Court decisions for restricting freedom of speech,
        particularly in regard to material considered pornographic. The Nixon and Ford administrations
        are also condemned as enemies of free speech.

115.   "American Plastic: The Matter of Fiction."
    a.   *New York Review of Books* 23, no. 12 (15 July 1976): 31–39.
    b.   In A.36.
    c.   In A.56.
        Essay on the New Novel as practiced in the United States, especially such writers as Donald
        Barthelme, William Gass, John Barth, John Gardner, and Thomas Pynchon, whose work is
        characterized by poor prose, narrow focus, and excessive self-consciousness.

116.   "Who Makes the Movies?"
    a.   *New York Review of Books* 23, no. 19 (25 November 1976): 35–39.
    b.   In A.42.
    c.   In A.56.
    d.   In A.62.
        Vidal contends that during the 1950s, when he was in the film industry, the director played a
        relatively small role in the making of a film. The notion of the director as *auteur* is absurd, and
        more credit should be given to screenwriters. Vidal discusses his role in rewriting the screenplay
        of *Ben-Hur.*

117.   "Christopher Isherwood's Kind."
    a.   *New York Review of Books* 23, no. 20 (9 December 1976): 10, 12, 14, 16, 18 (as "Art,
        Sex and Isherwood").
    b.   In A.42.
    c.   In Christopher Isherwood. *Where Joy Resides: An Isherwood Reader.* Ed. Don
        Bachardy and James P. White. London: Methuen, 1989; New York: Farrar, Straus &
        Giroux, 1989, 1991; Minneapolis: University of Minnesota Press, 2003, pp. ix–xix (as
        "Introduction").
    d.   In A.56.
    e.   In A.63.
        Memoir of Christopher Isherwood (nominally a review of Isherwood's *Christopher Isherwood
        and His Kind*), a discussion of his work as novelist and autobiographer, and a study of his
        homosexuality.

118.   "Note."
    a.   In A.36.
        Vidal briefly explains why he has divided the essays in this volume into those concerned with
        "fact" and those concerned with "fiction." A long quotation from Sainte-Beuve is included.

119. "The Oz Books."
   a. *New York Review of Books* 24, no. 15 (29 September 1977): 10, 12–15 (as "The Wizard of the 'Wizard'"); 24, no. 16 (13 October 1977): 38–42 (as "On Rereading the Oz Books").
   b. In A.42.
   c. In A.56.
      Affectionate essay on L. Frank Baum's Oz books, which Vidal read in youth, an account of Baum's life and work, and a discussion of their role in stimulating the imagination of children.

120. "Introduction."
   a. In *Great American Families* by Gore Vidal and others. London: Times Books, 1977; New York: W. W. Norton & Co., 1977, pp. 6–7.
      Brief discussion of the social theories of the Founding Fathers. The first few paragraphs of the introduction were incorporated into "The Four Generations of the Adams Family" (item 110 above).

121. "Preface."
   a. In Rudolf Augstein. *Jesus Son of Man.* New York: Urizen Books, 1977, pp. 7–8.
      Briefly discusses how Augstein's radical book on Christianity is a "highly useful and informative record of continuing human folly."

122. "Introduction."
   a. *Atlantic Monthly* 241, no. 2 (February 1978): 64–67 (abridged; as "Of Writers and Class: In Praise of Edith Wharton").
   b. In Edith Wharton. *The Edith Wharton Omnibus.* Garden City, NY: Nelson Doubleday, 1978, pp. vii–xiii.
      Vidal believes that Wharton is a major American novelist but that she has not been given credit for her achievement because of her sex and because she discusses the issue of class, always an uneasy topic for Americans. Vidal briefly describes the three works in the volume: *Ethan Frome, The Age of Innocence,* and *Old New York.*

123. "Rich Kids."
   a. *New York Review of Books* 25, no. 1 (9 February 1978): 9–10, 12, 14.
   b. In A.42.
   c. In A.56.
      A review of *Priviledged Ones* by Robert Coles (part of his "Children of Crisis" series), as Vidal studies how Coles conducted his research and adds his own insights of a wealthy and privileged upbringing.

124. "On Prettiness."
   a. *New Statesman* 95 (no. 2452) (17 March 1978): 380, 382–83 (as "He Dwells with Beauty").
   b. In A.42.
   c. In A.56.
      A review of *The Parting Years* by Sir Cecil Beaton, the diary of a photographer. Vidal notes that Beaton is "a good travel-writer" and speaks interestingly of the celebrities he has known.

125. "How to Find God and Make Money."
   a. *New York Review of Books* 25, no. 11 (29 June 1978): 17–18, 20–22 ("Bert and LaBelle and Jimmy and God").
   b. In A.42.
   c. In A.56.
      A satirical review of several religious volumes, notably *This Too Shall Pass* by Mrs. Bert (LaBelle) Lance, wife of an official in the Jimmy Carter administration who was accused of financial irregularities.

126. [Comment on Jack Kerouac.]
     a. In Barry Gifford and Lawrence Lee. *Jack's Book: An Oral Biography of Jack Kerouac.* New York: St. Martin's Press, 1978, 1994; London: Hamish Hamilton, 1979; New York: Penguin, 1979; Edinburgh: Rebel Inc., 1999; New York: Thunder's Mouth Press, 2005, pp. 182–84.
     Vidal describes his relations with Kerouac (including going to bed with him in the Chelsea Hotel), with some discussion of Allen Ginsberg.

127. "Sex Is Politics."
     a. *Playboy* 26, no. 1 (January 1979): 174, 176–78, 214, 344–46 (as "Sex Is Politics and Vice Versa").
     b. A.39 (as *Sex Is Politics and Vice Versa*).
     c. In A.42.
     d. In A.56.
     e. In A.63.
     Notes that "the sexual attitudes of any given society are the result of political decisions," and notes the pernicious influence of fundamentalist religion and unscrupulous politics in restricting sexual freedom. Vidal attacks such critics as Alfred Kazin, Hilton Kramer, and Norman Podhoretz for their hostility to homosexuality.

128 "V. S. Pritchett as 'Critic.'"
     a. *New York Review of Books* 26, no. 11 (28 June 1979): 6, 8 (as "Secrets of the Shell").
     b. In A.42.
     c. In A.56.
     Appreciative essay on the British critic, noting that Pritchett is good on French and Russian novelists and that he fulfills "the first job of a critic": "to describe what he has read."

129. "Sciascia's Italy."
     a. *New York Review of Books* 26, no. 16 (25 October 1979): 17–23 (as "On the Assassins' Trail").
     b. In A.42.
     c. In A.56.
     Study of Leonardo Sciascia, a Sicilian writer whose novels discuss the Mafia and other aspects of Italian society, politics, and culture.

130. "Afterword."
     a. In Wendy Leigh. *What Makes a Man G.I.B. (Good in Bed).* New York: New American Library (Signet), November 1979; London: Frederick Muller, 1980; St. Albans, UK: Panther Books, 1980, pp. 223–24.
     Brief article asserting that "Sex is both all the same and infinitely various."

131. "Lessing's Science Fiction."
     a. *New York Review of Books* 26, no. 20 (20 December 1979): 3–4 (as "Paradise Regained").
     b. In A.42.
     c. In Claire Sprague and Virginia Tiger, ed. *Critical Essays on Doris Lessing.* Boston: G. K. Hall, 1986, pp. 200–204 (as "Paradise Regained"; extract).
     d. In A.56.
     Review of Lessing's *Shikasta*, which Vidal likens to Milton or the Old Testament, concluding that it is "a fairy tale about good and bad extraterrestrial forces who take some obscure pleasure in manipulating a passive ant-like human race."

132. "Paul Bowles's Stories."
     a. In Paul Bowles. *Collected Stories 1939–1976.* Santa Barbara, CA: Black Sparrow Press, 1979, 1985, 1989, 1994, 1996, 1997, pp. [5]–[9] (as "Introduction").
     b. In A.48.

    c.   In A.49.

    d.   In A.56.

    Warm appreciation of a writer and friend whom Vidal believed to be insufficiently recognized.

133. "Foreword."

    a.   In Peggy Guggenheim. *Out of This Century: Confessions of an Art Addict.* New York: Universe Books, 1979, 1987; Garden City, NY: Anchor Books, 1980; London: Andre Deutsch, 1980, 1983, 2005, pp. xi–xiv.

    b.   In Peggy Guggenheim. *Confessions of an Art Addict.* Hopewell, NJ: Ecco Press, 1997, pp. 7–10.

    Vidal tells of meeting Guggenheim at a party and records his impressions of her. In b. the foreword appears in a reprint of a book originally published in 1960.

134. "F. Scott Fitzgerald's Case."

    a.   *New York Review of Books* 27, no. 7 (1 May 1980): 12–20 (as "Scott's Case").

    b.   In A.42.

    c.   In A.56.

    Nominally a review of *The Notebooks and F. Scott Fitzgerald* and *Correspondence of F. Scott Fitzgerald,* allowing Vidal to conduct a survey and evaluation of Fitzgerald's work and his place in American literature. Vidal also studies Fitzgerald's work in film.

135. "The State of the Union: 1980."

    a.   *Esquire* 94, no. 2 (August 1980): 62–63, 65–69 (as "The State of the Union, 1980").

    b.   In A.42 (as "The State of the Union Revisited (1980)").

    c.   In A.56.

    d.   In A.69.

    Vidal asserts that America has fallen entirely under the rulership of corporations and proposes that a new constitutional convention be convened to ensure individual liberties, tax churches, and abolish the CIA and the National Security Agency.

136. "Edmund Wilson: This Critic and This Gin and These Shoes."

    a.   *New York Review of Books* 27, no. 14 (25 September 1980): 4, 6, 8, 10 (as "This Critic and This Gin and These Shoes").

    b.   In A.42.

    c.   In A.56.

    d.   In A.62.

    Nominally a review of Wilson's *The Thirties.* Vidal studies Wilson's sexual adventures, his flirtation with communism, and his involvements with writers of the period (Thornton Wilder, F. Scott Fitzgerald, and others).

137. "The Real Two-Party System."

    a.   *Los Angeles Times* (26 October 1980): Part VII, pp. 1, 3 (as "In This Dismal Year, Not Casting a Vote Is the Sane Political Act").

    b.   In A.42.

    c.   In A.56.

    Brief essay (originally an op-ed article) discussing why so many Americans choose not to vote and arguing that, in the 1980 election, where religious conservatives and other fanatics are "on a rampage," it is best not to vote at all.

138. "Thomas Love Peacock: The Novel of Ideas."

    a.   *New York Review of Books* 27, no. 19 (4 December 1980): 10, 12, 14, 16, 18–19 (as "The Thinking Man's Novel").

    b.   In A.42.

    c.   In A.56.

    d.   In A.62.

    Study of the nineteenth-century British novelist and his use of social satire.

139. "The Second American Revolution."
      a. *New York Review of Books* 28, no. 1 (5 February 1981): 36–42 (as "The Second American Revolution?").
      b. In A.42.
      c. In A.56.
      d. In A.69.
          Vidal suggests that a second American revolution occurred in 1978 when Californians passed Proposition 13, restricting property taxes. Vidal then studies the Founding Fathers' views of the Constitution (by way of Ferdinand Lundberg's *Cracks in the Constitution*), suggesting that the Supreme Court has arrogated to itself powers that the Founders never intended. The president has now become a dictator, and Vidal suggests that the United States adopt the British parliamentary system.

140. "First Note on Abraham Lincoln."
      a. *Los Angeles Times* (8 February 1981): Part V, pp. 1, 6 (as "Lincoln: 'His Ambition Was a Little Engine That Knew No Rest'").
      b. In A.42 (as "A Note on Abraham Lincoln").
      c. In A.56.
          Brief study of Lincoln through his own writings, concluding that "The actual Lincoln was cold and deliberate, reflective and brilliant." He reports William Herndon's views that Lincoln wrote a treatise against Christianity (later destroyed) and that Lincoln may have given his wife syphilis.

141. "Theodore Roosevelt: An American Sissy."
      a. *New York Review of Books* 28, no. 13 (13 August 1981): 19–23 (as "An American Sissy").
      b. In A.42.
      c. In A.56.
      d. In A.62.
          Review of David McCullough's *Mornings on Horseback*. Vidal studies the political power of the entire Roosevelt family, asserting that it was Theodore Roosevelt's personal deficiencies that led him to assert himself in war and politics.

142. "Pink Triangle and Yellow Star."
      a. *Nation* 233, no. 16 (14 November 1981): 489, 509–12, 515–17 (as "*Some* Jews and *the* Gays").
      b. In A.42.
      c. In A.56.
      d. In A.62.
      e. In A.63.
      f. *Advocate* (14 September 1999): 87 (extract; as "Relax, It's Just Sex").
      g. In Chris Bull, ed. *Come Out Fighting: A Century of Essential Writing on Gay and Lesbian Liberation*. New York: Thunder's Mouth Press/Nation Books, 2001, pp. 189–205.
          Important and controversial essays asserting that some Jewish leaders have made a dangerous pact with evangelical Christians, leading some of them to become gay-baiters. Vidal singles out Midge Decter (wife of Norman Podhoretz) and Joseph Epstein, submitting Decter's work to careful and lengthy analysis.

143. "He Is a Leader for Our Times, Tom Mix on a Trojan Horse."
      a. *Los Angeles Times* (10 January 1982): Sec. 4, pp. 1, 3.
          Op-ed article about Ronald Reagan, noting that unemployment and the deficit have gone up during his first year in office and asserting that Reagan will be forced to raise taxes.

144. "At Home in Washington, D.C."
      a. *New York Review of Books* 29, no. 7 (29 April 1982): 10 (as "The Ruins of Washington").

b. In Derry Moore. *Washington: Houses of the Capital.* Photographs by Derry Moore.
    Text by Henry Mitchell. New York: Viking Press, 1982, pp. 6–8 (as "Foreword").
c. In A.48.
d. In A.49.
e. In A.56.
f. In A.62.
    Brief account of the history of the city and some memories of Vidal's upbringing there.

145. "Hollywood!"
  a. *New York Review of Books* 29, no. 14 (23 September 1982): 6, 9–10 (as "Monkey
      Business").
  b. In A.48.
  c. In A.49.
  d. In A.56.
      Review of *Indecent Exposure* by David McClintock, a study of David Begelman, chief of
      production at Columbia Pictures, accused of financial irregularities.

146. "Tennessee Williams: A Personal Appreciation."
  a. *Los Angeles Times* (27 February 1983): Sec. 4, p. 3.
      Brief appreciation of Williams shortly after his death: "I doubt that we'll see anything like him
      again." Vidal speaks of the last time he saw Williams, a year and a half previously on a
      television appearance in Chicago.

147. "Mongolia!"
  a. *Vanity Fair* 46, no. 1 (March 1983): 72–76, 226, 229, 236 (as "Our Man in
      Mongolia").
  b. In A.48.
  c. In A.49.
  d. In A.56.
      Vidal takes a trip to Mongolia to report on a national park created by the government in the Gobi
      desert.

148. "Frederic Prokosch: The European Connection."
  a. *New York Review of Books* 30, no. 8 (12 May 1983): 14, 16, 18, 20–21 (as "The
      Collector").
  b. In A.48.
  c. In A.49.
  d. In A.56.
      Appreciation of a friend and novelist (nominally a review of Prokosch's memoir, *Voices*),
      leading to Vidal's reminiscences of him and an evaluation of his work.

149. "Ronnie and Nancy: A Life in Pictures."
  a. *New York Review of Books* 30, no. 14 (29 September 1983): 28–32 (as "The Best Years
      of Our Lives").
  b. In A.48.
  c. In A.49.
  d. In A.56.
  e. In A.62.
      Satirical essay on Ronald and Nancy Reagan (nominally a review of Laurence Leamer's *Make-
      Believe: The Story of Nancy and Ronald Reagan*), examining their personal and political
      backgrounds and likening Reagan to Warren G. Harding.

150. "William Dean Howells."
  a. *New York Review of Books* 30, no. 16 (27 October 1983): 45–47, 50–55 (as "'The
      Peculiar American Stamp'").
  b. In A.48.

    c.   In A.49.

    d.   In A.56.

    e.   In A.62.

    Review of the Library of America edition of Howells's early novels, allowing Vidal to survey Howells's life and career, finding him a worthy writer of social realism.

151. "Richard Nixon: Not *The Best Man*'s Best Man."

    a.   *Esquire* 100, no. 6 (December 1983): 66, 68, 70 (as "Nixon without Knives").

    b.   In A.48.

    c.   In A.49.

    d.   In A.56.

    Study of Nixon's presidency and the books that Nixon wrote after he resigned.

152. "Preface."

    a.   In John S. Friedman, ed. *First Harvest: The Institute for Policy Studies, 1963–1983.* New York: Grove Press, 1983, pp. ix–x.

    Vidal claims that "The United States is now in serious disrepair" but that the scholars of the Institute for Policy Studies are doing good work to "bring ideas into American politics."

153. "The Golden Bowl of Henry James."

    a.   *New York Review of Books* 30, Nos. 21 & 22 (19 January 1984): 8–12 (as "Return to 'The Golden Bowl'").

    b.   In Henry James. *The Golden Bowl.* New York: Penguin, 1985, pp. 7–18 (as "Introduction").

    c.   In A.48.

    d.   In A.49.

    e.   In A.56.

    Study of *The Golden Bowl,* seeing the bowl as a symbol for "the relations between the lovers and their legal mates."

154. "Logan Pearsall Smith Loves the Adverb."

    a.   *New York Review of Books* 31, no. 5 (29 March 1984): 20–21 (as "In Love with the Adverb").

    b.   In Logan Pearsall Smith. *All Trivia: Trivia, More Trivia, Afterthoughts, Last Words.* New York: Ticknor & Fields, 1984; London: Viking, 1985; Harmondsworth, UK: Penguin, 1986, pp. xiii–xxi (as "Introduction").

    b.   In A.48.

    c.   In A.49.

    d.   In A.56.

    Study of the American-born British writer whose books are curious collections of literary miscellany.

155. "Introduction."

    a.   In A.44.a.

    Brief account of the writing of *Lincoln.*

156. "On Flying."

    a.   *New York Review of Books* 31, Nos. 21 & 22 (17 January 1985): 14–20 (as "Love of Flying").

    b.   In A.48.

    c.   In A.49.

    d.   In A.56.

    e.   In Robert B. Silvers, ed. *The First Anthology (New York Review of Books).* New York: New York Review of Books, 1993, 2001, pp. 317–35 (as "Love of Flying").

    f.   In A.62.

Account of the early history of flight, including a discussion of his father, Eugene Vidal (director of the Bureau of Air Commerce in the Franklin D. Roosevelt administration), and of his own solo flight in the spring of 1936.

157. "Tennessee Williams: Someone to Laugh at the Squares With."
   a. *New York Review of Books* 32, no. 10 (13 June 1985): 5–6, 8–10 (as "Immortal Bird").
   b. In Tennessee Williams. *Collected Stories.* New York: New Directions, 1985, 1994, 1996; London: Secker & Warburg, 1986; London: Pan Books, 1988; London: Minerva, 1993, 1996, pp. xix–xxv; New York: Bantam Books, 1986, 1992, pp. xxi–xxviii (as "Introduction").
   c. In A.48.
   d. In A.49.
   e. In A.56.
   f. In A.63.
   Survey of Williams's life, with recollections of Vidal's association with him.

158. "At Home in a Roman Street."
   a. *Architectural Digest* 42, no. 10 (October 1985): 144, 146, 148–49 (as "Sempre Roma").
   b. In A.48.
   c. In A.49.
   d. In A.56.
   Brief article about Vidal's apartment in Rome.

159. *Vidal in Venice* (extracts).
   a. *House and Garden* 157, no. 11 (November 1985): 48–50 ("Preface"; as "In Aunt Fenita's Footsteps").
   b. *Washington Post* (20 April 1986): E1, 10 ("Preface"; as "Gore Vidal's 'The Face of Venice'").
   c. In Alice Leccese Powers, ed. *Italy in Mind.* New York: Vintage Books, 1997, pp. 318–23 (ch. 10; as "The City Today").
   In c., the chapter reprinted is not by Vidal. See A.45.

160. "Calvino's Death."
   a. *New York Review of Books* 32, no. 18 (21 November 1985): 3, 6, 8–10 (as "On Italo Calvino").
   b. In Elizabeth Hardwick, ed. *The Best American Essays 1986.* New York: Ticknor & Fields, 1986, pp. 254–66 (as "On Italo Calvino").
   c. In A.48.
   d. In A.49.
   e. In A.56.
   f. In A.62.
   Vidal recounts attending Calvino's funeral, assesses his later work, and provides recollections of his meetings with Calvino.

161. "The Day the American Empire Ran out of Gas."
   a. *Nation* 242, no. 1 (11 January 1986): 1, 15–19 (as "Requiem for the American Empire").
   b. In A.48.
   c. In A.49.
   d. In Ian Angus and Sut Jhally, eds. *Cultural Politics in Contemporary America.* New York: Routledge, 1989, pp. 17–25 (as "Requiem for the American Empire").
   e. In A.55.
   f. In A.56.
   g. In A.62.

h. In A.69.
    Celebrated and notorious essay in which Vidal contends that, with America now a debtor nation, the American Empire is officially over. He traces the development of American imperialism from the Theodore Roosevelt era to the present day and suggests that, with the growing economic power of China and Japan, an alliance with the Soviet Union will be necessary.

162. "A Cheerful Response."
    a. *Nation* 242, no. 11 (22 March 1986): 350, 352–53 (as "The Empire Lovers Strike Back").
    b. In A.48.
    c. In A.49.
    d. In A.56.
    e. In A.69.
        Response to criticisms by Norman Podhoretz (III.E.256) and Midge Decter (III.C.90) of item 161, asserting controversially that "In order to get military and economic support for Israel, a small number of American Jews . . . have made common cause with every sort of reactionary and anti-Semitic group in the United States, from the corridors of the Pentagon to the TV studios of the evangelical Jesus Christers," and that the first loyalty of these Jews is not to the United States but to Israel.

163. "The Bookchat of Henry James."
    a. *New York Review of Books* 23, no. 17 (6 November 1986): 7–10 (as "Lessons of the Master").
    b. In A.48.
    c. In A.49.
    d. In A.56.
    e. In A.62.
        Review of the Library of America edition of James's essays and reviews, exhibiting both the strengths and the weaknesses of James's critical method and practice.

164. "Why I Am Eight Years Younger Than Anthony Burgess."
    a. *New York Review of Books* 34, no. 8 (7 May 1987): 3, 6, 8 (as "Obsession").
    b. In A.48.
    c. In A.49.
    d. In A.56.
        Review of Burgess's *Little Wilson and Big God,* an autobiography, which allows Vidal to reminisce about his encounters with Burgess and to discuss his overall literary output.

165. "Reconvene the Convention and Rewrite the Document."
    a. *Los Angeles Times* (7 June 1987): Sec. 5, pp. 1, 3.
    b. *Newsday* (18 June 1987): 97 (as "Let's Scrap Our Antique Charter and Try Again").
    c. *San Francisco Chronicle* (5 July 1987): 20 (as "Refreshing the Tree of Liberty").
        Op-ed article in which Vidal recommends (as he has done before) holding a new constitutional convention and rewriting he constitution to reflect the altered condition of the United States from the time of the constitution's original writing.

166. "Ollie."
    a. *Newsweek* 110, no. 2 (13 July 1987): 20 (as "The Con-Man as Peck's Bad Boy").
    b. In A.49.
    c. In A.51.
        Brief article on Oliver North and his fleeting celebrity in the wake of the Iran-contra hearings.

167. "The Rise and Fall of the American Empire."
    a. *U.S. News and World Report* 103, no. 2 (13 July 1987): 62.
        Vidal discusses the writing of his new novel, *Empire,* the research he conducts for his historical novels, and the two further novels he has planned, *Harding* (i.e., *Hollywood*) and *The Golden Age.*

168. "Oscar Wilde: On the Skids Again."
   a. *Times Literary Supplement* no. 4409 (2–8 October 1987): 1063–64 (as "A Good Man and a Perfect Play").
   b. In A.49.
   c. In A.51.
   d. In A.56.
   e. In A.63.
       Review of Richard Ellmann's biography of Oscar Wilde. Vidal finds Ellmann good on Wilde's "intellectual progress" and sound in his literary criticism, but deficient in his understanding of Wilde's homosexuality.

169. "Dawn Powell: The American Writer."
   a. *New York Review of Books* 34, no. 17 (5 November 1987): 52–60 (as "Dawn Powell, the American Writer").
   b. In A.49.
   c. In Dawn Powell. *Angels on Toast; The Wicked Pavilion; The Golden Spur.* New York: Quality Paperback Book Club, 1989, pp. vii–xvii (as "Dawn Powell, the American Writer").
   d. In Dawn Powell. *Angels on Toast.* New York: Vintage Books, 1990, pp. vii–xxi (as "Dawn Powell, the American Writer").
   e. In Dawn Powell. *The Wicked Pavilion.* New York: Vintage Books, 1990, pp. vii–xxi (as "Dawn Powell, the American Writer").
   f. In A.51.
   g. In A.56.
       Significant essay on Dawn Powell, an American novelist and playwright whose work Vidal champions as an important contribution to the literature of its time, especially in its use of satire and its portrayal of New York life. Vidal's work led to the reissuance of Powell's work in a number of editions.

170. "Armageddon?"
   a. *Observer* (London) no. 10232 (15 November 1987): 21–22 (as "Battling for the Lord").
   b. *Sydney Morning Herald* (12 December 1987): 63 (as "Reagan's Holy War").
   c. In A.48.
   d. In A.49.
   e. In A.56.
   f. In A.69.
       Study of the Christian fundamentalism of Ronald Reagan, Jerry Falwell, and others, who look forward to an Armageddon of nuclear war as justifying biblical prophecy.

171. "Italian Footnote."
   a. *Times* (London) (17 November 1987) (as "Italian Genius: Put It Down to Curiosity").
   b. *Los Angeles Times* (1 May 1988): Part 5, pp. 1–2 (revised; as "Rebirth of a Nation: Why Italy Works").
   c. In A.51.
       Praise of Italian culture and society, especially in regard to fashion, literature, and journalism. In a., the article appears in a special supplement on Italy, but this supplement is not included in the microfilm edition of the *Times*. The text (no page number cited) is available in the online edition of the *Times*.

172. "Preface."
   a. In A.48.
       Vidal briefly justifies gathering his essays and reviews into this volume.

173. "An Ancient Equilibrium."
    a. In *Thailand: Seven Days in the Kingdom.* Text by William Warren. Singapore: Times Editions, 1987; Mississagua, Ontario: Cupress, 1987; Bangkok: Asia Books, 1995, pp. [12–13].
    Brief introduction to a volume of photographs about Thailand, supplying some notes on the Thai temperament in light of their adherence to Buddhism.

174. "Gore Vidal's 'Lincoln'?: An Exchange."
    a. *Los Angeles Times* (20 March 1988): Sec. 5, pp. 1, 6 (as "Of History and Hagiography").
    b. *Chicago Sun-Times* (24 March 1988): 49 (as "The Gods and Kings of Literature Came Tumbling Down . . .").
    c. *New York Review of Books* 35, no. 7 (28 April 1988): 56–58 (revised).
    d. In A.49 (incorporated into "How I Do What I Do If Not Why").
    e. In William Zinsser, ed. *The Art and Craft of the Political Novel.* Boston: Houghton Mifflin, 1989, pp. 125–52 (revised; as "The Agreed-Upon Facts").
    f. In A.51 (incorporated into "How I Do What I Do If Not Why").
    g. In A.56 (incorporated into "Lincoln, *Lincoln,* and the Priests of Academe").
    Strong response (in the form of an essay, not a letter) to C. Vann Woodward (III.E.313), who had cited various critics questioning the historical accuracy of *Lincoln,* particularly Richard N. Current (III.E.84) and Roy P. Basler (III.E.28). In c. there is a brief response by Woodward.

175. "The National Security State."
    a. *Nation* 246, no. 22 (4 June 1988): 281–83 (as "How to Take Back Our Country").
    b. In A.49.
    c. In A.51.
    d. In A.55.
    e. In A.56 (with addendum).
    f. In A.69.
    Blames Harry S Truman for establishing the National Security Agency in 1947, which set up an unaccountable shadow government and skewed the federal budget toward "defense."

176. "Pen Pals: Henry Miller and Lawrence Durrell."
    a. *Times Literary Supplement* no. 4458 (9–15 September 1988): 979–80 (as "From Outlaws to Intriguers").
    b. In A.51.
    c. In A.56.
    Review of *The Durrell-Miller Letters 1935–80,* which exhibits the literary and personal relationship between the American and the British writer.

177. "Every Eckermann His Own Man."
    a. *New York Review of Books* 35, no. 16 (27 October 1988): 82–83.
    b. In A.51.
    c. In A.56.
    Dialogue in which Johann Peter Eckermann (author of *Conversations with Goethe*) interviews a "Visitor" about the twenty-fifth anniversary of the *New York Review of Books.* Vidal discusses the contributions in *Selections from the First Two Issues of the New York Review of Books* (see item 45.c above).

178. "Preface."
    a. In A.49.
    Briefly discusses the essays contained in *At Home.*

179. "How I Do What I Do If Not Why."
    a. In A.49.
    b. In A.51.

A fusion of C.174 and F.30.

180. "Remembering Orson Welles."
    a. *New York Review of Books* 36, no. 9 (1 June 1989): 12–16.
    b. In A.51.
    c. In A.56.
    d. In A.62.
    e. In Mark W. Estrin, ed. *Orson Welles: Interviews.* Jackson: University Press of Mississippi, 2002, pp. 210–22.
        Vidal surveys Welles's career in film, recounts his own meetings with Welles, and provides a detailed analysis of Welles's screenplay of *The Big Brass Ring.*

181. "Cue the Green God, Ted."
    a. *Nation* 249, no. 5 (7–14 August 1989): 153, 170–74.
    b. In A.51.
    c. In A.55.
    d. In A.56.
        Critical account of Ted Koppel, the ABC newsman whom Vidal labels "the principal dispenser of the national religion" (i.e., corporate America).

182. "God & Greens."
    a. *Observer* (London) no. 10324 (27 August 1989): 29–30.
    b. In A.51.
    c. In A.56.
        Shows how, with the collapse of the Soviet Union, the United States is proceeding to create a new enemy—"the one billion Muslims in general and the Arabs in particular"—to justify continued expenditures in defense.

183. "On the Last Day of the 1980's."
    a. *Observer* (London) no. 10342 (31 December 1989): 25–26 (as "A New World on Prime-Time Television").
    b. In A.51.
        Survey of the state of Britain and the United States at the end of the 1980s, with a discussion of the dangers facing the world in regard to corporate control of resources, overpopulation, and lack of freedom.

184. "Maugham's Half & Half."
    a. *New York Review of Books* 37, no. 1 (1 February 1990): 39–44.
    b. In A.51.
    c. In A.56.
    d. In A.63.
    e. In W. Somerset Maugham. *Of Human Bondage.* New York: Modern Library, 1999, pp. xi–xxiii (as "Introduction").
        Review of Robert Calder's biography of W. Somerset Maugham. Vidal surveys Maugham's career as a writer and discusses elements of his character, including his homosexuality.

185. "Ford's Way."
    a. *Times Literary Supplement* no. 4551 (22–28 June 1990): 659–60 (as "Honourable Passions").
    b. In A.51.
    c. In A.56.
        Study of Ford Madox Ford by way of a review of Alan Judd's *Ford Madox Ford.* Vidal finds merit in Ford's historical novels and provides an assessment of Ford's overall achievement.

186. "Notes on Our Patriarchal State."
    a. *Nation* 251, no. 6 (27 August–3 September 1990): 185, 202–4.

    b.   In Victor Navasky and Katrina vanden Heuvel, eds. *The Best of* The Nation: *Selections from the Independent Magazine of Politics and Culture*. New York: Thunder's Mouth Press/Nation Books, 2000, 39–46.

    c.   In A.69.
       Study of the decline of freedom in the United States from the Declaration of Independence to the present day, with much of the blame resting on the militarization of the nation beginning with the Truman administration.

187. "Foreword."

    a.   In Alfred Chester. *Head of a Sad Angel: Stories 1953–1966*. Ed. Edward Field. Santa Rosa, CA: Black Sparrow Press, 1990, pp. 7–8.
       Brief discussion of Chester's short stories, many of which have as their theme "the quest for Love through Cock."

188. "Introduction."

    a.   In A.13.j.
    b.   In A.10.k.
    c.   In A.9.k.
    d.   *Armchair Detective* 27, no. 3 (Summer 1994): 322–24 (as "A Writer by Any Other Name . . ."; abridged).
       Vidal recounts the circumstances of his writing the three Edgar Box detective novels.

189. "Reflections on Glory Reflected and Otherwise."

    a.   *Threepenny Review* no. 45 (Spring 1991): 5–9 (as "Glorious Reflections upon *The Five of Hearts* and Other Wild Cards in the National Deck").
    b.   *Washington Post* (7 July 1991): B1, 4 (abridged; as "Reflections on Capital Glories").
    c.   In A.51.
    d.   In Wendy Lesser, ed. *Hiding in Plain Sight: Essays in Criticism and Autobiography*. San Francisco: Mercury House, 1993, pp. 247–64 (as "Glorious Reflections upon *The Five of Hearts* and Other Wild Cards in the National Deck").
    e.   In A.56.
       Review of *The Five of Hearts* by Patricia O'Toole, a discussion of the "eponymous coven of Henry and Clover Adams, of John and Clara Hay, of Clarence King" (discussed in *Empire*), with a particular discussion of the historical work of Henry Adams. Vidal begins the essay with a reminiscence of his stepfather, Hugh D. Auchincloss.

190. "Patriotism."

    a.   *Nation* 253, no. 3 (15–22 July 1991): 128, 130 (as part of symposium, "What Is Patriotism?").
    b.   In A.56.
       Vidal wonders how Americans can be patriotic "when there is no agreed-upon country to cherish, only warring tribes and, over all, a National Security State to keep the lid on." He mentions attending a gathering of the Gore family, including Al and Tipper Gore.

191. "Last Note on Lincoln."

    a.   *New York Review of Books* 38, no. 14 (15 August 1991): 21–22 (as "Lincoln Up Close").
    b.   In Susan Sontag, ed. *The Best American Essays 1992*. New York: Ticknor & Fields, 1992, pp. 314–20 (as "Lincoln Up Close").
    c.   In Abraham Lincoln. *Selected Speeches and Writings*. New York: Vintage Books/The Library of America, February 1992, pp. xxi–xxvii (as "Introduction").
    d.   In A.56.
       Rumination on the personal and literary character of Lincoln as revealed in his speeches and letters, and in the recollections of William Herndon.

192. "H. L. Mencken the Journalist."
    a. In H. L. Mencken. *The Impossible H. L. Mencken: A Selection of His Best Newspaper Stories.* Ed. Marion Elizabeth Rodgers. New York: Doubleday/Anchor, 1991, pp. xvii–xxxv (as "Foreword").
    b. *Nation* 253, no. 6 (26 August–2 September 1991): 228, 230, 232–33 (as "The Essential Mencken"; abridged).
    c. In A.51.
    d. In A.56.
    Enthusiastic essay on Mencken as an iconoclast and critic of American values. Vidal discusses Mencken's style, his hostility to religion, his opposition to Franklin D. Roosevelt, and his attitudes toward Jews.

193. "The Birds and the Bees."
    a. *Nation* 253, no. 14 (28 October 1991): 509–11.
    b. *New Statesman and Society* 5 (no. 215) (14 August 1992): 12–13 (as "Get Gay and Save the Planet").
    c. In A.56.
    d. In A.62.
    e. In A.63.
    Purportedly elementary essay on sex differences between men and women, with a discussion of sexual fantasies, bisexuality, and the "heterosexual dictatorship."

194. "Preface."
    a. In A.51.
    Explains the odd title to the book: in 1976 he had declined membership in the National Institute of Arts and Letters because "I was already a member of the Diners Club." He has "never written a book review for money," is proud of his championing of Dawn Powell, and shall "not write a memoir."

195. "E."
    a. In David Hockney. *Hockney's Alphabet.* Written Contributions Edited by Stephen Spender. London: Faber & Faber for the AIDS Crisis Trust, 1991; New York: Random House in Association with the American Friends of AIDS Crisis Trust, 1992, p. [27].
    Two-paragraph disquisition on the letter E.

196. "Et in Italia Ego."
    a. In Francesco Gandolfo et al. *Ravello.* Bologna: F. M. Ricci, 1991, pp. 9–12 (tr. Gianni Guadalupi).
    In Italian. Vidal discusses the long tradition of Americans visiting or living in Italy, including F. Marion Crawford and Tennessee Williams, and speaks of his own life there over the past thirty years.

197. "Time for a People's Convention."
    a. *Nation* 254, no. 3 (27 January 1992): 73, 88, 90–91, 94.
    b. In A.55.
    c. In A.59.
    d. In A.65.
    Discussion of the fiscal woes afflicting the United States and the consequent decline in the people's "inalienable" rights. Vidal repeats his frequent plea of calling a new constitutional convention. The essay is based on part on a speech given to the National Press Club.

198. "With Extreme Prejudice."
    a. *Nation* 254, no. 22 (8 June 1992): 784, 786 (as "Comments").
    b. In A.55 (as "Should Our Intelligence Services Be Abolished?").
    c. In A.59.
    d. In A.65.

    e.   In A.67.
        Brief essay asserting that the CIA and the Defense Intelligence Agency serve no useful purpose and should be abolished.

199. "Montaigne."
    a.   *Times Literary Supplement* no. 4656 (26 June 1992): 3–5 (as "Uncommon Sense").
    b.   In A.56.
    c.   In A.62.
        Review of a new translation of Montaigne's essays by M. A. Screech. Vidal surveys Montaigne's life and work, discussing his attitude toward learning, the body, politics, style, and other issues.

200. *Screening History* (extracts).
    a.   *Washington Post* (30 August 1992): C1, 4.
    b.   *American Heritage* 43, no. 5 (September 1992): 65–70, 72, 74–76.

201. "Monotheism and Its Discontents."
    a.   *New Statesman and Society* 5 (no. 208) (26 June 1992): 12–14 (as "Choking in Holy Smoke").
    b.   *Nation* 255, no. 2 (13 July 1992): 37, 54–56.
    c.   In A.55.
    d.   In A.56.
    e.   In Charles P. Cozic, ed. *American Values: Opposing Viewpoints.* San Diego: Greenhaven Press, 1995, pp. 219–26 (as "Judeo-Christian Values Deny Freedom in America"; abridged).
    f.   In S. T. Joshi, ed. *Atheism: A Reader.* Amherst, NY: Prometheus Books, 2000, pp. 303–10.
        Strong essay in which Vidal condemns the believers in the "sky-god" for infringing upon the rights of Americans' freedom of religion, for exacerbating race relations, and for prejudice against women. In e., the chaper in which Vidal's essay appears has been published separately (with identical pagination) as *How Do Religious Values Influence America?* (1995).

202. "Preface."
    a.   In A.55.
        Vidal explains that "I am trying to put into historical perspective the state of our union and what can still be done to salvage it."

203. "Truman."
    a.   *Independent Magazine* (3 October 1992): 62 (as "Harry S Truman").
    b.   In A.59.
    c.   In A.65.
        Brief condemnation of Truman for establishing the National Security Agency and the CIA.

204. "The Romance of Sinclair Lewis."
    a.   *New York Review of Books* 39, no. 16 (8 October 1992): 14, 16–20.
    b.   In A.59.
    c.   In A.65.
    d.   In Harold Bloom, ed. *George F. Babbitt.* Philadelphia: Chelsea House, 2004, pp. 69–85.
        Warm appreciation of Lewis as a novelist, especially *Main Street, Babbitt,* and *Elmer Gantry,* with considerable discussion of Lewis's upbringing in the Midwest.

205. "Clinton-Gore I."
    a.   *GQ* 62, no. 11 (November 1992): 226, 228–31 (as "Goin' South").
    b.   In A.59 (as "Goin' South: Clinton–Gore I").
    c.   In A.65.

Vidal assumes that Bill Clinton will be elected and makes predictions as to some of his policies.

206. "Foreword."
    a. In Robert McAlmon. *Miss Knight and Others*. Ed. Edward N. S. Lorusso. Albuquerque: University of New Mexico Press, 1992, pp. ix–xiv.
    Biographical and critical survey of this little-known American writer, one of whose short stories "one can place quite comfortably beside any of Sherwood Anderson's plain tales of that day."

207. "How We Missed the Saturday Dance."
    a. *Newsweek* 121, no. 2 (11 January 1993): 30–31 (as "Making a Mess of the American Empire").
    b. In A.59.
    c. In A.65.
    d. In A.67.
    Vidal speaks again of the "American Golden Age" (1945–1950) and the succession of misguided military ventures that followed.

208. "Author's Note."
    a. In A.56.
    Vidal briefly notes that *United States* collects approximately two-thirds of the essays he has written between 1952 and 1992.

209. "Lincoln, *Lincoln,* and the Priests of Academe."
    a. In A.56.
    Fusion of C.173, F.30, and F.32.

210. "Outer Limits."
    a. *Village Voice* 38, no. 24 (15 June 1993): 63.
    Review of *Queer in America* by Michelangelo Signorile, discussing such issues as ACT UP and Queer Nation (which "have always appealed to me"), the Christian Right, outing, and gays in the military.

211. "Pride."
    a. *New York Times Book Review* (4 July 1993): 3 (as "Pride: The Most Unnerving Sin").
    b. In Thomas Pynchon et al. *Deadly Sins*. New York: William Morrow, 1994, pp. 64–72.
    c. In A.59.
    d. In A.65.
    Brief essay on one of the seven deadly sins, commissioned by the *New York Times*. Vidal wonders whether pride is a sin at all and discusses instances of pride in his family history.

212. "Race against Time."
    a. *Sunday Telegraph* (London) (10 October 1993): Review, p. 1.
    b. In A.59.
    c. In A.65.
    Essay on race, immigration, and racial prejudice. "I regard race as nonsense, but most of the world feels passionately otherwise."

213. "Edmund Wilson: Nineteenth-Century Man."
    a. *New York Review of Books* 40, no. 18 (4 November 1993): 57–59 (as "A Nineteenth-Century Man").
    b. In A.59.
    c. In A.65.
    Vidal's third essay on Wilson, this one a review of Wilson's *The Sixties*. Vidal discusses Wilson's treatise on the Civil War, *Patriotic Gore,* and his involvement with Anaïs Nin, W. H. Auden, and others.

214. "JFK's War Games."
    a.   *New Statesman and Society* 6 (no. 280) (26 November 1993): 24.
        A characterization of John F. Kennedy and his administration, especially as concerns his military policy. The article is based upon a documentary, "JFK: A Personal Memory by Gore Vidal" (see I.ii.8).

215. "Anthony Burgess."
    a.   *Observer* (London) (28 November 1993): 2 (as "Anthony Burgess 1917–1993—Not So Poor Burgess").
    b.   In A.59.
    c.   In A.65.
        Brief obituary of Burgess, with notes on Vidal's meetings with him.

216. "Nixon R.I.P."
    a.   *New Statesman and Society* 7 (no. 301) (6 May 1994): 11 (as "Letter from America").
    b.   *Nation* 258, no. 19 (16 May 1994): 652–53 (as "R.I.P., R.M.N.").
    c.   In A.59 (as "R.I.P., R.M.N.").
    d.   In A.65.
        Very brief obituary of Nixon, a "ruthless Plantagenet king."

217. "Bedfellows Make Strange Politics."
    a.   *New York Times Book Review* (18 September 1994): 1, 24.
    b.   In A.59.
    c.   In A.65.
        Review of *All's Fair* by Mary Matalin and James Carville, a husband-wife political team of whom one, a conservative, is working for George Bush, and the other, a liberal, is working for Bill Clinton.

218. "The Union of the State."
    a.   *Nation* 259, no. 22 (26 December 1994): 789–90, 792.
    b.   *New Statesman and Society* 8 (no. 334)   (6 January 1995): 20–21.
    c.   In A.59.
    d.   In A.65.
    e.   In A.67.
        Vidal ponders the possibility of breaking up the United States into smaller geopolitical units.

219. "Foreword."
    a.   In Israel Shahak. *Jewish History, Jewish Religion: The Weight of Three Thousand Years.* London: Pluto Press, 1994, 1997, 2002, pp. vii–viii.
        Vidal again deplores the power of the Jewish lobby in the United States, who have made common cause with Christian fundamentalists and other unsavory groups. But a few voices of sanity remain in Israel, and Israel Shahak is one of them.

220. "FDR: Love on the Hudson."
    a.   *New York Review of Books* 42, no. 8 (11 May 1995): 4–6 (as "Love on the Hudson").
    b.   In A.59.
    c.   In A.65.
        Review of *Closest Companion* by Geoffrey C. Ward, a study of Franklin D. Roosevelt's relations with his cousin, Margaret (Daisy) Stuckey. The book offers new insights on Eleanor Roosevelt, on FDR's presidency, and on his conduct of World War II.

221. "In the Lair of the Octopus."
    a.   *Nation* 260, no. 22 (5 June 1995): 792, 794–95.
    b.   In A.59.
    c.   In A.65.
    d.   In A.67.

A study of American involvement in Guatemala in the 1950s, the subject of Vidal's early novel *Dark Green, Bright Red.*

222. "Kopkind."
   a. *Nation* 260, no. 23 (12 June 1995): 832, 834–36 (as "Andy Kopkind, 1935–94").
   b. In A.59.
   c. In A.65.
      Both an obituary of Andrew Kopkind, an American journalist, and a review of his posthumous volume, *Dispatches and Diversions of a Radical Journalist 1965–1994.* Vidal speaks of Kopkind's writings during the turbulent 1960s, including discussions of the Vietnam War and Eugene McCarthy, and his later writings on sexual politics.

223. "A Note on *The City and the Pillar* and Thomas Mann."
   a. *Threepenny Review* no. 61 (Summer 1995): 12–13 (as "The City and the Pillar").
   b. In A.57 (as "Preface").
   c. In A.59.
   d. In A.65.
      Notes Mann's appreciation of *The City and the Pillar,* as exhibited in his journals; Vidal's novel may have partially inspired Mann's *Felix Krull.*

224. *Palimpsest* (extracts).
   a. *New Yorker* 71, no. 30 (2 October 1995): 62, 64–68, 70–73, 75–76 (as "How I Survived the Fifties").
   b. *Advocate* no. 693 (31 October 1995): 40 (as "Unfinished Business").
   c. *New York Review of Books* 41, no. 17 (2 November 1995): 12–16 (as "Dah").
   d. *Psychology Today* 29, no. 1 (January–February 1996): 26–28 (as "The Pursuit of the Whole").
   e. *Cosmopolitan* (March 1996): 248–50, 252, 258, 261.
   f. In Jay Parini, ed. *The Norton Book of American Autobiography.* New York: W. W. Norton & Co., 1999, pp. 450–65.
   g. In Regina Marler, ed. *Queer Beats: How the Beats Turned America on to Sex.* San Francisco: Cleis Press, 2004, pp. 35–37 (as "We owed it to literary history . . ."), p. 39 (as "Norman wanted to know what had really happened . . .").

225. "Foreword."
   a. In Jonathan Ned Katz. *The Invention of Heterosexuality.* New York: Dutton, 1995; London: Penguin, 1995; New York: Plume, 1996, pp. vii–xi.
      Examines Freud's influence on the concept of heterosexuality and the artificiality of the distinction between heterosexuals and homosexuals.

226. "Foreword."
   a. In Bill Kauffman. *America First! Its History, Culture, and Politics.* Amherst, NY: Prometheus Books, 1995, pp. 9–13.
      Vidal maintains that the words "liberal" and "conservative" have become reversed in meaning in the course of the past century; he also addresses the issue of "isolationism."

227. *"Sullivan's Island."*
   a. In Ted Mico, John Miller-Monzon, and David Rubel, eds. *Past Imperfect: History According to the Movies.* New York: Henry Holt & Co., 1995; Markham, Ontario: Fitzhenry & Whiteside, 1996; London: Cassell, 1996; New York: Random House, 1998, pp. 216, 219.
      A discussion of the film (1941), concerning a chain gang in the South.

228. "Dawn Powell: Queen of the Golden Age."
   a. *New York Review of Books* 43, no. 5 (21 March 1996): 4–8 (as "Queen of the Golden Age").

b. In A.59.
c. In A.65.
Vidal's second essay on Dawn Powell, discussing Powell's relations with Edmund Wilson and the cultural life of the 1940s as found in her diaries.

229. "Rabbit's Own Burrow."
a. *Times Literary Supplement* no. 4856 (26 April 1996): 3–7.
b. In A.59.
c. In A.65.
Lengthy and harsh survey of the life and work of John Updike, upbraiding him for supporting American involvement in Vietnam and castigating his recent writings for their "ignorance of history and politics and of people unlike himself."

230. "Twain on the Grand Tour."
a. *New York Review of Books* 43, no. 9 (23 May 1996): 25–28.
b. In Mark Twain. *Following the Equator and Other Anti-Imperialist Essays.* New York: Oxford University Press, 1996, pp. xxxi–xl (as "Introduction").
c. In A.59.
d. In A.65.
Overview of Mark Twain's work, with a focus on his attitudes toward American and European imperialism and its adverse effect upon the foreign cultures it has affected.

231. "U.S. out of UN—UN out of U.S."
a. *Sunday Telegraph* (London) (11 August 1996): 29 (as "Why the U.S. Should Be Expelled from the U.N.").
b. In A.59.
c. In A.65.
Response to an article by the conservatives William Kristol and Robert Kagan, who wish for a more vigorous American military and foreign policy, something Vidal feels is both unwise and unfeasible.

232. "Mickey Mouse, Historian."
a. *Nation* 263, no. 9 (30 September 1996): 11–12, 14, 16, 18 (as "The End of History").
b. In A.59.
c. In A.65.
d. In A.67.
Vidal speaks of the television shows he had prepared for British television on the American presidency (see I.ii.11), and how they were watered down when presented on the History Channel, which set up a panel of "experts," including Arthur Schlesinger Jr., Roger Mudd, and Richard Slotkin, to dispute Vidal's conclusions.

233. "Clinton-Gore II."
a. *GQ* 66, no. 10 (October 1996): 184, 186–89 (as "Bubba Rules").
b. In A.59 (as "Bubba Rules: Clinton-Gore II").
c. In A.65.
Vidal predicts that Clinton will win reelection easily over Bob Dole, but that he will not be allowed to accomplish very much in his second term. He speaks of Hillary Clinton visiting him in Ravello in late 1994.

234. "International Books of the Year" [symposium].
a. *Times Literary Supplement* no. 4887 (29 November 1996): 16.
Vidal briefly endorses Muriel Spark's *Reality and Dreams.*

235. "Chaos."
a. In Chris Miller, ed. *The Dissident Word: The Oxford Amnesty Lectures 1995.* New York: Basic Books, 1996, pp. 131–50 (as "On Chaos").
b. In A.59.

c. *New York Review of Books* 46, no. 20 (16 December 1999): 39–40.

d. *Observer* (2 January 2000): 25 (abridged; as "Let the Old Gods Arise").

e. In A.65.

Vidal speaks of Giambattisa Vico's theory that empire-republics inevitably descend into chaos, leading to a new theocratic age. "Great centrifugal forces are at work all around the earth, and why resist them?"

236. "Foreword."

a. In Claiborne Davis. *Demon-Queller's Journey: Eight Stories.* Washington, D.C.: [Privately printed,] 1996, pp. [ix–xi].

Vidal finds Claiborne's stories "startling, to say the least." Several deal with school life at St. Albans Academy, which Vidal attended.

237. "Twain's Letters."

a. *Sunday Times* (London) (11 May 1997): Sec. 8, pp. 1–2 (as "Yankee's Doodles").

b. In A.65.

A review of *Mark Twain's Letters,* covering letters he wrote from England in 1872–1873, which display his involvement in the social and literary world of London.

238 "Blair."

a. *Nation* 264, no. 20 (26 May 1997): 5–6 (as "Through a Vote, Darkly").

b. In A.59 (as "Stop Press: Through a Vote, Darkly").

c. In A.65.

Vidal speaks of being invited by the BBC to cover the British election of 1997, in which the Labour candidate Tony Blair won in a landslide.

239. "Clare Boothe Luce."

a. *New Yorker* 73, no. 13 (26 May 1997): 70, 72–76 (as "The Woman Behind the Women").

b. In A.65.

Lengthy recollection of Clare Boothe Luce, by way of reviewing Sylvia Jukes Morris's biography, *Rage for Fame.* Vidal notes that "Clare was easily the most hated woman of her time." He tells of her acting career, her work on magazines, and her marriage to Henry R. Luce, founder of *Time.*

240. "Appendix."

a. In A.59.

A chart of American expenditures on the United Kingdom for the year 1995, especially in the area of military spending.

241. "The New Theocrats."

a. *Nation* 265, no. 3 (21 July 1997): 19–21.

b. In A.65.

c. In A.66.

Condemnation of the religious right for their obsession with sexual morality.

242. "Preface."

a. In A.59.

Vidal explains that the title *Virgin Islands: A Dependency of* United States suggests that this book is a pendant to his large omnibus of essays (A.56).

243. "George."

a. In A.59.

b. In A.65.

Rumination on George Washington and what he symbolizes today ("He is ever present in our decaying institutions").

244. "The Last Empire."
   a. *Vanity Fair* no. 447 (November 1997): 219–21, 224, 230, 245–47, 251, 255, 262–63, 276.
   b. *Observer* (15 February 1998): Review, p. 3 (abridged; as "The Sailor's Lament").
   c. *Progressive* 62, no. 5 (May 1998): 18–21 (abridged; as "The Menopause of Empire").
   d. In A.65.
   e. In A.67.
   Extensive survey of American history from 1945 to the present day, showing how the United States sought to take advantage of the end of World War II to establish a worldwide empire, especially through its domination of NATO.

245. "Amistad."
   a. *New Yorker* 73, no. 34 (10 November 1997): 112, 115–16, 119–20 (as "Reel History").
   b. In A.65.
   Reflections on Steven Spielberg's film *Amistad*, about a mutiny on a slave ship, in the subsequent trial for which ex-President John Quincy Adams acted as attorney for the defense.

246. "The View from the Amalfi Coast."
   a. *Forbes*, Special Issue (1 December 1997): 111.
   Vidal speaks of his writing habits and the role of the computer and the Internet in contemporary literature.

247. "Hersh's JFK."
   a. *New Yorker* 73, no. 37 (1 December 1997): 85–92 (as "Coached by Camelot").
   b. In A.65.
   Review of Seymour Hersh's *The Dark Side of Camelot*, an unflattering portrayal of John F. Kennedy and his family. Vidal studies the press reaction to the book, especially in its revelations of Kennedy's sexual activities.

248. "Lost New York."
   a. *New York Review of Books* 44, no. 20 (18 December 1997): 24–26, 28 (as "A Lost World").
   b. In A.65.
   A review of Isabel Bolton's *New York Mosaic*, an omnibus of the novels she wrote in the 1940s. Vidal reflects on the image of New York as seen in these novels.

249. "Bad History."
   a. *Nation* 266, no. 14 (20 April 1998): 11–15 (as by "G. V.").
   b. In A.62.
   c. In A.65.
   Harsh review of *America in Black and White* by Stephen Thernstrom and Abigail Thernstrom. Vidal condemns the book as both bad history and bad faith in its analysis of black-white relations.

250. "Sinatra."
   a. *Observer* (London) (17 May 1998): 28 (as "Behind the Smooth Sound, All Was Painfully Off-Key").
   b. In A.65.
   Eulogy to Frank Sinatra.

251. "I Fired Capra."
   a. *Newsweek* 131, no. 25A (Summer 1998): 74, 76.
   b. In Peter Bogdonavich, ed. *The Best American Movie Writing 1999*. New York: St. Martin's Griffin, 1999, pp. 25–30.
   Vidal recounts (as he did in brief compass in *Palimpsest*) rejecting Frank Capra's offer to direct the film version of *The Best Man*.

252. "Starr Conspiracy."
:   a. *Observer* (London) (9 August 1998): 20 (as "Big Business Doesn't Care for Bill Clinton or the People").
    b. *Los Angeles Times* (12 August 1998): B7 (as "The Real Crime Is Going Against the Will of We the People").
    c. *International Herald Tribune* (18 August 1998): 7 (as "A Willful and Malicious Conspiracy Against 'We the People'").
    d. In A.65.
    Vidal finds that Kenneth W. Starr's investigation of President Clinton is symptomatic of the "right-wing conspiracy" that Hillary Clinton identified. In A.65 Vidal erroneously gives the first appearance of this essay as the *International Herald Tribune* for 11 August 1998.

253. "Oh What a Lovely Thing Is War. How Diverting. How Uniting. How American."
:   a. *Observer* (23 August 1998): 20.
    Vidal reviews the history of American wars over the last half-century as a means of drumming up patriotic sentiment.

254. *The American Presidency* (extract).
:   b. *Progressive* 62, no. 10 (October 1998): 20–21 (as "To: Bill; Fr: Management; Re: Mind Your Place").

255. "Coup de Starr."
:   a. *Nation* 267, no. 13 (26 October 1998): 6.
    b. In A.65.
    Further brief notes on Kenneth W. Starr's investigation of President Clinton.

256. "Lindbergh: The Eagle Is Grounded."
:   a. *Times Literary Supplement* no. 4987 (30 October 1998): 3–6 (as "The Eagle Is Grounded").
    b. In A.65.
    Review of several books about British and American involvement in World War II, focusing on the role of Charles Lindbergh. Vidal surveys Lindbergh's career (including his father Eugene Vidal's involvement with him in the airline industry) and Lindbergh's controversial role in the war.

257. "Shredding the Bill of Rights."
:   a. *Vanity Fair* no. 459 (November 1998): 96, 98, 100, 102–4, 106, 110, 112 (as "The War at Home").
    b. In A.65.
    c. In A.66.
    Substantial essay on the increasing infringement of personal liberties by a government obsessed with "terrorism." Vidal surveys the war on drugs, corporate mergers, the "disintegration" of the Fourth Amendment, the government attack on the Branch Davidians, and Timothy McVeigh.

258. "J'Accuse!"
:   a. *Advocate* no. 773 (24 November 1998): 9.
    b. In A.63.
    c. In Chris Bull, ed. *Come Out Fighting: A Century of Essential Writing on Gay and Lesbian Liberation.* New York: Thunder's Mouth Press/Nation Books, 2001, pp. 303–4.
    Condemnation of right-wing politicians, notably Senator Trent Lott and Gary Bauer, for inciting hatred against homosexuals.

259. "Honorable Albert A. Gore, Junior."
:   a. *GQ* 68, no. 12 (December 1998): 246, 248–52, 301–2 (as "Blood and Gore").
    b. In A.65.

Discussion of Al Gore and the Gore family, including Vidal's grandfather, Thomas P. Gore, and Albert Gore Sr., as representative of Southern politicians.

260. "Gore Vidal on the Sex Trap."
   a. *Independent* (20 December 1998): 1, 2.
   A discussion of the furor surrounding the revelation of Bill Clinton's sexual dalliances.

261. "Birds and Bees and Clinton."
   a. *Nation* 267, no. 22 (28 December 1998): 5–6.
   b. In A.65.
   Further reflections on Bill Clinton's sexual peccadilloes and the hypocritical outrage they evoked.

262. "Preface."
   a. In A.63.
   Brief discussion of the artificial distinction between heterosexuals and homosexuals.

263. "A Biographer Writes Himself into the Picture."
   a. *New York Times* (26 September 1999): Sec. 4, p. 17.
   Rumination on Edmund Morris's *Dutch,* a "fictional biography" of Ronald Reagan. Vidal feels that Morris's methodology was the only feasible way to treat Reagan, who was himself a creation of the media.

264. "Wiretapping the Oval Office."
   a. *Nation* 269, no. 9 (27 September 1999): 25–26, 28, 30 (as "Candid in Camera").
   b. In A.65.
   Review of *Inside the Oval Office* by William Doyle, a history of White House wiretapping from FDR to Clinton. Vidal believes the tapes reveal that the FDR administration "had several days' warning that Pearl Harbor would be hit." He also finds interest in the Kennedy and Johnson tapes.

265. "Amalfi Coast."
   a. *National Geographic Traveler* (October 1999): 148.
   A one-paragraph description of his coming to the Amalfi coast, "the most beautiful spot on Earth."

266. "Preface."
   a. In Jay Parini, ed. *The Norton Book of American Autobiography.* New York: W. W. Norton & Co., 1999, p. 9.
   Brief preface noting some of the highlights in the volume, including autobiographical writings by Henry Adams and James Baldwin.

267. "Foreword."
   a. In David Donnelly, Janice Fine, and Ellen S. Miller. *Money and Politics: Financing Our Elections Democratically.* Ed. Joshua Cohen and Joel Rogers. Boston: Beacon Press, 1999, 2001 (as *Are Elections for Sale?*), pp. vii–xii.
   Vidal asserts that those in power have found many ways to suppress popular opinion: "the United States was never intended to be a democracy." The essays in this volume address the issue of campaign finance reform.

268. "Clearer Than Truth."
   a. *Forbes ASAP* 166, no. 9 (2 October 2000): 146, 148.
   A history of American political deceit from Franklin D. Roosevelt to Bill Clinton, largely focusing on the Truman administration.

269. "Three Lies to Rule By."
   a. *Times Literary Supplement* no. 5093 (10 November 2000): 16–17 (as "The Greater the Lie . . .").

b. In A.65.
c. In A.67.
    The three lies are: 1) that the Japanese attack on Pearl Harbor was unprovoked; 2) that Truman
    had to drop the atomic bomb on Japan to prevent immense American casualties; and 3) that the
    Soviets began the Cold War.

270. "After Four Lean Years, Wait for Hillary's Golden Age."
    a. *Observer* (12 November 2000): US Election 2000, p. 14.
    b. *Cleveland Plain Dealer* (14 November 2000): 9B (as "A Bush Win Might Put Hillary
        (and Bill) Back in the White House").
        Suggests that a George W. Bush presidency, with Dick Cheney "pledged to governing in the
        name of corporate America," will trigger such a wave of nostalgia for the Clintons that Hillary
        Clinton will be elected in 2004, with Bill as vice president.

271. "A Letter to Be Delivered."
    a. *Vanity Fair* no. 484 (December 2000): 136, 138, 140 (as "Washington, We Have a
        Problem").
    b. In A.65.
    c. In A.66.
        Vidal writes a letter on 7 November 2000 (when the outcome of the presidential election was still
        undecided), asserting that the new president will have to restrain defense spending and increase
        taxes on corporate profits.

272. "Foreword."
    a. In Victor Navasky and Katrina vanden Heuvel, eds. *The Best of* The Nation: *Selections
        from the Independent Magazine of Politics and Culture.* New York: Thunder's Mouth
        Press/Nation Books, 2000, xvii–xx.
        Vidal examines the long history of the *Nation* and its coverage of current political events.

273. "Democratic Vistas."
    a. *Independent* (15 December 2000): Friday Review, p. 5 (as "The Iron Law of Oligarchy
        Prevails").
    b. *Toronto Star* (29 December 2000): 1 (as "How George W. Pulled It Off").
    c. *Nation* 272, no. 2 (8–15 January 2001): 2, 4–5.
    d. In A.65.
    e. In A.67.
        Vidal states that the result of the Supreme Court awarding George W. Bush the presidency shows
        the court's "dedication to the 1 percent that own the country"; he predicts four years of political
        gridlock.

274. "Obituary: Memories of Venus in Flight" (with Faith Evans, Doris Lessing, and Snoo
      Wilson).
    a. *Guardian* (13 January 2001): 22.
        Vidal and others record their memories of Lorna Sage.

275. "The Meaning of Timothy McVeigh."
    a. *Vanity Fair* no. 493 (September 2001): 347–48, 350–53, 409–13, 415.
    b. In A.66.
    c. In Stephen Jay Gould, ed. *The Best American Essays 2002.* Boston: Houghton Mifflin,
        2002, pp. 309–30.
        Long essay in which Vidal examines the circumstances around the raid on the Branch Davidians
        in Waco, Texas, and explains how Timothy McVeigh read Vidal's earlier account of the incident
        (see item 257 above) and began a correspondence with Vidal (his letters are quoted at length).
        Vidal wonders whether McVeigh is in fact guilty of the crime with which he was convicted.

276. "*Times* Cries Eke! Buries Al Gore."
    a. *Nation* 273, no. 20 (17 December 2001): 13–15.

Excoriates a *New York Times* report discussing the recount of votes in Florida following the 2000 presidential election.

277.   *"Burr:* The Historical Novel."

     a.   In Mark C. Carnes, ed. *Novel History: Historians and Novelists Confront America's Past (and Each Other).* New York: Simon & Schuster, 2001, pp. 39–44.

        Vidal discusses the difference between writing history and writing a historical novel and discusses Joanne B. Freedman's essay on *Burr* (see III.E.117), addressing the factual errors Freedman found in the novel.

278.   "C. P. Cavafy."

     a.   In Constantine P. Cavafy. *Before Time Could Change Them: The Complete Poems of Constantine P. Cavafy.* Translated, with an Introduction and Notes, by Theoharis Constantine Theoharis. New York: Harcourt, 2001, pp. xv–xxi (as "Foreword").

     b.   In A.65.

        An overview of the life and work of Cavafy (1863–1933), the Greek poet.

279.   "'Everything Is Yesterday.'"

     a.   *New York Review of Books* 49, no. 3 (28 February 2002): 22–23.

        Review of *More Was Lost* by Eleanor Perenyi, a memoir of the early years of World War II first published in 1946.

280.   "Introduction."

     a.   In A.66.

        Discusses the Oklahoma City bombing of 1995, the terrorist attacks on 9/11, and the possibility that the United States has itself been conducting (in the words of Arno J. Mayer) "'preemptive' state terror" on Third World nations.

281.   "September 11, 2001 (A Tuesday)."

     a.   In A.66.

     b.   *Guardian* (27 April 2002): Saturday Review, p. 1 (as "Taking Liberties").

     c.   *Index on Censorship* 31, no. 2 (2002): 70–81 (as "The End of Liberty").

        Substantial discussion of the political background behind the 9/11 attacks and the reaction of the United States government and the press to the attacks. In an appendix Vidal presents a lengthy list of military operations conducted by the American military from 1948 to 1999. The article was commissioned by the *Daily Mail* (London), but was rejected by that newspaper and several other newspapers in England. It first appeared in Italian (II.A.xvi.30).

282.   "How I Became Interested in Timothy McVeigh and Vice Versa."

     a.   In A.66.

        Brief essay on Vidal's reaction to the Oklahoma City bombing and his following of the subsequent trial of Timothy McVeigh.

283.   "Fallout."

     a.   In A.66.

        Brief preface to a long letter by Vidal to Robert S. Mueller III, director of the FBI, urging him to consider evidence exculpating Timothy McVeigh. Vidal then presents McVeigh's ten additions to the Bill of Rights.

284.   "Goat Song: Unanswered Questions—Before, During, After 9/11."

     a.   *Observer* (London) (27 October 2002): Review, pp. 1–4 (as "The Enemy Within").

     b.   In A.67.

        Lengthy examination of the American government's reaction to the 9/11 attacks, asserting that the Bush administration used the attacks as an excuse to establish geopolitical control over the Middle East. Vidal also examines the Bush family's economic relations with the bin Laden family in Saudi Arabia, discusses the invasion of Afghanistan, and Pakistan's role in the attacks.

285. "Are Iraq's Vast Oil Reserves Worth a War?"
     a.   *Scotland on Sunday* (13 October 2002): 27.
     b.   *Nation* 275, no. 14 (28 October 2002): 7 (as "Blood for Oil").
          Brief article on how the Bush administration shifted its attention from Osama bin Laden to
          Saddam Hussein in its "war on terrorism."

286. "Note."
     a.   In A.67.
          Vidal briefly explains why he has "turned to the oldest form of American political discourse, the
          pamphlet."

287. "Meandering toward Armageddon."
     a.   In A.67.
          Vidal takes issue with Louis Menand's review of *Perpetual War for Perpetual Peace*
          (III.F.60.g), defending both himself and Noam Chomsky from Menand's assertion that they are
          "America-haters."

288. "Foreword."
     a.   In Kristina Borjesson, ed. *Into the Buzzsaw: Leading Journalists Expose the Myth of a
          Free Press.* Amherst, NY: Prometheus Books, 2002, pp. 5–7.
          Vidal praises the essays in the book, dealing with freedom of speech as well as "a close scrutiny
          of things political and—alas—religious." The conclusion (presenting a long quotation from Arno
          J. Mayer) is taken from the introduction to *Perpetual War for Perpetual Peace* (item 280 above).

289. "Author's Note 2002."
     a.   In A.41.g.
          Vidal speaks of the restoration of *Creation* to its original state and criticizes his editor at Random
          House, Jason Epstein (never mentioned by name, but cited merely as "an overly busy editor who
          mistakenly thought that he understood the public taste"), for forcing him to make cuts in the
          original edition.

290. "We Are the Patriots."
     a.   *Nation* 276, no. 21 (2 June 2003): 11–14.
     b.   In A.69.
          Vidal speaks of the reckless military ventures in which the United States has recently engaged
          and the infringements upon civil liberties represented by the Patriot Act.

291. "Introduction."
     a.   In Karl Bissinger. *The Luminous Years: Portraits at Mid-Century.* New York: Harry N.
          Abrams, 2003, pp. [8–11].
          In describing Bissinger's photographs, Vidal reminisces about Tennessee Williams, Truman
          Capote, Paul Bowles, Tallulah Bankhead, and other figures of a half-century before.

292. "Interim Report: Election 2004."
     a.   *Independent* (18 January 2004): 25 (as "The War against Lies").
     b.   In A.69.
          Brief article on the 2004 presidential campaign, written prior to the primaries on 2 March 2004.

293. "State of the Union: 2004."
     a.   In A.69.
     b.   *Independent* (10 June 2004): Review, pp. 2–4.
          Vidal tells of the difference between 1972 (when he first began giving annual "State of the
          Union" speeches) and today, in regard to the economy, sexual practices, drug use, and other
          subjects.

294. "The Privatizing of the American Election."
     a.   In A.69.

Vidal examines George W. Bush's state of the union messages of 2001, 2002, and 2003, enumerating the several lies Vidal claims to find in them. He also studies the possibility of vote-rigging in recent elections and primaries.

295. "Iran Next, Then Who?"
    a. *Independent* (23 January 2005): 27.
Vidal wonders if the Bush administration wants to attack Iran on the pretext of battling terrorism, but predicts that the United States will lose if it does so.

296. "Gore Vidal on the Couch with Dr Kinsey."
    a. *Independent* (24 February 2005): Review, p. 3.
Vidal speaks of being interviewed by Alfred Kinsey in 1948 as part of Kinsey's sex research project.

297. "James Purdy: The Novelist as Outlaw."
    a. *New York Times Book Review* (27 February 2005): 6–7.
Overview of Purdy's work as novelist and short story writer, with some biographical notes.

298. "Something Rotten in Ohio."
    a. *Nation* 280, no. 25 (27 June 2005): 6, 8–9.
    b. In Anita Miller, ed. *What Went Wrong in Ohio.* The Conyers Report on the 2004 Presidential Election. Chicago: Academy Chicago, 2005, pp. ix–xii (as "Introduction"; revised and abridged).
Vidal asserts that the "swing state of Ohio was carefully set up to deliver an apparent victory for Bush even though [John] Kerry appears to have been the popular winner."

299. "Introduction."
    a. In Timothy Greenfield-Sanders. *XXX 30 Porn Star Portraits.* Boston: Bulfinch, 2004; London: Time Warner, 2005, pp. [9–10].
Vidal briefly discusses "why pornography exists" and why political and religious conservatives are hostile to sexual freedom.

300. "Barbara Epstein" [symposium].
    a. *New York Review of Books* 53, no. 13 (10 August 2006): 8.
Vidal speaks briefly of his dealings with Epstein, a coeditor of the *New York Review of Books,* and her skill and understanding as an editor.

D. Plays

i. Theatrical Plays

1. *Visit to a Small Planet.*
   a. A.17.
   b. In Louis Kronenberger, ed. *The Best Plays of 1956–1957.* New York: Dodd, Mead, 1957; New York: Arno Press, 1975, pp. 227–47 (extracts).
   c. *Theatre Arts* 42, no. 2 (February 1958): 32–54.
   d. In A.22.
   e. In Richard H. Goldstone and Abraham H. Lass, ed. *The Mentor Book of Short Plays.* New York: New American Library (Signet), 1969; Garden City, NY: Fireside Theatre, 1992 (as *Twelve Short Plays*), pp. 73–107.
   f. *Harper's Magazine* 273, no. 5 (November 1986): 45 (extract).
   g. In Kathleen Nolan Monahan, ed. *Technology in American Literature.* Lanham, MD: University Press of America, 2000, pp. 184–203 (abridged).
      Premiere: Produced by George Axelrod and Clinton Wilder at the Booth Theatre, New York, 7 February–14 December 1957 (388 performances). Directed by Cyril Ritchard. Starring Cyril Ritchard, Eddie Mayehoff, Philip Coolidge, Sibyl Bowan, Sarah Marshall, and Conrad Janis.
      Revivals:
      1. Westport County Playhouse (Westport, CT), 11 August 1958. Directed by Pat Chandler. Starring Bert Lahr, Kenny Delmar, Stanley Tackney, and Josephine Nichols.
      2. Westminster Theatre (London), 25 February 1960 (12 performances). Directed by Charles Hickman. Starring Alan Badel, Frank Pettingell, Jerry Desmonde, and Brian Murray.
      3. Appleseed Productions (Syracuse, NY), 25 January 2005. Directed by Greg J. Hipius. Starring Doug Rougeaux, Tom Minion, William Edward White, and Binaifer Dabu.
      Vidal's first theatrical play and first Broadway success, a science fiction farce about an extraterrestrial, Kreton (Cyril Ritchard), seeking to incite a war among the members of the human race, purely for his own amusement, and is unwittingly abetted by a hawkish but bumbling general, Tom Powers (Eddie Mayehoff). In a departure from the television play (see ii.10 below) upon which it is based, the world is saved accidentally by a young woman, Ellen Spelding.

2. *The Best Man.*
   a. A.18.
   b. In Louis Kronenberger, ed. *The Best Plays of 1959–1960.* New York: Dodd, Mead, 1960; New York: Arno Press, 1975, pp. 183–206.
   c. *Theatre Arts* 45, No. 9 (September 1961): 25–56.
   d. In A.22.
   e. In John Gassner, ed. *Best American Plays: Fifth Series 1957–1963.* New York: Crown, 1963, pp. 635–74.
   f. In A.62.
      Premiere: Produced by the Playwrights' Company at the Morosco Theatre, New York, 31 March 1960–8 July 1961 (520 performances). Directed by Joseph Anthony. Starring Karl Weber, Melvyn Douglas, Leora Dana, Lee Tracy, Martin Fried, and Frank Lovejoy.
      Revivals:
      1. Alley Theatre (Houston, TX), beginning 8 April 1964 (42 performances). Directed by John Wylie. Starring Maury Cooper, Franklin Cover, and John Wardwell.
      2. Asolo Theatre Festival (Sarasota, FL), beginning 25 February 1972 (17 performances). Directed by Bradford Wallace. Starring Robert Lanchester, Bill E. Noone, William Leach, and Polly Holliday.

3.   New Jersey Shakespeare Festival (Madison, NJ), 23 July 1976 (19 performances). Directed by Paul Barry. Starring Kenneth Gray, J. C. Hoyt, Ronald Steelman, and Patricia Kilgarriff.

4.   Actors' Theater of Louisville (Louisville, KY), 7 October 1976 (28 performances). Directed by John Jory. Starring William Cain, Marji Dodrill, Victor Jory, and John Newton.

5.   American Century Theater (Washington, DC), 15 October–9 November 1996. Directed by Michael Repogle. Starring Joe Jenckes, Michael Thornton, and Maura McGinn.

6.   Produced by Jeffrey Richards et al. at the Virginia Theatre, New York, 17 September–31 December 2000 (as *Gore Vidal's The Best Man*) (121 performances). Directed by Ethan McSweeny. Starring Spalding Gray, Michael Learned, Mark Blum, Chris Noth, Christine Ebersol, and Charles Durning.

7.   Olney Theatre Centre (Washington, DC), 20 July 2004ff. Directed by Richard Romagnoli. Starring Paul Morella, Nigel Reed, and Vivienne Shub.

8.   Remy Bumppo Theatre Company (Chicago), 5 October–5 November 2006. Directed by James Bohnen. Starring David Darlow, James Krag, Gene Johnson, Annabel Armour, and Linda Gillum.

Vidal's greatest Broadway triumph, running for more than a year. A richly dramatic account of an intellectual politician, William Russell (Melvyn Douglas) caught in a power struggle with an unscrupulous rival, Joe Cantwell (Frank Lovejoy), at a political convention; the party's ex-President, Art Hockstader (Lee Tracy), attempts to act as intermediary. Many contemporary critics believed that the scenario reproduced the battle between Adlai Stevenson, Richard Nixon, and Harry S Truman.

3.   *On the March to the Sea.*

     a.   In A.22.

       Premiere: Hyde Park Playhouse (Hyde Park, NY), August 1960. Produced and directed by David Samples. No further information available.

     1.   *Revival:* Bonn, Germany, 14 November 1961 (as *Fire to the Sea*). Adapted for German theater by Eric Burger. No further information available.

       Revised version:

     2.   *Revival* (staged reading). Hartford Stage (Hartford, CT), 30 October 2004. Directed by Warner Shook. Starring Chris Noth.

     3.   *Revival* (staged reading). Reynolds Theater, Duke University (Durham, NC), 22 February–6 March 2005. Directed by Warner Shook. Starring Michael Learned, Isabel Keating, Charles Durning, and Chris Noth.

An elaboration of the television play *Honor* (D.ii.16), set in the time of the Civil War.

4.   *Romulus.*

     a.   *Esquire* 57, no. 1 (January 1962): 47–54 (extracts).

     b.   A.19.

       Premiere: Produced by Roger L. Stevens, in association with Henry Guettel, at the Music Box Theatre, New York, 10 January–10 March 1962 (69 performances). Directed by Joseph Anthony. Starring Cyril Ritchard, James Olson, Francis Compton, Cathleen Nesbitt, and George S. Irving. A farce adapted from a play by Friedrich Duerrenmatt, set in the waning days of the Roman Empire, with Cyril Ritchard playing the emperor Romulus.

5.   *Weekend.*

     a.   A.26.

       Premiere: Produced by Saint-Subber and Lester Osterman at the Broadhurst Theater, New York, 13–30 March 1968 (21 performances). Directed by Joseph Anthony. Starring John Marriott, Kim Hunter, John Forsythe, Rosemary Murphy, Staats Cotsworth, and Eleanor Wilson. A drawing room comedy about a conservative politician, Senator Charles MacGruder (John Forsythe), whose son brings home his African American fiancée (Kim Hunter), and the awkwardness it causes.

6.   *An Evening with Richard Nixon.*
      a.   A.30.
            Premiere: Produced by Hillard Elkins at the Sam S. Shubert Theater, New York, 30 April–13
            May 1972 (16 performances). Directed by Edwin Sherin. Starring George S. Irving, Stephen D.
            Newman, Robert Christian, Philip Sterling, and Robert King. An ingenious lampoon in which
            every word uttered by Nixon (George S. Irving) is taken from actual speeches and interviews.

ii. Television Plays

1.   "Janet Dean, Registered Nurse."
      Cornwall Productions, 1954–1955.
      Vidal wrote one episode (date of airing unknown), entitled "The Case of the Jinx Nurse" (see
      G.11). He later testified that this was his first television play.

2.   *Dark Possession.*
      a.   In A.15.
      b.   In [Katherine Robinson, ed.] *The Red-Headed League and Other Mystery Plays.* New
            York: Scholastic, 1986, pp. 61–82.
            Presented on "Studio One" (CBS), 15 February 1954. Produced by Felix Jackson; directed by
            Franklin Schaffner. Starring Geraldine Fitzgerald, Bramwell Fletcher, Leslie Nielsen, and
            Barbara O'Neal. Also shown on the BBC, 14 May 1959. Directed by Barbara Burnham. Starring
            Pamela Brown. A grim play about a household in which a murder has been committed.

3.   *Smoke.*
      a.   In A.15.
            Presented on "Suspense" (CBS), 4 May 1954. Adapted from the story by William Faulkner.
            Produced by Martin Manulis; directed by Robert Mulligan. Starring E. G. Marshall and George
            Mitchell. An adaptation of a tale of murder by Faulkner.

4.   *Barn Burning.*
      a.   In A.15.
            Presented on "Suspense" (CBS), 17 August 1954. Adapted from the story by William Faulkner.
            Produced by David Heilweil; directed by Robert Mulligan. Starring E. G. Marshall and Charles
            Taylor. A tale of revenge in the rural South.

5.   *The Contrast.*
      Presented on "Omnibus" (CBS), 12 December 1954. Adapted from a play by Royall Tyler. No
      further information available. Tyler's play, often thought to mark the beginning of American
      drama, deals with the contrast between a sophisticated manservant, Jessamy, and a rustic
      peasant, Jonathan, whom Jessamy tries to educate.

6.   *A Sense of Justice.*
      a.   In A.15.
            Presented on "Philco Television Playhouse" (NBC), 6 February 1955. Produced by Gordon Duff;
            associate producer Robert Alan Aurther; directed by Robert Mulligan. Starring John Hudson and
            E. G. Marshall. A play involving politics and gambling.

7.   *The Turn of the Screw.*
      a.   In A.15.
            Presented on "Omnibus" (CBS), 13 February 1955. Adapted from the story by Henry James.
            Produced by Paul Feigay; directed by Seymour Robie. Starring Geraldine Page, Cathleen
            Nesbitt, Rex Thompson, and Nina Reeder. An adaptation of Henry James's story about ghosts
            plaguing two young children.

8.   *The Blue Hotel.*
      Presented on "Danger" (CBS), 22 February 1955. Adapted from the story by Stephen Crane.
      Starring Henry Hull.

9. *Stage Door.*

   Presented on "The Best of Broadway" (CBS), 6 April 1955. Adapted from the Broadway comedy by George S. Kaufman and Edna Ferber. Produced by Felix Jackson; directed by Sidney Lumet. Starring Rhonda Fleming, Elsa Lanchester, and Charles Drake.

10. *Summer Pavilion.*

    a. In A.15.

    Presented on "Studio One" (CBS), 2 May 1955. Produced by Felix Jackson; directed by Paul Nickell. Starring Wyatt Cooper, Charles Drake, Miriam Hopkins, and Elizabeth Montgomery. Also presented on ITV (British television), 26 June 1959. Starring Margaret Vines, Mary Ellis, and Patricia English. A play about a woman rebelling against her excessively decorous upbringing.

11. *Visit to a Small Planet.*

    a. In A.14.
    b. In A.15.
    c. *Magazine of Fantasy and Science Fiction* no. 70 (March 1957): 103–27.
    d. *Cosmopolitan* 143, no. 2 (August 1957): 59–64.
    e. In Richard L. Loughlin, ed. *Journeys in Science Fiction.* New York: Globe Book Co., 1961, pp. 507–44.
    f. In M. Jerry Weiss, ed. *10 Short Plays.* New York: Dell, 1963, 1966, 1978, pp. 285–344.
    g. In Mark Van Doren, Arno Jewett, Olga Achtenhagen, and Margaret Early, ed. *Insights into Literature.* New York: Houghton Mifflin, 1965, 1968, pp. 459–76.
    h. In E. W. Johnson, ed. *Contemporary American Thought: A College Reader.* New York: Free Press, 1968, pp. 445–72.
    i. In James A. MacNeill, R. Garnet Colborne, and Jonathan Kaplan, ed. *Front Row: An Anthology of Plays.* Scarborough, Ontario: Nelson Canada, 1984, pp. 173–92.
    j. In M. Jerry Weiss, ed. *The Signet Book of Short Plays.* New York: Signet Classics, 2004, pp. 249–97.

    Presented on "Goodyear Television Playhouse" (NBC), 8 May 1955. Produced by Gordon Duff; associate producer Robert Alan Aurther; directed by Jack Smight. Starring Cyril Ritchard, Alan Reed, Edward Andrews, and Theodore Bikel. The original version of Vidal's play about an extraterrestrial coming to earth to engender the destruction of the human race for his own amusement; later expanded into a full-length stage play (see i.1 above).

12. *A Farewell to Arms.*

    Presented on "Climax Mystery Theatre" (CBS), 26 May 1955. Adapted from the novel by Ernest Hemingway. Directed by Allen Reisner. Starring Nicky Blair, Diana Lynn, and Martin Brooks. An adaptation of Hemingway's war novel.

13. *The Death of Billy the Kid.*

    a. In A.15.

    Presented on "Philco Television Playhouse" (NBC), 24 July 1955. Produced by Gordon Duff; associate producer Robert Alan Aurther; directed by Robert Mulligan. Starring Paul Newman, Michael Conrad, and Jason Robards Jr. A sympathetic portrayal of Billy the Kid. The basic plot was reworked into a TV movie (E.ii.4).

14. *Dr. Jekyll and Mr. Hyde.*

    Presented on "Climax Mystery Theatre" (CBS), 28 July 1955. Adapted from the novel by Robert Louis Stevenson. Directed by Allen Reisner. Starring Michael Rennie, Lowell Gilmore, and Cedric Hardwicke. An adaptation of Stevenson's classic tale of a psychic double.

15. *State of Confusion.*

    Presented on "The Milton Berle Show" (NBC), 18 October 1955. No further information available.

16.   *Portrait of a Ballerina* (as by Edgar Box).
      Presented on CBS, 1 January 1956. Adapted from Vidal's novel *Death in the Fifth Position.*

17.   *Honor.*
      a.   In A. S. Burack, ed. *Television Plays for Writers.* Boston: The Writer, Inc., 1957, pp. 361–93 (with "Author's Comment," pp. 394–96).
      b.   In *Journeys: What We Discover.* [Mahwah, NJ:] Troll Communications, 1998, pp. 38–60.
      Presented on "Playwrights 56" (NBC), 19 June 1956. Produced by Fred Coe; directed by Vincent J. Donahue. Starring Ralph Bellamy, Glenn Cannon, Carol Goodner, and Frieda Holloway. A grim play of the Civil War; later expanded into a full-length stage play, *On the March to the Sea* (see i.3 above).

18.   *The Indestructible Mr. Gore.*
      Presented on "Sunday Showcase" (NBC), 13 December 1959. Starring William Shatner, Inger Stevens, and Gore Vidal (as narrator). A play about Vidal's grandfather, Thomas P. Gore, relating an actual incident in his political career in which he was the target of political blackmail.

19.   *Dear Arthur.*
      Presented on "Ford Startime" (NBC), 22 March 1960. Adaptation of the romantic comedy by Ferenc Molnár. Produced and directed by Bretaigne Windust. Starring Hermione Baddeley, Robert Dryden, and Rex Harrison.

E. Screenplays

i. Film

1. *The Catered Affair.*
    MGM, 1956. 95 minutes. Released 14 June 1956. Produced by Sam Zimbalist. Directed by Richard Brooks. Screenplay by Gore Vidal, adapted from a television play by Paddy Chayefsky. Starring Bette Davis, Ernest Borgnine, Debbie Reynolds, Barry Fitzgerald, and Rod Taylor. Released 1 May 1956.
    Culver City, CA: MGM Home Video, 1990. 1 videocassette (VHS).
    A grim tale of lower-middle-class life in Brooklyn, where a couple planning a small wedding find that their parents are pressuring them to have a lavish wedding that will consume their modest savings.

2. *I Accuse!*
    MGM, 1958. 99 minutes. Released 5 March 1958. Produced by Sam Zimbalist. Directed by José Ferrer. Screenplay by Gore Vidal, adapted from a book by Nicholas Halasz. Starring José Ferrer, Anton Walbrook, Viveca Lindfors, and Emlyn Williams.
    Saskatoon, Canada: Robert's Hard to Find Videos, [2005?]. 1 videocassette (VHS).
    A dramatization of the Dreyfus affair, in which a Jewish officer in the French army is falsely accused of treason.

3. *The Scapegoat.*
    MGM, 1959. 91 minutes. Released 6 August 1959. Produced by Michael Balcon. Directed by Robert Hamer. Screenplay by Robert Hamer, based on an adaptation by Gore Vidal of the novel by Daphne du Maurier. Starring Alec Guinness, Bette Davis, and Nicole Maurey.
    Adaptation of du Maurier's novel about a French count who seeks to murder his wife and pin the murder on a British schoolteacher.

4. *Ben-Hur.*
    MGM, 1959. 212 minutes. Released 18 November 1959. Produced by Sam Zimbalist. Directed by William Wyler. Screenplay by Karl Tunberg [and Gore Vidal (uncredited)], adapted from the novel by Lew Wallace. Starring Charlton Heston, Jack Hawkins, Haya Harareet, and Stephen Boyd.
    Culver City, CA: MGM/UA Home Video, 1988. 2 videocassettes (VHS). Burbank, CA: Warner Home Video, 2000. 1 videodisc (DVD).
    The well-known and lavish film of ancient Rome, focusing on the conflict between a Jewish merchant in Jerusalem, Judah Ben-Hur, and the Roman governor of the province, Messala.

5. *Suddenly, Last Summer.*
    Columbia Pictures, 1959. 114 minutes. Released 22 December 1959. Produced by Sam Spiegel. Directed by Joseph L. Mankiewicz. Screenplay by Gore Vidal, adapted from the play by Tennessee Williams. Starring Elizabeth Taylor, Katharine Hepburn, Montgomery Clift, Albert Dekker, and Mercedes McCambridge.
    Burbank, CA: RCA/Columbia Pictures Home Video, 1984. 1 videocassette (VHS). Burbank, CA: Columbia TriStar Home Video, 1992. 1 videocassette (VHS). Burbank, CA: Columbia TriStar Home Video, 2000. 1 videodisc (DVD).
    A woman, Mrs. Venable (Katharine Hepburn), seeks to bribe a doctor to perform a lobotomy on her niece, as she is jealous of the niece's attentions to her deceased son, Sebastian.

6. *The Best Man.*
    United Artists, 1964. 102 minutes. Released 6 April 1964. Produced by Stuart Millar and Lawrence Turman. Directed by Franklin J. Schaffner. Screenplay by Gore Vidal, adapted from his play. Starring Henry Fonda, Cliff Robertson, Edie Adams, and Margaret Leighton.
    MGM/UA, 1989. 1 videocassette (VHS).

    Publications:
    a. In George Garrett, O. B. Hardison Jr., and Jane Gelfman, eds. *Film Scripts Four.* New York: Appleton-Century-Crofts, 1972; New York: Irvington, 1989, pp. 146–296.
        An effective adaptation of Vidal's play (D.i.2), with Henry Fonda playing William Russell and Cliff Robertson playing Joe Cantwell.

7. *Is Paris Burning?*
    Paramount/Seven Arts, 1966. 173 minutes. Released 10 November 1966. Produced by Paul Graetz. Directed by René Clément. Screenplay by Gore Vidal, Francis Ford Coppola, Jean Aurenche, Pierre Bost, and Claude Brulé, adapted from the book by Larry Collins and Dominique Lapierre. Starring Jean-Paul Belmondo, Charles Boyer, Leslie Caron, Kirk Douglas, and Glenn Ford.
    Hollywood, CA: Paramount, 1991. 2 videocassettes (VHS). Hollywood, CA: Paramount, 2003. 1 videodisc (DVD).
    Set in Paris at the close of World War II, focusing on the French resistance and the quandary of a Nazi general as to whether he should burn Paris if the Allies get too close.

8. *Night of the Generals.*
    Columbia Pictures, 1967. 148 minutes. Released February 1967. Produced by Sam Spiegel. Directed by Anatole Litvak. Screenplay by Joseph Kessel and Paul Dehn [revised by Gore Vidal (uncredited)]. Adapted from the novel by Hans Hellmut Kirst. Starring Peter O'Toole, Omar Sharif, Tom Courtenay, and Donald Pleasance.
    Burbank, CA: RCA/Columbia Pictures Home Video, 1985. 1 videocassette (VHS). New York: Goodtimes Home Video, 1989. 1 videocassette (VHS). Culver City, CA: Columbia Tristar Home Video, 1995. 1 videocassette (VHS).
    A film involving the plot by Nazi generals to kill Hitler in 1944.

9. *The Last of the Mobile Hot-Shots.*
    Warner Brothers/Seven Arts, 1970. 108 minutes. Released 14 January 1970. Produced and directed by Sidney Lumet. Screenplay by Gore Vidal, adapted from Tennessee Williams's play *The Seven Descents of Myrtle.* Starring James Coburn, Lynn Redgrave, and Robert Hooks.
    New York: Warner Home Video, 1994. 1 videocassette (VHS).
    A love triangle involving a man, his wife, and his half-brother, set on a Southern plantation about to be inundated by an overflowing river.

10. *The Sicilian.*
    Twentieth-Century Fox/Gladden Entertainment, 1987. 148 minutes. Released 23 October 1987. Produced by Michael Cimino and Joann Carelli. Directed by Michael Cimino. Screenplay by Steve Shagan [and Gore Vidal—uncredited], adapted from the novel by Mario Puzo. Starring Christopher Lambert, Terence Stamp, Joss Ackland, and John Turturro.
    [California?:] Artisan Home Entertainment, [2001?]. 1 videodisc (DVD).
    Giuliano, who has gained a reputation as a Robin Hood by robbing money from rich landowners and giving it to poor peasants, vaunts himself before his Mafia backers, who then seek to kill him. Vidal sued the Writers Guild of America to receive screenwriting credit for the film.

11.   *Dimenticare Palermo.*
      Gaumont, 1990. 100 minutes. Directed by Francesco Rosi. Written by Francesco Rosi,
      Tonino Guerra, and Gore Vidal, adapted from the novel *Oublier Palermo* by Edmonde
      Charles-Roux. Starring James Belushi, Mimi Rogers, and Joss Ackland. Shown in the
      United States as *The Palermo Connection.*
            [S.l.:] ARD, 1989. 1 videocassette. Van Nuys, CA: Live Home Video, 1991. 1
      videocassette (VHS) (as *The Palermo Connection*).
      Carmine Bonavia, who has just won election as mayor of New York on a campaign to legalize
      drugs, goes to Sicily and learns that the Mafia will go to any lengths to prevent the legalization
      of drugs, which threatens their profits.

12.   *Trailer for a Remake of Gore Vidal's Caligula.*
      Crossroads, 2005. 5 minutes. Directed by Francesco Vezzoli. Written by Gore Vidal.
      Starring Courtney Love, Karen Black, Milla Jovovich, and Helen Mirren.
      A short film featuring stylized costumes and female actors playing male roles and vice versa.
      Made for the Venice Biennale. It is not in fact a trailer for a future full-length film, but a film in
      its own right. It is presumably meant to suggest what the film *Caligula* (H.ii.4) would have been
      like had Vidal's original screenplay been followed.

ii. Television

1.   *On the March to the Sea.*
      BBC, 17 July 1966. Produced by Cedric Messina. Directed by Alan Gibson.
      Screenplay by Gore Vidal, adapted from his play. Starring Joss Ackland, Tony Bill,
      and Barrie Ingham.
      An adaptation of his stage play (see D.i.3).

2.   *Vidal in Venice.*
      BBC (Channel 4), 27–28 December 1984. Also shown on "National Geographic
      Explorer" (Nickelodeon), 11 August 1985; PBS, 30 June 1986. 110 minutes. Executive
      producer Peter Montagnon. Directed by Mischa Shorer. Written and presented by Gore
      Vidal.
            New York: A. C. Video, 1987. 2 videocassettes (VHS). New York: VPI/AC
      Video, 1988. 2 videocassettes (VHS). [S.l.:] Artful Journeys, 1991. 1 videodisc (DVD)
      (as *Venice*).
      A documentary of the history and topography of Venice, with Vidal as narrator. See the book
      version (I.A.45), of which Vidal wrote only the preface.

3.   *Dress Gray.*
      NBC, 9–10 March 1986. 192 minutes. Produced and directed by Glenn Jordan.
      Teleplay by Gore Vidal, adapted from the book by Lucian K. Truscott IV. Starring Hal
      Holbrook, Lloyd Bridges, and Alec Baldwin.
            Burbank, CA: Warner Home Video, 1993. 2 videocassettes (VHS).
      Set during the Vietnam War, the film focuses on the cover-up of a murder at a prestigious
      military academy (manifestly based on West Point), the dead soldier having clearly had sexual
      relations with a man.

4.   *Gore Vidal's Billy the Kid.*
      TNT, 10 May 1989. 96 minutes. Executive producers Frank Von Zerneck and Robert
      M. Sertner. Directed by William A. Graham. Written by Gore Vidal. Starring Val
      Kilmer, Duncan Regehr, Julie Carmen, Rene Auberjonois.
            Turner Home Entertainment, 1989. 1 videocassette (VHS). Chatworth, CA:
      Image Entertainment, 1991. 1 videodisc (DVD).
      An elaboration of Vidal's television play (see D.ii.13), a sympathetic portrait of the outlaw.

F. Published Letters

1. "Communication."
   a. *Exonian* (1 March 1941): 2 (as by "Gene Vidal").
      A letter of comment on a letter by a "Mr. Gunnar" in a previous issue of the *Exonian*, pertaining to the British and American role in World War II. Evidently Vidal's first appearance in print.

2. "Post-war Writers."
   a. *New York Times Book Review* (19 August 1962): 24.
      Response to John W. Aldridge's article "What Became of Our Postwar Hopes?" (III.E.10), defending his work in film and television and asserting that he has not abandoned the novel. For Aldridge's response, see III.E.8.

3. "Julian."
   a. *New York Times Book Review* (5 July 1964): 20–21.
      Response to Dudley Fitts's review of *Julian* (III.F.21.m), defending the Emperor Julian's criticisms of Christianity. For Fitts's brief response see III.E.110.

4. "Pornography."
   a. *New York Review of Books* 6, no. 8 (12 May 1966): 30.
      Response to a letter by Maurice Girodias (see III.E.127), asserting that Vidal is not an enemy of pornography, but the reverse.

5. "One Reader Writes."
   a. *New York Times Book Review* (4 May 1969): 44.
      Comment on Wilfrid Sheed's review of *Reflections upon a Sinking Ship* (III.F.26.o) and Josh Greenfield's review of *Washington, D.C.* (III.F.22.m).

6. "Vidal's Brow."
   a. *New Statesman* 78 (no. 2002) (25 July 1969): 115.
      Comment on Julian Mitchell's review of *Reflections upon a Sinking Ship* (III.F.26.l), sarcastically agreeing that his essays are not "interesting."

7. "Mishima."
   a. *New York Review of Books* 17, no. 10 (16 December 1971): 42.
      Response to a letter by Ivan Morris (III.E.223) on "The Death of Mishima" (C.87).

8. "Setting It Straight."
   a. *New York Review of Books* 18, no. 2 (10 February 1972): 34.
      Response to a letter by Ivan Morris (III.E.224).

9. "Vidal Blue."
   a. *Atlantic Monthly* 229, no. 5 (May 1972): 27.
      Response to a letter by William Styron (III.E.283).

10. "The Fever Breaks."
    a. *New York Review of Books* 20, no. 14 (20 September 1973): 45.
       Response to a letter by Robert Crichton (III.E.82) on "The Top Ten Best Sellers . . ." (C.96).

11. "The Kapstein Konnection."
    a. *New York Review of Books* 21, no. 2 (21 February 1974): 34.
       Response to a letter by I. J. Kapstein (III.E.170) on "The Art and Arts of E. Howard Hunt" (C.100).

12. "Solved!"
    a. *New York Review of Books* 23, no. 3 (4 March 1976): 38.
       Response to a letter by Donald Windham (III.E.310).

13. "Freedom When?"
    a. *New York Review of Books* 23, no. 10 (10 June 1976): 44.
       Response to a letter by Fred A. Crane (III.E.79) on Vidal's essay on the Adams family (C.110).

14. "The 'Excelsior' Affair" (with others).
    a. *New York Review of Books* 23, no. 13 (5 August 1976): 45.
       Vidal is one of eleven signers of a letter protesting the takeover of the Mexican daily, the *Excelsior,* by conservative employees backed by the Mexican government.

15. "Vidal for Driberg."
    a. *New Statesman* 92 (no. 2373) (10 September 1976): 341.
       Letter responding to A. J. P. Taylor's "London Diary" (20 August 1976), in which Tom Driberg was discussed. Vidal criticizes Taylor for homophobia and for unjustly disparaging Driberg's intellect.

16. "Plastic Fiction."
    a. *New York Review of Books* 23, no. 17 (28 October 1976): 45–46.
       Response to letters by James W. Earl, Name Withheld, and Paul Illert (III.E.99) on Vidal's article "American Plastic: The Matter of Fiction" (C.115).

17. "Who Makes Movies?"
    a. *New York Review of Books* 24, no. 1 (3 February 1977): 45.
       Response to letters by Peter Bogdonavich (III.E.39) and John Bernard Myers (III.E.226) on Vidal's article, "Who Makes the Movies?" (C.116).

18. "For the Record."
    a. *New York Review of Books* 24, no. 12 (14 July 1977): 42.
       Vidal prints a letter responding to the *New York Times* review of *Matters of Fact and of Fiction* (III.F.33.i), which the *Times* did not print.

19. "Killer Bees."
    a. *Esquire* 88, no. 6 (December 1977): 94–95.
       Vidal responds to John Simon's "The Good and Bad of Gore Vidal" (III.33.o). Simon has appended a reply (p. 95).

20. "Hard Maker."
    a. *New York Review of Books* 26, no. 15 (11 October 1979): 53.
       Response to letters by Victor Brombert et al. (III.E.43) on "V. S. Pritchett as 'Critic'" (C.128).

21. "The Wisdom of the East."
    a. *New York Review of Books* 27, no. 2 (21 February 1980): 44.
       Response to a letter by Ramsay Wood (III.E.311) on "Paradise Regained" (C.131.a).

22. "Verifying Genocide."
    a. *New York Review of Books* 28, no. 16 (22 October 1981): 59–60.
       Response to a letter by Robert Creamer (III.E.81) on "An American Sissy" (C.141).

23. "Death in the Philippines."
    a. *New York Review of Books* 28, no. 20 (17 December 1981): 69–70.
       Response to letters by John M. Gates et al. (III.E.122) on "An American Sissy" (C.141).

24. "Death in the Philippines."
    a. *New York Review of Books* 29, no. 3 (4 March 1982): 44.

Response to letters by Stephen Rosskam Shalom and John M. Gates (III.E.278) on "An American Sissy" (C.141).

25.   "Cracking 'The Golden Bowl.'"
      a.   *New York Review of Books* 31, no. 3 (1 March 1984): 49.
           Response to a letter by John Bayley (III.E.29) on "The Golden Bowl of Henry James" (C.153).

26.   "Caring for the Bird."
      a.   *New York Review of Books* 32, no. 13 (15 August 1985): 44.
           Response to a letter by Theodore Lidz, M.D. (III.E.190) on "Tennessee Williams: Someone to Laugh at the Squares With" (C.157).

27.   "Exchange."
      a.   *Nation* 242, no. 17 (26 April 1986): 570, 588, 596; 242, no. 18 (3 May 1986): 602, 628.
           Brief responses to letters by Joseph Wershba et al. (III.E.299 and 2) on Vidal's essay "The Empire Lovers Strike Back" (C.162.a).

28.   "A Mind So Free."
      a.   *New York Review of Books* 33, no. 20 (18 December 1986): 76.
           Response to a letter by Eleanor Cook (III.E.74) on "Lessons of the Master" (C.163.a).

29.   "Powell's People."
      a.   *New York Review of Books* 35, no. 6 (14 April 1988): 45.
           Response to a letter by Diana Trilling (III.E.291) on "Dawn Powell: The American Writer" (C.169).

30.   "Vidal's 'Lincoln': An Exchange."
      a.   *New York Review of Books* 35, no. 13 (18 August 1988): 67–69.
      b.   In A.49 (incorporated into "How I Do What I Do If Not Why").
      c.   In A.56 (incorporated into "Lincoln, *Lincoln,* and the Priests of Academe").
           Response to letters by Harold Holzer and Richard N. Current (III.E.157) on the historical accuracy of *Lincoln.*

31.   "Rosebud."
      a.   *New York Review of Books* 36, no. 13 (17 August 1989): 60.
           Response to a letter by Jay Topkin (III.E.290) on "Remembering Orson Welles" (C.180).

32.   "Communications."
      a.   *American Historical Review* 96, no. 1 (February 1991): 324–26.
      b.   In A.56 (incorporated into "Lincoln, *Lincoln,* and the Priests of Academe").
           Response to Don E. Fehrenbacher's essay (see III.E.107) on the supposed historical errors in *Lincoln.* For Fehrenbacher's response, see III.E.106.

33.   "Lincoln Addendum."
      a.   *New York Review of Books* 38, no. 19 (21 November 1991): 58.
           Letter discussing Lincoln's psychological state as revealed in manuscript letters consulted by Vidal at Brown University.

34.   "Vidal Replies."
      a.   *Nation* 255, no. 10 (5 October 1992): 346.
           Two separate replies to letters (see III.E.89 and 192) commenting on Vidal's essay "Monotheism and Its Discontents" (C.201).

35.   "Vidal Replies."
      a.   *Nation* 261, no. 3 (17–24 July 1995): 74.
           Brief response to a letter by Joseph A. Palermo (III.E.241) on "Kopkind" (C.222).

36.   "Vidal and Buckley, Calley and My Lai."
       a.   *New York Times Book Review* (17 September 1995): 4.
             Discusses William F. Buckley's lawsuit against him and Vidal's accusations of Buckley's anti-
             Semitism.

37.   "The Angel in the Story."
       a.   *New York Review of Books* 43, no. 10 (6 June 1996): 65.
             Response to a letter by Claire DeSilver (see III.E.91) on "Dawn Powell: Queen of the Golden
             Age" (C.228).

38.   "Dinner with the Princess."
       a.   *New Yorker* 72 (24 June–1 July 1996): 121.
             A letter to Louis Auchincloss (1965) about a visit from Princess Margaret.

39.   "Reply to a Critic."
       a.   *New York Review of Books* 43, no. 14 (19 September 1996): 80–81 (as part of "Mark
             Twain's Reputation").
       b.   In A.59.
       c.   In A.65.
             Response to a letter by Guy Cardwell (III.E.59), chiefly dealing with Twain's sex life.

40.   "Vidal Replies."
       a.   *Nation* 263, no. 16 (18 November 1996): 2, 24.
             Response to letters by Larry Adelman and Arthur Schlesinger Jr. (III.E.5) on "The End of
             History" (C.232.a).

41.   "Pleased to Have Been Your Contemporary."
       a.   *Times Literary Supplement* no. 4890 (20 December 1996): 14–15.
             Contents: Letters by Gore Vidal to Christopher Isherwood, November 1958 (14-15); September
             1960 (15); 1962 (15); May 1962 (15); August 1984 (15); Christopher Isherwood to Gore Vidal,
             19 December 1947 (14); 4 November 1948 (14); 7 December 1960 (15); 12 August 1967 (15);
             21 August 1967 (15). Edited by Fred Kaplan. The letters discuss *The City and the Pillar*, Allen
             Ginsberg, Jack Kerouac, Vidal's 1960 campaign, various works by Isherwood, *Washington,
             D.C., Myra Breckinridge,* and Truman Capote.

42.   "Just Between Cousins" (with Louis Auchincloss).
       a.   *New Yorker* 73, no. 15 (9 June 1997): 76, 78–82, 84–85.
             Contents: Letters between Vidal and Louis Auchincloss. Auchincloss to Vidal, 7 April 1952
             (76); Auchincloss to Vidal, 1952 (76); Vidal to Auchincloss, 1952 (76, 78); Vidal to
             Auchincloss, 28 September 1955 (78); Auchincloss to Vidal, 25 July 1957 (78); Vidal to
             Auchincloss, 1957 (78); Vidal to Auchincloss, 1962 (78–79); Auchincloss to Vidal, 1962 (79);
             Auchincloss to Vidal, 12 March 1963 (79); Vidal to Auchincloss, March 1963 (79–80);
             Auchincloss to Vidal, 8 November 1963 (80); Vidal to Auchincloss, November 1963 (80);
             Auchincloss to Vidal, November 1963 (80); Vidal to Auchincloss, 10 January 1964 (80–81);
             Auchincloss to Vidal, 17 January 1964 (81); Auchincloss to Vidal, 3 May 1965 (81); Vidal to
             Auchincloss, 1965 (81); Vidal to Auchincloss, 1965 (81–82); Auchincloss to Vidal, 7 April 1967
             (82); Vidal to Auchincloss, 1967 (82); Auchincloss to Vidal, 22 May 1967 (82, 84); Vidal to
             Auchincloss, 1968 (84); Auchincloss to Vidal, 20 November 1974 (84–85); Vidal to
             Auchincloss, 1974 (85); Auchincloss to Vidal, 9 November 1990 (85); Vidal to Auchincloss,
             December 1990 (85). The letters discuss *The Judgment of Paris,* contemporary literature, *The
             Catered Affair, Visit to a Small Planet, Julian,* the Kennedys, Edmund Wilson, the death of John
             F. Kennedy, *Washington, D.C.,* and Norman Mailer.

43.   "'The Last Party.'"
       a.   *New York Times Book Review* (8 August 1997): 4.
             Objects to a remark attributed to him in Adele Miller's *The Last Party,* about Norman Mailer.

44.   "Historians—Good, Bad and Ugly."
       a.   *Nation* 266, no. 18 (18 May 1998): 24.
             Response to letters (III.E.287) commenting on his essay "Bad History" (C.249).

45.   "'GV' Replies."
       a.   *Nation* 267, no. 1 (6 July 1998): 2, 30.
             Response to a letter by John Haber (III.E.136) commenting on "Bad History" (C.249), also discussing Vidal's foreword to Israel Shahak's *Jewish History, Jewish Religion.*

46.   "Epistle-ing Match."
       a.   *Nation* 267, no. 19 (7 December 1998): 2.
             Response to Christopher Hitchens's "An Open Letter to Gore Vidal" (III.E.154), concerning a right-wing conspiracy to destroy Bill Clinton.

47.   "The Literary Psyche."
       a.   *New York Times Book Review* (5 December 1999): 4.
             Brief letter explaining his work with Fred Kaplan on Kaplan's biography.

48.   "Vidal Replies."
       a.   *Nation* 270, no. 22 (5 June 2000): 2.
             Response to a letter by Greg Geddes (III.E.123), who had mocked Vidal's running for office in 1960 and 1982.

49.   "Japanese Intentions in the Second World War."
       a.   *Times Literary Supplement* no. 5098 (15 December 2000): 15.
       b.   In A.65.
       c.   In A.67.
             Response to a letter by Clive James (see III.E.162) as to whether Japan would have surrendered without the United States' dropping the atomic bomb. For James's response, see III.E.163.

50.   "The American Republic."
       a.   *Times Literary Supplement* no. 5100 (29 December 2000): 15.
             Response to Clive James's second letter (III.E.163) about Japanese involvement in World War II.

51.   "Pearl Harbor: An Exchange."
       a.   *New York Review of Books* 48, no. 8 (17 May 2001): 67.
             Letter commenting on Ian Buruma's "The Emperor's Secrets" (*New York Review of Books,* 25 March 2001), asserting that Franklin D. Roosevelt really did encourage the Japanese to launch their attack on Pearl Harbor. For Buruma's response, see III.E.54.

52.   ". . . And Apple Pie."
       a.   *Nation* 272, no. 25 (25 June 2001): 2.
             Response to Katha Pollitt's article "Happy Mother's Day" (*Nation,* 28 May 2001), which discussed Vidal's plan to attend the execution of Timothy McVeigh.

53.   "A Letter from 18 Writers" (with others).
       a.   *Nation* 283, no. 6 (28 August–4 September 2006): 38.
             Letter discussing the latest conflict between Israel and Palestine, claiming that Israel is on a long-term mission toward the "liquidation of the Palestinian nation." The letter appeared in a number of newspapers worldwide.

G. Manuscripts

1. Bernard and Rebecca Reis Papers. Getty Research Institute (Los Angeles, CA)
    Contains: 1 letter by Vidal to the Reises (n.d.).

2. University of California at Los Angeles Library (Los Angeles, CA)
    Stanley Chase Papers.
        Contains: Drafts of the play *Fire to the Sea* and materials relating to its attempted production.
    Norman Cousins Papers.
        Contains: Letters by Vidal to Cousins.
    NBC Matinee Theater Collection of Scripts and Production Material.
        Contains: Draft of *Dark Possession*.
    Anaïs Nin Papers.
        Contains: Notes and letters by Vidal to Nin.
    Lawrence Turman Papers.
        Contains: Drafts of the screenplay for *The Best Man*, with annotations by Vidal.
    William Wyler Papers.
        Contains: Draft of the screenplay for *Ben-Hur* (with additions and revisions by Vidal); correspondence between Vidal and Wyler.

3. Christopher Isherwood Papers. Huntington Library and Art Gallery (San Marino, CA)
    Contains: Letters by Vidal to Isherwood; 1 letter by Vidal to Sara S. Hodson (2002).

4. Stanford University (Stanford, CA)
    Don Edward Fehrenbacher Papers.
        Contains: Letters by Vidal to Fehrenbacher.
    Alfred M. Lilienthal Papers. Hoover Institution Archives.
        Contains: Letters by Vidal to Lilienthal (1993).

5. Beinecke Rare Book and Manuscript Library, Yale University (New Haven, CT)
    William A. Graham Collection of Television Scripts.
        Contains: Ms. of *The Light in the Dark*.
    Mabel Dodge Luhan Papers.
        Contains: Letter by Vidal to Luhan (1952).
    New World Writing MSS. Survey.
        Contains: Mss. of "Erlinda and Mr. Coffin"; "Notes on Television"; letters by Vidal pertaining to the editing of *New World Writing*.
    Steven H. Scheuer Collection of Television Program Scripts.
        Contains: Mss. of *A Farewell to Arms, Murder Me Gently* [= *Please Murder Me?*], *Smoke, Summer Pavilion, Dark Possession, Honor, A Sense of Justice*.
    Betsy Beinecke Shirley Collection of American Children's Literature.
        Contains: Letter by Gore Vidal to Polly Goodwin.
    Theatre Guild Correspondence.
        Contains: Letters by Vidal.
    Virgil Thomson Papers. Irving S. Gilmore Music Library.
        Contains: Letters by Vidal to Thomson.
    Carl Van Vechten MSS. Survey.
        Contains: Letters by Vidal to Van Vechten.
    Glenway Wescott Papers.
        Contains: Letters by Vidal to Wescott.
    Edmund White Papers.
        Contains: Letters by Vidal to White.
    Thornton Wilder Collection.

Contains: Letters by Vidal to Wilder (1967–1975).
ZA Letter File.
Contains: 9 letters by Vidal to F. H. Markoe (June–November 1952).

6.   Dwight Macdonald Papers. Manuscripts and Archives, Yale University Library (New Haven, CT)
Contains: Letters by Vidal to Macdonald.

7.   University of Delaware Library (Newark, DE)
Paul Bowles Papers.
Contains: 18 letters by Vidal to Bowles (1969–1985, n.d.).
Christopher Sawyer-Lauçanno Papers Related to Paul Bowles.
Contains: 1 letter by Vidal Sawyer-Lauçanno (1986).

8.   Library of Congress (Washington, DC)
James M. Cain Papers.
Contains: Letters by Vidal to Cain (1975).
Huntington Cairns Collection.
Contains: Letters by Vidal to Cairns.
Maurice Rosenblatt Papers.
Contains: Letters by Vidal to Rosenblatt (1960).

9.   Smithsonian Institution (Washington, DC)
Albert Christ-Janer Papers.
Contains: Letters by Vidal to Christ-Janer.
Edward Melcarth Papers.
Contains: Letters by Vidal to Melcarth.

10. Howard Gotlieb Archival Research Center, Boston University (Boston, MA)
F. Sherman Baker Collection.
Contains: 1 letter by Vidal to Baker (n.d.).
Claire Bloom Collection.
Contains: 8 letters by Vidal to Bloom (1972–1992).
Abraham Burack Collection.
Contains: Letters and postcards from Vidal to Burack.
Douglas Fairbanks Jr. Collection.
Contains: 1 letter by Vidal to Fairbanks.
Myrick Land Collection.
Contains: Copy of a letter by Vidal to Land.
Christopher Lehmann-Haupt Collection.
Contains: Cable by Vidal to Lehmann-Haupt (1977).
Herbert Ross and Nora Kaye Collection.
Contains: Typescript of treatment by Vidal; 2 letters (1975, n.d.).

11. Houghton Library, Harvard University (Cambridge, MA)
Osbert Sitwell Papers.
Contains: 2 letters by Vidal to Sitwell.
Gore Vidal Papers.
Contains:
Novels: The City and the Pillar; The City and the Pillar and Seven Early Stories; Dark Green, Bright Red; Death Before Bedtime; Death in the Fifth Position; Ghost of a Rose (fragment); *In a Yellow Wood; The Judgment of Paris; Julian; Messiah; Myra Breckinridge; The Season of Comfort; A Search for the King; Some Desperate Adventure; Washington, D.C.; Williwaw;* [early mystery novel (fragment)]; [untitled novel (c. 1942–1943)]; [untitled novel (c. 1944)].
Theatrical Plays: The Best Man; Different Journey; Do You Know the Milky Way (by Karl Wittlinger; revised by Vidal); *Drawing Room Comedy; Heavenly Hosts; The Independent Mourner; On the March to the Sea; Romulus; Time of Darkness; Visit to a Small Planet; Ways*

of Love; Weekend; Wings of the Eagle: A Political Farce; [untitled play about a retired World War II pilot]; [untitled musical set in the South Pacific].

Television Plays: Barn Burning; Blue Hotel; The Case of the Jinx Nurse (as by Cameron Kay); *The Contrast; The Copper Cage; The Deadly Lady; Dear Arthur; The Death of Billy the Kid; Dr. Jekyll and Mr. Hyde; Honor; The Indestructible Mr. Gore; Lord Byron* (treatment); *Louisa Pallant; Magical Monarch of Mo; A Man and Two Gods; Monograph with Gore Vidal; The Monument* (treatment); *Norman Ross at Work; Portrait of a Ballerina; Private Relations; Queen Aurelia; Sincerely, Willis Wayde; Smoke; Stage Door; State of Confusion; Tall, Dark Man* (treatment); *Traveler in Time; The Turn of the Screw; Visit to a Small Planet;* [untitled science fiction satire].

Screenplays: America the Beautiful; Ben-Hur; The Best Man; The Cardinal (by Robert Dozier; revised by Vidal?); *Casanova; The Catered Affair; The Doctor and the Devils; The Girl of the Golden East; The Golden Age of Pericles; I Accuse!; Is Paris Burning?* (with Francis Ford Coppola); *The Left-Handed Gun; Love Is a Horse Named Gladys* (treatment; with John Latouche); *Night of the Generals; Reunion; Rumble in the Street* (treatment); *The Scapegoat; Suddenly, Last Summer* (with Tennessee Williams).

Essays: "Appointment with O'Hara"; "Bermuda Letter"; "The Best Man 1968"; "Book Report"; "But Is It Legal?"; "Byzantine Mosaic"; "Citizen Ken"; "*The City and the Pillar* After Twenty Years"; "Comment" (*Esquire,* August 1962); "The Commercialites"; "Communication" (F.1); "A Comparison between a Dynastic Ruler and a Totalitarian Ruler"; "The Couch in the Shrine"; "A Day in Geneva"; "Debate in the Moonlight"; "Did a Machine Write *Moby-Dick?*"; "Disaster and Flight"; "E. Nesbit"; "French Letters: The Theory of the New Novel"; "[The] Future of Conservatism"; "God's Country"; "Gore Vidal's Quick Start" (C.1); "Guatemala"; "The Holy Family"; "In the Shadow of the Scales"; "Indicting the Piper"; "An Inside View on the Politician . . ." (= "Comment," *Esquire,* November 1961); "John Blessington Parks" (unpublished); "John Kennedy: A Translation for the English"; "Julian" (F.3); "Ladders to Heaven"; "The Late Show"; "The Liberal Dilemma"; "A Liberal Meets Mr. Conservative"; "Love, Love, Love"; "The Making of a Hero and a Legend"; "A Manifesto"; "Modest Proposals for the Provision of Adequate Shelter in Case of Nuclear War"; "Night of the Vigilantes"; "[The] Norman Mailer Syndrome"; "Notes on Television"; "The Novel in the Age of Science"; "Oh Henry"; "On a Few Personal Horizons"; "On Pornography"; "A Passage to Egypt"; "Pederasty, Plato, and Mr. Burdett"; "The Perils and Rewards of Going into Trade"; "Post-war Writers"; "Primary Vote for a 'Best Man'"; "The Race into Grace, or the Civilization Gap"; "Robert Graves and the Twelve Caesars"; *Rocking the Boat;* "The Satiric World of Evelyn Waugh"; "See It Later"; "Sir John, by a Nose"; "Social Climbing, and How"; "Somber Lunacy, Stern Illogic"; "Some Notes on What Happened at the Cow Palace"; "Speaking of Books" (C.8); "Speaking of Books: John Horne Burns"; "Speaking of Books: Making and Remaking"; "Strangers at Breakfast"; "The Subject Doesn't Object"; "Tarzan Revisited"; "Television Drama, circa 1956"; "Tenacity"; "Tennessee Williams"; "Traveltalks"; "Turn Left, or Right, to More Vivacious Matters" (= "Comment," *Esquire,* May 1962); "A Twist of History"; "Un-American Activities"; "The Unrocked Boat"; "Vidal to Vidal: On Misusing the Past" (= III.C.129); "W. Somerset Maugham"; "The Whole Sordid History"; "Why and How the Russians Came Out Second in the Space Race"; "The World Outside"; "The Wrath of the Radical Right"; "The Writer as Cannibal"; "Writers in the Public Eye"; [statement on Vietnam] (= C.73); [untitled essay on running for Congress in 1960]; [untitled essay on Constantinople]; [untitled essay on filming *The Catered Affair* and *I Accuse!*]; [untitled essay on Tennessee Williams and Time, Inc.]; [untitled essay on *Visit to a Small Planet*].

Poetry: "Allegory of the Three Enemies"; "Beyond this lawn, among the tender trees"; *Clocks in the Granite* (poetry collection; includes "Protagonist"; "Something Remembered"; "Barracks"; "Concerning Dreams"; "Personnel"; "Bivouac"; "Weariness"; "What Exists"; "Change"; "B-25"; "First Flight"; "Furlough"; "Troop Train"; "Port of Embarkation"; "Crossing"; "Arrival"; "Base"; "Summertime"; "Rome"; "Thinking"; "Longing"; "Florence"; "Acclimation"; "Departure"; "Clocks in the Granite"; "Plane"; "Walking"; "The Eagles"; "Modernity"; "Hedges"; "The Secret"; "Void"; "The Lover and the Juniper Tree"); *Exercises in Typing with the Right Hand* (poetry collection; includes "Awareness"; "Without Doubt"; "Names"; "Riders and Watchers"; "Effect"; "Prescience"; "A Prayer"; "For Bob"; "Youth etc."; "The Game 1943"; "For Aesthetes"; "Talking Bishop"; "Semi Sonnet I"; "Semi Sonnet II"; "This and No More"); "Haunted by that young Duke of Buckingham"; *Litany for the Living* (poetry collection; includes "Georgian Town"; "Spring Soon Goes"; "Dark Night"; "Tower of Stone"; "The 8th Went By";

"Night Heat"; "The Lady of Ill-Repute"; "Union Station"; "Roman Sword"; "Parallel Construction"; "On Drugstores"; "Looking Down at Chartres"; "Haroun al Raschid"; "The Stream"; "Summer Garden"; "Day in December"; "The Yesteryear"; "This Passing Shadow"; "Hidden Valley"; "Semisonnet I"; "Semisonnet II"; "Semisonnet III"; "Litany for Living"); [Poems] (poetry collection; includes "For R. R."; "Throne to Exile"; "He had loved him far too much"; "From Olympus"; "In Our Time: War"; "Mostly Rain"; "Thoughts for Aesthetes"; "For Bob"; "This and No More"; "Preferences"; "From Other Places"; "Then***"; "A House in the Woods"; "Our Waiting"; "The Emperor Stirred upon His Bed"; "The Mighty One"; "The sun sinks slowly behind a cloud"; "The heavens are shot with red and gold"); [Poems] (includes "Throne to Exile"; "Pauper King"; "Alhambra"); [Poems] (includes "Rupert Brooke" and "Concerning Memory"; "Void" and "Questions"); "The Present" and "The Glass"; *Recreation Period and Other Poems* (poetry collection; includes "First Dream"; "Recreation Period"; "Void"; "Modernity"; "Change"; "Chain"; "Medley"; "Sonnet"; "Painting"; "Without Doubt"; "Type"; "Rupert Brooke"; "Aesthetes"; "Later"; "Sub Species"; "Dreamer"; "The Winter Wind"; "For Bob"; "Landing at LA"; "Scene"; "Irish Sea"; "Girl"; "Creation"; "Commencement"; "No More"; "A Painter"; "Names"; "Night Heat"; "Believing"; "Effect"; "American Legion"; "By Dark"; "Dream"; "Mistake"; "New Mexican Moment"; "Memory"; "Union Station"; "Question"; "Episode"; "Price Paid"; "This Wind"; "Hedges"; "Plane"; "Pathos"; "Fragments"; "Sentimentality"; "The Last One"); "Seven"; [Sonnets]; "Suicide Twice"; "Times Rhetoric"; "To R. K. B.'s Lost Generation"; "Tower of Stone"; "Twenty-three Poems" (23 untitled poems); "Unyielding to Adversity."

Short Stories: "The Bivouac"; "Boredom"; "The Borgias"; "The Bride Wore a Business Suit"; "Clouds and Eclipses"; "The Counted Eggs"; "The Dancer"; "Gerald the Pseudo-Mugger"; "Ghosts"; "The Great Actor"; "The Ladies in the Library"; "Look Downward Angel"; "The Mistake"; "A Moment of Green Laurel"; "Mostly about Geoffrey"; "Mr. Smythe's First Murder"; "Mrs. Marsten and the End of the World"; "Out of the Mouths of Babes Comes Babble"; "The Robin"; "Roses and Rings"; "The Royalist"; "Secret Agent X2"; "Sex through the Ages of My Life and Times"; "The Splendid Gesture"; "Three Stratagems"; "Untitled Screen Original" (fragment); "Weather and a Death at Sea"; "The Whisperer"; "The Zenner Trophy"; [eight untitled stories]; [unidentified partial drafts].

Miscellaneous Works: [three speeches written at Phillips Exeter Academy]; [Writers of the 40's]; "Satire and the Novel" (notecards); [On the novel] (speech); [On writing for film] (notecards); [On writing for television] (notecards); [The contemporary American novel] (speech); [Gustave Flaubert] (speech); [History of the novel] (speech); [Julian] (speech); [Speech written for Dwight D. Eisenhower, 1957]; [The role of the government] (speech); [The senatorial candidacy of Robert F. Kennedy] (speech); [Television and politics] (notecards).

Letters: Large holdings of correspondence to and from Vidal.

By far the single largest collection of papers and manuscripts by Vidal. The collection was originally donated to the State Historical Society of Wisconsin, but in 2002 Vidal withdrew it and donated it to Harvard. The collection has not been fully catalogued, and the above listing derives largely from what was catalogued by Wisconsin.

12.   Jeannette Rankin Papers. Radcliffe College, Harvard University (Cambridge, MA)
       Contains: Letters by Vidal to Rankin.

13.   University of Michigan Library (Ann Arbor, MI)
       Esquire, Inc., Papers.
       Contains: Mss. by Vidal and letters by him to *Esquire.*
       Henry Van Dyke Papers.
       Contains: Letters by Vidal to Van Dyke.

14.   Firestone Library, Princeton University (Princeton, NJ)
       Kimon Friar Papers.
       Contains: 9 letters by Vidal to Friar (1945–1980).
       Stanley Kunitz Papers.
       Contains: 1 letter to Kunitz (n.d.).
       Lehmann Family Papers.
       Contains: Letters by Vidal to John Lehmann (1943–1966).

Quarterly Review of Literature Archives.
> Contains: 3 letters by Vidal to Theodore Weiss (1953–1958).

Archives of *Story* Magazine and Story Press.
> Contains: 4 letters by Vidal to *Story* magazine (1968–1969).

Arthur H. Thornhill Papers.
> Contains: 1 letter by Vidal to Thornhill (1970).

15. Columbia University Library (New York, NY)
    Robert Halsband Papers.
    > Contains: Letters by Vidal to Halsband.

    John Latouche Papers.
    > Contains: Letters by Vidal to Latouche.

    Jerome Moross Papers.
    > Contains: Letters by Vidal to Moross.

    Sitwell Family Papers.
    > Contains: 1 letter by Vidal to Geoffrey Elborn (1978).

16. Billy Rose Theatre Collection, New York Public Library (New York, NY)
    Theatre Special Collections
    > Contains: Typescript of *Blood Kin* (original title for *The Last of the Mobile Hot-Shots*).

    Richard Barr–Clinton Wilder Papers.
    > Contains: Production book for *Visit to a Small Planet;* miscellaneous correspondence pertaining to the production and other matter.

    Montgomery Clift Papers.
    > Contains: TMs. of the screenplay of *Suddenly, Last Summer*.

    Cheryl Crawford Papers.
    > Contains: 1 letter by Vidal to Crawford.

    Vincent J. Donahue Papers.
    > Contains: Correspondence concerning the production of *Honor*.

    Ruth and Augustus Goetz Papers.
    > Contains: Letters by Vidal to Ruth Goetz.

    Jo Mielziner Papers.
    > Contains: Letters by Vidal to Mielziner.

17. Lincoln Kirstein Papers. Jerome Robbins Dance Division, New York Public Library (New York, NY)
    > Contains: 1 letter by Vidal to Kirstein (n.d.).

18. Joyce Carol Oates Papers. Syracuse University Library (Syracuse, NY)
    > Contains: Letters by Vidal to Oates.

19. Robert Coles Papers. University of North Carolina (Chapel Hill, NC)
    > Contains: Letters by Vidal to Coles (1978).

20. Frank Whitson Fetter Papers. Duke University Library (Durham, NC)
    > Contains: Letters by Vidal to Fetter.

21. Thomas P. Gore Papers. Carl Albert Congressional Research and Studies Center, University of Oklahoma (Norman, OK)
    > Contains: Letters by Vidal to Thomas P. Gore (1939–1947).

22. *The American Poetry Review* Office Files. University of Pennsylvania Library (Philadelphia, PA)
    > Contains: Essay by Vidal on Abraham Lincoln; extract from *Screening History*.

23. Ann Morrissett Davidon and William C. Davidon Papers. Swarthmore College Library (Swarthmore, PA)
    > Contains: Letters by Vidal to Ann Morrissett Davidon.

24.   Harry Ransom Humanities Research Center, University of Texas (Austin, TX)
       Paul Bowles Collection.
              Contains: Letters by Vidal to Bowles.
       Millicent Dillon Papers.
              Contains: Letters by Vidal to Dillon.
       Noël Riley Fitch Papers.
              Contains: Letters by Vidal to Fitch.
       Elizabeth Hardwick Papers.
              Contains: Letters by Vidal to Hardwick.
       Carson McCullers Collection.
              Contains: Letters by Vidal to McCullers.
       James Roose-Evans Papers.
              Contains: Letters by Vidal to Roose-Evans (Hempstead Theatre).
       Nancy Wilson Ross Papers.
              Contains: Letters by Vidal to Ross.
       C. P. Snow Collection.
              Contains: Letters by Vidal to Snow.

25.   Richard Halworth Rovere Papers. Wisconsin Historical Society (Madison, WI)
              Contains: 2 letters by Vidal to Rovere (1965, n.d.).

26.   Wendy Beckett Papers. National Library of Australia (Canberra, Australia)
              Contains: Letters by Vidal to Beckett.

27.   Patricia Highsmith Papers. Swiss National Library (Berne, Switzerland)
              Contains: Letters by Vidal to Highsmith.

H. Media Adaptations

i. Audiobooks and eBooks

1. *Lincoln*
   a. New York: Random House Audiobooks, 1985. 2 sound cassettes.

2. *Kalki*
   a. New York: Warner Audio, 1985. 2 sound cassettes. Abridged.
   b. New Fairfield, CT: Homespun Audio, 1996. 4 sound cassettes. Read by Diana Canova.

3. *Empire*
   a. New York: Random House, 1987. 2 sound cassettes. Read by Kathryn Walker.
   b. Newport Beach, CA: Books on Tape, 1993. 14 sound cassettes. Read by Grover Gardner.

4. *Hollywood*
   a. New York: Random House Audio, 1989. 2 sound cassettes. Read by Kathryn Walker.
   b. Washington, DC: Library of Congress, 1990. 11 sound discs. For use by the blind and handicapped. Narrated by Mitzi Friedlander.
   c. Newport Beach, CA: Books on Tape, 1993. 13 sound cassettes. Read by Grover Gardner.

5. *Washington, D.C.*
   a. Pittsburgh, PA: Association, Pleasant Hills Community Church, 1991. Sound cassettes.
   b. Newport Beach, CA: Books on Tape, 1993. 9 sound cassettes. Read by Grover Gardner.

6. *Live from Golgotha*
   a. New York: Random House Audio, 1992. 2 sound cassettes. Read by B. D. Wong.

7. *Burr*
   a. Newport Beach, CA: Books on Tape, 1993. 13 sound cassettes. Read by Grover Gardner.

8. *1876*
   a. Newport Beach, CA: Books on tape, 1993. 9 sound cassettes. Read by Grover Gardner.

9. *The Smithsonian Institution*
   a. Novato, CA: Soundelux Audio, 1998. 2 sound cassettes. Read by Steve Pietrofesa.
   b. Newport Beach, CA: Books on Tape, 1999. 6 sound cassettes. Read by Grover Gardner.

10. *The Golden Age*
    a. New York: Random House, 2000. 4 sound cassettes. Read by Kathryn Walker.
    b. New York: BDD Audio, 2000. 10 sound cassettes. Read by Anne Twomey.

11. *The Last Empire: Essays 1992–2000*
    a. Beverly Hills, CA: New Millennium Audio, 2001. 12 sound cassettes. Read by Dan Cushman.

12. *Inventing a Nation*
     a.   Frederick, MD: Recorded Books, 2003. 4 sound cassettes. Narrated by Paul Hecht and
          Gore Vidal.

13. *Lincoln*
     a.   New York: RosettaBooks, 2004. Electronic Book.

14. *Burr*
     a.   New York: RosettaBooks, 2004. Electronic book.

15. *Empire*
     a.   New York: RosettaBooks, 2004. Electronic book.

16. *Hollywood*
     a.   New York: RosettaBooks, 2004. Electronic book.

ii. Films

1.   *The Left-Handed Gun.*
          Warner Brothers, 1958. 102 minutes. Released 7 May 1958. Produced by Fred Coe.
          Directed by Arthur Penn. Screenplay by Leslie Stevens from a play [*The Death of Billy
          the Kid*] by Gore Vidal. Starring Paul Newman, Lita Milan, John Dehner, and Hurd
          Hatfield.
               Burbank, CA: Warner Home Video, 1986. 1 videocassette (VHS).
          Adaptation of Vidal's television play (D.ii.13).

2.   *Visit to a Small Planet.*
          Paramount, 1960. 85 minutes. Released 4 February 1960. Produced by Hal B. Wallis.
          Directed by Norman Taurog. Screenplay by Edmund Beloin and Henry Garson,
          adapted from the play by Gore Vidal. Starring Jerry Lewis, Joan Blackman, Earl
          Holliman, Fred Clark, and John Williams.
               Farmington Hills, MI: Magnetic Video Corp., 1978. 1 videocassette (VHS).
          Middling adaptation of Vidal's stage play (D.i.1).

3.   *Gore Vidal's Myra Breckinridge.*
          Twentieth-Century-Fox, 1970. 94 minutes. Released 23 June 1970. Produced by
          Robert Fryer. Directed by Michael Sarne. Screenplay by Michael Sarne and David
          Giler from the novel by Gore Vidal. Starring Mae West, Raquel Welch, Rex Reed,
          Farrah Fawcett, and John Huston.
               Farmington Hills, MI: Magnetic Video Corp., 1980. 1 videocassette (VHS).
          Twentieth-Century-Fox Home Entertainment, 2003. 1 videodisc (DVD).
          Pungently satirical adaptation of Vidal's novel (A.25).

4.   *Caligula.*
          Penthouse Productions, 1979. 105 minutes. Released 14 August 1979 (Italy), 1
          February 1980 (US). Produced by Bob Guccione and Franco Rossellini. Adapted from
          an original screenplay by Gore Vidal. Starring Malcolm McDowell, Teresa Ann Savoy,
          Peter O'Toole, Helen Mirren, and Sir John Gielgud.
               Stamford, CT: Vestron Video, 1984. 1 videodisc (LaserVision). New York:
          Penthouse Films International, 1991. 1 videocassette (VHS). New York: Penthouse
          Films International, 1999. 1 videodisc (DVD).
          Flamboyant and pornographic depiction of the life of the Roman emperor Caligula (Malcolm
          McDowell). The film was directed by Tinto Brass, but he later disavowed it and demanded that
          his name be removed from the credits. Vidal's screenplay was evidently significantly altered, to
          the extent that he also sought to have his name removed.

iii. Television

1.   *Please Murder Me.*
        Presented on "Armchair Theatre" (UK), 16 November 1958. Adaptation by Sarrett
        Rudley of an episode in *The Judgment of Paris.* Starring Eric Pohlmann and Beryl
        Measor.
        Dramatizes the scene where a hugely fat man wishes someone to kill him, but the job is bungled
        by a female detective novelist.

2.   *Gore Vidal's Lincoln.*
        NBC, 27 and 28 March 1988. 4 hours. Chris/Rose Productions. Produced by Bob
        Christiansen and Rick Resenberg. Directed by Lamont Johnson. Screenplay by Ernest
        Kinoy based on the novel by Gore Vidal. Starring Sam Waterston, Mary Tyler Moore,
        Richard Mulligan, Deborah Adair, and Tom Brennan.
             New York: Vision Entertainment, 1993. 2 videocassettes (VHS). La Crosse, WI:
        Platinum Disc Corp., 2004. 1 videodisc (DVD).
        Moving and faithful adaptation of Vidal's novel (A.44).

iv. Theater

1.   *Live from Golgotha.*
        Directed by Malcolm Sutherland. Adapted from the novel by Gore Vidal. Starring
        David de Keyser, Sylvester McCoy, and William Hope. *Premiere:* Drill Hall, London,
        15 November 2002.

v. Recordings

1.   *Visit to a Small Planet.*
        1 sound tape reel. Broadcast on WQZR Stereo Theatre, 1963. With Cyril Ritchard,
        Dina Merrill, Richard Hurd, and Ed Zimmerman.

2.   *Gore Vidal's An Evening with Richard Nixon.*
        Hollywood, CA: A & M Records, 1972. 1 sound disc.

3.   *The Best Man.*
        [Venice, CA:] L. A. Theatre Works, 2003. 2 sound discs. Starring Marsha Mason and
        Fred Thompson. Directed by Nick Olcott.

I. Vidal in the Media

i. Vidal as Actor in Film, Television, and Theater

1. *Ritual in Transfigured Time.*
    [Privately produced], 1946. Directed by Maya Deren. Starring Anaïs Nin and Frank Westbrook.
    Vidal plays himself at a party given by Nin.

2. *The Indestructible Mr. Gore.*
    "Sunday Showcase" (NBC), 13 December 1959.
    Vidal is the narrator. See D.ii.16.

3. *Suddenly, Last Summer.*
    Columbia Pictures, 1959.
    Vidal is in the audience during an operation. See E.i.4.

4. *The Best Man.*
    United Artists, 1964.
    Vidal is a delegate at the convention. See E.i.5.

5. "Hot Line."
    WPIX (Channel 11, New York), December 1964.
    Vidal served as host on this talk show.

6. "Mary Hartman, Mary Hartman."
    1976–1977.
    Vidal played himself on six episodes of this parody of a soap opera.

7. *Gore Vidal's Billy the Kid.*
    TNT, 10 May 1989.
    Vidal is a preacher. See D.ii.4.

8. *Bob Roberts.*
    Paramount, 1992. 103 minutes. Released September 1992. Produced by Forrest Murray. Written and directed by Tim Robbins. Starring Tim Robbins, Giancarlo Esposito, Ray Wise, and Rebecca Jenkins.
    Vidal plays Senator Brickley Paiste, a liberal senator who is ousted by a clever, young far-right politician, Bob Roberts (Tim Robbins), who uses folk songs and other devices to attract a cadre of devoted young followers. Many of the political views uttered by Vidal in the film—e.g., on defense spending and the national security state—are direct echoes of his essays.

9. *With Honors.*
    Warner Brothers, 1994. 101 minutes. Released May 1994. Produced by Paula Weinstein and Amy Robinson. Directed by Alek Keshishian. Screenplay by William Mastrosimone. Starring Joe Pesci, Brendan Fraser, Moira Kelly, and Patrick Dempsey.
    Vidal plays Professor Pitkannan, in a film about Simon Wilder (Joe Pesci), a student who loses his thesis and is beholden to a squatter, Monty Kessler (Brendan Fraser), who finds it.

10. *Shadow Conspiracy.*
    Hollywood Pictures, 1997. 103 minutes. Released 31 January 1997. Produced by Terry Collis. Directed by George P. Cosmatos. Screenplay by Adi Hasak and Ric Gibbs. Starring Charlie Sheen, Linda Hamilton, Donald Sutherland, and Sam Waterston.

Vidal plays Congressman Page in a film about Bobby Bishop (Martin Sheen), an assistant to the president who learns of a plot against the White House and strives to combat it.

11. *Gattaca.*
     Columbia, 1997. 108 minutes. Released 24 October 1997. Produced by Danny DeVito, Michael Shamberg, and Stacy Sher. Written and directed by Andrew Niccol. Starring Ethan Hawke, Uma Thurman, Alan Arkin, and Jude Law.
     Vidal plays Director Josef in a science fiction thriller about the last natural man, Vincent Freeman (Ethan Hawke), in a genetically engineered world.

12. *Igby Goes Down.*
     MGM, 2002. 99 minutes. Released 23 May 2002. Produced by Lisa Tornell and Marco Weber. Written and directed by Burr Steers. Starring Kieran Culkin, Claire Danes, and Jeff Goldblum.
     Vidal plays the First School Headmaster in a film about a teenager, Igby Slocumb Jr. (Kieran Culkin), who rebels against his upper-class upbringing and enters the bohemian underworld of Manhattan.

13. *Trumbo* by Christopher Trumbo.
     Westside Theatre (New York), November 2003. Directed by Peter Askin.
     Vidal played the lead role in what is essentially a one-man show in which Dalton Trumbo's blacklisting in the 1940s and 1950s is portrayed, chiefly through his letters. Other actors, such as Nathan Lane, F. Murray Abraham, and Christopher Lloyd, also portrayed Trumbo.

14. "Jack & Bobby."
     WB Television Network, Episode 22 (11 May 2005). Starring Matt Long, Logan Lerman, and Christine Lahti.
     Vidal is a host of a fake documentary set in the year 2049 about Bobby McCallister (Logan Lerman), president of the United States, and his older brother, Jack (Matt Long).

15. "Middle Sexes: Redfining He and She."
     HBO, 6 December 2005.
     Vidal is the narrator of a documentary probing homosexuality, bisexuality, and related issues.

16. "The Simpsons."
     Fox TV, 19 November 2006.
     Vidal plays himself on this animated television show (i.e., a figure representing him appears, along with his voice). Also appearing are writers Michael Chabon and Jonathan Franzen.

ii. Media Programs by or about Vidal

1. *The Novel in the Age of Science.*
    1 sound tape reel. Recorded 11 January 1965 at the Coolidge Auditorium of the Library of Congress. Vidal introduced by L. Quincy Mumford. The lecture was later published (see I.C.58).

2. *Gore Vidal.*
    Sydney, Australia: A.B.C., 1975. 1 sound cassette.

3. *Gore Vidal.*
    Washington, DC: Tapes for Readers, 1978. 1 sound cassette.
    Vidal is interviewed by Stephen Banker. He discusses *1876* and U.S. political corruption.

4. *Gore Vidal: Schriftseller, Politiker, Weltmann.*
    [Framingham, MA:] Home Vision, 1979. 1 videocassette (58 minutes).
    A program broadcast on Bayerischer Rundfunk, Munich. Vidal discusses his literary and religious views, the Kennedys, and other writers such as Norman Mailer and Truman Capote.

5.   *Profile of a Writer.*
       [Chicago:] Home Vision, 1979. 6 videocassettes. No. 4 about Vidal (55 minutes).
       A London Weekend Television coproduction with RM Arts.

6.   *Gore Vidal: The Man Who Said No.*
       New York: Mystic Fire Video, 1984. 1 videocassette. Produced and directed by Gary
       Conklin. 99 minutes.
       A program about Vidal's campaign for the U.S. Senate in 1982.

7.   "The South Bank Show."
       BBC1, 15 November 1987.
       An hour-long show about Vidal, hosted by Melvyn Bragg.

8.   "JFK: A Personal Memory by Gore Vidal."
       BBC2, 21 November 1993.
       See "JFK's War Games" (C.214).

9.   "Gore Vidal's Gore Vidal."
       BBC1, 12 October 1995.

10.   "Gore Vidal's Washington, D.C."
       Disney Channel, 23 July 1996. A segment of the series "Urban Heartlands."

11.   *Gore Vidal's American Presidency: Heroes or Villains?*
       BBC (Channel 4), [date unknown]. History Channel, 11 August 1996.
       Englewood, NJ: American Home Treasures, 1996. 1 videocassette.
       Later written up as *The American Presidency* (A.61).

12.   *The Education of Gore Vidal.*
       WNET, New York, 30 July 2003. Produced by Matt Kapp. Directed by Deborah
       Dickson.

13.   *Gore Vidal: Novelist, Playwright, Essayist, Book Reviewer.*
       [n.d.] Sound recording.
       Michael Barber interviews Vidal.

14.   *Gore Vidal: When National Security Rules.*
       National Public Radio, [n.d.]. 1 audio cassette.

iii. Filmed or Taped Interviews

1.   "Ten Year Old Boy Flies Airplane."
       Pathé News of the Week, May 1936.
       Presumably Vidal's first appearance on the screen, during which he flies an airplane solo to
       demonstrate the ease and practicality of airline travel. The stunt was arranged by Vidal's father,
       Eugene, who was at this time in the Commerce Department of the Franklin D. Roosevelt
       administration.

2.   "What's My Line?"
       CBS, 15 May 1960.
       Vidal is a guest panelist.

3.   "New York Forum."
       WCBS (Channel 2, New York), 21 August 1960.
       Vidal, in the midst of his campaign for Congress, discusses the low state of television. Robert L.
       Tofel, Andrew Connick, and Lawrence C. McQuade are questioners; Ned Calmer is moderator.
       See III.B.85.

4.   [Interview with Studs Terkel, 1961.]
    a.   In Studs Terkel. *Voices of Our Time.* Minneapolis, MN: HighBridge Co., 2005. 6 sound discs (DVD).
    b.   St. Paul, MN: HighBridge Co., 1993 (as *Four Decades with Studs Terkel*). 4 sound cassettes.
          Includes an interview with Vidal.

5.   "Open End."
        WNEW (Channel 5, New York), 23 September 1962.
        Vidal debates for two hours with William F. Buckley Jr., with David Susskind moderating.

6.   *The Writer Speaks.*
        1 sound tape reel.
        Vidal is interviewed by Maurice Dolbier, 1963. Produced and directed by Abby Brown.

7.   "The Les Crane Show."
        ABC, 9 April 1964.
        Vidal is interviewed.

8.   "What's My Line?"
        CBS, 12 April 1964.
        Vidal is a guest panelist.

9.   Republican National Convention.
        Westinghouse Broadcasting Co., 13–16 June 1964.
        Vidal is a commentator.

10.   "The Steve Allen Show."
        ABC, 21 August 1964.
        Vidal is guest along with Nanette Fabray, Frank Gorshin, and Della Reese. Guest host: Eddie Albert.

11.   Democratic National Convention.
        Westinghouse Broadcasting Co., 24–27 August 1964.
        Vidal is a commentator.

12.   "Late Night Line-Up."
        BBC2, September 1968. See III.C.38.

13.   "Face to Face."
        WNEW (Channel 5, New York), 11 June 1967.
        Vidal and Marya Mannes discuss the Vietnam War and other issues. See III.B.31.

14.   Republican National Convention.
        ABC, 5–8 August 1968.
        Vidal and William F. Buckley, Jr., are commentators.

15.   Democratic National Convention.
        ABC, 25–28 August 1968.
        Vidal and William F. Buckley, Jr., are commentators. It was on 28 August that Vidal and Buckley engaged in their celebrated feud, Vidal calling Buckley a "crypto-Nazi" and Buckley heatedly replying, "You queer!"

16.   "Playboy After Dark."
        Playboy Productions, Inc., 28 March 1969.
        Vidal is interviewed.

17.   "The Tonight Show Starring Johnny Carson."
         NBC, 4 May 1970.
         Vidal is a guest.

18.   "The Tonight Show Starring Johnny Carson."
         NBC, 30 September 1970.
         Vidal is a guest.

19.   "Rowan & Martin's Laugh-In."
         NBC, 11 January 1971.
         Vidal makes an appearance. He was repeatedly parodied on the show by Lily Tomlin (playing a telephone operator) as "Mr. Veedle."

20.   "The Dick Cavett Show."
         ABC, 1 December 1971.
         Vidal has his celebrated confrontation with Norman Mailer, with Janet Flanner looking on.

21.   "The Tonight Show Starring Johnny Carson."
         NBC, 18 April 1972.
         Vidal is a guest.

22.   *Fellini's Roma.*
         Francese/United Artists, 1972. Produced by Turi Vasile. Directed by Federico Fellini. Written by Federico Fellini and Bernardino Zapponi.
         Vidal gives a cynical interview at a sidewalk café in Rome.

23.   *Gore Vidal Talks about the U.S. Two-Party System.*
         1973. 1 cassette (5 minutes).
         Interview conducted 8 November 1973 by Mike Wallace.

24.   "Argument."
         BBC2, March 1974.
         Vidal is interviewed along with the Earl of Longford. See III.C.39.

25.   "Argument."
         BBC2, 1 August 1974.
         Vidal is interviewed along with Malcolm Muggeridge. See III.C.41.

26.   "60 Minutes."
         CBS, 27 July 1975.
         Vidal is interviewed by Mike Wallace.

27.   "Success Story."
         BBC1, 6 August 1975.
         Vidal is interviewed. See III.C.28.

28.   "The 48th Annual Academy Awards."
         ABC, 29 March 1976.
         Vidal presents an award.

29.   "Dinah."
         CBS, 22 October 1976.
         Vidal is interviewed by Dinah Shore. He discusses 1968 Democratic National Convention.

30.   *Gore Vidal Interviewed by Dennis Altman.*
         Sydney, Australia: A.B.C., 1977.

31. "The Dick Cavett Show."
     PBS, 2 January 1978.
     Vidal appears for a second time with Norman Mailer.

32. [Interview by Joan Bakewell.]
     At Edinburgh Festival Writers' Conference, 1980. Published as *Maxwell Perkins, Editor of Genius; Gore Vidal*. London: BBC Cassettes, 1983. 1 videocassette.

33. "The Tonight Show Starring Johnny Carson."
     NBC, 31 October 1980.
     Vidal is a guest.

34. *Gore Vidal with Lorna Sage.*
     a. Northbrook, IL: Anthony Roland Collection of Films on Art, [198-]. 1 videocassette.
     b. Northbrook, IL: ICA Video, 1989. 1 videocassette.
     [Interview on ICA TV?]

35. *A Documentary on the Making of "Gore Vidal's Caligula."*
     Cinemedia West Corp., 1981. Directed by Giancarlo Lui. Written by Alan Wallis.
     Vidal is interviewed.

36. *Great American Writers/Three: As Reported in the New York Times.*
     Sanford, NC: Microfilming Corp. of America, 1983. 40 microfiches.
     Contains a segment on Vidal.

37. "Wogan."
     BBC, 3 November 1984.
     Vidal in discussion with Beryl Reid.

38. *Memory and Imagination: New Pathways to the Library of Congress.*
     Krainin Productions, 1990. Written, directed, and produced by Julian Krainin and Michael R. Lawrence. 1 videocassette.
     Includes a segment with Vidal.

39. "The Clive James Interview."
     BBC1, 17 March 1991.
     Vidal is interviewed.

40. "Clive Anderson Talks Back."
     BBC (Channel 4), 15 November 1991.
     Vidal and Edward Heath are in a debate.

41. *In Search of Oz.*
     BBC2, 29 January 1994. A&E, 16 June 1994. ABC (Australia), 12 August 1996.
     Directed by Brian Skeet.
     Vidal is interviewed about the Oz books.

42. *Ben-Hur: The Making of an Epic.*
     Warner Home Video, 1993. Directed by Scott Benson. Written by Mary Adair Kaiser.
     Vidal is interviewed about his participation in the film.

43. "Clive Anderson Talks Back."
     BBC (Channel 4), 15 October 1993.
     Vidal in discussion with David Frost and Mandy Smith.

44.   *The Great Depression.*
> PBS, 25 October 1993. Produced by Lyn Goldfarb and Terry Kay Rockefeller. Directed by Jon Else, Lyn Goldfarb, and Stephen Stept. Written by Jon Else, Lyn Goldfarb, Stephen Stept, and Steve Fayer.
> Vidal is interviewed.

45.   *Tennessee Williams: Orpheus of the American Stage.*
> International Cultural Programming, Inc., 1994. Produced and directed by Merrill Brockway. Written by Jerry Pantzer.
> Vidal is interviewed about Williams.

46.   "Clive Anderson Talks Back."
> BBC (Channel 4), 20 October 1995.
> Vidal in discussion with David Baddiel, Frank Skinner, and Paula Yates.

47.   *The Celluloid Closet.*
> Brillstein-Grey Entertainment, 1995. Produced by Rob Epstein and Jeffrey Friedman. Written by Rob Epstein, Jeffrey Friedman, and Sharon Wood.
> Vidal is interviewed in this documentary about gays in Hollywood.

48.   "Lo + plus."
> Canal+España, 3 December 1996.
> Vidal is interviewed.

49.   *Democracy University.*
> a.   Los Angeles: JusticeVision, 1998. 9 videocassettes.
> No. 4 has Vidal in conversation with Christopher Hitchens.

50.   *On Writing.*
> a.   Princeton, NJ: Films for the Humanities and Sciences, 1999. 1 videocassette.
> b.   Princeton, NJ: Films for the Humanities and Sciences, 2003. 1 videodisc (DVD).
> Includes an interview with Vidal. Produced by Sylvène Gilchrist.

51.   *Rescued from the Closet.*
> Automat Pictures, 2001. Produced by Jeffrey Schwartz.
> Vidal is interviewed.

52.   *The Private Dirk Bogarde.*
> BBC Films, 2001. Directed by Adam Low. Written by Nicholas Shakespeare. Produced by Anthony Wall.
> Vidal is interviewed in this documentary about Bogarde.

53.   *Understanding America's Terrorist Crisis: What Should Be Done?*
> Oakland, CA: Independent Insitute, 2003. 1 videotape.
> Tape of panel discussion at Herbst Theatre, San Francisco, 18 April 2002, with Vidal, Barton J. Bernstein, Robert Higgs, and Thomas Gale Moore. Moderator: Lewis H. Lapham. Opening and closing remarks by David J. Theroux.

54.   *The Homosexuals.*
> Princeton: Films for the Humanities and Sciences, 2003. 1 videodisc (DVD).
> A documentary by Mike Wallace on homosexuality; includes an interchange between Vidal and Albert Goldman on the effects of homosexuality on society. Originally an episode of "CBS Reports."

55.   *XXI Century, Part 1: The Dawn.*
> Thecatsdream.com, 2003. 1 videodisc (DVD).
> Includes a segment with Vidal.

56. *XXI Century, Part 2: And the Pursuit of Happiness.*
     Thecatsdream.com, 2003. 1 videodisc (DVD).
     Includes a segment with Vidal.

57. *XXI Century, Part 3: And Nothing But the Truth.*
     Thecatsdream.com, 2003. 1 videodisc (DVD).
     Includes a segment with Vidal.

58. *XXI Century, Part 6: Blood and Oil.*
     Thecatsdream.com, 2003. 1 videodisc (DVD).
     Includes a segment with Vidal.

59. *XXI Century, Part 7: Pax Americana.*
     Thecatsdream.com, 2003. 1 videodisc (DVD).
     Includes commentary by Vidal.

60. *Federico Fellini—Mit den Augen der Anderen.*
     Bayerischer Rundfunk, 2003. Written, directed, and produced by Eckhardt Schmidt.
     Vidal is interviewed in this documentary about Fellini.

61. "Real Time with Bill Maher."
     HBO, 19 March 2004.
     Vidal in discussion with Howard Dean, David Frum, Eddie Izzard, and Russell Simmons.

62. *Duel: Hamilton vs. Burr with Richard Dreyfus.*
     History Channel, 29 August 2004.
     New York: New Video, 2004. 1 videocassette.
     Vidal is interviewed about Aaron Burr and Alexander Hamilton.

63. "Da Ali G Show."
     HBO, 15 August 2004.
     Vidal is interviewed.

64. *Thinking XXX.*
     HBO, 29 October 2004. Produced and directed by Timothy Greenfield-Sanders.
     Vidal is interviewed. See C.299.

65. "The Late Late Show with Craig Kilborn."
     CBS, 17 December 2004.
     Vidal in discussion with Jennifer Coolidge, Sarah McLachlan, Tim Robbins, and Susan Sarandon.

66. *Why We Fight.*
     Charlotte Street Films, 2005. Produced by Eugene Jarecki and Susannah Shipman.
     Written and Directed by Eugene Jarecki.
     Vidal is interviewed.

67. *Inside Deep Throat.*
     HBO Documentary Films, 2005. Produced by Fenton Bailey, Randy Barbato, and Brian Grazer. Written and directed by Fenton Bailey and Randy Barbato.
     Vidal is interviewed.

68. *USA: The Movie.*
     Mantic Eye, 2005. 1 videodisc (DVD). Released as motion picture, 2005.
     Vidal is interviewed.

69. "Real Time with Bill Maher."
     HBO, 13 May 2005.

Vidal in discussion with Charles Barkley, Senator Norm Coleman, Al Franken, and Liz Marlantes.

70.   *Garbo.*
      Turner Classic Movies, 6 September 2005. Produced by Carl Davis. Directed by Christopher Bird, Kevin Brownlow, and Patrick Stanbury. Written by Patrick Stanbury.
      Vidal is interviewed about Greta Garbo.

71.   *One Bright Shining Moment.*
      Street Legal Cinema, 2005. Produced by Stephen Vittoria and Frank Fischer. Written and directed by Stephen Vittoria.
      Vidal is interviewed.

72.   *L'Isola di Calvino.*
      Rai Tre Radiotelevisione Italiana, 2005. Directed by Roberto Giannarelli. Written by Pierpaolo Andriani and Roberto Giannarelli. Produced by Roberto Giannarelli and Massimo Lipari.
      Vidal is interviewed in this documentary about Italo Calvino.

73.   *Peace!*
      Cinema Libre Distribution; Doc Workers, 2005. 1 videodisc (DVD). Written and directed by Gabriele Zamparini. Produced by Lorenzo Meccoli and Gabriele Zamparini. Edited by Lorenzo Meccoli.
      Vidal is interviewed.

74.   *Global Haywire.*
      Bruce Petty Films, 2006. Written and directed by Bruce Petty. Produced by Claude Gonzalez.
      Vidal is interviewed, along with Noam Chomsky, Tariq Ali, and others, in this Australian film about the current geopolitical situation.

75.   *The U.S. vs. John Lennon.*
      Lions Gate Films, 2006. Written and directed by David Leaf and John Scheinfeld.
      Vidal is interviewed in this documentary about the life of John Lennon, which focuses on his antiwar activities.

iv. Radio

1.   *A State of the Union.*
      Los Angeles: Pacifica Tape Library, 1981. 1 sound cassette.
      Tape of Vidal's essay "The State of the Union: 1980" (C.135).

2.   *"Meeting the Challenge": March 10–13, 1988.*
      Alexandria, VA: Audio Transcripts, [1988?]. 33 sound cassettes. Produced by the American-Arab Anti-Discrimination Committee.
      Vidal is brunch speaker (cassette 18). See III.E.303.

3.   *The National Security State.*
      Washington, DC: National Public Radio, 1988. Recorded at National Press Club, 16 March 1988.
      Tape of Vidal's essay "The National Security State" (C.175).

4.   *The Patriarchal State of the Union: The Nation Turns 125.*
      North Hollywood, CA: Pacifica Radio Archives, [200-].
      Speech by Vidal at Zellerbach Audorium, University of California at Berkeley. KPFA broadcast, 30 June 1990. Tape of Vidal's essay "Notes on Our Patriarchal State" (C.186).

5.   *Down to the Deadline.*
         North Hollywood, CA: Pacifica Radio Archive, 1991. 1 sound cassette.
         Vidal discusses President George Bush's actions in the Persian Gulf, 15 January 1991.

6.   *The Best of Radio Nation: Volume 1.*
         New York: Radio Nation, [199-]. 3 sound cassettes. Broadcast edition of the *Nation* magazine. Vidal is a guest.

7.   *On the State of the Union.*
         North Hollywood, CA: Pacifica Radio Archives, 1994. 1 sound cassette.

8.   *Voices from the Left.*
         North Hollywood, CA: Pacifica Radio Archives, 1996. 4 sound discs.
         Disc 4 includes Vidal's speech on 30 June 1990. Originally broadcast on Pacifica Radio.

9.   "In the Psychiatrist's Chair."
         BBC radio, 8 October 2000.
         Vidal is interviewed. For a transcript, see III.C.29.

10.   *Not in Our Name.*
         Relentless Pursuit Records, 2002. 1 sound disc.
         One segment includes Vidal.

II. Gore Vidal in Translation

A. Books and Pamphlets

i. Albanian

1. *Uashington, Distrikti Kolumbia.*
    a. Tiranë: Naim Frashëri, 1973. Tr. V. Kokona.
        Translation of *Washington, D.C.*

ii. Bulgarian

1. *Julian.*
    a. Sofia: Kultura, 1970. Tr. Vasil Atanasov.
    b. Sofia: OF, 1981.
    c. Sofia: Savremennik, 1993.

2. *Viceprezidentăt Bar.*
    a. Sofia: OF, 1979. Tr. Ivanka Tomova.
        Translation of *Burr.*

3. *Kalki.*
    a. Sofia: Narodna Kultura, 1979. Tr. Pavel Glavusanov.
    b. Sofia: D. Jakov, 1994.

4. *Vašington, okrăg Kolumbija.*
    a. Plovdiv: Hristo G. Danov, 1984. Tr. Jordan Kosturkov.
        Translation of *Washington, D.C.*

5. *Sătvorenieto.*
    a. Sofia: Narodna Kultura, 1989. Tr. Nezabravka Mihajlova.
        Translation of *Creation.*

6. *Holivud.*
    a. Sofia: Interprint, 1992. Tr. Veneta Marinova.
        Translation of *Hollywood.*

7. *Na živo ot Golgota.*
    a. Sofia: Hemus, 1993. Tr. Vera Georgieva.
        Translation of *Live from Golgotha.*

8. *Smitsăn.*
    a. Sofia: Zvedzna kasta, 1999. Tr. Emilija Maslarova.
        Translation of *The Smithsonian Institution.*

9. *Linkăln.*
    a. Sofia: Mojri, 2002. Tr. Boris Daljanov.
        Translation of *Lincoln.*

10. *1876.*
    a. Sofia: Mojri, 2002. Jordan Kosturkov.

11. *Večna vojna za večen mir: Mečtanata vojna.*
    a. Sofia: Animar, 2003. Tr. Elka Videnova.
        Translation of *Perpetual War for Perpetual Peace.*

iii. Catalan

1. *Washington, D.C.*
   a. Barcelona: Proa, 1985. Tr. Jordi Arbonès.

2. *La institutió smithsoniana.*
   a. Barcelona: Proa, 1999. Tr. Cristina Mallol.
   Translation of *The Smithsonian Institution.*

3. *L'edat d'or.*
   a.1. Barcelona: Edicions 62, 2001. Tr. Ramon Monton.
   a.2. Barcelona: Edicions 62, 2001. 2 vols.
   Translation of *The Golden Age.*

4. *Julià apòstata.*
   a. Barcelona: Edicions 62, 2002. Tr. Joan Puntí i Recasens.

iv. Chinese

1. *Fong heng de Mei-la.*
   a. [No information available]
   Translation of *Myra Breckinridge.*

2. *Cheng t'an yu huo.*
   a. [No information available]
   Translation of *Washington, D.C.*

3. *Luan Shi Da Zong Tong Lin Ken.*
   a. [No information available]
   Translation of *Lincoln.*

v. Czech

1. *Ten nejlepši.*
   a. Prague: Dilia, 1976. Tr. Šimon Pellar.
   Translation of *The Best Man.*

2. *Skandální zivot Aarona Burra.*
   a. Prague: Odeon, 1990. Tr. Miroslav Jindra.
   Translation of *Burr.*

3. *Julianus.*
   a. Prague: Svoboda, 1992. Tr. Jiří Hanuš.
   Translation of *Julian.*

4. *Amerika! (Duluth): Parodie na televizní seriál Dallas.*
   a. Prague: Dita, 1993. Tr. Miroslav Janda and Miroslav Fulín.
   Translation of *Duluth.*

5. *Prímý prenos z Golgotha.*
   a. Prague: Naše vojsko, 1995. Tr. Jaroslav Holba.
   Translation of *Live from Golgotha.*

vi. Danish

1. *En nat i New York.*
    a. Copenhagen: Wangel, 1948. Tr. George Gjedde.
        Translation of *In a Yellow Wood.*

2. *Byen og søjlen.*
    a. Copenhagen: Wangel, 1949. Tr. George Gjedde.
        Translation of *The City and the Pillar.*

3. *Richard Løvehjerte.*
    a. Copenhagen: Wangel, 1951. Tr. George Gjedde.
        Translation of *A Search for the King.*

4. *Troldmandens Lærling.*
    a. Copenhagen: Wangel, 1956. Tr. Helga Vang Lauridsen.
        Translation of *Messiah.*

5. *Washington, D.C.*
    a. Copenhagen: Grafisk Forlag, 1968. Tr. Vibeke Willumsen.

vii. Dutch

1. *De vesting en de zoutpilaar.*
    a. 's-Graveland: De Driehoek, 1950. Tr. Jo Boer.
        Translation of *The City and the Pillar.*

2. *Myra Breckinridge.*
    a. Amsterdam: J. M. Meulenhoff, 1970. Tr. Dolf Koning.

3. *Twee zusters.*
    a. Amsterdam: J. M. Meulenhoff, 1971. Tr. Dolf Koning.
        Translation of *Two Sisters.*

4. *Myra Myron.*
    a. Baarn: Hollandia, 1975. Tr. Winifred Touwen.
        Translation of *Myron.*

5. *Direct van Golgotha.*
    a. Amsterdam: De Arbeiderspers, 1994. Tr. Tinke Davids.
        Translation of *Live from Golgotha.*

6. *Permanente oorlog voor permanente vrede: De nachtzijde van Amerika's politiek.*
    a. Amsterdam: De Arbeiderspers, 2003. Tr. Florence Tonk.
        Translation of *Perpetual War for Perpetual Peace.*

7. *Droomoorlog: Bloed voor olie en de Cheney-Bushjunta.*
    a. Amsterdam: De Arbeiderspers, 2003. Willy Hemelrijk.
        Translation of *Dreaming War.*

viii. Estonian

1. *Vashington, Columbia ringkond.*
    a. Tallinn: Eesti Raamat, 1972. Tr. Vilma Jürisalu.
        Translation of *Washington, D.C.*

2. *Kuningat otsimas.*
    a. Tallinn: Eesti Raamat, 1994. Tr. Helje Heinoja.
        Translation of *A Search for the King.*

ix. Finnish

1. *Myra.*
    a. Jyväskylä: Gummerus, 1970. Tr. Juhani Koskinen.
        Translation of *Myra Breckinridge.*

2. *Myron.*
    a. Jyväskylä: Gummerus, 1976. Tr. Aarne T. K. Lahtinen.

3. *Naiset kirjastossa ja muita kertomuksia.*
    a. Helsinki: Eurographica, 1986. Tr. Merja Lindroos and Timothy Binham.
        Translation of an unspecified work by Vidal.

x. French

1. *Ouragon.*
    a. Paris: Albin Michel, 1949. Tr. L. Rostain and F. Romieu.
        Translation of *Williwaw.*

2. *Un Garçon près de la rivière.*
    a. Paris: Editions des Deux-Rives, 1949. Tr. Gilbert Martineau.
        Translation of *The City and the Pillar.*

3. *La Saison du confort.*
    a. Paris: Calmann-Lévy, 1951. Tr. Emy Molinié.
        Translation of *The Season of Comfort.*

4. *La Mort en cinquième position.*
    a. Paris: Presses de la Cité, 1953. Tr. Maurice Bernard Derbene (pseud. of Maurice-Bernard Endrèbe).
        Translation of *Death in the Fifth Position.*

5. *Feu d'enfer* (as by Edgar Box).
    a. Paris: Presses de la Cité, 1955. Tr. Michel Tyl.
    b. Montreal: Cerce de Roman Policier, 1955.
        Translation of *Death Likes It Hot.*

6. *Julien.*
    a. Paris: Robert Laffont, 1966. Tr. Jean Rosenthal.
    b. Paris: Julliard, 1987.
    c. Lausanne: L'Age d'Homme, 1987.
    d. Paris: Editions Galaade, 2006.
        Translation of *Julian.*

7. *La Mauvaise Pente.*
    a. Paris: Robert Laffont, 1966. Tr. Jean Rosenthal.
        Translation of *A Thirsty Evil.*

8. *Myra Breckinridge.*
    a. Paris: Robert Laffont, 1970. Tr. Jean Rosenthal.

9.   *Burr.*
   a.   Paris: Pierre Belfond, 1978. Tr. Antoine Berman.

10.   *Les Faits et la fiction: Essais de littérature et d'histoire.*
   a.   Paris: Pierre Belfond, 1980. Tr. Antoine Berman.
        Translation of *Matters of Fact and of Fiction.*

11.   *Messiah.*
   a.1. Paris: Pierre Belfond, 1980. Tr. Philippe Mikriammos.
   a.2. Paris: Pierre Belfond, 1982.

12.   *Un Garçon près de la rivière.*
   a.   Paris: Persona, 1981. Tr. Philippe Mikriammos.
   b.   Payot et Rivages, 1999.
        Translation of *The City and the Pillar.*

13.   *Création.*
   a.   Paris: B. Grasset, 1983. Tr. Brice Matthieussent.
   b.   Paris: Grasset et Fasquelle, 1998.
        Translation of *Creation.*

14.   *Duluth.*
   a.   Paris: Julliard, 1984. Tr. Philippe Mikriammos.
   b.   Lausanne: L'Age d'Homme, 1984.
   c.   Paris: Christian Bourgois, 1989.

15.   *Lincoln.*
   a.   Paris: Julliard, 1985. Tr. Gérard Joulié.
   b.   Lausanne: L'Age d'Homme, 1985.

16.   *Myra Breckinridge; Myron.*
   a.   Lausanne: L'Age d'Homme, 1988. Tr. Gérard Joulié.
   b.   Paris: Payot et Rivages, 2002.

17.   *Hollywood.*
   a.   Paris: Éditions de Fallois, 1990. Tr. Gérard Joulié.

18.   *Kalki.*
   a.   Lausanne: L'Age d'Homme, 1991. Tr. Ian Dasey.
   b.   Paris: Editions Galaade, 2006.

19.   *Empire.*
   a.   Lausanne: L'Age d'Homme, 1993. Tr. Gérard Joulié.
   b.   Paris: Éditions de Fallois, 1993.

20.   *L'Histoire à l'écran.*
   a.   Paris: Fayard, 1994. Tr. Pierre-Emmanuel Dauzat.
        Translation of *Screening History.*

21.   *En direct du Golgotha.*
   a.   Paris: Fayard, 1994. Tr. Pierre-Emmanuel Dauzat.
        Translation of *Live from Golgotha.*

22.   *La Mort en tenue de soirée* (as by Edgar Box).
   a.   Paris: Fayard, 1994. Tr. Denise Meunier.
   b.   Paris: France Loisirs, 1994.
   c.   Paris: Fayard, 1998.

Translation of *Death Before Bedtime.*

23.   *La Mort l'aime chaud* (as by Edgar Box).
      a.   Paris: Le Grand Livre du Mois, 1995. Tr. Denise Meunier.
      b.1. Paris: Fayard, 1996.
      b.2. Paris: Fayard, 1998.
           Translation of *Death Likes It Hot.*

24.   *La Mort en cinquième position.*
      a.   Paris: Fayard, 1995. Tr. Pierre-Emmanuel Dauzat.
      b.   Paris: Librairie Générale Française, 2001.
           Translation of *Death in the Fifth Position.*

25.   *La Ménagerie des hommes illustres.*
      a.   Paris: Payot et Rivages, 1999. Tr. Florence Lévy-Paoloni.
           Translation of *The Smithsonian Institution.*

26.   *Dawn Powell: La romancière américaine par excellence.*
      a.   Paris: Quai Voltaire, 2000. Tr. Marèse Akar.
           Translation of "Dawn Powell: The American Writer."

27.   *La Fin de la liberté: Vers un nouveau totalitarisme?*
      a.   Paris: Payot et Rivages, 2002. Tr. Florence Lévy-Paoloni.
           Translation of *Il fine del libertà* (see item xvi.30 below), itself later published in English as
           Perpetual War for Perpetual Peace (I.A.66).

28.   *En direct du Golgotha.*
      a.   Paris: Payot et Rivages, 2003. Tr. Jean-Bernard Blandenier.
           Translation of *Live from Golgotha.*

29.   *Palimpseste: Memoires.*
      a.   Paris: Editions Galaade, 2006. Tr. Lydia Lakel.
           Translation of *Palimpsest.*

xi. German

1.   *Besuch auf einem Kleinen Planeten.*
     a.   Berlin: Ahn und Simrock, 1958. Tr. Eric Burger.
     b.   Pfarrkirchen: Sessler, [1970?].
          Translation of *Visit to a Small Planet.*

2.   *Tod in der fünften Position* (as by Edgar Box).
     a.1. Reinbek: Rowohlt, 1962. Tr. Gesa Gross.
     a.2. Reinbek: Rowohlt, 1978.
     b.   Berlin: Tiamat, 1990.
          Translation of *Death in the Fifth Position.*

3.   *Tod vorm Schlafengehen* (as by Edgar Box).
     a.1. Reinbek: Rowohlt, 1963. Tr. Kurt Wagenseil.
     a.2. Reinbek: Rowohlt, 1977.
     b.   Berlin: Tiamat, 1991.
          Translation of *Death Before Bedtime.*

4.   *Immer diese Morde* (as by Edgar Box).
     a.1. Reinbek: Rowohlt, 1963. Tr. Gottfried Beutel.
     a.2. Reinbek: Rowohlt, 1979.
          Translation of *Death Likes It Hot.*

5.   *Julian.*
     a.1. Cologne: Kiepenheuer und Witsch, 1965. Tr. Philip Weiler.
     a.2. Cologne: Kiepenheuer und Witsch, 1970.
     b.   Frankfurt am Main: Büchergilde Gutenberg, 1967.
     c.   Frankfurt am Main: Deutscher Bücherbund, 1967.
     d.   Geneva: Edito-Service, 1974.
     e.   Hamburg: Hoffmann und Campe, 1988.
     e.1. Munich: Goldmann, 1993.
     e.2. Munich: Goldmann, 1999.

6.   *Washington, D.C.*
     a.   Cologne: Kiepenheuer und Witsch, 1967. Tr. Philip Weiler.
     b.   Frankfurt am Main: Büchergilde Gutenberg, 1969.
     c.1. Bergisch Gladbach: Bastei-Lübbe, 1971.
     c.2. Bergisch Gladbach: Bastei-Lübbe, 1971 (as *Nacht über Washington*).

7.   *Myra Breckinridge.*
     a.   Cologne: Kiepenheuer und Witsch, 1969. Tr. Philip Weiler.
     b.   Reinbek: Rowohlt, 1970.

8.   *Betrachtungen auf einem sinkenden Schiff.*
     a.   Cologne: Kiepenheuer und Witsch, 1971. Tr. Eric Burger.
          Translation of *Reflections upon a Sinking Ship.*

9.   *Gesellschafts-Komödie.*
     a.   Vienna: TSV, GMV, WVA Bühnenverlag, 1972. Tr. Eric Burger.
          Translation of *Weekend.*

10. *Burr.*
     a.   Munich: Bertelsmann, 1975. Tr. Günter Panske.
     b.   Munich: Wilhelm Heyne, 1977.
     c.   Munich: Goldmann, 2001.

11. *Die Sirene von Babylon.*
     a.   Munich: Bertelsmann, 1976. Tr. Eric Burger.
     b.   Munich: Wilhelm Heyne, 1979.
          Translation of *Myron.*

12. *Messias.*
     a.1. Frankfurt am Main: Suhrkamp, 1977. Tr. Helga and Peter von Tramin.
     a.2. Frankfurt am Main: Suhrkamp, 1997.
          Translation of *Messiah.*

13. *1876: Roman aus Amerikas Belle Epoque.*
     a.   Munich: Bertelsmann, 1978. Tr. Dieter Dörr and Eric Burger.
     b.   Munich: Wilhelm Heyne, 1982.

14. *Kalki.*
     a.   Munich: Steinhausen, 1980. Tr. Helmut Kossodo.
     b.   Rastatt: Moewig, 1982.
     c.1. Munich: Goldmann, 1997.
     c.2. Munich: Goldmann, 2000.

15. *Duluth wie Dallas.*
     a.   Hamburg: Hoffmann und Campe, 1984. Tr. Günter Panske.
     b.   Munich: Goldmann, 1996.

Translation of *Duluth*.

16. *Lincoln.*
    a. Hamburg: Hoffmann und Campe, 1985. Tr. Christian Spiel and Rudolf Hermstein.
    b. Munich: Goldmann, 1993.
    c. Munich: Goldmann, 2002. Rev. ed.

17. *American Plastics: Über Literatur und Politik.*
    a. Hamburg: Hoffmann und Campe, 1986. Tr. Helmut Winter.
    Translation of *Matters of Fact and of Fiction.*

18. *Geschlossener Kreis.*
    a. Munich: Droemer Knaur, 1986. Tr. Peter Kobbe.
    Translation of *The City and the Pillar.*

19. *Ich, Cyrus: Enkel des Zarathustra.*
    a. Munich: Hoffmann und Campe, 1986. Tr. Günter Panske.
    b. Munich: Goldmann, 1993.
    Translation of *Creation.*

20. *Empire.*
    a. Hamburg: Hoffmann und Campe, 1989. Tr. Günter Panske.
    b. Munich: Goldmann, 1994.

21. *Hollywood.*
    a. Hamburg: Hoffmann und Campe, 1991. Tr. Günter Panske.
    b. Munich: Goldmann, 1995.

22. *Golgotha live oder das fünfte Testament.*
    a. Hamburg: Hoffmann und Campe, 1993. Tr. Pocaio.
    b. Munich: Goldmann, 1996.
    Translation of *Live from Golgotha.*

23. *Palimpsest: Memoiren.*
    a. Hamburg; Hoffmann und Campe, 1996. Tr. Friedrich Griese.
    b. Munich: Goldmann, 1998.

24. *Das ist nichts Amerika! Essays.*
    a. Munich: Knaus, 2000. Tr. Ulrich Blumenbach, Veronica Cordes, Thomas Piltz, Elke Schönfeld, Nikolaus Stingl, Maja Überle-Pfaff, and Willi Winkler.
    Contents unknown.

25. *Die Goldene Zeitalter.*
    a. Munich: Knaus, 2001. Tr. Silvia Morawetz.
    Translation of *The Golden Age.*

26. *Ewiger Krieg für ewigen Frieden: Wie Amerika den Hass erntet, den es gesät hat.*
    a. Hamburg: Europäische Verlags-Anstalt, 2002. Tr. Bernhard Jendricke and Barbara Steckhan.
    Translation of *Perpetual War for Perpetual Peace.*

27. *Bocksgesang: Antworten und Fragen vor und nach dem 11. September.*
    a. Hamburg: Europäische Verlagsanstalt, 2003. Tr. Bernhard Jendricke and Rita Seuss.
    Abridged translation of *Dreaming War.*

28. *Die vergessliche Nation: Wie die Amerikaner ihr politisches Gedächtnis verkaufen.*
    a. Hamburg: Europ. Verl.-Anst., 2004. Tr. Bernard Jendricke et al.

    b.   Remagen-Oberwinter: Europäische Ideen, 2004 (abridged; as *God Bless America oder: Wie Amerikaner ihr politisches Gedächtnis verkaufen*).
         Translation of *Imperial America.*

29.   *Amerikas Traum vom Fliegen.*
    a.   Munich: Müller und Nerding Verlag, 2004. Tr. Stefan Dornuf.
         Translation of *Dreaming War.*

xii. Greek

1.   *Ousinkton D.C.*
    a.   Athens: Ekdoseis Karre, 1985. Tr. Nestor Chounos.
         Translation of *Washington, D.C.*

2.   *Maira Brekinritz.*
    a.   Athens: Ekdoseis "Nea Synora," 1986. Tr. Alina Paschalidou.
         Translation of *Myra Breckinridge.*

3.   *Dimiourgia.*
    a.   Athens: Exadas, 1994. Tr. Vasilis Tomanas.
         Translation of *Creation.*

4.   *Se zontani metadosi ap'to Golgotha.*
    a.   Athens: Metamesonykties Ekdosis, 1997. Tr. Spyros Vretos.
         Translation of *Live from Golgotha.*

5.   *Diarkīs polemos gia diarkī eirīni: Pōs kataferame na ginoume toso misītoi.*
    a.   Athens: Scripta, 2003. Tr. Nektarios Kalaitzis.
         Translation of *Perpetual War for Perpetual Peace.*

6.   *I chrysī epochī.*
    a.   Athens: Scripta, 2002. Tr. Rena Chatchout.
         Translation of *The Golden Age.*

xiii. Hebrew

1.   *Beria.*
    a.   Hod Ha-sharon: Astrolog, 1999. Tr. Hadas Weiss.
         Translation of *Creation.*

xiv. Hungarian

1.   *Julianus.*
    a.   Budapest: Goldolat, 1969. Tr. Ilona Róna.
         Translation of *Julian.*

2.   *Washington, D.C.*
    a.   Budapest: Magvetü, 1973. Tr. Tibor Szilágyi.

3.   *Burr ezredes utolsó kalandja.*
    a.   Budapest: Európa, 1978. Tr. Ilona Róna.
         Translation of *Burr.*

4.   *Amerikai komédia: 1876.*
    a.   Budapest: Európa, 1981. Tr. Tibor Szilágyi.
         Translation of *1876.*

5.   *Irók, gengszterek, profeszszorok: Esszék.*
     a.   Budapest: Európa, 1984. Tr. Zsuzsa Kiss and György Novák.
          Contents unknown.

6.   *Teremtés.*
     a.   Budapest: Európa, 1985. Tr. János Betlen.
          Translation of *Creation.*

7.   *Élõ adas a Golgotáról.*
     a.   Budapest: Novella, 1993. Tr. Ferenc Takács.
          Translation of *Live from Golgotha.*

8.   *A Smithson pincéi.*
     a.   Szegad: LAZI, 2002. Tr. Katalin Sóvágó.
          Translation of *The Smithsonian Institution.*

xv. Icelandic

1.   *Feginn mun ég fylgja Þér.*
     a.   Reykjavik: Skerpla, 1995. Tr. Björgvin G. Kemp.
          Translation of *A Search for the King.*

xvi. Italian

1.   *La città perversa.*
     a.   Milan: Elmo, 1949. Tr. G. Monicelli.
          Translation of *The City and the Pillar.*

2.   *L'uragano.*
     a.   Milan: Elmo, 1950. Tr. Stanis La Bruna.
          Translation of *Williwaw.*

3.   *Alla ricerca del re.*
     a.   Milan: Garzanti, 1951. Tr. Maria Galli De Furlani.
          Translation of *A Search for the King.*

4.   *La morte in agguato* (as by Edgar Box).
     a.   Milan: Garzanti, 1955. Tr. Carlo Bernheimer.
          Translation of *Death Before Bedtime.*

5.   *Alla morte piace il caldo* (as by Edgar Box).
     a.   Milan: Garzanti, 1956. Tr. Lucio Trevisan.
          Translation of *Death Likes It Hot.*

6.   *Morte al volo* (as by Edgar Box).
     a.   Milan: Sugar, 1962. Tr. Donatella Pini.
          Translation of *Death in the Fifth Position.*

7.   *Washington, D.C.*
     a.   Milan: Bompiani, 1968. Tr. Luciano Bianciardi.

8.   *Myra Breckinridge.*
     a.1. Milan: Bompiani, 1969. Tr. Vincenzo Mantovani.
     a.2. Milan: Bompiani, 1973.
     a.3. Milan: Bompiani, 1989.

9. *Giuliano.*
   a. Milan: Rizzoli, 1969. Tr. Ida Omboni.
   b. Milan: Bompiani, 1990.
   Translation of *Julian.*

10. *Una nave che affonda.*
    a. Milan: Bompiani, 1971. Tr. Luciana Bulgheroni.
    Translation of *Reflections upon a Sinking Ship.*

11. *Due sorelle.*
    a. Milan: Bompiani, 1971. Tr. Ida Omboni.
    Translation of *Two Sisters.*

12. *Jim.*
    a.1. Milan: Bompiani, 1972. Tr. Vincenzo Mantovani.
    a.2. Milan: Bompiani, 1979.
    Translation of *The City and the Pillar.*

13. *Il mondo di Watergate: Personaggi, figure, situazioni nello scandale del seculo.*
    a. Milan: Bompiani, 1974. Tr. Pier Francesco Paolini.
    Contents: "The Art and Arts of E. Howard Hunt" (I.C.100); "Politics, Washington, D.C." (I.C.95.a); "Linkage Is All" (I.C.97.a); "West Point and the Third Loyalty" (I.C.99.a); "The Ashes of Hollywood" (I.C.96.a); "Interview" (i.e., *Playboy* interview [III.C.144]).

14. *Burr.*
    a. Milan: Bompiani, 1975. Tr. Pier Francesco Paolini.

15. *Myron.*
    a.1. Milan: Bompiani, 1976. Tr. Marisa Caramella.
    a.2. Milan: Bompiani, 1985.

16. *1876.*
    a. Milan: Bompiani, 1977. Tr. Pier Francesco Paolini.

17. *La parole e i fatti.*
    a. Milan: Bompiani, 1978. Tr. Pier Francesco Paolini.
    Translation of *Matters of Fact and of Fiction.*

18. *Kalki.*
    a. Milan: Bompiani, 1980. Tr. Pier Francesco Paolini.

19. *Creazione.*
    a. Milan: Garzanti, 1983. Tr. Pier Francesco Paolini.
    Translation of *Creation.*

20. *Duluth: Tutta America in una città*
    a. Milan: Garzanti, 1984. Tr. Pier Francesco Paolini.

21. *Intrigo a Washington.*
    a. Milan: Feltrinelli, 1988. Tr. Lucio Trevisan.
    Translation of *Death Before Bedtime.*

22. *Lincoln.*
    a. Milan: Bompiani, 1988. Tr. Pier Francesco Paolini.

23. *Hollywood.*
    a. Milan: Bompiani, 1991. Tr. Adriana Dell'Orto.

24. *La fine dell'impero.*
     a. Rome: Editori Riuniti, 1992. Tr. Gianfranco Corsini.
         Translation of *The Decline and Fall of the American Empire.*

25. *In diretta dal Golgota.*
     a. Milan: Longanesi, 1992. Tr. Pier Francesco Paolini.
         Translation of *Live from Golgotha.*

26. *Remotamente su questi schermi.*
     a. Milan: Anabasi, 1993. Tr. Claudio Mussolini.
         Translation of *Screening History.*

27. *La statua di sale.*
     a. Rome: Fazi, 1998. Tr. Alessandra Osti.
         Translation of *The City and the Pillar.*

28. *Palinsesto.*
     a. Rome: Fazi, 2000. Tr. Mauricio Bartocci.
         Translation of *Palimpsest.*

29. *L'età dell'oro.*
     a. Rome: Fazi, 2001. Tr. Luca Scarlini.
     a. Barcelona: MDS Books/Mediasat, 2003.
         Translation of *The Golden Age.*

30. *La fine della libertà: Verso un nuovo totalitarismo?*
     a. Romo: Fazi, 2001. Tr. Laura Pugno.
         Contents: "September 11th, 2001 (A Tuesday)" (C.281); "The Meaning of Timothy McVeigh"
         (C.275); "Shredding the Bill of Rights" (C.257); "The New Theocrats" (C.241). An expanded
         edition was later published in English under the title *Perpetual War for Perpetual Peace* (I.A.66).

31. *Impero.*
     a. Rome: Fazi, 2002. Tr. Benedetta Marietti.
         Translation of *Empire.*

32. *La menzogne dell'impero e altri tristi verità: Perché la junto petrolifera Cheney-Bush vuole
     la guerra con l'Iraq e altri saggi.*
     a. Rome: Fazi, 2002. Tr. Luca Scarlini and Laura Pugno.
         Contents: "Goat Song" (I.C.284); "How We Missed the Saturday Dance" (I.C.207); "The Last
         Empire" (I.C.244); "In the Lair of the Octopus" (I.C.221); "With Extreme Prejudice" (I.C.198);
         "The Union of the State" (I.C.218); "Mickey Mouse, Historian" (I.C.232); "A Letter to Be
         Delivered" (I.C.271); "Democratic Vistas" (I.C.273); "Three Lies to Rule By" (I.C.269);
         "Japanese Intentions in the Second World War" (I.F.49).

33. *Giuliano.*
     a. Rome: Fazi, 2003. Tr. Chiara Vatteroni.
         Translation of *Julian.*

34. *Il canarino e la maniera: Saggi letterari 1956–2000.*
     a. Rome: Fazi, 2003. Tr. Luciana Bulgheroni Spallino, Stefano Tummolini, Alessandra
         Osti, Pier Francesco Paolini, Chiara Vatteroni.
         Contents: "Twain on the Grand Tour" (I.C.230); "Reply to a Critic" (F.39); "Twain's Letters"
         (C.237); "The Bookchat of Henry James" (C.163); "The Golden Bowl of Henry James" (C.153);
         "Oscar Wilde: On the Skids Again" (C.168); "A Note on the Novel" (C.8); "Satire in the 1950's"
         (C.14); "Writers and the World" (C.61); "The *Sexus* of Henry Miller" (C.56); "Pen Pals: Henry
         Miller and Lawrence Durrell" (C.176); "F. Scott Fitzgerald's Case" (C.134); "Dawn Powell: The
         American Writer" (C.169); "Frederic Prokosch: The European Connection" (C.148); "Tennessee
         Williams: Someone to Laugh at the Squares With" (C.157); "Why I Am Eight Years Younger

Than Anthony Burgess" (C.164); "The Great World and Louis Auchincloss" (C.104); "American Plastic: The Matter of Fiction" (C.115); "Montaigne" (C.199); "French Letters: Theories of the New Novel" (C.70); "Sciascia's Italy" (C.129); "Calvino's Novels" (C.103); "Calvino's Death" (C.160); "The Death of Mishima" (C.87); "C. P. Cavafy" (C.278).

35. *Creazione.*
   a. Rome: Fazi, 2005. Tr. Stefano Tummolini.
      Translation of *Creation.*

36. *L'Invenzione degli Stati Uniti.*
   a. Rome: Fazi, 2005. Tr. Marina Astrologo.
      Translation of *Inventing a Nation.*

37. *Il giudizio di Paride.*
   a. Rome: Fazi, 2006. Tr. Caterina Cartolano.
      Translation of *The Judgment of Paris.*

xvii. Japanese

1. *Shi wa atsui no ga osuki.*
   a. Tokyo: Hayakawa Shobo, 1960. Tr. Motoichi Kuraki.
      Translation of *Death Likes It Hot.*

2. *Washington D.C.*
   a. Tokyo: Hayakawa Shobo, 1968. Tr. Uno Toshiyasu.

3. *Myra.*
   a. Tokyo: Hayakawa Shobo, 1969. Tr. Nagai Jun.
      Translation of *Myra Breckinridge.*

4. *Sen happyaku shichijûroku.*
   a. Tokyo: Hayakawa Shobo, 1978. Tr. Seijiro Tanaka.
      Translation of *1876.*

5. *Daiyogensha Kalki.*
   a. Tokyo: Sanrio, 1980. Tr. Hinatsu Hibiki.
      Translation of *Kalki.*

6. *Aaron Burr no eiyūteki shôgei.*
   a. Hayakawa Shobo, 1981. Tr. Seijiro Tanaka.
      Translation of *Burr.*

7. *Myron.*
   a. Tokyo: Sanrio, 1982. Tr. Kan Sawamura.

8. *Rinkan.*
   a. Tokyo: Honnotomo sya, 1998. Tr. Nakamura Koiti. 3 vols.
      Translation of *Lincoln.*

9. *Tosi to hasira.*
   a. Tokyo: Honnotomo sya, 1998. Tr. Hongo Akira.
      Translation of *The City and the Pillar.*

xviii. Latvian

1. *Vašingtona, Kulumbijas apgabals.*
   a. Riga: Liesma, 1971. Tr. Vanda Vikane.
   Translation of *Washington, D.C.*

xix. Lithuanian

1. *Vašingtonas, Kolumbijos apygarda.*
   a. Vilnius: Vaga, 1973. Tr. Juozas Subativičius.
   Translation of *Washington, D.C.*

xx. Norwegian

1. *Livet er mitt eget.*
   a. Stavanger, Norway: Stabelfeldt, 1947. Tr. Sigmund Strømme.
   Translation of *In a Yellow Wood.*

2. *Evig krig for evig fred: Hvorfor verden hater oss.*
   a. Oslo: Kagge, 2002. Tr. Gunnar Kagge.
   Translation of *Perpetual War for Perpetual Peace.*

xxi. Persian

1. *Afarinash.*
   a. Teheran: The Author, 1991. 2 vols. Tr. Abd al-Hamid Sultaniah.
   Translation of *Creation.*

2. *Setīz Khodāyān.*
   a. Teheran: Nashr-e Kārang, 1999. Tr. K. Karīmī.
   Translation of *Julian.*

xxii. Polish

1. *Trubadur króla Ryszarda.*
   a. Warsaw: Czytelnik, 1960. Tr. ?
   Translation of *A Search for the King.*

2. *Julian.*
   a. Warsaw: Pánstwowy Instytut Wydawniczy, 1970. Tr. Bronisław Zieliński.

3. *Stworzenie świata.*
   a.1. Warsaw: Państwowy Instytut Wydawniczy, 1988. Tr. Mira Michałowska.
   a.2. Warsaw: Pánstwowy Instytut Wydawniczy, 1997.
   Translation of *Creation.*

4. *Nie oglądaj się w stronę Sodomy.*
   a. Warsaw: Dom Księgarski i Wydawniczy Fundacji Polonia, 1990. Tr. Andrzej Selerowicz.
   Translation of *The City and the Pillar.*

5. *Myra Breckinridge.*
   a. Poznan: Obserwator, 1992. Tr. Jan Kornel Paygert.

6.   *Mesjasz.*
-     a.   Poznan: SAWW, 1993. Tr. ?
  - Translation of *Messiah.*

7.   *Na żywo z Golgoty.*
-     a.   Poznan: Kantor Wydawniczy, 1993. Tr. Jędrzej Polak.
  - Translation of *Live from Golgotha.*

8.   *Waszyngton.*
-     a.   Warsaw: MUSA SA, 1994. Tr. Elzbieta Zychowicz.
  - Translation of *Washington, D.C.*

xxiii. Portuguese

1.   *A longa espera do passado.*
-     a.   Rio de Janeiro: Artenova. 1971. Tr. Wilson Cunha.
  - Translation of *The City and the Pillar.*

2.   *Kalki.*
-     a.   São Paulo: Circulo do Livro, 1980. Tr. Luiz Horácio de Mata.

3.   *Criação.*
-     a.1. Rio de Janeiro: Nova Fronteira, 1984. Tr. Newton Goldman.
-     a.2. Rio de Janeiro: Nova Fronteira, n.d.
-     a.3. Rio de Janeiro: Nova Fronteira, n.d.
-     a.4. Rio de Janeiro: Nova Fronteira, n.d.
-     a.5. Rio de Janeiro: Nova Fronteira, 1986.
-     a.6. Rio de Janeiro: Nova Fronteira, 1987.
-     a.7. Rio de Janeiro: Nova Fronteira, n.d.
-     a.8. Rio de Janeiro: Nova Fronteira, 1990.
-     b.   São Paulo: Circulo do Livro, 1989.
  - Translation of *Creation.*

4.   *Um momento de louros verdes.*
-     a.   Rio de Janeiro: Rocco, 1986. Tr. Donaldson M. Garschagen.
  - Translation of *A Thirsty Evil.*

5.   *De fato e de ficção: Ensaios contra a corrente.*
-     a.   São Paulo: Companhia das Letras, 1987. Ed. Michael Hall and Paulo Sérgio Pinheiro. Tr. Heloisa Jahn.
  - Translation of *Matters of Fact and of Fiction.*

6.   *Juliano.*
-     a.   São Paulo: Circulo do Livro, 1987. Tr. Aulyde Soares Rodrigues.
  - Translation of *Julian.*

7.   *Kalki.*
-     a.1. Rio de Janeiro: Rocco, 1987. Tr. Roberto Grey.
-     a.2. Rio de Janeiro: Rocco, 2000.

8.   *À procura do rei.*
-     a.   Rio de Janeiro: Rocco, 1988? 1991? Tr. Eliana Sabino.
  - Translation of *A Search for the King.*

9. *A cidade e o pilar.*
   a.   Rio de Janeiro: Rocco, 1989. Tr. Eliana Valadares Sabino.
       Translation of *The City and the Pillar.*

10. *Hollywood.*
    a.   Rio de Janeiro: Rocco, 1990. Tr. Eliana Valadares Sabino.

11. *Messias.*
    a.   Rio de Janeiro: Rocco, 1990. Tr. Paulo Azevedo.
        Translation of *Messiah.*

12. *O julgamento de Paris.*
    a.   Rio de Janeiro: Record, 1991. Tr. Raul de Sa Barbosa.
        Translation of *The Judgment of Paris.*

13. *Myron.*
    a.   Rio de Janeiro: Rocco, 1991. Tr. Fabio Fernandes.

14. *Washington, D.C.*
    a.1. Rio de Janeiro: Rocco, 1992. Tr. Haroldo Netto.
    a.2. Rio de Janeiro: Rocco, 1993.

15. *Ao vivo do calvario: O evangelho segundo Gore Vidal.*
    a.   Rio de Janeiro: Rocco, 1993. Tr. Lia Wyler.
        Translation of *Live from Golgotha.*

16. *Em directo do Calvário: O evangelho segundo Gore Vidal.*
    a.   Lisbon: Piblicações Dom Quixote, 1994. Tr. José Luis Lima.
        Translation of *Live from Golgotha.*

17. *Palimpsesto.*
    a.   Rio de Janeiro: Rocco, 1996. Tr. Roberto Grey.
        Translation of *Palimpsest.*

18. *Burr.*
    a.   Rio de Janeiro: Rocco, 1999. Tr. Haroldo Netto.

19. *A era dourada: Narrativas do império.*
    a.   Rio de Janeiro: Rocco, 2001. Tr. Paulo Reis.
        Translation of *The Golden Age.*

20. *Imperio.*
    a.   [Madrid:] Mediasat, 2002. Tr. Paula Vitória and Manuela Madureira.

21. *Williwaw.*
    a.   São Paulo: Ediouro, 2004. Tr. ?

xxiv. Romanian

1. *Iulian.*
   a.   Bucharest: Univers, 1993. Tr. Gherasim Țic.
       Translation of *Julian.*

2. *În căutarea regelui.*
   a.   Bucharest: Univers, 1993. Tr. George Volceanov.
       Translation of *A Search for the King.*

3. *Adio, domnule general!*
   a. Bucharest: Editura Z, 1995. Tr. George Volceanov.
   Translation of *Dark Green, Bright Red.*

4. *Oraşul şi stilpul.*
   a. Bucharest: Univers, 1996. Tr. ?
   Translation of *The City and the Pillar.*

xxv. Russian

1. *Vašington, okrug Kolumbija.*
   a. Erevan: Ajastan, 1972. Tr. D. Saribekjan.
   b. Moscow: Progress, 1989 (as *Demokratiia;* with *Democracy* by Henry Adams and *Democracy* by Joan Didion).
   Translation of *Washington, D.C.*

2. *Vitse-prezident Berr.*
   a. Moscow: Progress, 1977. Tr. M. I. Bruk and A. A. Faingara.
   Translation of *Burr.*

3. *Iulian.*
   a. St. Petersburg: Akademicheskii proekt, 1994. Tr. E. Tsypina.
   Translation of *Julian.*

4. *1876.*
   a. Moscow: Progress, 1986. Tr. A. A. Faingara.
   b. Moscow: Zakharov, 1999.

5. *Smert' v piatoi pozitsii.*
   a. Gomel': Sigma, 1992 (with novels by Carter Brown and Matt Gatsden). Tr. I. V. Torubarov.
   b. Moscow: Izd. dom "RIPOL KLASSIK," 2002.
   Translation of *Death in the Fifth Position.*

6. *Imperija.*
   a. Moscow: Zakharov, 1999. Tr. A. A. Faingara.
   Translation of *Empire.*

7. *Sotvorenie mira.*
   a. Moscow: Terra-Kn. Klub, 1999. Tr. ?.
   Translation of an unspecified work by Vidal.

8. *Kalki.*
   a. Moscow: EKSMO-Press, 2000. Tr. E. Katsa.

9. *Maira i Mairon.*
   a. Moscow: EKSMO-Press, 2002.1 Tr. V. Petrischeva and Z. Artemovoi.
   Translation of *Myra Breckinridge* and *Myron.*

10. *Pochemu nas nenavidiat? Vechnaia voina radi vechnogo mira.*
    a. Moscow: AST, 2003. Tr. T. A. Kudriavtsevoi and A. A. Faingara.
    Translation of *Perpetual War for Perpetual Peace.*

xxvi. Serbo-Croatian

1. *Burr.*
   a. Zagreb: Znanje, 1978. Tr. Antun Jurčič.

2. *1876.*
   a. Zagreb: Znanje, 1980. Tr. Josip Katalanić.

3. *Slabljenje i pad američke imperije.*
   a. Beograd: Verzal Press, 1999. Tr. Branka Dinić.
   Translation of *The Decline and Fall of the American Empire.*

xxvii. Slovenian

1. *Julijan.*
   a. Ljubljana: Cankarjeva založba, 1971. Tr. Alenka Puharjeva.
   Translation of *Julian.*

2. *Myra Breckinridge.*
   a. Ljubljana: Cankarjeva založba, 2001. Tr. Jure Potokar and Marcel Štefančič.

xxviii. Spanish

1. *El juicio de Paris.*
   a. Buenos Aires: Goyanarte, 1956. Tr. Patricio Canto.
   Translation of *The Judgment of Paris.*

2. *Juliano el apóstata.*
   a. Buenos Aires: Editorial Sudamericana, 1966. Tr. Eduardo Masullo.
   b.1. Barcelona: Edhasa, 1983.
   b.2. Barcelona: Edhasa, 1984.
   b.3. Barcelona: Edhasa, 1986.
   b.4. Barcelona: Edhasa, 1987.
   b.5. Barcelona: Edhasa, 1988.
   b.6. Barcelona: Edhasa, 2000.
   b.7. Barcelona: Edhasa, 2002.
   c. Barcelona: Edhasa, 2004.
   d. Barcelona: Orbis, 1988.
   e. Barcelona: Circulo de Lectores, 1992.
   f. Barcelona: Salvat, 1994.
   g. Barcelona: Altaya, 1996.
   h. Madrid: El Pais, 2005.
   Translation of *Julian.*

3. *Myra Breckinridge.*
   a.1. Barcelona: Ediciones Grijalbo, 1968. Tr. Rosendo Castillo.
   a.2. Barcelona: Ediciones Grijalbo, 1978.
   a.3. Barcelona: Ediciones Grijalbo, 1986.
   a.4. Barcelona: Ediciones Grijalbo, 1987.
   a.5. Barcelona: Grijalbo Mondadori, 2000.
   b. Barcelona: Debolsillo, 2006.

4. *Los honorables de Washington, D.C.*
   a. Madrid: Rodas, 1974. Tr. Hena Eck.

Translation of *Washington, D.C.*

5. *Burr.*
    a. Barcelona: Ediciones Grijalbo, 1975. Tr. Horacio and Margarita González Trejo.

6. *Mil ochocientos setenta y seis.*
    a. Barcelona: Ediciones Grijalbo, 1977. Tr. ?
        Translation of *1876.*

7. *Myron.*
    a.1. Barcelona: Ediciones Grijalbo, 1977. Tr. Ramón Alonso.
    a.2. Barcelona: Ediciones Grijalbo, 1977.
    a.3. Barcelona: Ediciones Grijalbo, 1986.
    b. Barcelona: Grijalbo Mondadori, 2000.
    c. Barcelona: Debolsillo, 2006.

8. *Kalki.*
    a. Barcelona: Edhasa, 1979. Tr. Enrique Pezzoni.

9. *Muerte en la quinta posición* (as by Edgar Box).
    a. Buenos Aires: Sudamerica, 1980. Tr. Carlos Gardini.
    b. Barcelona: Edhasa, 1986.
    c. Bogotá: Círculo de Lectores, 1988.

10. *Creación.*
    a.1. Barcelona: Edhasa, 1982. Tr. Carlos Peralta.
    a.2. Barcelona: Edhasa, 1984.
    a.3. Barcelona: Edhasa, 1986.
    a.4. Barcelona: Edhasa, 1988.
    a.5. Barcelona: Edhasa, 1996.
    a.6. Barcelona: Edhasa, 1999.
    a.7. Barcelona: Edhasa, 2003.
    b. Buenos Aires: Editorial Sudamericana, 1983.
    c. Barcelona: Orbis, 1988. 2 vols.
    d. Barcelona: Círculo de Lectores, 1993.
    e. Barcelona: Salvat, 1994. 2 vols.
    f. Barcelona: Altaya, 1997. 2 vols.
    g. Madrid: El Pais, 2005.
        Translation of *Creation.*

11. *Duluth.*
    a. Barcelona: Plaza & Janés, 1984. Tr. Adolfo Martín.
    b. Barcelona: Debolsillo, 2006.

12. *En busca del rey.*
    a.1. Barcelona: Edhasa, 1984. Tr. Juan Carlos Gardini.
    a.2. Barcelona: Edhasa, 1984.
    a.3. Barcelona: Edhasa, 1995 (with subtitle: *Ricardo corazón de león*).
    a.4. Barcelona: Edhasa, 2003.
    a.5. Barcelona: Edhasa, 2006 (with subtitle: *Ricardo corazón de león*).
    b. Barcelona: Salvat, 1995.
    c. Barcelona: Santa Perpetua de Mogoda; Buenos Aires: Planeta Argentina, 1998.
    d. Barcelona: Planeta-De Agostini, 1999.
    e. Barcelona: RBA Promociones Editoriales, 2001.
    f. Barcelona: Edhasa, 2003.
        Translation of *A Search for the King.*

13. *Lincoln.*
    a. Barcelona: Edhasa, 1985. Tr. Carlos Peralta.
    b. Barcelona: Orbis, 1988. 3 vols.
    c. Barcelona: Ediciones B, 1994.

14. *El juicio de Paris.*
    a. Barcelona: Edhasa, 1985. Tr. Carlos Peralta.
    Translation of *The Judgment of Paris.*

15. *Muerta en la noche* (as by Edgar Box).
    a. Barclona: Edhasa, 1986. Tr. Carlos Gardini.
    Translation of *Death Before Bedtime.*

16. *Muerte improvisada* (as by Edgar Box).
    a.1. Barcelona: Edhasa, 1986. Tr. Maria Asunción Osés.
    a.2. Barcelona: Edhasa, 1987.
    Translation of *Death Likes It Hot.*

17. *Verde oscure, roho vivo.*
    a. Barcelona: Edhasa, 1986. Tr. Carlos Peralta.
    Translation of *Dark Green, Bright Red.*

18. *Imperio.*
    a.1. Barcelona: Edhasa, 1988. Tr. Angela Pérez and M. J. Alvares Flórez.
    a.2. Barcelona: Edhasa, 2003.
    b. Buenos Aires: Editorial Sudamericana, 1988.
    Translation of *Empire.*

19. *Hollywood.*
    a. Barcelona: Edhasa, 1990. Tr. Maria Asunción Osés.
    b. Barcelona: Ediciones B, 1994.

20. *Washington D.C.*
    a. Barcelona: Edhasa, 1990. Tr. Maria Asunción Osés.
    b. Barcelona: Ediciones B, 1994.

21. *Mesias.*
    a.1. Barcelona: Minotauro, 1990. Tr. Aurora Bernárdez.
    a.2. Barcelona: Minotauro, 2004.
    Translation of *Messiah.*

22. *Ensayos 1982–1988.*
    a. Barcelona: Edhasa, 1991. Tr. Pedro del Carril.
    Translation of *At Home.*

23. *En directo del Gólgota: El evangelio según Gore Vidal.*
    a. Madrid: Anaya & Mario Muchnik, 1995. Tr. Richard Charles Guggenheimer.
    Translation of *Live from Golgotha.*

24. *La ciudad y el pilar de sal y siete relatos de juventud.*
    a. Madrid: Anaya & Mario Muchnik, 1997. Tr. Richard Guggenheimer.
    b. Barcelona: Mondadori, 1999.
    c. Barcelona: Debolsillo, 2003.
    Translation of *The City and the Pillar and Seven Early Stories.*

25. *La Institución Smithsoniana.*
    a.1. Barcelona: Proa, 1999. Tr. Cristina Mallol.

a.2. Barcelona: Proa, 1999.
   Translation of The Smithsonian Institution.

26. *La Institución Smithsoniana.*
   a. Barcelona: Mondadori, 1999. Tr. Jaime Zulaika.
   b. Barcelona: RBA Coleccionables, 2001.
   Translation of The Smithsonian Institution.

27. *Una memoria.*
   a. Barcelona: Mondadori, 1999. Tr. Richard Guggenheimer.
   b. Madrid: Anaya & Mario Muchnik, 1996.
   Translation of Palimpsest.

28. *Patria e imperio: Ensayos políticos.*
   a. Barcelona: Edhasa, 2001. Tr. Eduardo Iriarte. Prologue by Manuel Vázquez Montalbán.
   Contents unknown.

29. *Sexualmente hablando.*
   a. Barcelona: Grijalbo Mondadori, 2001. Tr. Aurora Echevarría.
   b. Barcelona: Debolsillo, 2004.
   Translation of Sexually Speaking.

30. *El último imperio: ensayos 1992–2001 [sic].*
   a. Madrid: Síntesis, 2002. Tr. Eduardo Iriarte.
   Translation of The Last Empire: Essays 1992–2000.

31. *La edad de oro.*
   a. Barcelona: Mondadori, 2002. Tr. Aurora Echevarria.

32. *Soñando la guerra: Sangre por petróleo y la junta Cheney-Bush.*
   a. Barcelona: Anagrama, 2003. Tr. Jaime Zulaika.
   Translation of Dreaming War.

33. *La invención de una nación: Washington, Adams, Jefferson.*
   a. Barcelona: Editorial Anagrama, 2004. Tr. Jaime Zulaika.
   Translation of Inventing a Nation.

xxix. Swedish

1. *Mord in femte positionen* (as by Edgar Box).
   a. Stockholm: Bonnier, 1955. Tr. Ann-Sofi and Sten Rein.
   Translation of Death in the Fifth Position.

2. *Julianus.*
   a. Stockholm: Bonnier, 1966. Tr. Alvar Zacke.
   Translation of Julian.

3. *Messias.*
   a. Jönköping, Sweden: Kindberg, 1979. Tr. Peter Carlsson.
   Translation of Messiah.

4. *Revolutionen.*
   a. Lund: RA, 1982. Tr. Mats Dannewitz Linder.
   Translation of Dark Green, Bright Red.

xxx. Thai

1.   *Kali.*
   - a.   Bangkok: Bannakit, 1979. Tr. Klum 22.
     Translation of *Kalki.*

xxxi. Turkish

1.   *Dişi.*
   - a.   Ankara: Adam Yayinevi, 1972. Tr. Selâmi Sargut.
     Translation of an unspecified work by Vidal.

2.   *Hükümdar.*
   - a.   Istanbul: Üçler Matbaasi, 1974. Tr. Cahit Uzel.
     Translation of *Julian.*

3.   *Imparator Julian.*
   - a.   Istanbul: Bakiş Yayinlari, 2000. Tr. Nafiz Ovacikli.
     Translation of *Julian.*

4.   *Son imparatorluk.*
   - a.   Istanbul: Gendas A.S., 2005. Ed. Zerrin Yilmaz. Tr. Fahri Pamakçu.
     Translation of *Empire.*

5.   *Yaratilis.*
   - a.   Istanbul: Literatur, 2005. Tr. Latif Byaci.
     Translation of *Creation.*

B. Contributions to Books and Periodicals

i. Chinese

1. ["Pride."]
   a. In *Ren xing ba wu.* Taibei Shi: Lian jing chu ban shi ye gong si, 1997. Tr. ?
   Translation of *Deadly Sins* (see I.C.211).

ii. French

1. *Visite à une petite planète.*
   a. *Fiction* no. 51 (1958): 3–31. Tr. Roger Durand.
   Translation of *Visit to a Small Planet* (I.D.ii.11).

2. "Introduction."
   a. In Paul Bowles. *Le Scorpion: Nouvelles.* Tr. Chantal Mairot. Paris: Rivages, 1987, 1989, 1996, 1998.
   Translation of I.C.132.a.

3. "Introduction."
   a. In Tennessee Williams. *Toutes les nouvelles.* Tr. Jean Lambert. Paris: Robert Laffont, 1989.
   Translation of I.C.157.b.

4. "Avant-Propos."
   a. In Logan Pearsall Smith. *Trivia.* Tr. Michèle Hechter and Philippe Neel. Paris: Le Promeneur, 1991.
   Translation of I.C.154.b.

5. "Preface."
   a. In Jonathan Ned Katz. *L'Invention de l'hétérosexualité.* Tr. ? Paris: EPEL, 2001.
   Translation of I.C.225.

iii. German

1. "Frau Lehrerin hält Sprechstunde."
   a. In Hermann Kinder, ed. *Die klassische Sau.* Zurich: Haffmans, 1986, 1987, pp. 98–100 (tr. ?). Munich: Goldmann, 1994. Erftstadt: Area, 2004.
   An extract from *Myra Breckinridge.*

2. "Über das Chaos."
   a. In Chris Miller, ed. *Das rebellische Wort: Oxford Amnesty Lectures.* Tr. ? Berlin: Ch. Links Verlag, 1997.
   Translation of "Chaos" (I.C.235).

3. ["Foreword."]
   a. In Israel Shahak. *Jüdische Geschichte, jüdische Religion.* Tr. Friedel Wiezorek and Harm Menkens. Süderbrarup: Lühe-Verlag, 1998.
   Translation of I.C.219.

iv. Italian

1.   "Prefazione."
      a.   In Roloff Beny. *Italia.* Milan: Mondadori, 1975, p. 428.
            Translation of I.C.106.

2.   "Prefazione."
      a.   In Peggy Guggenheim. *Una vita per l'arte: Confessioni di una donna che ha amato l'arte e gli artisti.* Tr. Giovanni Piccioni. Milan: Rizzoli, 1999, p. 404.
            Translation of I.C.133.

v. Russian

1.   *Washington, D.C.*
      a.   *Inostrannaja literatura* no. 11 (1968); no. 12 (1968).

vi. Spanish

1.   "Orgullo."
      a.   In *Pecados capitales.* Tr. ? Buenos Aires: Editorial Atlántida, 1996.
            Translation of "Pride" (I.C.211).

2.   "Prólogo."
      a.   In Peggy Guggenheim. *Confesiones de una adicta al arte.* Tr. Daniel Aguirre Oteiza. Barcelona: Lumen, 2002.
            Translation of I.C.133.

3.   "Prólogo."
      a.   In H. L. Mencken. *En defensa de las mujeres.* Tr. Miguel Martínez-Lage and Eugenia Vázquez Nacarino. Madrid: La Fábrica, 2003.
            Translation of I.C.192.a. The work by Mencken translated is *In Defense of Women* (1918).

4.   "Prólogo."
      a.   In Israel Shahak. *Historia judía, religión judía.* Tr. Juan Aranzadi and Celia Montolio. Barcelona: Circolo de Lectores, 2004.
            Translation of I.C.219.

vii. Ukrainian

1.   *Sotvorenie svitu.*
      a.   *Universe* (January–April 1989).
            Translation of *Creation.*

III. Works about Gore Vidal

A. Bibliographies

1. Gilliam, Loretta Murrell. "Gore Vidal: A Checklist, 1945–1969." *Bulletin of Bibliography* 30, no. 1 (January–March 1973): 1–9, 44.

    An impressive attempt at a preliminary bibliography, exhaustively listing both primary and secondary works, although with some omissions and errors.

2. Stanton, Robert J. *Gore Vidal: A Primary and Secondary Bibliography.* Boston: G. K. Hall, 1978.

    Sound and thorough bibliography, but hampered by the clumsy format of the G. K. Hall bibliography series, whereby all material is listed in chronological sequence, thereby making it difficult to identify significant works of criticism. The great majority of secondary sources listed are reviews. The bibliography proceeds to the end of 1977.

B. News Items and Encyclopedias

i. News Items

1. Abrams, Garry. "Vidal's Vitriol Spills on Many in *The Nation.*" *Los Angeles Times* (4 August 1989): Sec. 5, pp. 1, 5.
    Account of Vidal's essay "Cue the Green God, Ted" (I.C.180) and its attack on politicians and journalists, especially Ted Koppel.

2. Adams, Val. "News and Notes Gathered from the Studios." *New York Times* (13 February 1955): Sec. 2, p. 13.
    Reports Vidal's involvement with a TV show, "The Devil's Theatre," developed by the Theatre Guild and ABC.

3. ———. "C.B.S. Finds Spot for Thomas Films." *New York Times* (30 December 1964): 51.
    Part of the article deals with Vidal's departure as host of "Hot Line," on Channel 11.

4. ———. "Vidal Will Cover Conventions for Westinghouse." *New York Times* (13 June 1964): 53.
    Vidal will serve as commentator for both political conventions for Westinghouse Broadcasting Company.

5. Alberge, Dalya. "Vidal Continues to Press the Case for McVeigh." *Times* (London) (17 August 2001).
    Vidal sympathizes with Timothy McVeigh's criticisms of an overbearing United States government. The article does not appear in the microfilm edition of the *Times,* only on the online edition.

6. Altman, Dennis. "How I Fought the Censors and (Partly) Won." *Meanjin Quarterly* 29, no. 2 (Winter 1970): 236–39.
    Discusses his battles with Australian censors in regard to *Myra Breckinridge.*

7. Apple, R. W., Jr. "Mayor Considering Delay in Endorsing Kennedy for Senate." *New York Times* (13 August 1964): 1, 15.
    Notes that Vidal's article in *Esquire* ("The Best Man 1968" [I.C.46]) is influencing Democratic attacks on Robert F. Kennedy, and that some Democrats are circulating the article.

8. Barron, James. "Simple Exchange, Complex Memories." *New York Times* (27 September 2000): B2.
    Reports Vidal's recollection of his first encounter with Robert F. Kennedy.

9. Billiter, Bill. "2 Candidates Doubt Results of Vidal's Poll." *Los Angeles Times* (18 March 1982): Sec. 1, p. 11.
    Politicians doubt that Vidal will receive 6 percent of the vote in the Democratic primary for the Senate, a figure larger than that for several other candidates.

10. ———. "Vidal Campaign Draws Volunteers." *Los Angeles Times* (16 March 1982): Sec. 1, pp. 13, 20.
    Vidal is attracting hundreds of volunteers to help on his campaign for the Senate, and is also receiving many unsolicited donations.

11. ———. "Vidal Rides Momentum of Celebrity." *Los Angeles Times* (4 April 1982): Sec. 1, pp. 3, 31.
    Vidal's celebrity is aiding his senatorial campaign; polls show him receiving 10 percent of the vote. Vidal states his campaign themes and policies.

12.   Brown, Les. "C.B.S. Slates '60 Minutes' for Summer Prime Time." *New York Times* (8 May 1974): 90.
      Part of the article deals with ABC's purchasing the television rights to *Burr.*

13.   ———. "TV Unions Threaten to Boycott British Version of Vidal's 'Burr.'" *New York Times* (24 October 1974): 83.
      Reports a planned protest by the National Conference of Motion Picture and Television Unions if ABC proceeds with its plan to film *Burr* in the UK. See further item 119.

14.   Bumiller, Elisabeth. "Straight Talk in the Upper Strata." *Washington Post* (18 April 1981): D1, 9.
      Article on Merrywood, the house outside of Washington, D.C., where Vidal grew up, with some discussion of Vidal's fictional version of it (Laurel House in *Washington, D.C.*) and an interview with Nina Straight, Vidal's half-sister.

15.   Calta, Louis. "Tone Quits Lead in Ibsen Revival." *New York Times* (20 September 1960): 46.
      Part of the article deals with a protest by a Philadelphia city official against a remark about the city's drinking water in a staging of *The Best Man.*

16.   ———. "Vidal Satire, 'Evening with Nixon,' Set for Broadway." *New York Times* (22 December 1971): 26.
      Reports that Vidal's play is being prepared for Broadway presentation by Hillard Elkins.

17.   Cheshire, Maxine. "VIP." *Washington Post* (21 October 1979): H1, 8.
      Part of the article discusses a dinner party at L'Ermitage in Los Angeles hosted by Vidal, with Paul Newman, Jason Epstein, and Howard Austen.

18.   Clarity, James F. "The Diverse Roles of Mrs. Agnew." *New York Times* (4 December 1971): 28.
      Reports that Dr. Benjamin Spock of the People's Party would wish Vidal for secretary of state if he were president.

19.   Davis, Clive. "Out for Blood and Gore." *Times* (London) (30 October 1989): 20.
      Reports the dismay of historians—notably Stephen Oates and Arthur Schlesinger Jr.—over the success of *Lincoln* and other historical novels that, in their judgment, are marred by errors and "outmoded interpretations."

20.   Dugdale, John. "Gore Vidal vs Charlton Heston." *Sunday Times* (London) (23 June 1996): Sec. 9, p. 16.
      Discusses the debate between Vidal and Heston over screenwriting credits on *Ben-Hur.*

21.   Endicott, William. "Bradley Strongly Favored for Governor." *Los Angeles Times* (26 January 1982): Sec. 4, pp. 1, 3.
      Part of the article records a poll showing that Vidal would receive only 4 percent of the vote if the Democratic primary for Senate were held that day.

22.   ———. "Vidal Becoming Serious about Senate Campaign." *Los Angeles Times* (20 April 1982): Sec. 1, pp. 3, 23.
      Vidal has hired a campaign manager, his raising money, and claims to be serious about his candidacy for the Senate. "The only thing in my way . . . is Jerry Brown. I don't think that's so formidable."

23.   ———. "Vidal Ventures into High-Rent Grass Roots." *Los Angeles Times* (14 April 1982): Sec. 1, pp. 3, 19.
      Vidal campaigns at the Century City shopping complex. The article also reports Vidal's tax reform policies.

24.   Farber, Stephen. "With Mini-series, Vidal Returns to TV Writing." *New York Times* (19 December 1985): C29.
      Vidal is working on *Dress Gray* for NBC. The article incorporates comments by Vidal from an interview.

25.   Fein, Esther B. "Book Notes." *New York Times* (29 July 1992): C20.
      One section deals with the fact that Random House is keeping *Live from Golgotha* "under wraps" because Vidal does not want the novel to be prejudged by reviewers.

26.   Fleischer, Leonore. "Letter from New York." *Washington Post Book World* (24 February 1980): 15.
      Explains how *Views from a Window* (D.15) came to be published by Lyle Stuart.

27.   Gelb, Arthur. "A Man Who Plays Ex-President Meets a Man Who Is One." *New York Times* (21 April 1960): 23.
      Reports Harry S Truman's enjoyment of *The Best Man* at the Morosco Theatre.

27A. Geracimos, Ann. "Georgetown Celebrates Vidal." *Washington Times* (20 November 2006): B8.
      Vidal has a party in his honor at Gore Dean, an antiques emporium, to celebrate the publication of *Point to Point Navigation.*

28.   Gerhart, Ann. "1 Gore Vidal + 2 Magazines = 2 Exclusives." *Washington Post* (13 October 1995): F3.
      Reports on the nearly simultaneous "exclusive" interviews that Vidal gave following the publication of *Palimpsest,* one in the *New York Times* (C.123) and one in *Vanity Fair* (C.65).

29.   Gilder, Joshua. "Gore Vidal's Latest Escapade." *Saturday Review* 9, no. 5 (May 1982): 20–21.
      Report on Vidal's running for U.S. Senate against Jerry Brown.

30.   Glaser, Alice. "Making It." *Washington Post Book World* (13 April 1969): 8.
      Wonders why Vidal wrote *Myra Breckinridge* and recommends Virginia Woolf's *Orlando* as embodying the original "sex-change girl."

31.   Gould, Jack. "TV: Gore Vidal and Marya Mannes Debate Politics." *New York Times* (12 June 1967): 91.
      Reports a debate between Vidal and Marya Mannes on the Channel 5 show "Face to Face," discussing the Vietnam War, religion, and other issues.

32.   Harlow, John, and Hilary Clarke. "Gore Vidal Quits Italian Sun for Hollywood Feuds." *Sunday Times* (London) (23 February 2003): 27.
      Vidal leaves his villa in Ravello to live full-time in Los Angeles. Numerous quotations from an interview are cited.

33.   Harris, Amanda. "The Very Low-Down." *More* 6, no. 5 (May 1976): 25.
      Brief article on the Vidal-Capote litigation.

34.   Hendrix, Kathleen. "The Active Political Stance of Gore Vidal." *Los Angeles Times* (7 April 1981): Sec. 5, p. 1.
      Discusses Vidal's delivery of a "State of the Union" address at the Beverly Wilshire and provides an overview of his career. With some comments by Vidal from an interview.

35.   Higgins, Bill. "They Were Hungry for More Gore." *Los Angeles Times* (29 September 1995): E10.
      Report of a party given at L'Orangerie to celebrate the publication of *Palimpsest,* hosted by Tina Brown and Harold Evans (publisher of Random House).

36. Holt, Patricia. "Vidal Supports Hersh's 'Dark Side.'" *San Francisco Chronicle* (7 December 1997): Sunday Review, p. 2.
     Reports Vidal's agreement with Seymour Hersh's exposé of the Kennedy administration (see I.C.247).

37. James, Caryn. "Chicago, Tugging the Sleeve and Heart." *New York Times* (16 July 1996): C13, 16.
     Notes the imminent appearance of the segment "Gore Vidal's Washington, D.C." (I.I.ii.10) on the series "Urban Heartlands."

38. Johnston, Laurie. "Stafford Is Leaving Astronauts." *New York Times* (28 August 1975): 39.
     Reports a writer in the Russian newspaper *Pravda* who quotes Vidal in regard to the exploitative films being produced in the United States.

39. Kakutani, Michiko. "Mailer and Vidal at PEN Celebration." *New York Times* (18 November 1985): C15.
     Vidal and Mailer seemingly make peace at a PEN meeting, lambasting the Reagan administration.

40. Kastor, Elizabeth. "Vidal on the Go." *Washington Post* (21 June 1984): B1, 9.
     Reports Vidal's numerous appearances following the publication of *Lincoln,* including a party thrown for him by his half-sister, Nina Straight, at the Georgetown club Pisces.

41. Kaufman, David. "Vidal Gores Conceited Directors Who Fancy Themselves 'Auteurs.'" *Variety* 282, no. 8 (31 March 1976): 2, 126.
     Report of a speech given by Vidal at the Writers Guild dinner-dance at the Bev-Hilton. Presumably the basis for the essay "Who Makes the Movies?" (I.C.116).

42. Keil, Beth Landman, and Deborah Mitchell. "*George* Gore'd by Kennedy Kin." *New York* (22 June 1998): 11–12.
     Reports that John F. Kennedy Jr. commissioned an essay by Vidal for his magazine, *George,* but then rejected it. The article was "George" (I.C.243).

43. ———. "Gore Vidal Plans for His *Golden Age.*" *New York* 32, no. 15 (19 April 1999): 9.
     Tells of Vidal's hiring Lynn Nesbit as his agent and his move to Doubleday from Random House.

44. Koncius, Jura. "One for the Books." *Washington Post* (8 April 1981): B8.
     Vidal, along with Toni Morrison, Robin Cook, and Evan Hunter, appear at the Washington Post Book and Author Luncheon at the Sheraton Washington Hotel.

45. Kornbluth, Jesse. "Live from Macy's: The Dick and Gore Show." *New Times* 3, no. 12 (13 December 1974): 50–51.
     Discussion of Vidal and Dick Cavett, both of whom have published new books (*Myron* and *Cavett,* respectively) and are giving joint book tours.

46. Krebs, Albin. "Holton, Out of Governor's Job, Due for Federal Post." *New York Times* (16 January 1974): 45.
     Reports that Vidal spoke at the Pontifical Gregorian University in Rome and stated that he did not believe in God.

47. ———. "Shift at Rockefeller Foundation." *New York Times* (15 May 1971): 18.
     Reports on the Buckley-Vidal litigation.

48. Lawrence, W. H. "Kennedy Pledges a Drive to Widen Social Security." *New York Times* (15 August 1960): 1, 15.
     Reports Vidal's running for Congress.

49.   ———. "Kennedy Will Meet U.N. Chief Today; Sees a Show Here." *New York Times* (7 December 1960): 1, 46.
>   Reports president-elect John F. Kennedy and New York City mayor Robert F. Wagner seeing *The Best Man* at the Morosco Theatre.

50.   Lee, Linda. "Enter Characters and an Author." *New York Times* (8 October 2000): Sec. 9, p. 5.
>   Vidal shows up toward the end of a performance of *The Best Man* at the Virginia Theater, then goes to Sardi's and meets the cast.

51.   Lewin, Leonard C. "While on the Other Side of the Town . . ." *New York Times* (30 April 1972): Sec. 4, p. 9.
>   Reports Vidal attending a "counter-convention" in New York (Vidal is cited only in a photo and accompanying caption).

52.   Lindsey, Robert. "Democratic Liberals in California Are Assisting Anderson Campaign." *New York Times* (22 January 1980): A17.
>   Vidal is one of several writers and intellectuals supporting John Anderson, then running as a Republican candidate for president.

53.   Louie, Elaine. "A Reign of Words." *New York Times* (26 August 2004): F5.
>   Reports on the famous visitors to Vidal's villa in Ravello, including Erica Jong, Harold Evans (publisher of Random House), and Susan Sarandon.

54.   Love, Keith. "Author Vidal Returns to Hitting the Books." *Los Angeles Times* (11 June 1982): Sec. 1, pp. 3, 24.
>   Sums up Vidal's spotty campaign for the Senate, showing that he never mounted a serious challenge to Jerry Brown. But Vidal is glad he ran, and he also "might run for office again and he may write about his experience."

55.   ———. "Brown Takes Playful Swat at Editorial Cartoonists." *Los Angeles Times* (28 May 1982): Sec. 1, pp. 3, 20.
>   Jerry Brown and Vidal appear at a banquet of the Association of American Editorial Cartoonists in San Francisco. Brown is full of jokes and witticisms, but Vidal is unwontedly somber.

56.   ———. "TV Veteran Vidal in an Embarrassing Spot: His Own Campaign Ad." *Los Angeles Times* (12 May 1982): Sec. 1, pp. 3, 28.
>   Vidal seems flustered and unsure of himself in a television ad for his senatorial campaign.

57.   ———. "Vidal Challenges Brown on UC Funding." *Los Angeles Times* (29 April 1982): Sec. 1, pp. 3, 24.
>   In a speech at UCLA, Vidal accuses Jerry Brown of not paying enough attention to higher education and underfunding the University of California system.

58.   ———. "Vidal Takes Attack into the Lion's (Arco's) Den." *Los Angeles Times* (7 May 1982): Sec. 1, pp. 3, 17.
>   Vidal goes to the offices of Atlantic Richfield to speak to employees at the Arco Tower. He wants Arco to pay more taxes on profits.

59.   ———. "Vidal Wants PUC Members to Quit." *Los Angeles Times* (11 May 1982): Sec. 1, p. 3.
>   Vidal wants the five members of the Public Utilities Commission to resign "because they have allowed the state's major utilities to greatly increase their rates in recent months."

60.   McKinley, Jesse. "On Stage and Off." *New York Times* (31 March 2000): E2.
>   Reports plans for a revival of *The Best Man* on Broadway.

61.   ———. "On Stage and Off." *New York Times* (2 June 2000): E2.
>   Plans for a revival of *The Best Man* are moving forward, with many of the cast members in place.

62.   ———. "On Stage and Off." *New York Times* (30 June 2000): E2.
       Chris Noth is to make his Broadway debute as Joe Cantwell in *The Best Man.*

63.   ———. "On Stage and Off." *New York Times* (1 December 2000): E2.
       Reports that Vidal is writing a play about Aaron Burr.

64.   Mann, Roderick. "Vidal Sues to Get Credit on 'Sicilian.'" *Los Angeles Times* (14 February
       1987): Sec. 6, pp. 1, 10.
       Vidal takes the extraordinary step of suing the Writers Guild of America and writer Steve
       Shagan to receive screenwriting credit for *The Sicilian* (I.E.i.10). Vidal states: "I was defrauded
       of my work."

65.   Mehren, Elizabeth. "Homecoming at Ancestral Manse." *Los Angeles Times* (20 April
       1981): Sec. 5, pp. 1, 2.
       Vidal returns to Merrywood, his home outside Washington, D.C., now owned by Nancy
       Dickerson.

66.   Miller, Russell. "Driberg's Time-Bomb: 70,000 Saucy Words." *Sunday Times* (London) (15
       August 1976): 3.
       Reports Vidal's enjoyment of the memoirs of Tom Driberg, a former Labour M.P. who discussed
       his homosexuality frankly.

67.   Nichols, Lewis. "American Notebook." *New York Times Book Review* (28 January 1968): 32.
       An advance notice of *Myra Breckinridge.* Copies will not be given to reviewers in advance of
       publication because (in Vidal's words) "there's a considerable surprise in the plot" and he does
       not want reviewers to give it away.

68.   O'Connell, Alex. "Bright Minds Ignore Books, Says Vidal." *Times* (London) (13 October
       1997): 6.
       In a panel discussion prior to the awarding of the Booker Prize, Vidal states that even the brightest
       students do not take much interest in literature, especially the novel. Other panelists disagree.

69.   Parker, Jerry. "Avalanche of Abuse Could Help President." *Los Angeles Times* (2 January
       1972): Sec. E, pp. 1, 2.
       Reports that the number of satirical barbs being directed at Richard Nixon, including Vidal's *An
       Evening with Richard Nixon,* could help Nixon in his reelection campaign by generating
       sympathy for him.

70.   Peek, Laura. "Vidal to Be a Witness at McVeigh's Execution." *Times* (London) (7 May
       2001): 11.
       McVeigh asks Vidal to be a witness at his execution. Remarks by Vidal are quoted.

71.   Pooter [*pseud.*]. *Times* (London) (14 March 1970): IV.
       Reports bountiful sales of Vidal's books through the bookseller W. H. Smith.

72.   Reese, Michael, and Martin Kasindorf. "Gore Vidal, Candidate." *Newsweek* 99, no. 17 (26
       April 1982): 37.
       Report on Vidal's campaign for U.S. Senate against Jerry Brown.

73.   Reich, Kenneth. "Gore Vidal, Critic of Voting, May Seek Office." *Los Angeles Times* (25
       January 1981): Sec. 1, pp. 3, 22.
       Vidal contemplates running for the Senate. Some of his views on contemporary politics
       (especially the Reagan administration) are recorded.

74.   ———. "Vidal Enters U.S. Senate Race." *Los Angeles Times* (9 March 1982): Sec. 1, p. 3.
       Vidal declares himself a candidate for the Senate. The article includes numerous comments by
       Vidal about his opponent, Jerry Brown, and his policy stances.

75. Roberts, Steven V. "A Dissident Party Formed in Dallas." *New York Times* (28 November 1971): 33.
    Reports Vidal's attendance at the People's Party convention in Dallas, organized by Dr. Benjamin Spock, and quotes a comment by him.

76. Robinson, Laymond. "Democrats Form a Keating Group." *New York Times* (13 September 1964): Sec. 1, p. 60.
    Reports Vidal's role in organizing a group of Democrats to support Republican senator Kenneth S. Keating in opposition to Robert F. Kennedy.

77. ———. "Democrats Form a Keating Group." *New York Times* (29 September 1964): 1, 37.
    Reports Vidal reading a statement at a gathering of Democrats supporting Kenneth S. Keating and opposed to Robert F. Kennedy.

78. Romano, Lois. "Vidal's Role at McVeigh Execution is Decried." *Washington Post* (6 May 2001): A13.
    Relatives of those who died in the Oklahoma City bombing are upset that Vidal will be allowed to witness the execution, but McVeigh was allowed to pick five witnesses and Vidal was one of them. Vidal is briefly quoted.

79. Rutten, Tim. "Novel Is Restored, But the Grudge Continues." *Los Angeles Times* (13 September 2002): E1, 3.
    Tells of the restored edition of *Creation* (I.A.41.g), but notes that Vidal retains anger at Jason Epstein for ordering cuts in the original edition.

80. ———. "Vidal's War of Words with Editor Continues." *Los Angeles Times* (18 September 2002): E1, 12.
    Notes the continuing feud between Vidal and Jason Epstein over *Creation.*

81. Ryon, Ruth. "Scribe Bids *Addio* to Italian Villa." *Los Angeles Times* (23 May 2004): K1, 2.
    Vidal leaves his villa in Ravello.

82. Sarne, Mike. "For Love of Myra." *Films and Filming* 17, no. 5 (February 1971): 26–27.
    The director of *Myra Breckinridge* discussses working on the film. Vidal is mentioned in passing.

83. Schaffner, Franklin. "The Best and the Worst of It." *Films and Filming* 11, no. 1 (October 1964): 9–11.
    Discusses how he came to direct *The Best Man.* Vidal is mentioned briefly.

84. Shanley, John P. "New Area for Actress." *New York Times* (20 March 1960): Sec. 2, p. 13.
    Reports British actress Hermione Baddeley's appearance in a play by Ferenc Molnar, *Dear Arthur,* adapted by Vidal (see I.D.ii.19).

85. ———. "T.V.: Negative Thinking." *New York Times* (22 August 1960): 47.
    Reports Vidal's opinion (in an interview on "The New York Forum," Channel 2) of television as "dreadful," and that TV advertising is false and misleading.

86. Sisario, Ben. "A Gore Vidal Rarity, with Shades of Tennessee Williams." *New York Times* (7 November 2005): E2.
    Announces the discovery of the lost short story "Clouds and Eclipses" (I.B.31).

87. Thompson, Howard. "Gore Vidal to Guide 'Myra' Film Career as Writer-Producer." *New York Times* (8 March 1968): 50.
    Reports that Vidal will cowrite the screenplay to *Myra Breckinridge* with Robert Fryer. The screen rights were purchased by Twentieth-Century-Fox for $750,000.

88. ———. "Mae West, 76, Still Finding New Generations of Fans." *New York Times* (25 June 1970): 54.
Reports Mae West's view of the film *Myra Breckinridge*.

89. Trebbe, Ann L. "Personalities." *Washington Post* (9 March 1982): B2.
Brief article about Vidal entering the race for U.S. Senate in California.

90. Trueheart, Charles. "Gore Vidal, with Knife Sharpened." *Washington Post* (3 November 1987): D7.
Brief notice of Vidal's interview in *Playboy* (C.145).

91. ———. "Vidal and Buchanan, Scandalized." *Washington Post* (7 July 1987): C7.
Brief notice of Vidal's article on Oliver North (I.C.166).

92. Usborne, David. "Gore Vidal: 'What I Like about Timothy McVeigh.'" *Independent* (13 May 2001): 20.
Speaks of how Vidal came into contact with McVeigh and his opinion of McVeigh's political beliefs, which have aroused "a tsunami of opprobrium."

93. Viorst, Milton. "The Skeptics." *Esquire* 70, no. 5 (November 1968): 123–29, 194, 196–98.
Discusses Vidal's opposition to Robert F. Kennedy.

94. Walls, Jeannette. "Life of Gore: Vidal and Clemons Clash." *New York* 26, no. 20 (17 May 1993): 10.
Vidal expresses dissatisfaction with the slow pace of Walter Clemons's work on his biography, so he is writing his own memoir.

95. Weber, Bruce. "The Devil and the Commander." *New York Times* (19 February 1993): B2.
Vidal, Norman Mailer, and others are at Weill Recital Hall in Carnegie Hall, reading Shaw's *Don Juan in Hell*. Vidal plays the Devil.

96. Weiler, A. H. "Scientific Sizzler to Be Filmed: Gould Buys Rights to Sex Book." *Houston Chronicle* (2 June 1970): 11.
Vidal is planning to adapt *Rabelais* from the stage production by Jean-Louis Berrault.

97. Wolcott, James. "Medium Cool." *Village Voice* 23, no. 2 (9 January 1978): 41.
Account of the second appearance of Vidal and Norman Mailer on "The Dick Cavett Show" (see I.I.iii.31).

98. Wright, Robert A. "Broad Spectrum of Writers Attack Obscenity Ruling." *New York Times* (21 August 1973): 38.
Reports Vidal deploring the recent Supreme Court ruling on obscenity, establishing "community standards" as the basis for judging obscenity.

99. [Unsigned.] "Playwright Enters Race for House Seat Upstate." *New York Times* (4 April 1960): 44.
Reports Vidal entering the race for U.S. Congress as a Democrat; no opposition in a party primary is expected.

100. [Unsigned.] "'The Best Man' Wins in Berlin." *New York Times* (5 October 1960): 44.
Reports the successful European premiere of *The Best Man*.

101. [Unsigned.] "Nehru Is Applauded on Visit to Theatre." *New York Times* (9 October 1960): Sec. 1, p. 35.
Reports Indian prime minister Jawaharlal Nehru attending a performance of *The Best Man* at the Morosco Theatre.

102. [Unsigned.] "Vidal Play Has Bonn Premiere." *New York Times* (15 November 1961): 20.
Reports the staging of *On the March to the Sea* (now titled *Fire to the Sea*).

103.   [Unsigned.] "What Are the Magazines Saying, Dear?" *Time* 81, no. 9 (1 March 1963): 37.
       Brief account of Vidal's article in *Esquire* ("The Best Man 1968" [I.C.46]).

104.   [Unsigned.] "Gore Vidal Finds Wilson and Johnson Unpopular." *New York Times* (6
       October 1966): 56.
       Reports a BBC interview in which Vidal states that Prime Minister Harold Wilson is almost as
       unpopular among Britons as Lyndon Johnson is in the United States.

105.   [Unsigned.] "C.B.S. Seeks Scripts by Vidal and Pinter." *New York Times* (4 November
       1967): 66.
       Vidal and Harold Pinter are asked to write original plays for the "C.B.S. Playhouse" series.

106.   [Unsigned.] "Miss Kitt Defends Remarks on War; Denies Rudeness." *New York Times* (23
       January 1968): 21.
       Reports Vidal supporting Eartha Kitt's statement at a White House luncheon that juvenile
       delinquency is linked to the Vietnam War.

107.   [Unsigned.] "Vidal's Comedy 'Weekend' May Close on Saturday." *New York Times* (28
       March 1968): 55.
       Reports that *Weekend* will close "unless business improves."

108.   [Unsigned.] "Buckley, in Defamation Case, Sues *Esquire* for $1 Million." *New York Times*
       (14 August 1969): 55.
       Brief notice of the initiation of the Buckley-Vidal litigation.

109.   [Unsigned.] "Feuds: Wasted Talent." *Time* 94, no. 8 (22 August 1969): 49.
       Extensive article on the Buckley-Vidal litigation.

110.   [Unsigned.] "Vidal Is Sued by Buckley; a 'Nazi' Libel Is Charged." *New York Times* (7
       May 1969): 44.
       Brief notice of Buckley's suit against Vidal for calling him a "crypto-Nazi" during the televised
       debate at the Democratic National Convention.

111.   [Unsigned.] "Misses West and Welch Mobbed at Film Debut." *New York Times* (24 June
       1970): 43.
       Reports Raquel Welch and Mae West being greeted by two thousand fans at the Criterion
       Theater after the premiere of *Myra Breckinridge*.

112.   [Unsigned.] "Top Tip." *Listener* 83 (no. 2317) (12 March 1970): 345.
       One section concerns Vidal's appearance on the television show "The World This Weekend,"
       discussing the Nixon administration and American politics.

113.   [Unsigned.] "Hollywood Triangle: What's the Connection?" *Film* 61, no. 1 (Spring 1971):
       10–11.
       Reports comments by several of the crew members of the film *Myra Breckinridge.*

114.   [Unsigned.] "Leftist Parties Planning a Strong, Joint Presidential Ticket in '72." *New York
       Times* (6 July 1971): 27.
       Quotes Vidal as saying that Ralph Nader would be the ideal presidential candidate for 1972.
       Vidal also recommends Eugene McCarthy.

115.   [Unsigned.] "Vidal to Act in His Play." *New York Times* (8 May 1972): 47.
       Reports that Vidal will play the role of "Con" in the prologue of *An Evening with Richard Nixon*
       for one week.

116.   [Unsigned.] "Buckley Drops Vidal Suit, Settles with *Esquire.*" *New York Times* (26
       September 1972): 40.
       Reports the end of the Buckley-Vidal litigation with an out-of-court settlement.

117. [Unsigned.] "Canberra Senators Chided over Morosi Affair." *Times* (London) (11 December 1974): 9.
Quotes Vidal in Melbourne about the poor quality of Australia's newspapers.

118. [Unsigned.] "Finding a Word for It." *Sunday Times* (London) (20 October 1974): 34.
Notes Vidal's use of the names of Supreme Court justices in *Myron*.

119. [Unsigned.] "ABC-TV Shifts Plan, to Do 'Burr' in U.S." *New York Times* (13 March 1975): 79.
Reports that ABC has decided to film *Burr* in the United States, not in the UK, as previously planned.

120. [Unsigned.] "Vidal's 'Decline and Filmization of the Roman Empire.'" *Variety* 282, no. 10 (14 April 1976): 41.
Reports Vidal's treatment for *Caligula* and speculates about the adaptation of *Julian* into a film.

121. [Unsigned.] "Will the Real Caligula Stand Up?" *Time* 109, no. 1 (3 January 1977): 64–65.
Reports Vidal's disenchantment with the filming of *Caligula*.

122. [Unsigned.] "Nina Gore Olds, 745, Socialite, Kin to U.S. Senator, Novelist." *Washington Post* (6 April 1978): C8.
Obituary of Vidal's mother.

123. [Unsigned.] "Gore Vidal Challenges Brown for Hayakawa's Senate Seat." *New York Times* (9 March 1981): A17.
Vidal will challenge former California governor Jerry Brown for the Democratic nomination for U.S. Senate.

124. [Unsigned.] "California Returns." *Los Angeles Times* (10 June 1982): Sec. 1, p. 16.
Tabulation showing that Jerry Brown received 1,352,179 votes (51%) in the Democratic primary for the Senate; Vidal came in second with 401,754 votes (15%).

125. [Unsigned.] "Vidal Sues WGA for 'Sicilian' Credit." *Variety* 326, no. 4 (18 February 1987): 3, 44.
Vidal sues the Writers Guild of America for screenwriting credit for *The Sicilian*.

126. [Unsigned.] "L.A. Ruling Favors Vidal in WGA/'Sicilian' Suit." *Variety* 329, no. 3 (11 November 1987): 6.
Vidal prevails in his suit against the Writers Guild of America for screenwriting credit for *The Sicilian*.

127. [Unsigned.] "No Gore on Television." *Esquire* 123, no. 1 (January 1995): 13.
Reports that Vidal is unhappy after an unsatisfactory appearance on "The Late Show with David Letterman."

128. [Unsigned.] "Vidal Is to Witness McVeigh's Execution." *New York Times* (7 May 2001): A14.
Vidal states that he and Timothy McVeigh "had similar views about the erosion of constitutional rights."

129. [Unsigned.] "Harold [*sic*] Austen." *Times* (London) (13 October 2003): 29.
Obituary of Vidal's longtime companion, Howard Austen.

130. [Unsigned.] "For the Record from *Esquire* Magazine." *National Review* 56, no. 24 (31 December 2004): 16.
The magazine continues to dispute Vidal's explanation of the resolution of the Buckley-Vidal litigation.

ii. Encyclopedias

1.   Barker, Julie. *"1876."* In Frank N. Magill, ed. *Magill's Literary Annual 1977.* Englewood Cliffs, NJ: Salem Press, 1977, Vol. 1, pp. 256–59.

2.   Benét, William Rose. "Vidal, Gore." In *The Reader's Encyclopedia.* 2nd ed. New York: Thomas Y. Crowell Co., 1975, p. 1059. 3rd ed. New York: Harper & Row, 1987, pp. 1029–30.
     Not to be confused with *The Reader's Encyclopedia of American Literature* (item 21 below).

3.   Blank, Gary B. *"Creation."* In Frank N. Magill, ed. *Magill's Literary Annual 1982.* Englewood Cliffs, NJ: Salem Press, 1982, pp. 151–55.

4.   Bloom, Harold, ed. "Gore Vidal." In *Twentieth-Century American Literature.* New York: Chelsea House, 1988, Vol. 7, pp. 4042–72.
     Contents: Tennessee Williams, "Gore Vidal" (E.306); John W. Aldridge, "Three Tempted Him" (F.8.a); Peter Green, "Resuscitated Emperor" (F.21.o); Wilfrid Sheed, "Affairs of State" (F.22.aa); Brigid Brophy, "The Tang of Uncertainty" (F.23.c); John Leonard, "Vidal—Another Opinion" (E.187); Francis Wyndham, "Hooray for Hollywood" (F.31.x); Ann Morrissett Davidon, "Doing Well by Doing Wrong" (F.32.l); John Simon, "Vishnu as Double Agent" (F.34.cc); J. D. O'Hara, "The Winds of Vidal" (F.36.u); Anthony Burgess, "Honest Abe's Obsession" (F.39.g); Michael Hayes, "The Ministers without Portfolio" (F.16.o); John Simon, "Dapper Gore" (F.24.j); Roger Sale, [review of *Homage to Daniel Shays*] (F.29.k); Clive James, "The Left-Handed Gun" (F.33.g); Seymour Krim, "Reflections on a Ship That's Not Sinking at All" (E.179); Stephen Spender, "Private Eye" (F.29.m); Peter Conrad, "Re-inventing America" (F.32.i); Harold Bloom, "The Central Man" (F.39.c).

5.   Bordman, Gerald. *The Oxford Companion to American Theatre.* New York: Oxford University Press, 1984. 2nd ed. New York: Oxford University Press, 1992. 3rd ed. New York: Oxford University Press, 2004.
     Includes: *"Best Man, The"* (77–78 [1st ed.]; 77 [2nd ed.]; 74 [3rd ed.]); "Vidal, Gore" (691–92 [1st ed.]; 692 [2nd ed.]; 639 [3rd ed.]; *"Visit to a Small Planet"* (693 [1st ed.]; 694 [2nd ed.]; 641 [3rd ed.]).

6.   Borklund, Elmer. "Vidal, Gore." In *Contemporary Novelists.* James Vinson, Editor. London: St. James Press; New York: St. Martin's Press, 1972, pp. 1281–83. 2nd ed. James Vinson, Editor. D. L. Kirkpatrick, Associate Editor. London: St. James Press; New York: St. Martin's Press, 1976, pp. 1409–12. 3rd ed. James Vinson, Editor. D. L. Kirkpatrick, Associate Editor. London: St. James Press; New York: St. Martin's Press, 1982, pp. 655–56.
     For other editions, see item 24 below.

7.   Brink, Jeanie. *"The Second American Revolution and Other Essays (1976–1982.)"* In Frank N. Magill, ed. *Magill's Literary Annual 1983.* Englewood Cliffs, NJ: Salem Press, 1983, Vol. 2, pp. 700–704.

8.   Bronner, Edwin. *The Encyclopedia of the American Theatre 1900–1975.* San Diego: A. S. Barnes & Co., 1980.
     Includes: *"Best Man, The"* (48–49); *"Visit to a Small Planet"* (506); *"Weekend"* (513).

9.   Burke, W. J., and Will D. Howe. "Vidal, Gore (1925–   )." In *American Authors and Books: 1640 to the Present Day.* Second ed., augmented and revised by Irving R. Weiss. New York: Crown, 1962, p. 767. Third rev. ed., revised by Irving Weiss and Anne Weiss. New York: Crown, 1972, p. 662.

10. Cerniglia, Ken. "Gore Vidal (1925–   )." In *Contemporary Gay American Poets and Playwrights,* ed. Emmanuel S. Nelson. Westport, CT: Greenwood Press, 2003, pp. 427–37.

11. Dasgupta, Gautam. "Vidal, Gore (1925–   )." In *McGraw Hill Encyclopedia of World Drama*, ed. Stanley Hochman. 2nd ed. New York: McGraw Hill, 1984, Vol. 5, pp. 105–6.

12. Davis, Paxton. *"Burr: A Novel."* In Frank N. Magill and Henry Taylor, eds. *Masterplots 1974 Annual*. Englewood Cliffs, NJ: Salem Press, 1975, pp. 44–46.

13. DeAndrea, William L. "Box, Edgar." In *Encyclopedia Mysteriosa*. New York: Prentice Hall, 1994, pp. 36–37.

14. Drabble, Margaret, ed. "Vidal Gore (Eugene Luther Jr) (1925–   )." In *The Oxford Companion to English Literature*. 6th ed. Oxford: Oxford University Press, 2000, p. 1060.

15. Edgar, Kathleen J., ed. "Vidal, Gore." In *Contemporary Theatre, Film and Television*. Detroit: Gale Research, 1999, Vol. 20, pp. 422–25.

16. Eisner, Douglas. "Vidal, Gore (1925–   )." In George E. Haggerty, ed. *Gay Histories and Cultures: An Encyclopedia*. New York: Garland, 2000, pp. 933–34.

17. Falconieri, John V. "Vidal, Gore (Eugene Luther Vidal, Jr.)." In James Vinson, ed. *Contemporary Dramatists*. London: St. James Press; New York: St. Martin's Press, 1973, pp. 777–80. 2nd ed. James Vinson, Editor. D. L. Kirkpatrick, Associate Editor. London: St. James Press; New York: St. Martin's Press, 1977, pp. 806–9. 3rd ed. James Vinson, Editor. D. L. Kirkpatrick, Associate Editor. London: St. James Press; New York: St. Martin's Press, 1982, pp. 801–4. 4th ed. D. L. Kirkpatrick, Editor. James Vinson, Consulting Editor. Chicago & London: St. James Press, 1988, pp. 537–39. 5th ed. K. A. Berney, Editor. London: St. James Press, 1993, pp. 673–75. 6th ed. Ed. Thomas Riggs. Detroit: St. James Press, 1999, pp. 707–10.

18. Graalman, Robert. "Gore Vidal (1925–   )." In James E. Kibler Jr., ed. *American Novelists Since World War II: Second Series*. (Dictionary of Literary Biography 6.) Detroit: Gale Research Co., 1980, pp. 345–50.

19. Hart, James D. "Vidal, Gore (1925–   )." In *The Oxford Companion to American Literature*. 4th Edition. New York: Oxford University Press, 1965, p. 864. 5th ed. New York: Oxford University Press, 1983, p. 791. 6th ed., with revisions by Phillip W. Leininger. New York: Oxford University Press, 1995, p. 692.

20. Harte, Barbara, and Carolyn Riley, ed. "Vidal, Gore 1925–   ." In *Contemporary Authors*. Detroit: Gale Research Co., 1969, Vols. 5–8, pp. 1185–87. Rpt. in *200 Contemporary Authors*. Detroit: Gale Research Co., 1969, pp. 285–87.

21. Herzberg, Max J., and the staff of the Thomas Y. Crowell Company. "Vidal, Gore." In *The Reader's Encyclopedia of American Literature*. New York: Thomas Y. Crowell Co., 1962, p. 1181. Rev. ed. as *Benet's Reader's Encyclopedia of American Literature*. Ed. George Perkins, Barbara Perkins, and Philip Leininger. New York: HarperCollins, 1991, p. 1089. Rev. ed. as *HarperCollins Readers' Encyclopedia of American Literature*. New York: HarperResource, 2002, p. 1039.

22. Jens, Walter, ed. *Kindlers Neues Literatur Lexikon*. Munich: Kindler Verlag, 1988, Vol. 17. Includes: M[ichael] Ma[tzer], *"Burr"* (131–32); J[erôme] v[on] Ge[bsattel], *"The City and the Pillar"* (132); M[ichael] Ma[tzer], *"Messiah"* (132–33); M[ichael] Ma[tzer], *"Myra Breckinridge"* (133–35).

23. Kellman, Steven G. *"Lincoln."* In Frank N. Magill, ed. *Magill's Literary Annual 1985*. Englewood Cliffs, NJ: Salem Press, 1985, Vol. 1, pp. 570–73.

24.   Kiernan, Robert F. "Vidal, Gore." In *Contemporary Novelists*. 4th ed. D. L. Kirkpatrick, Editor. Associate Editor, James Vinson. London: St. James Press; New York: St. Martin's Press, 1986, pp. 834–37. 5th ed. Lesley Henderson, Editor. Noelle Watson, Associate Editor. Chicago & London: St. James Press, 1991, pp. 904–6. 6th ed. Susan Windisch Brown, Editor. Detroit: St. James Press, 1996, pp. 1011–13. 7th ed. Neil Schlager, Editor. Josh Lauer, Associate Editor. Detroit: St. James Press, 2001, pp. 1007–9 (updated by Hedwig Gorski).

      For earlier editions, see item 6 above.

25.   ———. "Gore Vidal (1925–   )." In James R. Giles and Wanda H. Giles, eds. *American Novelists Since World War II: Fourth Series*. (Dictionary of Literary Biography 152.) Detroit: Gale Research Co., 1995, pp. 232–47.

26.   ———. "Vidal, Gore." In *Encyclopedia of World Literature in the 20th Century,* ed. Leonard S. Klein. Rev. ed. New York: Frederick Ungar Publishing Co., 1984, Vol. 4, pp. 558–59. Rpt. in *Encyclopedia of American Literature*. Steven R. Serafin, General Editor. Alfred Bendixen, Associate Editor. New York: Continuum, 1999, p. 1176.

27.   Kloman, Harry B. "Vidal, Gore (1925–   )." In Philip K. Jason and Mark A. Graves, eds. *Encyclopedia of American War Literature*. Westport, CT: Greenwood Press, 2001, pp. 347–48.

28.   Kunitz, Stanley J., and Vineta Colby, eds. "Vidal, Gore." In *Twentieth-Century Authors: First Supplement*. New York: H. W. Wilson Co., 1955, pp. 1031–32.

29.   Levin, James. "Vidal, (Eugene Luther) Gore." In Sharon Malinowski, ed. *Gay and Lesbian Literature*. Detroit and London: St. James Press, 1994, pp. 379–82.

30.   Matlaw, Myron. "Vidal, Gore." In *Modern World Drama: An Encyclopedia*. New York: E. P. Dutton, 1972, pp. 793–94.

31.   Miller, Edmund. "Gore Vidal." In Kirk H. Beetz, ed. *Beacham's Encyclopedia of Popular Fiction*. Osprey, FL: Beacham Publishing Corp., 1996, Vol. 3, pp. 1865–68.

32.   ———. "Vidal, Gore (b. 1925)." In Claude J. Summers, ed. *The Gay and Lesbian Literary Heritage*. New York: Henry Holt & Co., 1995, pp. 714–15.

33.   M[iller], T[ice] L. "Vidal, Gore," In Don B. Wilmeth and Tice L. Miller, ed. *Cambridge Guide to American Theatre*. Cambridge: Cambridge University Press, 1993, p. 480.

34.   Mo[nk], D. E. "Vidal, Gore." In S. H. Cassell, ed. *Cassell's Encyclopaedia of World Literature*. Rev. ed. by J. Buchanan-Brown. London: Cassell & Co.; New York: William Morrow, 1973, Vol. 3, p. 692.

35.   Moritz, Charles. "Vidal, Gore." In *Current Biography Yearbook 1965*. New York: H. W. Wilson Co., 1965, pp. 431–34.

36.   Morrison, Kristin. "Vidal, Gore." In Michael Anderson et al., eds. *Crowell's Handbook of Contemporary Literature*. New York: Thomas Y. Crowell Co., 1971, p. 460.

37.   Mottram, Eric. "Vidal, Gore." In Malcolm Bradbury, Eric Mottram, and Jean Franco, eds. *The Penguin Companion to American Literature*. New York: McGraw-Hill Book Co., 1971, p. 256.

38.   Murphy, Bruce. "Box, Edgar." In *The Encyclopedia of Murder and Mystery*. New York: St. Martin's Minotaur, 1999, p. 56.

39.   Nevins, Francis M., Jr. "Box, Edgar." In John M. Reilly, ed. *Twentieth-Century Crime and Mystery Writers.* New York: St. Martin's Press, 1976, pp. 159–61. 2nd ed. New York: St. Martin's Press, 1985, pp. 91–93. 3rd ed. Lesley Henderson, Editor. Chicago and London: St. James Press, 1991, pp. 112–13. 4th ed. Jay P. Pederson, Editor. Taryn Benbow-Pfalzgraf, Associate Editor. Detroit: St. James Press, 1996, pp. 93–95.

40.   Ousby, Ian. "Vidal, Gore." In *The Cambridge Guide to Literature in English.* 2nd ed. Cambridge: Cambridge University Press, 1993, pp. 797–80. 3rd ed., ed. Dominic Head. Cambridge: Cambridge University Press, 2006, p. 1155.
      For the first edition, see item 48 below.

41.   Parini, Jay. "Gore Vidal." In *American Writers: A Collection of Literary Biographies.* A. Walton Litz, Editor in Chief. Molly Weigel, Assistant Editor. New York: Charles Scribner's Sons, 1996, Supplement IV, Part 2, pp. 677–96.

42.   Pearse, Richard. "Vidal, Gore." In Wolfgang Bernard Fleischmann, ed. *Encyclopedia of World Literature in the 20th Century.* New York: Frederick Ungar Publishing Co., 1971, pp. 474–75.

43.   Pollard, Arthur, ed. "Vidal, Gore (1925–   )." In *Webster's New World Companion to English and American Literature.* New York: World Publishing Co., 1973, p. 696.

44.   Richardson, Kenneth, ed. "Vidal, Gore." In *Twentieth Century Writing: A Reader's Guide to Contemporary Literature.* London: Newnes Books, 1969, p. 626.

45.   Seymour-Smith, Martin. "Vidal, Gore." In *Who's Who in Twentieth Century Literature.* London: Weidenfeld & Nicolson, 1976, pp. 380–81.

46.   Shatzky, Joel. "Gore Vidal" (1925–   ). In *Contemporary Gay American Novelists,* ed. Emmanuel S. Nelson. Westport, CT: Greenwood Press, 1993, pp. 375–80.

47.   Stapleton, Michael. "Vidal, Gore." In *The Cambridge Guide to English Literature.* Cambridge: Cambridge University Press; Feltham, UK: Newnes Books, 1983, p. 919.

48.   Stringer, Jenny, ed. "Vidal, Gore (1925–   )." In *The Oxford Companion to Twentieth-Century Literature in English.* Oxford: Oxford University Press, 1996, p. 690.

49.   Tietjen, Heidi A. "Vidal, Gore 1925–   ." In Linda Metzger, ed. *Contemporary Authors.* New Revision Series, Vol. 13. Detroit: Gale Research Co., 1984, pp. 496–503, 506–7.

50.   Tilghman, Tench Francis. *"Julian."* In *Masterplots Annual 1965.* New York: Salem Press, 1966, pp. 155–58. In Frank N. Magill and Dayton Kohler, eds. *Survey of Contemporary Literature.* New York: Salem Press, 1971, Vol. 4, pp. 2387–90.

51.   Trenz, Brandon. "Vidal, Gore 1925–   ." In James P. Draper and Susan M. Trosky, eds. *Contemporary Authors.* New Revision Series, Vol. 45. Detroit: Gale Research, 1995, pp. 450–60. Rev. ed. in Daniel Jones and John D. Jorgenson, eds. *Contemporary Authors.* New Revision Series, Vol. 65. Detroit: Gale Research, 1998, pp. 388–99 (unsigned). Rev. ed. in *Contemporary Authors.* New Revision Series, Vol. 100. Detroit: Gale Group, 2002, pp. 439–51 (unsigned).

52.   Van Doren, Charles, and Robert McHenry, eds. "Vidal, Gore." In *Webster's American Biographies.* Springfield, MA: G. & C. Merriam Co., 1974, p. 1076.

53.   Warfel, Harry R. "Gore Vidal." In *American Novelists of Today.* New York: American Book Co., 1951, pp. 436–37.

54. Weiss, Irving, and Anne de la Vergne Weiss. *Thesaurus of Book Digests 1950–1980.* New York: Crown, 1981.

   Includes: *"The City and the Pillar"* (87); *"Kalki"* (240–41); *"Matters of Fact and Fiction"* [*sic*] (291); *"Messiah"* (298); *"Myra Breckenridge"* [*sic*] (310).

55. Westfahl, Gary. "Gore Vidal." In Michael J. Tyrkus, ed. *Gay and Lesbian Biography.* Detroit: St. James Press, 1997, pp. 442–43.

56. [Unsigned.] *"The Best Man."* In Frank N. Magill, ed. *Masterplots Annual 1961.* New York: Salem Press, 1962, pp. 19–21. Rpt. in Frank N. Magill and Dayton Kohler, eds. *Survey of Contemporary Literature.* New York: Salem Press, 1971, pp. 386–88.

57. [Unsigned.] "Box, Edgar." In Chris Steinbrunner et al., eds. *Encyclopedia of Mystery and Detection.* New York: McGraw-Hill Book Co., 1976, pp. 43–44.

58. [Unsigned.] "Vidal, Gore." In *Who's Who in America: Volume 32 (1962–1963).* Chicago: Marquis–Who's Who, 1962, p. 3224.

   Revised versions appear in every edition down to the most current one (2006).

59. [Unsigned.] "Vidal, Gore." In *The International Who's Who 1976–1977.* 40th ed. London: Europa Publications, 1976, p. 1785.

60. [Unsigned.] "Vidal, Gore." In Nancy Duin et al., eds. *The Writers Directory 1976–78.* London: St. James Press; New York: St. Martin's Press, 1976, p. 1105.

61. [Unsigned.] "Vidal, Gore." In *Notable Names in the American Theatre.* Clifton, NJ: James T. White & Co., 1976, p. 1197.

62. [Unsigned.] "Vidal, Gore." In *Who's Who 1976: An Annual Biographical Dictionary.* London: Adam & Charles Black, 1976, p. 2443.

63. [Unsigned.] "Vidal, Gore." In *Merriam-Webster's Encyclopedia of Literature.* Springfield, MA: Merriam-Webster, 1995, p. 1166.

C. Interviews

1. Abbott, Steven, and John Mitzel. "Gore Vidal: The *Fag Rag* Interview." *Fag Rag* nos. 7/8 (Winter–Spring 1974): 1, 3–9. In D.12. In D.14. In D.15 (extracts). In I.A.63.
   Vidal discusses sex and politics, his preference for the term "faggot" over "gay," sex and writing, his upbringing, John Horne Burns, Norman Mailer, his Edgar Box novels, Paul Goodman, and literature ("American literature has always been second-rate").

2. Abbott, Steven, and Thom Willenbecher. "Gore Vidal: The *Gay Sunshine* Interview." *Gay Sunshine* nos. 26/27 (Winter 1975–1976): 20–25. In I.A.63. Spanish trans. in Winston Leyland, ed. *Cónsules de Sodoma*. Tr. Eduardo Wards Simon and Homero Alsina Thevenet. Barcelona: Tusquets, 2004.
   Vidal discusses love, life in America, sex and the law, gay liberation, the women's movement, Henry Kissinger, Gerald Ford, the economy, Nelson Rockefeller, the Catholic church and homosexuality, *Myron, Two Sisters,* the film of *Myra Breckinridge* (which he hasn't seen), and the demise of the novel.

3. Abowitz, Richard. "America's Biographer: An Interview with Gore Vidal." *Gadfly* 3, no. 7 (July 1999). In D.14.
   Vidal discusses reading, Al Gore, drinking, the literary status of the historical novel, being an actor, and historical scholarship. *Gadfly* was an online journal, now defunct.

4. Alexander, Max. "Chariots of Fire." *Variety* 363 (15–21 July 1996): 6, 50.
   Vidal discusses politics, the movie business, current directors, and his acting career.

5. A[li], T[ariq], and B[lackburn], R[obin]. "Surrealism and Patriotism: The Education of an American Patriot." *New Left Review* no. 149 (January–February 1985): 95–107.
   Vidal discusses his early influences, *The City and the Pillar,* his historical novels, *Creation, Duluth,* Ronald Reagan, the media and politics, his running for office, *Lincoln,* deconstruction, and his readings.

6. [Alpert, Hollis.] "Dialogue on Film: Gore Vidal." *American Film* 2, no. 6 (April 1977): 33–48. In D.14. In D.15 (extracts).
   Lengthy interview. Vidal discusses film, directors, his work in Hollywood, the theater, Francis Ford Coppola, Fellini, Hitchcock, Lina Wertmüller, *Caligula,* Fellini's *Casanova, The Best Man* (film), movie actors, adapting literature into film, film's effect on writing, Norman Mailer, his writing habits, television, his appearances on television (including "Mary Hartman, Mary Hartman"), and talk shows.

7. Altman, Dennis. "An Interview with Gore Vidal." *Christopher Street* 2, no. 7 (January 1978): 4–10. In D.15 (extracts).
   Vidal discusses the term "homosexual," prejudice against gays, Christianity, and gay literature.

8. Amis, Martin. "Mr Vidal: Unpatriotic Gore." *Sunday Telegraph* (London), 1977. In Amis's *The Moronic Inferno and Other Visits to America.* London: Jonathan Cape, 1986; New York: Viking Press, 1987; Harmondsworth, UK: Penguin, 1987, pp. 97–106.
   Vidal discusses Norman Mailer, his family and upbringing, his career in the army, his ventures into politics, and *Caligula.* Amis also appends some words by Norman Mailer on Vidal.

9. [Anderson, Christopher P.] "Don't Worry That Vidal Is out of Oxen to Gore: He Says He's Running for the U.S. Senate." *People* 15, no. 12 (30 March 1981): 52–53, 56.
   Vidal discusses running for the Senate, Ronald Reagan, William F. Buckley, Truman Capote, Norman Mailer, and homosexuality.

10.   Anderson, Michael. "'J. F. K.' Is Not What He Had in Mind." *New York Times Book Review* (30 August 1992): 27.
        Interview timed for the publication of *Screening History*. Vidal states that Oliver Stone's *JFK* "is a royal mess by someone who has not grasped the history of that day."

11.   Aronson, Steven M. L. "Gore Vidal: 'Creation.'" *Interview* 11, no. 5 (May 1981): 46–47.
        Vidal discusses friendship, the American Academy and Institute of Arts and Letters, *Ben-Hur*, Tennessee Williams and *Suddenly, Last Summer*, Jackie Onassis, and John F. Kennedy.

12.   Auchincloss, Eve, and Nancy Lynch. "Disturber of the Peace: Gore Vidal." *Mademoiselle* 53, no. 3 (September 1961): 132–33, 176–79.
        Vidal discusses sex and marriage, sexual freedom, loneliness, his attitude toward society, politics, John F. Kennedy, and history.

13.   Bailey, Geoffrey. "Gore Vidal on Where We're Headed." *Mother Jones* 14, no. 4 (May 1989): 13.
        Vidal expresses his belief that over the next ten to fifteen years "the nation-state dissolves" and the multinational corporations will run everything.

14.   Bailey, Jeffrey. "Vidal: Patrician Gadfly as Popular Conscience." *Advocate* no. 291 (1 May 1980): 19–23.
        Vidal discusses his celebrity, his supposed pessimism, the American ruling class, the genesis of his books, the "heterosexual dictatorship," gay rights, *The City and the Pillar*, and being a popular writer.

15.   Bannon, Barbara A. "Gore Vidal." *Publishers' Weekly* 204, no. 18 (29 October 1973): 12–13.
        Vidal discusses *Burr*, Richard M. Nixon, and the current political climate.

16.   Barber, Michael. "Crusader against Cant." *Books and Bookmen* 19, no. 8 (May 1974): 65–69.
        Barber supplies an overview of Vidal's career. Vidal discusses *The City and the Pillar*, his bisexuality, writing for television and film, his political philosophy, American culture, and a comparison of the British and American literary scenes.

17.   Barkham, John. "The Author." *Saturday Review* 45, no. 31 (4 August 1962): 19.
        Vidal discusses his plays, especially *Romulus*, his novel-in-progress (*Julian*), and his running for office.

18.   Barnes, Susan. "Behind the Face of the Gifted Bitch." *Sunday Times* (London) *Magazine* (16 September 1973): 44–45, 47, 49, 51, 53. *Biography News* 1, no. 1 (January 1974): 106–9 (as "The Irreverent Gospel of Gore Vidal"). In Barbara Nykoruk, ed. *Authors in the News*. Detroit: Gale Research Co., 1976, Vol. 1, pp. 480–83.
        Vidal discusses his views on love and sex, his upbringing, Jackie Kennedy, John F. Kennedy, Robert F. Kennedy, homosexuality, and his relations with Howard Austen. Barnes includes discussions of Vidal by Stephen Spender, Claire Bloom, and others.

19.   Barsamian, David. "Gore Vidal: The *Progressive* Interview." *Progressive* 70, no. 8 (August 2006): 33–36.
        Vidal discusses George W. Bush, the American wars in Afghanistan and Iraq, the armed forces, the media, the Democrats, and the future of the United States.

20.   Bergquist, Laura. "Gore Vidal: The Elegant White Knife." *Look* 33, no. 15 (29 July 1969): 73–78.
        Vidal dscusses running for office, the Kennedys, Norman Mailer, Tuman Capote, *Myra Breckinridge*, young people, and his feud with William F. Buckley.

21. Birnbaum, Jesse. "In Ravello, as in *Duluth*, Gore Vidal's Bile Is Still Flowing." *People* 20, no. 7 (15 August 1983): 46, 49.
     Vidal discusses the American presidency, the literary establishment, and Hollywood.

22. Bone, James. "Vidal Casts McVeigh as a Hero." *Times* (London) (8 August 2001): 13.
     Vidal discusses his correspondence with Timothy McVeigh and their ideas about the erosion of civil liberties in the United States.

23. Boylan, Nuala. "Rebel Rebel." *Harper's Bazaar* no. 3373 (January 1994): 90–93.
     Discussion between Vidal and Susan Sarandon, discussing films, religion, contemporary politics, and their relations with each other.

24. Breit, Harvey. "Talk with Gore Vidal." *New York Times Book Review* (22 January 1950): 14.
     Vidal discusses his visit to George Santayana, contemporary literary criticism, his preference for the short novel, and travel.

25. Brussel, David. "The World According to Gore." *Interview* 26, no. 1 (January 1996): 22.
     Vidal discusses gossip, Jackie Kennedy, Andy Warhol, homosexuality, honesty, and being a cult figure.

26. Carroll, Rory. "'We Don't Know Where We're Going.'" *Guardian* (6 December 2001): Supplement, p. 4.
     Vidal discusses the American war in Afghanistan, his writings on terrorism, and George W. Bush's restriction of civil liberties.

27. Cheatham, Richard. "A Visit to a Young Success." *Diplomat* no. 91 (July 1957): 22.
     Rapid survey of Vidal's youth and career, with Vidal's comments on his life and beliefs. "I believe it possible—in fact, mandatory, to function without absolutes."

28. Cheshire, David. "Gore Vidal: On Success, Legends and Reality." *Listener* 94 (no. 2418) (7 August 1975): 167–68.
     An interview conducted on "Success Story" (BBC1). Vidal discusses his early writing career, his life in Italy, best sellers, and the future of the novel.

29. Clare, Anthony. "Gore Vidal: American Psyche." *Independent* (8 October 2000): Culture, p. 1.
     Vidal discusses the notion of duality, his childhood, his mother, love, and dying.

30. Clarke, Gerald. "The Art of Fiction L: Gore Vidal." *Paris Review* 15 (no. 59) (Fall 1974): 130–65. In D.14. In D.15 (extracts). In George Plimpton, ed. *Writers at Work: The* Paris Review *Interviews: Fifth Series.* New York: Viking Press, 1981, pp. 281–311.
     Extensive interview conducted in Rome. Vidal discusses his early writing (including juvenilia), *The City and the Pillar,* his literary contemporaries, E. M. Forster, Ernest Hemingway, education, *Two Sisters,* his "interest in Western civilization," his work habits, his life abroad, literature and politics, love ("love is not my bag"), movies, and reading.

31. Clement, Michel, and Lorenzo Codelli. "Une Soirée avec Gore Vidal." *Positif* no. 363 (May 1991): 75–85.
     In French. Vidal discusses many of the films he has worked on (*Dimenticare Palermo, The Sicilian, The Catered Affair, The Death of Billy the Kid, Ben-Hur, The Last of the Mobile Hot-Shots, Caligula*), his general work in Hollywood, his early writings, the theater, and Joseph L. Mankiewicz.

32. Coleman, Terry. "Old Style Religion." *Guardian* (16 October 1964): 11.
     Interview timed for the British release of *Julian.* Vidal discusses his return to novel writing and his political and religious views.

33. [Cooper, Arthur.] "Gore Vidal on . . . Gore Vidal." *Newsweek* 84, no. 21 (18 November 1974): 97–99. In D.15 (extracts).
    Vidal discusses his place among novelists, his celebrity status, the state of the novel, current politics, and sexual freedom.

34. Cooper, Marc. "Gore Vidal, Octocontrarian." *Nation* 281, no. 15 (7 November 2005): 26–28.
    Vidal discusses contemporary American politics, including Tom DeLay and Dick Cheney, taxation, the military, and 9/11.

35. ———. "The Last Defender of the American Republic? An Interview with Gore Vidal." In I.A.67.
    Vidal discusses the terrorist attacks on 9/11, the duplicity of the American government, the erosion of civil liberties in the United States, the American media, George W. Bush, and American liberalism.

36. [Coyle, Joseph S.] "The Rewards of Alienation." *Money* 7, no. 6 (June 1978): 74–75, 77–79. In D.15 (extracts).
    Vidal discusses his popular success, his various residences, his payment of taxes, his interest (or lack of it) in money, and socialism.

37. De Masi, Domenico. "Devoti al dio Pan." In De Masi's *Ravello: Un petit tour*. Naples: Avagliano, 2003, pp. 143–55.
    Vidal discusses the relationship between foreign intellectuals and Ravello (Richard Wagner, André Gide, E. M. Forster), his own relations with Ravello, his villa there, and its role in inspiring his creativity.

38. Dean, Michael. "Gore Vidal on His Latest Novel—in Conversation with Michael Dean." *Listener* 80 (no. 2061) (26 September 1968): 401–2. In D.15 (extracts).
    Interview on "Late Night Line-Up" (BBC2). Vidal discusses the writing of *Myra Breckinridge*, André Malraux, Norman Mailer, and America's future.

39. ———. "The Private Life of Public Men—Lord Longford and Gore Vidal in Conversation with Michael Dean." *Listener* 91 (no. 2346) (14 March 1974): 336–38. In D.15 (extracts).
    Interview on "Argument" (BBC2). Vidal discusses sex, politics, Bertrand Russell (Vidal has read him extensively), the sexual life of politicians, Christianity in England, and the family.

40. ———. "Talking for the Camera—1. Muggeridge and Gore Vidal." *Listener* 92 (no. 2367) (8 August 1974): 172–73. In D.15 (extracts).
    Interview on "Argument" (BBC2). Vidal discusses overpopulation, Eleanor Roosevelt, sex, the pursuit of pleasure, and censorship.

41. Delaney, Frank. "An All-American Apostate: Gore Vidal." *Sunday Times* (London) (29 October 1989): G8–9.
    Vidal discusses *Hollywood*, films and politics, George Bush, and his next novel (*The Golden Age*).

42. Dougary, Ginny. "The Wasp's Tale—Gore Vidal." *Times* (London) (7 October 1995): Magazine, pp. 22–23, 25–26.
    Extensive interview timed for the release of *Palimpsest*. Vidal discusses his father and upbringing, T. P. Gore, his early career, contemporary politics, Anaïs Nin, his mother, and Jimmie Trimble.

43. Dreifus, Claudia. "Gore Vidal: The Writer as Citizen." *Progressive* 50, no. 9 (September 1986): 36–39.
    Vidal discusses his views on American politics and society, sex, AIDS, and other subjects.

44.   Dutka, Elaine. "Hey, Maybe Leslie Nielsen Could Star in the Next Gore Vidal Script." *Los Angeles Times* (3 July 1994): Calendar, pp. 25–26.

    Vidal, having concluded a deal with Twentieth-Century-Fox to adapt Edith Wharton's *The Buccaneers,* discusses the state of the film industry, Edith Wharton, the screenplay to *Theodora* (written for Universal and Martin Scorsese), and *Bob Roberts.*

45.   Dzieduszycki, Michele. "Noi Americani siamo colpevoli di imperialismo involontario: Conversazione con Gore Vidal." *Fiera Letteraria* 43, no. 43 (24 October 1968): 2–4.

    In Italian. Vidal discusses his interest in literature, *The City and the Pillar,* living in Italy, American writers who have influenced him, Marcel Proust, the "Beats," *Julian, Myra Breckinridge,* his involvement in politics, African Americans, Eugene McCarthy, Nixon and Vietnam, the USSR, Latin America, Japan, and the Kennedys.

46.   Epstein, Fred. "Gore Vidal: Why Is This Man So Serious?" *Rolling Stone* no. 370 (27 May 1982): 12, 68.

    Vidal discusses his running for the U.S. Senate and his opponent, Jerry Brown.

47.   Epstein, Jacob. "The Candidates." *New Review* 2 (no. 24) (March 1976): 59–64. In D.15 (extracts).

    On the eve of the New Hampshire primary, Vidal discusses the candidates, Norman Podhoretz, American political history, life in Rome, university education, and his "advice to young America."

48.   Freeman, Ira Henry. "The Playwright, the Lawyer and the Voters." *New York Times* (15 September 1960): 20.

    Vidal, as candidate for Congress, discusses the issues of the campaign and the state of the Democratic party. Vidal's opponent, J. Ernest Wharton, is also interviewed.

48A.   Gannett, Lewis. "Gore Stories: U.S. History, Popular Film and the Life of Gore Vidal." *Gay Community News* 19, no. 6 (24 August 1991): 8.

    Vidal discusses American politics, fending off biographers, American history, film, and the Gulf War.

49.   Gardner, Paul. "Views of a 'Professional Meddler.'" *New York Times* (28 June 1964): Sec. 2, p. 15.

    Vidal discusses talk shows, his impending appearance on "Hot Line," and his role as political commentator for Westinghouse Broadcasting Company.

50.   Gent, George. "'C.B.S. Playhouse' Signs Gore Vidal." *New York Times* (9 November 1967): 95.

    Vidal discusses his plans to write an original play, tentatively titled *Uptight,* for "CBS Playhouse." The play was never written.

51.   Goldstein, William. "PW Interviews: Gore Vidal." *Publishers Weekly* 226, no. 2 (13 July 1984): 52–53.

    Vidal discusses his writing ("I'm a natural writer"), his historical novels, and contemporary politics and literature.

52.   Goodfriend, Arthur. "The Cognoscenti Abroad: Gore Vidal's Rome." *Saturday Review* 52, no. 4 (25 January 1969): 36–39.

    Vidal discusses living in Rome and many of the noteworthy sites in the city.

53.   Grenier, Richard. "Gore Vidal: What It's Like to Be Talented, Rich, and Bisexual." *Cosmopolitan* 179, no. 5 (November 1975): 164–67, 184–85. In D.15 (extracts).

    Interview conducted at La Rondinaia. Vidal is writing *1876.* He discusses his family and friends, including Paul Newman, the Kennedys, bisexuality and homosexuality, his political campaigns, and Jewish attitudes toward gays. He wonders why he is popular.

54. Gussow, Mel. "Vidal Warming Up His 'Act of Politics.'" *New York Times* (28 April 1972): 32.
     Vidal discusses the purpose of his play, *An Evening with Richard Nixon,* and his forthcoming novel, *Burr.*

55. Hallowell, John. "Gore Vidal on Homosexuality: 'I'm Given Credit for Having Invented It.'" *Advocate* 4, no. 19 (11–24 November 1970): 16, 19.
     Vidal discusses Phillips Exeter Academy, the film *Myra Breckinridge,* homosexuality, and the Italians.

56. Halpern, Daniel. "Interview with Gore Vidal." *Antaeus* no. 1 (Summer 1970): 67–76. In D.15 (extracts).
     Vidal discusses the contemporary literary scene, the poor quality of present-day English, contemporary writers (Thomas Pynchon, Harold Robbins, John Barth, John Updike), journalism, the avant-garde, his assessment of his own work, Ken Kesey, Jack Kerouac, modern civilization, Susan Sontag, and James Baldwin.

57. Harrison, Barbara. "Pure Gore." *Los Angeles Times Magazine* (28 January 1990): 8–13, 15–16, 38.
     Extensive interview in which Vidal discusses *Hollywood,* his life in Italy, his ventures into politics, his political views, and celebrities he has known.

58. Harvey, Mary Kersey. "The Author." *Saturday Review* 47, no. 23 (6 June 1964): 32.
     Vidal discusses his political stance (he is a "correctionist"), his running for office, John F. Kennedy, and his house on the Hudson.

59. Heilpern, John. "The Gospel According to Gore." *Observer* (London) no. 9896 (26 April 1981): 30.
     Interview timed for the publication of *Creation.* Vidal discusses the novel, his impressions of England, his contemplated run for the Senate, and his political ambitions.

60. Heimer, Mel. "Jack-of-All-Crafts." *Pictorial TView* (2 June 1957): 14.
     Not seen. Information taken from Stanton, who states that the interview concentrates on Vidal's work in television.

61. Hendrix, Kathleen. "Decline and Vidal." *Los Angeles Times* (5 December 1988): Sec. 5, pp. 1, 2.
     Vidal, returning to the U.S. for a visit, believes the nation has become a police state. He also discusses his future books (including *Hollywood*), Walter Clemons's planned biography of him, New York City, his refusal to vote, his controversy with Norman Podhoretz, and his other feuds.

62. Hill, Logan. "Vidal Statistics." *New York* 33, no. 35 (11 September 2000): 112, 114–15.
     Vidal discusses Fred Kaplan's biography (which "just ripped off *Palimpsest* . . . and turned it into dull, bureaucratic, academic prose") and states that *The Golden Age* is in effect Volume 2 of his memoirs.

63. Hill, Michael E. "'Lincoln': A Fast-Forward through Vidal's Historical Saga." *Washington Post* (27 March 1988): TV Week, pp. 7–8.
     Vidal discusses growing up in Washington, D.C., the writing of *Lincoln,* the television adaptation, and Lincoln the man and politician.

64. H[irschberg], L[ynn]. "How to Feud: Gore Vidal's Eight Great Tips." *Spy* (November 1988): 71.
     Vidal briefly discusses how to conduct literary feuds in print and in the media.

65. Hitchens, Christopher. "La Dolce Vidal." *Vanity Fair* no. 423 (November 1995): 60, 62, 64, 66–68.
     Vidal discusses his early sexual experiences, his relations with Anaïs Nin, the Kennedys, his writings (especially *Myra Breckinridge* and *Messiah*), Christianity, Al Gore, William F. Buckley, and current films.

66.   Hopcraft, Arthur. "Mr. Vidal Takes Pleasure in Ambiguity." *Nova* (January 1969): 78–79.
    Vidal discusses being a politician, the United States in transition, literary criticism, and Tennessee Williams.

67.   [Hutchings, David.] "Gospel According to Gore." *People* 38, no. 17 (2 November 1992): 103–4.
    Vidal discusses his appearance in the film *Bob Roberts,* contemporary political and social issues, and Ross Perot.

68.   Johnson, Diane. "Gore Vidal, Scorekeeper." *New York Times Book Review* (17 April 1977): 47. In D.15 (extracts).
    Vidal discusses his role as literary critic, the practice of criticism, Oscar Wilde, and "the relation of literature to culture."

69.   Johnson, Reed. "On War and Empire: Vidal Strikes Back." *Los Angeles Times* (1 April 2003): E1, 12.
    Vidal discusses the Iraq war as vindicating his ideas about the American Empire. "I'd say by and large it is not a good thing to mix in the internal affairs of other countries."

70.   Jones, Malcolm. "A Titan Takes the Stage." *Newsweek* 136, no. 13 (25 September 2000): 70.
    Brief interview timed for the opening of the revival of *The Best Man* and the publication of *The Golden Age.* Vidal discusses both works and his writing as a whole.

71.   Kaiser, Robert Blair. "Gore Vidal Is Not Amused." *Playgirl* 2, no. 10 (March 1975): 52–54, 56, 121.
    Vidal discusses Nelson Rockefeller, American politics, college students, pessimism, the "heterosexual dictatorship," love (Vidal doesn't believe in it), and the planned TV movie of *Burr.*

72.   Kakutani, Michiko. "Vidal: 'I'm at the Top of a Very Tiny Heap.'" *New York Times* (12 March 1981): C17.
    Vidal discusses his just-completed novel (*Creation*), the younger generation, the American ruling class, and middlebrow fiction and film.

73.   Katz, Robert. "Gore Goes to War." *American Film* 13, no. 2 (November 1987): 43–46.
    Vidal discusses his suit against the Writers Guild of America over *The Sicilian* and his other work in film.

74.   [Kelley, Ken.] "*Penthouse* Interview: Gore Vidal." *Penthouse* 6, no. 8 (April 1975): 97–98, 104–6.
    Vidal discusses *The City and the Pillar,* John F. Kennedy, running for office, homosexuality, the "tyranny of the female orgasm," psychiatry, his literary reputation, Ralph Nader, Lincoln, sexual fantasies, orgies, and prostitutes.

75.   [Kempton, Beverly.] "Conversation with Gore Vidal." *Oui* 4, no. 4 (April 1975): 72–74, 82, 134–38. In III.D.15 (extracts).
    Vidal discusses his move to Italy, academic writers, *The City and the Pillar,* the "heterosexual dictatorship," *Myra Breckinridge,* American writers, injustice in America, living in Rome, sex, bisexuality, pornography ("it's particularly useful to the young"), Americans vs. Europeans, politics, society, John F. Kennedy, Adlai Stevenson, success and envy, and happiness in life.

76.   Kinsella, Bridget. "The World According to Gore Vidal." *Publishers Weekly* 247, no. 38 (18 September 2000): 28, 30.
    Vidal discusses *The Golden Age, The Best Man,* and Fred Kaplan's biography (which he hasn't read).

77.   Kopkind, Andrew. "The Importance of Being Gore." *Nation* 257, no. 1 (5 July 1993): 16, 18–20.
    Vidal discusses *The City and the Pillar,* homosexuality, and sexuality in his historical novels.

78. Kramer, Larry. "The Sadness of Gore Vidal." *QW* no. 49 (11 October 1992): 26–31, 67–69. *Harper's Magazine* 286, no. 2 (February 1993): 24 (extract; as "Was George Washington Gay?"). In D.14. In I.A.63 (as "The Sadness of Gore Vidal: An Interview").
   Vidal discusses homosexuality and heterosexuality, ACT UP, AIDS, bisexuality, his youth, his new book (*Live from Golgotha*), and the historical novel ("I'm done with it").

78A. Lacayo, Richard. "10 Questions for Gore Vidal." *Time* 168, no. 21 (20 November 2006): 10.
   Vidal discusses being a famous novelist, Johnny Carson, his political views, gay marriage, and the assassination of John F. Kennedy.

79. Lasky, Michael S. "His Workings." *Writer's Digest* 55, no. 3 (March 1975): 20–26. In D.15 (extracts).
   Part of a cover story (see E.139). Vidal discusses his literary career, Tennessee Williams, *The City and the Pillar, Burr,* film adaptations of his works, his revision of his early novels, his work as critic and reviewer, William F. Buckley, political writing, advice to young writers, and his work on *1876.*

80. Leone, Domenica Winda. "Intervista con Gore Vidal." In Roberto Andò and David James. *Il Siciliano nel film di Michael Cimino.* Palermo: Novecento Editrice, 1987.
   In Italian. Vidal discusses his contribution to the film *The Sicilian* (I.E.i.10), for which he was initially denied credit.

81. Levey, Stanley. "Playwright with a Political Perspective." *New York Times* (27 March 1960): Sec. 2, pp. 1, 3.
   Vidal discusses *The Best Man,* soon to open, and the expected declaration of his candidacy for Congress.

82. Lynch, Eamon. "Golf: A Tedious Menace." *Golf Magazine* 46, no. 4 (April 2004): 138.
   Brief responses to queries about golf, including discussions of Eisenhower as a golfer.

83. McGrath, Charles. "Truer Than History." *New York Times Book Review* (1 October 2000): 14.
   Brief interview timed for the publication of *The Golden Age.* Vidal speaks of writing historical novels and of the "hugely expensive" political conventions.

84. McLellan, Joseph. "The World According to Gore." *Washington Post* (4 May 1981): B1, 13.
   Vidal discusses Ronald Reagan the politician and actor, *Creation,* the future of the human race, Confucius, and Abraham Lincoln (who "had syphilis . . . and presumably he gave it to Mary Todd Lincoln").

85. Mallory, Carole. "Mailer and Vidal: The Big Schmooze." *Esquire* 115, no. 5 (May 1991): 105–6, 108–12.
   Interview with both Mailer and Vidal, in which they discuss their own writing, their opinion of each other's work, the Kennedys, their supposed feud, John Cheever, Truman Capote, Tennessee Williams, *The City and the Pillar,* current politics, and warfare.

86. Mann, Roderick. "Gore Vidal: Making an Appearance on the Film Scene." *Los Angeles Times* (18 December 1979): Sec. 5, p. 22.
   Vidal discusses being in Los Angeles after completing the first draft of *Dress Gray* as well as his planned miniseries on Lincoln.

87. ———. "Repartee Laced with a Bit of Gore." *Los Angeles Times* (4 March 1979): Calendar, p. 27.
   Vidal discusses new projects (including *Dress Gray* and *Lincoln,* then conceived as a television miniseries), conversation in Los Angeles, literary feuds, Truman Capote, show business, and politics.

88. ———. "Vidal's Lincoln May Disturb Some." *Los Angeles Times* (18 December 1980): Sec. 6, pp. 2, 9.
   Vidal discusses the filming of *Dress Gray* and his planned miniseries on Lincoln.

89. Martinac, Paula. "Gore in All His Glory." *Lambda Book Report* 8, no. 7 (February 2000): 20–21.
     Vidal discusses reviews of his books, his essays, his favorites among his works, Edmund Morris's *Dutch,* actors as politicians, Al Gore, gay rights, and gay marriage.

90. Maxa, Rudy. "Politics on Wry: Vidal Eyes Senate." *Washington Post Magazine* (18 April 1982): 2.
     Vidal discusses why he is running for the Senate, his wit, raising money, his controversial reputation, and the main issues in the campaign.

91. Mills, Kay. "Gore Vidal: His Life Is an Opened Book." *Los Angeles Times* (15 July 1984): Sec. 8, pp. 1, 10, 11.
     Vidal discusses Abraham and Mary Todd Lincoln, politicians, Ronald Reagan, "university writers," T. P. Gore, and his future books.

92. Mitgang, Herbert. "Gore Vidal." *New York Times Book Review* (18 June 1978): 31.
     Vidal discusses living in Italy, Richard Nixon, *Kalki,* and his new novel-in-progress (*Creation*).

93. ———. "Grandson of a 'Populist Demagogue.'" *New York Times Book Review* (14 June 1987): 42.
     Brief interview timed for the publication of *Empire.*

94. Mitzel, John. "Live from Salerno." *Gay and Lesbian Review Worldwide* 7, no. 1 (Winter 1999–2000): 9–11.
     Vidal discusses Fred Kaplan's biography, his early writing career, Jason Epstein, the current publishing world, John F. Kennedy, Bill Clinton, and contemporary politics.

95. Monmany, Mercedes. "Gore Vidal: Mesías, apóstata ye expiador." *Insula* no. 468 (November 1985): 1, 10.
     Interview in Spanish. Vidal discusses his life in Italy, his admiration of Italo Calvino, his relations with other writers (Anaïs Nin, Paul Bowles, Norman Mailer, Truman Capote), and the writing of his historical novels.

96. Moorehead, Caroline. "The Writer Who Might Have Been President of the United States." *Times* (London) (12 March 1976): 12.
     Vidal discusses his recent works, *Caligula,* American politics, his cold temperament, and his wish to be president.

97. Mulligan, Hugh A. "Gore Vidal Still After Skeletons." *Los Angeles Times* (3 July 1980): Sec. 5, p. 11.
     Vidal discusses his planned six-part TV miniseries on Lincoln, *Dress Gray,* living in Italy, his running for office in 1960, and his literary feuds.

98. Neilson, Heather. "Encountering Gore Vidal." *Antithesis* 1, no. 2 (1987): 41–58.
     Vidal discusses his historical novels, his "inventions," *Lincoln,* his essays, *Messiah,* his role as "a Puritan moralist," Nathaniel Hawthorne, classical literature, Milton, Flaubert, Italo Calvino, literary criticism, Jack Kerouac, canonicity, *Duluth,* his political campaigns, and his recent work in television.

99. [Oakes, Philip.] "Tiding of Bad Cheer." *Sunday Times* (London) (14 December 1975): 32.
     Vidal discusses Caligula as an historical figure, the film *Caligula,* his bleak outlook, and his passion for American history.

100. Oliansky, Joel. "What Are Television Writers Made Of? Gore Vidal Tells of the Trials, Tribulations and Pleasures of Writing for TV." *Intro Bulletin* 2, no. 1 (1957): 1, 8.
     Vidal discusses his work for television.

101. Parini, Jay. "An Interview with Gore Vidal." *New England Review* 14, no. 1 (Fall 1991): 93–101. In D.13. In D.14.

Vidal discusses criticism about him, his two different kinds of novels, satire, his readings, his work in television, his popularity, American novelists, movies, his historical novels, his early works, his research on his historical novels, Italo Calvino, his essays, and the future of American writing.

102. Peck, Abe. "Vidal Created a Cult Hero—and Then Along Came Jones." *Feature* no. 95 (April 1979): 18.

Vidal discusses the parallels between *Kalki* and the mass suicides at Jonestown. He notes other cults as emblematic of cultural backsliding.

103. Pepper, Curtis Bill. "The Truth about Gore Vidal—Right from Gore Vidal." *Vogue* 164, no. 6 (December 1974): 176–79, 211. In III.D.15 (extracts).

Vidal discusses American writers living abroad, his partner Howard Austen, his work habits, the purpose of art, his relations to Anaïs Nin, and love.

104. PHS. "The Times Diary: Gore Vidal Attacks W. H. Smith." *Times* (London) (4 March 1970): 10.

Vidal discusses the partial ban of *Myra Breckinridge* in the UK by the book chain W. H. Smith.

105. Pilcher, Joseph. "His Work Habits." *Writer's Digest* 55, no. 3 (March 1975): 17–19.

Part of a cover story (see E.139). Vidal discusses his work habits, his early literary career, the "new journalism," and advice to young writers.

106. Pooter [*pseud.*]. "Vidal on Mailer on Vidal." *Times* (London) (21 September 1968): 21.

Vidal discusses the upcoming election ("Nixon will win"), and Norman Mailer. There is a brief interview of Mailer also.

107. Rosenfield, Paul. "A Literary Lancer Returns to the Lists." *Los Angeles Times Book Review* (30 April 1978): 3, 13.

Interview timed for the release of *Kalki*. Vidal discusses reviews of that book, American society, Los Angeles and its people, filmmakers, American history, his early writings, and retirement.

108. Ross, Jean W. [Interview.] In Linda Metzger, ed. *Contemporary Authors*. New Revision Series, Vol. 13. Detroit: Gale Research Co., 1984, pp. 503–6.

Vidal discusses *Williwaw, The City and the Pillar*, his Edgar Box novels, researching his historical novels, his knowledge of languages, book reviewing, contemporary writers, and modern culture.

109. Ruas, Charles. "Gore Vidal." In Ruas's *Conversations with American Writers*. New York: Knopf, 1985, pp. 57–74. In D.14.

Vidal discusses American history, his childhood, his early writing, his running for office, his celebrity, Tennessee Williams, *The City and the Pillar*, Anaïs Nin, his Edgar Box novels, American writers (including Henry James, Hawthorne, and Faulkner), films, whether his imagination is verbal or visual, and the possibility of writing an autobiography.

110. Saint-Phalle, Thérèse de. "Un Ermite aux allures de playboy." *Revue de Paris* 73 (July–August 1966): 147–50.

In French. Vidal discusses his early novels, his dichotomy between literature and politics, his lack of belief in God, and *Julian*.

111. Sanoff, Alvin P. "The Rise and Fall of the American Empire." *U.S. News and World Report* 103, no. 2 (13 July 1987): 62.

Vidal discusses his new book, *Empire*, his research on his historical novels, and a future work tentatively called *Harding* (i.e., *Hollywood*).

112. Scheer, Robert. "Gore Vidal: Novelist of U.S. Sees an Empire Replacing Republic He So Admired." *Los Angeles Times* (15 December 1991): M3.

    Vidal discusses the Bill of Rights, the Founding Fathers, the future of the Constitution, the melting pot, and the year 1950.

113. Scobie, W. I. "The Judgment of Vidal." *Advocate* no. 211 (9 March 1977): 24–27.

    Vidal discusses Jimmy Carter, Richard Nixon, *Caligula,* working in film, *Ben-Hur,* bisexuality, *The City and the Pillar,* Anaïs Nin, Tennessee Williams, Christopher Isherwood, Alfred Kinsey, Cardinal Spellman, and his historical novels.

114. ———. "Senator Vidal?" *Advocate* no. 337 (4 March 1982): 27–30.

    Vidal discusses his running for the Senate, his World War II experiences, his popularity among the young (he feels he has none), bisexuality, Ronald Reagan, Truman Capote, Tennessee Williams, Christianity, defense spending, the next war, the new administration, taxing religions, and government spending.

115. Segell, Michael. "Low Blows against the Empire: The Highbrow Railings of Gore Vidal, America's Most Irreverent Man of Letters." *Rolling Stone* no. 317 (15 May 1980): 40–43.

    Vidal discusses films (including his work on *Caligula*), television, Ronald Reagan (who "has no chance of being elected president"), third-party candidates (including John Anderson), legalization of drugs, and his litigation with William F. Buckley and Truman Capote.

116. Sheahan, Denis. "Gore Vidal . . . Talking Up a Storm." *Chicago Tribune* (9 January 1972): Sec. 5, p. 9.

    Vidal discusses his interest in politics, William F. Buckley, John Simon, *An Evening with Richard Nixon,* American youth, Norman Mailer, his reading habits, and his income.

117. Shenker, Israel. "Portrait of a Man Reading XIX: Gore Vidal." *Washington Post Book World* (4 August 1968): 2. In Shenker's *Words and Their Makers.* Garden City, NY: Doubleday, 1974, pp. 271–76. In D.15 (extracts).

    Vidal discusses his readings, Flaubert, Nabokov, John Horne Burns, Malcolm Lowry, and the "new novel."

118. Shepard, Richard F. "What Makes a Television Play?" *New York Times* (17 June 1956): Sec. II, p. 11.

    Vidal discusses the writing of television plays and the theater.

119. Shipman, Tim. "Gore Vidal." *Sunday Express* (London) (2 February 2003): 47.

    Vidal discusses the Iraq war, the British Left, and the collapse of the American Empire.

120. Shuster, Alvin. "Gore Vidal Loses Weight But Gains a New Novel." *New York Times* (24 February 1976): 30. In D.15 (extracts).

    Vidal discusses losing weight while in Miami, his research for his books, *1876,* and the future of America.

121. Smith, Margaret. "Gore Vidal and Hollywood." *Cinema Papers* no. 115 (April 1997): 4.

    Vidal discusses his attitude to Hollywood, Ronald Reagan as an actor, Bill Clinton, screenwriting, acting, and John F. Kennedy's assassination.

122. Smith, Richard. "An Unprincipled Interview with Gore Vidal." *Harvard Advocate* 109, no. 5 (April 1976): 20–25.

    Vidal discusses his upbringing and education, homosexuality and heterosexuality, *Myron,* religion, current political figures, the Kennedys, Nixon, *Myra Breckinridge,* and Truman Capote.

123. Solomon, Andrew. "Gore Vidal Receives a Visitor." *New York Times Magazine* (15 October 1995): 40–43.

    Extensive interview following the publication of *Palimpsest.* Vidal discusses John F. Kennedy, the American ruling class, his mimicry, Truman Capote, Greta Garbo, Norman Mailer, *The City and the Pillar,* sex, Jimmie Trimble, François Mitterand, and writing.

124. Stabnikov, Vladimir. "'We Enter a Change of the Weather.'" *Soviet Literature* no. 472 ([July] 1987): 112–14.

> Vidal discusses his views of Russian literature, changes in the Soviet Union between his first visit (1982) and his second (1987), and his impressions of the Moscow Forum "For a Nuclear-Free World, for the Survival of Mankind."

125. Suplee, Curt. "Gore Vidal, into the Fray Again." *Washington Post* (4 July 1984): C1, 4.

> Vidal discusses the controversy among historians caused by *Lincoln,* John Updike, his research on *Lincoln,* American political history, the need for reform, his return to Washington, D.C., his upbringing and education, contemporary literature, and Jonathan Swift.

125A. Svetkey, Benjamin. "Vidal's Last Stand." *Entertainment Weekly* no. 906 (10 November 2006): 46.

> Vidal discusses his new memoir, *Point to Point Navigation,* his literary habits, his move from Ravello, his celebrity, and George W. Bush.

125B. Taylor, Alan. "The World According to Gore: Alan Taylor Talks to a Literary Legend." *Sunday Herald* (Sydney) (12 November 2006): 12.

> Vidal discusses the Iraq war, the U.S. media, Howard Austen, and the assassination of John F. Kennedy.

126. Taylor, Clarke. "The State of Politics Vidal-Style." *Los Angeles Times* (7 October 1987): Sec. 6, pp. 1. 4.

> Vidal discusses a revival of *The Best Man* in Los Angeles and his writing of the play, a draft of which he showed to John F. and Jackie Kennedy.

127. Trueheart, Charles. "Vidal, with a Vengeance." *Washington Post* (21 June 1987): F1, 6.

> Vidal discusses the end of the American empire, the Iran-contra affair, his controversy with Norman Podhoretz and Midge Decter, his running for office, American presidents, journalists (including Tom Brokaw), and his future novels (*Hollywood* and *The Golden Age*).

128. Van Vooren, [Monique]. "Vidal." *Andy Warhol's Interview* 5, no. 4 (April 1976): 10–12. In D.15 (extracts).

> Vidal discusses his political ambitions, research for his novels, America vs. Europe, contemporary politics, American newspapers, Italo Calvino, Italy, cynicism, aging, Truman Capote, *Caligula,* Paul Newman, John Simon, films, television, bisexuality, and marriage.

129. [Vidal, Gore.] "Vidal to Vidal: On Misusing the Past." *Harper's Magazine* 231, no. 4 (October 1965): 162–64. In D.15 (extracts).

> Vidal interviews himself about the writing of *Julian.*

130. [Vidal, Gore.] "A Conversation with Myself." *Book-of-the-Month Club News* (November 1973): 4–5, 24. A.33. In D.15 (extracts).

> Vidal interviews himself about the writing of *Burr* and American history.

131. Villien, B. "Gore Vidal." *Cinematographe* no. 96 (January 1984): 46–50.

> Not seen.

132. Walker, Gerald. "Interview: Gore Vidal." *Writer's Year Book* no. 36 (1965): 63–67, 134.

> Vidal discusses his early work, his work in television and film, his writing habits, *The City and the Pillar, Julian,* a new play (*A Drawing Room Comedy*), contemporary writers, the Kennedys, Norman Mailer, sex, and his plays.

133. Walsh, Barbara. "Vidal on His Love Affair with Ravello." *Times* (London) (13 May 1988): 34.

> Vidal tells of his fascination with the Italian village. Historical background on the village is provided.

134. Walter, Eugene. "Conversations with Gore Vidal." *Transatlantic Review* no. 4 (Summer 1960): 5–17. In Joseph F. McCrindle, ed. *Behind the Scenes: Theater and Film Interviews*

from the Transatlantic Review. New York: Holt, Rinehart & Winston, 1971, pp. 327–41. In D.14. In D.15 (extracts).

Vidal discusses his youth, his early writing, *The City and the Pillar,* his preference for novels over plays, his interest in politics and religion, his work habits, and the state of the novel.

135. Weeks, Linton. "Coming Soon, Epilogue by Gore Vidal." *Washington Post* (7 May 2001): C1, 14.

Vidal discusses Timothy McVeigh and his own relations with McVeigh.

136. Wicker, Tom. "MM Interview: Gore Vidal." *Modern Maturity* 37, no. 2 (April–May 1994): 62–64, 66, 68, 70.

Vidal discusses modern art and literature, education, the lack of good readers, sex, religion, contemporary politics, what Vidal would have done if he had become president, and the national security state.

137. Wiener, Jon. "The Scholar Squirrels and the National Security State: An Interview with Gore Vidal." *Radical History Review* no. 44 (April 1989): 109–37. *Harper's Magazine* 278, no. 3 (March 1989): 24 (extract; as "Casting Presidents"). In D.14.

Vidal discusses Americans' knowledge of history, historical scholarship, T. P. Gore, his youthful politics, his early writings, his 1960 campaign, the year 1968, Lincoln, slavery, Norman Podhoretz, John F. Kennedy and Vietnam, the national security state, intellectuals, the "golden age" of 1945–1950, and Ronald Reagan.

138. Williams, Christian. "Pilgrim with a Grenade." *Washington Post* (5 April 1978): B1, 5.

Vidal discusses his feud with Norman Mailer, his work in television and film, his plays, actors (including Marlon Brando and Alec Guinness), and his new novel, *Kalki.*

139. [Windham, Donald.] "Vidal." *New Yorker* 36, no. 10 (23 April 1960): 38–39.

Vidal discusses running for office and the important issues in the campaign.

140. Wright, Colin. "Tug of War." *New Statesman and Society* 2 (no. 74) (3 November 1989): 43–44.

Vidal discusses *Hollywood,* American politicians, the 1992 election, and living in Italy.

141. [Unsigned.] "Outsider: American." *Observer* (London) no. 9042 (18 October 1964): 23.

Interview timed to coincide with the British release of *Julian.* Vidal discusses his earlier career as a novelist and playwright. "I'm awfully American . . . I go abroad to keep my blood pressure down."

142. [Unsigned.] "L'Écrivain et la politique—une interview de Gore Vidal." *Informations et Documents* 234 (1 December 1966): 42–47.

In French. Vidal discusses writing, politics, and the differences between French and American attitudes on these issues.

143. [Unsigned.] "Great Gore." *Listener* 80 (no. 2063) (10 October 1968): 471.

Vidal discusses Americans, politicians (including Eugene McCarthy), and the Kennedys.

144. [Unsigned.] "*Playboy* Interview: Gore Vidal." *Playboy* 16, no. 6 (June 1969): 77–80, 82, 84, 86, 90, 92–93, 96, 238. In D.15 (extracts).

Extensive interview in which Vidal discusses the Nixon administration, the Vietnam War, liberalism, violence in the United States, the presidential debates, political reform, overpopulation, the family, "the people," Eugene McCarthy, Robert F. Kennedy, the assassination of John F. Kennedy, the Kennedy administration, Edward Kennedy, money and politics, Lyndon Baines Johnson, Eisenhower, legalization of marijuana, *Myra Breckinridge,* homosexuality, *The City and the Pillar,* Norman Mailer, writers and politics, Truman Capote, *Julian,* and his temperament.

145.   [Unsigned.] "*Playboy* Interview Gore Vidal." *Playboy* 34, no. 12 (December 1987): 51–53,
       56–60, 62, 64–66, 68, 72–74.
           Unprecedented second interview in *Playboy,* in which Vidal discusses Ronald Reagan, the Iran-
       contra affair, Oliver North, George Bush, Gary Hart, John F. Kennedy, the American ruling
       class, the Soviet Union, Latin America, Lyndon Baines Johnson, the Vietnam War, his 1960
       campaign, Jackie Kennedy, education, world politics, Israel, Gorbachev, population,
       pornography, AIDS, his health and sexuality, reading, his novels vs. his essays, Truman Capote,
       Saul Bellow, Voltaire, and being an expatriate.

146.   [Unsigned.] "Gore Vidal." *Vanity Fair* 57, no. 4 (October 1994): 276.
           Vidal's one-sentence replies to a series of personal questions.

147.   [Unsigned.] "New World Ordure." *Observer* (25 January 1998): 26.
           Vidal discusses the sexual peccadilloes of Bill Clinton and the attempts by right-wingers to
       destroy him.

D. Books about Vidal

1. Altman, Dennis. *Gore Vidal's America.* Cambridge, MA: Polity, 2005.
   Reviews:
   a. Danchev, Alex. "He's a Genius—He Says So Himself." *Times Higher Education Supplement* no. 1747 (16 June 2006): 29.
   b. Polchin, James. "America's Gore Vidal." *Gay and Lesbian Review Worldwide* 13, no. 6 (November–December 2006): 34–35.
      Chiefly designed as a guide to Vidal's thought, especially in the areas of sexuality, religion, American history and imperialism, and the like. Some celebrated aspects of Vidal's life and career (e.g., his notorious debate with William F. Buckley) get very short shrift. Altman sees Vidal as an iconoclast who is deliberately attempting to subvert American "triumphalism."

2. Baker, Susan, and Curtis S. Gibson. *Gore Vidal: A Critical Companion.* Westport, CT: Greenwood Press, 1997.
   Reviews:
   a. Murray, Pius. *Catholic Library World* 68, no. 2 (December 1997): 77–78.
   b. [Unsigned.] *AB Bookman's Weekly* 99, no. 21 (26 May 1997): 1704, 1706.
      The book, part of a series of "critical companions," contains a brief chapter on Vidal's life, a discussion of his early novels, then separate chapters on the major historical novels and on Vidal's "inventions." The analysis combines plot summary with a variety of critical approaches, including feminist, new historicist, psychoanalytic, etc.

3. Behrendt, Jörg. *Homosexuality in the Work of Gore Vidal.* Münster: Lit, 2002.
   Somewhat dry and mechanical study of Vidal's attitudes toward homosexuality, examining statements on the subject in his essays and interviews and tracing the theme in his novels, especially *The City and the Pillar, Two Sisters, Myra Breckinridge/Myron,* and *In a Yellow Wood.* Behrendt concludes that, by "denying homosexual identity, Vidal stands diametrically opposed to most homosexual writers, fictional and non-fictional alike."

4. Bensoussan, Nicole. *Gore Vidal, l'iconoclaste.* Nanterre, France: Publidix/Université Paris X-Nanterre, 1997.
   A revision of her dissertation (see I.2). A study of Vidal's political, social, and religious thought as expressed in both his essays and his novels. The main focus is on Vidal's views on homosexuality, on the founding fathers, and on a "decadent" American society.

5. Dick, Bernard F. *The Apostate Angel: A Critical Study of Gore Vidal.* New York: Random House, 1974.
   Reviews:
   a. Detweiler, Robert. "Recent Books on Modern Fiction." *Modern Fiction Studies* 21, no. 2 (Summer 1975): 291–92.
   b. Jones, Arthur E., Jr. *Library Journal* 99, no. 9 (1 May 1974): 1302.
   c. [Unsigned.] *Booklist* 70, no. 18 (15 May 1974): 1027.
   d. [Unsigned.] *Choice* 11, nos. 5–6 (July–August 1974): 756–57.
   e. [Unsigned.] *Kirkus Reviews* 42, no. 6 (15 March 1974): 339.
   f. [Unsigned.] *Publishers Weekly* 205, no. 12 (25 March 1974): 53.
      A book based on extensive interviews, but a poorly conceived bio-critical study that proceeds chronologically over Vidal's career and provides lengthy plot summaries of his novels up to *Burr.*

6. Frank, Marcie. *How to Be an Intellectual in the Age of TV: The Lessons of Gore Vidal.* Durham, NC: Duke University Press, 2005.
    Slim monograph studying Vidal's use of television to establish himself in the public eye as a contrarian intellectual, including Vidal's contretemps with Norman Mailer on "The Dick Cavett Show," the use of media in Vidal's novels, and Vidal's promotion of sexual freedom.

7. Harris, Stephen. *The Fiction of Gore Vidal and E. L. Doctorow: Writing the Historical Self.* Bern: Peter Lang, 2002.
    Study of Vidal's historical novels as compared to those of E. L. Doctorow, including an extensive section on *Burr.* "It is a meausre of Vidal's success in his portrayal of Burr that he retains his importance in terms of the actual drama of the narrative despite the doubt he inspires."

8. ———. *Gore Vidal's Historical Novels and the Shaping of American Political Consciousness.* Preface by Heather Neilson. Lewiston, NY: Edwin Mellen Press, 2005.
    Philosophical study addressing Vidal's skepticism in regard to the understanding of history and tracing this element through his historical novels, especially *Burr* and *1876.*

9. *An Integrated Teaching Unit on Gore Vidal's* Visit to a Small Planet *Developed at Purdue University.* Skokie, IL: National Textbook Co., 1972.
    Not seen.

10. Kaplan, Fred. *Gore Vidal: A Biography.* New York: Doubleday, 1999. London: Bloomsbury, 1999. New York: Anchor Books, 2000.
    Reviews:
    a. Biswell, Andrew. "Gay Pride." *New Statesman* 128 (1 November 1999): 58.
    b. Clark, Alex. "Pick of the Week." *Sunday Times* (London) (19 November 2000): Sec. 9, p. 54.
    c. Davenport-Hines, Richard. "Glasses Tinkled, Facts Mangled." *Times Literary Supplement* no. 5067 (12 May 2000): 18.
    d. Deresiewicz, William. "His Cigar Is Just a Cigar." *New York Times Book Review* (14 November 1999): 42.
    e. Dyer, Richard. "A Writer's Rich Life, Under a Haystack of Detail." *Boston Globe* (10 November 1999): F7.
    f. Eder, Richard. "The Long and Short of an Author's Life." *New York Times* (15 October 1999): E47.
    g. Greig, Geordie. "Just Adore Gore." *Times* (London) (14 October 1999): 44.
    h. Henderson, David W. *Library Journal* 124, no. 17 (15 October 2000): 71.
    i. Hooper, Brad. *Booklist* 96, no. 2 (15 September 1999): 196.
    j. Keates, Jonathan. "Easy Rider along the Glamour Trail." *Spectator* 283 (no. 8937) (20 November 1999): 57.
    k. Leckie, Ross. "New Non-fiction." *Times* (London) (11 November 2000): Play, p. 21.
    l. Mackinnon, Lachlan. "Come On, Let's Have All the Gorey Details." *Observer* (London) (7 November 1999): Review, p. 12.
    m. Marks, Jim. "Favored Grandson." *Lambda Book Report* 8, no. 7 (February 2000): 18–19.
    n. Marler, Regina. "An American Institution." *Los Angeles Times Book Review* (7 November 1999): 1, 2.
    o. Meyers, Jeffrey. "Fighting, Fornication and Fiction." *Times Higher Education Supplement* no. 1437 (26 May 2000): 29.
    p. Miller, Karl. "A Dance Round the Totem Pole: Gore Vidal and Other Stories." *Raritan* 20, no. 1 (Summer 2000): 43–54 (esp. 43–50).
    q. Pela, Robert L. "Veni, Vidi, Vidal." *Advocate* (9 November 1999): 102.
    r. Perry, Jane. "Paperbacks." *Observer* (London) (15 October 2000): 14.
    s. Raphael, Frederic. "Cross Him If You Dare." *Sunday Times* (London) (17 October 1999): Sec. 9, pp. 34–35.

t.   Rigelhof, T. F. "Vidal Statistics." *Globe and Mail* (Toronto) (20 December 1999): D12.

u.   Rorem, Ned. "The Sage of Ravello." *Washington Post Book World* (21 November 1999): 1, 3.

v.   Rubin, Martin. "Life Story of Writer and Gadfly Whom We Have Met Before." *Washington Times* (7 November 1999): B8.

w.   Sheiner, Marcy. *Book* no. 7 (November–December 1999): 79.

x.   Smith, Patrick. "'Our' Gide?" *Nation* 269, no. 20 (13 December 1999): 22–25.

y.   Wallace, Jennifer. "The Lives and Loves of the Ubiquitous Gore Vidal." *Times Higher Education Supplement* no. 1423 (18 February 2000): 18–19.

z.   [Unsigned.] *Kirkus Reviews* 67 (15 September 1999): 1472.

aa.   [Unsigned.] "Comeback Kid." *Economist* no. 8149 (11 December 1999): 78.

bb.   [Unsigned.] "Paperbacks." *Observer* (London) (15 October 2000): Review, p. 14.

cc.   [Unsigned.] *Publishers Weekly* 246, no. 43 (25 October 1999): 65–66.

        Exhaustive biography, the product of years of research (undertaken only after Walter Clemons, previously named Vidal's biographer, died before even beginning the work after years of research). Vidal's early life, and his relations with both his grandfather (T. P. Gore) and his mother, are discussed in detail, as is his early literary career; but later portions tend to be sketchy. Vidal's own views of the work are mixed (see C.62, 94).

11.   Kiernan, Robert F. *Gore Vidal.* New York: Frederick Ungar Publishing Co., 1982. Tr. as *El mundo de Gore Vidal.* Trans. Luz del Carmen Rodriguez Martínez and Elisa Moreno C.; revised by Enrique Diaz Montes. Mexico City: Noema Editores, 1984.

     Reviews:

a.   Dick, B[ernard] F. *World Literature Today* 57, no. 2 (Spring 1983): 296.

b.   Guzlowski, John E. *Modern Fiction Studies* 29, no. 4 (Winter 1983): 737–41 (esp. 740).

c.   Pavese, Michael. *Best Sellers* 42, no. 6 (September 1982): 246–47.

d.   [Unsigned.] *Booklist* 78, no. 16 (15 April 1982): 1060.

e.   [Unsigned.] *Choice* 21, no. 5 (January 1984): 705–6.

        Routine study of Vidal's life and a survey of his major works, including *The Judgment of Paris, Two Sisters, Kalki, Williwaw, The City and the Pillar, Julian, Creation, Washington, D.C., 1876,* and *Myra Breckinridge/Myron.* Vidal's essays and "minor works" are also dealt with. "The great charm of Vidal's writing is its auctorial audacity."

12.   Mitzel, John, and Steven Abbott. *Myra and Gore: A New View of* Myra Breckinridge *and a Candid Interview with Gore Vidal; a Book for Vidalophiles.* Dorchester, MA: Manifest Destiny Books, 1974.

        Contents: John Mitzel[, Steven Abbott, and Gay Study Group], "Patriarchy vs. 'Pornography': Some Notes on Myra B." (E.222) (5–44); John Wieners, "Three Carols for Myra Breckinridge" (45–48); John Mitzel and Steven Abbott, "An Interview with Gore Vidal" (C.1) (51–90). Small-press publication. Wieners's contribution is a series of poems inspired by *Myra Breckinridge.*

13.   Parini, Jay, ed. *Gore Vidal: Writer against the Grain.* New York: Columbia University Press, 1992.

        Contents: "Gore Vidal: A Chronology of His Works" (vii–viii); Jay Parini, "Gore Vidal: The Writer and His Critics" (1–30); Italo Calvino, "Imagining Vidal" (E.56) (31–36); David Price, "*Williwaw:* Gore Vidal's First Novel" (37–55); Claude J. Summers, "*The City and the Pillar* as Gay Fiction" (56–75); "Bernard F. Dick, "Gore Vidal: The Entertainer" (extract from D.5) (76–84); Robert F. Kiernan, "The Vidalian Manner: *The Judgment of Paris, Two Sisters, Kalki*" (extract from D.11) (85–101); Alan Cheuse, "A Note on Vidal's *Messiah*" (102–5); Heather Neilson, "The Fiction of History in Gore Vidal's *Messiah*" (extract from I.10) (106–19); Ray Lewis White, "Vidal as Playwright: In Gentlest Heresy" (extract from D.16) (120–36); William H. Pritchard, "Vidal's Satiric Voices" (137–46); Samuel F. Pickering, "Living Appropriately: Vidal and the Essay" (146–57); Robert Boyers, "On Gore Vidal: Wit and the Work of Criticism" (158–70); Thomas M. Disch, "Vidal as Essayist: The Man Who Has Everything" (F.37.e) (171–

74); Stephen Spender, "Gore Vidal: Private Eye" (F.29.m) (175–82); Catharine R. Stimpson, "My O My O Myra" (E.282) (183–98); James Tatum, "The *Romanitas* of Gore Vidal" (E.286) (199–220); Harold Bloom, "The Central Man: On Gore Vidal's *Lincoln*" (F.39.c); (221–29); Richard Poirier, "Vidal's *Empire*" (F.42.y) (239–36); Louis Auchincloss, "Babylon Revisited" (F.45.a) (239–46); Donald E. Pease, "America and the Vidal Chronicles" (247–77); Jay Parini, "An Interview with Gore Vidal" (C.101) (278–90); "Notes" (291–306); "Selected Bibliography" (307–10); "Contributors" (311–13); "Index" (315–21).

Reviews:
a.   Corber, Robert J. *Modern Fiction Studies* 40, no. 2 (Summer 1994): 377–78.
b.   Cumming, Laura. "The Gospel According to Gore Vidal." *Manchester Guardian Weekly* 147, no. 17 (25 October 1992): 25.
c.   Cummings, Katherine. *Australian Book Review* no. 150 (May 1993): 53–54.
d.   LaHood, Marvin J. *World Literature Today* 70, no. 1 (Winter 1996): 191–92.
e.   Moran, Joe. *Journal of American Studies* 30, no. 1 (April 1996): 160–61.
f.   Sage, Lorna. "Carnival at the Cross." *Observer* (London) no. 10485 (27 September 1992): 50.
g.   Taylor, Robert. "Gorefoolery." *Boston Globe* (6 September 1992): A10.
h.   [Unsigned.] *American Literature* 65, no. 2 (June 1993): 402.
i.   [Unsigned.] *Lambda Book Report* 3, no. 6 (September–October 1992): 46.
     A substantial collection of essays and reviews, some original and some reprinted. Of the original contributions, Parini's introduction is an overview of Vidal's life and career and an attempt to justify his rank as a major American writer. Price writes a detailed study of *Williwaw*, quoting from it extensively and concluding that it is "a candid, revealing, provocative, and psychologically realistic novel." Cheuse writes a brief essay on *Messiah*, concluding that it is "an authentic American novel of ideas using the genre of science fiction to achieve its ends." Pritchard studies the varieties of satiric voices in Vidal's novels and essays. Pickering analyzes Vidal's essays, both as to style and as to substance. Boyers studies the element of criticism in both novels and essays, focusing on Vidal's portrait of American culture. Pease studies Vidal's historical novels from *Julian* to *Lincoln*, with some discussion of earlier works, stating that these novels "undermine the assumptions constructive of Literature as a discipline separable from History."

14.   Peabody, Richard, and Lucinda Ebersole, [ed.]. *Conversations with Gore Vidal.* Jackson: University Press of Mississippi, 2005.
      Contents: Peabody and Ebersole, "Introduction" (xi–xvii); "Chronology" (xix–xxiv); Eugene Walter, "Conversations with Gore Vidal" (C.134) (3–15); John Mitzel and Steve Abbott, "Gore Vidal: The *Fag Rag* Interview" (C.1) (16–35); Gerald Clarke, "The Art of Fiction L: Gore Vidal" (C.30) (36–59); Hollis Alpert, "Dialogue on Film: Gore Vidal" (C.6) (60–84); Charles Ruas, "Gore Vidal" (C.109) (85–99); Jon Wiener, "The Scholar Squirrels and the National Security Scare [*sic*]: An Interview with Gore Vidal" (C.137) (100–126); Jay Parini, "An Interview with Gore Vidal" (C.101) (127–38); Harry Kloman, "An Interview with Gore Vidal" (139–55); Larry Kramer, "The Sadness of Gore Vidal" (C.78) (156–72); Richard Abowitz, "America's Biographer: Interview with Gore Vidal" (C.3) (173–87); "Index" (189–96).

Reviews:
a.   Nickels, Thom. "When Vidal Spoke, People Taped." *Gay and Lesbian Review Worldwide* 12, no. 6 (November–December 2005): 37–38.
     Anthology of previously published interviews. The Kloman interview is from his website (H.1).

15.   Stanton, Robert J., ed. *Views from a Window: Conversations with Gore Vidal.* Secaucus, NJ: Lyle Stuart, 1980. Tr. by Horacio Vázquez Rial as *Conversaciones con Gore Vidal.* Barcelona: Edhasa, 1983. Tr. by Gérard Joulié as *Artistes et barbares: Entretiens.* Lausanne: L'Age d'Homme, 1985.
      Contents: Excerpts from interviews: Eugene Walter (C.134); Steven Abbott and John Mitzel (C.1); Beverly Kempton (C.75); Hollis Alpert (C.6); Jacob Epstein (C.47); Alvin Shuster (C.120); Monique Van Vooren (C.128); Arthur Cooper (C.33); [Unsigned (*Playboy*)] (C.144); Curtis Bill Pepper (C.103); Gerald Clarke (C.30); Joseph S. Coyle (C.36); Michael S. Lasky (C.79); Israel Shenker (C.117); Eve Auchincloss and Nancy Lynch (C.12); Michael Dean (C.38);

Gore Vidal (C.129); Gore Vidal (C.130); Daniel Halpern (C.56); Diane Johnson (C.68); Dennis Altman (C.7); Richard Grenier (C.53); Michael Dean (C.39). Also includes excerpts from unpublished correspondence between Vidal and Judy Halfpenny and a succession of unpublished interviews with Robert J. Stanton from 1977 to 1979.

Reviews:

a. Dirda, Michael. "Pros of Prose: Gore Vidal, Edmund Wilson, Peter Quennell." *Washington Post Book World* (18 January 1981): 3. *Guardian Weekly* 124, no. 15 (12 April 1981): 18.

b. Doyle, P. A. *Best Sellers* 40, no. 9 (December 1980): 338–39.

c. Jacoby, Susan. "Nonfiction in Brief." *New York Times Book Review* (21 December 1980): 12.

d. Mitchel, Duncan. "The Searchlight of Passionate Interests." *Gay Community News* no. 37 (11 April 1981): 2.

e. Rechy, John. "20 Years of Gore Vidal: A Candidate for Canonization?" *Los Angeles Times Book Review* (21 December 1980): 10.

f. Rovit, Earl. *Library Journal* 106, no. 3 (1 February 1981): 356.

g. [Unsigned.] *Booklist* 77, no. 4 (15 October 1980): 287.
A skillful stitching together of many of the interviews that Vidal had given up to this time, arranged by categories (e.g., politics, sexuality, art and literature), to present a kind of running conversation with Vidal on a wide array of subjects, including his own work.

16. White, Ray Lewis. *Gore Vidal.* New York: Twayne, 1968.
Reviews:

a. Vidal, Gore. "The Subject Doesn't Object." *New York Times Book Review* (1 September 1968): 1, 19. [See I.C.74.]

b. Waldmeir, Joseph. "Recent Books on Modern Fiction: American." *Modern Fiction Studies* 15, No. 2 (Summer 1969): 270–80.

c. [Unsigned.] *Choice* 6, nos. 5–6 (July–August 1969): 649–50.
First book-length study of Vidal, with an introductory biographical chapter followed by a discussion of his works, arranged largely biographically. "Vidal speaks as the voice of involvement to his age." Vidal's own review of the book is surprisingly charitable.

E. Criticism in Books and Periodicals

1. Abbott, Steven, and Thom Willenbecher. "Myra, Myron and Gore." *New York Review of Books* 22, no. 1 (6 February 1975): 38.
   Letters on Mazzocco's review of *Myron* (F.31.q), finding the novel "a sustained satirical performance."

2. Abrams, Floyd; Paul M. Weyrich; Evans Chan; and Arthur Herzberg. "Exchange." *Nation* 242, no. 18 (3 May 1986): 602, 628.
   More letters commenting on "The Empire Lovers Strike Back" (I.C.162.a); for an earlier batch of letters, see item 299 below. For Vidal's response, see I.F.27.

3. Acton, Harold. *More Memoirs of an Aesthete.* London: Methuen, 1970; New York: Viking Press, 1971 (as *Memoirs of an Aesthete 1939–1969*), pp. 211–12.
   Brief discussion of Acton's meeting Vidal, Tennessee Williams, and Frederick Prokosch in Rome.

4. Adams, Jon Robert. "'The Great General Was a Has-Been': Homoerotic Re-definitions of Masculinity in 1950s Conformist Culture." *Huntington Gay Men's Fiction Quarterly* 6, no. 3 (2004): 115–35.
   Part of the article discusses *The City and the Pillar* in the context of other novels of the 1950s; these novels "reflect the apprehension of a culture at war with itself over definitions of masculinity."

5. Adelman, Larry, and Arthur Schlesinger Jr. "Out of the Dustbin, into the Fire." *Nation* 263, no. 16 (18 November 1996): 2.
   Letters commenting on "The End of History" (I.C.232.a). For Vidal's response see I.F.40.

6. Aldridge, John W. *After the Lost Generation: A Critical Study of the Writers of Two Wars.* New York: McGraw-Hill Book Co., 1951; New York: Noonday Press, 1958, pp. 89, 99–101, 103, 133, 163, 170–84, 240, 251, 253, 256.
   Important early discussion of Vidal. Aldridge refers to *The City and the Pillar* as "purely a social document." The chapter on Vidal ("Gore Vidal: The Search for a King," 170–84) gives an overview of the novels from *Williwaw* to *A Search for the King.* He concludes that Vidal, like his characters, is still searching for a "center of life."

7. ———. "America's Young Novelists: Uneasy Inheritors of a Revolution." *Saturday Review of Literature* 32, no. 7 (12 February 1949): 6–8, 36–37, 42.
   Discussion of *Williwaw, In a Yellow Wood,* and *The City and the Pillar,* praising all three novels.

8. ———. Letter to the Editor. *New York Times Book Review* (2 September 1962): 15.
   Long reply to Vidal's letter (I.F.2) commenting on "What Became of Our Postwar Hopes?" (item 10 below).

9. ———. "The New Generation of Writers: With Some Reflections on the Older Ones." *Harper's Magazine* 195, no. 5 (November 1947): 423–32.
   Brief discussion of *In a Yellow Wood* (431–32).

10. ———. "What Became of Our Postwar Hopes?" *New York Times Book Review* (29 July 1962): 1, 24. In Harry T. Moore, ed. *Contemporary American Novelists.* Carbondale: Southern Illinois University Press, 1964, pp. 32–40 (as "The War Writers Ten Years Later"). In Aldridge's *Time to Murder and Create: The Contemporary Novel in Crisis.* New York: David McKay Co., 1966, pp. 139–48 (as "The War Writers Ten Years Later"). In Aldridge's *The Devil in the Fire: Retrospective Essays on American Literature and Culture*

1951–1972. New York: Harper & Row, 1972, pp. 73–80 (as "The War Writers Ten Years Later").

> Maintains that many of the post–World War II writers, including Vidal, have "reached a creative impasse of one kind or another." There is very little specific discussion of Vidal.

11. Alexander, Edward. "Gore Vidal's Anti-Jewish Nationalism." *Society* 25, no. 3 (March–April 1988): 71–80.

> Hostile article asserting that Vidal "hates" America and the Jews, as revealed in his discussions of sex, religion, and other subjects.

12. Allen, Walter. *Tradition and Dream: The English and American Novel from the Twenties to Our Time*. London: Phoenix, 1964; New York: E. P. Dutton, 1964 (as *The Modern Novel in Britain and the United States*); London: Hogarth Press, 1986, pp. 293–94, 295, 299–300. Harmondsworth, UK: Penguin Books, 1965, pp. 313–14, 315, 319.

> Brief discussion of *Williwaw* and *The City and the Pillar* in the context of post–World War II American literature.

13. Amiel, Barbara. "Lament of an American Patrician." *Maclean's* 99, no. 41 (13 October 1986): 11.

> Hostile report of the battle between Vidal and Norman Podhoretz and Midge Decter over Vidal's "Requiem for the American Empire" (I.C.161.a), asserting that "It utterly confounds me that . . . the American literary community has not risen up as one to censure Vidal."

14. Amis, Martin. "Vidal v. Falwell." *Observer* (London), 1982. In Amis's *The Moronic Inferno and Other Visits to America*. London: Jonathan Cape, 1986; New York: Viking Press, 1987; Harmondsworth, UK: Penguin, 1987, pp. 120–24.

> Report on a speech by Vidal at Lynchburg College, near the home of Jerry Falwell, leading to a comparison of the relative influence of Vidal and Falwell on American politics.

15. Antonioni, Giacomo. "Gore Vidal e la gioventú smarrita." *Fiera Letteraria* 8 (29 September 1953): 1, 6.

> In Italian. Antonioni, discussing Vidal's early novels, asserts that Vidal is one of a new generation of writers replacing the Lost Generation.

16. Armstrong, T. D. "An Old Philosopher in Rome: George Santayana and His Visitors." *Journal of American Studies* 19, no. 3 (December 1985): 349–68.

> Briefly discusses Vidal's visits to Santayana (esp. pp. 357–59).

17. Arthur, Anthony. "*Les Enfants Terribles:* Truman Capote and Gore Vidal." In Arthur's *Literary Feuds: A Century of Celebrated Quarrels—from Mark Twain to Tom Wolfe*. New York: St. Martin's Press, 2002, pp. 159–85.

> Detailed examination of the dispute between Capote and Vidal, including their ensuing litigation and an evaluation of the two writers' relative merits.

18. Atlas, James. "The Laureates of Lewd." *GQ* 63, no. 4 (April 1993): 202–7, 242.

> Article on Vidal, Philip Roth, and John Updike and their role in the sexual revolution of the 1960s.

19. Austen, Roger. "Gore Vidal and His All-Male Eden." In Austen's *Playing the Game: The Homosexual Novel in America*. Indianapolis: Bobbs-Merrill, 1977, pp. 118–25.

> A study of *The City and the Pillar* and its reception, asserting that "Vidal was quite right in charging his detractors with homophobia."

20. Bachman, Ruth. "Vidal and Nostradamus." *Esquire* 59, no. 6 (June 1963): 14.

> A letter commenting upon Vidal's "The Best Man 1968" (I.C.46).

21. Bair, Deirdre. *Anaïs Nin: A Biography*. New York: G. P. Putnam's Sons, 1995, pp. 307, 308–11, 314, 315, 316, 317, 318, 319, 323–24, 326, 327–28, 330, 356, 367, 368, 411–13, 414–16, 426, 430, 439, 447, 454, 472, 491, 580nn3–5, 585n21.
     Extensive discussion of Vidal's relations with Nin.

22. Baker, Russell. "Unmet by the Gods." *New York Times* (7 May 1996): A23.
     Op-ed article in which Baker reacts to the memoirs by Vidal (*Palimpsest*) and Alfred Kazin, two writers he "admire[s] extravagantly." But he gains the impression that both writers knew only famous people.

23. Balakian, Nona. "Topics: Style and the New Economy." *New York Times* (27 November 1965): 30.
     Discusses a passage on punctuation in Vidal's "On Revising One's Own Work" (I.C.60).

24. Balfe, John T. "No Drug Prohibition." *New York Times* (6 October 1970): 46.
     Letter commenting on Vidal's "Drugs" (I.C.85), supporting Vidal's plea for legalization of marijuana.

25. Bargainnier, Earl F. "The Mysteries of Edgar Box (aka Gore Vidal)." *Clues* 2, no. 1 (Spring–Summer 1981): 45–52.
     Survey of the three Edgar Box novels in the context of the conventions of detective fiction, with some discussion of the element of satire in them.

26. Barnouw, Erik. *The Television Writer*. New York: Hill & Wang, 1962, pp. 5, 35, 36, 96, 130.
     Random discussions of Vidal as a television writer, with an extract from *Honor* analyzed as exemplifying the technique of "transition."

27. Barton, David. "Narrative Patterns in the Novels of Gore Vidal." *Notes on Contemporary Literature* 11, no. 4 (September 1981): 3–5.
     Brief article identifying such "narrative patterns" in Vidal's novels as "the idealization of a particular character, his demise, and the attendant eulogy on the part of the narrator which usually closes the book." *Messiah, Julian, Myra Breckinridge,* and *Myron* are briefly discussed.

28. Basler, Roy Prentice. "Lincoln and American Writers." *Papers of the Abraham Lincoln Association* 7 (1985): 7–17.
     Maintains that "about 25 percent" of *Lincoln* "is made up of episodes that might have happened, but never as they are told by Vidal." "What seems to me most reprehensible in Vidal's narrative is his loftily cynical, and sometimes snide, portrayal of historical persons . . . wholly out of focus with historical fact and character." For Vidal's response, see I.C.174.

29. Bayley, John. "Cracking 'The Golden Bowl.'" *New York Review of Books* 31, no. 3 (1 March 1984): 49.
     Letter commenting on "The Golden Bowl of Henry James" (I.C.153). For Vidal's response, see I.F.25.

30. Beerman, Leonard I.; Marguerite Rothwell; and Laurence McMillan. "Lincoln Portrait." *Los Angeles Times* (12 February 1981): Sec. 2, p. 10.
     Letters commenting on "First Note on Abraham Lincoln" (I.C.140).

31. Benson, Sheila. "Wit, Wisdom of Candidate Vidal." *Los Angeles Times* (25 January 1982): Sec. 6, p. 2.
     Review of *Gore Vidal: The Man Who Said No* (I.I.ii.6), a documentary of his 1982 senatorial campaign. It is "at once stimulating and sad . . . sad because our political system seems to favor bland nonentities. . . . Vidal is never boring."

32. Bensoussan, Nicole. "Gore Vidal ou la pensée visuelle." *Revue Française d'Etudes Américaines* 12 (no. 32) (April 1987): 163–68.
     In French. Bensoussan notes the cinematic quality of much of Vidal's work, especially in *Myra Breckinridge* (which is compared to Sartre's *La Nausée*) and *Messiah.*

33.   Berman, Ronald. *America in the Sixties: An Intellectual History.* New York: Harper & Row; London: Collier-Macmillan, 1968, pp. 255–57.
> Discussion of *The City and the Pillar* and Vidal's essays on sex.

34.   Bernard, Bina. "Gore Vidal's 'Myron' Misses, But He Is Unperturbed—and Rich." *People* 3, no. 3 (27 January 1975): 28–29.
> Bernard notes the generally unfavorable reception of *Myron* and provides a superficial overview of Vidal's career. There are four large photographs.

35.   Berryman, Charles. "Satire in Gore Vidal's *Kalki.*" *Critique: Studies in Modern Fiction* 22, no. 2 (1980): 88–96.
> Probes the attack on religion in *Messiah, Julian,* and *Kalki* by the use of the "skeptical narrator." *Kalki* is Vidal's "latest and best attack on religious superstition." He finds that "Vidal is especially good at satirizing the final stages of a dying culture."

36.   Bertonneau, Thomas F. "Intellectualism and the Gnostic Debate: Julian the Apostate in the Modern Literary Imagination." *Anthropoetics* 10, no. 1 (Spring–Summer 2004).
> Part of the article studies Vidal's portrayal of Julian in *Julian* in light of his hostility to monotheism. *Anthropoetics* is an electronic journal with no page numbers.

37.   Bird, Kai. "Gore Vidal's America." *New York Times Book Review* (22 October 2000): 4.
> Letter commenting on Andrew Sullivan's review of *The Golden Age* (III.F.58.z), stating that Vidal is correct that the United States' dropping of the atomic bomb on Japan was unnecessary.

38.   Blume, Mary. "Gore Vidal: Taking American History Personally." *International Herald Tribune* (27 March 1999): 24.
> A biographical overview that discusses Fred Kaplan's biography in progress.

39.   Bogdonavich, Peter. "Who Makes Movies?" *New York Review of Books* 24, no. 1 (3 February 1977): 45.
> Letter responding to Vidal's essay "Who Makes the Movies?" (I.C.116), protesting that Vidal's remarks on Orson Welles are "pretty silly and not worthy of a fellow as smart as Gore Vidal." For Vidal's response, see I.F.17.

40.   Bowers, A. Joan. "Leonie Hargrave: Gore Vidal Exposed." *Prairie Schooner* 50, no. 1 (Spring 1976): 78–83.
> Presents the erroneous theory that Vidal is the pseudonymous author of the historical novel *Clara Reeve* (1985) by Leonie Hargrave.

41.   Bowles, Paul. *Without Stopping: An Autobiography.* New York: G. P. Putnam's Sons, 1972; London: Owen, 1972; New York: Ecco Press, 1985, pp. 184, 288, 291, 342.
> Brief discussions of Bowles's encounters with Vidal.

42.   Boyette, Purvis E. "'Myra Breckinridge' and Imitative Form." *Modern Fiction Studies* 17, no. 2 (Summer 1971): 229–38.
> *Myra Breckinridge* is not a novel at all but a Menippean satire. Vidal has launched a "frontal attack" on the novel form. He is appealing to the educated reader who will be able to perceive his use of satire and parody.

43.   Brombert, Victor; Irving Younger; and Peter N. Dunn. "Hard Maker." *New York Review of Books* 26, no. 15 (11 October 1979): 51, 53.
> Letters in response to "V. S. Pritchett as 'Critic'" (I.C.128). Brombert objects to Vidal's quoting Pritchett on Brombert's *The Novels of Flaubert.* Younger claims that Vidal has misused the phrase "negative capability." Dunn mentions a parallel between Borges and Lewis Carroll. For Vidal's response see I.F.20.

44.   Brower, Montgomery, and Logan Bentley. "In Memory of His Grandfather, the Senator, Gore Vidal Offers Hope to a Little Blind Girl." *People* 30, no. 11 (12 September 1988): 53–54.

Vidal, recalling his blind grandfather, is providing money and other assistance to give sight to an Italian girl born blind.

45. Buckley, William F., Jr. "Buckley vs. Vidal." *New York Times Book Review* (24 September 1995): 4.
    Response to Vidal's letter (I.F.35) discussing his lawsuit against Vidal and again accusing Vidal of anti-Semitism.

46. ———. "Gore Vidal on JFK." In Buckley's *The Jeweler's Eye.* New York: G. P. Putnam's Sons, 1968, pp. 221–25.
    Comments on Vidal's "The Holy Family" (I.C.67).

47. ———. "In Search of Anti-Semitism." *National Review* 43, no. 24 (30 December 1991): 2–20. Rpt. in Buckley's *In Search of Anti-Semitism.* New York: Continuum, 1992.
    Discussion of four cases of supposed anti-Semitism, three of them (Joe Sobran, Pat Buchanan, the *Dartmouth Review*) on the right, and one (Vidal and the *Nation*) on the left. In the latter case (pp. 47–56), Buckley states that Vidal was "genuinely and derisively anti-Semitic by whatever definition of the term" in regard to his article in the *Nation* (I.C.162). He records Norman Podhoretz's response to it and the responses by letter writers in the *Nation.*

48. ———. "On Experiencing Gore Vidal." *Esquire* 72, no. 2 (August 1969): 108–13, 122, 124, 126, 128, 131–32. In Harold Hayes, ed. *Smiling through the Apocalypse: Esquire's History of the Sixties.* New York: McCall Publishing Co., 1970, pp. 911–46. In Buckley's *The Governor Listeth: A Book of Inspired Political Revelations.* New York: G. P. Putnam's Sons, 1970, pp. 283–329.
    Immense, long-winded account of Buckley's confrontation with Vidal as commentators on ABC during the political conventions of 1968, beginning with previous encounters from 1962 onward. Buckley admits that he sent a telegram to Jack Paar calling Vidal a "pinko queer." He reports reading *Myra Breckinridge* and quotes hostile reviews of it, saying that the book "giv[es] gratification only to sadist-homosexuals." Vidal called Buckley a "crypto-Nazi" on television and Buckley responded by calling Vidal, "You queer." He concludes the essay by saying: "I herewith apologize to Gore Vidal."

49. Buckley, William F., Jr., and John Kenneth Galbraith. "Buckley v. Vidal, *Esquire.*" *National Review* 24, no. 40 (13 October 1972): 1113–15. In Buckley's *Execution Eve and Other Contemporary Ballads.* New York: G. P. Putnam's Sons, 1975, pp. 322–28.
    A series of letters between the two writers on Buckley's libel suit against Vidal and *Esquire.* Galbraith believes the suit unwise. In conclusion, Buckley issues a statement claiming (falsely) that Vidal's article on him in *Esquire* was "libelous" and that the court "sustained" Buckley's suit.

50. Burgess, Anthony. "*Creation:* Gore Vidal [1981]." In Burgess's *Ninety-nine Novels: The Best in English Since 1939.* London: Allison & Busby, 1984; New York: Summit Books, 1984, p. 129. In Vidal's *Creation.* New York: Vintage International, 2002, p. [vii] (as "Foreword").
    Brief and favorable evaluation of Vidal's novel.

51. ———. *The Novel Now: A Student's Guide to Contemporary Fiction.* London: Faber & Faber, 1967; New York: W. W. Norton & Co., 1967, pp. 53–54, 59, 200.
    Brief discussion of *Williwaw, The City and the Pillar,* and *Julian.*

52. ———. "The Postwar American Novel: A View from the Periphery." *American Scholar* 35, no. 1 (Winter 1965–1966): 150, 152, 154, 156.
    Brief discussion of *Williwaw* and *The City and the Pillar.*

53. Burns, Thomas Laborie. "Gore Vidal's Hollywood: History, Fiction, and Film." *Ilha do Desterro* 33, no. 1 (1997): 99–111.
    Study of *Hollywood* and its portrayal of the film industry of the 1920s.

54.   Buruma, Ian. "Pearl Harbor: An Exchange." *New York Review of Books* 48, no. 8 (17 May 2001): 67–68.
       Response to a letter by Vidal (I.F.51) on whether Franklin D. Roosevelt encouraged the Japanese attack on Pearl Harbor.

55.   Byrd, Max. "Historical Novel." *American Heritage* 53, no. 5 (October 2002): 44–45.
       In a section titled "Overrated/Underrated," Byrd believes Vidal's *Lincoln* is underrated: it is "a great novel because in it Vidal, whose brilliant wit almost always comes at the expense of other people, finally found something he couldn't make fun of." He finds the novel structurally brilliant and notes that professional historians hate it.

56.   Calvino, Italo. "Imagining Vidal." Trans. George Armstrong. *Threepenny Review* 5, no. 1 (Spring 1984): 26–27. In D.13.
       Address delivered when Vidal was made an honorary citizen of Ravello, the first time such an honor was ever bestowed upon a non-Italian. Calvino discusses *Duluth* as a new kind of literature and speaks of his wish that Vidal would write of Italy.

57.   Capote, Truman. *Truman Capote: Conversations.* Ed. M. Thomas Inge. Jackson: University Press of Mississippi, 1987, pp. 112, 167, 187, 197–98, 199, 202, 205–6, 234–35, 312–13, 327, 340, 358.
       Random discussions of Vidal in various interviews.

58.   Capp, Al. "Comedy, Satire and Gore Vidal." *Spectator* 235 (no. 7672) (12 July 1975): 45.
       Studies the character of Richard Nixon as embodied in *The Best Man* and *An Evening with Richard Nixon.*

59.   Cardwell, Guy. "Mark Twain's Reputation." *New York Review of Books* 43, no. 14 (19 September 1996): 80.
       Letter on "Twain on the Grand Tour" (I.C.230), stating that Vidal has mischaracterized Cardwell's book, *The Man Who Was Mark Twain* (1991). For Vidal's response, see I.F.39.

60.   Carlson, Peter. "Gore Vidal: This Space for Rent." *Washington Post* (27 October 1998): D2.
       Response to Vidal's essay "The War at Home" (I.C.257.a), which, in Carlson's judgment, shows that Vidal is "mad. He's hopping mad. He's spitting mad. He may even be stark raving mad." Vidal's worries about the erosion of civil liberties in the United States are overblown and cranky.

61.   Carr, Virginia Spencer. *The Lonely Hunter: A Biography of Carson McCullers.* Garden City, NY: Doubleday, 1975, pp. 144, 158, 365, 386, 469.
       Scattered discussions of Vidal's relations with McCullers.

62.   Cater, Douglas. "Advice and Dissent about the Best Man." *New York Times Magazine* (22 May 1960): 27, 89.
       Discussion of *The Best Man,* asserting that Vidal's view that all politicians are immoral "results in caricature rather than convincing documentary." By stressing only the thirst for power, Vidal ignores the fact that political disputes can also be over principles.

63.   Cavett, Dick, and Christopher Porterfield. *Cavett.* New York: Harcourt Brace Jovanovich, 1974, pp. 282, 299–300.
       Brief discussion of the Vidal-Mailer contretemps.

64.   Chamberlain, John. "Critic Finds New Authors Work Things Out in Their Own Ways." *Life* 23, no. 22 (2 June 1947): 81–82.
       Brief discussion of *Williwaw.* The article includes a photo of Vidal.

65.   Chapman, John. "*The Best Man* by Gore Vidal." In Chapman's *Broadway's Best 1960.* Garden City, NY: Doubleday, 1960, pp. 119–29.
       A synopsis of the play.

66.   ———. "*A* [*sic*] *Visit to a Small Planet* by Gore Vidal." In Chapman's *Broadway's Best 1957*. Garden City, NY: Doubleday, 1957, pp. 100–108.
       A synopsis of the play.

67.   Clarke, Gerald. *Capote: A Biography*. New York: Simon & Schuster, 1988, pp. 97, 130, 131, 139–43, 163, 164, 167–68, 171, 183–84, 199–200, 294–95, 474, 479–80, 517–18, 520.
       Random discussions of Capote's relations with Vidal, including their feud and Capote's opinion of Vidal's writings.

68.   ———. "Checking In with Truman Capote." *Esquire* 78, no. 5 (November 1972): 136–37, 187–88, 190.
       Quotes a brief and disparaging remark by Capote on Vidal and one by Vidal on Capote.

69.   ———. "Petronius Americanus: The Ways of Gore Vidal." *Atlantic Monthly* 229, no. 3 (March 1972): 44–51. In III.D.15 (extracts).
       Based on an interview. Clarke discusses Vidal's relations with other American writers, including Truman Capote (Clarke interjects Capote's comments on Vidal), his family background, his early writing, Robert F. Kennedy, his "exile from the White House," the "long apprenticeship" of Vidal the novelist, his life in Rome, and his reputation.

70.   Clemons, Walter. "Gore Vidal's Chronicles of America." *Newsweek* 103, no. 24 (11 June 1984): 74–75, 78–79.
       An enthusiastic overview of Vidal's career, timed for the publication of *Lincoln*. Clemons sees Vidal the novelist as "the conservative classicist, an objective, non-autobiographical artist— disdainful, like Coriolanus, of displaying his wounds." He thinks Vidal's historical novels will cement his place in American literature.

71.   Connell, Edward A. "Élan Vidal." *Esquire* 68, no. 1 (July 1967): 10.
       Letter on "The Holy Family" (I.C.67): Connell believes that Vidal is resorting to stereotypes about the Irish.

72.   Conrad, Peter. "Halls of Mirrors: The Novels of Gore Vidal." *Sunday Times* (London) *Magazine* (27 March 1977): 35.
       Vidal "is the victim of his own versatility." Some of his novels are "contrived as parodies and as self-parodies"; others reveal "a ventriloquial gift of mimicry."

73.   Cook, Bruce. "Aquarius Rex." *National Observer* 11, no. 45 (4 November 1972): 1, 15. In Laura Adams, ed. *Will the Real Norman Mailer Please Stand Up?* Port Washington, NY: Kennikat Press, 1974, pp. 224–32.
       Article on Mailer with a brief discussion of the Vidal-Mailer confrontation on "The Dick Cavett Show."

74.   Cook, Eleanor. "A Mind So Free." *New York Review of Books* 33, no. 20 (18 December 1986): 76.
       Letter commenting on "Lessons of the Master" (I.C.163.a), regarding T. S. Eliot's comment on Henry James. For Vidal's response see I.F.28.

75.   Cooper, Marc. "Two Angry Men." *Premiere* 1, no. 5 (January 1988): 48–51.
       Part of the article deals with Vidal's suit against the Writers Guild of America over screenwriting credits for *The Sicilian*. The other "angry man" is Larry Ferguson, who is disputing screenwriting credits for *Beverly Hills Cop II*.

76.   Corber, Robert J. "Gore Vidal and the Erotics of Masculinity." *Western Humanities Review* 48, no. 1 (Spring 1994): 30–52. In Corber's *Homosexuality in Cold War America: Resistance and the Crisis of Masculinity*. Durham, NC: Duke University Press, 1997, pp. 135–59.

A study of *The City and the Pillar* and the response to it by Donald Webster Cory in *The Homosexual in America* (1951) and by Leslie Fiedler. These critics misread the novel because Vidal shattered the stereotype of the gay man as effeminate.

77.   Cory, Donald Webster. *The Homosexual in America: A Subjective Approach.* New York: Greenberg, 1951; New York: Castle Books, 1960; New York: Arno Press, 1975, pp. 21, 81, 94, 136, 169, 170, 172, 174, 176, 200–201, 205.
Random discussion of *The City and the Pillar,* concluding that it is a "disappointing failure."

78.   Costa, Horácio. "The Fundamental Re-Writing: Religious Texts and Contemporary Narrative." *Dedalus* [Portugal] no. 6 (1996): 245–53. *Poligrafías* 1 (1996): 189–98.
A study of *Live from Golgotha,* Salman Rushdie's *The Satanic Verses,* and José Saramago's *O Evangelho segundo Jesus Cristo.* Vidal's book "displays an astounding blasphemous leverage." The work combines the science fiction novel and the old hagiologic tale.

79.   Crane, Fred A. "Freedom When?" *New York Review of Books* 23, no. 10 (10 June 1976): 44.
Letter pointing out two apparent factual errors in Vidal's essay on the Adams family (I.C.110). For Vidal's response, see I.F.13.

80.   Crawford, Tad. *The Writer's Legal Guide.* New York: Hawthorn Books, 1977, pp. 50–51.
Brief discussion of one aspect of the Buckley-Vidal litigation.

81.   Creamer, Robert. "Verifying Genocide." *New York Review of Books* 28, no. 16 (22 October 1981): 59.
Letter commenting on "An American Sissy" (I.C.141), protesting that Vidal's figure of three million Filipinos killed during the Spanish-American War is erroneous. For Vidal's response, see I.F.22.

82.   Crichton, Robert. "The Fever Breaks." *New York Review of Books* 20, no. 14 (20 September 1973): 44.
Letter protesting against Vidal's characterization of his novel *The Camerons* in "The Top Ten Best Sellers . . ." (I.C.96). For Vidal's response see I.F.10.

83.   Crowley, John W. "A Writer in Duluth: Gore Vidal and W. D. Howells." *Notes on Contemporary Literature* 18, no. 4 (September 1988): 4–5.
Crowley finds the roots of *Duluth*'s satire in a comment by Howells on Dostoevsky in *Criticism and Fiction.*

84.   Current, Richard Nelson. "Fiction as History: A Review Essay." *Journal of Southern History* 52, no. 1 (February 1986): 77–90 (esp. 78–82). In Current's *Arguing with Historians: Essays on the Historical and the Unhistorical.* Middletown, CT: Wesleyan University Press, 1987, pp. 147–61 (as "Fiction as History: Vidal, Haley, Styron").
Attacks Vidal's *Lincoln* for its linguistic awkwardnesses and historical errors. "At many points it is hard to know whether his version of Lincoln's life and times is an outright invention, a dubious interpretation, or simply a mistake." Vidal is naïve for relying so much on the memories of William Herndon. See also item 157 below. For Vidal's response, see I.F.29.

85.   Davidon, Ann Morrissett. "Anaïs Nin vs. Gore Vidal: Bon Mots and Billets Doux." *Village Voice* 21, no. 3 (17 January 1977): 80–82.
Overview of the Vidal-Nin relationship.

86.   ———. "Gore Vidal and the Two-Headed Monster." *Nation* 218, no. 21 (25 May 1974): 661–63.
General survey of Vidal's early novels, especially *Williwaw, The Judgment of Paris,* and *The City and the Pillar.*

87.   Davidson, Ralph P. "A Letter from the Publisher." *Time* 107, no. 9 (1 March 1976): 2.
Reports Paul Gray's diligence in reading Vidal for the *Time* cover story (see item 134 below) and Gray's admiration for Vidal's work.

88. Davis, Jerry C. "A Roar at the Lore of Gore." *Esquire* 57, no. 2 (February 1962): 12.
     Letter accusing Vidal of using the same guilt-by-association tactics against the right that the House Un-American Activities Committee is said to have used.

89. Davis, Robert Gorham. "If This Is Tuesday, It Must Be Ephesus." *Nation* 255, no. 10 (5 October 1992): 346.
     Letter commenting on "Monotheism and Its Discontents" (I.C.201), asserting that Christianity is not monotheistic but trinitarian. For Vidal's response, see I.F.34.

90. Decter, Midge. "Gore Vidal's Requiem for a Former Heavyweight." *Contentions* (February 1986): 1–3.
     Lengthy response to "The Day the American Empire Ran out of Gas" (I.C.161), suggesting that Vidal is wrong in thinking that the American empire was a conscious invention of Theodore Roosevelt, Henry Cabot Lodge, and others, and that Vidal underestimates the evils of the Soviet Union.

91. DeSilver, Claire. "The Angel in the Story." *New York Review of Books* 43, no. 10 (6 June 1996): 64–65.
     Letter commenting on "Dawn Powell: Queen of the Golden Age" (I.C.228), asserting that Powell's friend Margaret DeSilver's views were not pro-Communist. For Vidal's response, see I.F.37.

92. Devlin, Albert J., ed. *Conversations with Tennessee Williams.* Jackson: University Press of Mississippi, 1986, pp. 70, 72, 148, 155–56, 185–86, 204, 207, 226, 233, 246, 304, 321, 348, 355.
     Collection of interviews of Williams, with sporadic discussions of Vidal.

93. Dick, Bernard F. "Anaïs Nin and Gore Vidal: A Study in Literary Incompatibility." *Mosaic* 11, no. 2 (Winter 1978): 153–62.
     Dick studies Vidal's and Nin's early personal and literary involvements, and their later falling out. He feels that they were "poles apart" in every aspect of literature. But he points out some similarities between *In a Yellow Wood* and Nin's *Children of the Albatross.* He sees Nin as partial inspiration for several of Vidal's women characters, especially Maria Verlaine in *The City and the Pillar* and Marietta Donegal in *Two Sisters.* The issue of *Mosaic* was devoted to Nin.

94. Donnaruma, Jay F. Letter to the Editor. *Esquire* 67, no. 6 (June 1967): 12.
     Letter on "The Holy Family" (I.C.67) claiming that the article is "filled with gross generalizations and false conclusions."

95. Douglas, Wallace B. "Bobby in '68." *Esquire* 59, no. 5 (May 1963): 8.
     Letter on "The Best Man 1968" (I.C.46), claiming that the humor in the article redounds to Vidal's discredit.

96. Duffy, Martha. "A Gadfly in Glorious, Angry Exile." *Time* 140, no. 13 (28 September 1992): 64, 66.
     Article about Vidal's appearance in the film *Bob Roberts* and his recent books, especially *Live from Golgotha.* Duffy provides a brief biographical overview. There is a photo of Vidal on p. 65.

97. Dunlap, William. "Bring Me the Head of Gore Vidal." *Washingtonian* 35, no. 2 (November 1999): 70–73.
     Speaks of going to Italy to make a bust of Vidal. The article is illustrated with photographs of the work in progress.

98. Dunne, Dominick. "Tabloid Trouble." *Vanity Fair* no. 499 (March 2002): 142, 144, 146, 149.
     Discusses meeting Vidal in Guatemala in 1947 and then at a recent party in Los Angeles where Vidal called Timothy McVeigh a "patriot."

99.   Earl, James W.; Name Withheld; and Paul Illert. "Plastic Fiction." *New York Review of Books* 23, no. 17 (28 October 1976): 44–45.
      Letters commenting on Vidal's "American Plastic: The Matter of Fiction" (I.C.115). Earl (a professor of English) believes that Vidal doesn't understand Pynchon and that he slanders the teaching profession. Name Withheld (also a professor) says that many professors don't teach or read the modern writers, including Vidal. Illert objects to Vidal's characterization of Heisenberg's Uncertainty Principle as "culturally deranging" and his application of it to literature. For Vidal's response, see I.F.16

100. Eisinger, Chester E. *Fiction of the Forties.* Chicago: University of Chicago Press, 1965, pp. 26, 29.
      Brief discussion of *Williwaw.*

101. Eisner, Douglas. "*Myra Breckinridge* and the Pathology of Heterosexuality." In Patricia Juliana Smith, ed. *The Queer Sixties.* New York: Routledge, 1999, pp. 255–70.
      Shows how *Myra Breckinridge* sums up many of the cultural concerns of the 1960s, including civil rights, sexual and gay liberation, political radicalism, and the use of camp.

102. Elliott, S. James. "Homosexuality in the Crucial Decade: Three Novelists' Views." In Louie Crew, ed. *The Gay Academic.* Palm Springs, CA: ETC Publications, 1978, 164–77.
      Studies Vidal, Norman Mailer, and Gordon Merrick's treatment of gay themes in the 1940s and 1950s. He focuses on *The City and the Pillar* and *The Best Man.*

103. Endres, Nikolai. "The Pillaged Pillar: *Hubris* and *Polis* in Gore Vidal's *The City and the Pillar.*" *Classical and Modern Literature* 24, no. 2 (Fall 2004): 47–78.
      An exhaustive and detailed discussion of the influence of Plato (especially the *Symposium* and the *Phaedrus*) on Vidal's novel.

104. Fallows, James. "The White Peril." *Atlantic Monthly* 259, no. 5 (May 1987): 18, 20.
      Discusses Vidal's "Requiem for the American Empire" (I.C.161.a), saying that Vidal is right that the United States is spending too much on defense.

105. Feeney, F. X. "Ben-Gore: Romancing the Word with Gore Vidal." *Written By* 2, no. 1 (December [1997]–January 1998): 66–73.
      Survey of Vidal's work in film and television, focusing on *Ben-Hur* and establishing that Vidal probably did contribute extensively to the final script, contrary to the assertions of Charlton Heston and others.

106. Fehrenbacher, Don E. "Communications." *American Historical Review* 96, no. 1 (February 1991): 326–28.
      Response to Vidal's letter (I.F.32) on "The Fictional Lincoln" (below).

107. ———. "The Fictional Lincoln." *Stanford Magazine* 14, no. 1 (Spring 1986): 32–36. Rev. ed. in Fehrenbacher's *Lincoln in Text and Context: Collected Essays.* Stanford, CA: Stanford University Press, 1987, pp. 228–45 (esp. 240–43). Rev. ed. as "Vidal's Lincoln." In Gabor S. Borritt and Norman O. Forness, eds. *The Historian's Lincoln: Pseudohistory, Psychohistory, and History.* Urbana: University of Illinois Press, 1988, pp. 387–92.
      States that Vidal's *Lincoln* has "a certain amount of factual error and other unreliable information," and that literary reviewers like Joyce Carol Oates and Harold Bloom are incapable of assessing its historicity. The work is "seductively unreliable as biography" but is nevrtheless "the most important novel written about Lincoln to date."

108. Fernandus, Giséla Manganelli. "A 'viagem' espácio-temporal pelo romance histórico: Os casos *Lincoln* e *Libra.*" *Revista de Letras* 39 (1999): 125–46.
      In Portuguese. A study of *Lincoln* and Don DeLillo's *Libra* and their use of postmodern techniques as applied to the historical novel.

109. Fitch, Noël Riley. *Anaïs: The Erotic Life of Anaïs Nin.* Boston: Little, Brown, 1993, pp. 5, 9, 261, 276–77, 269, 271, 275, 276, 278, 279, 280, 282, 284, 285, 287, 288, 296–97, 306, 381, 385–87, 388, 402.
    Extensive discussion of Vidal's relations with Nin.

110. Fitts, Dudley. "A Reply." *New York Times Book Review* (5 July 1964): 20.
    Reply to Vidal's letter (I.F.3) protesting Fitts's review of *Julian* (F.21.m).

111. Fletcher, Don, and Kate Feros. "*Live from Golgotha:* Gore Vidal and the Problem of Satire Reinscription." *Mosaic* 33, no. 1 (March 2000): 133–44.
    The authors show how "Vidal combines a number of strategies to launch a clever and complex attack on Christian morality" in *Live from Golgotha,* chiefly by undermining "the pretensions of Christianity to divine origins by exposing the failings of the major participants in early Christianity."

112. Fletcher, M. D. "Vidal's *Duluth* as 'Post-Modern' Political Satire." *Thalia: Studies in Literary Humor* 9, no. 1 (Spring–Summer 1986) 10–21.
    Studies how Vidal uses postmodern techiques to augment the political satire in the novel. Vidal's targets are the stereotyping of minorities, sexual stereotypes, police brutality, the FBI and CIA, specific political figures (Hubert Humphrey, Lyndon Baines Johnson, Ronald Reagan), the "gullibility of the American people," and the dominance of the media. Vidal uses parody as a chief weapon. Satire itself is satirized.

113. Fletcher, M. D., and Kate Feros. "Gore Vidal's Satire." *Studies in Contemporary Satire* 20 (1996): 160–64.
    Brief article studying the targets of Vidal's satire: sexual hypocrisy (*Myra Breckinridge* and *Myron*), religious hypocrisy (*Kalki* and *Live from Golgotha*), and general hypocrisy (*Duluth*).

114. Flynn, Daniel J. "Gore Vidal." In Flynn's *Intellectual Morons: How Ideology Makes Smart People Fall for Stupid Ideas.* New York: Crown Forum, 2004, pp. 116–24.
    Superficial and partisan attack on Vidal as an "anti-American," especially in regard to his relations with Timothy McVeigh.

115. Fraser, Hugh Russell. Letter to the Editor. *Esquire* 67, no. 6 (June 1967): 12.
    Letter on "The Holy Family" (I.C.67), claiming that Vidal has the same flaws that he attacks in John F. Kennedy.

116. Frattarola, Angela. "Frustration and Silence in Gore Vidal's *The City and the Pillar.*" In Michael J. Meyer, ed. *Literature and Homosexuality.* Amsterdam: Rodopi, 2000, pp. 35–54.
    Study of Jim Willard's frustration with language in the context of his homosexuality, embodied in his quest for "normality."

117. Freedman, Joanne B. "History as Told by the Devil Incarnate: Gore Vidal's *Burr.*" In Mark C. Carnes, ed. *Novel History: Historians and Novelists Confront America's Past (and Each Other).* New York: Simon & Schuster, 2001, pp. 29–39.
    Detailed examination of *Burr,* its use of historical sources, and its fundamental message. The essay was followed by Vidal's own essay on *Burr* (see I.C.277).

118. Freedman, Morris. "From Hellenism to Hebraism, The Essay in Our Time: Gore Vidal and Irving Kristol." *Virginia Quarterly Review* 74, no. 2 (Spring 1998): 251–62.
    Freedman believes that the essay "has become the preeminent genre of the later 20th century." He contrasts the style and subject matter of Vidal and Kristol, especially in their recent books, *Palimpsest* and Kristol's *Neoconservatism.* Whereas Vidal is lively and playful, Kristol is often serious and brooding.

119. Friedberg, Maurice. *A Decade of Euphoria: Western Literature in Post-Stalin Russia, 1954–1964.* Bloomington: Indiana University Press, 1977, pp. 21, 31, 34–36.

Discussion of the inaccurate Russian translation of *Washington, D.C.* as serialized in *Inostrannaja literatura* (II.B.vii.1).

120.   Frow, John. "The Uses of Terror and the Limits of Cultural Studies." *Symplokē* 11, nos. 1–2 (2003): 69–76.
Studies Vidal's essay "The Enemy Within" (I.C.284.a) and its suggestion that the Bush administration was either complicit in the 9/11 attacks or "used the occasion opportunistically to harvest a series of economic and political benefits."

121.   Gardella, Kay. "Television Climate Cools as Dem Curtain Is Dropped." *New York Daily News* (30 August 1968): 83.
A section of the article discusses the Vidal-Buckley debate.

122.   Gates, John M.; Russell Roth; and David Nielsen. "Death in the Philippines." *New York Review of Books* 28, no. 20 (17 December 1981): 69.
Further letters (see item 81 above) questioning the figure of three million Filipinos killed in the Spanish-American War. For Vidal's response, see I.F.23.

123.   Geddes, Greg. "A Gore of a Different Color." *Nation* 270, no. 22 (5 June 2000): 2.
Letter jeering at Vidal for his two political campaigns of 1960 and 1982. For Vidal's response see I.F.48.

124.   Gill, A. A. "Gore Blimey—Gore Vidal." *Sunday Times* (London) (15 October 1995): Sec. 10, pp. 2–3.
Review of "Gore Vidal's Gore Vidal" (I.I.ii.9). The documentary unwittingly suggests that Vidal "was just a garrulous, mumming, lemon-faced bitch."

125.   Giovannini, Joseph. "For Gore Vidal, a Last, Long Look from the Heights." *New York Times* (26 August 2004): F1, 5. *International Herald Tribune* (3 September 2004): 9 (as "Vidal's Reluctant Goodbye to a Storied Villa").
Reports Vidal's departure from La Rondinaia because his ailing knees prevent him from climbing the hill to the villa. The film *The Life Aquatic* used the villa as a location.

126.   Girlanda, Elio. "Hollywood Story." *Cinema Studio* 5–6 (January–June 1992): 74–75.
Study of *Hollywood* in conjunction with Charles Bukowski's *Hollywood.*

127.   Girodias, Maurice. "Pornography." *New York Review of Books* 6, no. 8 (12 May 1966): 29–30.
Long letter on "On Pornography" (I.C.64), "one of the most ungenerous pieces of writing which I have ever read." He protests against Vidal's descriptions of his work. For Vidal's response see I.F.4.

128.   Gladsky, Thomas. "Texts and Other Fictions in Gore Vidal's *Burr.*" *University of Mississippi Studies in English* 11–12 (1993–1995): 321–28.
In *Burr*, "Vidal seems bemused by texts, perplexed that words hide history even as they hope to reveal it." Gladsky studies Vidal's use of primary source materials on Burr, especially Matthew Davis's *Memoirs of Aaron Burr* (1836).

129.   Goodman, Paul. "The Best Man." *New York Review of Books* 11, no. 7 (24 October 1968): 37.
Letter responding to "The Late Show" (I.C.75.a), saying that Nixon is probably the "lesser evil."

130.   Goodman, Walter. "History as Fiction." *New Leader* 71, no. 9 (16–30 May 1988): 11–12.
Discusses Vidal's dispute with historians over the historicity of *Lincoln* and his historical novels generally, but concludes that they are "something different from history."

131.   ———. "Where Are the Hardy-Har-Hars of Yesteryear?" *New York Times* (26 September 2000): E2.
A rumination on the revival of *The Best Man,* saying that contemporary politicans have none of the wit and cleverness displayed in the play. Politicians today have become too cautious and fearful of offending anyone to tell jokes.

132. Gould, Jean. *Modern American Playwrights.* New York: Dodd, Mead, 1966, pp. 286–87.
     Brief discussion of Vidal's plays for the stage and television.

133. Gray, Paul. "The World According to Gore." *Time* 156, no. 13 (25 September 2000): 92, 94.
     Article timed for the publication of *The Golden Age* and the revival of *The Best Man.* Gray discusses Vidal's historical novels and the political point of view inherent in them.

134. Gray, Paul; Erik Amfitheatrof; and Ronald Flamini. "Gore Vidal: Laughing Cassandra." *Time* 107, no. 9 (1 March 1976): 59–64.
     Cover story; an important landmark in Vidal's recognition. The article was timed for the publication of *1876* (the cover headline reads: "Gore Vidal's New Novel '1876': Sins of the Fathers"). A discussion of the book is followed by an overview of Vidal's career, especially his ventures into politics and his relations with the Kennedys. His views on literature and politics are recorded.

135. Haag, Ernest van den. "Buckley and Vidal." *Encounter* 34, no. 5 (May 1970): 96.
     Letter disputing "R's" account of the Buckley-Vidal debate (see item 264 below), largely taking Buckley's side.

136. Haber, Jon. "Jeez, Maimonides . . ." *Nation* 267, no. 1 (6 July 1998): 2.
     Letter commenting on "Bad History" (I.C.249) and also addressing Vidal's foreword to Israel Shahak's *Jewish History, Jewish Religion,* which Haber believes to be full of errors. For Vidal's response see I.F.45.

137. Hackett, Alice Payne, and James Henry Burke. *80 Years of Best Sellers 1895–1975.* New York: R. R. Bowker, 1977, pp. 18, 41, 203, 204, 213, 214.
     Random discussions of Vidal's best-selling novels.

138. Haden-Guest, Anthony. "The Vidal-Capote Papers: A Tempest in Camelot." *New York* 12, no. 24 (11 June 1979): 53–56.
     A one-page summary of Vidal's lawsuit against Capote and three pages of excerpts from interviews with and other writings by Capote, Vidal, Arthur Schlesinger Jr., and Lee Radziwill about the White House party at the nucleus of the suit.

139. Halley, Russell. "The Complete Works on Gore Vidal: His Work." *Writer's Digest* 55, no. 3 (March 1975): 15–16.
     General overview of Vidal's career. Vidal is on the cover of the issue.

140. Halliday, Wallace. "Vidal Campaign." *Los Angeles Times* (2 April 1982): Sec. 2, p. 6.
     Letter protesting Vidal's abuse of his opponent for the Senate, Jerry Brown, as expressed in numerous interviews.

141. Hansen, Horacio L.; Robert Birch; R. W. Maruda; Marvin Petal; and Jon Oustead. "Gore Vidal's View of Ronald Reagan." *Los Angeles Times* (17 January 1982): Sec. 4, p. 4.
     Letters commenting on "He Is a Leader for Our Times . . ." (I.C.143).

142. Harvey, Keith. "Translating Camp Talk: Gay Identities and Cultural Transfer." *Translator* 4, no. 2 (November 1998): 295–320.
     The article is in part an analysis of *The City and the Pillar* and Philippe Mikriammos's translation (II.A.x.12).

143. Hassan, Ihab. *Radical Innocence: Studies in the Contemporary American Novel.* Princeton: Princeton University Press, 1961, pp. 76–77.
     Brief discussion of *The City and the Pillar,* a novel "as frank as it is pedestrian."

144. Hattersley, Roy. "Gore Vidal: Ice in the Soul." *Guardian* (17 February 1999): Saturday, pp. 6–7.
> Discusses Vidal's role as an intellectual gadfly, including some of his memorable appearances on British television. He notes Vidal's relations with the Kennedys and his work as essayist and playwright. The article contains numerous quotations from an interview.

145. Herberg, Will. "The 'Separation' of Church and State." *National Review* 13, no. 16 (23 October 1962): 315, 330.
> Disputes Vidal's statements (made on the TV show "Open End") that the First Amendment should be interpreted to mean that the government should not be in the "religion business."

146. Heston, Charlton. *The Actor's Life: Journals 1956–1976.* Edited by Hollis Alpert. New York: E. P. Dutton, 1978, pp. 46, 48, 49.
> Heston's journal for 1958 shows that Vidal was on the set of *Ben-Hur* for nearly a month, although Heston asserts in a note that Vidal has exaggerated his role in the screenplay.

147. ———. *In the Arena: An Autobiography.* New York: Simon & Schuster, 1995, pp. 187, 194.
> Denies that Vidal made any substantive contribution to the final shooting script of *Ben-Hur.*

148. ———. "Love and Chariots II: Heston Responds to Vidal." *Los Angeles Times* (24 June 1996): F4.
> Letter responding to item 180 below, claiming once again that Vidal "did not write any part of 'Ben-Hur' as shot, edited and still shown around the world." Appended are comments from readers: John R. Johnson, Bob Stock, Peter Levin, Karl Alexander, Thomas E. Braun, and Michael Roush.

149. Hewes, Henry. "Young Dramatists on Trial in the U.S.A." *World Theatre/Théatre dans le Monde* 8, No. 3 (Autumn 1959): 217–24.
> Random discussion of Vidal's work in theater and television. The article is bilingual (French-English).

150. Hill, Hamlin. "Black Humor and the Mass Audience." In O. M. Brack Jr., ed. *American Humor: Essays Presented to John C. Gerber.* Scottzdale, AZ: Arete Publications, 1977, pp. 1–11 (esp. 5–10).
> Discussion of *Myra Breckinridge* along with Richard Fariña's *Been Down So Long It Looks Like Up to Me* and Philip Roth's *Portnoy's Complaint.* These books are superficial because all action is on a purely physical level. "The major characters of the three recent books are presented at a level that makes serious concern about them difficult."

151. Hines, Samuel M., Jr. "Political Change in America: Perspectives from the Popular Historical Novels of Michener and Vidal." In Ernest J. Yanarella and Lee Sigelman, ed. *Political Mythology and Popular Fiction.* Westport, CT: Greenwood Press, 1988, pp. 81–99 (esp. 92–96).
> Hines writes: "There is a real sense of the weight of history in these novels. But even more is there a sense of the personal costs and psychological burdens of having been historically significant figures." Hines focuses on *Washington, D.C., Burr, 1876,* and *Lincoln.*

152. Hirschberg, Lynn. "Feuds!" *Spy* (November 1988): 68–70, 72, 74, 76, 78, 80, 83–84 (esp. 84).
> Part of the article deals with Vidal's various feuds with William F. Buckley, Norman Podhoretz, Truman Capote, and others; includes comments by Vidal from an interview.

153. ———. "Where All Feuds Began: *The Dick Cavett Show.*" *Spy* (November 1988): 80.
> Brief discussion of the Vidal-Mailer feud.

154. Hitchens, Christopher. "An Open Letter to Gore Vidal." *Nation* 267, no. 14 (2 November 1998): 9.
       Protests against Vidal's defense of the Clinton administration. For Vidal's response, see I.F.46.

155. ———. "Vidal's Last Laugh." *Vanity Fair* no. 482 (October 2000): 252.
       Brief article on Vidal's reaction to the upcoming presidential election and his disinclination to run again for office.

156. Hoffman, Stanton. "The Cities of Night: John Rechy's *City of Night* and the American Literature of Homosexuality." *Chicago Review* 17, nos. 2–3 (1964): 195–206.
       Studies *The City and the Pillar,* James Baldwin's *Giovanni's Room,* and John Rechy's *City of Night* as homosexual novels.

157. Holzer, Harold, and Richard N. Current. "Vidal's 'Lincoln': An Exchange." *New York Review of Books* 35, no. 13 (18 August 1988): 66–67.
       Letters on "Vidal's 'Lincoln'?: An Exchange" (I.C.174) on the historical accuracy of *Lincoln.*

158. Howe, Irving; Morris Dickstein; and Hilton Kramer. "New York and the National Culture: An Exchange." *Partisan Review* 44, no. 2 (1970): 173–208.
       Panel discussion in part focusing on whether Vidal and Garry Wills represent New York intellectual culture (see especially 195, 207–8).

159. Inge, M. Thomas. "Gore Vidal and the Professors." *Encounter* 30, no. 5 (May 1968): 91.
       Long letter from a professor objecting to Vidal's characterization of academic critics in "French Letters" (I.C.70) and other writings.

160. Isherwood, Christopher. *Diaries, Volume One: 1939–1960.* Edited by Katherine Bucknell. London: Methuen, 1996, pp. 386, 393, 401–2, 406, 479, 498, 511, 513, 514, 517, 518, 520–21, 524, 526, 527, 530, 531, 532–33, 694, 695, 700, 720–21, 777, 798, 825, 858–60, 883–84.
       Extensive discussion of Vidal—his visits to Isherwood, Vidal's comments on Tennessee Williams and John F. Kennedy, and Isherwood's comments on several of Vidal's works.

161. ———. *Lost Years: A Memoir 1945–1951.* Edited by Katherine Bucknell. London: Chatto & Windus, 2000; New York: HarperCollins, 2000, pp. xv, xvii, 140n, 142–43, 145–46, 225n.
       Random discussions of Isherwood's encounters with Vidal.

162. James, Clive. "Japanese Intentions in the Second World War." *Times Literary Supplement* no. 5095 (24 November 2000): 19.
       Letter taking issue with "Three Lies to Rule By" (I.C.269), as to why the Japanese entered World War II and whether they were on the verge of surrendering in the summer of 1945. For Vidal's response, see I.F.49.

163. James, Clive, and David Murray. "Japanese Intentions in the Second World War." *Times Literary Supplement* (22 December 2000): 15.
       Letters responding to Vidal's letter (I.F.48). For Vidal's response, see I.F.50.

164. Jochnowitz, George; Francis J. Rignery, M.D.; and Gideon Forsythe. "Tribal Sex War." *New York Review of Books* 15, no. 3 (13 August 1970): 36.
       Letters commenting on Vidal's "Doc Reuben" (I.C.84). Jochnowitz protests that Jews are not alone in prejudice against gays. Rignery says that Vidal unjustly attacks psychiatry. Forsythe believes that he has caught Vidal in an error in chemistry.

165. Jones, Arthur. "A Wry Scourge on the Attack." *National Catholic Reporter* 39, no. 35 (1 August 2003): 910.
       Presents a summary of Vidal's recent political views, including the Bush administration's war on terrorism and its threat to American democracy.

166. Jones, Walter Royal, Jr.; Francis Jennings; John P. Wesley; Allen Michael Turner; Robbin Henderson; Martha Avery; Anthony S. Schlaff; Charlotte Schubert; David Phillips; Leslie J. Matthews; Adah Maurer; William J. Meecham, M.D.; Marshal Alan Phillips; Payton Hart; and Penelope Gilbert. "Abuzz and Atwitter." *Nation* 254, no. 3 (27 January 1992): 74.
      Letters commenting on "The Birds and the Bees" (I.C.193).

167. Jong, Erica. "Into the Lion's Den." *Guardian* (26 October 2000): Supplement, pp. 2–3.
      Jong visits Vidal in his villa in Ravello. They discuss writing, Norman Mailer, the upcoming presidential election, and other subjects.

168. Kaplan, Fred. "Introduction." In Vidal's *The Essential Gore Vidal.* New York: Random House, 1999; London: Little, Brown, 1999; London: Abacus, 2000, pp. ix–xxx.
      Lengthy survey of Vidal's life and career and suggestions as to his importance as a writer and thinker.

169. ————. "The Literary Psyche." *New York Times Book Review* (5 December 1999): 4.
      Letter objecting to William Deresiewicz's review of Kaplan's biography of Vidal (D.10.d).

170. Kapstein, I. J. "The Kapstein Konnection." *New York Review of Books* 21, no. 2 (21 February 1974): 33–34.
      Letter protesting Vidal's treatment of him in his essay on E. Howard Hunt (I.C.100); he likens Vidal to a "rabid dog." For Vidal's response see I.F.11.

171. Kaufman, Dave. "On All Channels." *Daily Variety* (18 October 1955): 19.
      Notes that Vidal has agreed to write teleplays for the NBC series "Writers' Choice." Kaufman discusses Vidal's other work in film and television.

172. Kazin, Alfred. "The Writer as Sexual Show-Off, or: Making Press Agents Unnecessary." *New York* 8, no. 23 (9 June 1975): 36–40.
      Article on the supposed self-promotion of Mailer, Vidal, Erica Jong, and others, especially in regard to their sexual proclivities.

173. Kerby, Phil. "Those Liberal Defectors: What Do They Want?" *Los Angeles Times* (8 April 1982): Sec. 2, p. 1.
      Op-ed article pondering why liberals are attracted to Vidal's campaign for the Senate.

174. Knight, Damon. *In Search of Wonder: Essays on Modern Science Fiction.* Rev. ed. Chicago: Advent: Publishers, 1967, pp. 175–76.
      Brief discussion of *Messiah* as a work of science fiction: it has "conviction," but "in several ways this is an appallingly bad book."

175. Koch, Stephen. "Gore Vidal: Urbane Witness to History." *Saturday Review/World* 1, no. 8 (18 December 1973): 24, 27–29.
      Cover story on Vidal as historical novelist and essayist, in the wake of the publication of *Burr.*

176. [Kolatch, Myron.] "Between Issues." *New Leader* 69, no. 7 (7–21 April 1986): 2.
      Editorial discussing the controversy between Vidal and Norman Podhoretz, referring to Vidal's "A Cheerful Response" (I.C.162) as "slime" and "anti-Semitic gore."

177. Kopkind, Andrew. "Vidalgate." In I.A.48.
      Article discussing the contretemps between Vidal and Norman Podhoretz and Midge Decter. It first appeared in the Italian magazine *Il Manifesto* (not located).

178. Kostelanetz, Richard. *The End of Intelligent Writing: Literary Politics in America.* New York: Sheed & Ward, 1974, pp. 36, 64, 66, 114, 132.
      Random and generally disparaging comments on Vidal's essays, especially in the *New York Review of Books.*

179. Krim, Seymour. "Reflections on a Ship That's Not Sinking at All." *London Magazine* NS
      10, no. 2 (May 1970): 26–43.
          Important essay based on *Reflections upon a Sinking Ship*. Krim discusses Vidal's novels,
          especially *Washington, D.C.* and *Myra Breckinridge,* showing their closeness to Vidal's essays.
          He studies Vidal's satirical style in his essays, his political orientation, his homosexuality, and
          his gift for self-promotion.

180. Lacher, Irene. "A Critical Eye." *Los Angeles Times* (30 October 1995): E1, 4.
          Discusses Vidal's career, especially his relations with Norman Mailer, Truman Capote, Charlton
          Heston, Wallis Simpson, Jackie Kennedy, and Tennessee Williams. Lacher also discusses
          Vidal's writing of *Palimpsest.* Includes numerous comments by Vidal from an interview.

181. LaHood, Marvin J. "Gore Vidal: A Grandfather's Legacy." *World Literature Today* 64, no.
      3 (Summer 1990): 413–17.
          Discusses Vidal's relations with T. P. Gore, especially his correspondence with him and Gore's
          response to Vidal's early novels. LaHood supplies a survey of Vidal's historical novels.

182. Lasky, Victor. *J.F.K.: The Man and the Myth.* New York: Macmillan, 1963, pp. 159, 314–
      15, 389, 504, 557–58, 581.
          Sporadic discussions of Vidal's relations with John F. Kennedy.

183. ———. *Robert F. Kennedy: The Myth and the Man.* New York: Trident Press, 1968, pp.
      14, 26–27, 204, 216, 217, 375.
          Random discussions of Vidal's relations with Robert F. Kennedy and the Kennedy family.

184. Lawrence, Lauren. "Gore Vidal." In Lawrence's *Private Dreams of Public People.* New
      York: Assouline, 2002.
          Not seen.

185. Lehmann, John. *The Ample Proposition: Autobiography 3.* London: Eyre & Spottiswoode,
      1966, pp. 79–80, 148–49. Rpt. in Lehmann's *In My Own Time: Memoirs of a Literary Life.*
      Boston: Little, Brown, 1969, pp. 453, 489.
          Brief discussions of publishing Vidal's work in England.

186. Lemeunier, Yves. "Aaron Burr: The American Non-President." In *La Presidence
      americaine.* Aix-en-Provence: Actes du GRENA, Groupe de Récherches et d'Etudes Nord-
      Americaines, 1979, pp. 141–55.
          Not seen.

187. Leonard, John. "Vidal—Another Opinion." *New York Times Book Review* (28 October
      1973): 55.
          Defends *Burr* against George Dangerfield's negative review (III.F.30.l), saying the novel is
          "wicked entertainment of a very high order" and that it is "Mr. Vidal's witty revenge on an
          America he doesn't like very much."

188. Levin, Bernard. "An American Serpent." *Times* (London) (23 November 1987): 14.
          A review of "The South Bank Show" devoted to Vidal (see I.I.ii.7). Levin reports Vidal's views
          on American politics, defense spending, and Soviet communism, but says that he is "not to be
          taken seriously" as a political commentator.

189. Lewis, Allan. *American Plays and Playwrights of the Contemporary Theatre.* New York:
      Crown, 1965, pp. 184–87.
          Analysis of Vidal's plays *Visit to a Small Planet, The Best Man,* and *Romulus* ("his best play and
          only failure").

190. Lidz, Theodore, M.D. "Caring for the Bird." *New York Review of Books* 32, no. 13 (15 August 1985): 44.

> Letter on "Tennessee Williams: Someone to Laugh at the Squares With" (I.C.157), defending Dr. Lawrence Kubie's treatment of Tennessee Williams. For Vidal's response, see I.F.26.

191. Lodge, David. *The Novelist at the Crossroads and Other Essays on Fiction and Criticism.* Ithaca, NY: Cornell University Press, 1971, pp. 21–22.

> Brief discussion of *Myra Breckinridge*: a "complex and accomplished" novel, but "somehow sterile and despairing."

192. Lofton, John. "Vidals Rush In Where Loftons Fear to Tread." *Nation* 255, no. 10 (5 October 1992): 346.

> Letter commenting on "Monotheism and Its Discontents" (I.C.201), stating that Vidal is a "fool" for confronting God. Lofton is the editor of *The Lofton Letter*, "A Christian newsletter." For Vidal's reply, see I.F.34.

193. Long, Barbara. "In Cold Comfort." *Esquire* 65, no. 6 (June 1966): 124, 126, 128, 171–73, 175–76, 178–81.

> An article on Truman Capote that records his brief utterances about Vidal.

194. Lowry, Robert. "Gore Vidal." In Lowry's *XXIII Celebrities.* Toronto: [Privately printed,] 1990.

> Not seen.

195. Lubow, Arthur. "Gore's Lore." *Vanity Fair* 55, no. 3 (September 1992): 126, 132, 134, 136, 142, 145.

> Article (with some words by Vidal from an interview) timed for the publication of *Live from Golgotha* (which "will not endear Vidal to pious Christians"). Lubow discusses Vidal's leftist politics, his appearance in the film *Bob Roberts,* his family and upbringing, his ruinning for office, and his life in Italy.

196. Lynn, Elizabeth A. "Introduction." In Vidal's *Messiah.* Boston: Gregg Press, 1980, pp. v–xv.

> Studies *Messiah* in the context of science fiction.

197. Macaulay, Stephen. "Gore Vidal or A Vision from a Particular Position." *Rockford Papers* 7, no. 6 (November 1982): 1–31.

> Immense but partisan and on the whole superficial survey of Vidal's life and work from *Williwaw* to *Kalki,* seeing Vidal is merely a pseudo-intellectual and his novels flawed by treatment of unsavory topics or lacking in an "affirmation of rudimentary humanness."

198. Macdonald, Dwight. "I'm Just Riled about Harry." *Esquire* 57, no. 2 (February 1962): 12.

> Letter disputing Vidal's claim that Harry Truman disapproved of the House Un-American Activities Committee.

199. McGinty, Burke. "Sans Teeth, Sans Everything." *Esquire* 72, no. 4 (October 1969): 31, 34.

> Letter commenting on Buckley's "On Experiencing Gore Vidal" (item 48 above), hoping that Vidal apologizes to Buckley for calling him a "crypto-Nazi."

200. McGregor, Jane A. "Children's Books." *New York Review of Books* 4, no. 2 (25 February 1965): 27.

> Letter on "E. Nesbit" (I.C.54.a), protesting that children's librarians do in fact encourage children to read works of the imagination.

201. McLuckie, Craig W. "'Such a Charming Absence': A Note on American Influences on William McIlvanney's Writing." *Notes on Contemporary Literature* 31, no. 2 (March 2001): 11–12.

> On the influence of Vidal's essays and of his Edgar Box novels on the Scottish novelist and essayist.

202. Mailer, Norman. *Advertisements for Myself.* New York: G. P. Putnam's Sons, 1959; New York: Perigee Books, 1981; Cambridge, MA: Harvard University Press, 1992, pp. 469–70.
    Notes Vidal's help on Mailer's play *The Deer Park;* includes Mailer's comments on Vidal's work: in his essays "he is at his best."

203. ———. "The Big Bite." *Esquire* 59, no. 6 (June 1963): 23–24, 28, 32. Rpt. in Mailer's *Cannibals and Christians.* New York: Dial Press, 1966; London: Andre Deutsch, 1967, pp. 104–30 (as "Some Children of the Goddess").
    Reports a discussion with Vidal about the decline of the American novel.

204. ———. "Of a Small and Modest Malignancy, Wicked and Bristling with Dots." *Esquire* 88, no. 5 (November 1977): 125–48. In Mailer's *Pieces and Pontifications.* Boston: Little, Brown, 1982, pp. 13–81 (esp. 55–74).
    A long article about Mailer's experiences on television, including an exhaustive discussion of his encounter with Vidal on "The Dick Cavett Show."

205. Mann, Jona J. "Is There an Angel in the House?" *Iowa English Bulletin Yearbook* 21 (Fall 1971): 39–50.
    Part of the article is a study of *Myra Breckinridge* as a satire on the notion that sex is a "goddess."

206. Markham, Charles Lam. *The Buckleys: A Family Examined.* New York: William Morrow, 1973, pp. 4, 51, 96, 146, 172, 211, 272–75.
    Random discussion of Vidal's relations with William F. Buckley Jr.

207. Mathewson, Ruth. "A 'Book-Chat' with Michael Wood on Gore Vidal." *New Leader* 60, no. 11 (23 May 1977): 15–16.
    Wood states that he admires Vidal but objects to Vidal's dismissal of "academe" as unfair.

208. Maves, Karl. "Gay Basic Bookshelf: The Maves Raves." *Advocate* no. 242 (31 May 1978): 42–43.
    Cites *Myra Breckinridge* as "the campiest, wittiest, looniest drag queen in literature," and the book as "the finest Swiftian satire in the American language."

209. Mayer, Hans. *Aussenseiter.* Frankfurt am Main: Suhrkamp Verlag, 1975, pp. 277–28. Tr. by Denis M. Sweet as *Outsiders: A Study in Life and Letters.* Cambridge, MA: MIT Press, 1982, pp. 237–38.
    Notes Vidal's argument on pornography against Susan Sontag.

210. Mayer, Kurt Albert. "'History Is Gossip, But the Trick Was in Determining Which Gossip Is History': Gore Vidal's American Chronicles, Henry James and Henry Adams." In John G. Blair and Rheinhold Wagenleitner, ed. *Empire: American Studies.* Tübingen: Gunter Narr Verlag, 1997, pp. 251–66.
    Study of Vidal's American Chronicles from *Washington, D.C.* to *Hollywood,* relating them to the critical theories of Henry James and the historical theories of Henry Adams.

211. Mayersberg, Paul. "The Fantasy of Power." *Listener* 79 (no. 2026) (25 January 1968): 104–6.
    A discussion of political films, including *The Best Man.*

212. Mazzocco, Robert. Letter to the Editor. *New York Review of Books* 22, no. 1 (6 February 1975): 38.
    Response to letters by Steven Abbott and Thom Willenbecher (item 1 above), defending his review of *Myron* (III.F.31.q).

213. Medved, Harry, and Randy Dreyfuss. *"Myra Breckinridge."* In Medved and Dreyfuss's *The Fifty Worst Films of All Time (and How They Got That Way)*. New York: Popular Library, 1978, pp. 154–58.
Superficial account of the production problems plaguing the film *Myra Breckinridge* and why it is such a bad movie.

214. Merchant, Latona; James K. Pedley; Isabel Norby; Belle Marie Faheree; John Lanigan; Lee George; and George J. Perchak. "Vidal, with Wit and Class." *Time* 107, no. 10 (22 March 1976): 4.
Letters briefly praising or disparaging Vidal, in the wake of the *Time* cover story (see item 134 above).

215. Mewshaw, Michael. "Gore Vidal." In Mewshaw's *Do I Owe You Something? A Memoir of the Literary Life*. Baton Rouge: Louisiana State University Press, 2003, pp. 164–226.
Extensive discussion of Mewshaw's meetings with Vidal; an expansion of item 217 below.

216. ———. "Gore Vidal on High: The Author Retrenches at His Amalfi Coast Villa." *Architectural Digest* 51, no. 1 (January 1994): 94–103, 158.
Notes Vidal's giving up his apartment in Rome to live permanently at La Rondinaia. Mewshaw discusses Vidal's acquisition of the villa and its architectural and decorative highlights. With many color photographs of interiors and exteriors.

217. ———. "Vidal and Mailer." *South Central Review* 19, no. 1 (Spring 2002): 4–14.
Recalls meeting Vidal in Rome, during which Vidal discussed his writing habits, his youth, and his relations with Norman Mailer. Later Mewshaw meets Mailer.

218. ———. "Vidal in Ravello." *House and Garden* 162, no. 4 (April 1990): 202–5, 220.
Article on the gardens that Vidal has established around his villa in Ravello, with numerous photographs and some comments by Vidal.

219. Michener, James A. "A Writer's Public Image." *Esquire* 64, no. 6 (December 1965): 149, 264, 266, 270, 272, 274.
Response to Vidal's comment (made to Elaine Dundy) that he "regretted . . . that he had not been fortunate enough to have established early and strong a public image of himself."

220. Miles, Jack. "Gore Vidal as Teacher." *Los Angeles Times Book Review* (21 June 1987): 15.
Study of Vidal's historical novels as educational tools for readers, who oftentimes know little about the periods he is writing about. Miles discusses Vidal's forthcoming book, titled *Harding* (i.e., *Hollywood*).

221. Milic, Louis T. "Decline." *New York Times Book Review* (9 September 1956): 30.
Letter agreeing with Vidal's "A Note on the Novel" (I.C.8).

222. Mitzel, John; Steven Abbott; and Gay Study Group. "Some Notes on Myra B." *Fag Rag* no. 6 (Fall–Winter 1973): 21–25. In D.12 (as by Mitzel only).
An idiosyncratic and somewhat self-indulgent analysis of the characters of Myra and Myron Breckinridge, with random discussions of other characters.

223. Morris, Ivan. "Mishima." *New York Review of Books* 17, no. 10 (16 December 1971): 42.
Response to Vidal's "The Death of Mishima" (I.C.87), claiming to find "a dozen or so mistakes" in the essay. For Vidal's response, see I.F.7.

224. ———. "Setting It Straight." *New York Review of Books* 18, no. 2 (10 February 1972): 34.
Response to Vidal's response (I.F.7) to his previous letter. For Vidal's response, see I.F.8.

225. Murphy, John. "Queer Books." In Murphy's *Homosexual Liberation: A Personal View*. New York: Praeger, 1971, pp. 42–72. In Karla Jay and Allen Young, ed. *Out of the Closets: Voices of Gay Liberation*. New York: Douglas/Links, 1972, pp. 72–93.
Scattered discussion of *The City and the Pillar,* deemed a "classic of this genre."

226.   Myers, John Bernard. "Who Makes Movies?" *New York Review of Books* 24, no. 1 (3 February 1977): 45.
> Letter commenting on "Who Makes the Movies?" (I.C.116), asserting the value of directors in filmmaking. For Vidal's response, see I.F.17.

227.   Nagourney, Adam. "The Bard of American Politics, Still Campaigning." *New York Times* (3 September 2000): E8, 12.
> Article on Vidal timed for the revival of *The Best Man* on Broadway. Nagourney notes that Vidal has decided not to alter the script, and he discusses the original production of 1960, in which Ronald Reagan was almost cast as William Russell.

228.   Naughton, John. "All Gore and Vidal Statistics." *Observer* (London) (17 November 1991): 78.
> An account of Vidal on "The Late Show" (BBC2) with Michael Ignatieff.

229.   Neilson, Heather. "In Epic Times: Gore Vidal's *Creation* Reconsidered." *Australasian Journal of American Studies* 23, no. 1 (July 2004): 21–33.
> Studies the role of politics and religion in the novel, in the context of the epic tradition of the *Iliad*, the *Odyssey,* and Milton's *Paradise Lost.* Neilson points to parallels between events in the novel and recent geopolitical events, especially the two Gulf wars.

230.   ————. "Jack's Ghost: Reappearances of John F. Kennedy in the Work of Gore Vidal and Norman Mailer." *American Studies International* 35, no. 3 (October 1997): 23–41.
> Traces the treatment of Kennedy in Vidal's essays (especially "The Holy Family"), his novels (especially *Washington, D.C.*), and in the memoir *Palimpsest.*

231.   ————. "*Live from Golgotha:* Gore Vidal's Second 'Fifth Gospel.'" *LiNQ* [*Literature in North Queensland*] 22, no. 2 (October 1995): 79–91.
> Detailed discussion of *Live from Golgotha* in the context of Vidal's other novels on religion, especially *Messiah;* but whereas the earlier work combined satire with *gravitas,* the later work is a "light-hearted spoof."

232.   ————. "A Reflection on the 'Culture Wars': Harold Bloom, Gore Vidal, and the Resistance of the Philistines." *Sydney Studies in English* 22 (1996–97): 120–35.
> Study of Vidal in light of Harold Bloom's theories in *The Western Canon,* with a discussion of Vidal's own views on canonicity and the function of criticism.

233.   Neuhaus, Volker. *Typen Multiperspektivischen Erzählens.* Cologne: Bohlau Verlag, 1971, pp. 164–65.
> Brief discussion of the narrative strategies in *Julian.*

234.   Nin, Anaïs. *The Diary of Anais Nin: Volume IV, 1944–1947.* Ed. Gunther Stuhlmann. New York: Harcourt Brace Jovanovich, 1971. London: Peter Owen, 1972, pp. 104, 105–6, 107, 111, 112–17, 118, 119, 121, 123, 124, 125, 130, 131, 132, 133, 134, 135, 136, 137, 139, 140, 141, 142, 144, 145, 156, 157, 165, 167, 173–74, 175, 178, 182, 186, 187, 191, 192, 202.
> Extensive discussion of Nin's initial meetings with Vidal, with a letter by Nin to Vidal (173–74) about *The City and the Pillar,* and a letter by Vidal (March 1947) from Antigua (186). For Vidal's review of the book, see I.C.89.

235.   ————. *The Diary of Anaïs Nin: Volume VI, 1955–1966.* Ed. Gunther Stuhlmann. New York: Harcourt Brace Jovanovich, 1976; London: Peter Owen, 1977 (as *The Journals of Anaïs Nin: Volume VI, 1955–1966*), pp. 257, 258, 279.
> Brief discussions of Vidal, "who represents all I dislike in writing."

236.   ———. "Under the Star of Writing: Letters to and about Gore Vidal, 1946–1961." *Anais* 14 (1996): 42–54.

> Prints letters, mostly to Vidal, discussing Vidal's early novels and essays, Paul Bowles, Lawrence Durrell, and a final letter (dated "n.d. 1960s") explaining why "Your letter destroyed our relationship."

237.   ———. *A Woman Speaks: The Lectures, Seminars, and Interviews.* Ed. Evelyn J. Hinz. Chicago: Swallow Press, 1975, pp. 235, 255.

> Brief remarks on Vidal, who became "very arrogant, very sure of himself."

238.   Olds, Nina Gore. "Mother Love." *Time* 107, no. 14 (5 April 1976): 8, 12.

> Reply by Vidal's mother to the *Time* cover story (see item 134 above), disputing the assertion that she abandoned Vidal. "I feel so sorry for him, for one day he will have regrets and sorrow."

239.   O'Neill, Dan, and Elizabeth Hayes. "The Wisdom of Not Voting." *Los Angeles Times* (31 October 1980): Sec. 2, p. 6.

> Letters responding to "In This Dismal Year, Not Casting a Vote Is the Sane Political Act" (I.C.137.a).

240.   O'Neill, Dan; Rick Mitchell; and Dennis W. Radcliffe. "Senate Race between Brown and Vidal." *Los Angeles Times* (24 April 1982): Sec. 2, p. 2.

> Letters commenting on Phil Kerby's article on Vidal's senatorial campaign (item 173 above).

241.   Palermo, Joseph A. "His Ox Is Gored." *Nation* 261, no. 3 (17–24 July 1995): 74.

> Letter commenting on "Kopkind" (I.C.222), accusing Vidal of hostility toward Robert F. Kennedy. For Vidal's response, see I.F.35.

242.   Parini, Jay. "Choosing Fred Kaplan." *New York Times Book Review* (16 January 2000): 4.

> Letter explaining how Kaplan came to be chosen as Vidal's biographer.

243.   ———. "Mentors." In Parini's *Some Necessary Angels: Essays on Writing and Politics.* New York: Columbia University Press, 1997, pp. 3–17 (esp. 13–17).

> Discusses meeting Vidal in 1985 at La Rondinaia and the influence of his literary and political beliefs upon Parini's own work.

244.   Parker, Peter. *Isherwood: A Life Revealed.* London: Picador, 2004; New York: Random House, 2004, pp. 499–501, 503–4, 553, 633, 674, 695, 697, 728.

> Brief discussions of Vidal's relations with Isherwood, including Isherwood's reaction to *The City and the Pillar* and *Myra Breckinridge.*

245.   Peabody, Leonard. "Atlas Shrieked." *Esquire* 56, no. 4 (October 1961): 14, 20.

> Letter commenting on Vidal's essay on Orville Prescott and Ayn Rand (I.C.30), claiming that Vidal is merely abusing and misrepresenting Ayn Rand rather than assessing her philosophy analytically.

246.   Pease, Donald E. "Citizen Vidal and Mailer's America." *Raritan* 11, no. 4 (Spring 1992): 72–98.

> Pease studies Vidal's and Norman Mailer's differing approaches to post–World War II American culture, especially in regard to homosexuality, totalitarianism, and the Vietnam War. He discusses *Myra Breckinridge* and *Washington, D.C.* in light of the Vietnam War. Vidal's historical novels are "part of his demystification of the national mythology." He examines Vidal's controversy with historians over *Lincoln.*

247.   Peden, William. *The American Short Story: Front Line in the National Defense of Literature.* Boston: Houghton Mifflin, 1964, pp. 114–15. Rev. ed. as *The American Short Story: Continuity and Change 1940–1975.* Boston: Houghton Mifflin, 1975, pp. 112–13.

> Brief discussion (in a footnote) of Vidal's short stories in *A Thirsty Evil.*

248. Pedersen, Lyn. "Bitch Fight of the Year: Buckley vs. Vidal." *Los Angeles Advocate* 3, no. 9 (October 1969): 3, 5.
      Survey of the Buckley-Vidal contretemps and a discussion of Buckley's long article in *Esquire* (see item 48 above).

249. Penzler, Otto. "Collecting Mystery Fiction: Edgar Box (Gore Vidal)." *Armchair Detective* 22, no. 1 (Winter 1989): 38.
      The Box novels "have nothing to recommend them apart from the fact that they were written by Gore Vidal." Penzler discusses other mainstream authors who have written mystery novels, provides synopses of the Box novels, and gauges their current market value.

250. Peterfy, Margit. "Gore Vidal's 'Public': Satire and Political Reality in *Visit to a Small Planet, The Best Man,* and *An Evening with Richard Nixon.*" *Amerikastudien/American Studies* 45, no. 2 (2000): 201–18.
      Detailed analysis of the three plays—"one a satire-turned-vaudeville, the second a play in the realistic tradition, the third an exercise in satiric hyper-realism."

251. Phillips, Gene D. *The Films of Tennessee Williams.* Philadelphia: Art Alliance Press; London: Associated University Presses, 1980, pp. 184, 185, 187, 192, 194, 195, 196, 213, 217, 218, 224–25, 253.
      Sporadic discussion of Vidal's work on *Suddenly, Last Summer* and *The Last of the Mobile Hot-Shots.*

252. Phillips, Robert. "Gore Vidal's Greek Revival: 'The Ladies in the Library.'" *Notes on Modern American Literature* 6, no. 1 (Spring–Summer 1982): Item 3 (pp. [7–8]).
      A brief discussion of Vidal's use of the Aeneas myth in his story: Walter Bragnet is Aeneas, his cousin Sybil is Dido, and the three Parker sisters are the *Parcae* (Fates).

253. PHS. "The Times Diary: Not-So-Literary Punch Lines at VIP Party." *Times* (London) (27 October 1977): 18.
      Report of the Mailer-Vidal fisticuffs at a Washington dinner party in honor of Lord Weidenfeld.

254. Plimpton, George. *Truman Capote.* New York: Nan A. Talese/Doubleday, 1997, pp. 45, 47, 64–65, 87–90, 103, 240–43, 280, 295, 297, 301, 305–6, 308, 378–83, 411, 430, 443–44.
      Random discussions of Vidal's relations with Capote, including their feud and their opinion of each other's writings.

255. Podhoretz. Norman. "The Hate That Dare Not Speak Its Name." *Commentary* 82, no. 5 (November 1986): 21–32.
      Long-winded article in which Podhoretz thinks it is self-evident that Vidal's attack on himself and Midge Decter in "A Cheerful Response" (I.C.162) is anti-Semitic, not merely anti-Zionist. He also briefly discusses Vidal's earlier essay, "*Some* Jews and *the* Gays" (I.C.142.a). He is amazed at the relative lack of outrage over Vidal's article; he had in fact sent twenty-nine letters to various intellectuals asking them to condemn the article, but only a small number did so. He notes that the editorial in the *New Republic* attacking Vidal (item 325 below) had created a stir, but he remains unsatisfied that more intellectuals have not censured Vidal.

256. ———. "A Severe Case of Writers' Bloc." *New York Post* (3 December 1985): 29.
      Attack on Vidal and Norman Mailer as hostile to "the kind of country they imagine America has become in the past hundred years." It is unclear whether this brief article was written as a response to Vidal's as-yet-unpublished lecture, "Requiem for the American Empire" (I.C.161.a). It led to Vidal's celebrated rebuttal, "A Cheerful Response" (I.C.261).

257. [Podhoretz, Norman, ed.] "Anti-Semitism, Left and Right." *Commentary* 83, no. 3 (March 1987): 2, 4–6, 8–10.
      A collection of letters—by Arnold Beichman, Paul Sperry, David T. Fried, Martin Merson, Edward E. Ericson Jr., Lewis L. Kramer, John Gelles, Irving Gavrin, Zachary D. Fasman, Harold B. Aspis, Joe Weber, Leo Rettig, Albert E. Cohen, David Gertsman, James J. Carberry, Charles

Ansell, N. A. Mednick, Joseph R. Aziz, Ted Kaplan, Stephen Chapman, Irving Louis Horowitz, Steven A. Falk, Joel Bellman, Bernard Greenspan, David Isenberg, Philip Hochstein, Adolph Lusthaus, Léon Poliakov, and Gerhard Wolfgang Goldberg—commenting on Podhoretz's "The Hate That Dare Not Speak Its Name," the majority of them predictably condemning Vidal; with a final comment by Podhoretz.

258.   Poirier, Richard. "Mailer: Good Form and Bad." *Saturday Review* 55, no. 17 (22 April 1972): 42–46. In Laura Adams, ed. *Will the Real Norman Mailer Please Stand Up?* Port Washington, NY: Kennikat Press, 1974, pp. 233–43.
      Discusses the Mailer-Vidal relationship in the wake of their confrontation on "The Dick Cavett Show."

259.   Powell, Jody. "Gory Duel Leaves Vidal and Podhoretz Headless, Topless." *Los Angeles Times* (22 May 1986): Sec. 2, p. 7.
      Op-ed article presenting an overview of the feud between Gore Vidal and Norman Podhoretz/Midge Decter, concluding: "Here we have a trio of aging, self-righteous ideologues bent on exposing the absurdities of their intellectual configuration to all who can stomach the spectacle."

260.   Prideaux, Tom. "Author of Hit and a Candidate." *Life* 48, no. 16 (25 April 1960): 55, 57–58, 60.
      A biographical article focusing on Vidal's successful play, *The Best Man,* and his running for Congress. With several photographs of scenes from the play and of Vidal and his family.

261.   Pritchard, William H. "Vidal's Satiric Voices." In Pritchard's *Playing It by Ear: Literary Essays and Reviews.* Amherst: University of Massachusetts Press, 1994, pp. 161–68.
      Reprint of his essay in I.D.13.

262.   Purdom, Todd S. "A Grand Old Setting for Politics of the Imagination." *New York Times* (11 August 1996): B27.
      Discusses *The Best Man* (film) in the context of other films about political conventions. Vidal's "sparkling dialogue and the trenchancy of his political world view remain as fresh and relevant as ever."

263.   Quinn, Sally. "In Hot Blood." *Washington Post* (6 June 1979): B1, 3; (7 June 1979): C1, 7.
      Interview with Truman Capote in which he accuses Vidal and Lee Radziwill of "betraying" him, especially in regard to the incident at the White House that led to Vidal's suit against Capote. The second part of the article prints extensive comments by Vidal explaining his side of the incident.

264.   R. "Column." *Encounter* 33, no. 5 (November 1969): 43–45.
      Contains a discussion of the Buckley-Vidal contretemps in *Esquire.*

265.   Rader, Dotson. *Blood Dues.* New York: Alfred A. Knopf, 1973, pp. 53–54, 55, 64–65.
      Random discussions of Vidal as a leftist writer, and an examination of his relations with Tennessee Williams.

266.   Rense, Paige. "Gore Vidal." In Rense's *Celebrity Homes.* Los Angeles: Knapp Press, 1977, pp. 144–51.
      Description, with many photographs, of Vidal's villa in Ravello.

267.   Resetarits, C. R. "Gore Vidal, Henry James: Turning Another Jolly Corner." *Journal of Gender Studies* 14, no. 1 (March 2005): 61–64.
      On the possible influence of James's story "The Jolly Corner" on *Palimpsest,* especially in regard to Vidal's love of Jimmie Trimble and Spencer Dryden's looking back at his alter ego of thirty years before.

268. Richards, Peter. "Whose Hur?" *Film Comment* 35, no. 2 (March–April 1999): 38–42.
Discusses the controversy over the screenwriting credits for *Ben-Hur,* concluding that "many lines of dialogue have an authentically Vidalian, sardonic tone." But Richards doubts whether there is a covert homosexual subtext to the film, as Vidal maintains.

269. Rosenstein, Beverly B. "Flight from Reality." *New York Times* (6 October 1970): 46.
Letter commenting on Vidal's "Drugs" (I.C.85), claiming that the article is "replete with contradictions and superficial thoughts."

270. Ross, Mitchell S. "Gore Vidal." In Ross's *The Literary Politicians.* Garden City, NY: Doubleday, 1978, pp. 247–300.
Broad overview of Vidal's life and career, focusing on the political elements in his work and their controversial nature, especially *The City and the Pillar, The Judgment of Paris,* and the plays. Ross also discusses Vidal's satirical essays, his encounters with William F. Buckley, his attitudes toward sex (as seen through *Myra Breckinridge* and *Myron*), and his historical novels (which are "teasings on a grand scale").

271. Rothberg, S. H. "The Flawed Dream: American Novels of Politics." *London Magazine* 6, no. 1 (April 1966): 17–33.
Brief discussion of *The Best Man* (24–25).

272. Safier, Gloria; Leland Moss; Parker Tyler; Rabbi Samuel M. Silver; Audrey Clark; and Rosa Moline. "'Myra': Is She Naughty or Nice?" *New York Times* (19 July 1970): Sec. 2, pp. 4–5.
Letters commenting on the film *Myra Breckinridge.* Safier says the film is a "witless melange of street dirt." Moss defends both the book and the film, saying that they are about "the horrifying distortion of sexual values and definitions that exists in this country." Tyler objects to the portrayal of himself in both the book and the film. Silver believes he and the public have been "dragged through the mire." Clark says the film was "awful" but defends Mae West. Moline says the film is both "pretty dirty" and "pretty funny."

273. Safire, William. "Vidal, Waldheim, Grant." *New York Times* (19 May 1986): A21.
Op-ed article taking note of the controversy between Vidal and Norman Podhoretz. Safire states that Vidal's article is "silly" and compares his attitude toward Jews with that of Austrian premier Kurt Waldheim and American president U. S. Grant.

274. Schlanger, Murray. "Sans Teeth, Sans Everything." *Esquire* 72, no. 4 (October 1969): 31.
Letter on Buckley's "On Experiencing Gore Vidal" (item 48 above), saying that Buckley, Vidal, Capote, and Mailer are overrated as writers and thinkers.

275. Schlereth, Thomas J. "Fictions and Facts: Henry Adams's *Democracy* and Gore Vidal's *1876.*" *Southern Quarterly* 16, no. 3 (April 1978): 209–22.
Studies the relations between the two novels: both cover approximately the same time period, both create a fictional narrator to tell the story, both re-create historical personages, and both attempt, "with varying degrees of success, to re-create the ambience of an era more persuasively than if they were writing traditional narrative history."

276. Schlesinger, Arthur, Jr. "The Historical Mind and the Literary Imagination." *Atlantic Monthly* 233, no. 6 (June 1974): 54–59.
A comparison of Vidal and John Updike, especially in their treatments of history in *Burr* and Updike's play *Buchanan's Rising* (about James Buchanan), mostly about the latter.

277. Scott, Robert H.; Lois K. Vincent; amd Paul R. Jackson. "Vidal's Portrayal of Lincoln." *Los Angeles Times* (21 February 1981): Sec. 2, p. 4.
Letters, mostly critical, on "Lincoln: 'His Ambition Was a Little Engine That Knew No Rest'" (I.C.140.a).

278.　Shalom, Stephen Rosskam, and John M. Gates. "Death in the Philippines." *New York Review of Books* 29, no. 3 (4 March 1982): 44.
    Further letters (see items 81 and 122) questioning the death totals of Filipinos in the Spanish-American War. For Vidal's response, see I.F.24.

279.　Shively, Charely [*sic*]. "Interview Commentary." *Fag Rag* nos. 7/8 (Winter–Spring 1974): 9.
    Commentary on C.1. Vidal is popular "not in spite but because he does express sexist, racist and elitist sentiments that *Fag Rag* has been struggling to overcome." Vidal has no vision of change.

280.　Simon, John. "Waltz of the Toreadors." *New York* 18, no. 47 (2 December 1985): 33.
    Report of readings by Vidal and Norman Mailer at a PEN meeting, suggesting that they had made peace.

281.　Sternberg, Cecilia. *The Journey*. London: Collins, 1977; New York: Dial Press, 1977, pp. 313, 314.
    Brief account of meeting Vidal in the company of Albrecht Edward Bismarck.

282.　Stimpson, Catharine R. "My O My O Myra." *New England Review* 14, no. 1 (Fall 1991): 102–15. In D.13.
    Dense and sophisticated article studying Myra Breckinridge as a "self-willed woman and divinity, self-named 'eternal feminine' and goddess." Stimpson examines the use of Plato and of Petronius' *Satyricon* in *Myra Breckinridge* and *Myron*. She sees the novels as a parody of the "nouveau roman."

283.　Styron, William. "Vidal Blue." *Atlantic Monthly* 229, no. 5 (May 1972): 27.
    Letter on Gerald Clarke's "Petronius Americanus" (item 69 above), claiming that Styron never stated that Vidal was not among the "five big writers in the country today." For Vidal's response, see I.F.9.

284.　Sultan, Michael, M.D. Letter to the Editor. *Esquire* 67, no. 6 (June 1967): 12.
    Letter on "The Holy Family" (I.C.67), asserting that in the article "Inaccuracy is superseded only by arrogance."

285.　Summers, Claude J. "'The Cabin and the River': Gore Vidal's *The City and the Pillar*." In Summers's *Gay Fictions: From Wilde to Stonewall*. New York: Continuum, 1990, pp. 112–29. In D.13.
    Studies Vidal's portrayal of the post–World War II gay subculture in his novel; but "the novel has more than sociological interest," and Summers examines its use of the myth of Sodom as a structural device, as well as Vidal's revisions in the 1965 edition.

286.　Tatum, James. "The *Romanitas* of Gore Vidal." *Raritan* 11, no. 4 (Spring 1992): 99–122. In D.13.
    Lengthy article that studies Vidal's attitude toward the Latin language and Latin literature, the Roman-style monuments in Washington, D.C., and the parallels between the Roman Empire and the American empire.

287.　Thernstrom, Stephan and Abigail; Richard Sennett; J. Everet Green; Robert Paul Wolff. "Historians—Good, Bad and Ugly." *Nation* 266, no. 18 (18 May 1998): 2, 24.
    Letters commenting on "Bad History" (I.C.249). The Thernstroms protest that Vidal has distorted their views and that his lectures at Harvard (the basis for *Screening History*) were poorly attended. Wolff notes that in their college years the Thernstroms had been far-left liberals. For Vidal's response, see I.F.44.

288.　Thimmesch, Nick, and William Johnson. *Robert Kennedy at 40*. New York: W. W. Norton & Co., 1965, pp. 175, 197, 203–4, 216.
    Random discussions of Vidal's relations with Robert F. Kennedy.

289. Thomas, Julia. Letter to the Editor. *Esquire* 70, no. 6 (December 1968): 18.
A letter on "A Manifesto" (I.C.76), disputing Vidal's account of the economic origin of the family.

290. Topkin, Jay. "Rosebud." *New York Review of Books* 36, no. 13 (17 August 1989): 60.
Letter commenting on "Remembering Orson Welles" (I.C.180). For Vidal's response see I.F.31.

291. Trilling, Diana. "Powell's People." *New York Review of Books* 35, no. 6 (14 April 1988): 45.
Letter on "Dawn Powell: The American Writer" (I.C.169), quoting at length her review of Powell's *The Locusts Have No King* in the *Nation* (19 September 1942). For Vidal's response, see I.F.29.

292. Tucker, Ken. "Vidal Signs." *Entertainment Weekly* no. 720 (25 July 2003): 62.
Speaks generally favorably of a new documentary, *The Education of Gore Vidal*, on PBS's "American Masters" series.

293. Tyler, Parker. *Screening the Sexes: Homosexuality in the Movies*. New York: Holt, Rinehart & Winston, 1972, pp. 5, 6, 7–8, 10, 12–16, 69–70, 199–202, 204–5, 207–9.
Sporadic discussion of the film *Myra Breckinridge* and, incidentally, the novel.

294. Tyrrell, R. Emmett, Jr. "Pietistic Gore." *American Spectator* 25, no. 12 (December 1992): 14.
Editorial asserting that Vidal is in fact "haunted" by the Christianity he lampoons in *Live from Golgotha*.

295. Vespa, Mary. "Sued by Gore Vidal and Stung by Lee Radziwill, a Wounded Truman Capote Lashes Back at the Dastardly Duo." *People* 11, no. 25 (25 June 1979): 35–36.
Reports Vidal's lawsuit against Capote emerging from Capote's interview in *Playgirl* (item 318 below) and displays Capote's anger at Vidal and at Lee Radziwill and others for not confirming his account of the White House party at the heart of the suit.

296. Wakefield, Dan. "Gore Vidal: The Best Man." *Nation* 191, no. 11 (8 October 1960): 222–24.
Article on Vidal's running for Congress.

297. Ward, Geoffrey C. "Vidal's Lincoln." *American Heritage* 35, no. 5 (August–September 1984): 18–19.
Reports fears that Vidal's portrayal of Lincoln in *Lincoln* might be a scurrilous portrait, but in fact his Lincoln is not so different from the figure as depicted by modern scholarship. "Before anything else, Vidal's Lincoln is a skilled and subtle politician."

298. Weales, Gerald. *American Drama Since World War II*. New York: Harcourt, Brace & World, 1962, pp. 58, 59, 60, 61, 62, 64, 65–66, 71, 73, 107, 113–14, 159.
Sporadic discussion of *Visit to a Small Planet* and *The Best Man*, mostly the former.

299. Wershba, Joseph; Leonard Kriegel; Jack Stauder; Steven L. Rubinstein; Micah Morrison; Irving M. Levine; and Roger Wilkins. "Exchange." *Nation* 242, no. 17 (26 April 1986): 570, 588, 596.
Letters commenting on "The Empire Lovers Strike Back" (I.C.162.a), most of them accusing Vidal of anti-Semitism. For Vidal's response, see I.F.27.

300. Westfahl, Gary. *Science Fiction, Children's Literature, and Popular Culture: Coming of Age in Fantasyland*. Westport, CT: Greenwood Press, 2000, pp. 109–11.
Brief discussion of *Hollywood* and the variations it plays on the standard Hollywood novel.

301. Weyr, Rhoda. "Vidal vs. Kaplan." *New York Times Book Review* (2 January 2000): 2.
Letter from Fred Kaplan's wife objecting to Vidal's remarks (I.F.46) about how Kaplan came to be named Vidal's biographer.

302.   Whitaker, Rick. *The First Time I Met Frank O'Hara: Reading Gay American Writers.* New York: Four Walls Eight Windows, 2003, pp. 156–62.
A study of *The City and the Pillar,* with some discussion of homosexuality in *Palimpsest.*

303.   W[ieseltier], L[eon]. "Washington Diarist: Abu Vidal." *New Republic* 198, no. 14 (4 April 1988): 42.
Tells of attending a meeting of the American-Arab Anti-Discrimination League where Vidal gave a speech. Accuses Vidal of anti-Semitism.

304.   Wilhelm, John F., and Mary Ann Wilhelm. "'Myra Breckinridge': A Study of Identity." *Journal of Popular Culture* 3, no. 3 (Winter 1969): 590–99.
Studies the role of film in *Myra Breckinridge* as well as the major characters in the novel.

305.   Williams, Tennessee. *Five O'Clock Angel: Letters of Tennessee Williams to Maria St. Just 1948–1982.* New York: Alfred A. Knopf, 1990, pp. 7, 8, 9, 11, 12, 13, 14, 16, 104, 114, 157, 161, 164, 170, 183, 190, 202, 205, 215, 227, 257, 291, 293, 312, 325, 338, 357.
Sporadic discussion of encounters with Vidal, mostly in Europe, with some discussion of *Suddenly, Last Summer.*

306.   ———. "Gore Vidal." *McCall's* 94, no. 1 (October 1966): 107. Rpt. in Roddy McDowall, ed. *Double Exposure.* New York: Delacorte Press, 1966, p. 232.
One-paragraph characterization of Vidal as a person.

307.   ———. *Memoirs.* Garden City, NY: Doubleday, 1975, pp. xvi–xvii, 146–50, 158.
Random discussions of encounters with Vidal, mostly in Europe.

308.   ———. *Tennessee Williams' Letters to Donald Windham 1940–1965.* Ed. Donald Windham. New York: Holt, Rinehart & Winston, 1977, pp. 211, 213, 215–16, 221–23, 243, 245n, 246, 252, 255, 260, 264, 266n.
Sporadic discussion of Vidal in letters from 1948 to 1950.

309.   Wilson, Robert. "Gore Vidal Nibbles at Hollywood and Politics." *USA Today* (8 October 1992): 13D.
Reports Vidal's new books (*Live from Golgotha, Screening History,* and *The Decline and Fall of the American Empire*), his acting in *Bob Roberts,* and his various TV appearances.

310.   Windham, Donald. "Solved!" *New York Review of Books* 23, no. 3 (4 March 1976): 38.
Letter querying a point in Vidal's article on Tennessee Williams (I.C.112). For Vidal's response, see I.F.12.

311.   Wood, Ramsay. "The Wisdom of the East." *New York Review of Books* 27, no. 2 (21 February 1980): 44.
Letter commenting on "Paradise Regained" (I.C.131.a), defending Idries Shah. For Vidal's response, see I.F.21.

312.   Woodhouse, Reed. "Gore Vidal's *Myra Breckinridge.*" In Woodhouse's *Unlimited Embrace: A Canon of Gay Fiction, 1945–1995.* Amherst: University of Massachusetts Press, 1998, pp. 53–62.
Discusses Myra as a sexual dandy, her adoption of male characteristics, and her aristocratic arrogance.

313.   Woodward, C. Vann. "Gilding Lincoln's Lily." *New York Review of Books* 34, no. 14 (24 September 1987): 23–26 (esp. 23).
A review-essay on William Safire's historical novel about Lincoln, *Freedom,* with a brief aside on Vidal's *Lincoln* and the criticism of it by historians. This passage led to the first of Vidal's lengthy discussions on the issue (see C.174).

314. Yoder, Edwin M., Jr. "Is Distaste for Israeli Policy Anti-Semitism?" *Los Angeles Times* (22
      May 1986): Sec. 2, p. 7.
      Op-ed article on the Vidal/Podhoretz feud, generally taking Vidal's side: "Podhoretz seems blind to
      the extent to which U.S. dialectics on Israel have gotten out of hand." Podhoretz "asked for it."

315. ———. "The Shadow of Lincoln." *Washington Post* (30 June 1984): A19.
      Op-ed article on *Lincoln,* stating that Vidal has stuck too close to the facts and not allowed his
      imagination free play.

316. Zimmerman, Paul D. "Elan Vidal." *Newsweek* 71, No. 9 (26 February 1968): 88.
      Based on an interview. Zimmerman discusses *Myra Breckinridge, The Best Man,* and Vidal's
      versatility.

317. Ziolkowski, Theodore. *Fictional Transfigurations of Jesus.* Princeton: Princeton University
      Press, 1972, pp. 8, 226–28, 230–31, 250–57, 266, 275, 277, 286, 295–96.
      Studies the character John Cave in *Messiah* as a Christ figure.

318. Zoerink, Richard. "Truman Capote Talks about His Crowd." *Playgirl* 3, no. 4 (September
      1975): 50–51, 54, 80–81, 128.
      In part of this interview (pp. 54, 80), Capote makes his notorious claim that "Bobby [Kennedy]
      had Gore thrown out of the White House," leading to Vidal's lawsuit against Capote.

319. [Unsigned.] "Versatile Vidal." *Newsweek* 45, no. 25 (20 June 1955): 84–85.
      Notes Vidal's prolific work as a television playwright and tells of his future projects.

320. [Unsigned.] "Gore Vidal: Politician." *Nation* 190, no. 16 (16 April 1960): 326–27.
      Editorial endorsing Vidal in his campaign for the U.S. Congress.

321. [Unsigned.] "People Are Talking about . . . Gore Vidal." *Vogue* 136, no. 2 (1 August 1960):
      80–81.
      Shows Vidal in the octagon-shaped library in his house at Hyde Park and discusses his recent
      work in literature and film.

322. [Unsigned.] "Veni (Vidal) Vici." *National Review* 11, no. 14 (7 October 1961): 223.
      Editorial protesting that the magazine did not call Vidal a Communist when it referred to him as
      a "Stakhanovite Liberal."

323. [Unsigned.] "People Are Talking About . . . Gore Vidal." *Vogue* 156, no. 9 (15 November
      1970): 108–9.
      Discusses *Myra Breckinridge* and *Two Sisters.* A large photo of Vidal accompanies the article.

324. [Unsigned.] "Still Feuding After All These Years, Gore and Norman Stage Fight Night at
      Lally's." *People* 8, no. 20 (14 November 1977): 42–43.
      Quotes both Vidal and Norman Mailer in regard to the fight at a Washington dinner party.

325. [Unsigned.] "Patriotic Gore." *New Republic* 194, no. 17 (28 April 1986): 8–9.
      Editorial reporting on the debate between Vidal and Norman Podhoretz/Midge Decter, accusing
      Vidal of anti-Semitism ("This man is ready for the funny farm").

326. [Unsigned.] "Patriotic Gore: A Big-League Literary Feud." *Newsweek* 107, no. 20 (19 May
      1986): 25.
      Brief account of the debate between Vidal and Norman Podhoretz/Midge Decter.

327. [Unsigned.] "The Vidal Exemption." *National Review* 38, no. 10 (6 June 1986): 20.
      Editorial condemning Vidal's attack on Norman Podhoretz/Midge Decter.

328. [Unsigned.] "Buckley's Search." *Nation* 254, no. 1 (6–13 January 1992): 4–5.
      Editorial about Buckley's "In Search of Anti-Semitism" (item 47 above), disputing the charge of
      anti-Semitism directed by Buckley toward Vidal and the *Nation.*

F. Book Reviews

1. *Williwaw*
   a. Coleman, John. "Novels or Whatever." *Observer* (London) no. 9348 (13 September 1970): 28.
   b. Daniels, Jonathan. "Dirty Weather." *Saturday Review of Literature* 29, no. 27 (6 July 1946): 27–28.
   c. Fields, Arthur C. "Turbulence of the Sea." *New York Herald Tribune Weekly Book Review* (23 June 1946): 17.
   d. [Green, Peter.] "What's New, Pussycat?" *Times Literary Supplement* no. 3577 (18 September 1970): 1026.
   e. Kingery, Robert E. *Library Journal* 71, no. 11 (1 June 1946): 824.
   f. Morgan, Rhea M. "Gore Vidal's Novel of 'Big Wind' in Arctic." *Springfield Republican* (28 July 1946): 4D.
   g. Power, Chris. "Paperbacks." *Times* (London) (20 December 2003): Weekend Review, p. 16.
   h. Prescott, Orville. "Books of the Times." *New York Times* (17 June 1946): 19.
   i. Rees, David. "Big Northern Storm." *Spectator* 215 (no. 7170) (26 November 1965): 716.
   j. Schorer, Mark. "The American Novel." *Kenyon Review* 9, no. 4 (Autumn 1947): 628–36.
   k. S[tevens], A[ustin]. "Aleutian Twister." *New York Times Book Review* (23 June 1946): 4.
   l. Tahourdin, Adrian. *Times Literary Supplement* no. 5263 (13 February 2004): 23.
   m. [Unsigned.] *Kirkus* 14, no. 9 (1 May 1946): 203.

Coleman believes that the novel "tells a plain, holding tale. . . . It is not 'deceptively' simple, just simple." . . . **Daniels** finds *Williwaw* "a very simple and very masculine book . . . a novel of great promise." . . . **Fields** writes: "The foreboding atmosphere aboard the ship brings to the fore the lights and shadows of their [the characters'] beings," but too much plot has been crammed into the book. . . . **Green** feels that the novel is "so bogusly and brilliantly 'significant' . . . and so winsomely innocent in its prose rhythms that its author almost deserves the embarrassment of its re-issue." . . . **Morgan** states that Vidal "writes in brief clipped sentences with dramatic force. Much may well be expected" from him. . . . **Prescott** states that the novel is "a sound, craftsmanlike work that would do credit to a practiced novelist twice its author's age." The dialogue is "excellent, simple, spare and natural." The work "is occasionally humorous and continuously interesting." . . . **Rees** asserts that "The style is flat, nervous, bleak, with a Hemingwayesque patina matching the subject"; but the novel "works." . . . **Schorer**, in a multiple review, notes that the work is "an accomplished novel of action, somewhat in the manner of Stephen Crane." . . . **Stevens** declares that the book "exhibits little strain and lots of discipline." Vidal "writes carefully but without self-consciousness." . . . **Tahourdin**, in a review of a recent reprint, deems the work a "tight, well-crafted novel. The dialogue is sharp and the description of the barren Aleutians . . . vivid."

2. *In a Yellow Wood*
   a. Barr, Donald. "The Veteran's Choice." *New York Times Book Review* (16 March 1947): 10.
   b. Craig, Patricia. "Back to Reality." *New Statesman* 97 (no. 2507) (6 April 1979): 489.
   c. Kingery, Robert E. *Library Journal* 72, no. 6 (15 March 1947): 464.
   d. Lee, Hermione. "All in the Day's Work." *Observer* (London) no. 9787 (25 March 1979): 36.
   e. Rothman, Nathan L. "A Strange Sort of War Casualty." *Saturday Review of Literature* 30, no. 22 (31 May 1947): 21.
   f. Schorer, Mark. "The American Novel." *Kenyon Review* 9, no. 4 (Autumn 1947): 628–36.

g.   Stefanchev, Stephen. "Four Roads to Tomorrow." *New York Herald Tribune Weekly Book Review* (16 March 1947): 10.

h.   Textor, Clinton. "Returned Vet Wants Only Humdrum Life." *Chicago Sun Book Week* (27 April 1947): 2.

i.   Yanitelli, Victor R. *Best Sellers* 7, no. 1 (1 April 1947): 7.

j.   [Unsigned.] *Kirkus* 15, no. 2 (15 January 1947): 43.

k.   [Unsigned.] *New Yorker* 23, no. 5 (22 March 1947): 115.

Barr finds the novel a "brief and unpretentious story." But the central character is a cipher: "here there is less than the author believes." . . . **Craig** believes the novel is effective but limited in scope. . . . **Lee**, in a multiple review, notes that this is "a big, flatly and repetitively written Jeremiad on post-war New York, a wasteland of glitter and hollow men." . . . **Rothman** considers the book "a surprisingly effective novel . . . Mr. Vidal's writing is a first-rate example of controlled naturalism." . . . **Schorer**, in a multiple review, dismisses the novel as "trivial." . . . **Stefanchev** feels that "The novel demonstrates Mr. Vidal's psychological acuteness" but "its special virtue is its admirable structure." . . . **Textor** states that Vidal "writes simply and cleanly and with real reserve," but the hero is weak. . . . **Yanitelli**, in a disdainful review, writes: "Twenty-two pages of homosexualism have nothing to do with the case, and could well have been left in the gutter where they were found without affecting the plot one way or another."

3.   *The City and the Pillar*

a.   Dawson, Helen. "Briefing: Paperbacks." *Observer* (London) no. 9458 (5 November 1972): 35.

b.   Donahugh, Robert H. *Library Journal* 90, no. 10 (15 May 1965): 2289–90.

c.   Doyle, Edward Dermot. "An Honest Approach." *San Francisco Chronicle* (2 February 1948): 14.

d.   Fiedler, Leslie. "The Fate of the Novel." *Kenyon Review* 10, No. 3 (Summer 1948): 519–27.

e.   Gehman, Richard B. "Abnormal Doom." *New York Herald Tribune Weekly Book Review* (18 January 1948): 6.

f.   Haslett, Adam. "The Name of Love." *Nation* 277, no. 19 (8 December 2003): 26, 28–32.

g.   Kingery, Robert E. *Library Journal* 72, no. 2 (1 December 1947): 1686.

h.   Kramer, Hilton. "Queer Affirmations." *New Leader* 48, no. 17 (30 August 1965): 16–17.

i.   McLaughlin, Richard. "Precarious Status." *Saturday Review of Literature* 31, no. 2 (10 January 1948): 14–15.

j.   Marcus, Steven. "A Second Look at Sodom." *New York Herald Tribune Book Week* (20 June 1965): 5.

k.   Mayne, Richard. "Make 'Em Wait." *New Statesman* 70 (no. 1803) (1 October 1965): 488–89.

l.   Newby, P. H. "New Novels." *Listener* 41 (no. 1058) (5 May 1949): 774.

m.   Price, R. G. G. "New Novels." *Punch* 249 (no. 6526) (6 October 1965): 512–13 (esp. 512).

n.   Rolo, Charles J. "Reader's Choice." *Atlantic Monthly* 181, no. 2 (February 1948): 107–12 (esp. 110).

o.   Shrike, J. S. "Recent Phenomena." *Hudson Review* 1, no. 1 (Spring 1948): 136–38, 140, 142, 144 (esp. 137–38, 140).

p.   Strachey, Julia. "New Novels." *New Statesman and Nation* 37 (no. 949) (14 May 1949): 510, 512.

q.   Strong, L. A. G. "Fiction." *Spectator* 182 (no. 6305) (29 April 1949): 586, 588.

r.   Terry, C. V. *New York Times Book Review* (11 January 1948): 22.

s.   Woods, Gregory. "Don't Look Back." *Times Literary Supplement* no. 4765 (29 July 1994): 19.

t.   Zebrowski, Walter. "Polish Americans in Fiction." *Polish American Studies* 16, nos. 1–2 (January–June 1959): 63.

u.   [Unsigned.] *Books and Bookmen* 18, no. 3 (December 1972): 123.

v.   [Unsigned.] *Kirkus* 15, no. 23 (1 November 1947): 608.
w.   [Unsigned.] *New York Times Book Review* (10 February 1974): 18.
x.   [Unsigned.] *New Yorker* 23, no. 47 (10 January 1948): 81.

Doyle states that the book is a "straightforward, unimpassioned appeal for understanding of a subject that remains until now one of the major taboos." But the ending is melodramatic: "It is the only false note in the novel." . . . **Fiedler**, in a multiple review, believes that the novel is "self-effacing, underwritten, *dull*." But "there *is* a real honesty that gives the book a certain brute impact, accidental to its nature as a novel." . . . **Gehman** finds the book "frank, shocking, sensational and often embarrassing, but it is also extremely sympathetic, penetrating and exhortive." But the style is careless. . . . **Haslett**, in a long retrospective review, asserts that the novel "remains remarkably salient, capturing the anxieties of American masculinity." But "it would be a seriouis mistake to think it is an early literary banner for gay rights or a gay identity." . . . **Kramer**, in a multiple review, cautiously welcomes the end of "the era of guilt and dissimulation" in American homosexual literature. Speaking of the revised version, Kramer states: "Vidal, always the obliging literary jobber, has touched up his outmoded tale with exactly the stroke needed to excite new interest." . . . **McLaughlin** uses the book to urge "an intelligent, well-balanced revaluation of our present legal codes on sexual behavior, normal or otherwise." He thinks the book is more successful as a "social tract" than as a novel. . . . **Marcus**, reviewing the revised edition, writes that Vidal "has wrought considerable changes in the new version." All the revisions "move toward economy, toward irony, toward a kind of harshness and acerbity of tone." But the new version "does not work" because "it is not as interesting a book" as the original. . . . **Mayne** asserts that the book is a "documentary," but gives Vidal credit for broaching a taboo subject. . . . **Newby** maintains that even though the "first chapter is tedious," this is "a good novel," "a wise and sober book about homosexuality. . . . Mr. Vidal tells a good story and his narrative is charged with imagination." . . . **Price**, reviewing the revised edition in a multiple review, feels that the novel "suffers from the thinness of the characters. Many of them are nothing but homosexuals." . . . **Rolo**, in a multiple review, claims that the work is an "attempt to clarify the inner stresses of our time, of which the increase in homosexuality and divorce are symptoms. It should be added that Mr. Vidal has not neglected to provide an entertaining story." . . . **Shrike**, reviewing the book along with Kinsey's *Sexual Behavior in the Human Male* and Truman Capote's *Other Voices, Other Rooms*, writes: "Aside from its sociological demonstration, Mr. Vidal's book is undistinguished. It is humorless, and most of its scenes are faked, as are the house interiors, the natural landscapes, and all the characters. The hero . . . is a stiff automaton." . . . **Strong** declares that "the theme is most sensitively handled" but that the conclusion may be "a way out rather than a solution." . . . **Woods** notes that the moral of the novel is "Don't Look Back." The book is notable, but it "was completed before Vidal became witty." The revised edition is "a mess." . . . The ***New York Times Book Review***'s brief review finds Vidal's "approach is coldly clinical"; "there is no real attempt to involve the reader's emotions." The "overall picture is as unsensational as it is boring." The novel is "sterile." . . . The brief ***New Yorker*** review states that the book is "disappointing": it "represents the latest, and possibly ultimate, stage in the decline of the literature of homosexuality to the level of unadorned tabloid writing."

4.   *The Season of Comfort*
  a.   Aldridge, John W. "A Boy and His Mom." *Saturday Review of Literature* 32, no. 3 (15 January 1949): 19–20.
  b.   Broderick, John. "Strong Start, Weak Finish." *New Yorker* 24, no. 47 (15 January 1949): 77–78.
  c.   Cheatham, Richard. *Carolina Quarterly* 1, no. 2 (March 1949): 69–70.
  d.   Dedmon, Emmett. "Gore Vidal's Novel Gives Hint of What Young Writers Think." *Chicago Sun Book Week* (9 January 1949): 8X.
  e.   Doyle, Edward Dermot. "Some of the New Novels of the Month in Review." *San Francisco Chronicle* (13 February 1949): This World, p. 14.
  f.   Hobson, Will. "Paperbacks." *Observer* (London) (7 December 1997): 18.
  g.   Kingery, Robert E. *Library Journal* 74, no. 1 (1 January 1949): 60.
  h.   Klaw, Barbara. "A Dominating Mother." *New York Herald Tribune Weekly Book Review* (9 January 1949): 10.
  i.   Levin, Bernard. "Strong Wine from the Vintage of His Youth." *Times* (London) (7 March 1996): 35.
  j.   Rolo, Charles J. "Life with Mother." *Atlantic Monthly* 183, no. 2 (February 1949): 86.

    k.   Weaver, William Fense. "Mr. Vidal's Silver Cord." *New York Times Book Review* (6 February 1949): 12.

    l.   [Unsigned.] *Booklist* 45, no. 11 (1 February 1949): 193–94.

    m.   [Unsigned.] *Kirkus* 16, no. 23 (1 November 1948): 578.

Aldridge believes the book is "in many respects his weakest novel," having all the deficiencies and none of the virtues of its predecessors. . . . **Broderick** feels that the novel begins promisingly but declines into a "portrait of the artist having hell with his mother." Vidal has not made the central character sympathetic enough for readers to care about him. . . . **Cheatham**'s review is largely a plot summary. "The author's weary cynicism is sometimes fascinating, but in his new book it is a definite distraction." But the novel is "thoroughly readable." . . . **Dedmon** suggests that "Vidal . . . must learn to give the content of his books the same concentrated attention they have obviously given technique and modern findings of psychology." . . . **Doyle** finds that the novel is admirable but glib. "The author carries his reader along easily, breathlessly." But the book is poorer than Vidal's three earlier novels. . . . **Klaw** notes that this is "an interesting book," but the portrayal of the mother is an overdrawn caricature. . . . **Levin**, reviewing a recent reissue, declares that, although a youthful work, the novel shows much maturity in its portrayal of the protagonist. . . . **Rolo** states that "His story is deftly told . . . but no deep tensions, no deep emotions, are generated." . . . **Weaver** finds the novel "uninspired." The writing style is "filled with uninteresting, mismanaged sentences" and the plot is chaotic. "There is in the book a complete absence of anything honestly interesting."

5.   *A Search for the King*

    a.   Grauel, George E. *Best Sellers* 9, no. 22 (15 February 1950): 183–84.

    b.   H., D. *Times Literary Supplement* no. 4732 (10 December 1993): 20.

    c.   Kingery, Robert E. *Library Journal* 74, no. 21 (1 December 1949): 1819.

    d.   Langbaum, Robert. "The Questing Hero." *Nation* 170, no. 15 (15 April 1950): 352.

    e.   Lerman, Leo. "The Legend of Richard." *New York Times Book Review* (15 January 1950): 4, 16.

    f.   Litten, Frederic Nelson. "Delightful, Romantic Tale from Pen of a 'High-brow.'" *Chicago Sun-Times* (26 January 1950): 6S.

    g.   M., D. F. "Old Legend Revived." *Springfield Republican* (26 March 1950): 8C.

    h.   Maloney, John J. "Set in the Mold of Legend." *New York Herald Tribune Book Review* (15 January 1950): 8.

    i.   Miles, George. *Commonweal* 51, no. 16 (27 January 1950): 446.

    j.   Putnam, Samuel. "Animated Tapestry." *Saturday Review of Literature* 33, no. 2 (14 January 1950): 10.

    k.   Rugg, Winnifred King. "Bookshelf: New Novels." *Christian Science Monitor* (26 January 1950): 11.

    l.   Wagenknecht, Edward. "Brilliant 'Historical' by a 24 Year Old." *Chicago Sunday Tribune Magazine of Books* (15 January 1950): 3.

    m.   [Unsigned.] *Booklist* 46, no. 11 (1 February 1950): 150.

    n.   [Unsigned.] *Kirkus* 17, no. 24 (15 November 1949): 628.

    o.   [Unsigned.] *New Yorker* 25, no. 48 (21 January 1950): 97–98.

    p.   [Unsigned.] *Publishers Weekly* 193, no. 8 (19 February 1968): 102.

Grauel's review is largely a plot summary. Although it does not capture the atmosphere of the fairy tale, there is in the novel "much delight and a pleasant sense of escape for the reader." . . . **D. H.** notes that the "book shows that the appeal of a legend is not so much to the logical mind as to the unencumbered imagination." . . . **Langbaum** asserts that the novel shows Vidal "at his best—as a projector of myth old as the Grail legend, the myth of the questing hero." Vidal has no talent for realism. The vampire, Countess Valeria, is "Mr. Vidal's most unforgettable creation." . . . **Lerman** maintains that Vidal's "story . . . lacks persuasiveness. It is tedious because Mr. Vidal merely tells his readers." The book is "almost devoid of any magic." . . . **Litten** states that the novel contains "such first-rate guessing in the characterization of men of distinction, and such casual verisimilitude in the laying-in of scene, plus such generally felicitous prose, as to charm the most erudite and stuffy reader." . . . **D. F. M.** believes that the novel is "a strange, weird and wonderful story whose only counterpart is to be found in the great fairy-tales of the past." . . . **Maloney** feels that Vidal is "overawed by tradition" and "seems reluctant to breathe life into the remote and statuesque figures of history." . . . **Miles** writes that "The book is a trivial and pretentious thing which gives little evidence that the author has ability with words or images or rhythms." The novel "indicates an almost complete absence of taste and talent." . . . **Putnam** finds the book "a kind of dream fabric . . . the narrative conveys a feeling of reality without benefit of archaisms." . . . **Rugg** maintains that Vidal has "smooth control of language" and a "respect for words which is kin to the true craftsman's care of his tools." However, "the irony is far from gentle, in spite of all the superbly polished phrases." . . . **Wagenknecht** declares that Vidal "may be just the man to redeem the historical novel from the lushness and bad taste into which it is always in danger of falling." The story is told "in a chaste, spare, intelligent, and essentially pictorial style, which frequently achieves a vividness equal to that of the best of the imagist poets."

6. *A Star's Progress*
    a. Weiler, A. H. "Gold Coast Meteor." *New York Times Book Review* (19 February 1950): 35.

The review is largely a plot summary. "Grace [Carter], despite the galaxy of males who attract her on the highroad to success, . . . executes her own tragic finis to it all."

7. *Dark Green, Bright Red*
    a. Barr, Donald. "From Patio and Jungle." *New York Times Book Review* (8 October 1950): 4, 28.
    b. Brooks, John. "Fighting Somebody Else's Revolution." *Saturday Review of Literature* 33, no. 41 (14 October 1950): 15.
    c. Charques, R. D. "Fiction." *Spectator* 184 (no. 6374) (25 August 1950): 252.
    d. Derleth, August. "Vidal Writes Vivid Tale of Revolution." *Chicago Sunday Tribune Magazine of Books* (8 October 1950): 3.
    e. Kingery, Robert E. *Library Journal* 75, no. 17 (1 October 1950): 1662.
    f. [Maclaren-Ross, Julian.] "Men, Women and War." *Times Literary Supplement* no. 2534 (25 August 1950): 529.
    g. Match, Richard. "Loveless Life, Banana Land." *New York Herald Tribune Book Review* (15 October 1950): 10.
    h. Rolo, Charles J. "The Office; the Revolution." *Atlantic Monthly* 186, no. 5 (November 1950): 99–101.
    i. Shrapnel, Norman. "New Novels." *Manchester Guardian* (11 August 1950): 4.
    j. Theall, D. Bernard. *Best Sellers* 10, no. 15 (1 November 1950): 129–30.
    k. Wyndham, Francis. "New Novels." *Observer* (London) no. 8308 (27 August 1950): 7.
    l. [Unsigned.] *Booklist* 47, no. 5 (1 November 1950): 98.
    m. [Unsigned.] *Dublin Magazine* NS 25, no. 4 (October–December 1950): 63–64.
    n. [Unsigned.] *Kirkus* 18, no. 17 (1 September 1950): 527.
    o. [Unsigned.] *New Yorker* 26, no. 36 (28 October 1950): 115–16.

Barr feels that "there are passages of excellent draftsmanship and strong perception . . . The prose is tight and nervous but often too mannered." The novel is "a sad waste of real narrative gifts and wit." . . . **Brooks** thinks the novel is "a near miss . . . an interesting failure." He believes that various aspects of the book clash with one another. . . . **Charques** states that the novel is "a not very grown-up and rather pretentious piece of work"; "none of the characters in the story really carries conviction." . . . **Derleth** finds the book "an extremely accomplished narrative, vividly written, with the simplicity and directness which have characterized Mr. Vidal's previous works." . . . **Maclaren-Ross** remarks on "the shakiness of the author's structure and . . . his lack of success in handling a promising theme." . . . **Match** believes that Vidal has not fully elucidated the significance of the events he is describing, but that the novel is nonetheless an engaging read. . . . **Rolo** declares that the book "is credible but somewhat underplayed"; he would have liked to see more satire. . . . **Theall** writes: "There is not much to distinguish it from other recent handlings of the same sort of material." . . . **Wyndham**, in a multiple review, states: "Raw material for a farce, a thriller, a musical comedy or a boy's adventure story is here given an original treatment and made completely credible."

8.   *The Judgment of Paris*
   a.   Aldridge, John W. "Three Tempted Him." *New York Times Book Review* (9 March 1952): 4, 29.
   b.   C., J. C. "Novel by Gore Vidal." *Springfield Republican* (30 March 1952): 10D.
   c.   Crane, Milton. "Plundered Myth." *Saturday Review* 35, no. 12 (22 March 1952): 18.
   d.   Derleth, August. "Vidal's Latest Not His Best, Nor Poorest." *Chicago Sunday Tribune Magazine of Books* (9 March 1952): 4.
   e.   Kingery, Robert E. *Library Journal* 77, no. 2 (15 January 1952): 144.
   f.   Lean, Tangye. "Fiction." *Spectator* 190 (no. 6514) (1 May 1953): 556.
   g.   Peterson, Virgilia. "Finding Love in Paris." *New York Herald Tribune Book Review* (8 June 1952): 11.
   h.   Raven, Simon. "New Novels." *Listener* 49 (no. 1260) (23 April 1953): 695.
   i.   Rolo, Charles J. "Potpourri." *Atlantic Monthly* 189, no. 4 (April 1952): 85–86.
   j.   Scott, J. D. "New Novels." *New Statesman and Nation* 45 (no. 1154) (18 April 1953): 465–66.
   k.   Theall, D. Bernard. *Best Sellers* 11, no. 24 (15 March 1952): 256.
   l.   Tisdall, Julie. *Books and Bookmen* 12, no. 6 (March 1967): 30.
   m.   V[ogler], L[ewis]. "Among the New Books." *San Francisco Chronicle* (6 July 1952): This World, p. 10.
   n.   [Warren, Robert Penn.] *New Republic* 126, no. 16 (21 April 1952): 22.
   o.   Young, Vernon. "Ghosts and Flesh, Vinegar and Wine: Ten Recent Novels." *New Mexico Quarterly* 22, no. 3 (Autumn 1952): 322–30 (esp. 328–29).
   p.   [Unsigned.] *Best Sellers* 25, no. 3 (1 May 1965): 68.
   q.   [Unsigned.] *Kirkus* 19, no. 26 (15 December 1950): 711.
   r.   [Unsigned.] *New Yorker* 28, no. 36 (15 March 1952): 115–16.
   s.   [Unsigned.] "Plain or Coloured?" *Times* (London) (4 April 1953): 6.

Aldridge provides a summary of Vidal's career. Up to now his novels have seemed like "badly balanced darts thrown at a moving target." This novel "is the best and most ambitious of his novels, the richest in texture and the most carefully executed." . . . **J. C. C.** finds this "a novel of deep philosophical meaning, told in a fluid and masterful style." . . . **Crane** believes the novel fails because it does not precisely embody the myth that serves as its foundation. . . . **Derleth** rates the book an "excellent entertainment, but it is far from being the 'major novel' his publisher would have us believe it is." Only the protagonist, Philip Warren, "is excellently and fully realized." . . . **Lean** feels that the novel suggests the cultural power of the Old World on Americans. "Mr. Vidal writes with an engaging freshness, which is rarely naif, occasionally salacious and almost always entertaining." . . . **Peterson** maintains that "Mr. Vidal can write, but . . . he fails to achieve the seriousness of a philosophy of life." . . . **Raven**, in a multiple review, declares that the central character "doesn't exist." "He is a silly, vapid, tedious, self-centred young man, and he is a disgrace to a novel which, apart from him, is witty, informative and gay." . . . **Scott** states that the novel "an irritating and affected book" but states that it "does possess quite a bit of verve, is readable, and in patches entertaining." . . . **Theall** dismisses the novel by writing that "the reader [should] not waste the time required to cover 375 pages of balderdash." Most of the review is a sarcastic plot summary. . . . **Tisdall** notes that the book is "an amusing burlesque, very fluently written but already very dated." . . . **Vogler** finds the book a "disappointment." "More ambitious than its predecessors, it is somehow less mature. More pretentious, it strikes me as being considerably less promising." The female characters are not convincing, "and most of the other characters are either inadequately portrayed or a little overdrawn." . . . **Warren**'s brief and snippish review notes the jarring discontinuity between the "improbably prudish hero" and the lurid scenes in which he is placed. . . . **Young** asserts that the book "a tedious and shapeless romp in Sodom . . . and the unmitigated gall with which Vidal pretends classical-myth parallels is but a minor feature of his general pseudonymous character as a writer." . . . The *Times* (London) review states that although Vidal "has an egocentric shrewdness and unusual fluency of expression," "the novel as a whole is high-pitched and pretentious, and in the reading becomes increasingly tiresome."

9.   *Death in the Fifth Position*
   a.   Boucher, Anthony. "Criminals at Large." *New York Times Book Review* (22 June 1952): 11.

b. Callendar, Newgate [*pseud.*]. "Crime." *New York Times Book Review* (30 December 1979): 17.
c. Cuff, Sergeant [*pseud.*]. "The Criminal Record." *Saturday Review* 35, no. 37 (5 July 1952): 40.
d. Godfrey, Thomas. *Armchair Detective* 20, no. 2 (Spring 1987): 211–12.
e. Hawtree, Christopher. "Vidal's Thrillers." *Books and Bookmen* 25, no. 9 (June 1980): 27–28.
f. Offord, Lenore Glen. "The Gory Road." *San Francisco Chronicle* (8 June 1952): This World, p. 20.
g. Partridge, Ralph. "Detection and a Thriller." *New Statesman and Nation* 47 (no. 1206) (17 April 1954): 506, 508.
h. Pierce, Robert J. "Books in Review." *Dance Magazine* 47, no. 1 (January 1973): 89, 91 (esp. 91).
i. Richardson, Maurice. "Crime Ration." *Observer* (London) no. 8485 (17 January 1954): 9.
j. S., J. F. "Novel of the Ballet." *Springfield Republican* (10 August 1952): 6D.
k. Sandoe, James. "Mystery and Suspense." *New York Herald Tribune Book Review* (15 June 1952): 12.
l. [Unsigned.] *Kirkus* 20, no. 9 (1 May 1952): 291.
m. [Unsigned.] "New in Paperback." *Washington Post Book World* (30 December 1979): 13.

Boucher finds that "The telling is terse and lively," but Vidal fails in trying to outdo Mickey Spillane and Adam Knight.... **Godfrey**, reviewing all three Box novels, states that they are "entertaining, forward-looking in subject matter, and characteristic of the author." The books offer "culture, politics, and society, all served up with a generous dollop of sexual hijinks." But "None of the stories are inventively plotted." In this novel, "the plot machinery is crude and obvious." ... **Hawtree**, reviewing all three Box novels, notes that "Vidal uses these stories for pleasantly acerbic comments on the American way of life.... They are fun to read for more than the puzzle of who done it.... The box tales are certainly far more readable and important than the pretentious, monstrous verbiage or Barth and Pynchon." ... **Partridge** declares that "Mr. Box's style aspires to extreme sophistication: any depravity is grist to his mill"; but the actual detection is weak.... **Sandoe** feels that the book is overburdened with topical references; it "has what might be called a lurking, smudged promise."

10. *Death Before Bedtime*
a. Boucher, Anthony. "Criminals at Large." *New York Times Book Review* (19 April 1953): 27.
b. Callendar, Newgate [*pseud.*]. "Crime." *New York Times Book Review* (30 December 1979): 17.
c. Cuff, Sergeant [*pseud.*]. "The Criminal Record." *Saturday Review* 36, no. 23 (6 June 1953): 28.
d. Godfrey, Thomas. *Armchair Detective* 20, no. 2 (Spring 1987): 211–12.
e. Hawtree, Christopher. "Vidal's Thrillers." *Books and Bookmen* 25, no. 9 (June 1980): 27–28.
f. Offord, Lenore Glen. "The Gory Road." *San Francisco Chronicle* (12 April 1953): This World, p. 11.
g. Partridge, Ralph. "Detection." *New Statesman and Nation* 49 (no. 1257) (9 April 1955): 512–13.
h. Sandoe, James. "Mystery and Suspense." *New York Herald Tribune Book Review* (26 April 1953): 15.
i. [Unsigned.] *Kirkus* 21, no. 3 (1 February 1953): 84.
j. [Unsigned.] "New in Paperback." *Washington Post Book World* (30 December 1979): 13.

Boucher notes that the "writing is clever and lively," but the plot does not move crisply, making for "a tryingly dull book." ... For **Godfrey**'s general comments, see under *Death in the Fifth Position.* Of this novel he writes that "the construction is more sophisticated and less awkward." ... For **Hawtree**'s comments, see under *Death in the Fifth Position....* **Sandoe** believes that the novel fails because Sergeant "is a singularly smug and unattractive young person."

11. *Messiah*
     a. Davenport, John. "An East African Tragedy." *Observer* (London) no. 8558 (10 July 1955): 12.
     b. Dawson, Helen. "Briefing: Paperbacks." *Observer* (London) no. 9482 (22 April 1973): 29.
     c. Geismar, Maxwell. "Deadly Altar." *New York Times Book Review* (25 April 1954): 4.
     d. Hicks, Granville. "A Fictional Roundup, with Comments on Form, Meaning and Narrative." *New Leader* 37, no. 22 (31 May 1954): 17–18.
     e. McLaughlin, Richard. *Springfield Republican* (13 June 1954): 7C.
     f. Rugoff, Milton. "One Very Dark Look Ahead." *New York Herald Tribune Weekly Book Review* (25 April 1954): 16.
     g. Stone, Jerome. "Frightening Future." *Saturday Review* 37, no. 21 (22 May 1954): 34–35.
     h. Sullivan, Richard. "Vidal's Odd Refugee from the World." *Chicago Sunday Tribune Magazine of Books* (25 April 1954): 4.
     i. Vogler, Lewis. "A Mediocre Evangelist Fools His Fellow Men." *San Francisco Chronicle* (23 May 1954): This World, p. 17.
     j. [Unsigned.] *Books and Bookmen* 18, no. 11 (August 1973): 137.
     k. [Unsigned.] *Kirkus* 22, no. 4 (15 February 1954): 130.
     l. [Unsigned.] *Saturday Review* 48, no. 31 (31 July 1965): 26.
     m. [Unsigned.] *Virginia Kirkus Service* 33, no. 12 (15 June 1965): 590.

Davenport's review is largely a plot summary, but he notes the "excellence of much of the writing." . . . **Geismar** finds the novel "a flat disappointment." It reveals a "fundamental lack of concern for both people and genuine social values." . . . **Hicks**, in a multiple review, declares that the novel is "pretty disappointing" because "one feels no strong conviction in the book." . . . **McLaughlin** believes the novel lacks imagination and that the writing is "decorative, lush and seldom communicative." . . . **Rugoff** writes that the book is "a mordant, cleverly conceived account of the credulity of the masses," but Vidal's cool cynicism makes the novel "diverting rather than affecting, ingenious rather than profound." . . . **Stone** asserts that Vidal "writes with a facility and an easy authority unusual in one so young." . . . **Sullivan** observes that this a "brightly written and admirably constructed novel." "Yet the satire on our times, tho [*sic*] intermittently apt and amusing, is on the whole bleak and forced." . . . **Vogler** maintains that "As a satire on mass man's desperate credulity, or as a warning about modern techniques of communication, it is effective in many ways. Yet one cannot help feeling that the book as a whole is not quite a success." It "seems to have been written much more in the spirit of mockery than of concern."

12. *Death Likes It Hot*
     a. Boucher, Anthony. "Criminals at Large." *New York Times Book Review* (23 May 1954): 14.
     b. Callendar, Newgate [*pseud.*]. "Crime." *New York Times Book Review* (30 December 1979): 17.
     c. Cuff, Sergeant [*pseud.*]. "The Criminal Record." *Saturday Review* 37, no. 23 (5 June 1954): 29.
     d. Godfrey, Thomas. *Armchair Detective* 20, no. 2 (Spring 1987): 211–12.
     e. Hawtree, Christopher. "Vidal's Thrillers." *Books and Bookmen* 25, no. 9 (June 1980): 27–28.
     f. Houston, Penelope. "It's a Crime." *Spectator* 195 (no. 6641) (7 October 1955): 470.
     g. K., B. F. *Springfield Republican* (25 July 1954): 8C.
     h. Maclaren-Ross, J. "New Novels." *Listener* 54 (no. 1382) (25 August 1955): 307.
     i. Offord, Lenore Glen. "The Gory Road." *San Francisco Chronicle* (4 July 1954): This World, p. 16.

     j.   Richardson, Maurice. "Crime Ration." *Observer* (London) no. 8565 (28 August 1955): 9.

     k.   [Unsigned.] *Kirkus* 22, no. 5 (1 March 1954): 168.

     l.   [Unsigned.] "New in Paperback." *Washington Post Book World* (30 December 1974): 13.

Boucher believes this to be "a first-rate comedy of manners," but as a detective story "it's merely untidy." . . . For **Godfrey**'s general comments, see under *Death in the Fifth Position.* Of this novel, he remarks that it gets "close to an integrated mystery plot." . . . For **Hawtree**'s comments, see under *Death in the Fifth Position.* . . . **B. F. K.** states that this is "one of the goriest suspense thrillers" of the day. "The author weaves a fascinating yarn enhanced by sparkling repartee." . . . **Maclaren-Ross**, in a multiple review, writes that the book is "Witty, amusing, faintly salacious as usual," but "Mr. Box breaks an important rule in his anxiety to conceal the criminal's identity."

13.   *A Thirsty Evil*

     a.   Hicks, Granville. "The Prize Short Stories of the New Year and Three New Individual Collections." *New Leader* 40, no. 6 (11 February 1957): 21–22.

     b.   Hooper, Brad. *Booklist* 102, no. 22 (1 August 2006): 44–45.

     c.   Malcolm, Donald. "At Home in a Gray Rubber Sack." *New Republic* 136, no. 8 (25 February 1957): 20.

     d.   Peden, William. "On the Road to Self-Destruction." *New York Times Book Review* (27 January 1957): 33.

     e.   Quinton, Anthony. *London Magazine* 6, no. 6 (June 1959): 68–72 (esp. 71).

     f.   Raven, Simon. "Brother Mountebank." *Spectator* 201 (no. 6800) (24 October 1958): 560.

     g.   Scobie, W. I. *Advocate* no. 337 (4 March 1982): 40.

     h.   Spark, Muriel. "Short Stories." *Observer* (London) no. 8729 (19 October 1958): 20.

     i.   Woods, Gregory. "Don't Look Back." *Times Literary Supplement* no. 4765 (29 July 1994): 19.

     j.   [Unsigned.] *Kirkus Reviews* 74, no. 13 (1 July 2006): 654.

     k.   [Unsigned.] "Seven Stories by Gore Vidal." *New York Herald Tribune Book Review* (17 February 1957): 5.

     l.   [Unsigned.] *Publishers Weekly* 220, no. 18 (30 October 1981): 61.

     m.   [Unsigned.] *Publishers Weekly* 253, no. 27 (10 July 2006): 52.

Malcolm's substantial review claims that Vidal "dwells in a private realm, attending only fitfully to the world at large." But "Erlinda and Mr. Coffin" is "a wonderfully comic invention," and "A Moment of Green Laurel" is the best story in the collection. . . . **Peden** finds the book "a rather dreary landmark in the literature of homosexuality. . . . there is acute perception here, and sensitivity, and effective irony, but little to delight or entertain." . . . **Quinton** writes: "The better of these stories are ironical comments on the complex contrivances and mannerisms of the homosexual life. They are quite funny, a little sad, and, on the whole, distinctly artificial." . . . **Scobie**, reviewing a reissue, feels that Vidal writes short stories with "elegance and brilliance." He focuses on the stories involving homosexuality. . . . **Spark**, in a multiple review, notes Vidal's "sharp eye for experience." The effects are "delightfully achieved by suggestion and implication." . . . The bulk of **Woods**'s review is devoted to *The City and the Pillar.* . . . The ***New York Herald Tribune*** review finds some stories "quite lovely," but others full of "cynical sophistication and ironic worldliness."

14.   *Visit to a Small Planet* (I.D.i.1)

     a.   Alvarez, A. "Shakespeare's Labour Lost." *New Statesman* 59 (no. 1512) (5 March 1960): 328–29.

     b.   Atkinson, Brooks. "The Theatre: 'Visit to a Small Planet.'" *New York Times* (8 February 1957): 18. *New York Theatre Critics' Reviews* 18, no. 4 (11 February 1957): 359.

     c.   ———. "Frivolous Visitor." *New York Times* (24 February 1957): Sec. 2, p. 1.

d. Chapman, John. "'Visit to a Small Planet' Offers Crazy Humor and Performances." *New York Daily News* (8 February 1957): 48. *New York Theatre Critics' Reviews* 18, no. 4 (11 February 1957): 357.

e. Clurman, Harold. "Theatre." *Nation* 184, no. 8 (23 February 1957): 174.

f. Coleman, Robert. "'Visit to a Small Planet' Funny Science Satire." *New York Daily Mirror* (9 February 1957): 21. *New York Theatre Critics' Reviews* 18, no. 4 (11 February 1957): 358.

g. Donnelly, Tom. "A Superman Who Came to Dinner." *New York World-Telegram and The Sun* (8 February 1957): 20. *New York Theatre Critics' Reviews* 18, no. 4 (11 February 1957): 357.

h. Driver, Tom F. "Little Visit." *Christian Century* 74, no. 3 (31 July 1957): 918.

i. Gibbs, Wolcott. "Out of the Nowhere." *New Yorker* 32, no. 52 (16 February 1957): 78, 80.

j. Hayes, Richard. "Four Versions of Comedy." *Commonweal* 65, no. 25 (29 March 1957): 662–64.

k. Hewes, Henry. "Saucerian Humor." *Saturday Review* 40, no. 8 (23 February 1957): 29.

l. Kerr, Walter. *New York Herald Tribune* (8 February 1957): 12. *New York Theatre Critics' Reviews* 18, no. 4 (11 February 1957): 356.

m. McClain, John. "Mayehoff Plus Ritchard Total Million Laughs." *New York Journal American* (8 February 1957): 14. *New York Theatre Critics' Reviews* 18, no. 4 (11 February 1957): 358.

n. Mannes, Marya. "Tension, Fun, and Faith." *Reporter* 16, no. 5 (7 March 1957): 40–41.

o. Watts, Richard, Jr. "2 Funny Men, One from Outer Space." *New York Post* (8 February 1957): 45. *New York Theatre Critics' Reviews* 18, no. 5 (11 February 1957): 356.

p. Wyatt, Euphemia Van Rensselaer. "Theater." *Catholic World* 185 (no. 1105) (April 1957): 68.

q. [Unsigned.] "Peck's Bad Boy from Outer Space." *Life* 42, no. 9 (4 March 1957): 87–88.

r. [Unsigned.] "This Lovable Lunatic." *Newsweek* 49, no. 7 (18 February 1957): 95.

s. [Unsigned.] *Theatre Arts* 41, no. 4 (April 1957): 17.

t. [Unsigned.] "New Play in Manhattan." *Time* 69, no. 7 (18 February 1957): 60.

u. [Unsigned.] "Arrival from Outer Space: Near-Pantomime Humour." *Times* (London) (26 February 1960): 15.

Alvarez declares the work "an amusing talky-talky play with science fiction trimmings." . . . **Atkinson**'s first review (8 February 1957) finds the play "uproarious." Vidal "makes us look ridiculous in a low-down comedy carnival that has its own insane logic and never runs out of ideas." Cyril Ritchard is brilliant both as actor and director. . . . **Atkinson**'s second review (24 February 1957) notes that the play is "a farce, and extraordinarily refreshing"; but it "does have an intelligent point of view." The characters are all "much better defined" in the play than in the TV script. . . . **Chapman** notes "the defiency in the story line and the haziness of the point of view," but the play has "a delightful lot of screwball humor. . . . Vidal's idea is a bright one. Bright and satiric, too, are many of the scenes." . . . **Clurman** believes the play to be "a grab-bag of materials from the whole range of popular entertainment," but it is nonetheless disappointing because it "is chiefly a product of show business cleverness." . . . **Coleman** feels that this "mediocre little satire on science fiction" is made funny by Ritchard and Mayehoff. The play is "as thin and transparent as a sheet of cellophane." . . . **Donnelly** states that this is "a television play which has gained immeasurably in its transference to the stage." It "is less a play than a vaudeville." Ritchard and Mayehoff are brilliant, "but even the lesser lights . . . shine brightly." . . . **Driver** claims that the basic premise of the play is not new; "one still has the subconscious regret all evening that the potentialities of a good idea have been wasted." The satire is ineffective. . . . **Gibbs** writes that, although the play is too long for its comic substance, it "is a remarkably lively and agreeable piece of work" and provides a good vehicle for the talents of Cyril Ritchard and Eddie Mayehoff. . . . **Hayes** observes that Vidal "has a natty pen and a cool effrontery of wit; nonetheless, a marked, controlling sensibility is absent from 'Visit to a Small Planet,' and the play never quite sustains its initial momentum." . . . **Hewes** asserts that the play is "a comedy that for a full evening runs the risk of satire." Vidal "has seen to it that his play is usually at least one dimension beyond mere stage foolery." . . .

Kerr praises Ritchard's performance. Vidal's tone "makes his antic little parable seem impudently plausible," but he "hasn't . . . written a play that holds together of its own adhesive power." . . . **McClain** writes: "This had the feeling of one of those bright, TV-type ideas that would sustain for a hot half hour and then slowly subside . . . [But Vidal] keeps the ball in the air with amazing consistency." . . . **Mannes** believes that "The play is pervaded by such good humor and speeded by such inventive stage business that a number of genuine satirical pricks are gone almost before they draw blood." . . . **Watts** notes: "As a satire or even as a play, Gore Vidal's comedy . . . pretty much fades into thin air after the first act," but the comedy of Ritchard and Mayehoff entertains. "It seems rather a shame that [the play] turns into a series of vaudeville acts." . . . **Wyatt**'s review is largely a plot summary. . . . The enthusiastic *Life* review states that "Broadway is having the funniest, freshest invasion of the season." It prints several photographs of the production. . . . The *Newsweek* review emphasizes the comic brilliance of Cyril Ritchard and Eddie Mayehoff. . . . The *Theatre Arts* review praises Ritchard's performance and adds: "While the diabolically satiric possibilities of the author's highly ingenious central situation are not explored after a fashion that is going to make anyone think of Lewis Carroll, they are not altogether overlooked." . . . The *Time* review maintains that this is not a play but "a kind of vaudeville show." It is saved by the acting of Cyril Ritchard and Eddie Mayehoff. . . . The *Times* (London) review feels the work is "an anti-American play from America." But "the play is from time to time about so many things . . . that it disappoints by sacrificing them all to an easy brand of near-pantomime humour."

15. *Visit to a Small Planet and Other Television Plays*
    a. Fink, John. "A Novelist's Collection of His TV Plays." *Chicago Sunday Tribune Magazine of Books* (6 January 1957): 10.
    b. [Unsigned.] *Booklist* 53, no. 11 (1 February 1957): 274–75.
    c. [Unsigned.] *Wisconsin Library Bulletin* 53, no. 1 (January 1957): 284.

Fink supplies a brief description of several of the plays in the book. "The impressive thing in this collection . . . is the breadth of his experience and the variety of his subject matter."

16. *The Best Man*
    a. Ascoli, Max. "Satire Comes to Broadway." *Reporter* 22, no. 9 (28 April 1960): 38–39.
    b. Aston, Frank. "'The Best Man' Considers Politics in Election Year." *New York World-Telegram and The Sun* (1 April 1960): 30. *New York Theatre Critics' Reviews* 21, no. 9 (4 April 1960): 311.
    c. Atkinson, Brooks. "Theatre: 'The Best Man' Arrives." *New York Times* (1 April 1960): 39. *New York Theatre Critics' Reviews* 21, no. 9 (4 April 1960): 309.
    d. ———. "'The Best Man': Gore Vidal's Cartoon of American Politics." *New York Times* (10 April 1960): Sec. 2, p. 1.
    e. Beschloss, Michael. "Expert's Picks." *Washington Post Book World* (26 September 2004): 4.
    f. Blanchard, Jayne. "Vidal's 'Best Man' Still Taut, Incisive." *Washington Times* (24 July 2004): B3.
    g. Brantley, Ben. "A Timeless Morality Tale Cloaked in Politics." *New York Times* (18 September 2000): E1, 5.
    h. Brustein, Robert. "Politics and the Higher Gossip." *New Republic* 142, no. 16 (18 April 1960): 21–22. In Brustein's *Seasons of Discontent: Dramatic Opinions 1959–1965*. New York: Simon & Schuster, 1965, pp. 108–10.
    i. Chapman, John. "'Best Man' a Good Play, Horray." *New York Daily News* (1 April 1960): 59. *New York Theatre Critics' Reviews* 21, no. 9 (4 April 1960): 308.
    j. Clurman, Harold. "Theatre." *Nation* 190, no. 16 (16 April 1960): 343–44. *New York Theatre Critics' Reviews* 21, no. 9 (4 April 1960): 310.
    k. Coleman, Robert. "'The Best Man' Garners Our Vote." *New York Mirror* (1 April 1960): 28. *New York Theatre Critics' Reviews* 21, no. 9 (4 April 1960): 310.
    l. Cooke, Richard P. "'The Best Man' a Winner." *Wall Street Journal* (4 April 1960): 14.
    m. Gamerman, Amy. "Theatre: Another Gore in the Spotlight." *Wall Street Journal* (20 September 2000): A24.

n. Gardner, Elysa. "'Best Man' Needs Better Platform." *USA Today* (18 September 2000): 4D.

o. Hayes, Richard. "The Ministers without Portfolio." *Commonweal* 72, No. 5 (29 April 1960): 128–29.

p. Hewes, Henry. "November Song." *Saturday Review* 43, no. 16 (16 April 1960): 33.

q. Kanfer, Stefan. "French Dressing." *New Leader* 83, no. 5 (November–December 2000): 61–63.

r. Kerr, Walter. *New York Herald Tribune* (1 April 1960): 12. *New York Theatre Critics' Reviews* 21, no. 9 (4 April 1960): 310.

s. Lahr, John. "Way of the World." *New Yorker* 76 (2 October 2000): 140–42.

t. Lewis, Theophilus. *America* 103, no. 14 (2 July 1960): 422.

u. McClain, John. "Good Theatre Is This Play by Gore Vidal." *New York Journal American* (1 April 1960): 19. *New York Theatre Critics' Reviews* 21, no. 9 (4 April 1960): 308.

v. Morehouse, Ward, III. "Politics and Pokémon Light Up Broadway Marquees." *Christian Science Monitor* (29 September 2000): 19.

w. Pressley, Nelson. "'Best Man' Politicians Spar Predictably, Wanly." *Washington Times* (14 October 1996): C12.

x. ———. "Mini Reviews." *Washington Post* (23 July 2004): Weekend, p. 22.

y. ———. "Potomac's 'Best Man' Is a Winner." *Washington Post* (21 July 2004): C1, 8.

z. Rose, Lloyd. "Political Posturing." *Washington Post* (16 October 1996): B12.

aa. Shipley, Joseph T. "A French Brothel and an American Presidential Campaign." *New Leader* 43, no. 16 (18 April 1960): 28.

bb. Simon, John. "Pols in a Pickle." *New York* 33, no. 38 (2 October 2000): 86, 88.

cc. Steyn, Mark. "Playful, at Times Savage." *New Criterion* 19, no. 3 (November 2000): 43–47 (esp. 43–46).

dd. Tynan, Kenneth. "No Respect for the Conventions." *New Yorker* 36, no. 8 (9 April 1960): 88, 90–91.

ee. Watts, Richard, Jr. "Three Men in National Politics." *New York Post* (1 April 1960): 64. *New York Theatre Critics' Reviews* 21, no. 9 (4 April 1960): 380.

ff. [Unsigned.] *Booklist* 57, no. 1 (1 September 1960): 17.

gg. [Unsigned.] *Bookmark* 19, no. 10 (July 1960): 260.

hh. [Unsigned.] "A Tiger in the Streets." *Newsweek* 55, no. 15 (11 April 1960): 86.

ii. [Unsigned.] "New Play on Broadway." *Time* 75, no. 15 (11 April 1960): 85.

Ascoli feels that the play is full of "unlikely happenings," but they are effective theater. "Again and again, what makes for the success of the play is its artful transparency." Ascoli urges more satire in drama. . . . **Aston** notes that the "wit" of the play "runs to vinegar." It is "more than welcome. Its sharp, jabbing entertaining is ideally tailored for the party-conscious year." . . . **Atkinson**'s first review deems the play "a political melodrama that comes close enough to the truth to be both comic and exciting." Vidal "knows how to put together a plot that is both amusing and engrossing." All the leading actors excel. . . . **Atkinson**'s second review states that the play "does not pretend to be grander than it is." Joe Cantwell is the most carefully etched character. Vidal "has a sense of humor as well as a plot." . . . **Beschloss** finds that "The play benefits from Vidal's inside knowledge of the politics of the time and its players." . . . **Blanchard**, reviewing a 2004 revival, believes that the play is "perhaps the best of the genre, its wit and insight untarnished more than 40 years later." But the production is "wildly uneven." . . . **Brantley**, reviewing the 2000 revival, claims that "this morality tale of a national political convention still rings appealingly with the whip cracks of abiding worldly wisdom dispensed with quips." The casting is "sometimes wonderfully apt," although many of the actors' performances are flawed. . . . **Brustein**'s famously hostile review states that the play is "less an original drama than an uncannily precise recording of the Broadway spectator's most simplistic notions of politics and politicians." It "takes the form of melodrama, tailored with a smart sophistication appropriate to the times." . . . **Chapman** asserts that this is "a well-made, keen-witted play of contemporary interest." The lead characters are all excellent. "This is a good election-year show and it won't influence your vote a damn bit." . . . **Clurman** finds the play "a successfully slick affair," but it is "more spoof than satire." . . . **Coleman** states that the "characters may be a bit distorted, but they're fascinating to watch and hear in action. . . . While we wouldn't accept Vidal as our political mentor, a lot that he has to say about our national pastime come every four years is trenchant and true." . . . **Cooke** maintains that the play "fast, funny, perceptive, well-acted and vastly entertaining." Vidal "presents a portrait of two valid opposing political types"; he "blows no particular political horn, and his discussions are remarkably free from the stock phrases about conservatism and liberalism we are accustomed to hear." . . . **Gamerman**, reviewing the 2000 revival, writes: "Despite Mr. Vidal's schoolmarmish handwringing over the cardboard quality of politics today, his characters seem about as deep as the campaign posters that are scattered about John Arnone's set." The direction is "unfocused" and the acting seems half-hearted. . . . **Gardner**'s review is largely devoted to the details of the 2000 revival. "What is most depressing about this production . . . is its waste of talent." . . . **Hayes** writes that Vidal "has stewed up a *bouillabaise* of some rather raunchy fish heads . . . which will decidedly nourish the buffet crowd." But perhaps Vidal overlooks the possibility that political power can be a good thing. . . . **Hewes** notes that the play displays Vidal's "slow-burning contempt for the deteriorating ways of contemporary America," but feels that it is "a small visit to a big subject." . . . **Kanfer**, discussing the 2000 revival in a multiple review, states that Vidal writes "with an insider's knowledge and a gadfly's irreverence." He "is unfailingly entertaining and frequently wise." . . . **Kerr** declares that the play is "a piece of first-rate journalism, with a telling little editorial tucked into one corner." He recognizes that Cantwell "is not a hypocrite, and that is what makes him dangerous." . . . **Lahr**, reviewing the 2000 revival, provides an overview of Vidal's career. He calls the play "sophisticated, elegant, and damnably entertaining." It is, however, not a satire, but a "comedy of manners—or, rather, of bad political manners." The play suggests that we have replaced "the despotism of monarchy" with "the despotism of the consensus." . . . **Lewis** thinks that Vidal "pokes fun at the absurdities [of politics] without deriding the process. The result is the top political comedy of your observer's experience." The play is "a continuous flow of merriment, ranging from quiet chuckles to gales of belly laughs." . . . **McClain** sums up the play as "enormously good theatre." Vidal has conceived "the elements of a plausible and highly exciting political drama in our times, and it is wonderfully well exploited." . . . **Morehouse**, reviewing the 2000 revival, provides a lengthy plot summary. The play's "behind-the-scenes glimpses of deception and honor are not just intriguing, but electric, character-driven theater." . . . **Pressley**'s first review, concerning the 1996 revival, states: "Obviously, 'The Best Man' isn't irrelevant; it's just predictable." The performances are also sub-par. . . . **Pressley**'s second review, concerning the 2004 revival, states that this is "a high-minded melodrama." This production introduces the novelty of having a woman play the ex-President. . . . **Rose**, reviewing the 1996 revival, feels the production is "a creaky-kneed affair" and Vidal's script "an astonishingly poor piece of work." . . . **Shipley**, in a multiple review, provides largely a plot summary. "Around the vivid clash of the thoughtful intellectual and the unscrupulous self-made man, Gore Vidal has wrapped a keen examination of political maneuvers." . . . **Simon**, referring to the 2000 revival, calls this Vidal's "best play, and one of his shrewdest pieces of writing." But Ethan McSweeny's direction "is not up to snuff." The acting, however, is sound. . . . **Tynan**, in an extensive review, judges Vidal to be a "born mocker." He is best as a satirist; when he tries to be a serious moral philosopher, he becomes tedious. . . . **Steyn**, reviewing the 2000 revival, presents a long and sarcastic summary of Vidal's political views. His "anticipation of the bland telepap politics of our time is so prescient as to make the play feel oddly contemporary. . . . What makes the play is Vidal's refusal to condescend to his characters, a virtue sadly rare in American drama, particularly of a political bent." . . . **Watts** states that the play is written with "wit, vigor and considerable theatrical effectiveness." But the play "tends to run down in its final act," because the Hockstader character is gone. It is "a provocative study of the flora and fauna of national politics." . . . The *Newsweek* review notes that the play is "a lively, pungent, and highly articulate melodrama." Vidal has "created a great many solid characterizations." . . . The *Time* review finds the play "a lively theater piece. . . . A modern-angled political morality play, it yet never forgets that bad politics make good theater."

17. *Romulus*
   a. Brustein, Robert. "Hipster Dramatics, Square Spectators." *New Republic* 146, no. 5 (29 January 1962): 20, 22. In Brustein's *Seasons of Discontent: Dramatic Opinions 1959–1965.* New York: Simon & Schuster, 1965, pp. 130–33.
   b. Chapman, John. "'Romulus' a Puzzle and a Bore to One Member of the Audience." *New York Daily News* (11 January 1962): 66. *New York Theatre Critics' Reviews* 23, no. 1 (15 January 1962): 381.
   c. Clurman, Harold. "Theatre." *Nation* 194, no. 5 (3 February 1962): 106–7.
   d. Coleman, Robert. "'Romulus' Reaches the Mind." *New York Mirror* (12 January 1962): 32. *New York Theatre Critics' Reviews* 23, no. 1 (15 January 1962): 380.
   e. Cooke, Richard P. "Rome's Last Days." *Wall Street Journal* (12 January 1962): 8.
   f. Driver, Tom F. "Theatrical Miscellany." *Christian Century* 79, no. 8 (21 February 1962): 233.

g. Hewes, Henry. "Sunny Side Down." *Saturday Review* 45, no. 4 (27 January 1962): 29.

h. Kerr, Walter. *New York Herald Tribune* (11 January 1962): 14. *New York Theatre Critics' Reviews* 23, no. 1 (15 January 1962): 383.

i. Lewis, Theophilus. *America* 106, no. 22 (10 March 1962): 772–73.

j. McCarten, John. "Slow Decline and Gentle Fall." *New Yorker* 37, no. 49 (20 January 1962): 63–64.

k. McClain, John. "Polite New Comedy Deft and Enlightened." *New York Journal American* (11 January 1962): 17. *New York Theatre Critics' Reviews* 23, no. 1 (15 January 1962): 382–83.

l. McKittrick, Ryan. "'Romulus' Falters But Is Still an Effective Farce." *Boston Globe* (17 May 2003): D7.

m. Mannes, Marya. "Just Looking." *Reporter* 26, no. 3 (1 February 1962): 45–46.

n. Nadel, Norman. "'Romulus' at Music Box." *New York World-Telegram and The Sun* (11 January 1962): 16. *New York Theatre Critics' Reviews* 23, no. 1 (15 January 1962): 381.

o. Parmentel, Noel E., Jr. "Rome and a Fella." *National Review* 12, no. 10 (13 March 1962): 173–74.

p. Simon, John. *Theatre Arts* 46, no. 3 (March 1962): 62–63.

q. Taubman, Howard. "'Romulus' at Music Box." *New York Times* (11 January 1962): 27. *New York Theatre Critics' Reviews* 23, no. 1 (15 January 1962): 382.

r. Watts, Richard, Jr. "Delightful Comedy of Rome's Fall." *New York Post* (11 January 1962): 16. *New York Theatre Critics' Reviews* 23, no. 1 (15 January 1962): 380.

s. Wortis, Irving. *Library Journal* 91, no. 5 (1 March 1966): 1242.

t. [Unsigned.] *Booklist* 62, no. 20 (15 June 1966): 989.

u. [Unsigned.] *Choice* 3, no. 4 (June 1966): 325.

v. [Unsigned.] "Fun While Rome Falls." *Newsweek* 59, no. 4 (22 January 1962): 50.

w. [Unsigned.] "Decline and Fall." *Time* 79, no. 3 (19 January 1962): 68, 70.

x. [Unsigned.] "Swiss Comedy Adapted to the Cold War." *Times* (London) (19 February 1962): 14.

Brustein's harsh review maintains that the play is evidence of the "hipster's flourishing influence." Vidal has transformed Duerrenmatt's play into "an effeminate charade enacted by the theatrical smart set." The portrayal of Romans as homosexuals is "in bad taste." . . . **Chapman** deems this "a cynical and scenic fantasy about how things are no worse now than they were then." The play is "beautifully mounted and acted," but it is "a puzzle and a bore to me." "The play struck me as a satire without a point of view." . . . **Clurman** feels that Vidal's adaptation has "markedly diluted" Duerrenmatt's play. It sounds "like wise aleck political after-dinner chatter." . . . **Coleman** notes that "we suspect that there's as much Vidal as Duerrenmatt in 'Romulus.'" It is "an essentially cerebral play, masking ideas under persiflage." Ritchard gives a "hypnotic performance." . . . **Cooke** states that "the theatrical company is good, and the entertainment is better, for not only is the audience greatly amused, but in the second half of the play, also instructed." Romulus concludes that "Rome was utterly corrupt and ready for extinction." . . . **Hewes** believes that "the fun is sporadic, the satire is discursive." . . . **Kerr** finds that the play has "a dry, muted flavor—sometimes uncertain, sometimes impudent but most often bittersweet." . . . **Lewis** writes that this an "acetic comedy on the rise and decline of nations." The play reflects "the author's [i.e., Duerrenmatt's] view that all humankind is corrupt. . . . *Romulus* is the most rewarding play of the year." . . . **McCarten** asserts that the first act is tedious, but the play picks up thereafter. . . . **McClain** refers to the play as "a deft and enlightened frolic." Its message is that "the grass is apt to look greener on the other fellow's civilization—until you get there." Although the play is slow getting going, "it is certainly an intelligent and sophisticated offering, bristling with humor and performed to the hilt." . . . **McKittrick**, reviewing a 2003 revival, writes: "The play needs an ensemble that can entertain the audience only to catch it off guard. Beneath the cracks in Vidal's comic masks, the audience must see the deformed faces of imperial decay." . . . **Mannes** claims that the play "a feeble mish-mash of satire and farce which manages to engage neither the mind nor the emotion [*sic*]." . . . **Nadel** declares that the play "lowers the boom on the pompous, ridiculous history of civilized man." It is "one of those refreshing and welcome comedies that have something to say, and that say it well. . . . Along with weaving a wicked satire on history, 'Romulus' touches sensitively on the anguish of life in a turbulent world." . . . **Parmentel** maintains that the play is a "limp-wristed, high-flying, ersatz-Shavian rendition of the last days of Rome." The acting is also sub-par. The play is "boring when it is not offensive." . . . **Simon** notes that "there is nothing great about this evacuation on Dürrenmatt's remarkable original." Vidal has reduced Duerrenmatt's serious play to camp. "The performances are undistinguished or worse." . . . **Taubman** feels that much of the first half of the play "is flat and ponderous, filled with juvenile jests," but the second half is "fine, sharp-witted, sardonic. . . . **Watts** finds the play "an intelligent and thoroughgoing pleasure." It is "preoccupied with the play of a witty, neo-Shavian intelligence on the course of history." Watts praises Ritchard's performance. . . . The *Choice* review states that Vidal has made the play "more farcical and more ambiguous" than the original; accordingly, "it becomes more entertaining and less meaningful." . . . The *Newsweek* review declares that the play has "imperfections," but it is "one of the most literate and engaging comedies to reach Broadway in a pedestrian year." . . . The *Time* review states that "the first act seems to veil a point of view under a comic mask," but that "the second and last act strips away the mask to make points in dead, and deadly, earnest." The play's politics are shallow; Vidal has added only a few topical references. . . . The *Times* (London) review observes that Vidal "has made [*Romulus*] his own play by gagging it up, by filling Mr. Dürrenmatt's caustic examination of the fall of Rome with jocular reminders of the cold war." The play "provides a great deal of talk, which is by turns airily fanciful, desperately contemporary or simply filled with jokes. . . . Something in the nature of the play is just a little awkward."

18. *Rocking the Boat*
   a. Armin, Perry. *Library Journal* 87, no. 13 (July 1962): 2550.
   b. Barrett, William. "Novelists Taking Inventory." *Atlantic Monthly* 210, no. 2 (August 1962): 143–44.
   c. Bryden, Ronald. "Prophet on the Rocks." *New Statesman* 66 (no. 1706) (22 November 1963): 746–47.
   d. Chamberlain, John. "A Wacky Deltoid." *Wall Street Journal* (24 July 1962): 16.
   e. Dupee, F. W. "Pieces of the Hour." *Commentary* 34, No. 6 (December 1962): 549–52 (esp. 552). In Dupee's *"The King of the Cats" and Other Remarks on Writers and Writing.* New York: Farrar, Straus & Giroux, 1965, pp. 201–7.
   f. Gross, John. "Gory Details." *Observer* (London) no. 8979 (4 August 1963): 14.
   g. H., H. B. "A Collection by Gore Vidal." *Springfield Republican* (5 August 1962): 2D.
   h. Hicks, Granville. "Windward on a Sea of Indecision." *Saturday Review* 45, no. 31 (4 August 1962): 19–20.
   i. Hogan, William. "Gore Vidal Climbs onto the Soapbox." *San Francisco Chronicle* (26 July 1962): 33.
   j. Jackson, Katherine Gauss. *Harper's Magazine* 225, no. 2 (August 1962): 97–98.
   k. Lindsay, John V. "From JFK to Love Love Love." *New York Times Book Review* (12 August 1962): 5.
   l. Mahoney, John J. *Best Sellers* 22, no. 11 (1 September 1962): 222–23.
   m. Morgenstern, Joseph. "Advice and Dissent: Uncommon Common Sense." *New York Herald Tribune Books* (29 July 1962): 7.
   n. Mottram, Eric. "Rallying the Cynics." *Spectator* 211 (no. 7054) (6 September 1963): 299.
   o. Poore, Charles. "Books of The Times." *New York Times* (24 July 1962): 25.
   p. Seidenspinner, Clarence. "Serious and Sophisticated Views of U.S. Literature and Political Life." *Chicago Sunday Tribune Magazine of Books* (29 July 1962): 2.
   q. [Unsigned.] *Booklist* 58, no. 22 (15 July 1960): 780.
   r. [Unsigned.] *New Yorker* 38, no. 23 (28 July 1962): 80.
   s. [Unsigned.] "Geese Honks by Gore." *Newsweek* 60, no. 5 (30 July 1962): 78.
   t. [Unsigned.] "Assistant Executioner." *Time* 80, no. 4 (27 July 1962): 70.
   u. [Unsigned.] "Quick Guide to New Reading." *Times* (London) (24 October 1963): 17.
   v. [Unsigned.] "Facing All Ways." *Times Literary Supplement* no. 3216 (18 October 1963): 830.
   w. [Unsigned.] *Virginia Kirkus Service* 30, no. 10 (15 May 1962): 467–68.
   x. [Unsigned.] *Wisconsin Library Bulletin* 58, no. 5 (September 1962): 342.

Barrett appreciates Vidal's view that novelists and playwrights are obsessed with love and sex in lieu of politics and society; the book is "one of the most intelligent and pleasant collections of essays that I have read for some time." . . . **Bryden** feels that Vidal is an "elegant, melancholy figure"; in his literary essays "his aim is not to reform the world but to recall it to reality." . . . **Chamberlain** states that the book "contains a number of telling pieces that are written with great force and elegance"; but other pieces go awry, such as the essays on Dos Passos and Ayn Rand. "Whenever Mr. Vidal becomes involved in a purely social judgment, his genius for missing the point comes to the surface." . . . **Dupee**, in a multiple review, notes that Vidal's "role is that of the free spirit." "Power is Mr. Vidal's chief subject. . . . Some (but not all) of his best stuff is satirical." In spite of the variety of the contents, "the book does nonetheless have . . . a distinct unity of tone." . . . **Gross** writes that Vidal "emerges from these pages as an acute, serious-minded social critic." But he "overrates President Kennedy, in his relief at seeing the last of the man he calls the Great Golfer" (i.e., President Eisenhower). . . . **Hicks**, in a substantial review, provides a summary of Vidal's career and states that he "has ideas and he has wit." He believes his literary essays are the best feature of the book. . . . **Hogan** thinks that Vidal is "one of the most articulate, stimulating and fearless spectators on the American scene." He is "a healthy, optimistic critic." "The fact that most of these pieces are picked up from a variety of publications over the past decade does not make them less fresh and challenging today." . . . In an enthusiastic review, **Lindsay** (at this time a congressman) declares that Vidal is "an individual of rare accomplishment." He "is the most ingratiating of iconoclasts." He is best when discussing theater. The volume has "some of the best and least known of his critical writing." . . . **Mahoney** asserts that Vidal "directs his urbane charm, his acid wit, and his graceful style to the general areas of politics, the theater, and books." Vidal's views are "expressed with clarity, sanity, and good sense." . . . **Morgenstern** finds merit in both the political and the literary essays. Vidal "is almost always poised, working gently and gracefully and rhythmically, not trying to overturn things but just to keep them moving forward." . . . **Mottram** maintains that Vidal "proves himself one of the most entertaining pundits on the scene." "The art of power is Vidal's theme"; in politics, he strives against surrendering the will and intelligence to totalitarianism. . . . **Poore** labels the book "a political, theatrical and literary chowder." It is "full of paprika." Vidal, like many others, thinks he is a "self-appointed President [or] Secretary of State." . . . **Seidenspinner** observes that the book is a "serious and sophisticated collection." The literary essays are better than the political ones, "which tend to be partisan rather than objective." . . . The *Newsweek* review states that Vidal is "a notably unsettling, as well as a witty, cultivated, and markedly versatile writer." "He writes of politics with savvy, of the theatre and books with learning and energy, and of TV with loathing." . . . The *Time* review notes that Vidal is the "nation's foremost boy of letters." He "shows exceptional promise in a new literary line." The review finds the political essays pungent and the literary essays even better; but "no essay in the book glitters from beginning to end." . . . The ***Times Literary Supplement*** review finds a "liberal independence of mind" animating both the political and the literary pieces, but occasionally Vidal seems conceited and self-important.

19.   *Three Plays*
    a.   [Unsigned.] *Times Literary Supplement* no. 3165 (26 October 1962): 830.

The reviewer notes that the plays "make good reading." Vidal "is a witty dramatist," but the preface is one of the best things in the book.

20.   *Three*
    a.   Jackson, Katherine Gauss. *Harper's Magazine* 225, no. 2 (August 1962): 98.

21.   *Julian*
    a.   Airlie, Stuart. "Speaking Volumes." *Times Higher Education Supplement* no. 1306 (14 November 1997): 22.
    b.   Allen, Walter. "The Last Pagan." *New York Review of Books* 2, no. 12 (30 July 1964): 20–21.
    c.   Armstrong, David. "A Pagan Modern?" *Arion* 3, no. 4 (Winter 1964): 137–46.
    d.   Auchincloss, Louis. "The Best Man, Vintage 361 A.D." *Life* 56, no. 24 (12 June 1964): 19, 21.
    e.   Barrett, William. "Death of the Gods." *Atlantic Monthly* 214, no. 1 (July 1964): 134–35.
    f.   Buckmaster, Henrietta. "Gore Vidal's Roman Emperor." *Christian Science Monitor* (18 June 1964): 7.

g. Burgess, Anthony. "A Touch of the Apostasies." *Spectator* 213 (no. 7112) (16 October 1964): 518.

h. Copeland, Edith. *Books Abroad* 39, no. 2 (Spring 1965): 220.

i. Davenport, Guy. "Caution: Falling Prose." *National Review* 16, no. 28 (14 July 1964): 609–10.

j. Davis, Robert M. "Approach to the Apostate." *Critic* 23, no. 1 (August 1964): 70–71.

k. Dolbier, Maurice. "Gore Vidal's Good, Solid Historical Novel." *New York Herald Tribune* (8 June 1964): 19.

l. Donahugh, Robert H. *Library Journal* 89, no. 7 (1 April 1964): 1625–26.

m. Fitts, Dudley. "Engaged in Life and in a Pagan Past." *New York Times Book Review* (31 May 1964): 4.

n. Fuller, Edmund. "An Idealistic Pagan." *Wall Street Journal* (12 June 1964): 6.

o. Green, Peter. "Resuscitated Emperor." *New Republic* 150, no. 24 (13 June 1964): 21, 24.

p. Hicks, Granville. "No Cross on Olympus." *Saturday Review* 47, no. 23 (6 June 1964): 31–32.

q. Highet, Gilbert. *Book-of-the-Month Club News* (Midsummer 1964): 9.

r. Hill, William B. *America* 111, no. 22 (28 November 1964): 719.

s. ———. *Best Sellers* 24, no. 6 (15 June 1964): 113–14.

t. Hope, Francis. "I, Julian." *New Statesman* 68 (no. 1757) (13 November 1964): 741–42.

u. Leone, Arthur T. *Catholic World* 199 (no. 1194) (September 1964): 381–84.

v. McClellan, Joseph. "Back in Paper." *Washington Post Book World* (3 April 1977): E3.

w. Murphy, Martin. "Roman Romantic." *Tablet* 218 (no. 6492) (24 October 1964): 1200, 1202.

x. Parkinson, C. Northcote. "The Christian 'Barbarians.'" *Cosmopolitan* 156, no. 6 (June 1964): 32–33.

y. Pickrel, Paul. "The Gods: Their Exits and Their Entrances." *Harper's Magazine* 229, no. 1 (July 1964): 99–104.

z. Pomer, Belle. "Echoes." *Canadian Forum* 44, no. 6 (September 1964): 144.

aa. Prescott, Orville. "Books of The Times: The Apostate Emperor." *New York Times* (10 June 1964): 43.

bb. Squirru, Rafael. *Américas* 16, no. 8 (August 1964): 40–41.

cc. Steiner, George. "'Vicisti, Galilaee.'" *Reporter* 31, no. 2 (16 July 1964): 45, 47.

dd. Warner, Rex. "Philosopher King—and Imperial Eagle Scout." *New York Herald Tribune Book Week* (7 June 1964): 4.

ee. Welch, Patrick. *Chicago Sunday Tribune Books Today* (7 June 1964): 5.

ff. [Unsigned.] *New York Times Book Review* (10 February 1974): 19.

gg. [Unsigned.] "Vidality." *Newsweek* 63, no. 24 (15 June 1964): 106.

hh. [Unsigned.] *Saturday Review* 48, no. 3 (31 July 1965): 26.

ii. [Unsigned.] "The Ascetic Pagan." *Time* 83, no. 24 (12 June 1964): 122, 124–25.

jj. [Unsigned.] "New Fiction." *Times* (London) (15 October 1964): 15.

kk. [Unsigned.] "Lost in the Crowds." *Times Literary Supplement* no. 3272 (12 November 1964): 1013.

ll. [Unsigned.] *Virginia Quarterly Review* 40, no. 4 (Autumn 1964): cxlviii.

Airlie, in a retrospective review, recalls his first reading of the book. *Julian* "transformed my view of history and confirmed a vocation." The structure of the book is particularly impressive.... **Allen** feels the novel "brings together and dramatizes more effectively and with much greater authority than ever before preoccupations that have been present in [Vidal's] fiction almost from its beginnings." Specifically, it broaches the subject of "the twilight of the gods, or rather, of the Christian god," implicit in *The Judgment of Paris* and other works. But *Julian* "is fatally contaminated by the very factors that gave rise to Christianity itself." ... **Armstrong**, a classical scholar, writes an immense and learned review discussing the historicity of the novel but finds numerous deficiencies: "The effort at presenting the conflict of ideas in the late empire is not convincing." But the "priggish, slightly absurd hero is very well realized," even if "he is not Julian." ...

Auchincloss states that Vidal's "primary interest in life" is "what the struggle for power amounts to and what it does to men." Vidal's "Christians are narrow-minded, disputatious, savage to their enemies and devoid of any style or eloquence." The novel "is the achievement of a scholar, an artist, a politician and a man of the world." . . . **Barrett** finds in the novel a richness in evoking the period comparable to Robert Graves's *I, Claudius*. . . . **Buckmaster** observes that this a "remarkable book, noble and discreet in its Hellenic cast of mind yet accomplishing the provocative tour de force of an idiomatic modern style." It is "a long, subtle, provoking, enthralling book." Vidal's "ability to invoke a world is amazing." . . . **Burgess** maintains that "Vidal has dealt with [the subject] so comprehensively that no historical novel need ever deal with it again." . . . **Copeland** believes that Vidal is "no friend of Christianity." But "the cultural climate of the time and place is realistically, vividly projected." This is "a highly important novel of ideas." . . . **Davenport** thinks that Vidal "seems to have set himself the task of writing a sassy, anti-Christian book, come Hell or high water." "This is a novel that distrusts high office and sees little but grandiose folly in history." . . . **Davis** observes that the work, "while full of interesting information, is not very significant as a novel." Vidal tells rather than shows. His method "encourages summary rather than scene, recollections of triumphs rather than the clash of personalities." . . . **Dolbier** believes that the book is exemplary but lacks "spark": "there is no passion at all in this presentation." . . . **Fitts** notes that "the breathing actuality of his Julian is not to be denied"; "the texture and tone of his narrative are persuasively in character." But Vidal "is generally unsuccessful in his attempt to demonstrate Julian the theological controversialist in action." Vidal is out of his depth as a philosopher. [See I.F.3 for Vidal's reply.] . . . **Fuller** asserts that this is Vidal's "best" novel. It is "historical fiction in the true, honorable sense. . . . Vidal is cryptic about Christianity, though we feel he has small regard for it, with its sins and savage schismatic struggles. . . . Vidal evokes [Julian] persuasively in a book that says much about the dilemmas of belief and power." . . . **Green** claims that the novel owes a great debt to Robert Graves. "On the whole, Mr. Vidal succeeds far beyond reasonable expectations, and when he fails it is generally because he refuses to fudge or distort intractable history." Vidal is at his best in grasping "Fourth-Century *ideas*." . . . **Hicks** finds "some of the book instructive, some of it exciting, a good deal of it dull"; he doesn't understand why Vidal wrote the book. . . . **Highet** labels the novel a "heroic comedy." "Many Christian readers will be wounded by its savagely anti-Christian tone," but it is "both a thoughtful and a distinguished work of historical fiction." . . . **Hill** writes: "The novel does a highly imaginative job on Julian's short life of thirty-two years." But Vidal distorts Julian's religious views and his attitude toward Christianity. . . . **Hope** regards the book as "a large, easy-paced, entertaining piece of work suitable for long winter evenings." . . . **Leone** states that the novel "could very well read as an *apologia pro vita sua* for the modern pagan." Vidal has "created something of a minor triumph" in portraying the fourth-century world through Julian's eyes. But because of Vidal's anti-Christian bias, "Julian becomes a 19th-century liberal in 20th-century dress." . . . **Murphy** deems the novel "disappointingly unexciting. . . . Julian is credited by Mr. Vidal with all the wordy prolixity of a dull public servant." . . . **Parkinson** writes that Vidal "holds our attention throughout. He brings Julian to life as a person, does as much for the minor characters and more for some of the places described." . . . **Pickrel** thinks the novel is "more fictionalized history than historical novel." The cleverness of the earlier parts is lost in the later sections. . . . **Pomer**'s review is largely a discussion of the historical Julian. "The novel creates a rich picture of what was taking place in those changing times. . . . The portrait of Julian from uncertain youth to manhood is particularly fine, and minor characters are handled with deft, suggestive touch. Vidal's cool, matter-of-fact prose transmits a very real sense of the political and religious climate." But the novel also has relevance to present-day concerns. . . . **Prescott** declares the book a "competent and moderately interesting work enlivened by flashes of wit, but flawed by numerous dull passages and by much pedestrian prose." Vidal is good on Julian's military campaign, but the sex scenes are "disgusting enough to sicken many of his readers." . . . **Squirru** states that the novel "is far more than a revival of the past." Vidal "has not dealt with his subject lightly." The best parts are those that deal with "Julian the student and Julian the Caesar." "*Julian* deserves a place among the best novels that the writers of our generation have published." . . . **Steiner** maintains that Vidal "has established a lively authority over the facts and mood of a particularly tangled historical period." The best feature of the novel is its conveying of Julian's "Stoic gaiety." It is not as strong as Graves's *I, Claudius*, but "Vidal has written a novel full of wit and energy." . . . **Warner** feels that Vidal "has devised a clever piece of machinery," but Julian himself sometimes gets lost in the historical details. . . . **Welch** notes that Vidal "has achieved that more difficult task of the imagination: the re-creation of thoughts, behavior, standards, and values that motivated history-makers of the 4th century. He displays a formidable erudition." . . . The *Newsweek* review asserts that Vidal's is "the unmistakable voice of a contemporary Hellenist partisan." He "has an easy and fluent gift for narrative; a theatrical sense of scene and dramatic occasion; a revealing eye and ear for character delineation." But the novel is a bit too facile. . . . The *Time* review states that Vidal "has mastered the manner [of Robert Graves] to perfection. Only his subject eludes him." Vidal "is an energetic husker of wrappings. The weakness of his novel is that he seems uncertain, as is the reader, about what manner of animal he has discovered inside." . . . The *Times* (London) review, a multiple review, writes:

"The form of Mr. Vidal's novel is ingenious, at times ingenuous." The "novel is generally intelligent and illuminating." But Vidal fails to provide a "vision and rationale" for the work. . . . The *Times Literary Supplement* review comments that, although the novel has many virtues, the portrait of Julian "is in the end inadequate."

22. *Washington, D.C.*
   a. Ackroyd, Peter. "Blood, Thunder and Gore." *Spectator* 236 (no. 7709) (27 March 1976): 20.
   b. Baro, Gene. "Power and Its Price." *Reporter* 36, no. 13 (29 June 1967): 43–44.
   c. Binder, James. "Focus Wanders as Vidal Tunes In on Washington's Inner Circle." *National Observer* 6, no. 20 (15 May 1967): 21.
   d. Boston, Richard. "Capitol Punishment." *Times* (London) (27 July 1967): 5.
   e. Brendon, Piers. "Piers Brendon on Pompous Power." *Books and Bookmen* 12, no. 11 (August 1967): 49.
   f. Buckmaster, Henrietta. "Must It Be Exposé? Politics in the Novel." *Christian Science Monitor* (11 May 1967): 13.
   g. Buitenhuis, Peter. "New Novels: Hemingway Rides Again." *Harper's Magazine* 234, no. 6 (June 1967): 106–8 (esp. 106).
   h. Clive, George. "Potomac Blues." *Spectator* 219 (no. 7258) (4 August 1967): 137.
   i. Curtin, Anne. "Novels on Politics." *Progressive* 31, no. 6 (June 1967): 49–51 (esp. 50–51).
   j. Dolbier, Maurice. "Rome and Peyton Place on the Potomac." *New York World Journal Tribune* (28 April 1967): 29.
   k. Fremont-Smith, Eliot. "The Wise and the Shrewd." *New York Times* (1 May 1967): 35.
   l. Galbraith, John Kenneth. "Where the Action Is." *New York World Journal Tribune Book Week* (30 April 1967): 3.
   m. Greenfield, Josh. "A Skeleton in Every Closet." *New York Times Book Review* (30 April 1967): 4, 45.
   n. Hamilton, Ian. "Unearned Wisdom." *Listener* 78 (no. 2003) (17 August 1967): 217.
   o. Hill, William B. *America* 117, no. 22 (25 November 1967): 666.
   p. Hodgson, Geoffrey. "Corruption in the Capitol." *Observer* (London) no. 9184 (23 July 1967): 20.
   q. Kapp, Isa. "A Smooth Deal." *New Leader* 50, no. 16 (14 August 1967): 18–20.
   r. Lehan, Richard. "Fiction, 1967." *Contemporary Literature* 9, no. 4 (Autumn 1968): 538–53 (esp. 543–44).
   s. McLellan, Joseph. "Paperbacks: Fiction." *Washington Post Book World* (26 December 1976): E10.
   t. Mitgang, Herbert. "Trying to Stem the Tide of Corruption." *Chicago Tribune Books Today* (7 May 1967): 1.
   u. Mott, H. Wilmarth. *Library Journal* 92, no. 9 (1 May 1967): 1856.
   v. Norrie, Ian. "Antidote." *Books and Bookmen* 13, no. 1 (January 1968): 11.
   w. Oberbeck, S. K. "Capital Cameos." *Newsweek* 69, no. 19 (8 May 1967): 107–8.
   x. Raymond, John. "New Novels." *Punch* 253 (no. 6622) (9 August 1967): 218.
   y. St. John, Jeffrey. "Brutus on Capitol Hill." *Saturday Review* 50, no. 25 (24 June 1967): 32–33.
   z. Sharpe, David F. *Best Sellers* 27, no. 3 (1 May 1967): 45–46.
   aa. Sheed, Wilfred. "Affairs of State." *Commentary* 44, no. 3 (September 1967): 93–94.
   bb. Shrapnel, Norman. "The Coolly Observing Insider." *Manchester Guardian Weekly* 97, no. 5 (3 August 1967): 11.
   cc. Strauss, Victor. "Wasps and Hive." *New Statesman* 74 (no. 1898) (28 July 1967): 123.
   dd. Thompson, John. "The Professionals." *New York Review of Books* 8, no. 11 (15 June 1967): 14–17.

ee. Weeks, Edward. "Inside 'Inside Washington.'" *Atlantic Monthly* 220, no. 2 (August 1967): 98–99.

ff. [Unsigned.] *Antiquarian Bookman* 39, no. 15 (10 April 1967): 1504.

gg. [Unsigned.] *Booklist* 63, no. 19 (1 June 1967): 1035.

hh. [Unsigned.] *Choice* 4, no. 8 (October 1967): 837.

ii. [Unsigned.] *Kirkus Service* 35, no. 5 (1 March 1967): 300.

jj. [Unsigned.] *Observer* (London) no. 10571 (22 May 1994): Review, p. 21.

kk. [Unsigned.] *Publishers' Weekly* 191, no. 9 (27 February 1967): 101.

ll. [Unsigned.] *Publishers' Weekly* 193, no. 14 (1 April 1968): 40.

mm. [Unsigned.] "Short Notices." *Time* 89, no. 17 (28 April 1967): 116.

nn. [Unsigned.] "Seamy Senators." *Times Literary Supplement* no. 3413 (27 July 1967): 649.

Ackroyd's hostile review of *Washington, D.C., Burr,* and *1876* concludes that "far from being the sharp-eyed observer of human weaknesses, he is a writer who insists upon sentimentalising politics and politicians; his books are melodramas, and his characters are really only mouthpieces." . . . **Baro** writes: "Is Gore Vidal one of our genuine social novelists? He ought to be." The "book is an excellent one in most ways that novels now are not." It is well-written, has wit, and the theme is well developed. But the book may be "too neat." . . . **Binder** states that Vidal "does his usual first-rate job with dialog, but his most impoprtant people are generally wan and unconvincing." The book's greatest virtue may lie "in its hard, often devastating little stares at the restless, gossipy, ambitious inner circle that for one reason or another clusters around the seat of Government." . . . **Boston**, in a multiple review, feels that Vidal "clearly has an intimate knowledge of the American political scene and he is very good on all the intricacies of Washington, the gossip, backbiting, scandal and corruption." The "book is meticulously constructed and written with unusual skill." . . . **Brendon** notes that "what this book really illustrates with such frightening clarity is the inability of nearly all American novelists . . . to produce much more than variations on a theme by Grace Metalious." . . . **Buckmaster** observes that "it is a pity that this book is not better than it is," given Vidal's knowledge of politics. All the main characters are stereotypes. "The lack of stature or quality in these movers and shakers tends to make everything one-dimensional. They are cheap thinkers and doers, and pretty much of a bore." But Vidal "writes with sudden enchanting bursts of wit." . . . **Buitenhuis** thinks the novel is "written with an elegant, sharp clarity of style and wit . . . Mr. Vidal's historic sense is as sharp as his political insight." . . . **Clive** finds the characters well-rounded; "its subtleties of scene and characterisation make it a rewarding book." . . . **Curtin**'s review is largely a plot summary. "The humanity [in the novel] turns out to be much like the humanity in any other venue—good, bad, and confused." . . . **Dolbier** believes that Vidal is "writing again about Rome. . . . This is the New Rome . . . but it is peopled with a number of classical types." In this realm, "adultery is the norm, and homosexuality and incest are also present." But the work comes to "the deadest of dead ends." . . . **Fremont-Smith** remarks that the novel is Vidal's "most accomplished work to date." Vidal "has organized this extremely complex material with the lucid, suspenseful dexterity of a pro." It is superior to Allen Drury's *Advise and Consent.* . . . **Galbraith** states: "This is a superb story." Although Vidal "writes about only a limited corner of Washington," the story is "fascinating." Vidal's characters are "persuasive . . . and he handles the interplay of personality and power with rare skill." . . . **Greenfield** notes scornfully that the novel "is the stuff best-seller charts are made for." The characters are "all as flat as a losing candidate's bankroll." . . . **Hamilton**, in a multiple review, comments that "Vidal's writing is . . . mechanically slick and the characterisation . . . thinly pasteboard." . . . **Hodgson** feels the book is "disappointing, but interesting." "There are flashes of wit and moments of authentic tension in the book; but on the whole the writing is conventional where it is not downright pompous." But Vidal's bleak portrait of politicians is "neither frivolous nor altogether inaccurate." . . . **Kapp** states that Vidal seems more concerned with the social movements of his characters than with their political involvements. "If this book is not noticeably witty, it can still be said that the plot is laughable." . . . **Lehan**, in a multiple review, writes that "Vidal has the narrative control that [Philip] Roth [in *When She Was Good*] lacks. . . . Vidal does not substitute a personal for a public problem, or use a point of view that refracts rather than absorbs narrative meaning." . . . **Mitgang** finds that "In a real sense, [Vidal] is writing fiction and nonfiction at the same time." At the core of the novel are "ruthless ambition and corruption." "Thruout [*sic*] the story there are brilliant touches and observations about the Washington code and political scene." But the book has "many lifeless sections." . . . **Oberbeck** feels that Vidal's characters are "nicely chiseled but pale, formal and barely three-dimensional." "Much of Vidal's high-gloss commentary on the Washington scene comes off like half-smothered giggles." . . . **Raymond**, in a multiple review, remarks that, in addition to "good cut-and-thrust narrative, abundant surface irony, a talent for the working-out of near-credible melodrama," Vidal "joins an excellent sense of history." It is "the public, political reflections and touches in this novel that carry the weight of truth all the way." . . . **St. John** finds Vidal's cynicism about politics appalling. His "diagnosis of our democratic dilemma is too pat and all surface." . . . **Sharpe**'s review is largely a plot summary. He feels that the novel is "cluttered and confusing." "This causes slow and at times boring reading and a loss of force. . . . When he wants to, Vidal can write with admirable economy, insight and wit. For the most part, in this instance, he lacks these qualities." . . . **Sheed** thinks that Vidal "has set himself a brutal task: the play Trollope in the land of Alan [*sic*] Drury." But Vidal "has written a very plausible story." However, all the characters sound the same: "Everyone has arrived at the same plateau of intelligence and inner detachment as the author." . . . **Shrapnel**, in a multiple review, declares that the book, "irritatingly self-assured, is no masterpiece. It is just a goodish American example of what, for better or worse, the British have not got"—a knowledgeable dissection of the political scene. . . . **Strauss** believes that "everything is smoothly done," but he is puzzled as to the novel's focus and direction. . . . **Thompson** claims that the book is about "politics as character: to know what is good, to resist the altogether bad, which is lack of character." "The novel is intelligent, seems to be very knowing about social facts of Washington both public and hidden . . . and yet it is flat, as flat as it says the scene itself is." . . . **Weeks** expresses skepticism that politics can be quite as corrupt and lacking in principle as Vidal suggests. The novel, "like *The Comedians* by Graham Greene, is about adventures whose morals are dubious, but in Mr. Greene's story the people have fun and some of it rubs off on the reader, whereas in *Washington, D.C.* the scheming ends in tawdriness." . . . The ***Times Literary Supplement*** review refers to the novel as "a prodigiously skilled and clever performance." It goes on to say that "what is surprising in this novel is the ferocity of its disbelief in any human, let alone political, good."

23. *Myra Breckinridge*
   a. Barrett, Marvin. "The 100 Per Cent American Nightmare." *Reporter* 38, no. 7 (4 April 1968): 39–40.
   b. [Beaver, Harold.] "Pathetic Phallusy." *Times Literary Supplement* no. 3476 (10 October 1968): 1145.
   c. Brophy, Brigid. "The Tang of Uncertainty." *Listener* 80 (no. 2061) (26 September 1968): 412.
   d. Buckley, F. R. "Dirty Books: The Lay of the Land." *Triumph* 3, no. 7 (July 1968): 28–31 (esp. 28).
   e. Capitanchik, Maurice. "Rich and Rare." *Spectator* 221 (no. 7319) (4 October 1968): 476, 478.
   f. Dawson, Helen. "Briefing: Paperbacks." *Observer* (London) no. 9319 (22 February 1970): 30.
   g. Fremont-Smith, Eliot. "Like Fay Wray If the Light Is Right." *New York Times* (3 February 1968): 27.
   h. ———. "Second Prize in the Camp Sweepstakes." *New York* 7, no. 42 (21 October 1974): 90–91.
   i. Hentoff, Margot. "Growing Up Androgynous." *New York Review of Books* 10, no. 9 (9 May 1968): 32–33.
   j. King, Francis. "Old and New Prose from an Old Pro." *Spectator* 259 (no. 8315) (21 November 1987): 41, 43.
   k. MacBride, James. "What Did Myra Want?" *New York Times Book Review* (18 February 1968): 44–45.
   l. Montagnes, Anne. "In Brief." *Saturday Night* 83, no. 5 (May 1968): 43.
   m. Moon, Eric. *Library Journal* 93, no. 6 (15 March 1968): 1164.
   n. Muggeridge, Malcolm. "Books." *Esquire* 69, no. 5 (May 1968): 58, 60, 62 (esp. 62).
   o. Oberbeck, S. K. "That Was No Lady." *Washington Post Book World* (25 February 1968): 6.
   p. O'Malley, Michael. "Odds and Ends." *Critic* 26, no. 6 (June 1968): 76, 78.
   q. Peterson, Clarence. "Paperbacks: First Principles." *Washington Post Book World* (8 September 1968): 29.
   r. Price, R. G. G. "New Novels." *Punch* 255 (no. 6680) (18 September 1968): 418.

s.   Ratcliffe, Michael. "The Pagan and the Puritan." *Times* (London) (28 September 1968): 21.

t.   Sayre, Nora. "Anti-Matter." *New Statesman* 76 (no. 1958) (20 September 1968): 358–59.

u.   Shrapnel, Norman. "V is for Vidal, Vanity, Vitality, and a Superior Vulgarity." *Guardian Weekly* 99, no. 13 (26 September 1968): 15.

v.   Weightman, John. "Myth of the Butch Bitch." *Observer* (London) no. 9244 (15 September 1968): 29. In Weightman's *The Concept of the Avant-Garde: Explorations in Modernism.* LaSalle, IL: Library Press; London: Alcove Press, 1973, pp. 281–84.

w.   Zimmerman, Paul D. "Elan Vidal." *Newsweek* 71, no. 9 (26 February 1968): 88.

x.   [Unsigned.] *Choice* 5, no. 2 (April 1968): 200.

y.   [Unsigned.] *Kirkus Reviews* 36, no. 2 (15 January 1968): 74.

z.   [Unsigned.] *Publishers' Weekly* 193, no. 6 (5 February 1968): 63.

aa. [Unsigned.] *Publishers' Weekly* 197, no. 17 (27 April 1970): 80.

bb. [Unsigned.] "Myra the Messiah." *Time* 91, no. 7 (16 February 1968): E6, 96.

Barrett's review is largely a summary of Vidal's career. He finds some merit in the book, but "on most other counts it is pretty dreadful." "Despite a superficial coyness, it takes a stern, unfriendly view of the modern world." He thinks the novel is Vidal's "farewell performance as a novelist." . . . **Beaver** feels that "If this is pornography, it is also a metaphysical assault on an American holy of holies—the matriarchal cult." "Pornography . . . is exhibited as the final metamorphosis of Existentialism." . . . **Brophy**'s now celebrated review is dense and enthusiastic. For her, the novel is an example of the "high baroque comedy of bad taste." "For baroque is the art of wreaking an explosion deep inside the classical structure and re-assorting the classical elements into an incongruity grotesque, ironic, comic, barbarically majestic." . . . **Buckley** dispenses with the novel as "the latest effluence from the juvenile pen of Gore Vidal." "Not excluding the protagonist, the characters are all pasteboard cut-outs from some masochist's collection of clichés." . . . **Capitanchik**'s harshly critical review concludes that the book "is the latest piece of porno-puritan commercialism to be foisted on to us," and that Vidal himself is the true Puritan. . . . **Fremont-Smith** believes this is a novel about a "transvestite." The book is "repulsive both in graphic detail and in the exploitive snicker one detects at some real-life hang-ups." It is a "genuinely, brutally witty book, a parody of Hollywood, pop intellectualism, pornography and just about anything else you could name." . . . **Hentoff** thinks that Vidal has "written the first popular book of perverse pornography." The novel "is almost entirely a parody of present cultural attitudes and concerns." . . . **King** notes that the novel is "a macabre book [and] also an extremely funny one." . . . **MacBryde** finds the book "a mad and sometimes grotesque pastiche." It is "a shocker as artfully mechanized as a Keystone Kops chase sequence." . . . **Oberbeck** sees the book as a "slyly saturnalian" novel. It is "grimly humorous—full of the self-indulgent cinematic camp and flamboyant put-on that seems *de rigeur* [*sic*] these days." . . . **O'Malley** observes that the novel is the "Apotheosis of Juicy Fruit. A flittier, fruitier novel, a more quintessential fairy tale, I cannot imagine." The novel is "soaked in estrogen." "This is a novel about skin. There is no heart at all in it." . . . **Price** writes: "Not taking itself too seriously, the romp is fun. It is not vintage Vidal but anyone is entitled to time off." But the novel is "very lightweight." . . . **Ratcliffe** refers to the "ferocious and exhuberantly well-written novel." It is a parody whose point is that, "as an anthropological phenomenon, sex has become wildly overrated." . . . In an enthusiastic review, **Sayre** states that "Mr Vidal's most serious novel is also his lightest." She appreciates Vidal's wit and his send-ups of pop culture. . . . **Shrapnel**, in a multiple review, finds that Myra is "the most fabulous heroine of the year, a maneater as near as one could get to a cross between the goddess Kali and Mae West." Vidal has written "a superior kind of vulgarity that is elegantly, you could almost say fastidiously, applied." . . . **Weightman** declares that this is "a queer, queer book, a virtuoso exercise in kinkiness, a strikingly intelligent attempt to go as far as possible in outrageousness. . . . One of the charms of this book is the difficulty of deciding whether it is a pure spoof . . . or a spoof with a core of genuineness." . . . **Zimmerman** asserts that "The book is short on traditional character development, long on sex of all kinds and cinematic in method." It is "witty, imaginative, full of élan Vidal." The novel "becomes, in the end, a kind of erotic propaganda." The review proceeds with an overview of Vidal's career. . . . The ***Time*** review comments that the plot resembles "a stag film." "What makes the novel a little more than a flighty drag is Vidal's stylish and erudite sense of humor, his sharp pokes at intellectually provocative themes, and his spoofing of literary forms."

24.   *Weekend*
  a.   Barnes, Clive. "Theater: Vidal's Political 'Weekend.'" *New York Times* (14 March 1968): 50. *New York Theatre Critics' Reviews* 29, no. 7 (18 March 1968): 326.
  b.   Chapman, John. "Gore Vidal's 'Weekend' a Long One in Washington, with Jokes." *New York Daily News* (14 March 1968): 63. *New York Theatre Critics' Reviews* 29, no. 7 (18 March 1968): 327.
  c.   Clurman, Harold. "Theatre." *Nation* 206, no. 14 (1 April 1968): 454.
  d.   Cooke, Richard P. "Politics and No People." *Wall Street Journal* (15 March 1968): 16. *New York Theatre Critics' Reviews* 29, no. 7 (18 March 1968): 326–27.
  e.   Gill, Brendan. "Vile Bodies." *New Yorker* 44, no. 5 (23 March 1968): 101–2.
  f.   Gottfried, Martin. "Theatre." *Women's Wear Daily* (14 March 1968): 40. *New York Theatre Critics' Reviews* 29, no. 7 (18 March 1968): 327–28.
  g.   Hewes, Henry. "Anyone for Politics?" *Saturday Review* 51, no. 13 (30 March 1968): 20.
  h.   Kerr, Walter. "Ready, Aim, Fire—But at What?" *New York Times* (31 March 1968): Sec. 2, pp. 1, 3.
  i.   Kroll, Jack. "Lost Weekend." *Newsweek* 71, no. 13 (25 March 1968): 100.
  j.   Simon, John. "Dapper Gore." *Commonweal* 88, no. 3 (5 April 1968): 74–75.
  k.   Watts, Richard, Jr. "Two Who Came for the Weekend." *New York Post* (14 March 1968): 27. *New York Theatre Critics' Reviews* 29, no. 7 (18 March 1968): 328.
  l.   [Unsigned.] "New Plays." *Time* 91, no. 12 (22 March 1968): 64.

Barnes believes that Vidal "has erected a thin story line and hung on it every political joke he can dream up." The play is "timely and polished." Vidal "writes very well in an artificial, literary style." The acting and direction are exemplary.... **Chapman** states: "I found that 'Weekend' was quite tedious because I didn't believe in it and I don't think the author really believed in it either. It was spurious fiction." ... **Clurman** notes that this is "a trivial play" but the cast performs well.... **Cooke** calls the play "well acted, often witty, entirely cynical and eminently knowledgeable," but "its figures represent attitudes rather than individuals." "This reviewer couldn't really believe these people had blood and viscera." ... **Gill** finds the play "a trumpery collection of unpleasant domestic and political wisecracks." It "has the odd distinction of containing not a single character that one feels a sympathetic interest in." ... **Gottfried** claims that, although Vidal "is the only American playwright with the experience, the craft and the knowledgeability to write a sophisticated comedy on national politics," he has not done so here. The play "settles for familiar domestic humor. Instead of being crafty, it is merely mechanical; instead of being pertinent, it is merely relevant." It is full of theatricality and politically implausible details.... **Hewes** thinks that the play shows Vidal's "disenchantment with America." The plot "is all rather too predictable." ... **Kerr** declares that the play "sounds like the rattle of ice cubes in a long weak drink." Vidal adopts "theatrical dodges" that are now outmoded; "he has nothing to offer but his slickness." ... **Kroll** notes that "The play looses a mortar-barrage of set gags which clump heavily down upon the audience." "Why has a writer of Vidal's talent settled for this farrago of clichés?" The play reveals Vidal's pessimism and misanthropy.... **Simon** observes that Vidal "is a reliable farceur," but *Weekend* is "only bearable." The play "is neither deep nor devilish, only dapper." It is merely a mouthpiece for Vidal's opinions.... **Watts** finds the play "a predictable and rather desultory narrative.... there is hardly a thing in the entire evening that you can't call your shots on well in advance." The play seems directed more at Nixon than at LBJ.... The *Time* review, largely a plot summary, states that "the jokes are either juvenile or senile."

25.   *Sex, Death and Money*
  a.   Peterson, Clarence. "Paperbacks: Iceboxes for Eskimos." *Washington Post Book World* (10 November 1968): 21.
  b.   [Unsigned.] *Publishers' Weekly* 194, no. 13 (23 September 1968): 98.

Peterson feels the book may be "disappointing" to fans of *Myra Breckinridge*. But Vidal's "essays are typically provocative and serious but back from the brink of self-seriousness by his unfailing wit."

26.   *Reflections upon a Sinking Ship*
  a.   Adams, Phoebe. *Atlantic Monthly* 223, no. 4 (April 1969): 146.

b.   [Beaver, Harold.] "Polished Nightmares." *Times Literary Supplement* no. 3517 (24 July 1969): 804.

c.   Brophy, Brigid. "A Reasoned Pessimism." *Listener* 82 (no. 2104) (24 July 1969): 117–18.

d.   Friedenberg, Edgar Z. "Patriotic Gore." *New York Review of Books* 12, no. 12 (19 June 1969): 34–36.

e.   Gerrity, Diana. "Elegant Notes for a Floating Bottle." *Christian Science Monitor* (24 April 1969): 13.

f.   Grant, Annette. "Iconoclast." *Newsweek* 73, no. 13 (31 March 1969): 100, 102.

g.   Green, Martin. "Beau Vidal." *Guardian Weekly* 101, no. 7 (14 August 1969): 18.

h.   Higgins, John. "Going Down." *Spectator* 223 (no. 7362) (2 August 1969): 147.

i.   Lask, Thomas. "Keep Smiling." *New York Times* (25 March 1969): 45.

j.   McAleer, John J. *Best Sellers* 29, no. 1 (1 April 1969): 9.

k.   Martinetti, Ronald. "Visions of a Middle-Aged Cassandra." *Wall Street Journal* (3 April 1969): 12.

l.   Mitchell, Julian. "Glum Elegance." *New Statesman* 78 (no. 2000) (11 July 1969): 50.

m.   Nichols, Christopher. "Taking Up the Job God Bungled." *National Review* 21, no. 19 (20 May 1969): 497–99.

n.   Ringer, Agnes C. *Library Journal* 93, no. 16 (15 September 1968): 3142.

o.   Sheed, Wilfrid. *New York Times Book Review* (6 April 1969): 4, 26. In Sheed's *The Morning After: Selected Essays and Reviews*. New York: Farrar, Straus & Giroux, 1971, pp. 43–47 (as "Gore Vidal: *Reflections upon a Sinking Ship*").

p.   Theroux, Paul. "Shipping Water." *Times* (London) (9 August 1969): 18.

q.   Weales, Gerald. "While the Orchestra Plays 'Nearer My God to Thee.'" *Washington Post Book World* (30 March 1969): 6.

r.   [Unsigned.] *Booklist* 65, no. 19 (1 June 1969): 1106–7.

s.   [Unsigned.] *Choice* 7, no. 8 (October 1970): 1044.

t.   [Unsigned.] *Christian Century* 86, no. 13 (26 March 1969): 420.

u.   [Unsigned.] *Kirkus Reviews* 37, no. 2 (15 January 1969): 92.

v.   [Unsigned.] *Publishers' Weekly* 195, no. 2 (13 January 1969): 90.

w.   [Unsigned.] "Pangs and Needles." *Time* 93, no. 13 (28 March 1969): 90.

Beaver notes that much of the book is "astute, old-fashioned liberal journalism spiced with an old-fashioned urge to puncture the affluent, imperial, puritan pretentions of his fellow American-Way-of-Lifers." ... **Brophy**'s long, discursive review finds her agreeing with Vidal on many subjects. The essays "are unified by their multiple, reasoned pessimism and the spark of aesthetic optimism in which he counter-asserts 'yet.'" "In this volume Mr Vidal takes every chance of preaching literacy wittily." ... **Friedenberg** believes that Vidal's essays are "quite unlike anything else in American letters today." The book is unified by "a kind of elegiac conservatism." Vidal is "a conservative defender of personal liberty." He has "a genuinely aristocratic temper," but this sometimes leads him to be insufficiently decisive in attacking political and social ills. ... **Gerrity** writes that "the tenor of urbane melancholy pervading these articles provides a continuity all its own, both in theme and image. ... Yet for all its attempted tone of aloof objectivity, the book is finally a composite impression of Gore Vidal, Ego and Intellect, rather than a body of thought with weight and import of its own." ... **Grant** feels that Vidal is "not only a formidable political and literary critic, but a provocative and persuasive sociologist, psychologist and *philosophe*." ... **Green** states that Vidal as essayist is "an interesting case of a mere manner, a hollow surface, an unfulfilled promise." Vidal affects the voice of an insolent dandy. The essays "lack substance." Vidal is "dull," both about himself and his subject matter. ... **Higgins** declares that the book is an accurate reflection of Vidal's scorn of America. The political essays are "brilliant." ... **Lask** observes that the liteary essays allow us to see Vidal's own standards. But the essay on the Kennedys ("The Holy Family") is "one of the most tasteless political essays that this reader has come across." ... **McAleer** writes: "Vidal has just one theme, really—the world is a death ship, hellbent—with a simple corollary—anything we can do to dull the anguish is ethical." Vidal "calls for unrestricted pornography, unrestricted access to drugs, incest." ... **Martinetti** claims that the book shows that Vidal's "reforming zeal has faded into a passive pessimism." Vidal "is the favorite subject of his own essays"; his "writing [is] marked by a coolness of tone and precision of style." Vidal has been called an unpredictable writer, "but shrewd would be a better choice." . . . **Mitchell** believes the essays on politics are much more interesting than those on literature, since Vidal "does not, fundamentally, think literature is very important. . . . Vidal is altogether too glib." . . . **Nichols** states that Vidal "is best, very urbane and witty, when lashing cultural lightweights with his velvet glove," but when "writing hortatory polemic, he is unbearable." Nichols takes Vidal to task for his views on sex and overpopulation, which he sees as irreligious. "He should be stuffed and placed in the Smithsonian as our definitive example of a high degree of secular evolution." . . . **Sheed** comments that Vidal's "nonfiction is invariably more cautious than the fiction." His tone is distant and impersonal: "The favorite note is one of personal indifference." Sheed takes Vidal to task on his discussion of homosexuality, but appreciates the wit of his literary essays. . . . **Theroux** finds this a "superb book." It contains searing criticisms of the American way of life. "There are judgments and prophecies on every page, some [of] which already have proved sadly true." . . . **Weales** notes that the book is "much less a unit" than *Rocking the Boat.* Vidal's reputation as a wit "is not exactly justified." But "even his most trivial piece is likely to have substance, both material and moral." . . . The *Time* review remarks that Vidal is "more 'creative' at nonfiction than fiction." "A sort of well-informed aloofness is the secret of the Vidal all-purpose style." Vidal is "cheerfully disillusioned."

27. *Two Sisters*
   a. Avant, John Alfred. *Library Journal* 95, no. 13 (July 1970): 2521–22.
   b. Cole, Barry. "Only Connect." *Spectator* 225 (no. 7423) (3 October 1970): 370–71.
   c. Coleman, John. "Novels or Whatever." *Observer* (London) no. 9348 (13 September 1970): 28.
   d. Cook, Bruce. "Vidal Sports His Talk-Show Hat in a Gossipy and Strained Novel." *National Observer* 9, no. 28 (13 July 1970): 19.
   e. Cruttwell, Patrick. "Fiction Chronicle." *Hudson Review* 24, no. 1 (Spring 1971): 177–84 (esp. 184).
   f. Davenport, Guy. "A Nose-Holding Diatribe, Complete with Novel and Movie Script." *New York Times Book Review* (12 July 1970): 6–7.
   g. Enright, D. J. "A Mirror in the Form of a Book." *Listener* 84 (no. 2165) (24 September 1970): 416.
   h. Epstein, Joseph. "A Scandalmonger's Oversight." *Washington Post Book World* (5 July 1970): 1, 3.
   i. Gold, Herbert. "Why 'I'?" *Saturday Review/World* 2 (8 February 1975): 18–21.
   j. [Green, Peter.] "What's New, Pussycat?" *Times Literary Supplement* no. 3577 (18 September 1970): 1026.
   k. Hope, Francis. "Golden I." *New Statesman* 80 (no. 2069) (13 November 1970): 650–51.
   l. Leonard, John. "Books of The Times: Not Enough Blood, Not Enough Gore." *New York Times* (7 July 1970): 37.
   m. Macklin, F. Anthony. *America* 123, no. 5 (5 September 1970): 129.
   n. Maddocks, Melvin. "Wit Trying to Care." *Christian Science Monitor* (16 July 1970): 7.
   o. Peterson, Clarence. "Paperbacks." *Washington Post Book World* (19 September 1971): 13.
   p. Ratcliffe, Michael. "Dreams Preceding a Time of Fire." *Times* (London) (19 September 1970): 20.
   q. Rosselli, Aldo. "Pettegolezzi e altre quisquilie dell'ultimo Gore Vidal." *Nuovi Argomenti* 19 (July–September 1970): 230–34.
   r. Sheppard, R. Z. "Overrripeness Is All." *Time* 96, no. 2 (13 July 1970): 74.
   s. Thomas, Edward. *London Magazine* NS 10, no. 7 (October 1970): 95–98 (esp. 96–97).
   t. Wade, Rosalind. "Quarterly Fiction Review." *Contemporary Review* 218, no. 1 (January 1971): 45–49 (esp. 48).
   u. Yoder, Edwin M., Jr. *Harper's Magazine* 241, no. 3 (September 1970): 103.
   v. Zimmerman, Paul D. "Author Self-Trapped." *Newsweek* 76, no. 1 (6 July 1970): 83A, 84.
   w. [Unsigned.] *Kirkus Reviews* 38, no. 9 (1 May 1970): 528.
   x. [Unsigned.] *Publishers' Weekly* 197, no. 17 (27 April 1970): 78.

Cole thinks the book is "a splendid firework display" but marred by egotism. . . . **Coleman** believes that Vidal "may be a more interesting essayist than novelist." The book is "a genuine oddity." The best parts are "where the author lets rip on assorted malaises of our century." . . . **Cook** feels that what Vidal "communicates most plainly to the reader is the strain that he must have felt in writing" this novel. The book seems largely to be gossip "at the expense of Jacqueline Kennedy Onassis." But "it gets out of hand." . . . **Cruttwell**, in a hostile review, states that the book is "a shapeless mess of vulgar exhibitionism. . . . The whole thing stinks." . . . **Davenport** observes that the novel is really a "snippish little essay." "All the novelistic passages of this confusing concoction of a book are obviously à clef." The book reveals Vidal's disdain for American literature and society. His ideas are confused: "Nothing in his strictures quite makes sense." But there are nonetheless some "lovely pages." . . . **Enright** maintains that the novel is "an insolent performance . . . but it is a perfunctory one too." It is "a skimpy left-over from *Myra Breckinridge.*" The book has an air of triviality, but perhaps it is parodying triviality. . . . **Epstein** claims that Vidal is "the funniest writer in America." He "would make a wonderful gossip columnist," for gossip is at the heart of this novel. "This is a book that offers a great number of enjoyments, not all of them simple." The characters are magnificently portrayed: "Vidal's talent really is best geared for the high comic, the absurd, the grotesqueries of the human circus." But Vidal himself is the "most careful creation in the book." . . . **Green** states: "the whole affair is at once so accomplished and so effortless that although we may tire from chapter to chapter, we never flag from line to line." . . . **Hope** finds the novel wearying and self-indulgent; "much tiresome concertina-ing takes place with art, time, memory, fact and fiction." . . . **Leonard** remarks that "There is no reason why a writer as accomplished as he is couldn't have whipped these materials into convincing shape." The book is not really revelatory of Vidal, because "he presents himself under so many coats of lacquer that one knows reality will never soil him." . . . **Macklin** finds the book "a scrapbook held together with the dried glue of reminiscence. It hardly holds." "Vidal is a deceiver, and the new book is devious. . . . The true feeling of the book is the awareness of advancing age." . . . **Maddocks** praises the epigrams in the book, but the novel reveals another side of Vidal, one plagued by loneliness: "Here is a Vidal, not playing the neo-Roman stoic—not forever buffing up his sophistication." . . . **Ratcliffe** declares that "the man is now the work: Narcissus has thrown a firework into the archives." The "writing is beautifully clear." . . . **Rosselli**'s review, in Italian, is largely a plot summary. . . . **Sheppard** notes that "the thin veil of fiction that he swirls so adeptly around the pale data of his life is disappointing." The views expressed in the novel are repetitions of what Vidal has said in articles and TV talk shows. . . . **Yoder** thinks that Vidal is "literate, amusing and mordant"; the novel is full of "sex and sententiousness." . . . **Zimmerman** states that Vidal "is a novelist in search of a form." The book "tries to do too many things at once, with uneven results." It "suffers from artifice to the point of archness."

28.   *An Evening with Richard Nixon*
    a.   Barnes, Clive. "Stage: 'Evening with Nixon' Is for Radical Liberals." *New York Times* (1 May 1972): 41. *Times* (London) (10 May 1972): 19.
    b.   Bridges, Linda. "An Evening with Vidal." *National Review* 24, no. 22 (9 June 1972): 652–53.
    c.   Clurman, Harold. "Theatre." *Nation* 214, no. 2 (22 May 1972): 669–70 (esp. 669).
    d.   Gill, Brendan. "For the Prosecution." *New Yorker* 48, no. 11 (6 May 1972): 54, 56, 61.
    e.   Gottfried, Martin. "The Theatre." *Women's Wear Daily* (2 May 1972): 16. *New York Theatre Critics' Reviews* 33, no. 12 (22 May 1972): 291.
    f.   Harris, Leonard. *New York Theatre Critics' Reviews* 33, no. 12 (22 May 1972): 292. [Originally on WCBS TV, 30 April 1972.]
    g.   Hewes, Henry. "Distal and Proximal Bite." *Saturday Review* 55, no. 21 (20 May 1972): 62–63.
    h.   Kalem, T. E. "Small Favor." *Time* 99, no. 20 (15 May 1972): 59. *New York Theatre Critics' Reviews* 33, no. 12 (22 May 1972): 292.
    i.   Kauffmann, Stanley. "Right Down the Middle." *New Republic* 166, no. 22 (27 May 1972): 22, 34–35 (esp. 34).
    j.   Kerr, Walter. "'Nixon'—Reminding Us Doesn't Amuse Us." *New York Times* (7 May 1972): Sec. 2, pp. 1, 3.
    k.   Kroll, Jack. "Hail to the Chief." *Newsweek* 79, no. 20 (15 May 1972): 92. *New York Theatre Critics' Reviews* 33, no. 12 (22 May 1972): 291–92.
    l.   Marvel, Bill. "Vidal's Stylish Con Has All the Lines in Debate Waist Deep in Radical Chic." *National Observer* 11, no. 20 (13 May 1972): 22.

m. Ricklefs, Roger. "Vidal's Malice: Witty But Dated." *Wall Street Journal* (2 May 1972): 18. *New York Theatre Critics' Reviews* 33, no. 12 (22 May 1972): 290.

n. Rollin, Betty. *New York Theatre Critics' Reviews* 33, no. 12 (22 May 1972): 293. [Originally on WNBC TV, 30 April 1972.]

o. Sanders, Kevin. *New York Theatre Critics' Reviews* 33, no. 12 (22 May 1972): 292. [Originally on WABC TV, 30 April 1972.]

p. Simon, John. "Eloquence in Spite of Words." *New York* 5, no. 20 (15 May 1972): 70.

q. Watt, Douglas. "'Evening with Nixon' Falls Flat." *New York Daily News* (1 May 1972): 52. *New York Theatre Critics' Reviews* 33, no. 12 (22 May 1972): 290.

r. Watts, Richard. "Gore Vidal Dislikes Nixon." *New York Post* (1 May 1972): 21. *New York Theatre Critics' Reviews* 33, no. 12 (22 May 1972): 289.

s. Wimble, Barton. *Library Journal* 97, no. 7 (1 April 1972): 1342.

t. [Unsigned.] *Booklist* 68, no. 22 (15 July 1972): 967.

u. [Unsigned.] *Publishers' Weekly* 201, no. 5 (31 January 1972): 239.

Barnes feels that Vidal's "blast at the President sparkles with fierceness but generates more light than heat." Nixon is "made into a caricature of that caricature he normally seems to play in his public life." . . . **Bridges** finds the play "not terribly entertaining." ". . . there is too much . . . invective for it to be a convincing documentary . . . but too little of it to put across the outrageous, and outraged hatred of *Macbird!*" The statements by Nixon are taken out of context. . . . **Clurman** believes that the play is not "drama" but is nonetheless rewarding. Vidal's transcription of Nixon's words is "fascinating and frequently funny." The play "has more substance than most of the 'art' Broadway now has to offer." . . . **Cooper** states that, beyond presenting Nixon as "an opportunistic boob," the play's "larger vision is of America itself as a ship of corrupt fools." . . . **Gill** thinks the play "a needle-sharp and exceedingly funny pasquinade." Vidal sees Nixon as "a man devoid of any principle—or even any motive—save that of running for public office and winning by whatever means happen to be within his grasp." . . . **Gottfried** writes: "Instead of writing satire, [Vidal] has mounted a diatribe, humorless, relentless, abusive. In the end, it is not theatre but a harangue. . . . Because Vidal has been so unoriginal, so heavy-handed and so unartistic in putting together his attack, its net effect is self-defeating—we feel sorry for Nixon." . . . **Harris** observes that the play "is immensely political, and I enjoyed it immensely. . . . I suggest it's good theatre, whatever your feelings." . . . **Hewes** notes that Vidal "has made shameless use of political figures and his cynicism about them." . . . **Kalem** remarks that the work is a "non-play." Vidal "rather hysterically strafes some of his pet skunks. . . . He offers a nonstop diatribe, vitriolic and at times caustically amusing." . . . **Kauffmann** claims that Vidal "has produced an anti-Nixon polemic whose effect—at best—is to make anti-Nixonites feel better about themselves." But the "result is an ungainly, superheated pageant." . . . **Kerr** states that "Nixon, synthetic to the core, seems only one more jumping-jack in a torrent of toadies, in which he may even be seen as the national end-product of what all before him have done furtively." . . . **Marvel** writes: "Vidal's play kicks its subject around so much that after a while there isn't much fun to it, unless you enjoy that sort of thing." Many times "Vidal's points are lost in a vast wallow of specious moralizing." But the pacing is good. . . . **Ricklefs** sums up the play as "an amusing evening of malice," but the play "is surprisingly ineffective as a political hatchet job. The writer is trapped in his own gimmick," because many of the Nixon quotes are old and familiar. But "the pace is fast and the laughs are frequent." . . . **Rollin** maintains that this is not a play but "a thoroughly tiresome, only occasionally amusing, biased history lesson." But the play is well acted and is "a spiffy production." . . . **Sanders** refers to the play as "variously devastating, hilarious and, occasionally, frightening. . . . The play moves with pace, style and precision, and only occasionally does Vidal slip into letting the judges sermonize." . . . **Simon** notes that "this pasquinade has a measure of wit and an excess of surface. . . . It confirms Vidal as a member of that luckless band of lesser wits who have a knack for being right in the wrong way." But the production "has many felicities." . . . **Watt** refers to this as "an almost resolutely nontheatrical piece. . . . In order to succeed, political satire must have thrust and imagination. . . . But Vidal's tone rarely rises above the querulous." It is "a political satire lacking bite." . . . **Watts** declares that the "lampoon . . . proved to be astonishingly tepid and, to get right down to it, extremely flat and tiresome." Moreover, "there is little wit and small sense of what is effective dramatically" in this work. "It merely seems petty."

29. *Homage to Daniel Shays*

a. Bailey, Paul. "Special Notices." *London Magazine* NS 14, no. 5 (December 1974/January 1975): 133–34.

b. Brudnoy, D. J. C. "Books in Brief." *National Review* 25, no. 5 (2 February 1973): 162.

c.   Conrad, Peter. "Look at Us." *New Review* 2 (no. 16) (July 1975): 63–66.
d.   Cooper, Arthur. "Bristling and Bitching." *Newsweek* 80, no. 23 (4 December 1972): 106, 109.
e.   De Vree, Freddy. *Kunst en Cultuur* (19 September 1974): 22.
f.   Green, Benny. "Patriotic Gore." *Spectator* 233 (no. 7626) (24 August 1974): 247.
g.   James, Clive. "Private Roman Eye." *Observer* (London) no. 9548 (28 July 1974): 28.
h.   Muggeridge, Malcolm. "Books." *Esquire* 79, no. 4 (April 1973): 8, 10 (esp. 10).
i.   Padel, Ruth. "Their Wits about Them." *Times Literary Supplement* no. 3807 (21 February 1975): 188.
j.   Rabinowitz, Dorothy. "Books in Brief." *World* 1, no. 13 (19 December 1972): 73.
k.   Sale, Roger. *New York Times Book Review* (31 December 1972): 7.
l.   Sheppard, R. Z. "Unpatriotic Gore." *Time* 100, no. 24 (11 December 1972): 116.
m.   Spender, Stephen. "Private Eye." *New York Review of Books* 20, no. 4 (22 March 1973): 6–8. In III.D.13.
n.   [Unsigned.] *Kirkus Reviews* 40, no. 19 (1 October 1972): 1180–81.
o.   [Unsigned.] *Library Journal* 97, no. 21 (1 December 1972): 3893.
p.   [Unsigned.] *New Yorker* 48, no. 45 (30 December 1972) 72.
q.   [Unsigned.] *Psychology Today* 7, no. 1 (June 1973): 102.
r.   [Unsigned.] *Publishers Weekly* 202, no. 16 (16 October 1972): 48.
s.   [Unsigned.] *Saturday Review of the Arts* 55, no. 49 (2 December 1972): 78.
t.   [Unsigned.] "Shorter Reviews." *Saturday Review of the Society* 55, no. 51 (16 December 1972): 71.
u.   [Unsigned.] "Short List." *Sunday Times* (London) (18 August 1974): 33.
v.   [Unsigned.] "Briefly Noted." *Washington Post Book World* (10 December 1972): 15.

Bailey, reviewing the book in conjunction with Yvor Winters's *Uncollected Essays and Reviews,* writes that Vidal's "prose is so eloquent, so accurately pitched between the flippant and the grave, that it's all too easy to dismiss him as a good read. . . . He's a very courageous writer. He takes his single-mindedness into the marketplace . . . he writes like an angel." . . . **Brudnoy** feels that Vidal "is a superb stylist and essayist, utterly unfair when he sets out to do a number on someone politically wrong, er, Right, but brilliant especially in literary criticism." He concludes that "at his critical sharpest, he's very keen indeed, and almost likable." . . . **Conrad**, focusing on *Myron,* reads the essays in light of the character of Myra Breckinridge. . . . **Cooper** believes that "The essay has become the vehicle for Vidal's elegant, ironic proselytizing, and he has become a master of the form. . . . There is no denying that Vidal is as provocative and perceptive a social and literary critic as America has today." He is "an admitted hater," but "his coolness is not a passionate coolness . . . but seems like the chill that leaps onto a falling flame." . . . **Green** compares Vidal to Edmund Wilson in the breadth of his critical work: he is "honest, urbane, erudite and courageous." . . . **James** states that Vidal is "among the most substantial" of American essayists. But it is "a glib opinion" to say that he is a better essayist than a novelist. "He would be a teacher, were his tone more dry. . . . It is remarkable how often Vidal has been right" in his political prophecies. Vidal is "always diverting" when discussing sex. . . . **Muggeridge** writes: "There are so few writers as genuinely funny, intelligent, well-read and accomplished as he, and yet his performance goes wrong somewhere, lacks some essential quality." . . . **Padel**, reviewing the book in conjunction with Randall Jarrell's *The Third Book of Criticism,* maintains that Vidal's sense of history and "the sharp, flexible, funny style" makes his essays "so much more than the ego-pushing observations currently required of the genre." "Randall Jarrell and Gore Vidal are at opposite poles of American writing-about-writing." . . . **Rabinowitz**, in an enthusiastic review, notes that Vidal "has a gift of catching the tremors of the moment as they occur, and he does so with an alertness usually reserved for the beneficiaries of hindsight . . . there is a good deal of intellectual, as well as plain, old-fashioned literary, pleasure to be had" in nearly all the essays. . . . **Sale** declares that Vidal's essays are brilliant ("there isn't a clinker in the bunch"), but too relentlessly topical and contemporary, hence dated. His "essays are almost always good and his novels are not so good." But Vidal is "a writer without a center." . . . **Sheppard** remarks that "unpatriotic Gore thrives on repetition." He admires Vidal's "polished prose" and the "compact and provocative insight" of the essays. "Scintillating pessimism and imperial disdain have always been Vidal's stock in trade." . . . **Spender**, in an extensive review, states that "Not only are the individual essays excellent, the whole is more than the sum of its parts." The literary essays can be "painfully painstaking." Vidal is "better on writers than on writing," and "he is better on politicians than politics." "When he writes about power, one is impressed by something authoritative in Gore Vidal's manner."

30. *Burr*

a. Ackroyd, Peter. "Blood, Thunder and Gore." *Spectator* 236 (no. 7709) (27 March 1976): 20.

b. Axelrod, George. "George Axelrod on Gore, a Novelette without Parts." *Spectator* 232 (no. 7604) (23 March 1974): 362–63.

c. Beloff, Max. "A 'Founding Father': The Sally Hemings Affair." *Encounter* 43, no. 3 (September 1974): 52–56.

d. Biddle, Wayne. "American Mass Myth." *New Society* 27 (no. 599) (28 March 1974): 782–83.

e. Brendon, Piers. "American Treason Trial." *Books and Bookmen* 19, no. 8 (May 1974): 80–81.

f. Breslin, John B. *America* 129, no. 10 (6 October 1973): 250.

g. Brodie, Fawn M. "The Man Who Loved Women." *Psychology Today* 7, no. 10 (March 1974): 13, 92.

h. Chace, James. *Village Voice* 18, no. 46 (15 November 1973): 29–30.

i. Conrad, Peter. "Look at Us." *New Review* 2 (no. 16) (July 1975): 63–66.

j. Crain, Jane Larkin. "Above the Herd." *Commentary* 57, no. 3 (March 1974): 76, 78.

k. Cunliffe, Marcus. "Stranger Than Fiction." *Guardian Weekly* 110, no. 14 (6 April 1974): 21.

l. Dangerfield, George. "Less Than History and Less Than Fiction." *New York Times Book Review* (28 October 1973): 2.

m. Dworkin, Ronald. "Ghost of America's Future." *Sunday Times* (London) (24 March 1974): 40.

n. Fetherhof, Shirley. *Kliatt* 28, no. 3 (May 1994): 42.

o. Fremont-Smith, Eliot. "Burr and Gore." *New York* 6, no. 44 (29 October 1973): 86–87.

p. French, Philip. "Vice President." *New Statesman* 87 (no. 2244) (22 March 1974): 415.

q. Furbank, P. N. "Gore Vidal's Voltairean Gentleman." *Listener* 91 (no. 2347) (21 March 1974): 372.

r. Highet, Gilbert. "Report." *Book-of-the-Month Club News* (November 1973): 2–3.

s. Hogarty, Ken. "Recommended Historical Fiction." *English Journal* 78, no. 1 (January 1989): 86.

t. Kempton, Murray. "Discovering America." *New York Review of Books* 20, no. 18 (15 November 1973): 6–8.

u. Klein, Jeffrey. "Politics and the Self-Serving Imagination." *North American Review* 259, no. 2 (Summer 1974): 57–61 (esp. 57–58).

v. Lehmann-Haupt, Christopher. "Books of The Times: Back to the First Principles." *New York Times* (25 October 1973): 45.

w. McLellan, Joseph. "Paperbacks." *Washington Post Book World* (1 December 1974): 4.

x. Maloff, Saul. "A Fiction of History." *New Republic* 169, no. 19 (10 November 1973): 23–24.

y. Nelson, Barbara. *Library Journal* 98, no. 19 (1 November 1973): 3284.

z. Nicol, Charles. "Putting Catsup on the Founders." *National Review* 26, no. 9 (1 March 1974): 270–71.

aa. Poirier, Richard. "The Heart Has Its Treasons." *Washington Post Book World* (28 October 1973): 3.

bb. Prescott, Peter S. "Great American Monster." *Newsweek* 82, no. 19 (5 November 1973): 98.

cc. R. "Column." *Encounter* 42, no. 5 (May 1974): 25–27.

dd. Ratcliffe, Michael. "A Memorable Contest." *Times* (London) (21 March 1974): 10.

ee. Rogers, Michael. *Library Journal* 123, no. 7 (15 April 1998): 120.

ff.   Sheppard, R. Z. "Foundling Father." *Time* 102, no. 19 (5 November 1973): 109.
gg.   Simon, John. "Clinging to A. Burr." *New Leader* 56, no. 24 (10 December 1973): 10–12.
hh.   Snow, C. P. "Fallible Father." *Financial Times* (London) (21 March 1974): 15.
ii.   Toynbee, Philip. "An Ambiguous Hero." *Observer* (London) no. 9530 (24 March 1974): 39.
jj.   Weeks, Edward. *Atlantic Monthly* 232, no. 6 (December 1973): 134–35.
kk.   Wilkinson, Burke. "Aaron Burr: America's 'Dark Legend' Seen in a Different Light." *Christian Science Monitor* (12 December 1973): 17.
ll.   Williams, David. "Play It Again." *New Review* 1, no. 2 (May 1974): 93.
mm. [Unsigned.] *Booklist* 70, no. 8 (15 December 1973): 423.
nn.   [Unsigned.] *Booklist* 70, no. 10 (15 January 1974): 538.
oo.   [Unsigned.] *Booklist* 95, no. 15 (1 April 2000): 1443.
pp.   [Unsigned.] *Choice* 10, no. 12 (February 1974): 1870.
qq.   [Unsigned.] "Worlds Apart." *Economist* 251 (no. 6816) (13 April 1974): 72–73.
rr.   [Unsigned.] *Kirkus Reviews* 41, no. 17 (1 September 1973): 988.
ss.   [Unsigned.] *New Yorker* 49, no. 40 (26 November 1973): 198–99.
tt.   [Unsigned.] "Briefing: Paperbacks." *Observer* (London) no. 9631 (7 March 1976): 26.
uu.   [Unsigned.] "Paperbacks." *Observer* (London) no. 10574 (12 June 1994): Review, p. 20.
vv.   [Unsigned.] *Playboy* 20, no. 12 (December 1973): 62, 64.
ww. [Unsigned.] *Publishers Weekly* 204, no. 11 (10 September 1973): 41.
xx.   [Unsigned.] *Times Literary Supplement* no. 3759 (22 March 1974): 281.
yy.   [Unsigned.] *Virginia Quarterly Review* 50, no. 2 (Spring 1974): lv.

In a flamboyantly written review, **Axelrod** believes the novel shows that Vidal's "two principal pre-occupations, literature and politics, have come together." "It is Mr. Vidal's pleasure to use Burr as a rear view mirror into history." . . . **Beloff**, in a multiple review, finds *Burr* "admirable" but wishes Vidal had written "straightforward biography . . . so that the force of the argument could be tested in a more direct fashion." . . . **Biddle** states that this is "a virtuoso, self-assured performance. It is entertaining, instructive, subversive." American readers are enjoying the book because "it assures them that selfishness and ineptitude in high office are as American as Yankee Doodle Dandy." Vidal's main point is that "personalities are a stronger force in history than ideas." . . . **Brendon** observes that the book is "repetitive, superficial and boring." Aaron Burr "has been created in the author's image, [but] practically everything else in the novel bears a sickly resemblance to the rotten state of America today, so often vituperated by Vidal." . . . **Brodie**, a professional historian, maintains that Vidal had a splendid opportunity to write a lively historical novel, but he "has chosen instead to write about the systematic destruction of one man by another, a novel in which the two leading characters bear little resemblance to two men in history called Aaron Burr and Thomas Jefferson." Vidal's treatment of Jefferson is "outrageous." . . . **Chace** writes: "To read 'Burr' is to be altogether exasperated and charmed. . . . What Vidal shows is the often cruel venality of men who remain nevertheless of such magnitude that we are not likely to see their kind as our rulers for a long time to come, if ever." . . . **Crain** notes that "Burr emerges as a man of complex brilliance and vision, a kind of tragic hero undone by the intensity of his own ambition." "Burr was a man of moral imagination and intelligence too refined and subtle for the American herd." But the action is "sluggish" and the style is clumsy. The attempt to debunk American history "eventually becomes predictable and tedious." . . . **Cunliffe** declares that this is "a skilful pastiche-reconstruction." Vidal "is a gifted pro. Yet to my mind the book does not quite come off." Burr's career is hard to follow, and Vidal may be too clever. . . . **Dangerfield** remarks that in this book Vidal is calling upon "the historian's imagination" rather than "the imagination of the novelist." He believes that Vidal totally identifies himself with Burr (throughout the review he refers to him as "Vidal-Burr"), and that he "pulls everybody down to his own level." . . . **Dworkin** asserts that Vidal's novel is "distinguished" both as a novel and as history. Vidal "raise[s] some fascinating issues of historical judgment and even political theory." . . . **Fremont-Smith** states that "for great stretches, *Burr* is a bore. One comes away from the book as if from a long slog through history." But the novel "is constructed—expertly—on two levels," involving the real historical figures and the invented ones. . . . **French** believes that Vidal's purpose is "to burst away the myths, the cant and the clap-trap and penetrate to the reality of the times . . . This is not a cynical, debunking book, merely a realistic one." . . . **Furbank** thinks that Vidal "cheats" in this novel because he "make[s] Burr a 20th-century-style novelist, closely resembling Gore Vidal." "Vidal's Burr seems all in an attitude, a machine for manufacturing epigrams and Voltairean ironies." . . . **Highet** writes: "The novel is constructed with subtle elegance, like a Capablanca chess game. . . . It is a wonderful story, . . . a masterly satire on history, on convention, and on human credulity." . . . **Hogarty** explains how the novel inspired classroom discussion. . . . **Kempton** finds the novel "both dextrous and affecting." *Burr* "has . . . some elements of the prank, but it is more a serious attack on the notion of an original American innocence." The portraits of Jefferson and others seem accurate; but the historical Jefferson, for all his flaws, still seems a more admirable and impressive figure than Burr. . . . **Klein** remarks: "Vidal brings both the 1780s and the 1830s to life. . . . We leave this book as from a great dinner party: the gossip has been as good as the food. . . . Vidal is the one novelist today who feels patrician enough not to be intimidated by the founding fathers." But Burr offers no vision of what the United States can be. "Vidal's bitterness is unrelieved by insight." . . . **Lehmann-Haupt** feels that Vidal sticks close to the historical record. Yet "how alive and immediate everything seems!" "What an employment of the usable past! What a hagiography for the Nixon era!" *Burr* "remains a dazzling entertainment, a tour de force of historical imagination, a devastating analysis of America's first principles." . . . **Maloff** claims that "Jefferson is the villain of this piece." But "it is Burr who dominates the novel: Burr's voice, Burr's perspectives, Burr's presence." Burr "is everything our Fathers never were." . . . **Nicol** believes that Vidal's depiction of the Founding Fathers "seems to be the work of a gossip columnist; it spreads unpalatable innuendo like a small boy catsups his french fries. It isn't wicked, just catty." Alexander Hamilton is a cipher in the novel, which suffers from "a failure of vision" and a "lack of insight." . . . **Poirier** feels that this is the "best" of Vidal's novels. The real focus of the novel is the question: "To what does anything or anyone truly belong?" But "the main trouble with *Burr* is that it does not dare quite enough." . . . **Prescott** comments that Vidal is "a cartoonist, an excellent draftsman, a satirist fond of the bawdy and perverse." The book is "an extraordinarily intelligent and entertaining novel." . . . **R.** states that Aaron Burr "provides [Vidal] with a perfect medium through which he can develop his own idiosyncratic and iconoclastic views on American history and American politics." Vidal's "description of the United States in its formative period is a marvellously vivid, amusing and fascinating one." The novel suggests that American politics was corrupt from the beginning. . . . **Ratcliffe** supplies much discussion of Burr as an historical figure. Vidal's references to present-day political events are very indirect: "this really *is* a novel about the notorious third Vice-President." But although the novel is "beautifully craftsmanlike," we don't get a real idea of what Vidal really feels about Burr. . . . **Sheppard** feels that the timing of the novel (in an age of political scandal) is uncanny. "The kinship of author and subject goes beyond elegant barbs at the high and mighty." The review is largely an overview of Burr's career. . . . **Simon** denies literary value to the historical novel as a whole. *Burr* does have wit, "but the ultimate wit lies in the satirical, debunking, irreverent notions of the work as a whole." "I rather enjoyed this book and recommend it threequartersheartedly to America at large." . . . **Snow** finds that "*Burr* is a whole class better than anything else of his that I have seen." Vidal "has a concrete imagination for the physical life of the past." His "abnormal capacity for disrespect" works when considering the political figures of the past. Vidal "enjoys himself in turning some preconceptions on their heads." . . . **Toynbee** maintains that this is "a splendid fictionalised life of this ambiguous and fascinating figure." The book is "written with great skill, wit and elegance." It is not a mere exercise in iconoclasm. . . . **Weeks**'s review is largely a plot summary; he concludes, "What a fascinating book Vidal has made of [Aaron Burr]!" . . . **Wilkinson** notes that "Burr's voice is perforce a disenchanted one. He cannot but see the Founding Fathers with a jaundiced eye." Citing numerous quotations from the book, Wilkinson adds: "Burr's self-deprecatory wit . . . come[s] wonderfully alive to us . . . there is an *elan Vidal* here that is the author's very own." . . . **Williams** feels that Schuyler "is a Boswell figure, interposing himself between Vidal and the quarry—Burr—whom Vidal is stalking." This allows Vidal to go beyond the facts when he needs to. Burr "cuts all the grand figures of American folklore down to—and often below—size. . . . I found this an abundantly interesting, and important, novel." . . . The *Choice* review states that "The man and the period, so much in our minds now, are shaped by Vidal's imagination and artistry into a very full and entertaining book." . . . The *Economist* review, a multiple review, finds this "a splendid work." The purpose of the novel "seems to be to demonstrate that any rottenness in the State of the Union is neither new nor a cause for a collapse of morale." . . . The brief *New Yorker* review comments on the "dazzling but rather uneven book"; it is "always absorbing." . . . The brief *Playboy* review notes that "Purists and patriots are sure to consign the author and his work to the lowest circles of literary hell," but others will enjoy it. Vidal "is doing that most unhistorical thing—assigning narrow motives to historical figures who may have been guided by other and perhaps larger motives." . . . The *Times Literary Supplement* review observes that Vidal's focus on Charlie Schuyler results in "the real interest of the book—what a stern critic of the United States will make of his clean-up job of an alleged American traitor—is dissipated and eventually lost." "*Burr* is scrupulous about details . . . but is short on the divine spark; it is unspeakably heavy and congested. Dubious as history, it is heavy going as a novel."

31.   *Myron*
    a.   Adams, Phoebe. *Atlantic Monthly* 234, no. 6 (December 1974): 127.
    b.   Amis, Martin. "Left-Handed Backhand." *Observer* (London) (6 April 1975): 30.
    c.   Avant, John Alfred. *Library Journal* 100, no. 1 (1 January 1975): 66.
    d.   Boatwright, James. *New Republic* 171, no. 23 (7 December 1974): 20–21.
    e.   Cole, William. "Campy." *Saturday Review/World* 2, no. 3 (19 October 1974): 30.
    f.   Conrad, Peter. "Look at Us." *New Review* 2 (no. 16) (July 1975): 63–66.
    g.   Egremont, Max. "Inner Circle." *Books and Bookmen* 21, no. 1 (October 1975): 60–61.
    h.   Freedman, Richard. "Myra Returns—and She's a Pain in the Vidal." *National Observer* 13, no. 50 (14 December 1974): 25.
    i.   Fremont-Smith, Eliot. "Second Prize in the Camp Sweepstakes." *New York* 7, no. 42 (21 October 1974): 90–91.
    j.   French, Philip. "Unmanned." *New Statesman* 89 (no. 2299) (11 April 1975): 487–88.
    k.   King, Francis. "Old and New Prose from an Old Pro." *Spectator* 259 (no. 8315) (21 November 1987): 41, 43.
    l.   Lehmann-Haupt, Christopher. "Books of The Times: Enough Is as Good as a Feast." *New York Times* (26 November 1974): 37.
    m.   Lomas, Herbert. "American Fiction—1." *London Magazine* NS 15, no. 4 (October–November 1975): 105–13.
    n.   McLellan, Joseph. "Briefly Noted." *Washington Post Book World* (24 November 1974): 4.
    o.   Mano, D. Keith. "It's Adversary, But Is It Art?" *National Review* 27, no. 1 (17 January 1975): 51.
    p.   Maves, Karl. "Myron Trapped in the Late Show." *Advocate* no. 150 (16 November 1974): 41–42.
    q.   Mazzocco, Robert. "The Charm of Insolence." *New York Review of Books* 21, no. 18 (14 November 1974): 13–15.
    r.   Nye, Robert. "A Bit of a Drag." *Guardian Weekly* 112, no. 16 (19 April 1975): 21.
    s.   Pritchard, William H. "Novel Sex and Violence." *Hudson Review* 28, no. 1 (Spring 1975): 147–60 (esp. 153–54).
    t.   Rosenbaum, Jonathan. "More Vidal." *Village Voice* 19, no. 46 (14 November 1974): 46–47.
    u.   S[heppard], R. Z. "Myra Lives!" *Time* 104, no. 17 (21 October 1974): 119, K13, K17.
    v.   Simmons, Charles. "Gore Vidal Brings Myra Back to Depowell the World." *New York Times Book Review* (3 November 1974): 6.
    w.   Tennant, Emma. "Myraland." *Listener* 93 (no. 2401) (10 April 1975): 486.
    x.   Wyndham, Francis. "Hooray for Hollywood." *Times Literary Supplement* no. 3814 (11 April 1975): 389.
    y.   [Unsigned.] *Booklist* 71, no. 7 (15 December 1974): 407.
    z.   [Unsigned.] *Choice* 11, no. 12 (February 1975): 1782.
    aa.   [Unsigned.] *Kirkus Reviews* 42, no. 19 (1 October 1974): 1077.
    bb.   [Unsigned.] *Playboy* 22, no. 1 (January 1975): 32.
    cc.   [Unsigned.] *Publishers Weekly* 206, no. 15 (7 October 1974): 54. *Publishers Weekly* 207, no. 15 (14 April 1975): 56 (abridged).

Amis, in a multiple review, states that this is Vidal's "worst novel yet: it reveals a marooned talent in all its vulgar radiance." "What irks is not the dullness of the ideas so much as the insipidity of their execution." . . . **Boatwright** notes that some readers and critics think *Myra Breckinridge* is "Vidal's best book." But Vidal was not wise to write a sequel: "Even a goddess, alas, can become something of a bore." . . . **Conrad** believes that "*Myron* is the successor to *Burr* rather than to *Myra Breckinridge,* since it is also an exercise in tampering with history." . . . **Egremont**, in a multiple review, feels the novel was written with Vidal's "habitual elegance." The review is largely a plot summary. . . . **Freedman** declares that this is a "damp sequel." "Despite a good deal of physical detail, the sexchanges between Myra and Myron are dramatically unconvincing. . . . Vidal provides us with an occasional raisin of wit to keep us slopping down his bowl of lumpy, lukewarm oatmeal." . . . **Fremont-Smith** thinks that Myra is "at best a shadow of her former strident self." The novel shows that Vidal himself "no longer has the courage of her convictions." . . . **French** observes that the book is a "disappointment": "There are some good jokes of course, but mostly they come thin and slow." . . . **Lehmann-Haupt** believes that "cleverness takes over everything, and if the result is not so bad as to be dreadful, it is certainly a shade too much"; "too much of the cleverness is tiresome." . . . **Lomas**, in a multiple review, remarks that "The sickness of America seems to have driven Gore Vidal to cramps of anger and made him as mad as Swift." Vidal has "produced a novel that chiefly holds your attention through his intelligence." . . . **Mano** uses the novel to lash out against "liberal fiction, [which,] having no profound symbolic or spiritual roots, nourishes itself with institutionalized paranoia." *Myron* is "the fiction of neuters." . . . **Maves**'s review is largely a plot summary. He believes that the novel "isn't nearly as vital as its classic predecessor." "Myra still is unique, but her scope has been distinctly narrowed." But the novel "is still superior entertainment." . . . **Mazzocco** feels that Vidal "is a master farceur—vulgar, autocratic, quaint." But *Myron* "seems to me *vieux jeu.*" It is "no match for the ineffable ease and raunchy simplicity of its predecessor." The book is padded with "odd bits of self-cannibalization." "It's hard to know what, beyond his usual benevolent interest in the American Grotesque, Vidal is really after here." . . . **Nye** writes that this "is the book that no one has been waiting for." Vidal "has done it again, and . . . you're welcome to it. . . . The ventriloquial expertise is amazing." . . . **Pritchard** concludes that Vidal "has settled for less than he was capable of. . . . Vidal is not merely 'camp' because he is too knowing and funny and soaked in the 'forties to be exhausted by the category." . . . **Rosenbaum** states that although *Myra Breckinridge* was a clever stunt, *Myron* "is another kind of stunt—also good for a lot of giggles, but much less unified in its strategies, and clumsily stuck together compared with its predecessor. . . . It's fast and funny and full of surprises. It is also, for long stretches, abominably written." . . . **Sheppard** finds the novel "an insidiously amusing camp fantasy." "Once again, Gore Vidal proves that in a market crowded with literary hookers, he is a true courtesan." He is "the best—if not the most original—of our hard-core satirists." . . . **Simmons**, in a review written as if by Buck Loner, asserts that "this book isnt half so good" as *Myra Breckinridge*. . . . **Tennant** writes that Vidal is a "satyrist"; *Myron* "slices the balls off America." The novel "is both extremely funny and extremely serious." . . . **Wyndham** maintains that *Myron* is better than *Myra Breckinridge*: "its originality is undeniable." "The book's funniest effects come from the exalted lunacy of Myra's *Weltanschauung* and the prosaic briskness with which she translates it into action." . . . The relatively brief *Playboy* review notes that the novel "plays cattily with concepts that seem to have been lifted from a Pirandello play or a sluggish *roman nouveau.*" . . .

32. *1876*

    a.   Ackroyd, Peter. "Blood, Thunder and Gore." *Spectator* 236 (no. 7709) (27 March 1976): 20.

    b.   Amiel, Barbara. "My Country, Wrong or Wrong." *Maclean's* 89, no. 6 (5 April 1976): 72, 74.

    c.   Bardacke, Frances L. "The American Dream as Nightmare." *San Diego Magazine* 28, no. 8 (June 1976): 37–38.

    d.   Betsky, Celia. *New Republic* 174, no. 17 (24 April 1976): 20–22.

    e.   Bliven, Naomi. "Not Amused." *New Yorker* 52, no. 7 (5 April 1976): 130, 133–35.

    f.   Bowers, A. Joan. "Vidal's Centennial." *Prairie Schooner* 50, no. 3 (Fall 1976): 273–74.

    g.   Bradbury, Malcolm. "A Modern Mugwump." *Observer* (London) no. 9633 (21 March 1976): 31.

    h.   Breslin, Jimmy. "The Rule of Sentence." *Harper's Magazine* 252, no. 3 (March 1976): 106, 110–11.

    i.   Conrad, Peter. "Re-inventing America." *Times Literary Supplement* no. 3863 (26 March 1976): 347–48.

    j.   Cook, Kenneth. *Best Sellers* 36, no. 3 (June 1976): 74.

    k.   Cosgrave, Mary Silva. "Outlook Tower." *Horn Book Magazine* 52, no. 5 (October 1976): 530–31.

    l.   Davidon, Ann Morrissett. "Doing Well by Doing Wrong." *Nation* 222, no. 15 (17 April 1976): 474–75.

    m.   Flower, Dean. "Fiction Chronicle." *Hudson Review* 29, no. 2 (Summer 1976): 270–82 (esp. 272–74).

n.   Forrest, Alan. "A Year's Good Reading." *Books and Bookmen* 22, no. 4 (January 1977): 57–58.

o.   Fremont-Smith, Eliot. "Making Book." *Village Voice* 21, no. 8 (23 February 1976): 49.

p.   French, Philip. "Us and Them." *New Statesman* 91 (no. 2348) (19 March 1976): 376.

q.   Janeway, Michael. *Atlantic Monthly* 237, no. 4 (April 1976): 114–16.

r.   Kaplan, Justin. "Halfway to the Bicentennial." *Saturday Review* 3, no. 11 (6 March 1976): 24–25.

s.   Lehmann-Haupt, Christopher. "Books of The Times: The Worst of Times." *New York Times* (2 March 1976): 31.

t.   Levy, Paul. "Historical Truth v. Fiction." *Books and Bookmen* 21, no. 8 (June 1976): 21–24.

u.   Lombardi, John. "Bicentennial Gore." *Oui* 5, no. 7 (July 1976): 31–32.

v.   McPherson, William. "A Score for Gore." *Washington Post Book World* (14 March 1976): H7, 10.

w.   Mewshaw, Michael. "Only Yesterday." *Texas Monthly* 4, no. 6 (June 1976): 78–79, 81.

x.   Morgan, Edwin. "The Coils of Corruption." *Sunday Times* (London) (28 March 1976): 40.

y.   Moynahan, Julian. "A Centennial Novel for the Bicentennial." *New York Times Book Review* (7 March 1976): 3–4.

z.   Nelson, Barbara. *Library Journal* 101, no. 5 (1 March 1976): 740.

aa.   Potter, Gary. "Vidal Goes Wilde." *New Guard* 16, no. 4 (May 1976): 27–28.

bb.   Prescott, Peter S. "Centennial Acid." *Newsweek* 87, no. 10 (8 March 1976): 78.

cc.   Pusateri, C. Joseph. *America* 134, no. 20 (22 May 1976): 460.

dd.   R. "Column." *Encounter* 46, no. 5 (May 1976): 42–44.

ee.   Ratcliffe, Michael. "Some Centennial." *Times* (London) (1 April 1976): 14.

ff.   Remini, Robert V. *Commonweal* 104, no. 1 (7 January 1977): 25–27.

gg.   Silkenat, James R. *American Bar Association Journal* 62 (October 1976): 1250, 1252.

hh.   Snow, C. P. "Son of Burr." *Financial Times* (London) (1 April 1976): 28.

ii.   Tennant, Emma. "Centennial Scenes." *Listener* 95 (no. 2450) (25 March 1976): 375–76.

jj.   Trapkus, Chuck. *Kliatt* 27, no. 6 (November 1993): 56.

kk.   Weisberger, Bernard A. "Vidal and the Sadness of Satire." *National Observer* 15, no. 13 (27 March 1976): 19.

ll.   Williams, Gordon L. "Vidal's Demon Diarist in Centennial America." *Business Week* no. 2423 (15 March 1976): 10.

mm.   Wood, Michael. "Passion in Politics." *New York Review of Books* 23, no. 7 (29 April 1976): 30–31.

nn.   Wordsworth, Christopher. "Star-Spangled Manner." *Guardian Weekly* 114, no. 15 (11 April 1976): 22.

oo.   [Unsigned.] *Booklist* 72, no. 13 (1 March 1976): 960.

pp.   [Unsigned.] *Booklist* 72, no. 13 (1 March 1976): 971.

qq.   [Unsigned.] *Booklist* 73, no. 15 (1 April 1977): 1153.

rr.   [Unsigned.] *Booklist* 96, no. 15 (1 April 2000): 1443.

ss.   [Unsigned.] *BooksWest* 1 (June 1977): 21.

tt.   [Unsigned.] "Paperback Bookshelf." *Changing Times* 31, no. 6 (June 1977): 29.

uu.   [Unsigned.] *Choice* 13, no. 7 (September 1976): 829.

vv.   [Unsigned.] *Critic* 34, no. 4 (Summer 1976): 85–86.

ww.   [Unsigned.] *Kirkus Reviews* 44, no. 2 (15 January 1976): 94.

xx.   [Unsigned.] *Kirkus Reviews* 44, no. 3 (1 February 1976): 144.

yy.   [Unsigned.] "Paperbacks." *Observer* (London) no. 10581 (31 July 1994): Review, p. 21.

zz.   [Unsigned.] *Playboy* 23, no. 5 (May 1976): 26.

aaa. [Unsigned.] *Progressive* 40, no. 8 (August 1976): 45.

bbb. [Unsigned.] *Publishers Weekly* 209, no. 3 (19 January 1976): 99.

ccc. [Unsigned.] *Publishers Weekly* 211, no. 5 (31 January 1977): 74.

ddd. [Unsigned.] *Washington Post Book World* (12 December 1976): H6.

Ackroyd believes this is "a novel perfectly contrived, a solid bourgeois entertainment which avoids seriousness as remorselessly as Vidal once pursued it." . . . **Amiel**, although beginning her review with snide comments about Vidal ("Vidal's air of concern . . . masks his superficiality"), concludes: "With stunning effectiveness he re-creates the America of 100 years ago: a country of desperate excesses blithely existing in a moral vacuum. . . . *1876* is the most dazzling novel of many a publishing season." . . . **Bardacke** writes: "Th[e] theme that runs through all three novels [*Washington, D.C., Burr,* and *1876*] is the American Dream as nightmare . . . a democratic form of government that depends on an informed electorate is the worst of all possible worlds." . . . **Betsky** feels that "*1876* resembles but hardly lives up to the variegated brilliance of *Burr.*" "*1876* is as much about writing as it is about historical events, as much a consideration of political rhetoric as an analysis of statesmanship." But Charlie Schuyler is too remote a commentator to be effective. . . . **Bliven** states that "The book is unable to cope with the unalloyed rascals who dominated American life in the centennial year." She thinks that Vidal is merely poking fun at corruption, which is not funny. . . . **Bowers** observes that "much of Vidal's customary dazzle is missing." The most satisfactory aspect of the book is "occupied with colorful descriptions of American life in 1876. . . . Unfortunately, the sum of the parts . . . does not make a unified and aesthetically pleasing whole." . . . **Bradbury** maintains that this novel does not work as well as *Burr* because the historical characters are not as compelling. But Vidal "possesses the great gift of investing party politics with a direct reality, writing with an anxiously intrusive purpose." . . . **Breslin**, in an enthusiastic review, notes that "*1876* is a glorious piece of writing." Vidal is a master stylist and can rivet the reader even if the subject matter is of little intrinsic interest. . . . **Conrad** presents a survey of Vidal's career. His historical novels are "the result of a precarious, dazzling partnership between Gore the researcher and Vidal the frivolous meddler with history." *1876* is "Vidal's reminder . . . that the past is as sullied as the present." This long, richly detailed review also discusses *An Evening with Richard Nixon, Washington, D.C., Burr,* and Vidal's methodology of historical writing. . . . **Cook**'s review is mostly a plot summary. "One cannot but admire his effort and the effortless reading he provides in this work." . . . **Cosgrave**, in a multiple review, finds this a "captivating novel": "he mixes real and imaginary people with style and éclat." . . . **Davidon** remarks that Vidal's account "is more entertaining—and possibly more enlightening, if more disillusioning—than reading the dry record." His characterizations are "astute and credible," but his novels are aimed too exclusively toward the intellect. . . . **Flower** states that the novel is "an unusually crafted performance, but like so many of Vidal's narratives it misfires interestingly." The book lacks a vivid central figure around whom the action can revolve. "Nobody is better than Gore Vidal at a trenchant, sneering criticism; but in this novel it fails to sting often enough." . . . **Fremont-Smith**, reviewing the book along with Joan Samson's *The Auctioneer,* states: "It is not Vidal's greatest book . . . but it is awfully good, the work of a pro who knows exactly what he's doing and delivers. . . . What makes [*1876*] so good is not that it transcends its genre, but that it is so true to it." . . . **French** finds the novel "a rewarding and accomplished book" and a sensitive probing of its historical period. . . . **Janeway** believes Charlie Schuyler's cynicism to be a match for Vidal's; the novel is "wickedly wise, savagely funny, and on the mark." . . . **Kaplan** notes that the book has no central character as riveting as *Burr.* It is "thin on character but painstaking in backgrounds . . . his pastiche of fact and invention is engaging." . . . **Lehmann-Haupt** comments that the novel is "at least as successful as 'Burr,' if not considerably more so." "The effect of '1876' is as curiously refreshing as 'Burr' was maliciously impudent." . . . **Levy**, reviewing the book along with E. L. Doctorow's *Ragtime,* feels that *1876* "actually is history and it is vital that the facts and their interpretation are correct. . . . Fortunately it is not a rip-off but an historical contribution of large importance." "What Vidal has done . . . is to show that nothing much has changed in America's last hundred years." He states that "the rich texture of the book is almost palpable; *1876* confirms Gore Vidal's right to reign almost alone over the difficult territory he has marked out for himself." . . . **Lombardi** claims that Vidal's purpose is to show that "moral rot is as American as cherry pie." But "the people and events in *1876* aren't believable." . . . **McPherson** asserts that Vidal "is especially concerned in *1876* with money and property as the underpinnings of power." His "beautifully wrought—like a Botticelli dish—Italianate prose dazzles and glitters"; but "the prose . . . is paste, an artful, cunningly contrived reproduction of what Henry James would call the real thing." . . . **Mewshaw**'s review is largely plot summary. "Of course, any resemblance between the events of *1876* and Watergate is absolutely intentional, but Gore Vidal has the good sense not to drive home his point with a sledgehammer." The novel "is a delight at every level." . . . **Morgan** feels that although *Burr* is the best of the trilogy, "*1876* has virtues of its own. . . . Corruption, and what, if anything, one can do about it, is the theme that coils and twists throughout the book." But "British readers will find some of this novel hard going" because the historical figures are not familiar to them. The novel is "skilful, sharp, and assured." . . . **Moynahan** concludes that the novel is not as riveting as *Burr.* Part of the problem lies with the narrator, Charlie Schuyler, "grown old, befuddled and quite tiresome." The novel is "a lead sinker." There are too many characters, and no one for the novel to focus around. . . . **Potter** notes that Vidal is interested in "subverting liberal democratic pieties." Vidal "hates America, but he does not cry his hatred with a special passion. He hates *cooly.* He *resents.*" But because *1876* deals with obscure personalities, it fails "even as a corrosive agent." . . . **Prescott** states that the book has a "flaccid cleverness." Vidal's re-creation of the scene is pleasant; "it's the people and plot that are boring." The novel lacks a vivid central figure like Aaron Burr. . . . **R.** feels the novel is not as good as *Burr.* Vidal writes "with a light and cynical touch and not too much moralising and an admirably sure sense of direction." "Yet the picture that he draws is in the end a sombre one"—one of unrelieved greed. . . . **Ratcliffe** writes of the "trilogy of novels which explode the convenient myths of American historiography in order to entertain and instruct in the positive uses of history a people which prefers to ignore or homogenize it." "*1876* simmers away without ever quite coming to the boil. It ambles." The figure of Samuel J. Tilden is sketched incompletely. . . . **Remini**, in a multiple review, remarks that Vidal "is only concerned with the wealthy and influential. He has no skill in understanding or communicating the problems of the lower classes. Besides, he is rather naïve as to what history is all about. He wants truth." . . . **Snow**, in a multiple review, writes that Vidal "is becoming more accomplished and more authoritative." *1876* may be "even better" than *Burr.* The novel is "sharp with intelligence." . . . **Tennant** believes that "there is an overwhelming feeling, usually disastrously lacking from the historical novel, of the narrator having actually been there, of an uncanny rightness in every description, however slight." The real historical figures are more vivid than the invented ones. The novel "can go down in history as an outstanding book about history, rather than one that sends history up." . . . **Trapkus** writes: "As creative and delightful as the narrative is, I am always disturbed by not knowing which details are historical and which are figments of Vidal's abundant imagination." . . . **Weisberger** thinks that "the plot line of *1876* is as thin as Saran-Wrap and provides the same kind of see-through package. . . . Vidal's fiction is true to the spirit of 1876, an age that was unsqueamishly exploitive and loved the grand scale." Vidal "pokes fun, not so much at the American dream as at how far Americans fall short of it." . . . **Williams** states that Vidal uses a "'You Are There' technique." "His scholarship is superb, his writing skills as imposing as ever, his powers of observation simply splendid." But Vidal has "less raw material to work with than in *Burr.*" Grant, Tilden, and others can't compare with Burr, Jefferson, etc. But this is "a thoroughly grand book—must, must reading for everyone." . . . **Wood** finds the novel narrated in a cumbersome manner. "The suggestion is that virtue is simply impractical, that effective action in the real world must always take up the instruments of evil." . . . **Wordsworth**'s review is mostly a plot summary. The novel features "the underworld of Civil War cast-offs and the strange xenophobia of a nation dependent on cheap immigrant labour for its prosperity." . . . The relatively brief ***Playboy*** review feels that this "is subtler than a pie but no less cheerfully devastating to the notion that American history can be honestly looked at with a straight face."

33. *Matters of Fact and of Fiction*
    a. Clemons, Walter. "Witlash." *Newsweek* 89, no. 19 (9 May 1977): 102.
    b. Cole, William. "A Nasty Certitude." *Saturday Review* 4, no. 15 (16 April 1977): 50.
    c. Dick, Bernard F. *World Literature Today* 51, no. 4 (Autumn 1977): 619–20.
    d. Epstein, Joseph. "What Makes Vidal Run." *Commentary* 63, no. 6 (June 1977): 72–75.
    e. Green, Benny. "Joker." *Spectator* 239 (no. 7782) (3 September 1977): 20.
    f. Hounion, Morris A. *Library Journal* 102, no. 5 (1 March 1977): 610.
    g. James, Clive. "The Left-Handed Gun." *New Statesman* 94 (no. 2422) (19 August 1977): 245–46. In James's *From the Land of Shadows.* London: Jonathan Cape, 1982, pp. 81–85 (as "Hard-Core Gore"). In James's *As of This Writing: The Essential Essays, 1968–2000.* New York: W. W. Norton & Co., 2003, pp. 421–25 (with postscript, 425–26).
    h. Jordan, Francis X. *Best Sellers* 37, no. 4 (July 1977): 122.
    i. Lehmann-Haupt, Christopher. "Books of The Times." *New York Times* (20 April 1977): C23.
    j. Lipsius, Frank. "Patriotic Gore." *Books and Bookmen* 23, no. 1 (October 1977): 34.
    k. McPherson, William. "A Roman in the Gloaming." *Washington Post Book World* (1 May 1977): E5. *Guardian Weekly* 116, no. 22 (22 May 1977): 18.
    l. Maves, Karl. *Advocate* no. 220 (27 July 1977): 41–42.
    m. Pritchard, William H. "Two Critics." *Listener* 98 (no. 2527) (22 September 1977): 382.
    n. Pritchett, V. S. "How to Say Serious Things." *New York Review of Books* 24, no. 9 (26 May 1977): 8–9.
    o. Simon, John. "The Good and Bad of Gore Vidal." *Esquire* 88, no. 2 (August 1977): 22–24. In Simon's *Paradigms Lost.* New York: Clarkson N. Potter, 1980, pp. 105–10.

p.   Spender, Stephen. "Gore Vidal, Essayist." *New York Times Book Review* (17 April 1977): 1, 46.

q.   Symons, Julian. "In a Personal Connection." *Times Literary Supplement* no. 3940 (30 September 1977): 1105.

r.   Weightman, John. "Vital Vidal." *Observer* (London) no. 9705 (14 August 1977): 24.

s.   White, Edmund. "Aristocratic Rebel." *Harper's Magazine* 254, no. 5 (May 1977): 97–98.

t.   Wolcott, James. "Gore Bulls Through Again." *Village Voice* 22, no. 19 (9 May 1977): 77.

u.   [Unsigned.] *Booklist* 73, no. 13 (1 March 1977): 984.

v.   [Unsigned.] *Carleton Miscellany* 17, no. 1 (Winter 1977–78): 145.

w.   [Unsigned.] *Choice* 14, no. 8 (October 1977): 1029.

x.   [Unsigned.] *Journalism Quarterly* 54, no. 4 (Winter 1977): 838.

y.   [Unsigned.] *Kirkus Reviews* 45, no. 3 (1 February 1977): 151.

z.   [Unsigned.] "Paperbacks: New and Noteworthy." *New York Times Book Review* (2 April 1978): 41.

aa. [Unsigned.] *Publishers Weekly* 211, no. 6 (7 February 1977): 88. *Publishers Weekly* 213, no. 7 (13 February 1978): 126 (abridged).

bb. [Unsigned.] "Notes on Current Books." *Virginia Quarterly Review* 53, no. 3 (Summer 1977): 88.

Clemons maintains that Vidal "remains more interesting than his fictions . . . and his formidable powers are most steadily apparent in his essays." Vidal is "utterly fearless"; his "self-possession, intelligence and wolfish wit are everywhere visible." The best essay is the memoir of Tennessee Williams. . . . **Dick** notes that "There is only one character in his essays: himself." The political essays repeat what Vidal has said before, but "in the critical essays Vidal presides over the literary scene like a mandarin." . . . **Epstein**, in a long review, states that Vidal's "personality permeates all he writes." "As a literary critic, Vidal is much to be preferred on the attack." Vidal's politics have become predictable; he suggests that "to be heterosexual is to be, somehow, stunted if not sick." . . . **Green** again likens Vidal to Edmund Wilson. He rates the literary essays the best, particularly "The Hacks of Academe" ("an example of literary mayhem at its finest"). . . . In an extensive review, **James** believes that Vidal "is so dauntingly good at the literary essay that he is likely to arouse in other practitioners an inclination to take up a different line of work." James is particularly appreciative of Vidal's "perfectly disciplined, perfectly liberated English" and his political essays. . . . **Jordan** feels that these are "very opinionated essays." But "the book holds up well because its author is a man of wit and style." . . . **Lehmann-Haupt** asserts that the essays are "too often characterized by an affinity for the Single Explanation." Some might feel that "Mr. Vidal's animus toward everything from West Point to the American Establishment . . . boils down to an unresolved hostility to his father, further evidence of which, some would argue, is Mr. Vidal's cheerfully admitted homosexuality." But Lehmann-Haupt says that this is also a simplistic Single Explanation. Vidal "can be magnificently complex, yet altogether lucid." . . . **Lipsius** claims that "The sharpness of Vidal's tongue is more disarming than offensive. . . . Throughout his writing, Vidal takes pains to distance himself from other American intellectuals and academics." Vidal is an American patrician; but his "ultimate contempt . . . is for his readers." . . . **McPherson** thinks that the essays show that Vidal "is a genuinely funny man, likeable in spite of himself, an acute observer and almost never boring. . . . Technical virtuosity is what Vidal possesses to an extraordinary degree; and intelligence and erudition, irreverence, and an ability to cut through cant." . . . **Maves** writes: "At times Gore Vidal sounds as gloomy as Tacitus, a comparison he would probably relish." Most of his review is a description of the various essays. . . . **Pritchard** believes that the essays, "read when they came out, one at a time, were tonic, but taken in a lump rather less so." "As a political and cultural commentator, Vidal is knowing (if too knowing), practiced and entertaining." But as a literary critic he is too obsessed with not being "academic." . . . **Pritchett** declares that Vidal "is a glancing wit who has the good essayist's art of saying serious things personally and lightly." In his political essays "he has festive powers of candor and detection, in his studies of the ruling class and the rich, and done from the insider's alcove." . . . **Simon** writes: "I think that Gore Vidal's greatest service to this society could be in the proper packaging of his style and language." Vidal is neither a good novelist nor a good playwright. The book "contains some very good pieces, as weighty as anything in Oscar Wilde and easily as witty as the best of Matthew Arnold." He praises "The Top Ten Best Sellers," "The Hacks of Academe," "American Plastic," and the memoir of Tennessee Williams. . . . **Spender** observes that Vidal himself is always the real subject of his essays. "As a critic of manners as well as literature, Vidal is in the tradition of Matthew Arnold and Edmund Wilson." His literary essays are excellent; his political screeds less so. . . . **Symons** feels that Vidal's presence infuses the essays; it shows that Vidal "is more a journalist than a literary or social critic." Vidal's range is limited to the American novel and American social life. "He has at his best a brilliant turn of comic phrase, and he knows how to put the knife in where it will do most damage." Symons has high praise for "French Letters" and "American Plastic." . . . **Weightman** maintains that Vidal "sees himself as a dissident patrician, or half-patrician, in the decadent American Empire, upholding pagan decency . . . in a corrupt and hypocritical society." Vidal is excellent on "the badness of bad books and the meaningless pomposity of some academic criticism." . . . **White** remarks that Vidal is "always funny and often witty," but some of his views of politics are glib, and he is hostile to literary experimentation. . . . **Wolcott** comments that Vidal wastes effort attacking his literary inferiors; but "when writing of those he considers equals (Calvino, Nabokov), Vidal spins prose that is lucid and elegant, magisterially Shavian." The memoir of Tennessee Williams "is a masterpiece of tender malice." Vidal's disdain of media and their audience is unwarranted.

34. *Kalki*
   a.   Blow, Simon. "Vidal Divided." *Books and Bookmen* 23, no. 9 (July 1978): 32–33, 36.
   b.   Bodo, Maureen. "His Own Worst Enemy." *National Review* 30, no. 19 (12 May 1978): 600–601.
   c.   Burke, Jeffrey. "Books in Brief." *Harper's Magazine* 256, no. 5 (May 1978): 75–77 (esp. 76).
   d.   Carter, Angela. "Bored Vidal." *Guardian Weekly* 118, no. 18 (30 April 1978): 22.
   e.   Conrad, Andrée. "Books on Catastrophism." *Book Forum* 4, no. 2 (1978): 235–54 (esp. 244–47).
   f.   Delap, Richard. "Books." *Magazine of Fantasy and Science Fiction* 56, no. 4 (April 1979): 33–39 (esp. 34–35).
   g.   Fuller, Edmund. "The Buckley-Vidal Wars, Continued." *Wall Street Journal* (15 May 1978): 28.
   h.   Halio, Jay L. "Violence and After." *Southern Review* 15, no. 3 (July 1979): 702–10 (esp. 710).
   i.   Hall, Richard. "Calculating Kalpa-tating in *Kalki* But Gates of Fire Burns Bright." *Advocate* no. 248 (23 August 1978): 41.
   j.   James, Clive. "Pensée Persons." *New York Review of Books* 25, no. 6 (20 April 1978): 31–32.
   k.   Jefferson, Margo. "Apocalypse Now." *Newsweek* 91, no. 15 (10 April 1978): 90, 92.
   l.   Johnson, Diane. "Gilding the Lotus." *Washington Post Book World* (16 April 1978): E3.
   m.   Jones, D. A. N. "In the Age of Kali." *Listener* 99 (no. 2555) (13 April 1978): 482–83.
   n.   Jordan, Francis X. *Best Sellers* 38, no. 5 (August 1978): 149.
   o.   King, Francis. "The Last Act." *Spectator* 240 (no. 7816) (22 April 1978): 23.
   p.   Korn, Eric. "We Are for the Dark." *Times Literary Supplement* no. 3967 (14 April 1978): 405.
   q.   Lee, Hermione. "Curtains." *New Statesman* 95 (no. 2456) (14 April 1978): 500.
   r.   Lehmann-Haupt, Christopher. "Books of The Times." *New York Times* (30 March 1978): C19.
   s.   Levins, Wendy. *Library Journal* 103, no. 7 (1 April 1978): 778.
   t.   Marcus, Greil. "Worlds Apart: From Garp to Gore." *Rolling Stone* no. 270 (27 July 1978): 70.
   u.   May, John R. "Current Fiction." *America* 139, no. 15 (11 November 1978): 339.
   v.   Muggeridge, John. "They Just Don't Make Taboos Like They Used To." *Maclean's* 91, no. 8 (17 April 1978): 84, 86.
   w.   Paulin, Tom. "Fantastic Eschatologies." *Encounter* 51, no. 3 (September 1978): 73–78 (esp. 76–77).
   x.   Pritchard, William H. "Telling Stories." *Hudson Review* 31, no. 3 (Autumn 1978): 517–29 (esp. 517–18).
   y.   Reedy, Gerard. "This Is the Way the World Ends." *America* 138, no. 19 (20 May 1978): 410–11.

z. Romano, John. "The Camera Follows." *New York Times Book Review* (2 April 1978): 1, 22, 26.

aa. Sage, Lorna. "Farewell to the Future." *Observer* (London) no. 9738 (9 April 1978): 32.

bb. Sheppard, R. Z. "Elegant Hell." *Time* 111, no. 13 (27 March 1978): 98.

cc. Simon, John. "Vishnu as Double Agent." *Saturday Review* 5, no. 15 (29 April 1978): 31–33.

dd. Stelzmann, Rainulf A. "Major Themes in Recent American Novels." *Thought* 55, no. 4 (December 1980): 476–86 (esp. 478).

ee. Stewart, Ian. "Recent Fiction." *Illustrated London News* 266 (no. 6958) (May 1978): 61.

ff. S[wanbrow], D[iane] J. *West Coast Review of Books* 4, no. 4 (July 1978): 35.

gg. Williams, David. "A Couple of Tecs." *Punch* 277 (no. 7246) (29 August 1979): 338.

hh. [Unsigned.] *Booklist* 74, no. 15 (1 April 1978): 1241.

ii. [Unsigned.] *Carleton Miscellany* 17, nos. 2 & 3 (Spring 1979): 244.

jj. [Unsigned.] *Choice* 15, no. 7 (September 1976): 876.

kk. [Unsigned.] *Kirkus Reviews* 46, no. 3 (1 February 1978): 135.

ll. [Unsigned.] *New Yorker* 54, no. 9 (17 April 1978): 136–37.

mm. [Unsigned.] *Publishers Weekly* 213, no. 8 (20 February 1978): 106.

nn. [Unsigned.] *Publishers Weekly* 215, no. 1 (1 January 1979): 57.

oo. [Unsigned.] "Notes on Current Books." *Virginia Quarterly Review* 54, no. 3 (Summer 1978): 93.

Blow believes Vidal's work has suffered by his becoming a best-seller too early. "Nowadays his novels seem geared to amuse his fellow-countrymen." The review contains very little discussion of the novel. . . . **Bodo** feels that Vidal has become his own worst enemy "by letting his novels become essays with stories wrapped around them." *Kalki* pales compared to *Messiah*, a "genuinely apocalyptic novel." But this is "not a bad novel . . . it is disappointing." . . . **Burke** deems this to be an "unlikely mixture of jeremiad and satire." But the working out of the plot "dilutes whatever moral intention he may have had." . . . **Carter**'s review is largely a plot summary. "Vidal's apocalypse is as cosily flabby as yesterday's salad, the plotting looks like kittens got at the knitting wool and a bouquet of invincible boredom rises from the ill-conceived pages." . . . **Conrad**, in a multiple review, states that the book is in "Vidal's satiric tradition of finding something that irritates him and stamping on it until it dies of hemorrhage." Kalki himself is "proof that Vidal is fed up with the world's local manifestations of entropy." . . . **Delap**, in a harsh review, maintains that the book is "deliberately calculated in every way. . . . Vidal has here chosen to smash into the wall of cultural phobias hidden in a maze of current fashion trends." It is a "feeble parody of American bad taste." . . . **Fuller**, reviewing the book along with William F. Buckley's novel *Stained Glass,* states that the novel embodies "an essentially negative philosophy." Vidal "is impartially satirical, respecting neither persons nor institutions. He professes no moral positions to be ambiguous or ambivalent about." . . . **Halio**, in a multiple review, observes that "Vidal does not think much of our modern societies and therefore has developed a fiction to get rid of them." But the characters are "unmoved" by the destruction of the human race. . . . **Hall** contends that this novel shows "Gore Vidal at his worst." It "offers a slick and facile bit of sci-fi, leavened only occasionally by wit . . . there is little or no artistry on display." . . . **James** claims that the novel represents "Myra Breckinridge meets Messiah." ". . . it somehow manages to be a very enjoyable literature invention." "The book has many substantial pleasures." . . . **Jefferson** thinks that the novel "combines the political vision of Vidal's historical novels with the mythic sexual imaginings of 'Myra Breckinridge.'" It is "a fierce, striking book." . . . **Johnson** asserts that Vidal is "a singularly astute observer of human behavior and student of history." "It is art that accounts for this being a wise and charming, rather than a horrid book." . . . **Jones** claims that "the earlier chapters of the novel are extremely artificial . . . But, eventually, *Kalki* turns into a real novel." "This morbid and macabre romance is, surprisingly, a pleasure to read." . . . **Jordan** writes: "Those who dislike Vidal's writing and wit will undoubtedly regard *Kalki* as a potboiler, but with Vidal mixing the ingredients, it makes for better fare than the more serious efforts of many less gifted writers." . . . **King** states that in this novel "Mr Vidal shows his thin-lipped distaste of the kind of human garbage that the deluge will sweep away." . . . **Korn** compares *Kalki* to *Messiah*. "It's an ingeniously dusty fable, but uneven; tropes of virtuoso buffoonery . . . and tracts of slightly arid whimsy." . . . **Lee** feels that Vidal's jokes are "shiny as jet, with cruel malice and linguistic verve." . . . **Lehmann-Haupt** remarks that "the world as it appears in 'Kalki' probably deserves to be wiped out. At least we can be sure that Mr. Vidal thinks so." An "icy wind blows throughout the novel, and when all is said and done that wind has blasted the characters and plot of 'Kalki' into just so many opinions." . . . **Muggeridge**

believes that iconoclasm has now become so commonplace that this novel doesn't have much of a punch. "*Kalki* suffers above all from satire's kiss of death: predictability." But "there is more to this novel than warmed-over radicalism." . . . **Paulin**, in a multiple review, asserts the novel is "only remarkable for the beauty of its prose and for the way it demonstrates Vidal's cultivated intelligence." The "story seems curiously light and flimsy, as though he is writing elegantly on a paper tissue." . . . **Pritchard**, in a multiple review, asserts that the book reveals "Vidal's by now rather well-worn nastiness about how vulgar everybody is. . . . *Kalki* doesn't stand still long enough to explore anything." . . . **Reedy** thinks that "this pop novel is a book about writing pop novels. Only Vidal's coy dexterity and efficient plot prevent us from examining this silliness too closely." . . . **Romano** dismisses the novel as "a potboiler: subspecies, disaster movie." Teddy Ottinger's "sourness toward the emotional life is, without mitigation, her creator's own." As "an allegory of the Last Things . . . *Kalki* is worse than banal, it's irresponsible," because the portrayal of humanity is so cynical that we do not regret its passing. . . . **Sage**, reviewing the book along with Brian Aldiss's *A Rude Awakening,* writes that Vidal reveals "an almost monkish loathing of 'this world.'" Although Teddy Ottinger is "a nicely satiric creation," the novel is not one "meant to stir you into action before it's too late. It already is too late." . . . **Sheppard** finds the novel an "apocalyptic extravaganza." "*Kalki* is an amusing, brittle tissue of truths culled largely from the journalistic sources Vidal enjoys satirizing." . . . **Simon**'s substantial review states that the novel is "diabolically clever" but finds some of the satire "heavy and obvious." The book is "a receptacle for all of his personal gripes." . . . **Stelzmann**, in a multiple review, claims that "Vidal depicts man's last religion as an illusion which is totally pernicious. . . . According to Vidal, man destroys himself finally and irredeemably by mixing religion and science, two of his most favorite pursuits." . . . **Stewart**, in a multiple review, feels that the theme of the novel is suited to "so witty and caustic a critic of the American way of life" as Vidal. "This deadly joke of a cautionary tale . . . is brilliantly and entertainingly sustained." . . . **Williams** believes that the novel "begins as a modish, fantastic frolic then it deepens, becomes complicated and unbearably exciting, funny and savage all at once." . . . The *Choice* review finds the book "a novel ever poised on the edge of final silence . . . the paranoia of the powerless—the prophet of doom and conspiracy on the sidelines of reality—is beautifully captured here."

35.   *Three by Box*
    a.   B[lum], D[avid]. *New Republic* 179, no. 11 (9 September 1978): 46.
    b.   Breen, Jon L. "The World of Mysteries—Plus." *Wilson Library Bulletin* 53, no. 5 (January 1979): 376–77 (esp. 376).
    c.   S[chier], D[onald]. *Carleton Miscellany* 18, no. 2 (Summer 1980): 223.
    d.   [Unsigned.] *Booklist* 74, no. 22 (15 July 1978): 1717.
    e.   [Unsigned.] *Publishers Weekly* 213, no. 24 (12 June 1978): 73.

Blum states that "No good writer . . . need be ashamed of these three stories, each designed to keep the reader tingling wth apprehension." *Death in the Fifth Position* is the best.

36.   *Creation*
    a.   Ableman, Paul. "Back to the Cradle." *Spectator* 246 (no. 7973) (2 May 1981): 26–27.
    b.   Amiel, Barbara. "Rubbing Shoulders with the Riffraff." *Maclean's* 94, no. 15 (13 April 1981): 56.
    c.   Bragg, Melvyn. "In the Beginning." *Punch* 280 (no. 7333) (27 May 1981): 842–43.
    d.   Clemons, Walter. *Newsweek* 97, no. 16 (20 April 1981): 90, 92.
    e.   Conrad, Peter. "Back to the Drawing-Board." *Observer* (London) no. 9896 (26 April 1981): 32.
    f.   DeMott, Benjamin. "Vidal's History Lesson." *Saturday Review* 8, no. 3 (March 1981): 64–65.
    g.   Dick, Bernard F. *World Literature Today* 56, no. 2 (Spring 1982): 340.
    h.   Duvall, Elizabeth. *Atlantic Monthly* 247, no. 4 (April 1981): 120–21.
    i.   Emerson, Sally. "Recent Fiction." *Illustrated London News* 269 (no. 6996) (July 1981): 59.
    j.   Fuller, Edmund. "Two Recent Novels of Originality and Imagination." *Wall Street Journal* (23 March 1981): 22.
    k.   Gray, Paul. "Travelogue." *Time* 117, no. 13 (30 March 1981): 83–84.
    l.   Green, Randall. "Tinsel Wisdom." *New York Arts Journal* no. 22 (1981): 19–20.

m. Howes, Victor. "Endless Historic Tidbits But Not a Novel." *Christian Science Monitor* (13 April 1981): B2.

n. Kanfer, Stefan. "Two Cheers for Zoroaster." *New Republic* 184, no. 17 (25 April 1981): 34–36.

o. LaSalle, Peter. *America* 144, no. 20 (23 May 1981): 429.

p. Lemon, Lee T. "A Non-Vital Vidal." *Prairie Schooner* 56, no. 2 (Summer 1982): 98.

q. Lively, Penelope. "Wisdoms of Hindsight." *Encounter* 57, no. 5 (November 1981): 84–88 (esp. 86–88).

r. Michaud, Charles. *Library Journal* 106, no. 6 (15 March 1981): 683.

s. Murray, Oswyn. "Whoring After Strange Gods." *Times Literary Supplement* no. 4078 (29 May 1981): 595.

t. Newman, S. J. "No Ghost." *New Statesman* 101 (no. 2616) (8 May 1981): 21–22.

u. O'Hara, J. D. "The Winds of Vidal." *Nation* 232, no. 11 (21 March 1981): 343–45.

v. Renault, Mary. "The Wise Lord and the Lie." *New York Review of Books* 28, no. 8 (14 May 1981): 29–30.

w. Ross, Mitchell S. "In Search of History." *National Review* 33, no. 18 (18 September 1981): 1086.

x. Theroux, Paul. "Vidal's 5th Century B.C." *New York Times Book Review* (29 March 1981): 1, 32–33.

y. Warner, Rex. "Beware of Persians Dropping Names." *Washington Post Book World* (22 March 1981): 5.

z. Whitehead, Phillip. "Persian Version." *Listener* 105 (no. 2710) (30 April 1981): 585.

aa. Wolcott, James. "The Ancients According to Gore." *Esquire* 95, no. 4 (August 1981): 19–20.

bb. Wordsworth, Christopher. "Getting Around." *Guardian Weekly* 124, no. 19 (10 May 1981): 22.

cc. [Unsigned.] *Booklist* 77, no. 12 (15 February 1981): 775.

dd. [Unsigned.] *Christian Science Monitor* (12 March 1981): B3.

ee. [Unsigned.] *Kirkus Reviews* 49, no. 2 (15 January 1981): 102.

ff. [Unsigned.] "Paperbacks: New and Noteworthy." *New York Times Book Review* (24 January 1982): 31.

gg. [Unsigned.] *New Yorker* 57, no. 9 (20 April 1981): 152.

hh. [Unsigned.] "Paperback Choice." *Observer* (London) no. 9955 (20 June 1982): 31.

ii. [Unsigned.] *Publishers Weekly* 219, no 8 (20 February 1981): 88–89. *Publishers Weekly* 221, no. 1 (1 January 1982): 49 (abridged).

jj. [Unsigned.] "New in Paperback." *Washington Post Book World* (31 January 1982): 12.

Ableman feels that Vidal is "a fine writer and . . . a prodigious scholar," but the scope of the subject matter in this book overwhelms him. . . . **Amiel** writes: "Vidal is witty, aristocratic and erudite. He is also a bitch." These qualities are on display here. The novel is written by one "profoundly unsympathetic to the democratic ideal." But the book is "probably the finest he has written," and it proves Vidal "to be a master craftsman and, quite simply, a writer of beautiful compelling prose." . . . **Bragg** believes that the novel is "one of Vidal's best." "One of the most detailed strands of this novel is its consistent detailing of court politics. . . . The density of it is clearly meant to convince by that old fashioned method known as exhaustion. I gave in." . . . **Clemons** states: "I believe I have not read to the end a duller novel by an admired writer since Willa Cather's 'Sapphira and the Slave Girl.'" . . . **Conrad** maintains that this is "a mythical novel which describes . . . the end of the age of myth." It is "an historical novel of awesome scope and dense scholarship." It constitutes "a witty and ingenious campaign against history." . . . **DeMott**'s review (in the form of an interview of himself) contends that the book is difficult and tedious in its detailed discussions of the ancient world. . . . **Dick** claims that "Vidal piles layer after layer of meaning on his narrative as it branches out into politics, religion and morality." Vidal wears his learning "like an invisible mantle, with grace and style." . . . **Duvall** believes the novel has "a certain diffuseness that detracts from an otherwise stimulating book." . . . **Emerson**, in a multiple review, finds Cyrus a bore. "The novel provides an enormous quantity of information about the ancient world and its theories of creation . . . but few insights and no life." . . . **Fuller**, reviewing the book along with D. M. Thomas's *The White Hotel*, notes that this is Vidal's best novel after *Julian*. It "is essentially a philosophical novel preoccupied with First and Last Things." "The book is richly epigrammatic. . . . Ultimately 'Creation' is a pessimistic, world-weary book . . . Yet it is highly literate, stylish, entertaining and provocative." . . . **Gray** states that Vidal's target is "the Athens if Pericles, the cradle of western democracy." But the philosophical set-pieces "produce a peculiar lifelessness in the novel as a whole." . . . **Green** labels the novel "a dud." "Vastly learned, painstaking in its research, it never gets inside its subject." Green discusses Vidal's novels and essays. "Neither writerly nor readerly this is a teacherly treatise." Vidal's discussions of philosophy are simplistic. Italo Calvino seems to be the "tutelary spirit" of the novel. . . . **Howes** finds this "A sweet sour potpourri, appetizing, tantalizing, and more than a little indigestible." The novel is full of information; but "Does information—however tasty and inviting— constitute a novel? I'd say not." . . . **Kanfer** believes the book "dodges sensationalism and studiously avoids sex . . . and concentrates on an epoch remote to all but scholars and undergraduates." Vidal "writes with extraordinary concentration and little of the predictable reversals that mar much of his work." He has "written a book of grace and hope." . . . **LaSalle** observes that, although *Creation* makes a good read, "something about this novel is very pompous." "Cyrus' philosophizing . . . is basically of the dime-store variety. . . . The prose itself is lusterless and entirely unengaging." . . . **Lively**, in a multiple review, thinks that the "narrative voice is cool, civilised and persuasive." "The novel sparkles with detail" but "at times the reader has a queasy feeling of being among the pages, as it were, of a Cecil B. de Mille film." . . . **Murray** maintains that this is "a massive exercise in historical imagination, which seldom falters, and which is fuelled by an inexhaustible supply of learning." Vidal's "novel is essentially didactic, a massive enterprise in world education, based on detailed and accurate antiquarian knowledge." . . . **Newman** claims that Vidal's subject-matter needs poetic language, which he is unable to supply. . . . **O'Hara** writes: "His reconstruction of history is not at all bad, except as prose." The novel is pedantic and the philosophy is superficial. . . . **Renault** states that "To enormous research into Persian, Indian, and Chinese history, there has of course been added much fertile, vivid, and ingenious invention." The review is largely a deft plot summary. . . . **Ross** feels that the novel "suffers from a certain stiffness of language that is undoubtedly difficult to avoid in books of this type." The narrative is "admirably clear and sprinkled with wit." It "reads more like a travelogue than a novel." "Vidal's wit and erudition render this book, finally, a satisfying read." . . . **Theroux** deems the novel a "historical novel with knobs on." It is "a long novel, and an audacious one"; it is "a good [novel] that all too often fails to avoid the sort of patrician name-dropping that mars so many historical epics." . . . **Warner**'s review is largely a plot summary. He claims that Cyrus "cannot count either history or philosophy among his strong points." "What Cyrus Spitama is really good at is gossip-writing." . . . **Whitehead** asserts the novel is a "long, rambling, stream of consciousness." He notes "the immense research which has gone into this book." "The set-piece studies have a horrible power." . . . **Wolcott** finds the novel "a teeming gallery of plastic whiskers." It is "a sly exercise in comparative religion—Joseph Campbell for the young at heart." But Vidal has made the "catastrophic mistake" of telling the story through Cyrus, "hardly an enthralling narrator." The novel is "a curiously dry and lifeless academic affair. You can write your name in its dust." . . . **Wordsworth**'s review is largely a plot summary. "As a paradigm of beliefs and philosophies it [the voyage of Cyrus] has been highly absorbing, rich in history, irony and erudition . . . whatever else, it is a book that Montaigne might have enjoyed."

37. *The Second American Revolution (a.k.a. Pink Triangle and Yellow Star)*

    a. Amis, Martin. "Unpatriotic Gore." *Observer* (London) no. 9963 (15 August 1982): 30. In Amis's *The Moronic Inferno and Other Visits to America.* London: Jonathan Cape, 1986; New York: Viking Press, 1987; Harmondsworth, UK: Penguin, 1987, pp. 106–8.

    b. Anderson, A. J. *Library Journal* 107, no. 10 (15 May 1982): 996.

    c. Austen, Roger. *Advocate* no. 356 (25 November 1982): 30–31.

    d. Barber, Michael. "In Brief." *Books and Bookmen* no. 337 (October 1983): 37.

    e. Disch, Thomas M. "Gore Vidal: Essayist Extraordinaire." *Washington Post Book World* (25 April 1982): 1, 17. In III.D.13.

    f. Donoghue, Denis. "Odds and Ends by Gore Vidal." *New York Times Book Review* (2 May 1982): 7, 35.

    g. Fallowell, Duncan. "On the Warpath." *Spectator* 249 (no. 8041) (21 August 1982): 23.

    h. Jenkins, Lawrence A. *Best Sellers* 42, no. 5 (August 1982): 195.

    i. Johnson, Paul. "Pair-annoyed." *Listener* 108 (no. 2776) (2 September 1982): 22–23.

    j. Kress, Paul F. *Southern Humanities Review* 19, no. 1 (Winter 1985): 93–94.

    k. L., D. J. *Kliatt* 17, no. 6 (September 1993): 32.

    l. Landesman, Cosmo. *Books and Bookmen* no. 325 (October 1982): 35.

m. Lehmann-Haupt, Christopher. "Books of The Times." *New York Times* (27 April 1982): C13.

n. Mallon, Thomas. "Catching a Buzz." *National Review* 34, no. 16 (20 August 1982): 1035–36.

o. Montrose, David. "Riding His Hobby Horses." *New Statesman* 104 (no. 2683) (20 August 1982): 18.

p. Ross, Mitchell S. *American Spectator* 15, no. 6 (June 1982): 40–41.

q. Symons, Julian. "Fancy Footwork." *Times Literary Supplement* no. 4143 (27 August 1982): 916.

r. Wood, Michael. "Patriotic Gore." *London Review of Books* 5, no. 9 (19 May–1 June 1983): 13.

s. [Unsigned.] *Booklist* 78, no. 13 (1 March 1982): 803.

t. [Unsigned.] *Kirkus Reviews* 50, no. 3 (1 February 1982): 192–93.

u. [Unsigned.] "Paperbacks: New and Noteworthy." *New York Times Book Review* (15 May 1983): 39.

v. [Unsigned.] "Paperback Choice." *Observer* (London) no. 10020 (25 September 1983): 31.

w. [Unsigned.] *Publishers Weekly* 221, no. 9 (26 February 1982): 139–40.

x. [Unsigned.] *Publishers Weekly* 223, no. 7 (18 February 1983): 128.

y. [Unsigned.] "Notes on Current Books." *Virginia Quarterly Review* 58, no. 4 (Autumn 1982): 122.

Amis writes that Vidal is "probably the cleverest book-reviewer in the world." He is "the unchallengeable master of the droll stroll." In his political essays Vidal "sounds like the only grown-up in America." Part of the reason for this is that he is "incorrigibly anti-American. My, is Gore unpatriotic." . . . **Austen** finds that Vidal is "irrepressibly playful, he is provocatively mischievous . . . he just loves to tease." He expresses exasperation at Vidal's contention that there is no such thing as homosexuality. . . . **Disch** believes that Vidal "is most entertaining as a prosecuting attorney or a debunker of inflated reputations." ". . . that Vidal is one of our best essayists is undeniable, and his faults rarely bulk so large as even to be visible unless you squint." Disch expresses a wish that Vidal would write a memoir. . . . In a peculiarly snide review, **Donoghue** observes that in his political essays Vidal is suggesting "that the U.S.A. should adopt the British system of government." The book "is best read as a function of Vidal's personality." . . . **Fallowell**'s review is largely an archly written overview of Vidal's career. He remarks that the essays show a refreshing irony and wit. . . . **Jenkins** states that Vidal is a "learned and eccentric cynic." His "theories are strangely provocative." The book provides an "odd difficult ride over intellectual rapids." . . . **Johnson** maintains that "At his best [Vidal] is a wonderfully attractive writer." Vidal writes well about movies, but he is obsessed with homosexuality, which is "merely tiresome." . . . **Kress** concludes that Vidal's essays are "original, independent, waspish, Donish, and bitchy." Vidal's "range is impressive." But "for a man so politically-minded, Vidal becomes curiously unsure when he writes of public matters. . . . Despite the frequent brilliance and insight of his prose, Vidal is sometimes cloying . . . but this is an easily affordable price to pay for so much intelligence and wit so exuberantly expressed." . . . **Landesman** asserts that in these essays "body punches of erudition and wit abound, but alas, no K.O.'s." The "humour we expect from Vidal isn't up to par." There is "an anti-American strain so virulent and ubiquitous that it makes Pravda seem like The Voice of America." . . . **Lehmann-Haupt** contends that the book is "by turns outrageous, witty, nasty, amusing, poisonous, shrewd and silly, yet still leave[s] one feeling that it was written by a man of taste and seriousness." Vidal is an aesthetic traditionalist but a radical anti-elitist in politics. . . . **Mallon** writes: "No one else [in America] . . . can combine better sentences into more elegantly sustained demolition derbies." He praises the literary essays, but the political ones are repetitious of what Vidal has said before. . . . **Montrose** finds these essays repetitive of previous work and given to implausible conspiracy theories; but Vidal is "an astute literary critic . . . and a stimulating, if not entirely reliable, political pundit." . . . **Ross** notes: "Vidal the politician has always been Vidal at his worst, and the present collection of his essays offers additional evidence of this." But "whatever doubts one might entertain about him, one must recognize his talent." Ross praises the literary essays. . . . **Symons** writes: "Altogether, Vidal is a lightweight, but a sparky little fellow prepared to shadow-box twice his own size in the ring." He praises the essays on literature; but Vidal has "a passion for generalizations which will not stand five minutes' consideration." . . . **Wood** feels that most of the essays are merely "workmanlike." "Vidal the essayist moves about more freely than Vidal the novelist, is more creative when he doesn't have to be 'creative', and scatters insults and epigrams with fine abandon."

38.   *Duluth*

a.   Barber, Michael. "Nowhere City." *Books and Bookmen* no. 332 (May 1983): 13.

b.   ———. "Fine Fiction from Murdoch, Masters, Naipaul." *Books and Bookmen* no. 348 (September 1984): 36.

c.   Beatty, Jack. "A Rubber Chicken Novel." *New Republic* 188, no. 21 (30 May 1988): 37–38.

d.   Bell, Pearl K. "The End of the Highly Organized Zoo." *Times Literary Supplement* no. 4180 (13 May 1983): 481.

e.   Burgess, Anthony. "Tokyo Roses." *Punch* 284 (no. 7431) (27 April 1983): 76–77 (esp. 77).

f.   Clark, Jeff. *Library Journal* 108, no. 14 (August 1983): 1505–6.

g.   Conrad, Peter. "Not with a Bang." *Observer* (London) no. 9999 (1 May 1983): 28.

h.   Erlich, Richard D. *Fantasy Review* 8, no. 4 (April 1985): 28.

i.   Fremont-Smith, Eliot. "Three Ways to Sunday." *Village Voice* 28, no. 22 (31 May 1983): 54–55.

j.   Lehmann-Haupt, Christopher. "Books of The Times." *New York Times* (20 May 1983): C32.

k.   McCaffery, Larry. "Vidal's Signs of the Reality Rewritten into Satire." *Los Angeles Times Book Review* (3 July 1983): 8.

l.   McRobbie, Angela. "Sign Language." *New Statesman* 105 (6 May 1983): 24.

m.   Prescott, Peter S. "American Provincial." *Newsweek* 101, no. 21 (23 May 1983): 77, 80.

n.   R[ochmis], D[orothy] H. *West Coast Review of Books* 9, no. 5 (September–October 1983): 38.

o.   Sheppard, R. Z. "Shotgun Satire." *Time* 121, no. 24 (13 June 1983): 73.

p.   Stade, George. "The Duluth We Deserve?" *New York Times Book Review* (5 June 1983): 3, 37.

q.   Williams, R. V. *Best Sellers* 43, no. 5 (August 1983): 169.

r.   Wood, Michael. "Patriotic Gore." *London Review of Books* 5, no. 9 (19 May–1 June 1983): 13.

s.   Yardley, Jonathan. "Throwing Firecrackers Down Main Street." *Washington Post Book World* (15 May 1983): 3.

t.   [Unsigned.] *Booklist* 79, no. 19 (1 June 1983): 1246.

u.   [Unsigned.] *Kirkus Reviews* 51, no. 9 (1 May 1983): 547.

v.   [Unsigned.] "Paperbacks." *Punch* 287 (No. 7500) (29 August 1984): 53.

w.   [Unsigned.] "Notes on Current Books." *Virginia Quarterly Review* 59, no. 4 (Autumn 1983): 128.

Barber's first review is largely an attempt at a plot summary. The novel "is stunningly imaginative, with a whole warehouse full of special effects." . . . **Beatty** "find[s] no trace of any creative motive in [the novel] except political bitterness and the desire to produce a novel under the author's bankable name." It "was written in haste." It is simultaneously "a spoof of American political chicanery," "a parody of . . . the academic novel," and "a spoof of science fiction novels"—but in the end it is a "bomb." . . . **Bell** believes that the novel "fairly screams its satirical intentions on every page. . . . Vidal has a huge catch of satirical fish to fry"; but "every joke in *Duluth* lays an egg." The book is filled with "clumsily laboured sniggering." Many of Vidal's attacks on America seem outdated. . . . **Burgess**, in a multiple review, writes: "God's plenty? The book's too diabolic to be that, but its scurrility and wit are a large joy." . . . **Conrad** states that Vidal is here "writing a horror comic not a prophetic allegory" as in *Kalki*. Vidal displays his hatred both of the human race and of his fellow-novelists. He "laughingly debauches the novel with an anthology of skits, mimicking Regency romance, soap opera and science fiction." In his view, "Television seems . . . to have abolished the novel by its closure of circuitry." . . . **Erlich** observes that the novel is "a satire that easily incorporates the SF motifs of First Contact, bug takeover, and general holocaust." It is "of interest to students of SF, but SF isn't primarily what it's up to." . . . **Fremont-Smith**, in a multiple review, characterizes the book as a "travestoid." It is "just Vidal reshuffling his bag of tricks. He doesn't like America or the CIA or English studies or the overpopulation heterosexuality daily threatens. But he also thinks it's *funny.*" . . . **Lehmann-Haupt** feels that Vidal "has come up with a knockout." Vidal, "in madcap mood, . . . is kidding everything from heterosexuality to J. Edgar Hoover." But "by and by, the bright brittleness of 'Duluth' begins to pall a little." This is a "savagely inhuman comedy." . . . **McCaffery** notes that this is "a book so radical in approach (even for Vidal) that it is certain to delight and surprise some readers while boring or disgusting others." "Vidal demonstrates a keen eye for the trivialities and absurdities on which Americans spend so much of their emotional (and literal) currency." But McCaffery doesn't like the racist and sexist jokes. . . . **McRobbie** maintains that the book is "one of the most brilliant, most radical and most subversive pieces of writing to emerge from America in recent years," seeing it as an exposé of Americans' addiction to pop culture. . . . **Prescott** contends that the novel is "a satiric farce . . . The book is very funny: all tasteless froth and decadent, too." . . . **Rochmis** asserts that his is "an indulgence by Vidal, strained and tried by his convolutions and contrivances." . . . **Sheppard** deems the novel "clever throughout but only sporadically funny." . . . **Stade** feels that Duluth is a portrait of Middle America. "The main targets of Mr. Vidal's derision this time out, then, are Middle America's political and sexual practices, its cultural pretentions and its literary preferences." But Vidal "is not at his best here, mandibles clacking with venom and glee." . . . **Williams** writes that "there is abundant satire, heavy ironies, hyperbole, wildly outrageous scenes." Vidal "seems to be saying that Duluth is not a single city. It is a state of mind." . . . **Wood** finds this a "joky novel." "The irony is a bit hefty, but the effects can be eerie and funny. . . . There is . . . a glum, constant sense of history being erased by show business, or just business." But much of the lampooning is "mechanical." . . . **Yardley** believes that "There can be no question that Vidal had a grand time writing *Duluth,* and some of that pleasure is passed along to the reader." But Vidal, although accomplished, "relishes retailing a brand of witless, slapstick humor that would cause a sophomore to blush." The novel is "a long succession of gags, asides and invectives."

39. *Lincoln*
    a. Allen, Bruce. "'Lincoln' Awash with Detail, Lacking in Depth." *Christian Science Monitor* (25 July 1984): 19–20.
    b. Barber, Michael. "Paperbacks." *Books and Bookmen* no. 361 (November 1985): 38.
    c. Bloom, Harold. "The Central Man." *New York Review of Books* 31, no. 12 (19 July 1984): 5–6, 8. In III.D.13.
    d. Blue, Adrianne. "Facts of Life." *New Statesman* 108 (28 September 1984): 31–32.
    e. Bradbury, Malcolm. "In the Hot Seat." *Observer* (London) no. 10068 (23 September 1984): 22.
    f. Brown, Andrew. "Politic President." *Spectator* 253 (no. 8151) (22 September 1984): 28–29.
    g. Burgess, Anthony. "Honest Abe's Obsession." *Times Literary Supplement* no. 4252 (28 September 1984): 1082.
    h. Chipchase, Paul. "High Politics." *Books and Bookmen* no. 348 (September 1984): 15–16.
    i. Clayton, Sylvia. "Honest, Abe!" *Punch* 287 (no. 7506) (10 October 1984): 83.
    j. Coffey, Shelby, III. "Gore Vidal's Lincoln Log." *Washington Post Book World* (10 June 1984): 1, 14.
    k. Dick, Bernard F. *World Literature Today* 59, no. 2 (Spring 1985): 269.
    l. Eder, Richard. "The Honest Abe by This Artful Vidal." *Los Angeles Times Book Review* (24 June 1984): 1, 13.
    m. Edwards, Owen Dudley. "Fiction as History." *Encounter* 64, no. 1 (January 1985): 33–42.
    n. ———. *History Today* 34, no. 12 (December 1984): 55.
    o. Elam, Elizabeth. *School Library Journal* 31, no. 7 (March 1985): 185–86.
    p. Ferry, Richard. "Scary Monsters . . . Historic Gore . . . Terkel's Good War." *Quill and Quire* 52, no. 9 (September 1986): 78.
    q. Fielding, Ellen Wilson. "Honest, Yes, But No Pushover." *Wall Street Journal* (27 June 1984): 32.
    r. Fleming, John. "In Brief." *Saturday Review* 10, no. 2 (November–December 1984): 88.
    s. Gray, Paul. "Gone with the Winds of War." *Time* 123, no. 21 (21 May 1984): 87–88.
    t. Hoffman, Nicholas von. "Patriotic Gore." *Nation* 238, no. 23 (16 June 1984): 744–45.

u. Hooper, Brad. *Booklist* 97, no. 15 (1 April 2001): 1456.

v. Howard, Maureen. "Fiction in Review." *Yale Review* 74, no. 2 (Winter 1985): xvi.

w. J[onas], L[arry]. *West Coast Review of Books* 10, no. 6 (November–December 1984): 23.

x. Jones, D. A. N. "Royal Americans." *London Review of Books* 6, no. 18 (4–17 October 1984): 14–15.

y. Keneally, Thomas. "Bore Vidal." *New Republic* 191, no. 1 (2 July 1984): 32–34.

z. Lehmann-Haupt, Christopher. "Books of The Times." *New York Times* (30 May 1984): C20.

aa. Michaud, Charles. *Library Journal* 109, no. 10 (1 June 1984): 1146.

bb. Oates, Joyce Carol. "The Union Justified the Means." *New York Times Book Review* (3 June 1984): 1, 36–37.

cc. Robertson, Heather. "The Sad Legacy of a Liberator." *Maclean's* 97, no. 27 (2 July 1984): 54–55.

dd. Shrapnel, Norman. "Some American Cousins." *Guardian Weekly* 131, no. 7 (7 October 1984): 21.

ee. Trapkus, Chuck. *Kliatt* 27, no. 6 (November 1993): 56.

ff. Vanaria, Louis M. "For Summer Reading." *Social Education* 49, no. 5 (May 1985): 418.

gg. Whitehead, Phillip. "Evenings with the Ancient." *Listener* 112 (no. 2877) (27 September 1984): 30–31.

hh. [Unsigned.] *Booklist* 80, no. 16 (15 April 1984): 1130.

ii. [Unsigned.] *Booklist* 96, no. 15 (1 April 2000): 1443.

jj. [Unsigned.] *Kirkus Reviews* 52, no. 7 (1 April 1984): 323.

kk. [Unsigned.] "Paperback Choice." *Observer* (London) no. 10128 (17 November 1985): 31.

ll. [Unsigned.] "Paperbacks." *Observer* (London) no. 10578 (10 July 1994): Review, p. 21.

mm. [Unsigned.] *Publishers Weekly* 225, no. 18 (4 May 1984): 49. *Publishers Weekly* 227, no. 17 (26 April 1985): 81 (abridged).

Allen feels that the "book [is] packed with historical information transposed into drama and dialogue"; but the story, "brilliant as it often is, doesn't quite satisfy the expectations it raises." Allen praises the narrative strategy of the novel and finds several "striking characterizations," but the pace is sluggish, and Lincoln himself "is, essentially, the stone figure seated within that celebrated memorial." . . . In an extensive review, **Bloom** finds this a "superb novel." He provides an overview of Vidal's career. Vidal "is a masterly American historical novelist, now wholly matured, who has found his truest subject." "Vidal's imagination of American politics, then and now, is so powerful as to compel awe." Vidal's "Lincoln is an authentic image of authority." The subsidiary characters are rendered with "unfailing gusto." . . . **Blue** judges the novel to be "careful, competent, dismally uninspired." It is "too factual," and Lincoln himself gets lost in the crowd of characters. . . . **Bradbury** characterizes the novel as "a fictonalised American national history told from the standpoint of the State Rooms and the drawing rooms, and seen through the eyes of 'characters' who are personages from the history books." The best part of the book is the "telling portrait of Lincoln." . . . **Brown** believes the novel is a "partial failure," but the characterization of Lincoln is "extraordinarily good." "It is the best novel about politics that Vidal has written; but it is not his best novel about politicians." The style is curiously flat. . . . **Burgess** writes: "What skill there is in the novel resides precisely in the reduction of a tangle of complexities to a not over-long narrative in which the simple reader will learn the basic facts about Lincoln and the Civil War." But "the novel itself seems only to be a device for awakening wonder at the historical actuality; it points at history without heightening it through art." . . . **Chipchase** deems this "a detailed study in political genius. . . . It is hard . . . to recognize the delicate and malicious satirist Vidal in this long, sober and earnestly instructive book." The subsidiary characters are well rendered. It is "a dazzlingly efficient and well organized history lesson." . . . **Clayton** observes that the novel is a "well-organized, traditional narrative. . . . Vidal is in control of all the threads; he makes the book easy to read." "Almost everyone in *Lincoln* is driven by ambition." The novel "is a clever historical entertainment rather than a tragedy." . . . **Coffey** notes that the novel is "richly entertaining." He praises the portrayal of Seward and

Chase. "For the general reader the elegant explication of the issues gives hearty satisfaction: history with the blood still hot." The minor characters are "vivid as miniatures painted on ivory." . . . **Dick** writes: "Vidal's Lincoln portrait is amazingly compassionate, magnanimous by comparison with other historical sketches. . . . Vidal is reverential but not idolatrous toward Lincoln." . . . **Eder** calls the novel "lively but overstretched." "It is, in fact, like one of those museum panoramas where a few figures in the foreground are substantially rounded and the rest are painted flat." The portrayals of Lincoln, Chase, and Mary Todd are well done; but overall, "'Lincoln' is an uneven book." . . . **Edwards** (*Encounter*), in an immense multiple review of books about Lincoln and the Civil War, contends that the novel is "one of the literary events of our time. It is brilliant, moving, thoughtful." But Vidal is so tied to the historical record that "the fictional element is heavily imprisoned." "The book breathes of documentary evidence; but there is no halitosis to be warned against. Mr Vidal wears his learning very lightly." William Seward was not merely power-hungry, but a sincere reformer. Vidal wants to be taken seriously by historians. . . . **Fielding** finds the book "extraordinary." Vidal's "Lincoln is . . . the proponent of a great ideal: an indissoluble Union. . . . Characters are sharply and often sardonically drawn. . . . Readers of 'Lincoln' will find lots of intrigue, low politics and vaulting ambition, but they will also find a 'lovable' Lincoln." . . . **Gray** maintains that "The compulsion to drop facts overrides stylistic standards that Vidal once championed." Vidal does not capture "a consistent sense of the imagined past," but only offers "the never-lever land of convenient clichés." . . . **Hoffman**, in a strongly negative review, asserts that "what Vidal has brought forth is history as soap opera." Vidal "is too weighted down by respect for the facts." . . . **Jonas** concludes that the book is "manipulative and absorbing history, thanks to the adeptness of its author, and it's also a fascinating work of fiction." . . . **Jones**, reviewing the book along with William Boyd's *Stars and Bars,* notes that Vidal "is curbed by his subject-matter here." "Lincoln's grandeur and awesomeness must, for Vidal, be presented more discreetly, more stealthily. . . . Vidal's novel is largely about the way in which Lincoln became an image of 'greatness' to his people." . . . **Keneally** feels that the book is "literal, solid, and reverent." It is "a strangely dated piece of work lacking in the fancy, idiosyncrasy, and flashes of lightning for which we depend on fiction writers, not least on Gore Vidal." Vidal "has failed . . . to filter historic events through the peculiar sieve of a literary imagination." But the portrait of Lincoln himself is "fascinating and accessible." . . . **Lehmann-Haupt** finds this "a well-founded, complex, very nearly heroic portrait of Lincoln." But the novel is "sodden in its lack of pace or focus"; "compared to the author's usual fare, it is all so mellow and responsible, and, I am afraid, finally dull. One misses the hiss of acid." . . . In an expansive and favorable review, **Oates** remarks that Vidal's portrait of Lincoln "is reasoned, judicious, straightforward and utterly convincing." Lincoln is "not a debunked portrait by any means . . . and, as the novel runs its course, he emerges as a truly outstanding man." The portraits of Seward and Chase are also excellent, but Mary Todd Lincoln "is a collection of symptoms rather than a coherent personality." One of the best features of the book is Vidal's "presentation of the incalculable complexity of his subject." . . . **Robertson** comments that, because Vidal seems to like Lincoln, this novel is less irreverent than "humorless, ponderous and sad." Vidal's "obsession with Washington chitchat becomes tedious and irritatingly repetitive in the epic context of the Civil War." But "the portrait of Lincoln is entirely sympathetic and human." . . . **Shrapnel**, in a multiple review, believes that the novel inspires "awe at the sheer stamina involved." Lincoln "does come to life, in a galvanic sort of way that seems quaintly appropriate." . . . **Trapkus** feels that the novel is an "impressive fictionalization of Lincoln's presidential years." The telling is "absorbing" and the narration is "superb." . . . **Whitehead**'s review is largely a plot summary. He claims that Vidal has used Lincoln's words "to fuse together a novel which is also a work of history and a study in political psychology." "Vidal gives us Lincoln the politician, and does not bore us with Lincoln the saint." The portrait of Chase is "the best thing in the book."

40. *Vidal in Venice*
   a. Barber, Michael. *Books* no. 6 (September 1987): 25.
   b. Craft, Robert. "A New Year Roundup." *New York Review of Books* 33, no. 2 (13 February 1986): 28.
   c. Field, Carol. "A Vidal Concern." *San Francisco Chronicle* (29 December 1985): Review, p. 4.
   d. Glendenning, Victoria. "Having a Horrible Time." *Sunday Times* (Lond~ December 1985): 34.
   e. Hoelterhoff, Manuela. "Christmas Books: A Holiday Sampler." *Wall Street* December 1985): 28.
   f. Mironowicz, Margaret. "Gore Vidal Gives Engaging, Colorful Tour of Venice." *and Mail* (Toronto) (23 October 1985): C5.

    g.   Mitgang, Herbert. "Travel Bookshelf." *New York Times* (23 March 1986): Sec. 10, p. 21.

    h.   P[oole], S[hona] C[rawford]. "Travel Books." *Times* (London) (29 August 1987): 14.

    i.   Solomon, Charles. *Los Angeles Times Book Review* (12 January 1986): 4.

    j.   [Unsigned.] *Kirkus Reviews* 53, no. 21 (1 November 1985): 1192.

    k.   [Unsigned.] "New in Paperback." *Washington Post Book World* (20 September 1987): 16.

Craft sums up the book as "pert pocket-history, part waiting-room art, part tourist guyed." Vidal makes astute parallels between the Venetian and American republics; but "the weakest chapter is the one on the arts." . . . **Field** believes that Venice "has been wittily and provocatively described in Gore Vidal's essay." . . . **Mironowicz** notes that Vidal is a "thoroughly engaging and colorful host" to Venice. "Even when Mr. Vidal has nothing to say about Venice, he says something." . . . **Mitgang** writes that "this book adds up to little more than a pleasant side trip for [Vidal] and his devoted readers." . . . **Solomon** declares that Vidal "offers a superficial, anecdotal account of the city's long and curious history." . . . The ***Washington Post Book World*** review states that "Vidal is at his best when he can exercise his well-known wit and irony, but Venice—despite its crowds of tourists—calls forth affection and concern."

41.   *Myra Breckinridge; Myron*

    a.   Hitchens, Christopher. "Vidal Statistics." *Observer* (London) no. 10233 (22 November 1987): 25.

    b.   Kermode, Frank. "Reagan and the Venal Empire." *Manchester Guardian Weekly* 137, no. 23 (6 December 1987): 29.

    c.   [Unsigned.] "Paperbacks." *Manchester Guardian Weekly* 140, no. 10 (5 March 1989): 28.

Hitchens spends most of his time discussing *Empire* and *Armageddon?* . . . **Kermode** devotes most of his review to *Armageddon?* He notes that Vidal "disingenuously pretends not to understand why some moralists found [these novels] objectionable. . . . These gamesome books nevertheless don't neglect Vidal's serious preoccupations."

42.   *Empire*

    a.   Ackroyd, Peter. "Wit and Poet of Lost Time." *Times* (London) (19 November 1987): 19.

    b.   Baker, Brock. "Empire, the Novel." *New Criterion* 6, no. 8 (April 1988): 86–88.

    c.   Barber, Michael. *Books* 3, no. 1 (April 1989): 19.

    d.   Beschloss, Michael R. "Gore Vidal's 'Empire.'" *Chicago Tribune Books* (14 June 1987): 1, 4.

    e.   Brunet, Elena. "Current Paperbacks." *Los Angeles Times Book Review* (7 August 1988): 10.

    f.   Carson, Tom. "His Country, Right or Wrong: Gore Vidal Pledges Allegiance." *Village Voice* 32, no. 40 (6 October 1987): 53–55.

    g.   Cieri, Carol des Lauriers. "Gore Vidal's 'Empire' Offers a Morality Play without Morals." *Christian Science Monitor* (20 July 1987): 22.

    h.   Delbanco, Andrew. "The Bad and the Ugly." *New Republic* 197, nos. 11 and 12 (14 and 21 September 1987): 49–50, 52–55.

    i.   Eder, Richard. *Los Angeles Times Book Review* (24 May 1987): 1.

    j.   Fender, Stephen. "Remember Pound." *Listener* 118 (no. 3042) (17 and 24 December 1987): 50.

    k.   Gates, David. "A Tale of the Gilded Age." *Newsweek* 109, no. 24 (15 June 1987): 70.

    l.   Gray, Paul. "The Veneer of the Gilded Age." *Time* 129, no. 25 (22 June 1987): 73–74.

    m.   Hannan, Charles. *School Librarian* 36, no. 1 (February 1988): 36.

    n.   Hemesath, James B. *Library Journal* 112, no. 12 (July 1987): 99.

    o.   Hitchens, Christopher. "Vidal Statistics." *Observer* (London) no. 10233 (22 November 1987): 25.

    p.   Johnson, George. "New and Noteworthy." *New York Times Book Review* (17 July 1988): 34.

    q.   Kaplan, Justin. "A Fat and Hungry Nation." *New York Times Book Review* (14 June 1987): 1, 42.

r. Kemp, Peter. "Patrician Observer of Corruption." *Sunday Times* (London) (29 November 1987).

s. Kermode, Frank. "Reagan and the Venal Empire." *Manchester Guardian Weekly* 137, no. 23 (6 December 1987): 29.

t. King, Francis. "Old and New Prose from an Old Pro." *Spectator* 259 (no. 8315) (21 November 1987): 41, 43.

u. Leader, Zachary. "On the State of America." *Times Literary Supplement* no. 4416 (20 November 1987): 1271–72.

v. Lehmann-Haupt, Christopher. "Books of The Times." *New York Times* (11 June 1987): C24.

w. Lescaze, Lee. "As the Century Turned." *Wall Street Journal* (9 June 1987): 32.

x. MacCurtain, Austin. "Paperbacks." *Sunday Times* (London) (26 February 1989): G10.

y. Perrin, Noel. "Gore Vidal's American Glory." *Washington Post Book World* (24 May 1987): 1, 14.

z. Poirier, Richard. "American Emperors." *New York Review of Books* 34, no. 14 (24 September 1987): 31–33. In III.D.13. In Poirier's *Trying It out on America: Literary and Other Performances.* New York: Farrar, Straus & Giroux, 1999, pp. 145–54 (as "Vidal's American Empire").

aa. Reynolds, Stanley. "The American Balzac." *Punch* 293 (no. 7665) (25 November 1987): 90–91.

bb. Steel, Ronald. "Vidal Builds a Strong 'Empire.'" *USA Today* (29 May 1987): 7D.

cc. Towle, Philip. "The Last Days of the American Empire." *London Review of Books* 10, no. 10 (19 May 1988): 8.

dd. Waldman, Steven. "Making McKinley Sexy." *Washington Monthly* 19, no. 8 (September 1987): 45–46, 48–49.

ee. [Unsigned.] *Booklist* 83, no. 18 (15 May 1987): 1386.

ff. [Unsigned.] *Books* no. 8 (November 1987): 29.

gg. [Unsigned.] *Kirkus Reviews* 55, no. 8 (1 May 1987): 673.

hh. [Unsigned.] *Publishers Weekly* 231, no. 18 (1 May 1987): 53–54.

Ackroyd feels that the novel is "about personalities rather than about people, and as such it comes as a welcome relief." It is "a genuinely engaging book." . . . **Baker** believes that "The author has obviously done a great deal of research for his project," but "The invented heroine [Caroline Sanford] lacks charm and plausibility. . . . Mr. Vidal has chosen to tidy up the past, leaving out any complexities, in order to make it reflect his own narrowly focused and inveterately cynical temperament." . . . **Beschloss** writes: "We feel Vidal's delight in exposing political hypocrisy," but "hypocrisy is not unmixed with a sense of history." "In most respects, 'Empire' ranks alongside the strongest volumes in what is now Vidal's historical quintet." But the imagined characters are "monochromatic," and there is "little pace or plot" in the novel. . . . **Carson** notes that this novel is "entertaining, impressively engineered stuff." The connections with previous books make Vidal's historical novels "feel closer to a TV epic than a literary one." The portrait of Theodore Roosevelt is "first-rate." This long, complex review brings in other novels in the series to highlight Vidal's methodology of writing historical fiction. . . . **Cieri** states that the book's thesis is that "newspapers invent politics." But Vidal is tripped up by his own formula, for the novel offers "the 'Society Lady' angle on American history. . . . It is hard to know where fiction ends and facts begin." . . . In an enormous review, **Delbanco** observes that the novel "is composed with a comic technique made up largely of the grotesque." "As history, the novel is badly truncated"; "as fiction *Empire* is tired. The book is one long expression of disgust." He presents an overview of Vidal's career, emphasizing the political novels. "Whenever Vidal raises genuinely historical questions, he tends to answer them with unrelieved flippancy." Delbanco expresses admiration for *Lincoln,* but Vidal's other novels are merely exercises in cynicism and debunking. "Next to *Lincoln,* Vidal's new novel is a series of miniature lampoons." . . . **Eder** writes that the novel, "though witty and absorbing in parts, is weaker than its predecessors." The fictional characters take up too much of the attention. "Vidal makes his point that the spirit of American expansion was in conflict with the authentic qualities of the American character, and has tended to extinguish them." . . . **Fender** maintains that the novel "has too much of everything including history. . . . Yet the history is given a shape, moulded on the old Whig thesis that cultures begin to decline when they turn themselves from republics to empires." Vidal is too hard on

Theodore Roosevelt, but "is good on class." . . . **Gates** finds the novel rambling (like the history it depicts) but entertaining. . . . **Gray** thinks that the novel is "stronger on atmosphere than plot." It "offers many small pleasures in place of an absorbing whole." . . . **Hitchens** contends that Vidal "has been steadily raising a fictional edifice through which the growth of the United States into a global colossus can be appreciated and understood." Vidal "plainly believes that you can't have an empire without making hypocrisy into a civil religion." . . . **Kaplan** declares that "Vidal demonstrates a political imagination and insider's sagacity equaled by no other practicing fiction writer I can think of." The novel is "a wonderfully vivid documentary drama," but Vidal's prose has suffered a decline. . . . **Kemp**'s review is largely a plot summary. Vidal's "concern with the power of the press to elevate or destroy politicians—much apparent in earlier books—here becomes central." [The review appeared in a special "Books" section of the *Sunday Times,* but this section is not reproduced in the microfilm edition; the text is available only in the online edition.] . . . **Kermode** devotes most of his review to *Armageddon?* and supplies only a brief discussion of *Empire*. . . . **King** remarks that the novel has too many characters unfamiliar to a British audience. . . . **Leader** remarks that the novel "is a relative disappointment, at least in comparison to *Lincoln,* its immediate predecessor. . . . Too many of the characters in the novel are viewed *ab extra,* as collections of tags and tics." . . . **Lehmann-Haupt** asserts that Vidal "has surpassed himself in 'Empire' and written what now stands as the best in the series." The secret of the novel's success is the blending of foreground, middleground, and background. Caroline Sanford is Vidal's "best invention since Myra Breckinridge." . . . **Lescaze** claims that the problem with the novel is that it lacks "a towering central character." It is "a curiously plotless book, almost totally lacking drama." . . . **Perrin** writes that "Vidal handles his huge cast brilliantly" and that "Vidal has never been wittier." "This is a deeply serious novel, as well as a witty one." Nevertheless, there is "a thick layer of tinsel" on the novel. . . . **Poirier** feels that the aloof and cynical Henry James sets the tone of the book; Caroline Sanford is like Isabel Archer in *Portrait of a Lady.* "No American writer I know of has Vidal's sense of national proprietorship. He summons the entire American scene into his confident voice. . . . Vidal's prose is intended to strip American imperialism of its mystery." He likens Vidal to Santayana in his ambiguous response to empire: "he opposes the brutal and self-defeating ways of getting and managing an empire." . . . **Reynolds** deems the novel a "600-page story of pompous, late-Victorian American windbags." . . . **Steel** claims that "the cast of characters is as grand as the themes of greed, self-righteousness and imperial delusion that give the novel its shape." The tie that binds the historical characters is the fictional Caroline Sanford. "*Empire* is a compelling novel that brilliantly illuminates the critical moment when America was first seized by imperial dreams." . . . **Towle**'s essay discusses the novel only briefly, focusing on *Armageddon?* . . . **Waldman** comments that Vidal's "books are peppered with anecdotes that are as fun as they are revealing." Vidal's nonfiction and persona are off-putting, yet his "novels are so well executed that you forget he's the same loon you just saw on 'Dick Cavett.'" Vidal is the "Hugh Sidey of novelists—chronicling the leaders, the presidents, the power brokers, and the wealthy." "*Empire* would be as good a read in the classroom as on the beach."

43.   *Armageddon?*
    a.   Ackroyd, Peter. "Wit and Poet of Lost Time." *Times* (London) (19 November 1987): 19.
    b.   Barber, Mike. *Books* no. 8 (November 1987): 24.
    c.   Bradfield, Scott. "Paperbacks." *Times Educational Supplement* (24 February 1989): B8.
    d.   Fender, Stephen. "Remember Pound." *Listener* 118 (no. 3042) (17 and 24 December 1987): 50.
    e.   Glass, Charles. "Beat the Devil." *Spectator* 261 (no. 8363) (22 October 1988): 31–33.
    f.   Hitchens, Christopher. "Vidal Statistics." *Observer* (London) no. 10233 (22 November 1987): 25.
    g.   Kemp, Peter. "Patrician Observer of Corruption." *Sunday Times* (London) (29 November 1987).
    h.   Kermode, Frank. "Reagan and the Venal Empire." *Manchester Guardian Weekly* 137, no. 23 (6 December 1987): 29.
    i.   King, Francis. "Old and New Prose from an Old Pro." *Spectator* 259 (No. 8315) (21 November 1987): 41, 43.
    j.   Leader, Zachary. "On the State of America." *Times Literary Supplement* no. 4416 (20 November 1987): 12871–72.
    k.   Reynolds, Stanley. "The American Balzac." *Punch* 293 (no. 7665) (25 November 1987): 9091.

l. Towle, Philip. "The Last Days of the American Empire." *London Review of Books* 10, no. 10 (19 May 1988): 8.

m. [Unsigned.] *Books* 3, no. 3 (June 1989): 12.

Ackroyd feels that in this book Vidal "neatly outline[s]" the theme of *Empire*. . . . **Barber**, reviewing the book along with John Carey's *Original Copy*, believes that some of Vidal's views on politics seem "a bit too apocalyptic." But Vidal unleashes his "arsenal of irony, high camp and epigrammatic wit" against Ronald and Nancy Reagan. . . . **Fender** claims that Vidal's essays remind one of Ezra Pound, whose "opinions can be assigned to the rubbish pile of history's crackpots." . . . **Glass** notes that Vidal (along with Noam Chomsky and Alexander Cockburn) "stand outside the American political spectrum." Vidal's essays keenly dissect the age of Ronald Reagan. . . . **Hitchens** states that *Armageddon* complements the themes in *Empire*. Vidal's "hatred of the Reagans is more or less pure, and he chooses to express it in a sort of mocking, feline style." Vidal's "general contempt for Christianity . . . has now found its ideal target." . . . **Kemp** devotes most of his review to *Empire*. . . . **Kermode** observes that the "key to Gore Vidal, in both jest and earnest, is his disappointment with the United States," and the best essays in the book show how he came to this view. Vidal is particularly hard on Ronald Reagan, but blames his rise on the American people. . . . **King** appreciates the devastating essay "A Cheerful Response" and other items. . . . **Leader** discusses Vidal's attacks on Reagan and the religious right, and his controversy with Jewish figures. "Elsewhere, the volume is a treat, full of the many virtues, including a controlled and perceptive malice, characteristic of previous collections." . . . **Reynolds**'s review focuses on "The Day the American Empire Ran out of Gas." "Gore Vidal is the most thought-provoking and witty American journalist writing today." . . . **Towle**, reviewing this book and *Empire* along with Paul Johnson's *The Rise and Fall of the Great Powers*, declares that "many of Vidal's political essays should not be taken too seriously." Vidal is "master of the black joke," and many of his essays are merely intended to be provocative.

44. *At Home*

a. Bawer, Bruce. "Unpatriotic Gore: Advertisements for Himself." *Wall Street Journal* (11 January 1989): A15.

b. Caldwell, Gail. "A Podium for Vidal." *Boston Globe* (27 November 1988): B18.

c. Fitch, Robert. "What's Left to Write?" *Voice Literary Supplement* no. 74 (May 1989): 18–22 (esp. 21–22).

d. Gargan, William. *Library Journal* 113, no. 19 (15 November 1988): 75.

e. H[ooper], B[rad]. *Booklist* 85, no. 6 (15 November 1988): 533.

f. Johnson, George. "New and Noteworthy." *New York Times Book Review* (4 February 1990): 32.

g. Lehmann-Haupt, Christopher. "Books of The Times: Vidal's Specialty: The Good Deeds of Subversion." *New York Times* (14 November 1988): C16.

h. Peterson, Clarence. "Paperbacks." *Chicago Tribune Books* (28 January 1990): 8.

i. Raskin, Alex. "Nonfiction in brief." *Los Angeles Times Book Review* (8 January 1989): 4.

j. Solomon, Charles. "Current Paperbacks." *Los Angeles Times Book Review* (11 March 1990): 10.

k. Stuewe, Paul. "Of Some Import." *Quill and Quire* 55, no. 2 (February 1989): 27.

l. Yardley, Jonathan. "The Indian Summer of Gore Vidal." *Washington Post Book World* (20 November 1988): 3.

m. [Unsigned.] *Kirkus Reviews* 56, no. 20 (15 October 1988): 1520.

n. [Unsigned.] *Publishers Weekly* 234, no. 14 (30 September 1988): 53.

o. [Unsigned.] *Time* 132, no. 21 (21 November 1988): 139.

p. [Unsigned.] "Notes on Current Books." *Virginia Quarterly Review* 65, no. 2 (Spring 1989): 68.

q. [Unsigned.] "New in Paperback." *Washington Post Book World* (11 February 1990): 12.

Bawer states that although Vidal the novelist "hardly merits serious consideration," Vidal the essayist "demands notice." The essays are "at once forthright and mendacious, smart and demented . . . written (at best) with panache, vigor and a caustic, often perverse wit." Vidal's writing on literature is "sane and astute," but his political essays "are another story." "Vidal reveals hostility to America and American freedom." He is a braggart about his family and social connections. . . . **Caldwell** feels that the book "is funny, eyebrow-raising, self-referential and very smart, often passionate, in its reach." Vidal is engaging even when he is being narcissistic.... **Fitch**, in a multiple review, notes that Vidal "is seized by a seemingly uncontrollable need to mention himself or his distinguished family.... Vidal's self-referential universe is populated by two species: the members of 'our crowd' and the squares," as exemplified in the memoir of Tennessee Williams.... **Lehmann-Haupt** observes that the book is filled with Vidal's reflections as to "what is wrong with American society." Most of the views will be familiar to readers of Vidal's earlier essays. His literary essays (e.g., on Dawn Powell and William Dean Howells) can be dull.... **Raskin** declares that in these essays Vidal "harmoniousoly blend[s] pariotic fervor with irreverence." But Vidal's "hubris sometimes has led to exhibitionism." ... **Yardley** remarks that "Sometimes [Vidal] is petulant, at others pugnacious; he is by turns elegiac and sarcastic; he boils over with contempt, then offers high and heartfelt tribute." Vidal's "sorrow over our [i.e., Americans'] loss of purpose and seriousness cannot be dismissed as the maundering of a crank."

45. *Hollywood*
   a. Auchincloss, Louis. "Babylon Revisited." *New York Review of Books* 37, no. 5 (29 March 1990): 20–22. In D.13. In Auchincloss's *The Style's the Man: Reflections on Proust, Fitzgerald, Wharton, Vidal, and Others*. New York: Charles Scribner's Sons, 1994, pp. 53–67 (as "Babylon Revisited: Gore Vidal's American Trilogy").
   b. Barber, Michael. "The Parade Going By." *Listener* 122 (no. 3139) (9 November 1989): 35.
   c. Brosnahan, John. *Booklist* 86, no. 6 (15 November 1989): 619.
   d. Connarroe, Joel. "Klieg Lights on the Potomac." *New York Times Book Review* (21 January 1990): 1, 38.
   e. Davis, Clive. "Cynic's Eye View." *New Statesman and Society* 2 (no. 74) (3 November 1989): 35–36.
   f. Gilbert, Ruth. "The Hot Wire." *New York* 23, no. 5 (5 February 1990): 30.
   g. Gold, Victor. *American Spectator* 23, no. 5 (May 1990): 45–46.
   h. Green, Jonathan. "Hollywood from Upstairs." *Books* 3, no. 9 (December 1989): 7.
   i. King, Francis. "A Biography of the United States." *Spectator* 263 (no. 8415) (4 November 1989): 30–31.
   j. Leader, Zachary. "Where Everyone Thinks Like a Movie." *Observer* (London) no. 10334 (5 November 1989): 54.
   k. Parrinder, Patrick. "Acapulcalypse." *London Review of Books* 11, no. 22 (23 November 1989): 24–26.
   l. Reeves, Richard. "Politics Is—Surprise!—Show Biz." *Los Angeles Times Book Review* (18 February 1990): 4.
   m. See, Carolyn. "Gore Vidal and the Screening of America." *Washington Post Book World* (14 January 1990): 1, 2.
   n. Snider, Norman. "Movers and Movies." *Maclean's* 103, no. 10 (5 March 1990): 63.
   o. Tryon, Tom. "Vidal in Tinseltown." *Chicago Tribune Books* (28 January 1990): 1, 4.
   p. Wilkinson, Burke. "Vidal Puts Hardly Any 'Hollywood' into Novel." *Washington Times* (12 February 1990): E5.
   q. Wood, Michael. "Improvisations on the Fact of Force." *Times Literary Supplement* no. 4519 (10–16 November 1989): 1243.
   r. Woog, Adam. "Vidal's 'Hollywood' Hits Highs and Lows." *Seattle Times* (4 March 1990): K7.
   s. [Unsigned.] *Kirkus Reviews* 57, no. 21 (1 November 1989): 1561.
   t. [Unsigned.] *Publishers Weekly* 236, no. 24 (15 December 1989): 56.
   u. [Unsigned.] *Publishers Weekly* 237, no. 9 (2 March 1990): 60.
   v. [Unsigned.] "Passing Time." *Time* 135, no. 7 (12 February 1990): 66.

Auchincloss states that the novel forms a logical trilogy with *Lincoln* and *Empire*. It has "an entracing gallery of portraits, as funny as it is acute," notably Woodrow Wilson and Warren G. Harding. "In *Hollywood*, as in many of Vidal's novels (*Lincoln* and *Julian* excepted), the parts are greater than the whole." ... **Barber**'s review is largely a plot summary. "Like Suetonius, Vidal sugars the political pill with gossip, anecdote and unrelenting attention to physical detail." ... **Conarroe** believes this to be "a wonderfully literate and consistently impressive work that clearly belongs on a shelf with the author's best earlier efforts." The book is full of vivid characters, but Vidal is "determined not only to amuse but to enlighten." Washington, not Hollywood, is the real subject of the book. . . . **Davis** thinks the novel lacks focus and that the historical figures fail to come alive: "In the end, the book is submerged by its period accessories." . . . **Gold**, reviewing the book along with *Emperor of America* by Richard Condon, states that "the sonofabitch can write." Vidal's historical novels are "distinguished not so much for their broad sweep as their author's eye for detail." Parts of the novel show Vidal "at his satiric best," but other parts are tedious. . . . **Green** writes: "It is a Rosenkrantz and Guildenstern history, a backstage version, intermingled with the passage of great events." In Vidal's view, politicians "can fool all the people if not all the time, then as near as makes no difference." The book provides "great pleasure," But Vidal is a better essayist than novelist. . . . **King** feels that the portraits of Woodrow Wilson and Warren G. Harding are convincing; the "Hollywood" sections less so. . . . **Leader**'s review is largely a plot summary. "The best bits in the book [are] the historical confrontations and set pieces." The prose is "less distractingly literary" than in *Empire*, "its prevailing archness no longer antiquely mandarin." . . . **Parrinder**, in a multiple review, declares that the novel "fits rather curiously into Vidal's saga of American political history." Vidal has become "a C. P. Snow of the Potomac." This is "a well-made novel with much wit of the 'little did they know' sort." . . . **Reeves** claims that this is "not the best of Vidal's work by a long shot. . . . Vidal tries to show that Washington and Hollywood are both part of an American continuum or, as he sees it, an American decadence that inexorably led to an actor in the White House." . . . **See** observes that the novel is "a masterly blend of thought patterns." Its message is that "Corruption will always be covered up, however ineptly. Politicians, at the top level, are in the game for power, and, at the next level, for bucks." . . . **Snider** remarks that the book is "glacially paced." It "succeeds only partially." It fails to establish true links between Hollywood and Washington, D.C. "The Hollywood portion of the book . . . is an unlikely fantasy." Vidal's anti-democratic and misanthropic views come to the fore. . . . **Tryon** finds this a "sparkling work." "What this book does not fail to do is entertain . . . the author is ever naughty, wicked and provocative. . . . The narrative stream flows along, now bubbling and babbling, now sweeping as in a flood. . . . Vidal is a sort of literary Ed Murrow; he puts you there, in the picture, with effortless authenticity." . . . **Wilkinson** claims that the "heady blend of narrative drive and barbed wit" found in Vidal's other historical novels "is only intermittently in evidence" here. Vidal is more concerned with Washington, D.C., than Hollywood. The book is "only middling Gore Vidal." . . . **Wood**'s review is largely a plot summary. "A man of bright and waspish wit, Vidal is very restrained in this and other novels of the sequence. . . . The general effect is readable, but pretty bland." . . . **Woog** contends that "Some of this book is vivid . . . Some is very funny . . . Unfortunately, there's also dead weight in 'Hollywood' . . . a good deal of Vidal's prose is curiously, uncharacteristically wooden."

46. *A View from the Diners Club*
    a. Lefkowitz, Mary. "Tiresias' Truths." *Times Literary Supplement* no. 4627 (6 December 1991): 7.
    b. Mantel, Hilary. "How Pleasant to Be Enraged." *Spectator* 267 (No. 8523) (16 November 1991): 42–43.
    c. Morton, Brian. "American Graffiti." *New Statesman and Society* 4 (No. 177) (15 November 1991): 43–44.
    d. Wood, James. "Belles-Lettres from Italy." *Manchester Guardian Weekly* 145, no. 23 (8 December 1991): 27.
    e. [Unsigned.] "Hardback Briefs." *Observer* (London) (8 December 1991): 56.

Lefkowitz feels that the essays express "the formidable wit and wisdom of an author who, despite his lack of formal qualifications, has been, by his own admission, invariably right." She prefers the political essays to the literary ones. . . . **Mantel** finds Vidal's literary essays painfully thorough, but his political essays lively and on the mark. . . . **Morton** states that Vidal presents an image of "almost insouciant omniscience." . . . **Wood** writes that this is an "entertaining, but intellectually hasty, book of essays." The book has many "vices," among which is that Vidal "has a fear of real engagement." But Vidal is also "funny, shrewd, and intelligent." "Wherever people read about books, he will be read and enjoyed; those who live for books will turn elsewhere."

47. *Screening History*
    a. Adair, Gilbert. "Everlasting Watch, But Movieless." *Spectator* 269 (no. 8577) (28 November 1992): 49.

b.   Adams, Phoebe-Lou. *Atlantic Monthly* 270, no. 4 (October 1992): 123–24.

c.   Anderson, Jon. "A Little Sermon from Gore Vidal on the Best Way to Learn History." *Chicago Tribune Books* (20 September 1992): 5.

d.   Cawley, Marianne. *Library Journal* 117, no. 12 (July 1992): 94.

e.   Davidoff, Robert. "Revelations from Gore." *Advocate* no. 610 (25 August 1992): 81.

f.   Gates, David. "A Glitch in the Gospel." *Newsweek* 120, no. 9 (31 August 1992): 69.

g.   Goldstein, Laurence. "Film as Family History." *Michigan Quarterly Review* 32, no. 2 (Spring 1993): 285–95 (esp. 289–92).

h.   Graeber, Laurel. "New and Noteworthy Paperbacks." *New York Times Book Review* (27 March 1994): 24.

i.   Indiana, Gary. "Elan Vidal." *Artforum* 31, no. 3 (November 1992): 10. In Indiana's *Let It Bleed: Essays 1985–1995*. New York: Serpent's Tail, 1996, pp. 118–21 (as "Gore Vidal's *Screening History*").

j.   Johnson, Diane. "Star." *New York Review of Books* 40, no. 7 (8 April 1993): 24–25.

k.   Kammen, Michael. "What He Learned at the Movies." *New York Times Book Review* (30 August 1992): 1, 26–27.

l.   Kazin, Alfred. "Ecce Homo." *New Republic* 207, no. 15 (5 October 1992): 36–37.

m.   Kilday, Gregg. "A Puck and a Half." *Los Angeles Times Book Review* (13 September 1992): 2, 7.

n.   Klinghoffer, David. "Rotten Fruit." *National Review* 44, no. 23 (30 November 1992): 50–52.

o.   Lyons, Donald. "Gore Vidal on Gore Vidal, Al Gore and Jesus." *Wall Street Journal* (28 September 1992): A10.

p.   Mendelsohn, Jane. *Voice Literary Supplement* no. 108 (September 1992): 7–8.

q.   Mitgang, Herbert. "Books of The Times: One Affair with Movies and One with Sacrilege." *New York Times* (23 September 1992): C19.

r.   Prince, Stephen. *Film Quarterly* 47, no. 1 (Fall 1993): 70.

s.   Rosenbaum, Jonathan. *Cinéaste* 19, no. 4 (March 1993): 95–96.

t.   Schachtmann, Tom. *Variety* 348 (21 September 1992): 103.

u.   Schuman, Howard. "Memory Lapse." *Sight and Sound* 3, no. 4 (April 1993): 36.

v.   Sheed, Wilfrid. "Gore's Gospel." *New Yorker* 68 (26 October 1992): 130–34.

w.   Simon, John. *American Spectator* 26, no. 1 (January 1993): 78–82.

x.   Taylor, Robert. "Gorefoolery." *Boston Globe* (6 September 1992): A10.

y.   Tubridy, Michael. *Wilson Library Bulletin* 67, no. 4 (December 1992): 102–3.

z.   Yardley, Jonathan. "Vidal, Missing the Big Picture." *Washington Post Book World* (26 August 1992): C2.

aa.   [Unsigned.] *Chicago Tribune Books* (8 May 1994): 8.

bb.   [Unsinged.] *Lambda Book Report* 3, no. 7 (November–December 1992): 45.

cc.   [Unsigned.] *Lambda Book Report* 4, no. 4 (May–June 1994): 39.

dd.   [Unsigned.] *Publishers Weekly* 239, no. 29 (29 June 1992): 47.

ee.   [Unsigned.] *University Press Book News* 4 (September 1992): 35.

ff.   [Unsigned.] "New in Paperback." *Washington Post Book World* (27 March 1994): 12.

In a harsh review, **Adair** sees the book as "a rambling, inconsequential book that fails absolutely to do justice to its title." He feels that Vidal has no understanding of movies. . . . **Anderson** feels that Vidal puts "his quarrelsome skills to good use" here. The review is largely a summary of the book and of Vidal's life. . . . **Davidoff** writes: "The experience of having Vidal touch more explicitly on his own life than he usually does reveals how much more interesting he is than most people we get to listen to." . . . **Gates**'s review is almost entirely focused on *Live from Golgotha*. . . . **Goldstein**, in a multiple review, provides a summary of the book and of Vidal's views on film. "Vidal certainly knows his movie history, though one must be careful in trusting his generalizations." Vidal is not correct in thinking that there were no major films about the American Revolution in the 1930s. Vidal's "revisionism is fiercely partisan, and here as elsewhere, often very funny." But "the book keeps losing focus; the movies disappear for many pages at a time." . . . **Indiana** warmly records Vidal's devotion to film. "The book has even more than Vidal's usual tossed-off hilarity. The bemused, sardonic ring of his speaking voice is clearly audible throughout." . . . **Johnson** notes that the book is a "delightful, rather reticent memoir . . . the solitary and bookish boy-moviegoer emerges from behind his jokes as a surprisingly austere, scholarly intellectual with a disappointed romantic's impatience with his country." . . . **Kammen** believes that Vidal "emphasizes the significance of film as a basis for social interaction in the United States." Vidal is "Henry Adams redivivus . . . a historian, novelist and well-connected social critic." . . . **Kazin** finds that the book is Vidal's "largely charming and almost idyllic memories of life at the movies." . . . **Kilday**'s review is largely a summary of the book. "As an evocative reminiscence, it's most persuasive, even if Vidal's logic is not airtight." The book "can also be read simply for its rich load of acerbic Vidalian asides." . . . **Klinghoffer** contends that the book is an excuse to talk about his illustrious family. "His appreciation of old movies is . . . appealing." . . . **Lyons** thinks the book "offers a peekaboo autobiography. . . . The watery gravy of Vidalian contempt is ladeled" upon FDR, Truman, and Lincoln. "There are no positive values in the Vidal universe." . . . **Mendelsohn** finds the book "a charming, curmudgeonly collection of lectures. . . . Despite his bleak thoughts about present-day America, Vidal has a Puckish faith, and these essays are never dreary." . . . **Mitgang** remarks that the book "is unadulterated Vidal and a small gem." Most of his review is devoted to *Live from Golgotha.* . . . **Rosenbaum** states that "some of these highly subjective memories carry a certain novelistic density and suggestiveness." But Vidal "never settles down to . . . a disciplined, coherent program." The book is full of digressions, but Vidal "has plenty of interesting things to say." . . . **Schachtmann** declares that Vidal's points are presented "in a breezy manner that makes the reader wish the book were longer." . . . **Schuman** asserts that the book is characterized by "laziness and evasion." Vidal "treats every subject with equal superficiality." The book "is a catalogue of missed opportunities and fuzzy thinking." . . . **Sheed** finds merit in the book, but most of his review is devoted to *Live from Golgotha.* . . . **Simon**, in a long and hostile review, claims that Vidal is the real subject of the book. Vidal believes that his opinions are "of patent interest to all," as are his encounters with celebrities. Simon criticizes what he believes to be Vidal's factual errors and stylistic infelicites. "Still, Vidal is funny." . . . **Taylor** comments that the book "comes as close to autobiographical revelations as anything he's written so far." He adds: "the discourse tends to stray, but the epigrammatic personal style is far more inviting than a leaden treatise about film." . . . **Tubridy** feels that the book is "shamelessly padded." "To say that these essays are meandering is an understatement. . . . Vidal is the village atheist of the mass media age—clever, erudite, sardonic." . . . **Yardley** finds this "a peculiar and on the whole unsatisfactory book." He states that "it is so haphazard and self-indulgent that the reader comes to its end wondering what, precisely, is the point of it all." "Throughout, 'Screening History' has the air of the perfunctory and offhand."

48. *Live from Golgotha*
   a. Annichiarico, Mark. *Library Journal* 118, no. 3 (15 February 1993): 212.
   b. Batchelor, John Calvin. "Christianity, Vidal-Style." *Chicago Tribune Books* (6 September 1992): 3.
   c. Clifford, Andrew. "A Glimpse of the Future and Past Imperfect." *New Scientist* 137 (no. 1854 (2 January 1993): 42.
   d. Cumming, Laura. "The Gospel According to Gore Vidal." *Manchester Guardian Weekly* 147, no. 17 (25 October 1992): 25.
   e. Davidoff, Robert. "Revelations from Gore." *Advocate* no. 610 (25 August 1992): 81.
   f. Disch, Thomas M. "A Coke with Petronius." *Nation* 255, no. 16 (16 November 1992): 606–8.
   g. Drake, Robert. *Lambda Book Report* 3, no. 8 (January–February 1993): 35–36.
   h. Gates, David. "A Glitch in the Gospel." *Newsweek* 120, no. 9 (31 August 1992): 69.
   i. Graeber, Laurel. "New and Noteworthy Paperbacks." *New York Times Book Review* (3 October 1993): 36.
   j. Greeley, Andrew. "Is Nothing Sacred?" *Washington Post Book World* (20 September 1992): 2.
   k. Holt, Patricia. "We Interrupt This Era . . ." *San Francisco Chronicle* (30 August 1992): Sunday Review, p. 1.
   l. Humphrey, Clark. *Seattle Times* (18 October 1992): K6.
   m. Johnson, Diane. "Star." *New York Review of Books* 40, no. 7 (8 April 1993): 24–25.
   n. Kazin, Alfred. "Ecce Homo." *New Republic* 207, no. 15 (5 October 1992): 36–37.
   o. Kennedy, Douglas. "Further Revelations." *New Statesman and Society* 5 (no. 227) (6 November 1992): 50.

p.   King, Florence. "Vidal's Failed Satire Is Reader's 'Golgotha.'" *Washington Times* (11 October 1992): B7.

q.   Klinghoffer, David. "Rotten Fruit." *National Review* 44, no. 23 (30 November 1992): 50–52.

r.   Korn, Eric. "Meddling with Sacred History." *Times Literary Supplement* no. 4670 (2 October 1992): 20.

s.   Krist, Gary. "Hype." *Hudson Review* 46, no. 1 (Spring 1993): 239–46 (esp. 243–45).

t.   Lawson, Mark. "The Crucifixion as Crude Science Fiction." *Independent* (2 October 1992): 23.

u.   Lyons, Donald. "Gore Vidal on Gore Vidal, Al Gore and Jesus." *Wall Street Journal* (28 September 1992): A10.

v.   Malin, Irving. "A Fiendish Gospel." *Commonweal* 119, no. 19 (6 November 1992): 38–39.

w.   Mitgang, Herbert. "Books of The Times: One Affair with Movies and One with Sacrilege." *New York Times* (23 September 1992): C19.

x.   Moore, Caroline. "When the Saints Go Marching In Again." *Spectator* 269 (no. 8570) (10 October 1992): 32–33.

y.   Olson, Ray. *Booklist* 89, no. 2 (15 September 1992): 101.

z.   ———. *Booklist* 95, no. 3 (1 October 1998): 293.

aa.   Sage, Lorna. "Carnival at the Cross." *Observer* (London) no. 10485 (27 September 1992): 50.

bb.   Samway, Patrick H. *America* 168, no. 2 (23 January 1993): 18–19.

cc.   Schwarz, Walter. "Man and Myth—More Bad News for Believers." *Manchester Guardian Weekly* 147, no. 16 (18 October 1992): 28.

dd.   Sheed, Wilfrid. "Gore's Gospel." *New Yorker* 68 (26 October 1992): 130–34.

ee.   Taylor, Robert. "Gorefoolery." *Boston Globe* (6 September 1992): A10.

ff.   Thomas, D. M. "God's Own Media Event." *New York Times Book Review* (4 October 1992): 13.

gg.   Warner, Michael. "Crossover Dreams." *Village Voice* 37, no. 44 (2 November 1992): 67–68.

hh.   Weales, Gerald. "Jesus Who?" *Gettysburg Review* 6, no. 4 (Autumn 1993): 688–96.

ii.   Winnett, Scott. *Locus* 29, no. 5 (November 1992): 65.

jj.   [Unsigned.] *Lambda Book Report* 4, no. 2 (January–February 1994): 42.

kk.   [Unsigned.] *Publishers Weekly* 239, no. 44 (5 October 1992): 27–28.

Batchelor states that this is a "zesty new send-up of a novel about Chritianity." What Vidal achieves "is a serious argument about the birth and meaning of Christianity.... There is ... much to enjoy in watching Vidal pull the Gospels apart and rearrange them mischievously." ... **Clifford** finds this a "ruthless and obscene satire on modern American religion." The novel "is deadly dry, overwitty and incoherent.... Vidal himself comes across as a bit of a false Messiah." ... **Cumming** notes that Pat Robertson has denounced Vidal as the Antichrist, much to Vidal's delight. "The book's own viral infection is irksomely spoofish anachronism, consistent with the whole manipulative satire." ... **Davidoff** believes that the novel has "a wonderful premise and page after page of surprising, acute, and delightful writing." The book "calls to mind Voltaire, Mary Renault, Robert Graves, Swiftian satire, magic realism, and science fiction." ... **Disch** observes that Vidal "has produced the most sustained and programmatically outrageous blasphemy to tweak the nose of official piety since Monty Python's *Life of Brian*." But the book "does not come off well, overall, as satire." ... **Drake** feels that the book is a "mildly amusing, pseudo-intellectual science fiction romp through the core text of the Christian faith." But it says nothing new.... **Gates** claims that the book is Vidal's "most outrageous novel." Some readers will "find him entertaining company with his systematic subversion of every known value—except, of course, intelligence, wit and imagination." ... **Greeley**, a prominent Catholic, declares that "Vidal can fairly be charged with blasphemy." "It may well be said that Vidal's *jeu d'esprit* with blasphemy is witty, ingenious and frothy, with emphasis on the last adjective." ... **Holt** writes: "There's something to offend everyone in 'Live from Golgotha.' It's just too bad that much of it is boring." ... **Johnson** contends that in this novel Vidal "wants to undermine the Judeo-Christian tradition.... But the hope that he has done in monotheism ... seems literally optimistic." ... **Kazin** thinks that "though it tries to shock," the novel "is actually no dirtier than anything else these days." "The book is full of clowns, fools, and monsters, but its only villain is Jesus." . . . **Kennedy** asserts that Vidal "is gunning for the Rushdie prize for droll blasphemy." He finds much of the satire on target, and the novel "has a certain demented energy." . . . **King** claims that the book is a "hopelessly tangled, frequently incoherent and virtually impenetrable exercise in failed biblical satire. . . . The humor ranges from embarrassingly unfunny to just plain embarrassing." . . . In a malicious review, **Klinghoffer** remarks that Vidal "looks more and more like an oversized baby." The novel is "an occasion for him to indulge a range of perverse [sexual] fantasies," among which is the fact that "almost all the early Christians are depicted as ravenous gays." The novel "gives unrestrained expression" to Vidal's hostility to Jews. . . . **Korn** believes that the book is "a study of the inevitable and enjoyable corruption of texts and doctrines." The novel is "a romp, a Carry On Up To The Right Hand Of God . . . there's nobody sharper or more politically savvy than Gore Vidal." . . . **Krist**, in a multiple review, admits to not liking Vidal's "satiric comedies"; but this novel "strikes me as unworthy of Vidal." The satire in the novel "is all over the map. As a result, the book comes off as lame and sophomoric, hinting at a desperation to entertain at all costs." . . . **Lawson** concludes that the novel "can confidently be described as the most complicated American plot since Iran-Contra." But Vidal's satire misses its targets. "The prose works a single joke, though occasionally sweetly." . . . **Lyons** asserts that in this novel Vidal "indulges in some familiar impish fun. . . . But the tone turns nasty in the treatment of Jesus. We don't get salacity or blasphemy but political rancor." . . . **Malin** states that, like *Duluth* or *Myra Breckinridge*, the novel "is earthy, dirty, and obscene." "Although Vidal offers a *fiendish* gospel—a counter-gospel—he must be taken seriously." . . . **Mitgang** comments that the novel shows that "there is no denying Mr. Vidal's talent to entertain and outrage." The work "is too funny to be condemned simply as a blasphemous novel that should be added to the Vatican's Index of banned works and censored by the book police everywhere." . . . **Moore** feels that the elements of the novel are "tacky" but "are given surprising comic energy by Vidal." . . . **Sage** deems this is "a carnival *tour de force*. A travesty. . . . With manic cunning, Vidal spins a plot that twists and turns and brings things back to how they always were. . . . It's a marvellous specimen of parodic invention, anarchic and angry at the same time." . . . **Samway** finds the book "mostly adulterated whimsy." "In his attempt to shock and entice, Vidal has done just the opposite." The work is "a tired novel precisely because it lacks any genuine theological insight that would provide an axis upon which the novel could rotate." . . . **Schwarz**, in a multiple review, notes that the novel is "far more scabrous about the first Christians than the Satanic Verses is about Mohammed. . . . All this debunking probably leaves serious religion in better shape than before." . . . **Sheed** thinks the work exemplifies the death of the novel. It fails at blasphemy, and is "not satire but burlesque." . . . **Taylor** feels that the book's "zany spirit suggests Monty Python rather than Voltaire." He adds: "even at his most iconoclastic he provides genuine comic relief from the spectacular hypocrisy of our smiling public men." . . . **Thomas** concludes that the novel "is a wonderful idea," but the "savagery" of the satire "seems excessive, a product of the author's antireligious beliefs rather than a natural consequence of his artistic creation." It "might have been richer and more thought-provoking had it been written by someone less hostile to monotheistic religion." . . . **Warner** writes: "This is Vidal going mano a mano with monotheism. For about the umpteenth time." But the novel has "more than a whiff of th[e] crackpot grandeur" that makes *Myra Breckinridge* and *Myron* the best of Vidal. . . . **Weales**, reviewing the book along with A. N. Wilson's *Jesus*, states that Vidal's novel "does have a serious point to make." He studies Vidal's attitudes toward Christianity, especially in *Messiah* and *Julian*. But in this novel Vidal "is acting like a smartass college boy." . . . **Winnett** feels that "If Christianity-bashing is your cup of tea, this book is perfect. It's mean-spirited, ruthless, and very enjoyable."

49.   *The Decline and Fall of the American Empire*
     a.   Kazin, Alfred. "Ecce Homo." *New Republic* 207, no. 15 (5 October 1992): 36–37.
     b.   Solomon, Charles. "Paperbacks." *Los Angeles Times Book Review* (11 October 1992): 15.
     c.   Walton, David. *New York Times Book Review* (29 November 1992): 19.
     d.   Wulbert, Roland. *Booklist* 89, no. 5 (1 November 1992): 470.
     e.   [Unsigned.] *Lambda Book Report* 3, no. 8 (January–February 1993): 47.
     f.   [Unsigned.] *Publishers Weekly* 239, no. 43 (28 September 1992): 72.
     g.   [Unsigned.] "New in Paperback." *Washington Post Book World* (25 October 1992): 12.
     h.   [Unsigned.] "The Real Story Series." *Whole Earth Review* no. 87 (Fall 1995): 68.

Kazin feels that the essays show resentment against the Jews. . . . **Solomon** states that the book "reads like an 18th-Century political pamphlet." Vidal "draws a withering portrait of a government he perceives as utterly corrupt and in flagrant violation of the Constitution it's supposed to embody." . . . **Walton** believes that the book says what Vidal has been saying "for as long as anyone can remember."

50. *United States*

  a. Brookhiser, Richard. "The State of the Essay?" *New Criterion* 12, no. 1 (September 1993): 80–83.

  b. Burgess, Anthony. "Stating a Case for Gore." *Observer* (London) (10 October 1993): 17.

  c. Costes, Joseph. "Jaunty Jeremiah." *Chicago Tribune Books* (6 June 1993): 6–7.

  d. Dirda, Michael. "Gore Vidal: Views and Reviews." *Washington Post Book World* (30 May 1993): 1, 10. *Manchester Guardian Weekly* (18 July 1993): 20 (as "Partisan, Provocateur and Superior Essayist").

  e. Fraser, Brigitte. "The A-murrikin Way of Life." *Hungry Mind Review* no. 27 (Fall 1993): 5, 10–11.

  f. Hooper, Brad. *Booklist* 89, no. 16 (15 April 1993): 1488.

  g. Kaveney, Roz. "Gentleman's Relish." *New Statesman and Society* 6 (no. 273) (8 October 1993): 33–34.

  h. Keppler, Joseph F. *Seattle Times* (11 July 1993): F2.

  i. Koenig, Rhoda. "The Red, White, and True." *New York* 26, no. 22 (31 May 1993): 60, 63.

  j. Lanchester, John. "Styling." *London Review of Books* 15, no. 20 (21 October 1993): 12–13.

  k. Lewis, R. W. B. "Two Score of Gore." *New York Times Book Review* (20 June 1993): 11.

  l. Lezard, Nicholas. "Paperbacks." *Manchester Guardian Weekly* 151, no. 16 (16 October 1994): 28.

  m. MacIntyre, Ben. "The Vital Vidal." *Times Literary Supplement* no. 4727 (5 November 1993): 28.

  n. Packer, George. "Left Wing Snobs and the Style of Contempt." *Dissent* 43, no. 4 (Fall 1996): 123–28.

  o. Pells, Richard. *Journal of American History* 81, no. 2 (September 1994): 806–7.

  p. Raban, Jonathan. "Bolts from Mt. Olympus." *Los Angeles Times Book Review* (23 May 1993): 1, 7.

  q. Raphael, Frederic. "The Waspish Grandee." *Spectator* 271 (no. 8622) (9 October 1993): 31-32.

  r. Rogers, Michael. *Library Journal* 126, no. 14 (1 September 2001): 241.

  s. Self, David. "Paperbacks." *Times Educational Supplement* no. 4085 (14 October 1994): Part 2, p. 14.

  t. Shires, Nancy. *Library Journal* 118, no. 9 (15 May 1993): 69.

  u. [Unsigned.] *Booklist* 90, no. 10 (15 January 1994): 863.

  v. [Unsigned.] *Booklist* 90, no. 14 (15 March 1994): 1350.

  w. [Unsigned.] *Contemporary Review* 264, no. 2 (February 1994): 112.

  x. [Unsigned.] "The Puncturer." *Economist* 329 (no. 7836) (6 November 1993): 121–22.

  y. [Unsigned.] *Lambda Book Report* 3, no. 12 (September–October 1993): 47.

  z. [Unsigned.] "Paperbacks." *Observer* (London) (25 September 1994): 22.

  aa. [Unsigned.] *Publishers Weekly* 240, no. 14 (15 April 1993): 54.

  bb. [Unsigned.] *Publishers Weekly* 240, no. 44 (1 November 1993): 48.

  cc. [Unsigned.] *Rapport* 17 (May 1993): 10.

  dd. [Unsigned.] *San Francisco Review* 21, no. 5 (September–October 1996): 48.

Brookhiser, in a predictably hostile review, begins by summarizing Vidal's political views. But Vidal really "doesn't know very much." "When Vidal exerts himself, he rises to the average"; but the literary essays are above average. . . . **Burgess** feels that "Vidal's essays go back to the nineteenth century of Bagehot, Carlyle, even Macaulay, in respect of leisurely probing, pleasing irrelevance, anecdotalism. . . . Vidal's literary essays are much in the [Edmund] Wilsonian mode. They inform before they judge. . . . This volume has a considerable importance." . . . **Costes** emphasizes Vidal's resemblance to Henry Adams. For Vidal, Americans' puritanical views of sex have engendered a corresponding militancy by gays and others. Vidal is an "increasingly pessimistic, though ever-jaunty, Jeremiah" in regard to American politics. The literary section of the volume "contains some of the shrewdest and most useful assessments of literary reputations to be found between two covers." . . . **Dirda** believes that the volume is "spangled with glorious oldies . . . frequently unorthodox views of American presidents . . . and, best of all, a series of painstaking and affectionate introductions to underappreciated writers." "Vidal is himself . . . nothing less than an old-fashioned bookman. . . . Gore Vidal is the master-essayist of our age." . . . **Fraser**, in an enthusiastic review, writes that Vidal is "possessed of an uncommonly sound mind, a cold eye, and a murderous wit." His essays "exemplify the power of negative thinking." Vidal is a cross between H. L. Mencken and Henry James. He "has taken upon himself the task of tireless nag and civic conscience of American self-adulation." . . . **Kaveney** observes that Vidal is "America's greatest living belle-lettriste/agitator." "No one should forget that he has, for the past 40 years, been a powerful and witty force on the side of Us against Them." . . . **Koenig** praises Vidal for his "erudition, his uncompromising wit, and the way he dramatically throws out a poetic flourish as the cape swooshes over his exit." . . . **Lanchester**, in a multiple review, states that Vidal's essays "are unmistakably a performance—more of a self-celebration than a self-interrogation, and none the worse for that." Vidal reveals "a highly unusual degree of freedom from received ideas, especially from standard wisdoms about politics and from the moral axes of Judeo-Christianity." . . . **Lewis** contends that the essays are "animated by Mr. Vidal's sweeping, grasping prose style, with its mix of the elegant and the vernacular." He has praise for the literary essays on British writers and on such Americans as Howells, Dawn Powell, and Auchincloss. Of the essays on politics and sex, Vidal "writes more intelligently, knowingly, angrily, compassionately, entertainingly and downright smartly than anyone else around." But the collection "is a good deal too long." . . . **MacIntyre** states that Vidal's essays are "the vital Vidal, full of brio and braggadocio, sharply learned, wittily argued and beautifully written. . . . He is a supreme stylist, almost incapable of an inelegant sentence, an inapt allusion or a spongy metaphor." But MacIntyre doesn't know what Vidal's "beliefs and convictions" are. Vidal is also "rather a snob." . . . **Packer**, reviewing the book along with *Palimpsest* and two books by Lewis Lapham, concludes that they "show the corrosions of political contempt at work on an elegant and learned mind." The "note of apocalyptic ennui keeps intruding on his later essays whenever they turn from history the present." . . . **Pells** maintains that "the collection is a testimonial to Vidal's wit and remarkable erudition." Vidal's essays "are far livelier and often more personal than his novels." Vidal models himself on Henry Adams in emphasizing "the decline of the American republic—a spectacle of loss and decay he appears . . . to take as a personal affront." . . . **Raban** asserts that the volume "is like a lively picaresque novel in reverse," with Vidal as a character. He praises the satirical sting of Vidal's prose: "it is the style of a man who has spent a lifetime suffering fools unglady." But Vidal's acerbity has rendered him merely "outrageous," and thereby easily dismissed. But "Vidal is fearless and cogent." . . . **Raphael** declares that "there is a feeling of tiredness, afterthought, repetition" in the essays, but he admires the "sheer dogged consistency of his radicalism." . . . The relatively brief ***Contemporary Review*** review remarks that "This is a lifetime work from a writer of enormous intelligence, wit and style." . . . The ***Economist*** review finds this "a rich, almost dangerously digestible feast." Vidal's tastes are both American and European, but "he can be acerbic" when treating American writers. Vidal's writing is "usually interesting and intelligent," and also "refreshingly human." The unifying feature of the volume is "a fascination with greatness."

51.   *The City and the Pillar and Seven Early Stories*
      a.   Reynolds, Susan Salter. "In Brief." *Los Angeles Times Book Review* (23 July 1995): 6.
      b.   Schwendener, Peter. "Gore Vidal Revisited." *Chicago Tribune Books* (6 August 1995): 6.
      c.   [Unsigned.] *Lambda Book Report* 4, no. 12 (September–October 1995): 44.

Reynolds writes: "Back in 1948, [*The City and the Pillar*] may well have been a battering ram of a book." The short stories "have much more power." . . . **Schwendener** discusses Vidal's revision of *The City and the Pillar*. "The novel succeeds because it is poised between two very different consciousnesses that support each other . . . One is frequently aware of Vidal the moralist, to whom the social world, gay as well as straight, is mostly a brittle façade." There is no discussion of the short stories.

52.   *Palimpsest*
      a.   Amis, Martin. "A Talent to Abuse." *Sunday Times* (London) (22 October 1995): Sec.
           7, pp. 1–2. In Amis's *The War against Cliché: Essays and Reviews, 1971–2000*.
           London: Jonathan Cape, 2001, pp. 279–83 (as "Vidal's Mirror").

b. Bayley, John. "Class Act." *New York Review of Books* 44, no. 8 (15 May 1997): 45–48. In Bayley's *The Power of Delight: A Lifetime in Literature: Essays 1962–2002.* Ed. Les Carey. London: Duckworth, 2005, pp. 644–54.

c. Beschloss, Michael. "Washington Memoirs." *Washington Post Book World* (10 December 1995): 9.

d. Brogan, Hugh. "Private Faces, Public Places." *New Statesman and Society* 8 (no. 376): (27 October 1995): 44.

e. Carson, Tom. "Vidal Statistics." *Village Voice* 40, no. 48 (28 November 1995): 73–75.

f. Fialkoff, Francine. *Library Journal* 120, no. 18 (1 November 1995): 76.

g. Graeber, Laurel. "New and Noteworthy Paperbacks." *New York Times Book Review* (29 September 1996): 32.

h. Hillier, Bevis. "He Has Not Lived in Vain." *Spectator* 275 (no. 8727) (14 October 1995): 39–40.

i. Hitchens, Christopher. "After-Time." *London Review of Books* 17, no. 20 (19 October 1995): 8–9. In Hitchens's *Unacknowledged Legislation: Writers in the Public Sphere.* London: Verso, 2000, pp. 72–80.

j. King, Florence. "Crashing Gore." *National Review* 47, no. 25 (31 December 1995): 41–42.

k. Kroll, Jack. "Presidential Aspirations." *Newsweek* 126, no. 15 (9 October 1995): 82.

l. LaHood, Marvin J. *World Literature Today* 70, no. 3 (Summer 1996): 704.

m. Lehmann-Haupt, Christopher. "Books of The Times: Pithy Recollections and Hints of Revenge." *New York Times* (5 October 1995): C21. *International Herald Tribune* (20 October 1995): 11 (untitled).

n. Levin, Bernard. "A Butterfly Who Stings Like a Bee." *Times* (London) (26 October 1995): 41.

o. McCourt, James. "Isn't It Romantic?" *Los Angeles Times Book Review* (1 October 1995): 2, 9.

p. Mallon, Thomas. "The Best Man." *GQ* 65, no. 11 (November 1995): 72, 74, 76. In Mallon's *In Fact: Essays on Writers and Writing.* New York: Pantheon, 2001, pp. 40–45.

q. Miller, Karl. "The Cheerful Leper-Bell." *Times Literary Supplement* no. 4829 (20 October 1995): 7–8.

r. Mitzel[, John]. "The Book He Was Never Going to Write." *Harvard Gay and Lesbian Review* 3, no. 1 (Winter 1996): 41–42.

s. Ott, Bill. *Booklist* 92, no. 5 (1 November 1995): 434.

t. Packer, George. "Left-Wing Snobs and the Style of Contempt." *Dissent* 43, no. 4 (Fall 1996): 123–28.

u. Shively, Charley. "The Seductions of Autobiography." *Journal of Homosexuality* 37, no. 1 (1999): 146–51.

v. Simon, John. "What Gore Remembers." *New Criterion* 14, no. 4 (December 1995): 18–27.

w. Solomon, Charles. "Paperbacks." *Los Angeles Times Book Review* (8 September 1996): 11.

x. Stengel, Richard. "Unsentimental Journey." *Time* 146, no. 15 (9 October 1995): 76.

y. Taylor, Robert. "A Gossipy Vidal Offers Glimpse Beneath Veneer." *Boston Globe* (17 October 1995): 59.

z. Vaill, Amanda. "Gore Vidal's Mirror-like Memoir." *Chicago Tribune Books* (15 October 1995): 3.

aa. Vincent, David. "Paperbacks." *Observer* (London) (7 January 2001): 20.

bb. Weinberg, Steve. "True Lies." *American Book Review* 17, no. 3 (February–March 1996): 14.

cc. Weinberger, J. K. *Choice* 33, no. 7 (March 1996): 1138.

dd. Wolcott, James. "Gore unto Himself." *Observer* (London) (15 October 1995): 14.

ee. Wood, Michael. "Selective Memory." *New York Times Book Review* (8 October 1995): 7.

ff. Yardley, Jonathan. "The World, the Flesh and Vidal." *Washington Post Book World* (8 October 1995): 3.

gg. [Unsigned.] *Publishers Weekly* 243, no. 30 (22 July 1996): 235.

Bayley writes: "Brought so fascinatingly close to us, the Vidal world seems both exotic and domestic, glitzy and homely, and is presented with a deft economy that is itself highly droll." Moreover, "the reader feels himself becoming one with the characters in the book: a sure sign of a literary master at work." Bayley praises the portraits of T. P. Gore and Jimmie Trimble. "Every page of *Palimpsest* has some pleasurable absurdity, usually a good-natured one, that stays in the memory, and often with an aroma of poetry about it." . . . **Brogan** finds the work "a narrative of unflagging brilliance," full of entertaining stories and lively wit. . . . **Carson** feels that Vidal "dons the mask of candor for this book." Jimmie Trimble's "early death is made acutely poignant." The portrait of Jackie Kennedy is affecting. . . . **Hillier**, in a lengthy and favorable review, states that Vidal is (in his own words) an "objective narcissist"; "he is a vain man with a lot to be vain about." Hillier finds Vidal's candor about sex refreshing. . . . **Hitchens**, in a lengthy review, notes that the memoir makes explicit what had been hinted in previous works, in regard to Vidal's love of Jimmie Trimble and other issues. "We come to understand how divided a self he is; not just as between love and death but as between literature and politics, America and the world, the ancient and the modern, the sacred and the profane." The best passages are those that discuss the Kennedys. . . . In a predictably snide review, **King** claims that Vidal is "a misanthrope who knows everybody." The book is full of name-dropping, and the reader is left "with a picture of a worn-out Regency buck taking the waters at a German spa." . . . **Kroll** sees the book as a kind of "highbrow 'Lifestyles of the Rich and Famous'" in its name-dropping. "Behind its vivacity, 'Palimpsest' is a stoic confession of a brilliant but unfulfilled spirit." . . . **LaHood** deems this a "fascinating memoir" that swings "from a poignant humanity to a caustic cynicism." Vidal's memories are "informative, often delightful, and utterly fascinating." Vidal reveals a keen sense of place. "*Palimpsest* is Gore Vidal's testament to self-knowledge." . . . **Lehmann-Haupt** observes that "much cruelty is present . . . on the author's part, in varying degrees, toward most of the people he has ever known," but "none of it is gratuitous." Vidal, however, has a "two-dimensional view of politics." "Although this memoir appears to be crowded with people, they are merely shadows of the author's experience." . . . **Levin** remarks that, in spite of his air of being a "flaneur," Vidal reveals a more serious side: "we find him warm and generous among the poisoned arrows he also flings." . . . **McCourt** states: "I dislike most of 'Palimpsest''s cast of 'power people,'" but he likes the "great romance of his life" with Jimmie Trimble. "Although I believe that Gore Vidal often goes awry, I think he never deliberately lies, and that distinction is worth making." . . . **Mallon** discusses Vidal's relations to Jimmie Trimble ("the only real passion of Vidal's life"), T. P. Gore, the Kennedys, and his political views. . . . **Miller** provides a summary of Vidal's career. "The world is Gore's bad oyster. But you would have to be one of his worst enemies to deny that *Palimpsest* is packed with funny stories—some of them friendly." . . . **Mitzel** writes: "Vidal is very good on parts concerning his family," especially his grandfather and father. But Vidal is in fact "*not* the subject of his work." . . . **Ott**'s relatively brief review notes: "We all spend some of our most pleasurable hours talking about other people; Vidal makes that fundamental human activity into a minor art form." . . . **Packer**, focusing chiefly on *United States,* states that the memoir "puts its own spin on mendacity." . . . **Shively**, reviewing the book along with Alan Helms's *Young Man from the Provinces,* finds that "Vidal's memory gets right what matters most partly because he knows many worlds intimately." Shively discusses the homosexual passages in the book. . . . **Simon**, in an immense but petty and sniping review, claims that the book is "awesome as a catty gossip column." He speaks of Vidal's relations with himself and wonders: "How concerned *is* Vidal with the truth?" He accuses Vidal of "cavalier sloppiness about English and other tongues," discusses Vidal's relations with other writers (especially Jack Kerouac) and with the Kennedys, studies Vidal's attitudes toward sex, and ponders his relations with Howard Austen and Jimmie Trimble. . . . **Stengel** comments that Vidal is "Courtly but gossipy, chummy but not overfamiliar." The book "lacks the sharp, confident voice of his essays." . . . **Taylor** believes that the tone of the memoir "is amusing and worldly and depends to a large extent on name-dropping; it is also extremely well written, perhaps overly so, since style becomes a device for keeping potentially destructive emotions at bay." . . . **Vaill** declares that Vidal would have preferred not to have met most of the people in his life: "Vidal's portraits of them are frequently as devastating as they are brief. . . . The problem is that these acid-etched cameos, entertaining as they are, are so often arranged for artful effect around the central figure of the author." . . . **Weinberg** asserts that Vidal's memoir is not meant to be factually accurate. But it "is often accurate, susprisingly thorough . . . and breathtakingly original." He discusses Vidal's passages on the Kennedys. The scenes about Jimmie Trimble "are oddly touching in a memoir that is so often bloodless." . . . **Weinberger** finds the work a "loosely structured memoir charged with his iconoclastic wit. . . . Disappointing for students of literature, however, is Vidal's lack of reflection on his development as a writer." . . . **Wolcott** believes that the title indicates that "memory isn't a filing-cabinet with every person and event neatly labelled, but a puzzle board of jumbled impressions and overlapping images." The book "never sinks into mystification; it projects a cool steady objective light." It resembles *Two Sisters.* Wolcott discusses Vidal's sexual experiences and relations with Bobby Kennedy. "It is Vidal's comic timing . . . which keeps *Palimpsest* from going stale." . . . **Wood** contends that the book a "personal memoir . . . but it is also, for all its tilts and malice and wonderful jokes, an oddly disinterested work." He appreciates the portraits of Jack Kerouac and Tennessee Williams. . . . **Yardley** maintains that this "may well be the best book in his long, erratic and interesting career." The story is told "with Vidal's customary fluidity but with his malicious, or catty, side somewhat subdued."

53. *Virgin Islands*
   a. Cohen, Nick. "Vidal's Statistics." *Observer* (London) (31 August 1997): 14.
   b. Kennedy, Douglas. "A One-Man Institution." *Times* (London) (8 October 1998): 44.
   c. Raphael, Frederic. "His Cutting Edge." *Sunday Times* (London) (10 August 1997): Sec. 8, p. 4.

Cohen feels that Vidal is "the only American essayist good enough to reach a world audience." "There is a pleasure, which is not entirely malicious, in watching him fillet the bigots of the American right, time-serving academics, the powerful, corrupt, lazy and compromised. Vidal's combination of learning, wit and disdain gets into your blood." . . . **Douglas** believes that Vidal is "the best essayist alive today." In this volume he does a "demolition job" on Harry S Truman and John Updike. . . . **Raphael** notes that, "wild and woolworthy as some of these pieces are, Vidal is an irreplaceable voice when it comes to sticking it to opinions received from lofty addresses."

54. *The Smithsonian Institution*
   a. Allen, Brooke. "Creating a Führer." *New Criterion* 16, no. 9 (May 1998): 55–59 (esp. 55–57).
   b. Allen, Bruce. "A Washington Original Visits a Washington 'Institution.'" *Washington Times* (8 March 1998): B8.
   c. Bahr, David. "If Only . . ." *Advocate* no. 757 (14 April 1998): 74.
   d. Benfey, Christopher. "Dead Presidents Society." *New York Times Book Review* (1 March 1998): 8.
   e. Birkerts, Sven. "In Camp with History." *Boston Globe* (8 March 1998): E1.
   f. Bowman, James. "The Museum of Mischief and Mockery." *Wall Street Journal* (27 February 1998): A16.
   g. Butterworth, Alex. "Paperbacks." *Observer* (London) (10 October 1999): 15.
   h. Deveson, Tom. "Metaphysical Jerks." *Sunday Times* (London) (4 October 1998): Sec. 8, p. 8.
   i. Friedman, Vanessa V. *Entertainment Weekly* no. 424 (27 March 1998): 65.
   j. Hall, Linda. "The Writes of Spring." *New York* 31, no. 2 (19 January 1998): 83.
   k. Hitchens, Christopher. "The Cosmopolitan Man." *New York Review of Books* 46, no. 7 (22 April 1999): 29–32. In Hitchens's *Unacknowledged Legislation: Writers in the Public Sphere.* London: Verso, 2000, pp. 59–71.
   l. Hooper, Brad. *Booklist* 94, no. 11 (1 February 1998): 877.
   m. Kennedy, Douglas. "A One-Man Institution." *Times* (London) 8 October 1998): 44.
   n. Kloszewski, Marc A. *Library Journal* 123, no. 4 (1 March 1998): 130.
   o. LaHood, Marvin J. *World Literature Today* 74, no. 1 (Winter 2000): 174.
   p. Lehmann-Haupt, Christopher. "Books of The Times: Think History's Dull? Not Mrs. Grover Cleveland." *New York Times* (19 March 1998): E9.
   q. Marr, Andrew. "Gore and Peace." *Observer* (London) (11 October 1998): 13.
   r. Miller, Keith. "American Prodities." *Times Literary Supplement* no. 4985 (16 October 1998): 22.
   s. Novak, Ralph. *People* 49, no. 13 (6 April 1998): 34, 36.
   t. Rubin, Merle. "A Wrinkle in Time." *Los Angeles Times Book Review* (15 March 1998): 6.

u. Taylor, D. J. "High Jinks and Low Jokes in Never-Land." *Spectator* 281 (no. 8881) (24 October 1998): 54.

v. Veale, Scott. "New and Noteworthy Paperbacks." *New York Times Book Review* (24 October 1999): 48.

w. Woodcock, Susan H. *School Library Journal* 44, no. 7 (July 1998): 114.

x. [Unsigned.] *Kirkus Reviews* 66, no. 2 (15 January 1998): 79.

y. [Unsigned.] "Bookcase." *New Scientist* 160 (no. 2164) (12 December 1998): 55.

z. [Unsigned.] *Publishers Weekly* 245, no. 5 (2 February 1998): 82.

aa. [Unsigned.] "Notes on Current Books." *Virginia Quarterly Review* 74, no. 3 (Summer 1998): 96.

Brooke Allen assesses the book as "respectable if frequently silly." Vidal's "slight, rather goofy plot nearly gets buried under a morass of amateurish scientific speculation on the nature of time and other mysteries." The novel "never pretends to be much more than a facetious play on American politics and history." . . . **Bruce Allen** feels that the novel is "a rich sampling of [Vidal's] varied career's themes and interests." The protagonist, T., reflects "a quintessentially Vidalian distrust of history." . . . **Bahr** states that the novel is "doused with Vidal's rambling trademark wit." The book "is a succession of cartoonish skits disguised as a narrative." . . . **Benfey** finds the novel "a strange confection of science fiction, historical costume romance, political satire and veiled autobiography." It is a "light entertainment to while away a winter weekend." . . . **Birkerts** claims that the "characters are flat to the point of transparency and their encounters cannot begin to animate the plot." The novel is too campy to take seriously. . . . **Bowman** observes that Vidal's taste for science fiction "has had the unfortunate effect of liberating all his worst artistic impulses. . . . The only real point to the tedious tale of T is to serve as a platform for Mr. Vidal's occasionally amusing sallies on the subject of American history." . . . **Deveson** writes: "Among all the metaphysical fun, Vidal is making thoughtful and plausible observations about the promises and failures of history." The book "has great charm and readability." . . . **Hitchens**'s review is more a critical essay. He asserts that "Not the least achievement of this apparently unstrenuous work is the way that it mobilizes several dimensions of space and time without losing its narrative thread." The novel "revisits and refines seveal Vidalian tropes." . . . **Kennedy** declares that this novel "could probably be best described as a subversive vaudeville." It is "pretty damn inventive," but a serious message lurks under the playfulness. . . . **LaHood** notes that Vidal's "lifelong knowledge of and lifelong interest in American history add substance to the novel." But, as a whole, the work is thin. . . . **Lehmann-Haupt** states: "Despite its seeming zaniness," the novel "is appealing in several ways. . . . For all the novel's witty arabesques of plot, T.'s passion to make himself whole is what finally lends the story its substance." . . . **Marr**, referring to the work as a "strange little novel," maintains that it is "a jeu d'esprit, an iridescent bubble of a book. . . . The novelist gleefully rewrites history and fights old battles throughout." It is "a silly book that is strictly for grown-ups." . . . **Miller** provides a plot summary. Vidal "is not gravely preoccupied with plausibility"; he "is more excited about the poor man's time machine, history. . . . Vidal appreciates that hilarity and bewilderment are entirely appropriate responses to the ridiculous, appalling events at the heart of our century." . . . **Novak** contends that "Vidal spins this yarn glibly. It moves along . . . but the novel ends in a flurry of time-space mumbo-jumbo." . . . **Rubin** provides a survey of Vidal's career, stating that he is underappreciated as a novelist. "Vidal is a mordant satirist of American culture, but . . . his overriding aim—and strength—is clarity." The novel "is the *dernier cri* of many of the themes, tendencies and obsessions found in his previous work. . . . In a bad way, this is a very personal book. . . . By some mysterious defect of his usually fertile imagination, Vidal has managed to produce a book that is silly without being entertaining, faintly offensive without being provocative." . . . **Taylor** deems the novel "wretched": Vidal "imparts only a sort of sophisticated smirking" to the subject matter. . . . **Woodcock**, in a relatively brief review, finds the novel a "disjointed, lightweight page-turner." But it is "an enjoyable introduction to Vidal as well as enjoyable historical fiction."

55. *The American Presidency*

a. Thorpe, Peter. *Bloomsbury Review* 19, no. 2 (March/April 1999): 19.

b. [Unsigned.] *Kirkus Reviews* 66, no. 19 (1 October 1998): 1444.

c. [Unsigned.] *Publishers Weekly* 245, no. 43 (26 October 1998): 58.

d. [Unsigned.] "Who Owns the US?" *Whole Earth Review* no. 70 (Spring 1991): 27.

Thorpe believes that Vidal is presenting "a series of urbane satirical portraits" of the presidents. "A probable irony in this author's writings—and he is one of the greatest satirists of the century—is that he desperately needs the modern-day corruption, the ongoing evil in order to be a satirist in the first place." . . . The *Whole Earth Review* review, published years before the book appeared and based on an advance copy, titles the book *Who Owns the US?* The review consists mostly of extracts from the book.

56.   *The Essential Gore Vidal*
    a.   Brownrigg, Sylvia. "Witness for the Prosecution." *Times Literary Supplement* no. 5013 (30 April 1999): 26.
    b.   Caldwell, Christopher. "Hard-Core Gore." *National Review* 51, no. 8 (3 May 1999): 51–52.
    c.   Henderson, David W. *Library Journal* 124, no. 1 (January 1999): 97.
    d.   Hitchens, Christopher. "The Cosmopolitan Man." *New York Review of Books* 46, no. 7 (22 April 1999): 29–32.
    e.   Kirn, Walter. "Gore Text." *New York* 32, no. 1 (11 January 1999): 55–56.
    f.   Mattick, Paul. "Inventing History." *New York Times Book Review* (14 February 1999): 13.
    g.   Murphy, Rex. "Gore Vidal: A Writer Not Quite for the Ages." *Globe and Mail* (Toronto) (13 March 1999): D12.
    h.   Plunket, Robert. "Vital Vidal." *Advocate* no. 782 (30 March 1999): 76–77.
    i.   Sutherland, John. "All Blood and Gore." *Sunday Times* (London) (21 February 1999): Sec. 8, p. 6.
    j.   Wagner, Erica. "A Vast Monument to Plain Good Sense." *Times* (London) 11 February 1999): 38.
    k.   [Unsigned.] *Kirkus Reviews* 66, no. 24 (15 December 1998): 1760.
    l.   [Unsigned.] *Publishers Weekly* 245, no. 48 (30 November 1998): 58.

Brownrigg believes that the volume "provides an adventurous tour around the busy mind and improbable imagination of this gifted, incisive autodidact." But Fred Kaplan's commentary is "fairly pedestrian." On *Myra Breckinridge:* "Myra may be unreal, but she has a surreal presence and life force unmatched by Vidal's more plausible characters." Vidal "has always written . . . with a sense of the many imminent endings that face us." . . . **Caldwell** feels that Vidal's "contrarian turn of mind has served him well in his historical novels"; but his "great liability as a writer is that his worldview has only two dimensions: power and hate." In his essays "hate and contrariety get in the way of the spirit of inquiry." The essays are also filled with bad faith. . . . **Hitchens** claims that Fred Kaplan's "choices are excellently made, and partitioned by well-wrought passages of introduction from both editor and author." *Julian* "is his literary masterpiece, in my opinion." There is a lengthy discussion of Vidal's views on sex and on political isolationism. . . . **Kirn** declares that the book "seems less the product of a single writer circumscribed by space and time than the greatest hits of a score of authors existing on some cultural astral plane." He surveys Vidal's career as novelist and essayist. Vidal's "subject is always people, and his gift is to treat all of them, even dead near-deities, as peers." . . . **Mattick** praises Fred Kaplan's editing, saying that he has picked essays that illuminate Vidal's own fiction. He feels that *Julian* is "the best key to Vidal's productive contradictions." . . . **Murphy** admits that Vidal is both a writer and a "presence," but questions whether he is really "essential." He may have made a "dangerous barter" by becoming a celebrity. *Myra Breckinridge* is already dated. Vidal's essays are never uninteresting, but "he can be an irredeemable bore when he mounts one of his overstuffed hobby horses." . . . **Plunket** contends that Vidal's greatest accomplishment is that "he's always been right." Most reviewers have not noticed "Vidal's magnificent obsession with the male butt." The essays "are heaven indeed." . . . Wagner feels that Vidal is "serious but never sententious and—rare quality—unafraid to say what he thinks." But Kaplan's selections are open to question, although he has done a good job in choosing the essays. . . . **Sutherland** writes: "Outrageous and preposterous as he incorrigibly is, Vidal has been right surprisingly often."

57.   *Sexually Speaking*
    a.   Anton, Saul. *Salon.com* (20 August 1999).
    b.   Bailey, Paul. "Live and Let Live." *Sunday Times* (London) (12 August 2001): Sec. 9, p. 41.
    c.   Beard, William Randall. *Counterpoise* 4, no. 3 (July 2000): 51.

    d.   Murray, Douglas. "An Editor's Frustrating Titillation." *Spectator* 287 (no. 9031) (8 September 2001): 37.

    e.   Sheiner, Marcy. *Book* no. 6 (September–October 1999): 88.

    f.   Showalter, Elaine. "I Love Drag." *New Statesman* 130 (no. 4549) (6 August 2001): 40–41.

    g.   Smith, Patrick. "'Our' Gide?" *Nation* 269, no. 20 (13 December 1999): 22–25.

    h.   Woods, Gregory. *Times Literary Supplement* no. 5140 (5 October 2001): 34.

Anton's review is largely a summary of Vidal's views on sex, noting that his absorption of classical culture was important in their development. . . . **Bailey** speaks of the historical importance of Vidal's essays in breaking down the "bigotry" of the 1970s and 1980s in regard to sex. "Vidal is at elegant pains in his critical writings to emphasise the lasting importance of individual values." But the editing of the collection is poor. . . . **Beard** finds the book "highly entertaining. What it lacks in breadth, it makes up for in a unique and twisted perspective . . . this is sophisticated writing from a man who loves language and knows how to use it." . . . **Murray** believes that although "there is no doubting the joy of reading Gore Vidal at his finest," the book is filled with repetitive and inessential pieces. . . . **Sheiner**'s brief review notes: "Acerbic wit is Vidal's hallmark . . . even when you disagree with Vidal, he is always entertaining and provocative." . . . **Showalter** summarizes Vidal's views on sex but finds them dated, failing to take cognizance of AIDS, gay marriage, and other recent developments. . . . **Smith**, reviewing the book along with Fred Kaplan's biography, notes that "Vidal has been salient on human sexuality from his earliest days in print." But the book seems to be designed to identify Vidal as a "gay writer," which he is not. . . . **Woods** states that the essays "are considerably diminished by their removal from Vidal's lifelong attack on the American empire." The book is poorly edited, but it "is inevitably worth reading."

58.   *The Golden Age*

    a.   Allen, Bruce. "Washington's Poisonous Games: Gore Vidal Concludes His Cycle." *Washington Times* (8 October 2000): B8.

    b.   Baker, Kevin. "The World According to Gore." *Los Angeles Times Book Review* (17 September 2000): 3–4.

    c.   Barnacle, Hugh. "Novel of the Week." *New Statesman* (no. 4511) (6 November 2000): 52.

    d.   Barnes, Steve. *Wall Street Journal* (22 September 2000): W13.

    e.   Bernhard, Brendan. "Gore Vidal Skewers America's Elite of the '30s and '40s." *San Francisco Chronicle* (12 November 2000): Sunday Review, p. 5.

    f.   Carlevale, Edmund. "Nuggets Fuel Vidal's 'Golden Age.'" *Boston Globe* (29 October 2000): C3.

    g.   Charles, Ron. "Gore Vidal Concludes His Chronicle of America." *Christian Science Monitor* (21 September 2000): 17.

    h.   Fasman, Jonathan. "A Servant Problem." *Times Literary Supplement* no. 5091 (27 October 2000): 22.

    i.   Gray, Paul. "The World According to Gore." *Time* 156, no. 13 (25 September 2000): 92, 94.

    j.   Henderson, David W. *Library Journal* 125, no. 13 (August 2000): 163.

    k.   Hooper, Brad. *Booklist* 96, no. 21 (July 2000): 1977.

    l.   ———. *Booklist* 97, no. 15 (1 April 2001): 1452.

    m.   Johnson, Diane. "The Best Men?" *New York Review of Books* 47, no. 16 (19 October 2000): 21–22.

    n.   Kemp, Peter. "Delusions of Grandeur." *Sunday Times* (London) (22 October 2000): Sec. 9, p. 47.

    o.   Klepp, L. S. "A Gorey Story." *Entertainment Weekly* no. 564 (20 October 2000): 71.

    p.   LaHood, Marvin J. *World Literature Today* 75, no. 2 (Spring 2001): 335.

    q.   Leader, Zachary. "No Accident." *London Review of Books* 23, no. 12 (21 June 2001): 27–29.

    r.   MacLeish, Roderick. "Washington Confidential." *Washington Post Book World* (1 October 2000): 5.

s.   Maunsell, Jerome Boyd. "Paperback Fiction." *Times* (London) (5 January 2002): Play, p. 14.

t.   Minzesheimer, Bob. "Gore Vidal's Twist on History Is Just a Scandal." *USA Today* (5 October 2000): 6D.

u.   Ott, Bill. "Political Bios for the Apolitical." *American Libraries* 33, no. 11 (December 2002): 73.

v.   Pitt, David. "Listen Up!" *Globe and Mail* (Toronto) (25 November 2000): D40–41.

w.   Powers, Katherine A. "Audio Books." *Washington Post Book World* (10 December 2000): 12.

x.   Pritchard, William H. "Fiction Chronicle." *Hudson Review* 54, no. 2 (Summer 2001): 313–21 (esp. 320–21).

y.   Sheldon, Michael. "Bite the Hand." *Daily Telegraph* (London) (25 November 2000): 4.

z.   Sullivan, Andrew. "The Greatest Generation (Revised)." *New York Times Book Review* (1 October 2000): 14–15.

aa. Veale, Scott. "New and Noteworthy Paperbacks." *New York Times Book Review* (16 September 2001): 32.

bb. [Unsigned.] *Booklist* 97, nos. 9/10 (1–15 January 2001): 858.

cc. [Unsigned.] *Kirkus Reviews* 68, no. 14 (15 July 2000): 987–88.

dd. [Unsigned.] *New Yorker* 76 (30 October 2000): 99.

ee. [Unsigned.] *Publishers Weekly* 247, no. 30 (24 July 2000): 65.

ff. [Unsigned.] *Publishers Weekly* 247, no. 40 (2 October 2000): 45–46.

Allen writes: "Mr. Vidal loves American politics and politicians the way Jacobean dramatists loved court intrigues, poisonings and declamatory operatic demises." The plot is thin, but the book is carried along by "comic energy." . . . **Baker** feels that the novel fails because of Vidal's "decision to subordinate everything to a dubious political polemic." Vidal has become addicted to conspiracy theories, which "squeeze all the life" out of the novel. Baker maintains that Vidal's theory that FDR incited the Japanese to attack Pearl Harbor is false. . . . **Barnacle** believes the novel offers "an atmosphere of insider gossip, articulated and animated in style." . . . **Barnes** states: "The depiction of Franklin and Eleanor Roosevelt . . . is lively and compelling," as is that of Truman. But the fictional characters do not come off so well. The book is "one of the more lackluster entries in this major series of novels." . . . **Bernhard** notes that the subject of the book is "America's transformation from a country at least occasionally content to mind its own business" into an aggressive world empire. The characters are largely flat except when they have interesting views to express. . . . **Carlevale** writes: "Vidal is at the top of his talent in describing how the American imperialists have exploited the bogey of communism as a means to building the empire." But the book is often static, and the characters struggle to carry the plot forward. . . . **Charles** observes that the series of historical novels "ends not with a bang, but a whimper." The novel comes close to being "a series of lectures." The action seems to be at a remove. At the end "Vidal drops the wooden masks entirely and lectures to us directly." . . . **Fasman** notes: "At times, *The Golden Age* reads less like a novel than an extended lecture delivered by a professor with a passion for listening to himself talk about American history." Vidal "depicts Washington as a particularly nasty Jacobean court, in which ambition drives all. . . . Vidal's flat characters and bland, if occasionally eloquent, prose mirror the repetitious narrowness of his ideas." . . . **Gray** claims that the novel "coats its ethical inquiries with plenty of narrative sweeteners: the sweep of history, celebrity walk-ons, conspiracy theories and reams of conversation." . . . **Johnson** finds that the work "is Gore Vidal's elegiac historical novel about the twentieth century, and we seem to be in good hands." There is much discussion over whether FDR really incited the Pearl Harbor attack. . . . **Kemp** contends that Vidal sees himself as "a modern-day Suetonius: a suave patrician observer of the enormities and pettinesses of imperial power figures." But the book is marred by "slovenly inconsistency" and "an uninventive recycling of situations and devices that Vidal has used (and re-used) before." . . . **Klepp**'s brief review states that the book contains Vidal's "signature cynicism." "As usual, the conversation's good. Vidal's animated historical figures aren't farcically pompous, but they are, like Vidal himself, trenchant, sporadically wise, and routinely malicious." . . . **LaHood**'s review is largely a plot summary. Vidal "has a scorn, approaching hatred" for Franklin D. Roosevelt, and other historical characters fare little better. But "this novel suffers from too little analysis of America's place on the world stage." . . . **Leader**, in an extensive review, asserts that "the writing labours under the enormous task he has set himself." Leader surveys the previous novels in the series. This one focuses largely on FDR and Truman: "Little [creative energy] has been expended on difficulties of plot or structure." . . . **MacLeish** writes that the "principal charm" of the book "is its up-close view of American national politics in the years of war and upheaval between 1939 and 1954." "There are perhaps too many people, real and imaginary, crowding *The Golden Age.*" But Vidal has done "prodigious research" and there are "stretches of superb writing." . . . **Minzesheimer**'s review is largely a plot summary. "Vidal comes across as a writer who loves to show off—the people he knew, what he heard, what was left out of the official version. It's history as gossip, and gossip as history, as if there's no difference." . . . **Pritchard** declares that "the descriptions of public figures and events are terrific." The novel's perspective is "a disillusioned, but somehow genial, even godlike, one." . . . **Sheldon** writes: "when he is at his best, Vidal's satiric thrusts are enormous fun, but a little of it goes a long way . . . in this novel the relentless ridicule begins to wear down the reader's patience." . . . **Sullivan** maintains that the novel is "irresistibly diverting, if quite unreliable." Vidal "is best on the surface"—e.g., in depicting the political conventions of 1940. "But the broad picture Vidal paints is simply unconvincing." Sullivan takes offense at Vidal's suggestion that "Not only is Roosevelt as bad as Stalin, but the American people are worse than Hitler."

59.   *The Last Empire*
    a.   Applebaum, Anne. "Stylishly But Consistently Wrong." *Spectator* 288 (no. 9066) (11 May 2002): 41.
    b.   Berman, Paul. "Patriotic Gore." *New York Times Book Review* (1 July 2001): 7.
    c.   Daniels, Wayne. "Everybody's Ox Is Gored." *Globe and Mail* (Toronto) (21 July 2000): D4.
    d.   Finlayson, Iain. *Times* (London) (17 April 2002): T2, p. 19.
    e.   Jones, Mary Paumier. *Library Journal* 126, no. 9 (15 May 2001): 125.
    f.   LaHood, Marvin J. *World Literature Today* 76, no. 2 (Spring 2002): 160.
    g.   Levy, Lisa. *Entertainment Weekly* no. 600 (15 June 2001): 82.
    h.   Pritchard, William H. "Gore Vidal's Outrageous Rage." *Washington Times* (22 July 2001): B8.
    i.   Rigelhof, T. F. "America, America." *Books in Canada* 31, no. 1 (Winter 2002): 19–20.
    j.   Robinson, Judith. *Library Journal* 127, no. 5 (15 March 2002): 127.
    k.   Shafer, Jack. "Still Rocking the Boat." *Washington Post Book World* (9 September 2001): 9.
    l.   Veale, Scott. "New and Noteworthy Paperbacks." *New York Times Book Review* (9 June 2002): 32.
    m.   [Unsigned.] *Kirkus Reviews* 69, no. 9 (1 May 2001): 649.
    n.   [Unsigned.] *Publishers Weekly* 248, no. 22 (28 May 2001): 78–79.

Applebaum feels that, although Vidal "reads brilliantly," he is given to conspiracy theories and ignores the real threat that the Soviet Union posed to Europe and the World after World War II. . . . **Berman** thinks only "four of five" of the essays are meritorious. But even in these "Vidal can't help slipping . . . into what seems to be one or another obsessive mania." "Certain of Vidal's ideas strike me as singularly repulsive" (such as his supposed suggestion that racism had its origins in Judeo-Christianity). . . . **Daniels** writes that "Vidal's historical, political and social interests are every bit as encompassing as his literary ones, if sometimes a shade predictable." . . . **LaHood** believes that, taken with *United States,* the books "represent half a century of brilliant, acerbic, slanted, sophisticated and unmatched commentary on everything an extremely intelligent and witty person ought to know about Western civilization." . . . **Pritchard** asserts that Vidal is too tempted to confound his serious arguments with jokes. The essay on Updike is overly harsh. . . . In an enthusiastic review, **Rigelhof** maintains that Vidal "does not dislike his country but is deeply disappointed in it." He praises the literary essays, although "Vidal is always better on the attack than as a witness for the defence," such as the essay on Updike. Vidal's political essays are "a continuation of a worthy tradition of dissent against 'Received Opinion' that remains vital, accurate, and insightful." . . . **Shafer** notes that "Obviously, when it comes to geopolitics, Gore Vidal is cracked," because his views of the Soviet Union and China are naïve and ignore their tyrannies and savageries. "But Vidal is only half-cracked," and the literary essays reveal great substance. Vidal's "voice rings with originality."

60.   *Perpetual War for Perpetual Peace*
    a.   Cooper, Marc. "Against the American Grain." *Los Angeles Times Book Review* (12 May 2002): 8.

b. Gitlin, Todd. "America—Love It . . . or Dump on It." *Globe and Mail* (Toronto) (7 September 2002): D4–5. *Dissent* 50, no. 1 (Winter 2003): 103–6 (as "Anti-anti-Americanism").

c. Green, John. *Booklist* 98, no. 14 (15 March 2002): 1188.

d. Hunter, Joanna. "Paperbacks." *Observer* (London) (15 December 2002): 19.

e. LaHood, Marvin J. *World Literature Today* 77, no. 1 (April–June 2003): 107.

f. Mead, Walter Russell. "The United States." *Foreign Affairs* 81, no. 5 (September–October 2002): 205–7 (esp. 206).

g. Menand, Louis. "Faith, Hope, and Clarity." *New Yorker* 78 (16 September 2002): 98, 100–104 (esp. 100).

h. Morgan, Michael. *Naval War College Review* 56, no. 3 (Summer 2003): 163–65.

i. Ribadeneira, Diego. "Vidal Takes Dim View of Us in 'Perpetual War.'" *Boston Globe* (1 May 2002): D7.

j. Schwarz, Benjamin. "Fighting Spirits." *Washington Post Book World* (28 April 2002): 3.

k. [Unsigned.] *Kirkus Reviews* 70, no. 6 (15 March 2002): 398–99.

l. [Unsigned.] *Publishers Weekly* 249, no. 13 (1 April 2002): 63.

Cooper sums up the book as an "unevenly stitched together collection of essays." Vidal is "quite a patriot" and "writes not from hatred but from a profound love betrayed and defiled." But Cooper does not share Vidal's sympathy for Timothy McVeigh. Vidal is "a powerful, urgently needed and near lone voice of national conscience." . . . **Gitlin**, in a multiple review, feels that Vidal is now "a witless crank." The book is "skimpy and redundant at once." Vidal "dabbles in conspiracy theory." His sympathy for Timothy McVeigh is unconscionable. . . . **LaHood** finds the book "a bit of a disappointment"; "it features Vidal's most acerbic anti-Americanism." It is written in a "grumpy, shoot-from-the-hip style." . . . **Mead**, reviewing the book in conjunction with Noam Chomsky's *9/11*, writes: "Neither book represents its author's finest work. . . . Nevertheless, Chomsky and Vidal write with verve, passion and style that complement their controversial views." . . . **Menand** dismissively notes that "if you put Gore Vidal's name on the cover [of a book] people will buy it." . . . **Morgan**, in a surprisingly charitable review, states that he disagrees with "many of Vidal's assumptions and prepositions," but "the book is worthwhile because it challenges one to think about inconsistencies and issues in American foreign policy as well as domestic security." But the main theme of "how we got to be so hated" is not well developed. . . . **Ribadeneira** writes: "This is classic Vidal and it will infuriate many readers. But Vidal is a gifted and shrewd writer and an important voice in the debate over the shifting role of the United States in the world." . . . **Schwarz**, in a multiple review, claims that Vidal is "perhaps the finest American literary essayist alive" and is "a national treasure"; but "this book, like too much of his political writing, is snide rather than skeptical and extremely unreliable."

61. *Dreaming War*

a. Gould, Robert. *Ecologist* 33, no. 4 (May 2003): 60.

b. Green, John. *Booklist* 99, no. 11 (1 February 2003): 955.

c. Hari, Johann. "Day of Infamy." *New Statesman* 132 (no. 4630) (24 March 2003): 54–55.

d. Kingwell, Mark. "Three Intellectuals in Search of an Empire." *Globe and Mail* (Toronto) (12 July 2003): D3, 13.

e. Nickels, Thom. *Lambda Book Report* 12, nos. 5 and 6 (December 2003–January 2004): 37.

f. [Unsigned.] *Kirkus Reviews* 70, no. 24 (15 December 2002): 1836.

g. [Unsigned.] *Publishers Weekly* 250, no. 4 (27 January 2003): 250–51.

Hari thinks Vidal has "gone mad" and is addicted to conspiracy theories. . . . **Kingwell**, in a multiple review, writes that Vidal is "both brave and serious." He has "elegant turns of phrase and a fine disdain for stupidity, all backed up with solid evidence." He is both "historically acute" and "condescending." He is right on most of the points he discusses. . . . **Nickels** believes that this is an "intense but short overview of America's fall from Republic to Empire." Vidal "refrains from shocking predictions but manages to back up most of what he says with facts and statistics."

62. *Inventing a Nation*

   a.   Breen, T. H. "A Family Feud." *Times Literary Supplement* no. 5264 (20 February 2004): 5, 7.

   b.   Burstein, Andrew. "New Republic." *Washington Post Book World* (4 January 2004): 7.

   c.   Cogliano, Francis D. "Founders Chic." *History* 70 (no. 299) (July 2005): 411–19 (esp. 411–13).

   d.   Eder, Richard. "The Founding Fathers: For All Their Faults, Gore Vidal Loves Them Still." *New York Times* (27 November 2003): E18. *International Herald Tribune* (2 December 2003): 20.

   e.   Ellis, Joseph J. "The Right Men, But Not the Real Story." *Los Angeles Times Book Review* (16 November 2003): R3.

   f.   Hammersmith, James P. *Southern Humanities Review* 38, no. 4 (Fall 2004): 402–4.

   g.   Lazare, Daniel. "Skeletons in the Closet." *Nation* 278, no. 1 (5 January 2004): 28, 30–32, 34.

   h.   Lundegaard, Erik. "Vidal Looks at Nation's Messy Beginnings." *Seattle Times* (23 November 2003): K10.

   i.   Morgan, Edmund S. "A Tract for the Times." *New York Review of Books* 50, no. 20 (18 December 2003): 26, 28.

   j.   Morone, James. "The Triumph of Plunder." *London Review of Books* 26, no. 18 (23 September 2004): 32–33.

   k.   Mount, Ferdinand. "Gang of Three." *Sunday Times* (London) (16 November 2003): Sec. 9, p. 47.

   l.   Nichols, John. *Progressive* 67, no. 12 (December 2003): 41–42.

   m.   Piehl, Charles K. *Library Journal* 128, no. 18 (1 November 2003): 100, 108.

   n.   Pollard, Finn. *Journal of American Studies* 38, no. 3 (December 2004): 534–35.

   o.   Taylor, Gilbert. *Booklist* 100, no. 4 (15 October 2003): 387.

   p.   Taylor, Isahn. "Paperback Row." *New York Times Book Review* (3 October 2004): 34.

   q.   Wood, Gordon S. "Slaves in the Family." *New York Times Book Review* (14 December 2003): 10–11.

   r.   [Unsigned.] *History Today* 53, no. 11 (November 2003): 73.

   s.   [Unsigned.] *Publishers Weekly* 250, no. 36 (8 September 2003): 65.

Breen feels that Vidal "invites candid reappraisal of the achievements of the so-called Founding Fathers." Vidal "depicts the Founders as members of a somewhat dysfunctional family. . . . Vidal casts Franklin as the Cassandra of this political drama." . . . **Burstein** approves of Vidal's vaunting of John Adams and Benjamin Franklin, but Vidal is unable "to explain how the 18th century produced powerful thinkers whose combustible mix of idealism and caution gave muscle to the Revolution and set the two-party system in motion." . . . **Cogliano**, reviewing many books about the Founding Fathers, remarks that Vidal assumes "an insider's knowledge to present an intimate view of the founding of the American republic. . . . While [the book] is an entertaining read, it is not entirely clear why Vidal wrote the book." It "can be read as a less satisfying sequel to Vidal's 1973 novel, *Burr*." . . . **Ellis** writes: "Scholars are unlikely to take 'Inventing a Nation' seriously. . . . There are no larger-than-life heroes in the Vidal story because he believes, correctly I think, that such creatures do not exist." The book is "his edgy tribute to the way we were before the fall." . . . **Hammersmith** observes: "It isn't easy . . . to pinpoint exactly what Vidal is up to here. . . . It may justly be called history as political commentary. . . . The book is prickly with deftly aimed barbs" at present political corruption and chicanery. . . . **Lazare**, in a multiple review, states that the book is "not without wit and insight. Vidal knows his subjects well and paints each portrait with a few deft strokes." But "there is something a bit musty about the whole exercise." . . . **Lundegaard** contends that the book is "more of a booklong essay, whose dual purpose is to both humanize the founding fathers while demonizing the Bush administration, both worthy tasks in my mind." . . . **Morgan** provides a summary of Vidal's political views. He "delivers [his views] with the certitude we too easily associate with the paranoid. . . . Seemingly paranoid fears and conspiracy theories sometimes prove to be justified." The work is "a rambling, deceptively simple talk—there is no better word for it." It is "an unblinking view of our national heroes by one who cherishes them, warts and all . . . the recital of the Founders' views and achievements offers him the opportunity to invite his readers to recognize the present violation of everything they stood for." . . . **Morone** asserts that "for Vidal there never was a golden age—

quite the contrary—and he rudely exposes the clay feet hidden beneath those Federalist chairs. . . . The most sustained theme of *Inventing a Nation* might be tagged as tales of avarice." Vidal's entire vision of American history is based on class, economics, and religion. . . . **Mount** maintains that the book contains "bracing provocations." He doubts that Jefferson fathered any children from Sally Hemings. "No admirer of Vidal's work would wish to miss this sparkling historical excursion." . . . **Nichols** remarks that the book features Vidal's "remarkable historical insight, his irreverence, and his famously savage wit." He admires Vidal's use of Benjamin Franklin to reflect on the shortcomings of the Constitution. . . . **Pollard** comments: "Vidal's attempted subject is admirable; it is to be regretted that he does not quite succeed in bringing it off." The book's structure is erratic. "The chronology is loose and Vidal fails to offer a compelling substitute argument supporting his placing of material." . . . **Wood**, reviewing several books on early American history, finds that Vidal "has his usual sardonic fun with the creation of the nation." There are "some shrewd judgments," but at other times "Vidal's history reads as if it had been written by Dave Barry."

63.   *Imperial America*
   a.   Hall, Anthony J. "Patricians of Dissent." *Globe and Mail* (24 July 2004): D8–9.
   b.   Nardini, Bob. *Library Journal* 129, no. 12 (July 2004): 103–4.
   c.   Whitford, Sophie. *Ecologist* 34, no. 6 (July–August 2004): 53.
   d.   [Unsigned.] *Kirkus Reviews* 72, no. 8 (15 April 2004): 387.

Hall, reviewing the book along with Lewis Lapham's *Gag Rule,* notes that both writers are "patrician mavericks." "There is little doubt that Vidal will emerge in the intellectual histories of the future as one of the most original and enduring figures of 20th-century Americana." The book could be subtitled "I Told You So." But Vidal's reductionism can at times "strain credulity."

64.   *Point to Point Navigation*
   a.   Bigsby, Christopher. "Laughter and Forgetting." *Independent* (10 November 2006): 25.
   b.   Eyman, Scott. "The Last Hurrah." *Palm Beach Post* (19 November 2006): 6J.
   c.   Farndale, Nigel. "Nigel Farndale Marvels at Gore Vidal's Undiminished Gift for Writing and Feuding." *Daily Telegraph* (London) (19 November 2006): 47.
   d.   Greig, Geordie. "Not Going Gentle . . ." *Times* (London) (4 November 2006): Books, p. 10.
   e.   Haslam, Nicholas. "Around the World in Eighty Years." *Spectator* 302 (no. 9302) (18 November 2006): 58–59.
   f.   Healy, Benjamin, and Benjamin Schwarz. "Cover to Cover." *Atlantic Monthly* 298, no. 4 (November 2006): 124.
   g.   Hitchens, Christopher. "Leave-Taking." *New York Times Book Review* (26 November 2006): 12.
   h.   Hooper, Brad. *Booklist* 103, no. 1 (1 September 2006): 6.
   i.   Kirsch, Adam. "Making It." *New York Sun* (3 November 2006): 25.
   j.   Leonard, John. "New Books." *Harper's Magazine* 313, no. 5 (November 2006): 81–82.
   k.   Lidle, Rod. "The Glory That Is Gore." *Sunday Times* (London) (19 November 2006): Culture, p. 49.
   l.   McMurtry, Larry. "The Lives of Gore." *New York Review of Books* (30 November 2006): 23–25.
   m.   Marcus, James. "The Rest of the Story." *Los Angeles Times Book Review* (5 November 2006): 3.
   n.   Patterson, Troy. *Entertainment Weekly* no. 906 (10 November 2006): 87.
   o.   Pritchard, William H. "Gore Vidal Charts His Course, Witty to the End." *Washington Times* (19 November 2006): B8.
   p.   Robertson, Ray. "Valedictory Vidal." *Globe and Mail* (Toronto) (11 November 2006): D4.
   q.   [Unsigned.] *Kirkus Reviews* 74, no. 17 (1 September 2006): 894–95.
   r.   [Unsigned.] *Publishers Weekly* 253, no. 35 (4 September 2006): 47.

Bigsby asserts: "Perhaps the best that can be said . . . is that it is a testament to the depth of his commitment to [Howard] Austen." The book "has something of the quality of a dream." The criticisms of American politics, though repetitious, remain cogent. . . . **Eyman** feels that this is "a scattered book, in a more or less stream-of-consciousness vein." "As a writer, Vidal has always had a sense of pity, but life seems to have taught him compassion." . . . **Farndale** notes that Vidal has always been "waspish, snobby, a shameless dropper of names." But Vidal "does know how to write, and his pen portraits are beautifully crafted." The book is "a lighter, wittier read" than *Palimpsest,* "though it is no less elegantly written." . . . **Greig** concludes that "Death is the leitmotif" of the book. The "central tableau" is the death of Howard Austen. "An unmistakably patrician tone pervades this book at every turn. It is, at times, very funny." . . . **Haslam** observes that "In this navigation round the shores and shoals of his later life, Vidal nails up his true colours." The book is enlivened by Vidal's attacks on the Bush administration and others. . . . **Hitchens** notes that "much of [the memoir] is almost alarmingly laconic, as if offhandedly dictated." But the discussion of Howard Austen's death exhibits "the sort of stoicism we should all want to emulate." . . . **Kirsch,** in a harsh review, believes that the book is a "haughty, shoddy new memoir . . . even when it comes to Mr. Vidal's private life," the memoir "is a weary book, fragmentary and repetitive, stuffed with twice-told tales." . . . **Leonard** writes: "For a novelist, he's not really curious, has no patience for psychoanalysis . . . and has no use, either, for identity politics, refusing to be defined by his sexuality." The memoir is mournful in its elegy to Howard Austen. . . . **Lidle** believes that the theme of the book is: "how shall we remember him, when he is gone?" Vidal is, "heaven help us, . . . a man of letters. But such beautiful letters." But this is "a melancholy book, shaded by the death of his partner of five decades, Howard Austen." . . . **McMurtry,** in a lengthy review, ruminates on Vidal's life and career. While there are many poignant moments in the book, "I find myself wishing that the death of Howard Austen chapter could have been printed separately from the gossip and the gab." . . . **Marcus** claims that "This is a book of the dead." There are "witty evocations" of the many celebrities Vidal has known. "Despite some exquisite passages," the book "betrays a diminished attention span." . . . **Pritchard** notes that the book "has a highly improvised quality." Many "anecdotes, deflationary definitions, and turns of phrase . . . animate these pages. . . . One comes away from the book admiring Mr. Vidal's capacity for friendship." . . . **Robertson** maintains that the book is "not nearly as well written as its predecessor [*Palimpsest*]—in many ways, it isn't even strictly a memoir—but it is almost as enjoyable." The book is married by "an impatience with simple storytelling in favour of a cranky defence of Vidal's own status as a writer." The chapters on Howard Austen's death "are extremely moving but never maudlin."

G. Media Reviews

1. *Dark Possession* (I.D.ii.2)
   a. [Unsigned.] "Simple Psychology Plus Melodrama: Unhappy Mixture for Television Play." *Times* (London) (15 May 1959): 6.

The play is "unlikely to improve [Vidal's] reputation." In regard to Pamela Brown's performance: "there was as much embarrassment as pleasure in watching so distinguished an actress coming to terms with a wretchedly hack composition."

2. *A Sense of Justice* (I.D.ii.6)
   a. Gould, Jack. "Television: Anxiety." New York Times (16 February 1955): 40.

The play is "an incredibly contrived item by Gore Vidal."

3. *Stage Door* (I.D.ii.9)
   a. S[hanley], J[ohn] P. "Television: 'Stage Door.'" *New York Times* (8 April 1955): 29.

Vidal has "crammed a lot of script into the one-hour show." Shanley praises the acting of Diana Lynn, Peggy Ann Garner, and others.

4. *Visit to a Small Planet* (I.D.ii.11)
   a. Gould, Jack. "Television: Saucer Satire." *New York Times* (11 May 1955): 42.

The play is "welcome good fun, something off the beaten path in television drama." Vidal "got across his points of social commentary but never lost his sense of humor and light touch."

5. *A Farewell to Arms* (I.D.ii.12)
   a. S[hanley], J[ohn] P. "Devitalized 'Farewell to Arms' on 'Climax.'" *New York Times* (27 May 1955): 45.
   The play is an "unimaginative production"; the lead roles gave "routine performances."

6. *Dr. Jekyll and Mr. Hyde* (I.D.ii.14)
   a. Gould, Jack. "TV: 'Jekyll and Hyde.'" *New York Times* (29 July 1955): 35.

The play is "several megacycles away from Robert Louis Stevenson's classic." "Mr. Vidal's attorney must be grateful that his client took the precaution of massacring a work in the public domain."

7. *The Catered Affair* (I.E.i.1)
   a. B., R. B. *Village Voice* 1, no. 47 (24 October 1956): 8.
   b. B[aker], P[eter] G. *Films and Filming* 2, no. 11 (August 1956): 21.
   c. Bucklin, Mrs. Louise E. "Motion Picture Previews." *National Parent-Teacher* 50, no. 10 (June 1956): 37.
   d. Crowther, Bosley. "Screen: 'Catered Affair.'" *New York Times* (15 June 1956): 32.
   e. Hart, Henry. *Films in Review* 7, no. 5 (May 1956): 215–17.
   f. Hartung, Philip T. "Life Is Real, Life Is Earnest." *Commonweal* 64, no. 12 (22 June 1956): 300–301.
   g. Kass, Robert. "Film and TV." *Catholic World* 183 (no. 1905) (June 1956): 222.
   h. Knight, Arthur. "East India and West Bronx." *Saturday Review* 39, no. 22 (2 June 1956): 25–26.
   i. McCarten, John. "Paris to the Pacific, via the Bronx." *New Yorker* 32, no. 18 (23 June 1956): 64–65.
   j. Walsh, Moira. *America* 95, no. 11 (23 June 1956): 312.

    k.   [Unsigned.] "After 'Marty.'" *Newsweek* 47, no. 26 (25 June 1956): 94, 96.

    l.   [Unsigned.] *Time* 68, no. 1 (2 July 1956): 78.

R. B. B. states that the film "may not be very entertaining, but it certainly is loud, tasteless, shrill, and depressing." It is "one of the year's major disappointments." Vidal is mentioned only in passing. . . . **Baker** maintains that the film "turns out to be a substantial meal." Vidal is not mentioned. . . . **Crowther** believes that Vidal's "screen play . . . only gets a few more words in the design." The performances do not ring true. . . . **Hart** feels the film is not as good as Chayefsky's *Marty*. Sam Zimbalist's "choice of Gore Vidal to expand Cheyefsky's [*sic*] tv script was odd, but, it turns out, also efficacious." . . . **Hartung** declares that Vidal "has written a moving and literate script . . . But stretched to such lengths as it is, the unhappy incidents become repetitive and contrived." But the film is still "engrossing" and the cast is excellent. . . . **Kass** writes that the film "does possess a certain accuracy in pinpointing the drab lives of an Irish-Catholic family in the Bronx." But neither Chayefsky nor Vidal really know anything about Catholicism. . . . **McCarten** judges the film "a confused and wearisome account of a family squabble in the Bronx." The central conflict "hasn't much dramatic substance." . . . **Walsh** finds the film "an uninteresting story about drab and muddle-headed people made tolerable only by the young couple." Vidal is not mentioned. . . . The *Newsweek* review states that Vidal "shouldn't be too satisfied with his screen adaption." In the film "nothing spectacular has happened beyond a general house cleaning of the emotional atmosphere." . . . The *Time* review deems the film "another Bronx cheer . . . for the marital problems of the lower middle class." Vidal "has kept Chayefsky's sharply observed vignettes of Bronx life."

8.   *Honor* (I.D.ii.17)

    a.   S[hanley], J[ohn] P. "TV: Drama of Civil War." *New York Times* (20 June 1956): 63.

A brief review, noting that the work is "a routine job of playwriting." Only Dick York's performance is notable.

9.   *I Accuse!* (I.E.i.2)

    a.   Alpert, Hollis. "All's Ferrer." *Saturday Review* 41, no. 10 (8 March 1958): 41.

    b.   B[aker], P[eter]. *Films and Filming* 4, no. 6 (March 1958): 27–28.

    c.   Crowther, Bosley. "Screen: Dreyfus Affair." *New York Times* (6 March 1958): 32.

    d.   McCarten, John. "Wrong Focus." *New Yorker* 34, no. 4 (15 March 1958): 93–94.

    e.   Rich. *Variety* 209, no. 10 (5 February 1958): 20.

    f.   Walsh, Moira. *America* 98, no. 20 (22 February 1958): 615–16.

    g.   [Unsigned.] "After Disgrace, a Kiss." *Newsweek* 51, no. 10 (10 March 1958): 108.

Alpert refers to "the lackluster script by Gore Vidal." . . . **Baker** writes: "This is the most perfect piece of cinema I have seen for many a month." The script "has a clarity and simplicity that are unique in an era that demands 'gimmicks' or neuroses of its screenwriters." Vidal is not mentioned. . . . **Crowther** finds the film a "studious and generally valid re-enactment of the highlights of the [Dreyfus] case." But the film is not "dramatic [or] exciting." . . . **McCarten** feels that Vidal's script "doesn't give [José Ferrer] many opportunities to examine the major aspects of the affair." . . . **Rich** believes that the film "makes strong, if plodding, entertainment." There is "a literate screenplay by Gore Vidal." . . . **Walsh** states that the film is a "comparatively accurate and authoritative dramatization of the Dreyfus case." Vidal's "script is workmanlike rather than distinguished." . . . The *Newsweek* review notes that the film "is not only a sound denunciation of obdurate military injustice and a stimulating reminder of judicial fallibility but also an indelible profile of a tragic hero."

10.   *The Left-Handed Gun* (I.H.ii.1)

    a.   Bolas, Terry. *Screen* 10, no. 1 (January–February 1969): 15–23.

    b.   H. *Monthly Film Bulletin* (British Film Institute) no. 297 (October 1958): 128–29.

    c.   Hartung, Philip T. "What Makes Rita Run?" *Commonweal* 68, no. 8 (23 May 1958): 206–7 (esp. 207).

    d.   Moffitt, Jack. "Coe-Penn Pic Bio of Billy the Kid." *Hollywood Reporter* 149, no. 33 (23 April 1958): 3, 4.

    e.   Powe. *Variety* 210, no. 9 (30 April 1958): 6.

    f.   Roud, Richard. *Films and Filming* 5, no. 2 (November 1958): 24.

    g.   Thompson, Howard. *New York Times* (8 May 1968): 36.

    h.   Walsh, Moira. "Film and TV." *Catholic World* 187 (no. 1120) (July 1958): 307.

Bolas, in an immense review, provides a detailed analysis of the character of Billy the Kid. Vidal is not mentioned. . . . **Hartung** feels that the screenplay is "full of psychology and symbolism." The cast, especially Paul Newman, is outstanding. . . . **Moffitt** praises Paul Newman's performance, but "the rest of the picture is not as good as its main character or its plot line." Vidal is mentioned only in passing. . . . **Powe** writes: "There is plenty of action for western buffs and the added value of a psychological story for general appeal." Paul Newman "dominates the picture." Vidal is not mentioned. . . . **Roud** notes that "The film has many things in its favour. . . . the trouble with the film is that . . . it is just not a very efficiently put together Western." There is only a glancing mention of Vidal. . . . **Thompson** states: "A Gore Vidal script shaped a moody psychological vignette, long on reactions and short on motivations." The film "moves self-consciously, at a snail's pace." . . . In **Walsh**'s opinion, the film shows that effects that work on television do not always work on the big screen. Vidal is not mentioned.

11.   *Please Murder Me* (I.H.iii.1)

    a.   [Unsigned.] "*Please Murder Me*—Television Play of Unusual Polish." *Times* (London) (17 November 1958): 14.

The play is "a diverting comédie noire." "The production achieved its unusual success by outstanding teamwork from all concerned."

12.   *Summer Pavilion* (I.D.ii.10)

    a.   [Unsigned.] "A Familiar Mansion Re-explored: Mr. Gore Vidal's Play on Television." *Times* (London) (27 June 1959): 8.

The reviewer states "Mr. Vidal covers the ground again briskly and divertingly," noting that the theme of a decaying Southern mansion has become commonplace.

13.   *The Scapegoat* (I.E.i.3)

    a.   C[orbin], L[ouis]. *Films in Review* 10, no. 7 (August–September 1959): 423–24.

    b.   Robinson, David. "In Brief." *Sight and Sound* 28, nos. 3 and 4 (Summer–Autumn 1959): 172.

    c.   Rotha, Paul. *Films and Filming* 5, no. 12 (September 1959): 21.

Corbin's review does not mention Vidal. The film "is good in every department of filmaking [*sic*] except the script, which inadequately characterizes the leading parts and insufficiently motivates the major plot-turns." . . . **Robinson** notes that "one must still question whether *The Scapegoat* could ever have been much better than it now is." The film is "no more than superficial." Vidal is mentioned only in passing. . . . **Rotha** feels that "Gore Vidal's adaptation and Robert Hamer's screenplay is [*sic*] just about as unconvincing and preposterous as they come."

14.   *The Indestructible Mr. Gore* (I.D.ii.18)

    a.   Shanley, John P. "The Story of Oklahoma's Blind Senator." *New York Times* (14 December 1959): 63.

Vidal has written "a play that was moving and compassionate, witty and believable."

15.   *Suddenly, Last Summer* (I.E.i.5)

    a.   Baker, Peter. *Films and Filming* 6, no. 9 (June 1960): 21.

    b.   Crowther, Bosley. "The Screen: 'Suddenly, Last Summer.'" *New York Times* (23 December 1959): 22.

    c.   H[art], H[enry]. *Films in Review* 11, no. 1 (January 1960): 39–41.

    d.   Hartung, Philip T. "The Voice of the Turtles." *Commonweal* 71, no. 14 (1 January 1960): 396–97.

    e.   Hatch, Robert. "Films." *Nation* 190, no. 3 (16 January 1960): 59–60.

f.   Herbstman, Mandel. *Film Daily* 116, no. 116 (16 December 1959): 6.

g.   Jacobs, Jay. "Putting the Bite on Sebastian." *Reporter* 22, no. 3 (4 February 1960): 37–38.

h.   Johnson, Albert. *Film Quarterly* 13, no. 3 (Spring 1960): 40–42.

i.   Kauffmann, Stanley. "Arty Horror, Straight Suspense." *New Republic* 142, no. 3 (18 January 1960): 20–21 (esp. 20).

j.   Knight, Arthur. "Eating People Is Wrong." *Saturday Review* 43, no. 1 (2 January 1960): 31.

k.   McCarten, John. "Meagre Merriment." *New Yorker* 35, no. 47 (9 January 1960): 74–75.

l.   Marek, Richard. "Sight and Sound: Movies." *McCall's* 87, no. 5 (February 1960): 6, 8 (esp. 8).

m.   Moffitt, Jack. "'Suddenly, Last Summer' Electrifying, Absorbing." *Hollywood Reporter* 158, no. 5 (16 December 1959): 3.

n.   Powe. *Variety* 217, no. 3 (16 December 1959): 6.

o.   Walsh, Moira. *America* 102, no. 14 (9 January 1960): 428–29.

p.   [Unsigned.] "As It Should Be." *Newsweek* 54, no. 26 (28 December 1959): 64.

q.   [Unsigned.] "The New Pictures." *Time* 75, no. 2 (11 January 1960): 64, 66.

Baker feels the film "is false, phoney, and utterly lacking in human values." The relationship between mother and son "is fundamentally false." Vidal is not mentioned. . . . **Hart** believes the "script makes plain Mrs. Venable's emasculation of her son and her connivance in his sexual perversion in order to gain ascendancy over him." The review appears to reveal a tendency toward homophobia. . . . **Hartung** finds the script "skillful." "If the film was not well conceived and executed, it would seem no more than a horror thriller or a bad joke about perversion." . . . **Hatch** maintains that the director has "turned out a polished film, and one that deals boldly with the ugly theme," but it lacks subtlety. . . . **Jacobs** writes that the film is "a reasonable facsimile of the original play." The review is largely a sarcastic plot summary. . . . **Herbstman** feels that the screenplay "moves along powerfully, frequently touching exposed, sensitive nerves. And the depth and insight into characters is expressed in hard, resilient language that often reaches poetic grandeur." The acting is superb. . . . **Johnson**, in a substantial review, notes that "The film leaves audiences in mute astonishment, with their senses stunned; this is its intention. . . . Williams and Gore Vidal have written a strong screenplay." . . . **Kauffmann** finds this "a foolish, unrewarding work." The film "is further handicapped because censorship lets it only hint at the point on which it depends"—i.e., homosexuality. Vidal is not mentioned. . . . **McCarten** thinks the film is "a preposterous and monotonous potpourri of incest, homosexuality, psychiatry, and, so help me, cannibalism." . . . **Marek** describes the film as "a clinical, distasteful, morbid, extraordinarily shocking study of some of the most twisted psychological behavior ever shown on the screen." Yet "it is, in its total effect, remarkable; if you have the nerve for it, you're bound to be deeply shaken." Vidal is mentioned only in passing. . . . **Moffitt** states that the film's controversial subject "is done with a sensitivity and subtlety that absolves it from charges of crass commercial sensationalism." Tennessee Williams and Vidal have "done a taut and suspenseful script." . . . **Powe** writes: "it is like lifting the roof on Hell to see these characters in action. . . . Nothing that's been added [to the play] is an improvement on the original." But the film "has its redeeming aspects." . . . **Walsh** discusses the controversy over the film's content. It is "a psychiatric detective story . . . the picture builds skillfully, inexorably and believably to . . . [the] horrible revelation." Vidal is not mentioned. . . . The *Newsweek* review finds the script "beautiful" and the direction "penetrating and unhurried." "The result . . . is an absorbing, original, and often moving film." . . . The ***Time*** review notes that the film "undoubtedly tells a story that they [moviegoers] will shudder at." But it is too long: "it glides along so languidly that the audience has time to wonder what is happening." Vidal is not mentioned.

16.   *Visit to a Small Planet* (I.H.ii.2)

a.   B[aker], P[eter] G. *Films and Filming* 6, no. 9 (June 1960): 24.

b.   Hartung, Philip T. "Don't Miss the Scenery." *Commonweal* 72, no. 7 (13 May 1960): 180, 182.

c.   Quinn, Frank. "Jerry Stars in 'Small Planet.'" *New York Mirror* (31 March 1960): 23.

Baker believes that "The screenplay . . . plays it strictly for laughs"; there is no social satire. But the film has a "wonderful Hollywood gloss." . . . **Hartung** states that "Like the Gore Vidal play on which all this nonsense is based, the movie is only mildly amusing." The film "as a whole is rather ordinary." . . . **Quinn**

writes that the film "has some sharp, satirical thrusts. It is occasionally smartly sophisticated but mainly in the manner of [Jerry] Lewis' trademarked comedy." Vidal is mentioned in passing.

17.   *The Best Man* (I.E.i.6)
    a.   Alpert, Hollis. "Politics and Puppy Love." *Saturday Review* 47, no. 14 (4 April 1964): 36.
    b.   Breslow, Paul. "Movies." *Vogue* 143, no. 8 (15 April 1964): 52.
    c.   Crist, Judith. "'Best Man' Is First Rate: Bristling and Outspoken." *New York Herald Tribune* (7 April 1964): 14.
    d.   Crowther, Bosley. "Dirty Politics." *New York Times* (12 April 1964): Sec. 2, p. 1.
    e.   ———. "The Screen: Gore Vidal's 'Best Man.'" *New York Times* (7 April 1964): 29.
    f.   Durgnat, Raymond. "Raymond Durgnat Finds One to Vote For . . ." *Films and Filming* 11, no. 2 (November 1964): 24–25.
    g.   Gill, Brendan. "Another Writer." *New Yorker* 40, no. 9 (18 April 1964): 118, 120, 122.
    h.   Hart, Henry. *Films in Review* 15, no. 5 (May 1964): 301–3.
    i.   Hartung, Philip T. "Strange Bedfellows." *Commonweal* 80, no. 5 (24 April 1964): 147–48.
    j.   Herbstman, Mandel. *Film Daily* 124, no. 63 (1 April 1964): 4
    k.   Houston, Penelope. "Making of a President." *New Statesman* 68 (no. 1748) (11 September 1964): 370.
    l.   Kael, Pauline. "Film Notes." *New Yorker* 80 (6 September 2004): 46.
    m.   Kauffmann, Stanley. "Politics and Bedfellows." *New Republic* 150, no. 16 (18 April 1964): 24, 26, 28.
    n.   Macdonald, Dwight. *Esquire* 61, no. 6 (June 1964): 18, 20.
    o.   Oulahan, Richard. "All the Low-Down Appeal of Politics." *Life* 56, no. 16 (17 April 1964): 15.
    p.   S., E. *Monthly Film Bulletin* (British Film Institute) no. 369 (October 1964): 144.
    q.   Sarris, Andrew. "Films." *Village Voice* 9, no. 44 (20 August 1964): 11, 20.
    r.   Tube. *Variety* 234, no. 6 (1 April 1964): 6.
    s.   Wyndham, Francis. *Sight and Sound* 33, no. 4 (Autumn 1964): 198.

Breslow states that the film affords "moderate but undeniable" pleasure. The "comic moments are subordinated to a purpose that is plainly instructive." He praises Henry Fonda's performance. . . . **Crist** believes that the film is "still marked . . . by Mr. Vidal's brisk and biting commentary." It is a "caustic commentary on the facts of our political life." . . . **Crowther**'s first review (7 April 1964) finds the film "a razzle-dazzle rendering" of the play, "even more vivid, energetic and lacerating on the screen." Much of the credit goes to Schaffner's directing and the acting of Henry Fonda and Cliff Robertson. . . . **Crowther**'s second review (12 April 1964) notes that this is an "excitingly ruthless melodrama about the nature of American politics." Vidal has introduced some discussions of civil rights into the film. The best thing about the film is "that it comes to vivid grips with the ever more crucial question of ethics in politics." . . . **Durgnat** writes that "Gore Vidal's wisecracks . . . are wry, dry and edgy, and clear the air marvellously." . . . **Gill** believes that the film has a "brilliant screenplay." The cast is splendid and the film "has been directed with great verve and slickness by Franklin Schaffner." . . . **Hart** finds the film "an interesting, and even an important, motion picture." The lead actors (Henry Fonda and Cliff Robertson) are not quite right for their roles. "Schaffner's limitations, and Vidal's superficialities and biases . . . do not prevent *The Best Man* from being an engrossing experience." . . . **Hartung** takes note of Vidal's "popular and witty stage play," but states that the film "is even funnier than the original." "For all its bright satire and humor, 'The Best Man' is a very bitter and cynical affair." . . . **Herbstman** believes that the film is "charged with irreverent wit, insight and high-voltage drama." Vidal "has peppered [the screenplay] with bright and sparkling dialogue and telling characterizations of political types and followers." . . . **Houston** asserts that the dialogue "is sharp, accurate in its wit, and always in character"; the film is "highly recommended." . . . **Kauffmann** states that Vidal "has adapted [his play] to the screen with dexterity." But the film fails to satisfy on two counts: first, the political blackmail is unconvincing; second, the title is misleading: "This comedy about the need for intelligent idealism in politics ends up by calling down a plague on all the houses." . . . **Macdonald** maintains that Vidal has "written a screenplay which is as fast-moving and amusing as the original play," but the film is confusing in spots. It is not art but *kitsch. . . . .* **Oulahan** finds that the "transition" of the play to film "is a happy one." The real heart of the film is "the mortal conflict between political rivals." The film is "an excellent facsimile of the real thing." ... **E. S.** believes that what makes the film is "the wit, in both senses of the term, that consistently informs Gore Vidal's immensely entertaining script." Henry Fonda is "surely one of the very few actors who looks capable of inventing lines as good as those that Vidal has written for the leading player." ... **Sarris** declares that the play is "considerably improved" by conversion to film. The work is "a sample of middlebrow art, [but] it is surprisingly good middlebrow art." The portrayal of Russell as an Adlai Stevenson figure is unfair. "Nevertheless, 'The Best Man' is still above average screen entertainment." ... **Tube** states that Vidal's play "has been skillfully converted to film." Some viewers might be offended by the point of view of some of the characters. The film captures Vidal's "bold, tangy dialog, her [sic] perceptive, intelligent point-of-view, and his admirable hero." ... **Wyndham** feels that the film is "wittily written, has a good plot, and is directed ... with unpretentious efficiency." It is actually an "improvement" over the play. The film is "a civilised and well-constructed comedy of manners, in which the humour springs from restraint rather than exaggeration."

18.   *Is Paris Burning?* (I.E.i.7)
   a.   Alpert, Hollis. "Burnt Paris?" *Saturday Review* 49, no. 48 (26 November 1966): 59.
   b.   Arneel, Gene. *Film Daily* 129, no. 54 (9 November 1966): 3.
   c.   Coleman, John. "Saving the City." *New Statesman* 72 (no. 1865) (9 December 1966): 885–86.
   d.   Crowther, Bosley. "The Screen: 'Is Paris Burning?' Takes Great Documentary Material and Turns It into a Garble." *New York Times* (11 November 1966): 36.
   e.   Genêt. "Letter from Paris." *New Yorker* 42, no. 37 (5 November 1966): 158, 160, 162, 165–68 (esp. 167–68).
   f.   Gill, Brendan. "Gone Wrong." *New Yorker* 42, no. 39 (19 November 1966): 183–84 (esp. 183).
   g.   Gillett, Josh. *Sight and Sound* 36, no. 1 (Winter 1966–1967): 48.
   h.   Guy, Rory. "Is Paris Burning?" *Cinema* 3, no. 3 (July 1966): 4–7.
   i.   Hart, Henry. "Film Reviews." *Films in Review* 17, no. 10 (December 1966): 662–63.
   j.   Hartung, Philip T. "Screen." *Commonweal* 85, no. 9 (2 December 1966): 260, 262 (esp. 262).
   k.   Houston, Penelope. "Franco-American." *Spectator* 217 (no. 7225) (16 December 1966): 788.
   l.   Morgenstern, Joseph. "City of Dullness." *Newsweek* 68, no. 21 (21 November 1966): 126.
   m.   Mosk. *Variety* 244, no. 10 (26 October 1966): 6.
   n.   Russell, Francis. "Paris Warmed Up." *National Review* 19, no. 1 (10 January 1967): 47.
   o.   S., L. "'Is Paris Burning?' Arrives on Screen." *Christian Science Monitor* (11 November 1966): 8.
   p.   Simon, John. "No Thanks." *New Leader* 49, no. 23 (21 November 1966): 29–30. In Simon's *Private Screenings.* New York: Macmillan, 1967, pp. 255–60 (esp. 256–57).
   q.   Sklar, Robert. "Humdrum Epic." *Reporter* 36, no. 1 (12 January 1967): 56, 58.
   r.   W., D. *Monthly Film Bulletin* (British Film Institute) no. 396 (January 1967): 3–4.
   s.   Walsh, Moira. *America* 115, no. 22 (26 November 1966): 715–16.
   t.   [Unsigned.] "Movies." *Playboy* 14, no. 2 (February 1967): 19–22 (esp. 20).
   u.   [Unsigned.] "Bang-I-Gotcha!" *Time* 88, no. 22 (25 November 1966): 122, 125.
   v.   [Unsigned.] "When the Truth Fails to Convince." *Times* (London) (8 December 1966): 18.

Alpert notes that Vidal and Coppola "lacked the capacity to make military sense and human drama out of the ample material provided by the book." ... **Arneel** finds the film "a monumental recounting of a part of World War II"; but "the war is rendered impersonal by so large a cast of individuals." Vidal is mentioned only in passing. ... **Coleman** writes that the film "never *looks* like the Forties. It certainly nowhere penetrates into an ordinary interior of the time." Vidal is not mentioned. ... **Crowther** feels that the film is confusing, has too many characters, and lacks suspense. Vidal and Coppola "have come up wth badly fragmented and bewildering continuity." ... **Genêt** declares that the director "was noticeably at his best in his big, flowing scenes with nameless individuals." But Parisians were disappointed in the film. Vidal is not mentioned. ... **Gill** feels that the film "slowly, tiresomely dies of the disparity between its huge bulk and the tiny pinch of intelligence informing it. . . . I was obliged to lay much of the blame for its failure on Gore Vidal and Francis Ford Coppola." . . . **Gillett** rates the film "poor to middling." The plot is conveyed in "snatched, disconnected episodes." Vidal is not mentioned. . . . **Guy**'s notice is a detailed examination of the film prior to release. He discusses the genesis of the film and Vidal's work as screenwriter. . . . **Hart** believes that the film "makes us realize how destructive the hand of politics is of any form of art." The script— "written by Gore Vidal (!) and Francis Ford Coppola"—"is a tissue of inadequacies and falsifications." . . . **Hartung** finds the film "a pretentious mess." But some of the performances are good. . . . **Morgenstern** writes: "Incompetence, laziness or pressure from the producers led screenwriters Gore Vidal and Francis Ford Coppola to bulldoze the complexities of history. . . . So many ingredients are missing from this sorry stew, but the most obvious is poetry." . . . **Mosk** feels that the film has "ringing action, epic flavor, and fine production trappings." Most of the actors "acquit themselves well." "Perhaps the political aspects have been watered down so as not to create any polemics." Vidal is not mentioned. . . . **Russell** feels that "its parts are larger than the whole. Some parts manage to be quite good indeed." . . . **L. S.** states: "A certain lethargy, a lack of urgency, robs this film of the taut veracity of the book. It may be caused by the script, written by Gore Vidal and Francis Ford Coppola, or by the slack direction of a top-heavy cast." . . . **Simon** believes that the film "never catches fire. . . . It lacks both clarity and suspense." . . . **Sklar** writes a detailed review in which he claims that the film "fails as art." "The film makers committed their rarest of errors, an excess of fidelity to the book." . . . **D. W.** believes that the film "never really decides what it is setting out to do . . . only a few performances stand out." Vidal is not mentioned. . . . **Walsh** claims that the film is "made up of a multitude of only tenuously related incidents. . . . Much of the film . . . does not capture our attention as it should." Vidal is not mentioned. . . . The ***Playboy*** review states that the film, "with a clodhopping script by Gore Vidal and Francis Ford Coppola, disperses logic in an orgy of crosscutting." . . . The ***Time*** review maintains that this is "just possibly the most drastically disorganized war movie ever made." The script "tries to tell the story from about 60 points of view at once," with the result that the film is "a 161-minute non sequitur." The ***Times*** (London) review finds that the film "lacks any clear progression of cause and effect." Lacking believability, it has little to support its considerable length." Vidal is not mentioned.

19. *The Last of the Mobile Hot-Shots* (I.E.i.9)
     a. Canby, Vincent. "The Screen: 'Last of the Mobile Hot-Shots' Opens." *New York Times* (15 January 1970): 38.
     b. Sarris, Andrew. "Films in Focus." *Village Voice* 15, no. 5 (29 January 1970): 51.

Canby finds the film a "slapstick tragicomedy that looks and sounds and plays very much like cruel parody—of Tennessee Williams." . . . **Sarris** feels that Tennessee Williams's play is itself mediocre. "The movie loses ground to the play steadily as it seeks to transform a poetic swamp into a sociological puddle." Vidal is mentioned only in passing.

20. *Myra Breckinridge* (I.H.ii.3)
     a. Alpert, Hollis. "Beyond Belief." *Saturday Review* 53, no. 28 (11 July 1970): 40.
     b. Armstrong, Michael. *Films and Filming* 17, no. 7 (April 1971): 59.
     c. Britt, Gwenneth. *Films in Review* 21, no. 7 (August–September 1970): 442–43.
     d. Canby, Vincent. "Getting Beyond Myra and the Valley of the Junk." *New York Times* (5 July 1970): Sec. 2, pp. 1, 20.
     e. Champlin, Charles. "'Myra Breckinridge' Plays on Decadence." *Los Angeles Times* (25 June 1970): Part 4, p. 16.
     f. Fairbanks, Harold. "'Myra' Campiest Comedy in Years." *Advocate* 4, no. 9 (24 June–7 July 1970): 12, 15.
     g. Farber, Stephen. *Film Quarterly* 24, no. 2 (Winter 1970–71): 61–62.
     h. Gilliatt, Penelope. "This England, This Past." *New Yorker* 46, no. 20 (4 July 1970): 71– 72 (esp. 71).
     i. Graves, Ralph. "A Question of Values and Vulgarity." *Life* 69, no. 1 (4 July 1970): 1.
     j. Kauffmann, Stanley. "Myra Breckenridge [*sic*] and Other Disasters." *New Republic* 163, no. 3 (18 July 1970): 22, 34 (esp. 22).
     k. McGuinness, Richard. *Village Voice* 15, no. 27 (2 July 1970): 51.
     l. Morgenstern, Joseph. "Down for the Count." *Newsweek* 76, no. 1 (6 July 1970): 85. Rpt. in David Denby, ed. *Film 70/71*. New York: Simon & Schuster, 1971, pp. 263–64.

m. Murf. *Variety* 259, no. 6 (24 June 1970): 17.

n. O'Connor, John J. "Myra, Myron and Smiling Mae." *Wall Street Journal* (26 June 1970): 8.

o. Pittman, Bruce. *Take One: The Canadian Film Magazine* 2, no. 7 (1970): 21.

p. Russell, Francis. "Boys Will Be Girls." *National Review* 22, no. 33 (25 August 1970): 906, 909.

q. Shalit, Gene. "Raquel and Charlton, Russ and Mae, Five New York Movies, None OK." *Look* 34, no. 17 (25 August 1970): 10–11.

r. Simon, John. "Dirty Movies." *New Leader* 53, no. 14 (6 July 1970): 23–25 (esp. 24–25). In Simon's *Movies into Film: Film Criticism 1967–1970*. New York: Dial Press, 1971, pp. 151–60 (esp. 151–52) (as "*Myra Breckenridge* [sic]; *Freedom to Love; Censorship in Denmark; Beyond the Valley of the Dolls*").

s. Thompson, Howard. "'Myra Breckinridge' Unveiled on Screen." *New York Times* (25 June 1970): 54.

t. [Unsigned.] "Some Sort of Nadir." *Time* 96, no. 1 (6 July 1970): 70.

Alpert dismisses the film as "one long, relatively meaningless bore, filled with what in sports are known as cheap shots." The satire in the book is itself spotty, but in the film it "is nowhere to be found." **Armstrong** defends Sarne's previous films and writes that "under Sarne's direction [the film] has evolved into a brilliant and irreverently vicious attack on an America crumbling under the hypocrisy of its social and moral values. It is "a gaudy kaleidoscope of satirical images." He praises Raquel Welch's performance. . . . **Britt** believes the film is "lower than any respectable studio has hitherto gone in chasing a buck." He praises the acting of Rex Reed and Raquel Welch. . . . **Canby** maintains that the film is "a succession of desperate compromises." It is "just a series of disconnected jokes and personal appearances that have no particular point." . . . **Champlin** declares that the film is "both dirtier and more aberrant" than *Beyond the Valley of the Dolls*, also just released, especially in "its whole shaping view of existence." "What the existence and the nature of this movie say about the present and the future of this society is in fact appalling to contemplate." . . . **Fairbanks**, in an enthusiastic review, writes: "The film will be remembered for a long time to come." There is much discussion of Mae West's role in the film. It is a good adaptation, but some elements of the book are missing. . . . **Farber** notes that this is "admittedly not a well-made movie . . . the finished film looks as if it had been put together by the studio construction crew on a weekend lark." But "it does have some wit, style, and vitality." He adds that "the film offers a bizarre, grandiose satiric examination of Hollywood . . . the film is vulgar, uneven, desperate, and sometimes right on target." . . . **Graves**, writing in an editorial, feels that this is "an unforgivable movie, a consummate exercise in vulgarity." It is dirty, "but certainly not in any important or interesting way." . . . **Kaufmann** claims that the film "looks like an abandoned battlefield after a lot of studio forces tussled and nobody won. . . . *Myra* isn't even good opportunism." . . . **McGuinness** states that the film is "unpresentable, a mess." Raquel Welch is "called upon to embody Vidal's elaborate, pathetic, garish spite toward heterosexual pride." The male roles are "uninteresting." . . . **Morgenstern** finds this "a horrifying movie, but not because it's dirty"; rather, it is because "it's an entirely incompetent, impotent attempt at exploitation." . . . **Murf** asserts that the film "starts off promisingly, but after a couple of reels plunges straight downhill under the weight of artless direction." It "was an interesting try at a very elusive story." . . . **O'Connor** notes that the book "was generally labeled distasteful, offensive and dishonest." "There are, to be honest, one or two nice bits and pieces in the film," but the director "has failed to find a focus for the film on any level." . . . **Pittman** writes a flippant review largely consisting of quotations from the film. "Myra is an act of celluloid incest, a perverted exercise upon the American myths. The ones locked in film vaults." . . . **Russell** admits that he has not read the book. "The whole thing is a fag's dream following an auto accident." It is "a sequence of pornographic *longueurs.*" . . . **Shalit** finds the film "a new low in amateur squalor." . . . **Simon** believes that the film is "mid-obscenity." He has not read Vidal's novel. The film is a "witless, lip-smacking, consistently inept cop-out." It shows an eagerness to "make us squirm." . . . **Thompson** states that the film "starts strongly, dazzlingly and hilariously in a flow of rich color imagery and filthy language . . . But rot soon sets in." Thompson admits he has not read the book. . . . The **Time** review notes that the film "is about as funny as a child molester. It is an insult to intelligence, an affront to sensibility and an abomination to the eye. . . . There is a little something here to set everyone's gorge agurgling."

21. *Caligula* (I.H.ii.4)

a. Arnold, Gary. "All Rogues Lead to Rome." *Washington Post* (31 March 1980): B1, 11.

b. Covert, Colin. "'Caligula' a Decadent Waste of Talent." *Minneapolis Star Tribune* (1 October 1999): 40.
c. Overbey, David L. *Sight and Sound* 46, no. 1 (Winter 1976–77): 27–28.

Arnold believes this to be a "miserable cinematic toga party" and "an appalling bore." There is some discussion of Vidal's involvement in the film. . . . **Covert** writes: "This is a film that inspires benumbed shock among those hardy souls who can endure it at all." . . . **Overbey** notes that the film is in production. "Gore Vidal is very much a felt presence." He discusses purported changes in Vidal's screenplay as well as the costumes and the sets. "Vidal and Tinto Brass both seem to agree that this will be 'the first *realistic* film about ancient Rome.'"

22. *Vidal in Venice* (I.E.ii.2)
  a. Brayfield, Celia. "Vidal's Stimulating Cynicism." *Times* (London) (28 December 1984): 7.
  b. Corry, John. "'Vidal in Venice,' Two Works on 13." *New York Times* (30 June 1986): C18.
  c. Schneider, Steve. "More Movies, a Political Comic Strip and Gore Vidal." *New York Times* (11 August 1985): Sec. 2, p. 28.
  d. ———. *New York Times* (4 October 1987): B32.

Brayfield, reviewing the first installment, writes: "Despite the world-weary sophistication of Vidal's asides to the audience . . . a considerable amount of history was packed into the hour." . . . **Corry** believes that the show is a "costume ball," but he takes exception to some of Vidal's cynical reflections on government and politics. . . . **Schneider**'s first review is largely a summary of the broadcast.

23. *Gore Vidal's Lincoln* (I.H.iii.2)
  a. O'Connor, John J. "'Lincoln'—A Giant Seen as a Man." *New York Times* (27 March 1988): B37.
  b. Rosenberg, Howard. "'Gore Vidal's Lincoln' Puts History on the Irresistible List." *Los Angeles Times* (25 March 1988): Sec. 6, pp. 1, 33.
  c. Shales, Tom. "'Lincoln,' Incisive and Wise." *Washington Post* (26 March 1988): C1, 4.

O'Connor discusses the differences between the book and the adaptation, noting that the screenwriter, Ernest Kinoy, "forced to cram a huge historical novel into four hours . . . falls back on the device of having major developments described hurriedly in casual conversation." Sam Waterston "too often looks and sounds like a high-school thespian determined to play Lincoln." . . . **Rosenberg** states that the work is "superb—four hours you can't stop watching. . . . If ever an actor fit a character, it is Waterston here." The screenplay by Ernest Kinoy and the direction by Lamont Johnson are brilliant. "In 'Gore Vidal's Lincoln,' the past lives." . . . **Shales** writes that this is "Probably the most provocative historical mini-series ever, and one of the most beautifully photographed." Sam Waterston "plays Lincoln like a man and not a statue."

24. *Gore Vidal's Billy the Kid* (I.E.ii.4)
  a. Willman, Chris. "A Sympathetic But Overly Long 'Billy the Kid.'" *Los Angeles Times* (10 May 1989): Sec. 6, p. 8.

"Vidal's limitations as a dialogist are in fact much more revelatory than any light he has to shed on old cliches." The film is "not nearly brief enough."

25. *Live from Golgotha* (I.H.iv.1)
  a. Johns, Ian. *Times* (London) (16 November 2002): 27.

The production is a shambles and, aside from David de Keyser, the acting is poor. Some of the themes in the play come across as "anti-Semitic ramblings."

26. *Trailer for a Remake of Gore Vidal's Caligula*
  a. Nathan, Lee. *Film Comment* 42, no. 2 (March–April 2006): 17.

H. Websites

1. The Gore Vidal Index

    www.pitt.edu/~kloman/vidalframe.html

    The leading Vidal website, supplying a brief biographical overview, an original interview (see D.14), extensive information on Vidal's works (including foreign translations), a survey of Vidal criticism, and much other interesting matter. Run by Harry B. Kloman.

2. Gore Vidal

    www.kirjasto.sci.fi/vidal.htm

    A biographical overview and a selected bibliography.

3. American Masters: Gore Vidal

    www.pbs.org/americanmasters/database/vidal_g_homepage.html

    Information on Vidal related to the PBS documentary, *The Education of Gore Vidal* (I.I.ii.12). With a biography by Jay Parini, a brief bibliography, a "career timeline," additional video footage, and a conversation between the producer of the Vidal segment, Matt Kapp, and the director, Deborah Dickson.

4. Gore Vidal Quotes

    www.brainyquote.com/quotes/authors/g/gore_vidal.html

    A compilation of 56 quotations, mostly from Vidal's essays, but without any identifications as to source.

5. Gore Vidal: The Erosion of the American Dream

    www.counterpunch.org/vidal03142003.html

    Transcript of an interview with Mark Davis, presented on SBS TV (Australia) on 12 March 2003, in which Vidal discusses recent American history, the recklessness of George W. Bush, the "Bush-Cheney junta," the 2000 presidential election, the Iraq war, Norman Mailer, the clash of religions, and the inadequacy of American education.

6. The Undoing of America

    www.citypages.com/databank/26/1268/article13085.asp

    Transcript of an interview with Steve Perry of *Citypages* (Minneapolis/St. Paul), 23 March 2005, in which Vidal discusses the Iraq war, the American political system, the media, George W. Bush, Bill Clinton, the Democrats, the American empire, and the decline of public education.

7. Gore Vidal: Living Through History

    www.truthdig.com/interview/item/20061121_gore_vidal_living_through_history/

    Transcript of an interview with Robert Scheer on 21 November 2006, in which Vidal discusses *Point to Point Navigation*, his long life, his army career, Franklin D. Roosevelt, and his support of African American writers.

8. Gore Vidal Delivers His State of the Union

    www.democracynow.org/article.pl?sid=06/01/31/1532246

    Transcript of Vidal's "State of the Union" address of 31 January 2006, condemning the American government for warmongering around the world and likening the present administration to that of Tiberius in the Roman Empire.

9. The Salon Interview: Gore Vidal

    www.salon.com/books/int/1998/01/cov_si_14int.html

    Interview conducted by Chris Haines in January 1998, in which Vidal discusses American culture, the Internet and the American empire, pornography, his writing habits, *The Smithsonian Institution, The City and the Pillar,* "queer studies," gay marriage, the Scopes trial, Harry S Truman, John F. Kennedy, and Hollywood.

10.   Gore Vidal Interviewed

www.leftbusinessobserver.com/VidalTranscript.html

> Interview conducted by Doug Henwood on WBAI radio on 6 May 2002, in which Vidal discusses George W. Bush and 9/11, the Patriot Act, the "supine" character of the American public, American warmongering, corporate control of the United States, Timothy McVeigh, Enron, running for Congress, Pat Buchanan, and Christopher Hitchens.

11.   Uncensored Gore Vidal

www.alternet.org/story/17442/

> Interview by Marc Cooper on 30 December 2003, in which Vidal discusses *Inventing a Nation,* Thomas Jefferson, Enron, John Adams, Alexander Hamilton, the Patriot Act, George W. Bush, John Ashcroft, Lyndon Johnson, American democracy, and the Iraq war.

12.   Gore Vidal

www.christinesmith.us/id33.html

> Web page run by Christine Smith, in which she posts a review of *Point to Point Navigation,* an interview with Vidal (21 December 2005), a tribute to Vidal on his eightieth birthday, and other items.

I. Academic Papers

1. Barker, Andrew David. "Creating Art against the Sky-Gods: Gore Vidal's Manifesto and Didacticism." Ph.D diss.: University of Hong Kong, 2002.

2. Bensoussan, Nicole. "La Thème de la décadence dans l'oeuvre de Gore Vidal." Ph.D. thesis: Université Michel de Montaigne-Bordeaux III, 1991.

3. Bremer, Brian W. "Reading Camp: Gay Theory and *Myra Breckinridge.*" M.A. thesis: University of Kentucky, 1990.

4. Bryant, Christopher William. "The Cold War and the American Media in the Fiction of Gore Vidal." Ph.D. thesis: University of Edinburgh, 2001.

5. Eisner, Douglas J. "The Homophile Difference: Pathological Discourse and Communal Identity in Early Gay Novels." Ph.D. thesis: University of California at Riverside, 1996.

6. Launier, Eugene Scott. "History and Narrative: Challenging the Power of the Official Record in *Midnight's Children* and *Creation.*" M.A. thesis: St. Cloud State University, 1999.

7. Livesey, Matthew Jerald. "From This Moment On: The Homosexual Origins of the Gay Novel in America." Ph.D. diss.: University of Wisconsin, 1997.

8. Moncef, Salah. "Hysterical Labor: Formal Reproduction and the Rhetoric of Commodification in Three Narrative Moments of Postmodern America (Kesey, Updike, Vidal)." Ph.D. thesis: Indiana University, 1992.

9. Neal, Green B., II. "In(di)visible Men: The Problems of Defining Sexual Difference in the Novels of Gore Vidal and James Baldwin." Honors thesis: College of William and Mary, 1994.

10. Neilson, Heather Lucy Elizabeth. "The Fiction of History: Gore Vidal, from Creation to Armageddon." Ph.D. thesis: University of Oxford, 1990.

11. Osborne, Cindy. "Historical Fiction: The Representation and Misrepresentation of Fact and Fiction as an Approach to Writing History." M.A. thesis: Northern Michigan University, 2001.

12. Riggenbach, Jeff. "Witness to the Times: Gore Vidal's 'American Chronicle' Novels and the Revisionist Tradition of American Historiography." M.A. thesis: California State University, 2004.

13. Schultheis, Kathleen J. "Born for Combat: The Education of Gore Vidal." Ph.D. thesis: University of Southern California, 1993.

14. Simpson, Richard Hunter. "The Television Plays of Gore Vidal." M.S. thesis: University of Wisconsin, 1964.

15. Smithpeters, Jeffrey Neal. "'To the Last Generation': Cold War and Post Cold War U.S. Civil War Novels in Their Social Contexts." Ph.D. diss.: Louisiana State University, 2005.

16. Sullivan, Andrew George, Jr. "'Buckley v. Esquire': Libel and a Legendary Editor." Ph.D. diss.: Indiana University, 1999.

17. Wahler, Gloria Ann. "Gore Vidal: Journalist." M.A. thesis: University of Florida, 1985.

J. Miscellany

1. Barrio, Raymond. *The Devil's Apple Cart: A Trauma in Four Acts*. Guerneville, CA: Ventura Press, 1976.

   A play about Vidal and Howard Hughes.

2. [Galbraith, John Kenneth.] *The McLandress Dimension*. As by Mark Epernay. Boston: Houghton Mifflin, 1963, pp. 5, 47.

   Vidal is mentioned in passing in this parody of a sociological study of the United States. See Vidal's review (I.C.50).

3. Howard, William. *"Gore Vidal's Caligula": A Novel Based on Gore Vidal's Screenplay*. New York: Warner Books, 1979. London: Futura, 1980. Tr. as *Calígula*. Mexico City: Grijalbo, 1981 (translator unknown).

4. Kerouac, Jack. *The Subterraneans*. New York: Grove Press, 1958, pp. 52–54.

   Vidal is the model for character Arial Lavalina.

5. Knowles, John. *A Separate Peace*. New York: Macmillan, 1960.

   Vidal is the model for character Brinker Hadley.

6. Lee, Susan Previant, and Leonard Ross. "Bore." *Columbia Forum* NS 3, no. 1 (Spring 1974): 39–40.

   A parody in the form of journal entries written in the years 1994–1998.

7. Wells, John. "Matters of Great Pith." *Spectator* 225 (no. 7415) (8 August 1970): 141.

   A comic item purporting to report on an article in the *Warwickshire Tractor* written by "Gore Vudal" about President and Mrs. Nixon, in which Mrs. Nixon is revealed to be "a homosexual called Otto Pitz, long known for his compulsive transvestism and preference for blue-jowled men."

Index

A. Names

B. Titles by Vidal

United States: Essays 1952–1992 I.A.56, 59, 65; III.F.50

"Unrocked Boat, The" I.C.14.a, G.11

"Unrocked Boat: Satire in the 1950's, The" I.A.21, C.14.b

[Untitled] I.C.73

"Untitled Screen Original" I.G.11

"Unyielding to Adversity" I.G.11

Uptight III.C.50

Uragano, L II.A.xvi.2

"V. S. Pritchett as 'Critic'" I.A.42, 56, C.128, F.20; III.E.43

Vashington, Columbia ringkond II.A.viii.1

Vašington, okrǎg Kolumbija II.A.ii.4

Vašington, okrug Kolumbija II.A.xxv.1

Vašingtona, Kulumbijas apgabals II.A.xviii.1

Vašingtonas, Kolumbijos apygarda II.A.xix.1

Večna vojna za večen mir: Mečtanata vojna II.A.ii.11

Venice I.E.ii.2

Verde oscure, roho vivo II.A.xxviii.17

Vergessliche Nation: Wie die Amerikaner ihr politisches Gedächtnis verkaufen, Die II.A.xi.28

"Verifying Genocide" I.F.22

Vesting en de zoutpilaar, De II.A.vii.1

Viceprezidentǎt Bar II.A.ii.2

"Vidal and Buckley, Calley and My Lai" I.F.35

"Vidal Blue" I.F.9

"Vidal for Driberg" I.F.15

Vidal in Venice I.A.45, C.159, E.ii.2; III.F.40

Vidal in Venice (broadcast) I.E.ii.2; III.G.22

"Vidal Replies" I.F.34, 35, 40, 48

"Vidal to Vidal: On Misusing the Past" I.G.11

"Vidal's 'Lincoln': An Exchange" I.F.30

"Vidal's Brow" I.F.6

"View from the Amalfi Coast, The" I.C.246

View from the Diners Club: Essays 1987–1991, A I.A.51; III.F.46

Virgin Islands: A Dependency of United States: *Essays 1992–1997* I.A.59, 65, C.242; III.F.53

"Visit to a Small Planet" I.A.17, 22, 31, 56, C.12

Visit to a Small Planet (film) I.H.ii.2; III.G.16

Visit to a Small Planet (television play) I.A.14, 15, 17, D.ii.11, G.11; II.B.ii.1; III.G.4

Visit to a Small Planet: A Comedy Akin to a Vaudeville I.A.17, 21, D.i.1, F.42, G.11, 16, H.v.1; II.A.xi.1; III.B.ii.5, D.9, E.66, 189, 250, 298, F.14

Visit to a Small Planet and Other Television Plays I.A.15; III.F.15

Visite à une petite planète II.B.ii.1

Vitse-prezident Berr II.A.xxv.2

"Void" I.G.11

"W. Somerset Maugham" I.G.11

"Waking Dream: Tarzan Revisited, The" I.A.28, C.49.c

"Walking" I.B.9, G.11

"War against Lies, The" I.C.292.a

"War at Home, The" I.C.257.a; III.E.60

Washington, D.C. I.A.24, 62, B.21, C.95, F.41, 42, G.11, H.i.5; II.A.i.1, ii.4, iii.1, iv.2, vi.5, viii.1, xi.6, xii.1, xiv.2, xvi.7, xvii.2, xviii.1, xix.1, xxii.8, xxiii.14, xxv.1, xxviii.4, xxviii.20, B.v.1; III.B.i.14, D.11, E.119, 151, 179, 210, 230, 246, F.22, 32

"Washington, We Have a Problem" I.C.271.a

Waszyngton II.A.xxii.8

Ways of Love I.G.11

"We Are the Patriots" I.A.69, C.290

"We owed it to literary history . . ." I.C.224.f

"Weariness" I.G.11

"Weather and a Death at Sea" I.G.11

Weekend: A Comedy in Two Acts I.A.26, D.i.5, G.11; II.A.xi.9; III.B.i.107, F.24

"West Point" I.A.36, 56, 62, C.99

"West Point and the Third Loyalty" I.C.99.a; II.A.xvi.13

"What Exists" I.G.11

"What Robert Moses Did to New York City" I.A.36, 56, C.105

"Whisperer, The" I.G.11

"Who Makes Movies?" I.F.17

"Who Makes the Movies?" I.A.42, 56, 62, C.116, F.17; III.B.i.41, E.39, 226

Who Owns the US? III.F.55

"Whole Sordid Story, The" I.C.31.a, G.11

"Why and How the Russians Came Out Second in the Space Race" I.G.11

"Why I Am Eight Years Younger Than Anthony Burgess" I.A.48, 49, 56, C.164; II.A.xvi.34

"Why the U.S. Should Be Expelled from the U.N." I.C.231.a

"Willful and Malicious Conspiracy Against 'We, the People,' A" I.C.252.c

"William Dean Howells" I.A.48, 49, 56, 62, C.150

Williwaw I.A.1, 20, 40, G.11; II.A.x.1, xvi.2, xxiii.21; III.C.108, D.11, 13, E.6, 7, 12, 51, 52, 64, 86, 100, 197, F.1

Wings of the Eagle: A Political Farce I.G.11

"Winter River, The" I.B.13

"Winter Wind, The" I.G.11

"Wiretapping the Oval Office" I.A.65, C.264

"Wisdom of the East, The" I.F.21

"Wit and Wisdom of J. K. Galbraith, The" I.A.28, C.50

"With Extreme Prejudice" I.A.59, 65, 67, C.198; II.A.xvi.32

"Without Doubt" I.G.11

"Wizard of the 'Wizard,' The" I.C.119.a

"Woman Behind the Women, The" I.C.239.a

"Women's Liberation Meets Miller-Mailer-Manson Man" I.A.31, C.88.b, c

"Women's Liberation: Feminism and Its Discontents" I.A.56, 62, 63, C.88

"World Outside, The" I.C.33.a, G.11

"Wrath of the Radical Right, The" I.C.35.a., G.11

"Writer as Cannibal, The" I.C.69.a, G.11

"Writer by Any Other Name . . ., A" I.C.188.d

"Writers and the World" I.A.27, 28, 31, 56, C.61; II.A.xvi.34

"Writers in the Public Eye" I.C.61.a, G.11

"Writing Plays for Television" I.A.15, 21, 27, 31, 56, C.10

"Yankee's Doodles" I.C.237.a

Yaratilis II.A.xxxi.5

"Yesteryear, The" I.G.11

"Youth etc." I.G.11

"Zenner Trophy, The" I.A.16, 20, 57, B.16, G.11

C. Periodicals

AB Bookman's Weekly III.D.2.b

Advocate I.C.142.f, 224.b, 258.a; III.C.14, 55, 113, 114, D.10.q, E.208, F.13.g, 31.p, 33.l, 34.i, 37.c, 47.e, 48.e, 54.c, 56.h, G.20.f

America III.F.16.t, 17.i, 21.r, 22.o, 27.m, 30.f, 32.cc, 34.u, y, 36.o, 48.bb, G.7.j, 9.f, 15.o, 18.s

American Bar Association Journal III.F.32.gg

American Book Review III.F.52.bb

American Film III.C.6, 73

American Heritage I.C.200.b; III.E.55, 298

American Historical Review I.F.32.a; III.E.106

American Libraries III.F.58.u

American Literature III.D.13.h

American Poetry Review I.G.22

American Scholar III.E.52

American Spectator III.E.294, F.37.p, 45.g, 47.w

American Studies International III.E.230

Américas III.F.21.bb

Amerikastudien/American Studies III.E.250

Anais III.E.236

Andy Warhol's Interview III.C.128

Antaeus III.C.56

Anthropoetics III.E.36

Antiquarian Bookman III.F.22.ff

Antithesis III.C.98

Architectural Digest I.C.158.a; III.E.216

Arion III.F.21.c

Armchair Detective I.C.188.d; III.E.249, F.9.d, 10.d, 12.d

Artforum III.F.47.i

Atlantic Monthly I.B.25.a, C.122.a, F.9.a; III.E.69, 104, 276, 283, F.3.n, 4.j, 7.h, 8.i, 18.b, 21.e, 22.ee, 26.a, 30.jj, 31.a, 32.q, 36.h, 47.b, 64.f

Australasian Journal of American Studies III.E.229

Australian Book Review III.D.13.c

Best Sellers III.D.11.c, 15.b, F.2.i, 5.a, 7.j, 8.k, p, 18.l, 21.s, 22.z, 26.j, 32.j, 33.h, 34.n, 37.h, 38.q

About the Author

S. T. Joshi (A.B., A.M., Brown University) is a prolific author, critic, and bibliographer. He has prepared bibliographies of H. P. Lovecraft (1981), Lord Dunsany (Scarecrow Press, 1993), Ramsey Campbell (1995), and Ambrose Bierce (1999). He is the author of such critical and biographical studies as *The Weird Tale* (1990), *H. P. Lovecraft: A Life* (1996), and *The Modern Weird Tale* (2001), and has prepared editions of the work of H. P. Lovecraft, Ambrose Bierce, Lord Dunsany, Arthur Machen, H. L. Mencken, and other authors. He is also the editor of *Atheism: A Reader* (2000) and *In Her Place: A Documentary History of Prejudice against Women* (2006). His recent volumes, partially inspired by his study of Gore Vidal, are *God's Defenders: What They Believe and Why They Are Wrong* (2003) and *The Angry Right: Why Conservatives Keep Getting It Wrong* (2006).